Hitler

A Study In Tyranny

Hitler

A Study In Tyranny

By Alan Bullock

SMITHMARK

This edition published in 1995 by SMITHMARK Publishers, Inc.,
16 East 32nd Street, New York, NY 10016

SMITHMARK books are available for bulk purchase for sales
promotion and premium use. For details write or call the
manager of special sales, SMITHMARK Publishers, Inc.,
16 East 32nd Street, New York, NY 10016; (212) 532-6600.

This edition published by special arrangement with
W.S. Konecky Associates, Inc. and with HarperCollins
Publishers, Inc.

ISBN: 0-8317-5709-4

Printed in the United States of America

10 9 8 7 6 5 4 3 2

TO MY
MOTHER AND FATHER

CONTENTS

Men do not become tyrants in order to keep out the cold.

ARISTOTLE, *Politics*

PREFACE TO THE REVISED EDITION

I FIRST began this study with two questions in mind. The first, suggested by much that was said at the Nuremberg Trials, was to discover how great a part Hitler played in the history of the Third Reich and whether Göring and the other defendants were exaggerating when they claimed that under the Nazi régime the will of one man, and of one man alone, was decisive. This led to the second and larger question: if the picture of Hitler given at Nuremberg was substantially accurate, what were the gifts Hitler possessed which enabled him first to secure and then to maintain such power. I determined to reconstruct, so far as I was able, the course of his life from his birth in 1889 to his death in 1945, in the hope that this would enable me to offer an account of one of the most puzzling and remarkable careers in modern history.

The book is cast, therefore, in the form of a historical narrative, interrupted only at one point by a chapter in which I have tried to present a portrait of Hitler on the eve of his greatest triumphs (Chapter 7). I have not attempted to write a history of Germany, nor a study of government and society under the Nazi régime. My theme is not dictatorship, but the dictator, the personal power of one man, although it may be added that for most of the years between 1933 and 1945 this is identical with the most important part of the history of the Third Reich. Up to 1934 the interest lies in the means by which Hitler secured power in Germany. After 1934 the emphasis shifts to foreign policy and ultimately to war, the means by which Hitler sought to extend his power outside Germany. If at times, especially between 1938 and 1945, the figure of the man is submerged beneath the complicated narrative of politics and war, this corresponds to Hitler's own sacrifice of his private life (which was meagre and uninteresting at the best of times) to the demands of the position he had created for himself. In the last year of his life, however, as his empire begins to crumble, the true nature of the man is revealed again in all its harshness.

No man can sit down to write about the history of his own times
– or perhaps of any time – without bringing to the task the

preconceptions which spring out of his own character and experience. This is the inescapable condition of the historian's work, and the present study is no more exempt from these limitations than any other account of the events of the recent past. Nevertheless, I wrote this book without any particular axe to grind or case to argue. I have no simple formula to offer in explanation of the events I have described; few major historical events appear to me to be susceptible of simple explanations. Nor has it been my purpose either to rehabilitate or to indict Adolf Hitler. If I cannot claim the impartiality of a judge, I have not cast myself for the role of prosecuting counsel, still less for that of counsel for the defence. However disputable some of my interpretations may be, there is a solid substratum of fact – and the facts are eloquent enough.

The bibliography printed at the end sets out the sources on which this study is based. In the ten years since this book was first published much new material has appeared which throws light on the history of the Nazi Party and the Third Reich. I have taken the opportunity of a new edition to make a thorough revision of the whole text, taking this material into account and, where it seemed necessary, rewriting in order to make use of it.

The passage of ten years also means a change of perspective: this is more difficult to take into account. I have found no reason to alter substantially the picture I drew of Hitler when the book was first published. although I have not hesitated to change the emphasis where it no longer seemed right. It is in the account of the events leading up to the Second World War that I have made the most complete revision, partly because of the large number of new diplomatic documents that have been published, partly because it is here that my own views have been most affected by the longer perspective in which we are now able to see these events. I am indebted to Mr A. J. P. Taylor's *Origins of the Second World War* for stimulating me to re-read the whole of the documentary evidence for Hitler's foreign policy in the years 1933–9. The fact that I disagree with Mr Taylor in his view of Hitler and his foreign policy – more than ever, now that I have re-read the documents – does not reduce my debt to him for stirring me up to take a critical look at my own account.

Amongst many other writers from whom I have learned since this book was originally published, I should like to mention two other Oxford colleagues: Professor Trevor-Roper whose essay on *The Mind of Adolf Hitler* convinced me that Hitler's table talk would repay careful re-reading, and the Warden of St Antony's (Mr F. W. Deakin), the proofs of whose study of German–Italian relations, *The Brutal Friendship*, he was kind enough to let me see before publication. Franz Jetzinger's painstaking researches, recorded in his book *Hitler's Youth* (to the English translation of which I contributed a foreword), have enabled me to provide a fuller and more credible account of Hitler's early years. My other debts, too numerous to acknowledge here, I have indicated in the footnotes.

The bibliography as well as the text has been revised and brought up to date, but the number of publications on the history of these years has forced me to confine it to original sources and first-hand accounts, excluding secondary works except where these print or make use of unpublished material.

In the preface to the original edition I expressed my thanks to the friends who had helped me in a variety of ways, not least to Mr Stanley Hyland for his skill and patience in compiling the index. To these I must now add my thanks to Miss S. Buttar for the trouble she has taken in deciphering and typing the revised manuscript.

My debt to my wife remains the greatest of all, not only for the help she gave me in first undertaking this study, but for her good judgement and encouragement in facing the task of its revision.

St Catherine's College ALAN BULLOCK
Oxford

March 1962

ACKNOWLEDGEMENTS

I WISH to acknowledge the permission of the Controller H.M. Stationery Office to quote from publications issued by the British Government. I wish to express my gratitude to the authors, editors, publishers, and agents concerned for permission to quote from the following books: *Mein Kampf* (translated by James Murphy), and *My Part in Germany's Fight* – Hurst & Blackett Ltd. *The Speeches of Adolf Hitler* (ed. Norman H. Baynes); *Documents on International Affairs*, 1936 and 1939–46 – Oxford University Press and Royal Institute of International Affairs. *Hitler Directs His War* (ed. F. Gilbert) – Oxford University Press Inc., New York. *The French Yellow Book*; *The Polish White Book*; *The Last Attempt* by B. Dahlerus, and *My War Memories* by Gen. Ludendorff – Hutchinson & Co. (Publishers) Ltd. *Failure of a Mission* by Sir N. Henderson – Raymond Savage Ltd. *I Paid Hitler* by Fritz Thyssen – Hodder & Stoughton Ltd. *Hitler Speaks* by Herman Rauschning and *The Royal Family of Bayreuth* by F. Wagner – Eyre & Spottiswoode (Publishers) Ltd. *Hitler as War-Lord* by Franz Halder – Putnam & Co. Ltd. *Ciano's Diary, 1939–43* – Wm Heinemann Ltd. *Ciano's Diplomatic Papers* – Odhams Press Ltd. *Der Führer* by K. Heiden – Victor Gollancz Ltd, and the Houghton Mifflin Co. *A History of National Socialism* by K. Heiden – Methuen & Co. Ltd. *The Goebbels Diaries*, and *Berlin Diary* by W. L. Shirer – Hamish Hamilton Ltd. *The Last Days of Hitler* by H. R. Trevor-Roper, and *The Life of Neville Chamberlain* by K. Feiling – Macmillan & Co. Ltd. *Hitler and I* by Otto Strasser – International Press Alliance Corporation. *Hitlers Tischgespräche* and *Statist auf diplomatischer Bühne* by Paul Schmidt – Athenäum Verlag. *The Second World War*, vol. I by Winston S. Churchill – Cassell & Co. Ltd, and the Houghton Mifflin Co.; *Farewell Austria* by K. von Schuschnigg, and *The Other Side of the Hill* by B. H. Liddell-Hart – Cassell & Co. Ltd. *Defeat in the West* by Milton Shulman, and *Hitler and His Admirals* by A. Martiennsen – Secker & Warburg Ltd. *To the Bitter End* by H. B. Gisevius – Jonathan Cape Ltd, and the Houghton Mifflin Co. *Hitler the Pawn* by R. Olden – Victor Gollancz Ltd. *The Fateful Years* by A. François-Poncet – Victor Gollancz Ltd, and Harcourt, Brace & Co., Inc. *The Memoirs of Ernst von Weizsäcker* – Victor Gollancz Ltd, and the Henry Regnery Co. *Panzer Leader* by Heinz Guderian – Michael Joseph Ltd. *Hitler* by K. Heiden – Constable & Co. Ltd. *Account Settled* by H. Schacht – Weidenfeld & Nicolson Ltd. *The Errant Diplomat* by O. Dutch – Arnold & Co. *The Fall of the German Republic* – Allen & Unwin Ltd. *The Curtain Falls* by Count Bernadotte – Alfred Knopf Inc. *The Struggle for Europe* by Chester Wilmot, and *Rommel* by Desmond Young – Collins, Sons and Co. Ltd. *Hegel's Lectures on the Philosophy of History* – G. Bell & Sons Ltd. *Die deutsche Katastrophe* by Fr. Meinecke – Eberhard Brockhaus Verlag. *Rätsel um Deutschland* by B. Schwertreger – Carl Winter Universitätsverlag. *Les Lettres secrètes échangées par Hitler et Mussolini* – Éditions du Pavois. *Hitler Privat* by A. Zoller – Droste Verlag. *Austrian Requiem* by K. von Schuschnigg – Victor Gollancz Ltd, and G. P. Putnam's Sons. *Blue Print of*

17

the Nazi Underground by R. W. M. Kempner – Research Studies of the State College of Washington. 'Von Schleicher, von Papen et l'avènement de Hitler' by G. Castellan – *Cahiers d'Histoire de la Guerre*, Paris. 'Reichswehr and National Socialism' by Gordon A. Craig – *Political Science Quarterly*, N.Y. *My New Order* (ed. Count Roussy de Sales) – Harcourt, Brace & Co. Inc. *Der letzte Monat* by Karl Koller – Norbert Wohlgemuth Verlag. *Die letzten 30 Tage* by Joachim Schultz – Steingrüben Verlag. *Rosenberg's Memoirs* – Ziff-Davis Publishing Co. *I Knew Hitler* by K. Ludecke – Jarrolds, Publishers (London) Ltd, and *Hitler's Words* by Gordon W. Prange – Public Affairs Press, Washington. I am grateful to the following authors and publishers for permission to quote additional material in this revised edition: *Hitler's Table Talk* – Weidenfeld & Nicolson Ltd. *Hitler's Youth* by Franz Jetzinger – Hutchinson & Co. (Publishers) Ltd. *Hitler, the Missing Years* by Ernst Hanfstängl – Eyre & Spottiswoode (Publishers) Ltd. *Hitler was my Friend* by Heinrich Hoffmann – Burke Publishing Co. Ltd. *The Testament of Adolf Hitler* – Cassell & Co. Ltd, and *Memoirs* by Franz von Papen – André Deutsch Ltd.

Quotations have been made from a number of other books which lack of space prevents me from acknowledging individually. Full acknowledgement is, however, given in the bibliography at the end of the book and in the footnotes, and I am grateful to all those who have granted me permission to quote. In some cases it has proved impossible to locate sources of copyright property. If, therefore, any quotations have been incorrectly acknowledged I hope the persons concerned will accept my apologies.

ABBREVIATIONS

The following abbreviations have been used in the footnotes:

N.D. – Nuremberg Documents presented in evidence at the trial before the International Military Tribunal, Nuremberg, 1945–6. The reference numbers (e.g. 376-PS) are the same in all publications.

N.P. – Nuremberg Proceedings. *The Trial of German Major War Criminals. Proceedings of the International Military Tribunal Sitting at Nuremberg.* 22 Parts (H.M.S.O., London, 1946–50).

N.C.A. – *Nazi Conspiracy and Aggression*; 8 vols. plus 2 supp. vols. (U.S. Govt Printing Office, Washington, 1946–8).

Brit. Doc. – *Documents on British Foreign Policy, 1919–39*, edited by E. L. Woodward and Rohan Butler (H.M.S.O., London, 1946–).

G.D. – *Documents on German Foreign Policy, 1918–45. From the Archives of the German Foreign Ministry* (H.M.S.O., London, 1948–).

Baynes – *The Speeches of Adolf Hitler*, edited by Norman H. Baynes, 2 vols. (Oxford U.P. for R.I.I.A., 1942).

Prange – *Hitler's Words*, edited by Gordon W. Prange (American Council on Foreign Relations, Washington, 1944).

BOOK I

PARTY LEADER
1889–1933

CHAPTER ONE

THE FORMATIVE YEARS
1889–1918

I

ADOLF HITLER was born at half past six on the evening of 20 April 1889, in the Gasthof zum Pommer, an inn in the small town of Braunau on the River Inn which forms the frontier between Austria and Bavaria.

The Europe into which he was born and which he was to destroy gave an unusual impression of stability and permanence at the time of his birth. The Hapsburg Empire, of which his father was a minor official, had survived the storms of the 1860s, the loss of the Italian provinces, defeat by Prussia, even the transformation of the old Empire into the Dual Monarchy of Austria-Hungary. The Hapsburgs, the oldest of the great ruling houses, who had outlived the Turks, the French Revolution, and Napoleon, were a visible guarantee of continuity. The Emperor Franz Joseph had already celebrated the fortieth anniversary of his accession, and had still more than a quarter of a century left to reign.

The three republics Hitler was to destroy, the Austria of the Treaty of St Germain, Czechoslovakia, and Poland, were not yet in existence. Four great empires – the Hapsburg, the Hohenzollern, the Romanov, and the Ottoman – ruled over Central and Eastern Europe. The Bolshevik Revolution and the Soviet Union were not yet imagined: Russia was still the Holy Russia of the Tsars. In the summer of this same year, 1889, Lenin, a student of nineteen in trouble with the authorities, moved with his mother from Kazan to Samara. Stalin was a poor cobbler's son in Tiflis, Mussolini the six-year-old child of a blacksmith in the bleak Romagna.

Hitler's family, on both sides, came from the Waldviertel, a poor, remote country district, lying on the north side of the Danube, some fifty miles north-west of Vienna, between the Danube and the frontiers of Bohemia and Moravia. In this countryside of hills and woods, with few towns or railways, lived a peasant population cut off from the main arteries of Austrian life. It was from this country stock, with its frequent intermarriages, that Hitler sprang. The family name, possibly Czech in origin and spelled in a variety of ways, first appears in the Waldviertel in the first half of the fifteenth century.

The presumed grandfather of the future chancellor, Johann Georg Hiedler, seems to have been a wanderer who never settled down, but followed the trade of a miller in several places in Lower Austria. In the course of these wanderings he picked up with a peasant girl from the village of Strones, Maria Anna Schicklgruber, whom he married at Döllersheim in May 1842.

Five years earlier, in 1837, Maria had given birth to an illegitimate child, who was known by the name of Alois. According to the accepted tradition the father of this child was Johann Georg Hiedler. However, although Johann Georg married Maria, then forty-seven in 1842, he did not bother to legitimize the child, who continued to be known by his mother's maiden name of Schicklgruber until he was nearly forty and who was brought up at Spital in the house of his father's brother, Johann Nepomuk Hiedler.

In 1876 Johann Nepomuk took steps to legitimize the young man who had grown up in his house. He called on the parish priest at Döllersheim and persuaded him to cross out the word 'illegitimate' in the register and to append a statement signed by three witnesses that his brother Johann Georg Hiedler had accepted the paternity of the child Alois. This is by no means conclusive evidence, and, in all probability, we shall never know for certain who Adolf Hitler's grandfather, the father of Alois, really was. It has been suggested that he may have been a Jew, without definite proof one way or the other. However this may be, from the beginning of 1877, twelve years before Adolf was born, his father called himself Hitler and his son was never known by any other name until his opponents dug up this long-forgotten village scandal and tried, without justification, to label him with his grandmother's name of Schicklgruber.[1]

Alois left his uncle's home at the age of thirteen to serve as a cobbler's apprentice in Vienna. But he did not take to a trade and by the time he was eighteen he had joined the Imperial Customs Service. From 1855 to 1895 Alois served as a customs officer in Braunau and other towns of Upper Austria. He earned the normal promotion and as a minor state official he had certainly moved up several steps in the social scale from his peasant origins.

1. For a genealogical table setting out Hitler's ancestry, see pp. 28–9.

As an official in the resplendent imperial uniform of the Hapsburg service Alois Hitler appeared the image of respectability. But his private life belied appearances.

In 1864 he married Anna Glass, the adopted daughter of another customs collector. The marriage was not a success. There were no children and, after a separation, Alois's wife, who was considerably older and had long been ailing, died in 1883. A month later Alois married a young hotel servant, Franziska Matzelberger, who had already borne him a son out of wedlock and who gave birth to a daughter, Angela, three months after their marriage.

Alois had no better luck with his second marriage. Within a year of her daughter's birth, Franziska was dead of tuberculosis. This time he waited half a year before marrying again. His third wife, Klara Pölzl, twenty-three years younger than himself, came from the village of Spital, where the Hitlers had originated. The two families were already related by marriage, and Klara herself was the granddaughter of that Johann Nepomuk Hiedler in whose house Alois had been brought up as a child. She had even lived with Alois and his first wife for a time at Braunau, but at the age of twenty had gone off to Vienna to earn her living as a domestic servant. An episcopal dispensation had to be secured for such a marriage between second cousins, but finally, on 7 January 1885, Alois Hitler married his third wife, and on 17 May of the same year their first child, Gustav, was born at Braunau.

Adolf was the third child of Alois Hitler's third marriage. Gustav and Ida, both born before him, died in infancy; his younger brother, Edward, died when he was six; only his younger sister, Paula, born in 1896, lived to grow up. There were also, however, the two children of the second marriage with Franziska, Adolf Hitler's half-brother Alois, and his half-sister Angela. Angela was the only one of his relations with whom Hitler maintained any sort of friendship. She kept house for him at Berchtesgaden for a time, and it was her daughter, Geli Raubal, with whom Hitler fell in love.

When Adolf was born his father was over fifty and his mother was under thirty. Alois Hitler was not only very much older than Klara and her children, but hard, unsympathetic, and short-tempered. His domestic life – three wives, one fourteen years older than himself, one twenty-three years younger; a separation; and seven children, including one illegitimate child and two others born shortly after the wedding – suggest a difficult and passionate temperament. Towards the end of his life Alois Hitler seems to have become bitter over some disappointment, perhaps connected with another inheritance. He did not go back to his native district when he retired in 1895 at the age of fifty-eight. Instead he stayed in Upper Austria. From Passau, the German frontier town, where Alois Hitler held his last post, the family moved briefly to Hafeld-am-Traun and Lambach before they settled at Leonding, a village just outside Linz, overlooking the confluence of the Traun and the Danube. Here the retired customs official spent his remaining years, from 1899 to 1903, in a small house with a garden.

Hitler attempted to represent himself in *Mein Kampf*[1] as the child of poverty and privation. In fact, his father had a perfectly adequate pension and gave the boy the chance of a good education. After five years in primary schools, the eleven-year-old Adolf entered the Linz Realschule in September 1900. This was a secondary school designed to train boys for a technical or commercial career. At the beginning of 1903 Alois Hitler died, but his widow continued to draw a pension and was not left in need. Adolf left the Linz Realschule in 1904 not because his mother was too poor to pay the fees, but because his record at school was so indifferent that he had to accept a transfer to another school at Steyr, where he boarded out and finished his education at the age of sixteen. A year before, on Whit Sunday 1904, he had been confirmed in the Roman Catholic Cathedral at Linz at his mother's wish.

In *Mein Kampf* Hitler makes much of a dramatic conflict between himself and his father over his ambition to become an artist.

I did not want to become a civil servant, no, and again no. All attempt on my father's part to inspire me with love or pleasure in this profession by stories from his own life accomplished the exact opposite. . . . One day it became clear to me that I would become a painter, an artist. . . . My father was struck speechless. . . . 'Artist! No! Never as long as I live! . . .' My father would never depart from his 'Never!' And I intensified my 'Nevertheless!'[2]

There is no doubt that he did not get on well with his father, but it is unlikely that his ambition to become an artist (he was not fourteen when his father died) had much to do with it. A more

1. The edition referred to throughout this book is the unexpurgated translation by James Murphy (Hurst & Blackett, London, 1939).
2. *Mein Kampf*, p. 22.

probable explanation is that his father was dissatisfied with his school reports and made his dissatisfaction plain. Hitler glossed over his poor performance at school which he left without securing the customary Leaving Certificate. He found every possible excuse for himself, from illness and his father's tyranny to artistic ambition and political prejudice. It was a failure which rankled for a long time and found frequent expression in sneers at the 'educated gentlemen' with their diplomas and doctorates.

Forty years later, in the sessions at his Headquarters which produced the record of his table talk, Hitler several times recalled the teachers of his schooldays with contempt.

They had no sympathy with youth; their one object was to stuff our brains and turn us into erudite apes like themselves. If any pupil showed the slightest trace of originality, they persecuted him relentlessly, and the only model pupils whom I have ever known have all been failures in later-life.[1]

For their part they seem to have had no great opinion of their most famous pupil. One of his teachers, Dr Eduard Hümer, gave this description of the schoolboy Hitler at the time of his trial in 1923:

I can recall the gaunt, pale-faced youth pretty well. He had definite talent, though in a narrow field. But he lacked self-discipline, being notoriously cantankerous, wilful, arrogant, and bad-tempered. He had obvious difficulty in fitting in at school. Moreover he was lazy . . . his enthusiasm for hard work evaporated all too quickly. He reacted with ill-concealed hostility to advice or reproof; at the same time, he demanded of his fellow pupils their unqualified subservience, fancying himself in the role of leader. . . .[2]

For only one of his teachers had Hitler anything good to say. In *Mein Kampf* he went out of his way to praise Dr Leopold Pötsch, an ardent German nationalist who, Hitler claimed, had a decisive influence upon him:

There we sat, often aflame with enthusiasm, sometimes even moved to tears. . . . The national fervour which we felt in our own small way was used by him as an instrument of our education. . . . It was because I had such a professor that history became my favourite subject.[3]

1. 7 September 1942. *Hitler's Table Talk, 1941–4* (London, 1953), pp. 698–9.
2. Quoted in Franz Jetzinger: *Hitler's Youth* (London, 1958), pp. 68–9.
3. *Mein Kampf*, p. 26.

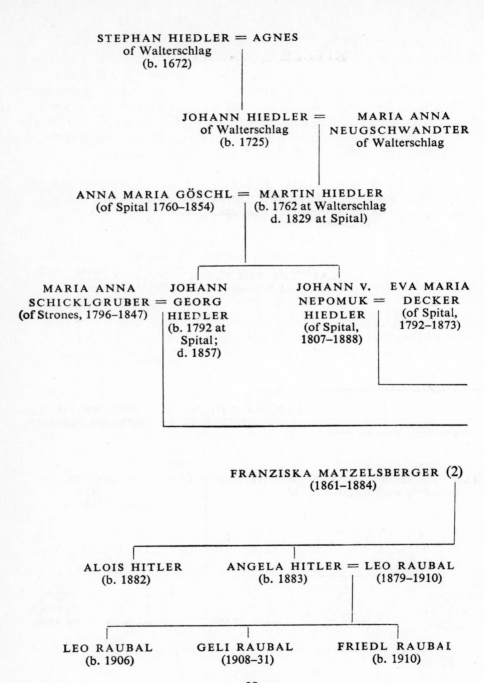

STEPHAN HIEDLER = AGNES
of Walterschlag
(b. 1672)

JOHANN HIEDLER =   MARIA ANNA
of Walterschlag   NEUGSCHWANDTER
(b. 1725)   of Walterschlag

ANNA MARIA GÖSCHL = MARTIN HIEDLER
(of Spital 1760–1854)   (b. 1762 at Walterschlag
                         d. 1829 at Spital)

MARIA ANNA   JOHANN   JOHANN V.   EVA MARIA
SCHICKLGRUBER = GEORG   NEPOMUK =   DECKER
(of Strones, 1796–1847) HIEDLER   HIEDLER   (of Spital,
                    (b. 1792 at   (of Spital,   1792–1873)
                    Spital;   1807–1888)
                    d. 1857)

FRANZISKA MATZELSBERGER (2)
(1861–1884)

ALOIS HITLER   ANGELA HITLER = LEO RAUBAL
(b. 1882)   (b. 1883)   (1879–1910)

LEO RAUBAL   GELI RAUBAL   FRIEDL RAUBAI
(b. 1906)   (1908–31)   (b. 1910)

28

HITLER'S ANCESTRY

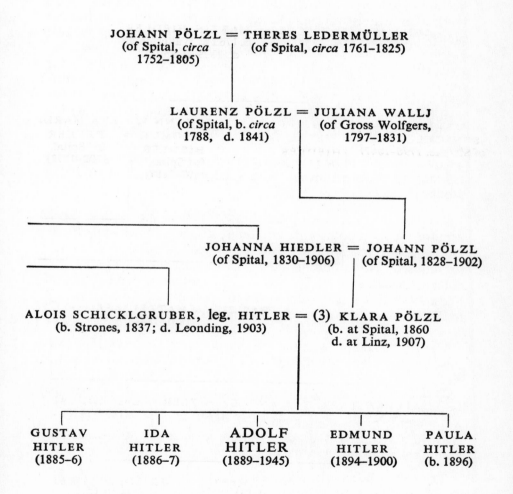

JOHANN PÖLZL = THERES LEDERMÜLLER
(of Spital, *circa*   (of Spital, *circa* 1761–1825)
1752–1805)

LAURENZ PÖLZL = JULIANA WALLJ
(of Spital, b. *circa*   (of Gross Wolfgers,
1788, d. 1841)   1797–1831)

JOHANNA HIEDLER = JOHANN PÖLZL
(of Spital, 1830–1906)   (of Spital, 1828–1902)

ALOIS SCHICKLGRUBER, leg. HITLER = (3) KLARA PÖLZL
(b. Strones, 1837; d. Leonding, 1903)   (b. at Spital, 1860
d. at Linz, 1907)

GUSTAV   IDA   ADOLF   EDMUND   PAULA
HITLER   HITLER   HITLER   HITLER   HITLER
(1885–6)   (1886–7)   (1889–1945)   (1894–1900)   (b. 1896)

When Adolf finally left school in 1905, his widowed mother, then forty-six, sold the house at Leonding. With the proceeds of the sale and a monthly pension of 140 kronen, she was not ill provided for and she moved to a small flat, first in the Humboldt-strasse in Linz, then in 1907 to Urfahr, a suburb of Linz. There is no doubt that Hitler was fond of his mother, but she had little control over her self-willed son who refused to settle down to earn his living and spent the next two years indulging in dreams of becoming an artist or architect, living at home, filling his sketch book with entirely unoriginal drawings and elaborating grandiose plans for the rebuilding of Linz. His one friend was August Kubizek, the son of a Linz upholsterer, eight months younger than Hitler, who provided a willing and awe-struck audience for the ambitions and enthusiasms which Hitler poured out in their walks round Linz. Together they visited the theatre where Hitler acquired a life-long passion for Wagner's opera. Wagnerian romanticism and vast dreams of his own success as an artist and Kubizek's as a musician filled his mind. He lived in a world of his own, content to let his mother provide for his needs, scornfully refusing to concern himself with such petty mundane affairs as money or a job.

A visit to Vienna in May and June 1906 fired him with enthusiasm for the splendour of its buildings, its art galleries and Opera. On his return to Linz, he was less inclined than ever to find a job for himself. His ambition now was to go back to Vienna and enter the Academy of Fine Arts. His mother was anxious and uneasy but finally capitulated. In the autumn of 1907 he set off for Vienna a second time with high hopes for the future.

His first attempt to enter the Academy in October 1907 was unsuccessful. The Academy's Classification List contains the entry:
The following took the test with insufficient results or were not admitted. . . .
Adolf Hitler, Braunau a.Inn, 20 April 1889.
German. Catholic. Father, civil servant. 4 classes in *Realschule*. Few heads. Test drawing unsatisfactory.[1]

The result, he says in *Mein Kampf*, came as a bitter shock. The Director advised him to try his talents in the direction of architecture: he was not cut out to be a painter. But Hitler refused to

1. Quoted in Konrad Heiden: *Der Führer* (London, 1944), p. 48.

admit defeat. Even his mother's illness (she was dying of cancer) did not bring him back to Linz. He returned only after her death (21 December 1907) in time for the funeral, and in February 1908 went back to Vienna, to resume his life as an 'art student'.

He was entitled to draw an orphan's pension and had the small savings left by his mother to fall back on. He was soon joined by his friend Kubizek whom he had prevailed upon to follow his example and seek a place at the Vienna Conservatoire. The two shared a room on the second floor of a house on the Stumpergasse, close to the West Station, in which there was hardly space for Kubizek's piano and Hitler's table.

Apart from Kubizek, Hitler lived a solitary life. He had no other friends. Women were attracted to him, but he showed complete indifference to them. Much of the time he spent dreaming or brooding. His moods alternated between abstracted preoccupation and outbursts of excited talk. He wandered for hours through the streets and parks, staring at buildings which he admired, or suddenly disappearing into the public library in pursuit of some new enthusiasm. Again and again, the two young men visited the Opera and the Burgtheater. But while Kubizek pursued his studies at the Conservatoire, Hitler was incapable of any disciplined or systematic work. He drew little, wrote more and even attempted to compose a music drama on the theme of Wieland the Smith. He had the artist's temperament without either talent, training, or creative energy.

In July 1908, Kubizek went back to Linz for the summer. A month later Hitler set out to visit two of his aunts in Spital. When they said good-bye, both young men expected to meet again in Vienna in the autumn. But when Kubizek returned to the capital, he could find no trace of his friend.

In mid-September Hitler had again applied for admission to the Academy of Art. This time, he was not even admitted to the examination. The Director advised him to apply to the School of Architecture, but there entry was barred by his lack of a school Leaving Certificate. Perhaps it was wounded pride that led him to avoid Kubizek. Whatever the reason, for the next five years he chose to bury himself in obscurity.

II

Vienna, at the beginning of 1909, was still an imperial city, capital of an Empire of fifty million souls stretching from the Rhine to the

Dniester, from Saxony to Montenegro. The aristrocratic baroque city of Mozart's time had become a great commercial and industrial centre with a population of two million people. Electric trams ran through its noisy and crowded streets. The massive, monumental buildings erected on the Ringstrasse in the last quarter of the nineteenth century reflected the prosperity and self-confidence of the Viennese middle class; the factories and poorer streets of the outer districts the rise of an industrial working class. To a young man of twenty, without a home, friends, or resources, it must have appeared a callous and unfriendly city: Vienna was no place to be without money or a job. The four years that now followed, from 1909 to 1913, Hitler himself says, were the unhappiest of his life. They were also in many ways the most important, the formative years in which his character and opinions were given definite shape.

Hitler speaks of his stay in Vienna as 'five years in which I had to earn my daily bread, first as a casual labourer then as a painter of little trifles.'[1] He writes with feeling of the poor boy from the country who discovers himself out of work. 'He loiters about and is hungry. Often he pawns or sells the last of his belongings. His clothes begin to get shabby – with the increasing poverty of his outward appearance he descends to a lower social level.'[2]

A little further on, Hitler gives another picture of his Vienna days. 'In the years 1909–10 I had so far improved my position that I no longer had to earn my daily bread as a manual labourer. I was now working independently as a draughtsman and painter in water-colours.' Hitler explains that he made very little money at this, but that he was master of his own time and felt that he was getting nearer to the profession he wanted to take up, that of an architect.

This is a very highly coloured account compared with the evidence of those who knew him then. Meagre though this is, it is enough to make nonsense of Hitler's picture of himself as a man who had once earned his living by his hands and then by hard work turned himself into an art student.

According to Konrad Heiden, who was the first man to piece together the scraps of independent evidence, in 1909, Hitler was obliged to give up the furnished room in which he had been living in the Simon Denk Gasse for lack of funds. In the summer he could sleep out, but with the coming of autumn he found a bed in a doss-house behind Meidling Station. At the end of the year,

1. *Mein Kampf*, p. 32.   2. ibid., p. 35.

Hitler moved to a hostel for men started by a charitable foundation at 27 Meldemannstrasse, in the 20th district of Vienna, over on the other side of the city, close to the Danube. Here he lived, for the remaining three years of his stay in Vienna, from 1910 to 1913.

A few others who knew Hitler at this time have been traced and questioned, amongst them a certain Reinhold Hanisch, a tramp from German Bohemia, who for a time knew Hitler well. Hanisch's testimony is partly confirmed by one of the few pieces of documentary evidence which have been discovered for the early years. For in 1910, after a quarrel, Hitler sued Hanisch for cheating him of a small sum of money, and the records of the Vienna police court have been published, including (besides Hitler's own affidavit) the statement of Siegfried Loffner, another inmate of the hostel in Meldemannstrasse who testified that Hanisch and Hitler always sat together and were friendly.

Hanisch describes his first meeting with Hitler in the doss-house in Meidling in 1909. 'On the very first day there sat next to the bed that had been allotted to me a man who had nothing on except an old torn pair of trousers – Hitler. His clothes were being cleaned of lice, since for days he had been wandering about without a roof and in a terribly neglected condition.'[1]

Hanisch and Hitler joined forces in looking for work; they beat carpets, carried bags outside the West Station, and did casual labouring jobs, on more than one occasion shovelling snow off the streets. As Hitler had no overcoat, he felt the cold badly. Then Hanisch had a better idea. He asked Hitler one day what trade he had learned. '"I am a painter", was the answer. Thinking that he was a house decorator, I said that it would surely be easy to make money at this trade. He was offended and answered that he was not that sort of painter, but an academician and an artist.' When the two moved to the Meldemannstrasse, 'we had to think out better ways of making money. Hitler proposed that we should fake pictures. He told me that already in Linz he had painted small landscapes in oil, had roasted them in an oven until they had become quite brown and had several times been successful in selling these pictures to traders as valuable old masters.' This sounds highly improbable, but in any case Hanisch, who had registered under another name as Walter Fritz, was afraid of the police. 'So I suggested to Hitler that it would be better to stay in an honest trade and paint postcards. I myself was to sell the

1. Quoted in Rudolf Olden: *Hitler the Pawn* (London, 1936), p. 45.

painted cards, we decided to work together and share the money we earned.'[1]

Hitler had enough money to buy a few cards, ink and paints. With these he produced little copies of views of Vienna, which Hanisch peddled in taverns and fairs, or to small traders who wanted something to fill their empty picture frames. In this way they made enough to keep them until, in the summer of 1910, Hanisch sold a copy which Hitler had made of a drawing of the Vienna Parliament for ten crowns. Hitler, who was sure it was worth far more – he valued it at fifty in his statement to the police – was convinced he had been cheated. When Hanisch failed to return to the hostel, Hitler brought a lawsuit against him which ended in Hanisch spending a week in prison and the break-up of their partnership.

This was in August 1910. For the remaining four years before the First World War, first in Vienna, later in Munich, Hitler continued to eke out a living in the same way. Some of Hitler's drawings, mostly stiff, lifeless copies of buildings in which his attempts to add human figures are a failure, were still to be found in Vienna in the 1930s, when they had acquired the value of collectors' pieces. More often he drew posters and crude advertisements for small shops – Teddy Perspiration Powder, Santa Claus selling coloured candles, or St Stefan's spire rising over a mountain of soap, with the signature 'A. Hitler' in the corner. Hitler himself later described these as years of great loneliness, in which his only contacts with other human beings were in the hostel where he continued to live and where, according to Hanisch, 'only tramps, drunkards, and such spent any time'.

After their quarrel Hanisch lost sight of Hitler, but he gives a description of Hitler as he knew him in 1910 at the age of twenty-one. He wore an ancient black overcoat, which had been given him by an old-clothes dealer in the hostel, a Hungarian Jew named Neumann, and which reached down over his knees. From under a greasy, black derby hat, his hair hung long over his coat collar. His thin and hungry face was covered with a black beard above which his large staring eyes were the one prominent feature. Altogether, Hanisch adds, 'an apparition such as rarely occurs among Christians'.[2]

From time to time Hitler had received financial help from his

1. Olden: p. 46.
2. Olden: p. 50; Heiden: *Der Führer*, p. 61.

aunt in Linz, Johanna Pölzl and, when she died in March 1911, it seems likely that he was left some small legacy. In May of that year his orphan's pension was stopped, but he still avoided any regular work.

Hanisch depicts him as lazy and moody, two characteristics which were often to reappear. He disliked regular work. If he earned a few crowns, he refused to draw for days and went off to a café to eat cream cakes and read newspapers. He had none of the common vices. He neither smoked nor drank and, according to Hanisch, was too shy and awkward to have any success with women. His passions were reading newspapers and talking politics. 'Over and over again,' Hanisch recalls, 'there were days on which he simply refused to work. Then he would hang around night shelters, living on the bread and soup that he got there, and discussing politics, often getting involved in heated controversies.'[1]

When he became excited in argument he would shout and wave his arms until the others in the room cursed him for disturbing them, or the porter came in to stop the noise. Sometimes people laughed at him, at other times they were oddly impressed. 'One evening,' Hanish relates, 'Hitler went to a cinema where Kellermann's *Tunnel* was being shown. In this piece an agitator appears who rouses the working masses by his speeches. Hitler almost went crazy. The impression it made on him was so strong that for days afterwards he spoke of nothing except the power of the spoken word.'[2] These outbursts of violent argument and denunciation alternated with moods of despondency.

Everyone who knew him was struck by the combination of ambition, energy, and indolence in Hitler. Hitler was not only desperately anxious to impress people but was full of clever ideas for making his fortune and fame – from water-divining to designing an aeroplane. In this mood he would talk exuberantly and begin to spend the fortune he was to make in anticipation, but he was incapable of the application and hard work needed to carry out his projects. His enthusiasm would flag, he would relapse into moodiness and disappear until he began to hare off after some new trick or short cut to success. His intellectual interests followed the same pattern. He spent much time in the public library, but his reading was indiscriminate and unsystematic. Ancient Rome, the Eastern religions, Yoga, Occultism, Hypnotism, Astrology, Protestantism, each in turn excited his interest

1. Olden: p. 51.   2. ibid.

for a moment. He started a score of jobs but failed to make anything of them and relapsed into the old hand-to-mouth existence, living by expedients and little spurts of activity, but never settling down to anything for long.

As time passed these habits became ingrained, and he became more eccentric, more turned in on himself. He struck people as 'queer', unbalanced. He gave rein to his hatreds – against the Jews, the priests, the Social Democrats, the Hapsburgs – without restraint. The few people with whom he had been friendly became tired of him, of his strange behaviour and wild talk. Neumann, the Jew, who had befriended him, was offended by the violence of his anti-Semitism; Kanya, who kept the hostel for men, thought him one of the oddest customers with whom he had had to deal. Yet these Vienna days stamped an indelible impression on his character and mind. 'During these years a view of life and a definite outlook on the world took shape in my mind. These became the granite basis of my conduct at that time. Since then I have extended that foundation very little, I have changed nothing in it . . . Vienna was a hard school for me, but it taught me the most profound lessons of my life.'[1] However pretentiously expressed, this is true. It is time to examine what these lessons were.

III

The idea of struggle is as old as life itself, for life is only preserved because other living things perish through struggle. . . . In this struggle, the stronger, the more able, win, while the less able, the weak, lose. Struggle is the father of all things. . . . It is not by the principles of humanity that man lives or is able to preserve himself above the animal world, but solely by means of the most brutal struggle. . . . If you do not fight for life, then life will never be won.[2]

This is the natural philosophy of the doss-house. In this struggle any trick or ruse, however unscrupulous, the use of any weapon or opportunity, however treacherous, are permissible. To quote another typical sentence from Hitler's speeches: 'Whatever goal man has reached is due to his originality plus his brutality.'[3] Astuteness; the ability to lie, twist, cheat and flatter; the elimination of sentimentality or loyalty in favour of ruthlessness, these were the qualities which enabled men to rise; above all, strength

1. *Mein Kampf*, pp. 32 and 116.
2. Hitler's speech at Kulmbach, 5 February 1928; G. W. Prange (ed.): *Hitler's Words* (Washington, 1944), p. 8.
3. Hitler at Chemnitz, 2 April 1928, ibid.

of will. Such were the principles which Hitler drew from his years in Vienna. Hitler never trusted anyone; he never committed himself to anyone, never admitted any loyalty. His lack of scruple later took by surprise even those who prided themselves on their unscrupulousness. He learned to lie with conviction and dissemble with candour. To the end he refused to admit defeat and still held to the belief that by the power of will alone he could transform events.

Distrust was matched by contempt. Men were moved by fear, greed, lust for power, envy, often by mean and petty motives. Politics, Hitler was later to conclude, is the art of knowing how to use these weaknesses for one's own ends. Already in Vienna Hitler admired Karl Lueger, the famous Burgomaster of Vienna and leader of the Christian Social Party, because 'he had a rare gift of insight into human nature and was very careful not to take men as something better than they were in reality.'[1] He felt particular contempt for the masses – 'everybody who properly estimates the political intelligence of the masses can easily see that this is not sufficiently developed to enable them to form general political judgements on their own account.'[2] Here again was material to be manipulated by a skilful politician. As yet Hitler had no idea of making a political career, but he spent a great deal of time reading and arguing politics, and what he learned was an important part of his political apprenticeship.

In the situation in which he found himself in Vienna, Hitler clung tenaciously to the conviction that he was better than the people with whom he was now driven to associate. 'Those among whom I passed my younger days belonged to the *petit bourgeois* class. . . . The ditch which separated that class, which is by no means well-off, from the manual labouring class is often deeper than people think. The reason for this division, which we may almost call enmity, lies in the fear that dominates a social group which has only just risen above the level of the manual labourer – a fear lest it may fall back into its old condition or at least be classed with the labourers. . . .'[3]

Although Hitler writes in *Mein Kampf* of the misery in which the Vienna working class lived at this time, it is evident from every line of the account that these conditions produced no feeling of sympathy in him. 'I do not know which appalled me most at that time: the economic misery of those who were then my companions, their crude customs and morals, or the low level of their

1. *Mein Kampf*, p. 94.　　2. ibid., p. 83.　　3. ibid., pp. 32–3.

intellectual culture.'[1] Least of all did he feel any sympathy with the attempts of the poor and the exploited to improve their position by their own efforts. Hitler's hatred was directed not so much against the rogues, beggars, bankrupt business men, and *déclassé* 'gentlemen' who were the flotsam and jetsam drifting in and out of the hostel in the Meldemannstrasse, as against the working men who belonged to organizations like the Social Democratic Party and the trade unions and who preached equality and the solidarity of the working classes. It was these, much more than the former, who threatened his claim to superiority. Solidarity was a virtue for which Hitler had no use. He passionately refused to join a trade union, or in any way to accept the status of a working man.

The whole ideology of the working-class movement was alien and hateful to him:

All that I heard had the effect of arousing the strongest antagonism in me. Everything was disparaged – the nation because it was held to be an invention of the capitalist class (how often I had to listen to that phrase!); the Fatherland, because it was held to be an instrument in the hand of the bourgeoisie for the exploitation of the working masses; the authority of the law, because this was a means of holding down the proletariat; religion, as a means of doping the people, so as to exploit them afterwards; morality, as a badge of stupid and sheepish docility. There was nothing that they did not drag in the mud. . . . Then I asked myself: are these men worthy to belong to a great people? The question was profoundly disturbing; for if the answer were 'Yes', then the struggle to defend one's nationality is no longer worth all the trouble and sacrifice we demand of our best elements if it be in the interest of such a rabble. On the other hand, if the answer had to be 'No', then our nation is poor indeed in men. During these days of mental anguish and deep meditation I saw before my mind the ever-increasing and menacing army of people who could no longer be reckoned as belonging to their own nation.[2]

Hitler found the solution of his dilemma in the 'discovery' that the working men were the victims of a deliberate system for corrupting and poisoning the popular mind, organized by the Social Democratic Party's leaders, who cynically exploited the distress of the masses for their own ends. Then came the crowning revelation: 'I discovered the relations existing between this destructive teaching and the specific character of a people, who up to that time had been almost unknown to me. Knowledge

1. *Mein Kampf*, p. 39.   2. ibid., pp. 46–7.

of the Jews is the only key whereby one may understand the inner nature and the real aims of Social Democracy.'[1]

There was nothing new in Hitler's anti-Semitism; it was endemic in Vienna, and everything he ever said or wrote about the Jews is only a reflection of the anti-Semitic periodicals and pamphlets he read in Vienna before 1914. In Linz there had been very few Jews – 'I do not remember ever having heard the word at home during my father's lifetime.' Even in Vienna Hitler had at first been repelled by the violence of the anti-Semitic Press. Then, 'one day, when passing through the Inner City, I suddenly encountered a phenomenon in a long caftan and wearing black sidelocks. My first thought was: is this a Jew? They certainly did not have this appearance in Linz, I watched the man stealthily and cautiously, but the longer I gazed at this strange countenance and examined it section by section, the more the question shaped itself in my brain: is this a German? I turned to books for help in removing my doubts. For the first time in my life I bought myself some anti-Semitic pamphlets for a few pence.'[2]

The language in which Hitler describes his discovery has the obscene taint to be found in most anti-Semitic literature: 'Was there any shady undertaking, any form of foulness, especially in cultural life, in which at least one Jew did not participate? On putting the probing knife carefully to that kind of abscess one immediately discovered, like a maggot in a putrescent body, a little Jew who was often blinded by the sudden light.'[3]

Especially characteristic of Viennese anti-Semitism was its sexuality. 'The black-haired Jewish youth lies in wait for hours on end, satanically glaring at and spying on the unsuspicious girl whom he plans to seduce, adulterating her blood and removing her from the bosom of her own people. ... The Jews were responsible for bringing negroes into the Rhineland with the ultimate idea of bastardizing the white race which they hate and thus lowering its cultural and political level so that the Jew might dominate.'[4] Elsewhere Hitler writes of 'the nightmare vision of the seduction of hundreds of thousands of girls by repulsive, crooked-legged Jew bastards'. More than one writer has suggested that some sexual experience – possibly the contraction of venereal disease – was at the back of Hitler's anti-Semitism.

In all the pages which Hitler devotes to the Jews in *Mein Kampf* he does not bring forward a single fact to support his wild

1. *Mein Kampf*, p. 55.   2. ibid., p. 59.
3. ibid., p. 60.   4. ibid., p. 273.

assertions. This was entirely right, for Hitler's anti-Semitism bore no relation to facts, it was pure fantasy: to read these pages is to enter the world of the insane, a world peopled by hideous and distorted shadows. The Jew is no longer a human being, he has become a mythical figure, a grimacing, leering devil invested with infernal powers, the incarnation of evil, into which Hitler projects all that he hates and fears – and desires. Like all obsessions, the Jew is not a partial, but a total explanation. The Jew is everywhere, responsible for everything – the Modernism in art and music Hitler disliked; pornography and prostitution; the antinational criticism of the Press; the exploitation of the masses by Capitalism, and its reverse, the exploitation of the masses by Socialism; not least for his own failure to get on. 'Thus I finally discovered who were the evil spirits leading our people astray. . . . My love for my own people increased correspondingly. Considering the satanic skill which these evil counsellors displayed, how could their unfortunate victims be blamed? . . . The more I came to know the Jew, the easier it was to excuse the workers.'[1]

Behind all this, Hitler soon convinced himself, lay a Jewish world conspiracy to destroy and subdue the Aryan peoples, as an act of revenge for their own inferiority. Their purpose was to weaken the nation by fomenting social divisions and class conflict, and by attacking the values of race, heroism, struggle, and authoritarian rule in favour of the false internationalist, humanitarian, pacifist, materialist ideals of democracy. 'The Jewish doctrine of Marxism repudiates the aristocratic principle of nature and substitutes for it and the eternal privilege of force and energy, numerical mass and its dead weight. Thus it denies the individual worth of the human personality, impugns the teaching that nationhood and race have a primary significance, and by doing this takes away the very foundations of human existence and human civilization.'[2]

In Hitler's eyes the inequality of individuals and of races was one of the laws of Nature. This poor wretch, often half-starved, without a job, family, or home, clung obstinately to any belief that would bolster up the claim of his own superiority. He belonged by right, he felt, to the *Herrenmenschen*. To preach equality was to threaten the belief which kept him going, that he was different from the labourers, the tramps, the Jews, and the Slavs with whom he rubbed shoulders in the streets.

1. *Mein Kampf*, pp. 63–4.   2. ibid., pp. 65–6.

Hitler had no use for any democratic institution: free speech, free press, or parliament. During the earlier part of his time in Vienna he had sometimes attended the sessions of the Reichsrat, the representative assembly of the Austrian half of the Empire, and he devotes fifteen pages of *Mein Kampf* to expressing his scorn for what he saw. Parliamentary democracy reduced government to political jobbery, it put a premium on mediocrity and was inimical to leadership, encouraged the avoidance of responsibility, and sacrificed decisions to party compromises. 'The majority represents not only ignorance but cowardice. ... The majority can never replace the man.'[1]

All his life Hitler was irritated by discussion. In the arguments into which he was drawn in the hostel for men or in cafés he showed no self-control in face of contradiction or debate. He began to shout and shower abuse on his opponents, with an hysterical note in his voice. It was precisely the same pattern of uncontrolled behaviour he displayed when he came to supreme power and found himself crossed or contradicted. This authoritarian temper developed with the exercise of power, but it was already there in his twenties, the instinct of tyranny.

Belief in equality between races was an even greater offence in Hitler's eyes than belief in equality between individuals. He had already become a passionate German nationalist while still at school. In Austria-Hungary this meant even more than it meant in Germany itself, and the fanatical quality of Hitler's nationalism throughout his life reflects his Austrian origin.

For several hundred years the Germans of Austria played the leading part in the politics and cultural life of Central Europe. Until 1871 there had been no single unified German state. Germans had lived under the rule of a score of different states – Bavaria, Prussia, Württemberg, Hanover, Saxony – loosely grouped together in the Holy Roman Empire, and then, after 1815, in the German Federation. Both in the Empire and in the Federation Austria had enjoyed a traditional hegemony as the leading German Power. In the middle of the nineteenth century it was still Vienna, not Berlin, which ranked as the first of German cities. Moreover, the Hapsburgs not only enjoyed a pre-eminent position among the German states, but also ruled over wide lands inhabited by many different peoples.

On both counts the Germans of Vienna and the Austrian lands,

1. *Mein Kampf*, p. 81.

who identified themselves with the Hapsburgs, looked on themselves as an imperial race, enjoying a position of political privilege and boasting of a cultural tradition which few other peoples in Europe could equal. From the middle of the nineteenth century, however, this position was first challenged and then undermined.

In place of the German Federation a unified German state was established by Prussia, from which the Germans of Austria were excluded. Prussia defeated Austria at Sadowa in 1866, and thereafter the new German Empire with its capital at Berlin increasingly took the place hitherto occupied by Austria and Vienna as the premier German state.

At the same time the pre-eminence of the Germans within the Hapsburg Empire itself was challenged, first by the Italians, who secured their independence in the 1860s; then by the Magyars of Hungary, to whom equality had to be conceded in 1867; finally by the Slav peoples. The growth of the demand for equal rights among the Slavs and other subject peoples was slower than with the Magyars, and uneven in its development. But especially in Bohemia and Moravia, where the most advanced of the Slav peoples, the Czechs, lived, it was bitterly resented by the Germans and fiercely resisted. This conflict of the nationalities dominated Austrian politics from 1870 to the break-up of the Empire in 1918.

In this conflict Hitler had no patience with concessions. The Germans should rule the Empire, at least the Austrian half of it, with an authoritarian and centralized administration; there should be only one official language – German – and the schools and universities should be used 'to inculcate a feeling of common citizenship', an ambiguous expression for Germanization. The representative assembly of the Reichsrat, in which the Germans (only thirty-five per cent of the population of Austria) were permanently outnumbered, should be suppressed. Here was a special reason for hatred of the Social Democratic Party, which refused to follow the nationalist lead of the Pan-Germans, and instead fostered class conflicts at the expense of national unity.

In September 1938, at the time of the Sudeten crisis, Hitler said in a newspaper interview: 'The Czechs have none of the characteristics of a nation, whether from the standpoint of ethnology, strategy, economics, or language. To set an intellectually inferior handful of Czechs to rule over minorities belonging to races like the Germans, Poles, Hungarians, with a thousand years of culture behind them, was a work of folly and ignorance.'[1] This was a view which Hitler first learned in Austria before 1914, and indeed the whole Czech crisis of 1938–9 was part of an old quarrel rooted deep in the history of the Hapsburg Empire from which Hitler came.

The influence of his Austrian origins is even more obvious in the case of the *Anschluss*, the incorporation of Austria in the German Reich, which Hitler carried out at the beginning of 1938. Long before 1914 extreme German nationalists in Austria had begun to talk openly of the break-up of the Hapsburg Empire and the reunion of the Germans of Austria with the German Empire. Habsburg policy in face of the national conflicts which divided their peoples had been uncertain and vacillating. To the Pan-German extremists this appeared as a betrayal of the German cause. In *Mein Kampf* Hitler asked:

How could one remain a faithful subject of the House of Hapsburg, whose past history and present conduct proved it to be ready ever and always to betray the interests of the German people? . . . The German Austrian had come to feel in the very depth of his being that the historical mission of the House of Hapsburg had come to an end. . . . Therefore I welcomed every movement that might lead towards the final disruption of that impossible State which had decreed that it would stamp out the German character in ten millions of people, this Babylonian Empire. That would mean the liberating of my German Austrian people and only then would it become possible for them to be reunited to the Motherland.[2]

When Hitler returned to Vienna after the *Anschluss* had been carried out and the dream of a Greater Germany which Bismarck had rejected had at last been fulfilled, he said with a touch of genuine exultation: 'I believe that it was God's will to send a boy from here into the Reich, to let him grow up and to raise him to be the leader of the nation so that he could lead back his homeland into the Reich.'[3] In March 1938, the Austrian-born Chancellor of Germany reversed the decision which Bismarck, a Prussian-born Chancellor, had made in the 1860s when he excluded the German Austrians from the new German Reich. The Babylonian captivity was at an end.

1. Interview with G. Ward Price, published in the *Daily Mail*, 19 September 1938.
2. *Mein Kampf*, pp. 26, 91, and 44.
3. Hitler's speech in Vienna, 9 April 1938, in Norman Baynes (ed.): *The Speeches of Adolf Hitler*, 2 vols. (Oxford, 1942); vol. ii, p. 1,457 (hereafter referred to as Baynes).

IV

The political ideas and programme which Hitler picked up in Vienna were entirely unoriginal. They were the clichés of radical and Pan-German gutter politics, the stock-in-trade of the anti-semitic and nationalist Press. The originality was to appear in Hitler's grasp of how to create a mass-movement and secure power on the basis of these ideas. Here, too, although he took no active part in politics, he owed much to observations drawn from his years in Vienna.

The three parties which interested Hitler were the Austrian Social Democrats, Georg von Schönerer's Pan-German Nationalists, and Karl Lueger's Christian Social Party.

From the Social Democrats Hitler derived the idea of a mass party and mass propaganda. In *Mein Kampf* he describes the impression made on him when 'I gazed on the interminable ranks, four abreast, of Viennese workmen parading at a mass demonstration. I stood dumb-founded for almost two hours, watching this enormous human dragon which slowly uncoiled itself before me.'[1]

Studying the Social Democratic Press and Party speeches, Hitler reached the conclusion that: 'the psyche of the broad masses is accessible only to what is strong and uncompromising. . . . The masses of the people prefer the ruler to the suppliant and are filled with a stronger sense of mental security by a teaching that brooks no rival than by a teaching which offers them a liberal choice. They have very little idea of how to make such a choice and thus are prone to feel that they have been abandoned. Whereas they feel very little shame at being terrorized intellectually and are scarcely conscious of the fact that their freedom as human beings is impudently abused. . . . I also came to understand that physical intimidation has its significance for the mass as well as the individual. . . . For the successes which are thus obtained are taken by the adherents as a triumphant symbol of the righteousness of their own cause; while the beaten opponent very often loses faith in the effectiveness of any further resistance.'[2]

From Schönerer Hitler took his extreme German Nationalism, his anti-Socialism, his anti-Semitism, his hatred of the Hapsburgs and his programme of reunion with Germany. But he learned as much from the mistakes which Schönerer and the Nationalists

1. *Mein Kampf*, p. 47.　　2. ibid., pp. 48–50.

committed in their political tactics. For Schönerer, Hitler believed, made three cardinal errors.

The Nationalists failed to grasp the importance of the social problem, directing their attention to the middle classes and neglecting the masses. They wasted their energy in a parliamentary struggle and failed to establish themselves as the leaders of a great movement. Finally they made the mistake of attacking the Catholic Church and split their forces instead of concentrating them. 'The art of leadership,' Hitler wrote, 'consists of consolidating the attention of the people against a single adversary and taking care that nothing will split up this attention. . . . The leader of genius must have the ability to make different opponents appear as if they belonged to one category.'[1]

It was in the third party, the Christian Socialists, and their remarkable leader, Karl Lueger, that Hitler found brilliantly displayed that grasp of political tactics, the lack of which hampered the success of the Nationalists. Lueger had made himself Burgomaster of Vienna – in many ways the most important elective post in Austria – and by 1907 the Christian Socialists under his leadership had become the strongest party in the Austrian parliament. Hitler saw much to criticize in Lueger's programme. His anti-Semitism was based on religious and economic, not on racial, grounds ('I decide who is a Jew,' Lueger once said), and he rejected the intransigent nationalism of the Pan-Germans, seeking to preserve and strengthen the Hapsburg State with its mixture of nationalities. But Hitler was prepared to overlook even this in his admiration for Lueger's leadership.

The strength of Lueger's following lay in the lower middle class of Vienna, the small shopkeepers, business men and artisans, the petty officials and municipal employees. 'He devoted the greatest part of his political activity', Hitler noted, 'to the task of winning over those sections of the population whose existence was in danger.'[2]

Years later Hitler was to show a brilliant appreciation of the importance of these same classes in German politics. From the beginning Lueger understood the importance both of social problems and of appealing to the masses. 'Their leaders recognized the value of propaganda on a large scale and they were veritable virtuosos in working up the spiritual instincts of the broad masses of their electorate.'[3]

1. *Mein Kampf*, p. 110.   2. ibid., p. 95.   3. ibid., p. 111.

Finally, instead of quarrelling with the Church, Lueger made it his ally and used to the full the traditional loyalty to crown and altar. In a sentence which again points forward to his later career, Hitler remarks: 'He was quick to adopt all available means for winning the support of long-established institutions, so as to be able to derive the greatest possible advantage for his movement from those old sources of power.'[1]

Hitler concludes his comparison of Schönerer's and Lueger's leadership with these words:

If the Christian Socialist Party, together with its shrewd judgement in regard to the worth of the popular masses, had only judged rightly also on the importance of the racial problem – which was properly grasped by the Pan-German movement – and if this party had been really nationalist; or if the Pan-German leaders, on the other hand, in addition to their correct judgement of the Jewish problem and of the national idea, had adopted the practical wisdom of the Christian-Socialist Party, and particularly their attitude towards Socialism – then a movement would have developed which might have successfully altered the course of German destiny.[2]

Here already is the idea of a party which should be both national and socialist. This was written a dozen years after he had left Vienna, and it would be an exaggeration to suppose that Hitler had already formulated clearly the ideas he set out in *Mein Kampf* in the middle of the 1920s. None the less the greater part of the experience on which he drew was already complete when he left Vienna, and to the end Hitler bore the stamp of his Austrian origins.

V

Hitler left Vienna for good in the spring of 1913. He was then twenty-four years old, awkward, moody and reserved, yet nursing a passion of hatred and fanaticism which from time to time broke out in a torrent of excited words. Years of failure had laid up a deep store of resentment in him, but had failed to weaken the conviction of his own superiority.

In *Mein Kampf* Hitler speaks of leaving Vienna in the spring of 1912, but the Vienna police records report him as living there until May 1913. Hitler is so careless about dates and facts in his book that the later date seems more likely to be correct. Hitler is equally evasive about the reasons which led him to leave. He writes in general terms of his dislike of Vienna and the state of affairs in Austria:

1. *Mein Kampf*, p. 95.   2. ibid., pp. 113–14.

My inner aversion to the Hapsburg State was increasing daily. . . . This motley of Czechs, Poles, Hungarians, Ruthenians, Serbs and Croats, and always the bacillus which is the solvent of human society, the Jew, here and there and everywhere – the whole spectacle was repugnant to me. . . . The longer I lived in that city the stronger became my hatred for the promiscuous swarm of foreign peoples which had begun to batten on that old nursery ground of German culture. All these considerations intensified my yearning to depart for that country for which my heart had been secretly longing since the days of my youth. I hoped that one day I might be able to make my mark as an architect and that I could devote my talents to the service of my country. A final reason was that I hoped to be among those who lived and worked in that land from which the movement should be launched, the object of which would be the fulfilment of what my heart had always longed for, the reunion of the country in which I was born with our common fatherland, the German Empire.[1]

All this, we may be sure, is true enough, but it gives no specific reason why, on one day rather than another, Hitler decided to go to the station, buy a ticket and at last leave the city he had come to detest.

The most likely explanation is that Hitler was anxious to escape military service, for which he had failed to report each year since 1910. Inquiries were being made by the police, and he may have found it necessary to slip over the frontier. Eventually he was located in Munich and ordered to present himself for examination at Linz. The correspondence between Hitler and the authorities at Linz has been published.[2] Hitler's explanation, with its half truths, lies, evasions and its characteristic mixture of the brazen and the sly, ranks as the first of a long series of similar 'explanations' with which the world was to become only too familiar. Hitler denied that he had left Vienna to avoid conscription, and asked, on account of his lack of means, to be allowed to report at Salzburg, which was nearer to Munich than Linz. His request was agreed to, and he duly presented himself for examination at Salzburg on 5 February 1914. He was rejected for military or auxiliary service on the grounds of poor health, and the incident was closed. But after the Germans marched into Austria in 1938 a very thorough search was made in Linz for the records connected with Hitler's military service and Hitler was furious when the Gestapo failed to discover them.

It was in the May of 1913 that Hitler moved to Munich, across

1. *Mein Kampf*, pp. 114–15.
2. By Franz Jetzinger, op. cit., c. 6.

the German frontier. He found lodgings with a tailor's family, by the name of Popp, which lived in the Schleissheimerstrasse, a poor quarter near the barracks. In retrospect, Hitler described this as 'by far the happiest time of my life. . . . I came to love that city more than any other place known to me. A German city. How different from Vienna.'[1]

It may be doubted if this represented Hitler's feelings at the time. His life followed much the same pattern as before. His dislike of hard work and regular employment had by now hardened into a habit. He made a precarious living by drawing advertisements and posters, or peddling sketches to dealers. He was perpetually short of money. Despite his enthusiasm for the architecture and paintings of Munich, he was not a step nearer making a career than he had been on the day when he was turned down by the Vienna Academy. In his new surroundings he appears to have lost touch with his relations, and to have made few, if any, friends.

The shadowy picture that emerges from the reminiscences of the few people who knew him in Munich is once again of a man living in his own world of fantasy. He gives the same impression of eccentricity and lack of balance, brooding and muttering to himself over his extravagant theories of race, anti-Semitism, and anti-Marxism, then bursting out in wild, sarcastic diatribes. He spent much time in cafés and beer-cellars, devouring the newspapers and arguing about politics. Frau Popp, his landlady, speaks of him as a voracious reader, an impression Hitler more than once tries to create in *Mein Kampf*. Yet nowhere is there any indication of the works he read. Nietzsche, Houston Stewart Chamberlain, Schopenhauer, Wagner, Gobineau? Perhaps. But Hitler's own comment on reading is illuminating. 'Reading had probably a different significance for me from that which it has for the average run of our so-called "intellectuals." I know people who read interminably, book after book, from page to page. . . . Of course they "know" an immense amount, but . . . they have not the faculty of distinguishing between what is useful and useless in a book; so that they may retain the former in their minds and if possible skip over the latter. . . . Reading is not an end in itself, but a means to an end. . . . One who has cultivated the art of reading will instantly discern, in a book or journal or pamphlet, what ought to be remembered

1. *Mein Kampf*, p. 117.

because it meets one's personal needs or is of value as general knowledge.'[1]

This is a picture of a man with a closed mind, reading only to confirm what he already believes, ignoring what does not fit in with his preconceived scheme. 'Otherwise,' Hitler says, 'only a confused jumble of chaotic notions will result from all this reading. . . . Such a person never succeeds in turning his knowledge to practical account when the opportune moment arrives; for his mental equipment is not ordered with a view to meeting the demands of everyday life.'[2] Hitler was speaking the truth when he said: 'Since then (i.e. since his days in Vienna) I have extended that foundation very little, and I have changed nothing in it.'[3]

Hitler retained his passionate interest in politics. He was indignant at the ignorance and indifference of people in Munich to the situation of the Germans in Austria. Since 1879 the two states, the German Empire and the Hapsburg Monarchy, had been bound together by a military alliance, which remained the foundation of German foreign policy up to the defeat of 1918. Hitler felt that this predisposed most Germans to refuse to listen to the exaggerated accounts he gave of the 'desperate' position of the German Austrians in the conflict of nationalities within the Monarchy.

Hitler's objection to the alliance of Germany and Austria was twofold. It crippled the Austrians in their resistance to what he regarded as the deliberate anti-German policy of the Hapsburgs. At the same time, for Germany herself it represented a dangerous commitment to the support of a state which, he was convinced, was on the verge of disintegration. Hitler would have agreed with the view expressed by Ludendorff in his memoirs: 'A Jew in Radom once said to one of my officers that he could not understand why so strong and vital a body as Germany should ally itself with a corpse. He was right.'[4]

When Franz Ferdinand was assassinated by Serbian students, at Sarajevo on 28 June 1914, Hitler's first reaction was confused. For, in his eyes, it was Franz Ferdinand, the heir to the Hapsburg throne, who had been more responsible than anyone else for that policy of concessions to the Slav peoples of the Monarchy which roused the anger of the German nationalists in Austria. But, as events moved towards the outbreak of a general European war, Hitler brushed aside his doubts. At least Austria would be

1. *Mein Kampf*, pp. 42–3.   2. ibid.   3. ibid., p. 32.
4. General Ludendorff: *My War Memoirs* (London, n.d.), vol. I, p. 117.

compelled to fight, and could not, as he had always feared, betray her ally Germany. In any case, 'I believed that it was not a case of Austria fighting to get satisfaction from Serbia, but rather a case of Germany fighting for her own existence – the German nation for its own to be or not to be, for its freedom and for its future. ... For me, as for every other German, the most memorable period of my life now began. Face to face with that mighty struggle all the past fell away into oblivion.'[1]

There were other, deeper and more personal reasons for his satisfaction. War meant to Hitler something more than the chance to express his nationalist ardour, it offered the opportunity to slough off the frustration, failure, and resentment of the past six years. Here was an escape from the tension and dissatisfaction of a lonely individuality into the excitement and warmth of a close, disciplined, collective life, in which he could identify himself with the power and purpose of a great organization. 'The war of 1914', he wrote in *Mein Kampf*, 'was certainly not forced on the masses; it was even desired by the whole people' – a remark which illustrates at least this man's state of mind. 'For me these hours came as a deliverance from the distress that had weighed upon me during the days of my youth. I am not ashamed to acknowledge today that I was carried away by the enthusiasm of the moment and that I sank down upon my knees and thanked Heaven out of the fullness of my heart for the favour of having been permitted to live in such a time.'[2]

On 1 August Hitler was in the cheering, singing crowd which gathered on the Odeons Platz to listen to the proclamation declaring war. In a chance photograph that has been preserved his face is clearly recognizable, his eyes excited and exultant; it is the face of a man who has come home at last. Two days later he addressed a formal petition to King Ludwig III of Bavaria, asking to be allowed to volunteer, although of Austrian nationality, for a Bavarian regiment. The reply granted his request. 'I opened the document with trembling hands; no words of mine can describe the satisfaction I felt. ... Within a few days I was wearing that uniform which I was not to put off again for nearly six years.'[3]

Together with a large number of other volunteers he was enrolled in the 1st Company of the 16th Bavarian Reserve Infantry

1. *Mein Kampf*, pp. 146–7.   2. ibid., p. 145.
3. ibid., p. 147.

Regiment, known from its original commander as the List Regiment. Another volunteer in the same regiment was Rudolf Hess; the regimental clerk was a Sergeant-major Max Amann, later to become business manager of the Nazi Party's paper and of the Party publishing house. After a period of initial training in Munich, they spent several weeks at Lechfeld, and then, on 21 October 1914, entrained for the Front.

After two days' journey they reached Lille and were sent up into the line as reinforcements for the 6th Bavarian Division of the Bavarian Crown Prince Rupprecht's VIth Army. Hitler's first experience of fighting was in one of the fiercest and most critical engagements of the war, the First Battle of Ypres, when the British succeeded in stemming an all-out effort by the Germans to burst through to the Channel coast. For four days and nights the List Regiment was in the thick of the fighting with the British round Becelaere and Gheluvelt. In a letter to his old Munich landlord, the tailor Herr Popp, Hitler reported that when they were pulled out of the line and sent into rest billets at Werwick, the regiment had been reduced in four days from three thousand five hundred to six hundred men; only thirty officers were left and four companies had to be broken up.

Throughout the war Hitler served as a *Meldegänger*, a runner whose job was to carry messages between Company and Regimental H.Q. His two closest comrades were Ernst Schmidt – one of the sources for this period of his life – and another *Meldegänger* called Bachmann, who was later killed in Rumania. Although Hitler was not actually in the trenches, there is little doubt that his was a dangerous enough job, and for the greater part of four years he was at the Front or not far in the rear.

In 1915, after a period at Tourcoing, the List Regiment was moved up towards Neuve Chapelle, again opposite British troops. In 1916 they took part in the heavy fighting on the Somme, and in October found themselves near Bapaume. Here on 7 October Hitler was wounded in the leg, and was sent back to Germany for the first time for two years.

After a period in hospital at Beelitz, near Berlin, and at Munich with the Reserve battalion of his regiment, he returned to the Front at the beginning of March 1917, now promoted to lance-corporal. He was in time to take part in the later stages of the Battle of Arras and in the Third Battle of Ypres in the summer. After two months at Hochstadt, in Alsace, the List Regiment was back in the line on the Aisne, near Lizy, for the winter. With the

rest of the regiment Hitler went forward in the last great German offensive in the spring of 1918.

In October 1918, the List Regiment found itself back near
Werwick, south of Ypres. During the night of 13–14 October the
British opened a gas attack. Hitler was caught on a hill south of
Werwick and his eyes were affected. By the time he got back to
Rear H.Q. he could no longer see. On the morning of 14 October
he collapsed and, temporarily blinded, was put into a hospital
train and sent back to a military hospital at Pasewalk, in Pomerania, not far from Stettin. He was still there, recovering from the
injury to his eyes, when the war ended with the capitulation of
11 November.

VI

What sort of a soldier was Hitler? As early as December 1914, he
had been awarded the Iron Cross, Second Class, and when Hitler,
in March 1932, brought a lawsuit against a newspaper which
had accused him of cowardice, his former commanding officer,
Lieutenant-Colonel Engelhardt, testified to his bravery in the
fighting of November 1914, when the regiment had first gone into
action. Much more interesting is the Iron Cross, First Class, an
uncommon decoration for a corporal, which Hitler was awarded
in 1918. The most varied and improbable accounts have been
given of the action for which he won this. The date on which he
received the award was 4 August 1918, but dates ranging over a
period from the autumn of 1915 to the summer of 1918 have been
suggested for the exploit for which it was given. According to one
witness, single-handed he took prisoner fifteen (others say ten or
twelve) Frenchmen; according to another they were Englishmen.
The official history of the List Regiment says nothing at all.
Whatever the occasion, it was certainly a decoration of which
Hitler was proud and which he habitually wore after he had
become Chancellor.

In view of his long service and the shortage of officers in the
German Army in the last months of the war, the fact that Hitler
never rose above the rank of corporal aroused curiosity and was
much discussed in the German Press before 1933. There is no
evidence that Hitler ever applied or was eager for promotion to the
rank of non-commissioned officer, leave alone a commission. He
appears to have been content with the job he had. It is probable,
also, that the impression of eccentricity which he continued to give

was no recommendation. Hans Mend, another of Hitler's fellow-soldiers in the List Regiment, wrote of him as 'a peculiar fellow. He sat in the corner of our mess holding his head between his hands, in deep contemplation. Suddenly he would leap up, and, running about excitedly, say that in spite of our big guns victory would be denied us, for the invisible foes of the German people were a greater danger than the biggest cannon of the enemy.' This led to violent attacks on the Marxists and Jews, in the old style of the Vienna hostel for men. On other occasions, Mend recalls, 'he sat in a corner, with his helmet on his head, buried deep in thought, and none of us was able to rouse him from his listlessness.'[1]

While not unpopular with his comrades, they felt that he did not share their interests or attitude to the war. He received no letters, no parcels from home. He did not care about leave or women. He was silent when the others grumbled about the time they had to spend in the trenches or the hardships. 'We all cursed him and found him intolerable. There was this white crow among us that didn't go along with us when we damned the war.'[2]

The few photographs of this time seem to bear this out – a solemn pale face, prematurely old, with staring eyes. He took the war seriously, feeling personally responsible for what happened and identifying himself with the failure or success of German arms. These were not endearing qualities, but they do not detract from Hitler's good record as a soldier, at least as brave as the next man and a good deal more conscientious.

Many years afterwards Hitler would still refer to 'the stupendous impression produced upon me by the war – the greatest of all experiences. For, that individual interest – the interest of one's own ego – could be subordinated to the common interest – that the great, heroic struggle of our people demonstrated in overwhelming fashion.'[3] Like many other Germans, Hitler regarded the comradeship, discipline and excitement of life at the Front as vastly more attractive than the obscurity, aimlessness, and dull placidity of peace. This was particularly true of Hitler, for he had neither family, wife, job, nor future to which to return: there was much greater warmth and friendliness in the orderlies' mess than he had known since he left Linz. This was his world: here he had a secure place such as he had never found in Vienna or

1. Olden: pp. 70–1.
2. Heiden: *Der Führer*, p. 74.
3. Speech at Hamburg, 17 August 1934. (Baynes: vol. I, p. 97).

Munich. In the years after the war it was from ex-servicemen like this who felt more at home in a uniform, living in a mess or barracks, men who could never settle down into the monotonous routine of life in 'Civvy Street' that the Freikorps,[1] the Nazis, and a score of extremist parties recruited their members. The war, and the impact of war upon the individual lives of millions of Germans, were among the essential conditions for the rise of Hitler and the Nazi Party.

It is surprising, in view of his later pretensions as a strategist in the Second World War, that Hitler has nothing to say in *Mein Kampf* about the conduct of the military operations. At the time he wrote his book he was still too anxious to secure the favour of the Army leaders to indulge in the attitude of contempt he later adopted towards the generals. In any case, Hitler followed the conventional Nationalist line of argument: the German Army had never been defeated, the war had been lost by the treachery and cowardice of the leaders at home, the capitulation of November 1918 was a failure of political not military leadership.

At the time of his stay in hospital at Beelitz and his visit to Munich (October 1916–March 1917) Hitler became indignant at the contrast between the spirit of the Army at the Front and the poor morale and lack of discipline at home. There he encountered shirkers who boasted of dodging military service, grumbling, profiteering, the black market, and other familiar accompaniments of wartime civilian life; it was with relief that he returned to the Front. Hitler had no use for a government which tolerated political discussion, covert anti-war propaganda and strikes in time of war. In *Mein Kampf* his contempt for parliamentary deputies and journalists is lavish: 'All decent men who had anything to say, said it point-blank in the enemy's face; or, failing this, kept their mouths shut and did their duty elsewhere. Uncompromising military measures should have been adopted to root out the evil. Parties should have been abolished and the Reichstag brought to its senses at the point of the bayonet, if necessary. It would have been still better if the Reichstag had been dissolved immediately.'[2]

This is no more than the common talk of any one of the ex-

1. Illegal armed bands which were an important feature of German life after the war and which were given covert support by the Army as a means of evading the demilitarization imposed by the Treaty of Versailles.

2. *Mein Kampf*, pp. 149 and 151.

servicemen's (*Frontkämpfer*) associations which sprang up after the war and comforted their wounded pride by blaming Socialist agitators, Jews, profiteers, and democratic politicians for the 'shameful treachery' of the 'Stab in the Back'. But Hitler adds a characteristic twist which shows once more the originality of his ideas as soon as he was faced with a question of political leadership. It was not enough, he concluded, to use force to suppress the Socialist and anti-national agitation to which he attributed the sapping of Germany's will to go on fighting. 'If force be used to combat a spiritual power, that force remains a defensive measure only, so long as the wielders of it are not the standard bearers and apostles of a new spiritual doctrine . . . It is only in the struggle between *Weltanschauungen*[1] that physical force, consistently and ruthlessly applied, will eventually turn the scale in its own favour.'[2] This was the reason for the failure of every attempt to combat Marxism hitherto, including the failure of Bismarck's anti-socialist legislation – 'it lacked the basis of a new *Weltanschauung*'.

Out of this grew the idea of creating a new movement, something more than a parliamentary party, which would fight Social Democracy with its own weapons. For power lay with the masses, and if the hold of the Jew-ridden Marxist parties on their allegiance was to be broken, a substitute had to be found. The key, Hitler became convinced, lay in propaganda, and the lesson Hitler had already drawn from the Social Democrats and Lueger's Christian Socialists in Vienna was completed by his observation of the success of English propaganda during the war, by contrast with the failure of German attempts. The chapter on War Propaganda in *Mein Kampf* is a masterly exercise in that psychological insight which was to prove Hitler's greatest gift as a politician.

There were two themes on which Hitler constantly played in the years that followed the war: Man of the People, and Unknown Soldier of the First World War. When he spoke to the first Congress of German Workers in Berlin on 10 May 1933, he assured them: 'Fate, in a moment of caprice or perhaps fulfilling the designs of Providence, cast me into the great mass of the people, amongst common folk. I myself was a labouring man for years in the building trade and had to earn my own bread. And for a

1. A favourite word of Hitler's, meaning: 'World view' or 'Philosophy of life'.
2. *Mein Kampf*, p. 153.

second time I took my place once again as an ordinary soldier amongst the masses.'[1] These were the twin foundations of his demagogy and, in however garbled a fashion, they correspond to the two formative experiences of his life, the years in Vienna and Munich, and the years at the Front.

Those years between the end of 1908 and the end of 1918 had hardened him, taught him to be self-reliant, confirmed his belief in himself, toughened the power of his will. From them he emerged with a stock of fixed ideas and prejudices which were to alter little in the rest of his life: hatred of the Jews; contempt for the ideals of democracy, internationalism, equality, and peace; a preference for authoritarian forms of government; an intolerant nationalism; a rooted belief in the inequality of races and individuals; and faith in the heroic virtues of war. Most important of all, in the experiences of those years he had already hit upon a conception of how political power was to be secured and exercised which, when fully developed, was to open the way to a career without parallel in history. Much of what he had learned remained to be formulated even in his own mind, and had still to be crystallized into the decision to become a politician. But the elements for such a decision were already complete; it required only a sudden shock to precipitate it. That shock was supplied by the end of the war, the capitulation of Germany, and the overthrow of the Empire.

1. Baynes: vol. I, p. 862.

CHAPTER TWO

THE YEARS OF STRUGGLE
1919–24

I

THE news that Germany had lost the war and was suing for peace came as a profound shock to the German people and the German Army. The first half of 1918 had seen some of the most spectacular German successes of the whole war. In March and May – only a few months before the capitulation – Germany had signed the Treaties of Brest-Litovsk and Bucharest, each marking massive accessions to German power in Eastern Europe. The defeat of Russia and Rumania, and the end of the 'war on two fronts', had been followed in the west by the opening of the greatest offensive of the war. On 21 March 1918, Ludendorff began a series of attacks in France in which he drove the British and French Armies back and advanced the German line within forty miles of Paris. In the early summer of 1918 the Germans believed themselves at last to be within sight of victory.

The swift reversal of this situation in August and September was kept from the German people, and the announcement at the beginning of October 1918, that the German Government had asked for terms of peace stunned and bewildered the nation. Not until 2 October were the leaders of the Reichstag parties informed of the seriousness of the military situation. In his *Memoirs*, Prince Max of Baden, the new Chancellor who was to negotiate the surrender, wrote: 'Up to this moment the Home Front had stood unbroken. . . . Now the spark leaped across to the people at home. There was panic in Berlin.'[1]

The situation of the German Army by November 1918 was in fact without hope. It was only a matter of time before it was driven back into Germany and destroyed. Yet, at the moment when the German Government signed the capitulation, the German Army still stood outside Germany's frontiers and still preserved an unbroken front in the west. Moreover, although the initiative for ending the war had come from the High Command, from General Ludendorff himself, this fact was concealed. The High Command not only left the civil government, hitherto

1. Prince Max of Baden: *Memoirs*, vol. II, p. 12.

denied any voice in the conduct of the war, to take the full
responsibility for ending it, but tried to dissociate itself from
the consequences of the decision into which it had rushed the
Government against the cooler judgement of men like Prince
Max. Here was the germ of the legend of the 'Stab in the Back'.

The end of the war brought the collapse of the Imperial régime
and the reluctant assumption of power by the democratic parties
in the Reichstag. The Republican Government had to bear the
odium of signing, first the surrender and then the peace terms. It
was easy for the embittered and unscrupulous to twist this into the
lie that the Social Democrats and the Republican Parties had
deliberately engineered the capitulation, betrayed Germany, and
stabbed the German Army in the back, in order to hoist themselves into power. The fact that the Provisional Government,
led by the Social Democrats, sacrificed party and class interests to
the patriotic duty of holding Germany together in a crisis not of
their making, was brushed aside. These were the 'November
criminals', the scapegoats who had to be found if the Army and
the Nationalists were to rescue anything from the wreck of their
hopes. Rarely has a more fraudulent lie been foisted on a people,
yet it was persistently repeated and widely believed – because so
many wanted to believe it.

Any society is bound to be shaken by the experience of violence
and sufferings involved in years of war. The effect was doubly
severe in Germany since war had led to defeat, sudden, unexpected
defeat. Throughout Central and Eastern Europe the end of the
war was marked by a series of revolutionary changes. The
Hapsburg, the Hohenzollern, and the Ottoman Empires followed
the Romanovs into oblivion. The political and social structure of
half Europe was thrown into the melting-pot. It was a time of
widespread unrest, insecurity and fear in all Europe east of the
Rhine. In Germany, where people now found themselves faced
with new sacrifices demanded by the Peace Treaty and Reparations, this condition lasted for five years, until the end of 1923. It
was during that restless and disturbed period that Hitler first made
his mark as a politician.

The threat to the stability of the new Republican régime came,
not only from the extremists of the Left who sought to carry out a
social revolution on a Communist pattern, but equally, perhaps
even more, from an intransigent Right, in whose eyes the
Republic was damned from birth. It was associated with the

surrender, a shameful and deliberate act of treachery, as most of them soon came to regard it. In 1919 the Republican Government signed a Peace Treaty the terms of which were universally resented in Germany; this was looked upon as a fresh act of betrayal, and the Government was henceforward branded as the agent of the Allies in despoiling and humiliating Germany. The fact that its institutions were democratic, that the Social Democratic Party and the working-class organizations supported it, and that there was a demand for more radical action from the Left – finding expression in workers' demonstrations, strikes, and, on occasion, street fighting – added to the hostility with which the extremists of the Right viewed the new régime. It was openly said that loyalty to the Fatherland required disloyalty to the Republic.

This mood was not only to be found among the classes which had hitherto ruled Germany, and ruled it in their own interests, the noble families, the Junkers, the industrialists, the big business men, and the German Officer Corps. It was also characteristic of many wartime officers and ex-servicemen, who resented what they regarded as the ingratitude and treachery of the Home Front and the Republic towards the *Frontkämpfer*. They identified their own personal grievances of unemployment, the loss of their privileged position as officers, their inability and reluctance to exchange their wartime life for a humdrum peacetime existence, with the losses and humiliations for Germany which were the inevitable consequences of defeat and which were accepted, as they had to be, by the Republican Government.

In this way the malaise which is the inevitable sequel to a long period of war found a political form. It was canalized into a campaign of agitation and conspiracy against the existing régime, a campaign in which free use was made of the habits of violence learned in the years of war. No one has described this frame of mind better than Hitler himself. In the speech of 13 July 1934, in which he justified his action in the Röhm Purge,[1] he spoke

of those revolutionaries whose former relation to the State was shattered by the events of 1918: they became uprooted and thereby lost altogether all sympathy with any ordered human society. They became revolutionaries who favoured revolution for its own sake and desired to see revolution established as a permanent condition. . . .

Amongst the documents which during the last week it was my duty to read, I have discovered a diary with the notes of a man who, in 1918, was thrown into the path of resistance to the law and who now lives in a

1. See below, c. 5.

world in which law in itself seems to be a provocation to resistance. It is
... an unbroken tale of conspiracy and continual plotting: it gives one
an insight into the mentality of men who, without realizing it, have
found in nihilism their final confession of faith.[1]

It was this mood of discontent which Hitler was to exploit, and
of which he himself at that time furnished a typical example.

When the war ended and the Republic was proclaimed, Hitler
was still in hospital at Pasewalk. The acknowledgement of Germany's defeat and the establishment of a democratic Republic, in
which the Social Democrats played the leading part, were both
intolerable to him. There is no reason to doubt his statement that
the shock of Germany's surrender was a decisive experience in his
life.

Everything went black before my eyes as I staggered back to my ward
and buried my aching head between the blankets and pillow. . . . The
following days were terrible to bear and the nights still worse. . . .
During these nights my hatred increased, hatred for the originators of
this dastardly crime.[2]

Everything with which he had identified himself seemed to be
defeated, swept aside in a torrent of events which had been released, as he had no doubt, by the same Jews who had always
desired the defeat and humiliation of Germany.

Like many others among the mob of demobilized men who
now found themselves flung on to the labour market at a time of
widespread unemployment, he had little prospect of finding a job.
The old problem of how to make a living, conveniently shelved for
four years, reappeared. Characteristically, Hitler turned his back
on it. 'I was forced now to scoff at the thought of any personal
future, which hitherto had been the cause of so much worry to
me. Was it not ludicrous to think of building up anything on
such a foundation?'[3] He was not interested in work, in finding a
steady job; he never had been. After all, what had he to lose in the
break-up of a world in which he had never found a place? Nothing. What had he to gain in the general unrest, confusion, and
disorder? Everything, if only he knew how to turn events to his
advantage. With a sure instinct, he saw in the distress of Germany
the opportunity he had been looking for but had so far failed to
find.

1. Speech to the Reichstag, 13 July 1934 (Baynes: vol. I, pp. 300–2).
2. *Mein Kampf*, pp. 176–8.   3. ibid., p. 178.

'At that juncture innumerable plans took shape in my mind. . . . Unfortunately, every project had to give way before the hard fact that I was quite unknown and therefore did not even have the first prerequisite necessary for effective action.'[1] None the less, he did not despair. With considerable naïvety, he wrote in *Mein Kampf*: 'Generally speaking, a man should not take part in politics before he has reached the age of thirty.'[2] Hitler was now in his thirtieth year, the time was ripe and the decision was taken: 'I resolved that I would take up political work.'

But how? Uncertain as yet of the answer, Hitler, after his discharge from hospital, made his way through a disorganized country back to Munich. He was still in uniform and still drew his rations and pay from the Army. In December 1918, he volunteered for guard duty in a prisoner-of-war camp at Traunstein near the Austrian frontier. By the end of January, however, the prisoners were sent home and the camp closed; Hitler had to return to Munich. It was there in the next few months that he found the answer to his question.

Few towns in the Reich were as sensitive to the mood of unrest as Munich: its political atmosphere was unstable and exaggerated towards one extreme or the other. During the war Hitler himself had remarked that bad morale and war-weariness were more pronounced in Munich than in the north. The revolution of 1918 broke out in Munich before Berlin, and the Wittelsbach King of Bavaria was the first to abdicate. In the first six months of 1919 political violence was an everyday occurrence in Munich. Kurt Eisner, the man who had led the Bavarian revolution of November 1918, was murdered in February. A Social Democratic government under Hoffman only lasted until 6 April, when, under the influence of Bela Kun's Communist régime in Hungary, a Soviet republic was proclaimed in Munich too. This in turn lasted less than a month, and was accompanied by quarrelling, uproar, and the utmost confusion, all of which left an indelible impression on the Bavarians. At the beginning of May, the Soviet regime was overthrown by a combined force of regular troops and Freikorps volunteers. A bloody revenge was exacted, and many people were shot in the wave of suppression which followed. Hoffman's government was nominally restored, but the events of May 1919 marked a decisive swing to the Right in Bavarian politics.

In Bavaria, ever since the unification of Germany, there had

1. *Mein Kampf*, p. 179.　　2. ibid., p. 67.

been a traditional dislike of government from Prussian and Protestant Berlin, a sentiment which found expression after the war in demands for greater autonomy, and even in a separatist programme for a complete break with Northern Germany in favour of a Catholic, South German Union with Austria. The constitution of the Weimar Republic afforded considerable opportunity for the expression of this Bavarian particularism, for, alongside the central Reich government in Berlin, the old German states – Bavaria, Prussia, Württemberg, Saxony, etc. – each retained its own State government and representative assembly (Landtag), which exercised powers of considerable importance, notably control of the police. In the disturbed and unstable condition of Germany between 1918 and 1923, the power of the central government in Berlin was weakened, and the Bavarian State Government was able to exploit a situation in which the orders of the Reich Government were only respected if they were backed by the support of the authorities in Munich.

This anomalous position became more marked after March 1920, when an attempt to overthrow the Reich Government in Berlin by force failed (the Kapp Putsch), but a simultaneous *coup d'état* succeeded in Bavaria. On the night of 13–14 March 1920, the District Commander of the Reichswehr (the German Regular Army), General Arnold von Möhl, presented the Social Democratic Premier of Bavaria, Johannes Hoffman, with an ultimatum which led to the establishment of a right-wing government under Gustav von Kahr, from which the parties of the Left were excluded. Bavaria was thenceforward ruled by a State government which had strong particularist leanings and a Right-wing bias quite out of sympathy with the policies pursued by the central government in Berlin. Bavaria thus became a natural centre for all those who were eager to get rid of the republican régime in Germany, and the Bavarian Government turned a blind eye to the treason and conspiracy against the legal government of the Reich which were being planned on its doorstep in Munich. It was in Bavaria that the irreconcilable elements of the Freikorps gathered, armed bands of volunteers formed under the patronage of the Reichswehr at the end of the war to maintain order and protect the eastern frontiers of Germany against the Poles and the Bolsheviks, but now just as willing to turn their guns against the Republic. Driven from Berlin by the failure of the Kapp Putsch, the notorious Captain Ehrhardt and his Ehrhardt Brigade found shelter in Bavaria, and here were arranged the murders of Erzberger, the man who had signed the Armistice of 1918, and Walther Rathenau, Germany's Jewish Foreign Minister, who had initiated the policy of fulfilling the provisions of the Peace Treaty. The Freikorps were the training schools for the political murder and terrorism which disfigured German life up to 1924, and again after 1929.

Among the regular officers of the VII District Command of the Army stationed in Munich were men like Major-General Ritter von Epp and his assistant, Captain Ernst Röhm, who were prepared to give protection and support to these activities as a way of evading the Treaty of Versailles' limitations upon Germany's military power. In the Freikorps and in the innumerable defence leagues, patriotic unions, and ex-servicemen's associations which sprang up in Bavaria, they saw the nucleus of that future German Army which should one day revenge the humiliations of 1918. When that day would come no one knew, but in the meantime it was essential to keep together, under one disguise or another, the men who had been the backbone of the old German Army, which was now reduced by the terms of the Treaty to a mere hundred thousand in numbers.

If necessary there were highly placed officials in most ministries who had served as reserve officers during the war, or entertained nationalist sympathies, to whom appeal could be made. It was Pöhner, the Police President of Munich, who gave the famous reply, when asked if he knew there were political murder gangs in Bavaria: 'Yes, but not enough of them.' Wilhelm Frick, later Hitler's Minister of the Interior, was Pöhner's assistant; one of his colleagues in the Bavarian Ministry of Justice was Franz Gürtner, later Hitler's Minister of Justice.

At the back of the minds of all these men was the dream which bewitched the German Right for twenty years, the dream of overthrowing the Republic, reversing the decision of 1918, restoring Germany to her rightful position as the greatest Power of continental Europe and restoring the Army to its rightful position in Germany. The obvious first step was to begin by weakening, obstructing and, if possible, getting rid of the government in power in Berlin. Such was the promising political setting in which Hitler began his career.

II

Hitler lived through the exciting days of April and May 1919 in Munich itself. What part he played, if any, is uncertain. Accord-

ing to his own account in *Mein Kampf*, he was to have been put
under arrest at the end of April, but drove off with his rifle the
three men who came to arrest him. Once the Communists had
been overthrown, he gave information before the Commission of
Inquiry set up by the 2nd Infantry Regiment, which tried and
shot those reported to have been active on the other side. He then
got a job in the Press and News Bureau of the Political Department of the Army's VII (Munich) District Command, a centre
for the activities of such men as Röhm. After attending a course
of 'political instruction' for the troops, Hitler was himself appointed a *Bildungsoffizier* (Instruction Officer) with the task of
inoculating the men against contagion by socialist, pacifist, or
democratic ideas. This was an important step for Hitler, since it
constituted the first recognition of the fact that he had any political ability at all. Then, in September, he was instructed by the
head of the Political Department to investigate a small group
meeting in Munich, the German Workers' Party, which might
possibly be of interest to the Army.

The German Workers' Party had its origins in a Committee of
Independent Workmen set up by a Munich locksmith, Anton
Drexler, on 7 March 1918. Drexler's idea was to create a party
which would be both working class and nationalist. He saw what
Hitler had also seen, that a middle-class movement like the Fatherland Front (to which Drexler belonged) was hopelessly out of
touch with the mood of the masses, and that these were coming
increasingly under the influence of anti-national and anti-
militarist propaganda. Drexler made little headway with his
committee, which recruited forty members, and in October 1918
he and Karl Harrer, a journalist, founded the Political Workers'
Circle which, in turn, was merged with the earlier organization
in January 1919 to form the German Workers' Party. Harrer
became the Party's first chairman. Its total membership was little
more than Drexler's original forty, activity was limited to discussions in Munich beer-halls, and the committee of six had no clear
idea of anything more ambitious. It can scarcely have been a very
impressive scene when, on the evening of 12 September 1919,
Hitler attended his first meeting in a room at the Sterneckerbräu,
a Munich beer-cellar in which a handful of twenty or twenty-five
people had gathered. One of the speakers was Gottfried Feder, an
economic crank well known in Munich, who had already impressed Hitler at one of the political courses arranged for the

Army. The other was a Bavarian separatist, whose proposals for the secession of Bavaria from the German Reich and a union with Austria brought Hitler to his feet in a fury. He spoke with such vehemence that when the meeting was over Drexler went up to him and gave him a copy of his autobiographical pamphlet, *Mein politisches Erwachen*.[1] A few days later Hitler received a postcard inviting him to attend a committee meeting of the German Workers' Party.

After some hesitation Hitler went. The committee met in an obscure beer-house, the Alte Rosenbad, in the Herrnstrasse. 'I went through the badly lighted guest-room, where not a single guest was to be seen, and searched for the door which led to the side room; and there I was face to face with the Committee. Under the dim light shed by a grimy gas-lamp I could see four people sitting round a table, one of them the author of the pamphlet.'[2]

The rest of the proceedings followed in the same key: the Party's funds were reported to total 7.50 marks, minutes were read and confirmed, three letters were received, three replies read and approved.

Yet, as Hitler frankly acknowledges, this very obscurity was an attraction. It was only in a party which, like himself, was beginning at the bottom that he had any prospect of playing a leading part and imposing his ideas. In the established parties there was no room for him, he would be a nobody. After two days' reflection he made up his mind and joined the Committee of the German Workers' Party as its seventh member.

The energy and ambition which had been hitherto unharnessed now found an outlet. Slowly and painfully he pushed the Party forward, and prodded his cautious and unimaginative colleagues on the committee into bolder methods of recruitment. A few invitations were multigraphed and distributed, a small advertisement inserted in the local paper, a larger hall secured for more frequent meetings. When Hitler himself spoke for the first time in the Hofbräuhaus in October, a hundred and eleven people were present. The result was to confirm the chairman, Karl Harrer, in his belief that Hitler had no talent for public speaking. But Hitler persisted and the numbers rose. In October there were a hundred and thirty when Hitler spoke on Brest-Litovsk and Versailles, a little later there were two hundred.

At the beginning of 1920 Hitler was put in charge of the Party's propaganda and promptly set to work to organize its first mass

1: *My Political Awakening.*   2. *Mein Kampf*, p. 189.

meeting. By the use of clever advertising he got nearly two thous-
and people into the *Festsaal* of the Hofbräuhaus on 24 February.
The principal speaker was a Dr Dingfelder, but it was Hitler who
captured the audience's attention and used the occasion to
announce the Party's new name, the National Socialist German
Workers' Party, and its twenty-five point programme. Angered by
the way in which Hitler was now forcing the pace, Harrer resigned
from the office of chairman. On 1 April 1920, Hitler at last left the
Army and devoted all his time to building up the Party, control
of which he now more and more arrogated to himself.

Hitler's and Drexler's group in Munich was not the only
National Socialist party. In Bavaria itself there were rival groups,
led by Streicher in Nuremberg and Dr Otto Dickel in Augsburg,
both nominally branches of the German Socialist Party founded
by Alfred Brunner in 1919. Across the frontier in Austria and in
the Sudentenland the pre-war German Social Workers' Party had
been reorganized and got in touch with the new Party in Munich.
A number of attempts had been made in Austria before 1914 to
combine a working-class movement with a Pan-German nationalist programme. The most successful was this Deutsch Arbeiter-
partei which, led by an Austrian lawyer, Walther Riehl, and a
railway employee named Rudolf Jung, won three seats in the
Reichsrat at the Austrian elections of 1911. The Party's programme
was formulated at the Moravian town of Iglau in 1913, and reflected the bitterness of the German struggle with the Czechs as
well as the attraction of Pan-German and anti-Semitic ideas.[1]

In May 1918, this Austrian party took the title of D.N.S.A.P.
– the German National Socialists Workers' Party – and began to
use the Hakenkreuz, the swastika, as its symbol. When the
Austro-Hungarian monarchy was broken up, and a separate
Czech State formed, the National Socialists set up an inter-State
bureau with one branch in Vienna, of which Riehl was chairman,
and another in the Sudetenland. It was this inter-State bureau
which now invited the cooperation of the Bavarian National
Socialists, and a Munich delegation attended the next joint
meeting at Salzburg in August 1920. Shortly afterwards the
Munich Party, too, adopted the name of the National Socialist
German Workers' Party.

Up to August 1923, when Hitler attended the last of the inter-
State meetings at Salzburg, there were fairly frequent contacts

1. cf. Andrew G. Whiteside: 'Nationaler Sozialismus in Osterreich vor
1918', *Vierteljahrshefte fur Zeitgeschichte*, October 1961.

between these different National Socialist groups, but little came
of them. Hitler was too jealous of his independence to submit to
interference from outside, and the last meeting of the conference,
at Salzburg in 1923, led to Riehl's resignation.

Much more important to Hitler was the support he received
from Captain Röhm, on the staff of the Army District Command
in Munich. Röhm, a tough, scar-faced soldier of fortune with
real organizing ability, exercised considerable influence in the
shadowy world of the Freikorps, Defence Leagues, and political
conspiracies. He had actually joined the German Workers' Party
before Hitler, for, like Hitler, he saw that it would be impossible
to re-create a strong, nationalist Germany until the alienation of
the mass of the people from their old loyalty to the Fatherland
and the Army could be overcome. Any party which could recapture the working classes for a nationalist and militarist
allegiance interested him. He admired the spirit and toughness of
the Communists, who were prepared to fight for what they believed in: what he wanted was working-class organizations with
the same qualities on his own side.

Röhm had little patience with the view that the Army should
keep out of politics. The Army, he believed, had to go into politics if it wanted to create the sort of State which would restore its
old privileged position, and break with the policy of fulfilling the
terms of the Peace Treaty. This was a view accepted by only a
part of the Officer Corps; others, especially among the senior
officers, viewed Röhm's activities with mistrust. But there was
sufficient sympathy with his aims to allow a determined man to
use the opportunities of his position to the full.

When Hitler began to build up the German Workers' Party,
Röhm pushed in ex-Freikorps men and ex-servicemen to swell
the Party's membership. From these elements the first 'strong-
arm' squads were formed, the nucleus of the S.A. In December
1920, Röhm had persuaded his commanding officer, Major-
General Ritter von Epp – himself a former Freikorps leader and
a member of the Party – to help raise the sixty thousand marks
needed to buy the Party a weekly paper, the *Völkischer Beobachter*.[1] Dietrich Eckart[2] provided half, but part of the rest came
from Army secret funds. Above all, Röhm was the indispensable
link in securing for Hitler the protection, or at least the tolerance,

1. Best translated as the 'Racist Observer'.
2. See below, pp. 78–9

of the Army and of the Bavarian Government, which depended on the local Army Command as the ultimate arbiter of public order. Without the unique position of the Army in German, and especially in Bavarian, politics – its ability to extend powerful support to the political groups and activities it favoured – Hitler would never have been able to exercise with impunity his methods of incitement, violence and intimidation. At every step from 1914 to 1945 Hitler's varying relationship to the Army was of the greatest importance to him: never more so than in these early years in Munich when, without the Army's patronage, Hitler would have found the greatest difficulty in climbing the first steps of his political career. Before his death the Army was to learn the full measure of his ingratitude.

Yet however important this help from outside, the foundation of Hitler's success was his own energy and ability as a political leader. Without this, the help would never have been forthcoming, or would have produced insignificant results. Hitler's genius as a politician lay in his unequalled grasp of what could be done by propaganda, and his flair for seeing how to do it. He had to learn in a hard school, on his feet night after night, arguing his case in every kind of hall, from the smoke-filled back room of a beer cellar to the huge auditorium of the Zirkus Krone; often, in the early days, in the face of opposition, indifference or amused contempt; learning to hold his audience's attention, to win them over; most important of all, learning to read the minds of his audiences, finding the sensitive spots on which to hammer. 'He could play like a virtuoso on the well-tempered piano of lower-middle-class hearts,' says Dr Schacht.[1] Behind that virtuosity lay years of experience as an agitator and mob orator. Hitler came to know Germany and the German people at first hand as few of Germany's other leaders ever had. By the time he came to power in 1933 there were few towns of any size in the Reich where he had not spoken. Here was one great advantage Hitler had over nearly all the politicians with whom he had to deal, his immense practical experience of politics, not in the Chancellery or the Reichstag, but in the street, the level at which elections are won, the level at which any politician must be effective if he is to carry a mass vote with him.

Hitler was the greatest demagogue in history. Those who add 'only a demagogue' fail to appreciate the nature of political power

1. Hjalmar Schacht: *Account Settled* (London, 1949), p. 206.

in an age of mass politics. As he himself said: 'To be a leader, means to be able to move masses.'[1]

The lessons which Hitler drew from the activities of the Austrian Social Democrats and Lueger's Christian Socialists were now tried out in Munich. Success was far from being automatic. Hitler made mistakes and had much to learn before he could persuade people to take him seriously, even on the small stage of Bavarian politics. By 1923 he was still only a provincial politician, who had not yet made any impact on national politics, and the end of 1923 saw the collapse of his movement in a fiasco. But Hitler learned from his mistakes, and by the time he came to write *Mein Kampf* in the middle of the 1920s he was able to set down quite clearly what he was trying to do, and what were the conditions of success. The pages in *Mein Kampf* in which he discusses the technique of mass propaganda and political leadership stand out in brilliant contrast with the turgid attempts to explain his entirely unoriginal political ideas.

The first and most important principle for political action laid down by Hitler is: Go to the masses. 'The movement must avoid everything which may lessen or weaken its power of influencing the masses . . . because of the simple fact that no great idea, no matter how sublime or exalted, can be realized in practice without the effective power which resides in the popular masses.'[2]

Since the masses have only a poor acquaintance with abstract ideas, their reactions lie more in the domain of the feelings, where the roots of their positive as well as their negative attitudes are implanted. . . . The emotional grounds of their attitude furnish the reason for their extraordinary stability. It is always more difficult to fight against faith than against knowledge. And the driving force which has brought about the most tremendous revolutions on this earth has never been a body of scientific teaching which has gained power over the masses, but always a devotion which has inspired them, and often a kind of hysteria which has urged them into action. Whoever wishes to win over the masses must know the key that will open the door to their hearts. It is not objectivity, which is a feckless attitude, but a determined will, backed up by power where necessary.[3]

Hitler is quite open in explaining how this is to be achieved. 'The receptive powers of the masses are very restricted, and their understanding is feeble. On the other hand, they quickly forget. Such being the case, all effective propaganda must be confined to a few bare necessities and then must be expressed in a few

1. *Mein Kampf*, p. 474. 2. ibid., p. 101. 3. ibid., p. 283.

stereotyped formulas.'[1] Hitler had nothing but scorn for the intellectuals who are always looking for something new. 'Only constant repetition will finally succeed in imprinting an idea on the memory of a crowd.'[2] For the same reason it is better to stick to a programme even when certain points in it become out of date: 'As soon as one point is removed from the sphere of dogmatic certainty, the discussion will not simply result in a new and better formulation, but may easily lead to endless debates and general confusion.'[3]

When you lie, tell big lies. This is what the Jews do, working on the principle, 'which is quite true in itself, that in the big lie there is always a certain force of credibility; because the broad masses of a nation are always more easily corrupted in the deeper strata of their emotional nature than consciously or voluntarily, and thus in the primitive simplicity of their minds they more readily fall victims to the big lie than the small lie, since they themselves often tell small lies in little matters, but would be ashamed to resort to large-scale falsehoods. It would never come into their heads to fabricate colossal untruths and they would not believe that others could have the impudence to distort the truth so infamously. . . . The grossly impudent lie always leaves traces behind it, even after it has been nailed down.'[4]

Above all, never hesitate, never qualify what you say, never concede an inch to the other side, paint all your contrasts in black and white. This is the 'very first condition which has to be fulfilled in every kind of propaganda: a systematically one-sided attitude towards every problem that has to be dealt with. . . . When they see an uncompromising onslaught against an adversary, the people have at all times taken this as proof that right is on the side of the active aggressor; but if the aggressor should go only halfway and fail to push home his success . . . the people will look upon this as a sign that he is uncertain of the justice of his own cause.'[5]

Vehemence, passion, fanaticism, these are 'the great magnetic forces which alone attract the great masses; for these masses always respond to the compelling force which emanates from absolute faith in the ideas put forward, combined with an indomitable zest to fight for and defend them. . . . The doom of a nation can be averted only by a storm of glowing passion; but only

1. *Mein Kampf,* p. 159.   2. ibid., p. 163.   3. ibid., p. 383.
4. ibid., pp. 198–9.   5. ibid., pp. 160–1 and 283.

those who are passionate themselves can arouse passion in others.'[1]

Hitler showed a marked preference for the spoken over the written word. 'The force which ever set in motion the great historical avalanches of religious and political movements is the magic power of the spoken word. The broad masses of a population are more amenable to the appeal of rhetoric than to any other force.'[2] The employment of verbal violence, the repetition of such words as 'smash', 'force', 'ruthless', 'hatred', was deliberate. Hitler's gestures and the emotional character of his speaking, lashing himself up to a pitch of near-hysteria in which he would scream and spit out his resentment, had the same effect on an audience. Many descriptions have been given of the way in which he succeeded in communicating passion to his listeners, so that men groaned or hissed and women sobbed involuntarily, if only to relieve the tension, caught up in the spell of powerful emotions of hatred and exaltation, from which all restraint had been removed.

It was to be years yet before Hitler was able to achieve this effect on the scale of the Berlin Sportpalast audiences of the 1930s, but he had already begun to develop extraordinary gifts as a speaker. It was in Munich that he learned to address mass audiences of several thousands. In *Mein Kampf* he remarks that the orator's relationship with his audience is the secret of his art. 'He will always follow the lead of the great mass in such a way that from the living emotion of his hearers the apt word which he needs will be suggested to him and in its turn this will go straight to the hearts of his hearers.'[3] A little later he speaks of the difficulty of overcoming emotional resistance: this cannot be done by argument, but only by an appeal to the 'hidden forces' in an audience, an appeal that the orator alone can make.

Propaganda was not confined to the spoken word. There were the posters, always in red, the revolutionary colour, chosen to provoke the Left; the swastika and the flag, with its black swastika in a white circle on a red background, a design to which Hitler devoted the utmost care; the salute, the uniform, and the hierarchy of ranks. Mass meetings and demonstrations were another device which Hitler borrowed from the Austrian Social Democrats. The essential purpose of such meetings was to create

1. *Mein Kampf*, pp. 317 and 100.   2. ibid., p. 100.
3. ibid., pp. 391–2.

a sense of power, of belonging to a movement whose success was irresistible. Hitler here hit upon a psychological fact which was to prove of great importance in the history of the Nazi movement: that violence and terror have their own propaganda value, and that the display of physical force attracts as many as it repels. 'When our political meetings first started,' Hitler writes, 'I made it a special point to organize a suitable defence squad. . . . Some of them were comrades who had seen active service with me, others were young Party members who right from the start had been trained and brought up to realize that only terror is capable of smashing terror.'[1] Defence is an ambiguous word to describe such activities, for, as Hitler adds, 'the best means of defence is attack, and the reputation of our hall-guard squads stamped us as a political fighting force and not as a debating society.'[2]

From the first these men were used, not to protect the Nazis' meetings, but to provoke disturbance, if necessary by breaking up other parties' meetings, and to beat-up political opponents as part of a deliberate campaign of intimidation. On 4 January 1921, Hitler told an audience in the Kindl Keller: 'The National Socialist Movement in Munich will in future ruthlessly prevent – if necessary by force – all meetings or lectures that are likely to distract the minds of our fellow countrymen.'[3] In September of the same year Hitler personally led his followers in storming the platform of a meeting addressed by Ballerstedt of the federalist Bavarian League. When examined by the police commission which inquired into the incident, Hitler replied: 'It's all right. We got what we wanted. Ballerstedt did not speak.'[4]

Far from using violence in a furtive underhand way, Hitler gave it the widest possible publicity. In this way people were forced to pay attention to what he was doing and they were impressed even against their will. No government of any determination would have tolerated such methods, but the Republican Government in Berlin had virtually no authority in Bavaria, and the Bavarian State Government showed remarkable complacence towards political terrorism, provided it was directed against the Left.

The 'strong-arm' squads were first formed in the summer of 1920, under the command of an ex-convict and watchmaker, Emil Maurice, but their definitive organization dates from

1. *Mein Kampf*, p. 406.   2. ibid., p. 406.
3. Heiden: *History of National Socialism* (London, 1934), p. 31, quoting the report in the *V.B.*   4. ibid.

August 1921, when a so-called 'Gymnastic and Sports Division' was set up inside the Party. 'It is intended,' said the Party proclamation, 'to serve as a means for bringing our youthful members together in a powerful organization for the purpose of utilizing their strength as an offensive force at the disposal of the movement.'[1] The German Government, under pressure from the Allies, had ordered the dissolution of the Freikorps and Defence Leagues, and the Nazi Gymnastic and Sports Division was one of many camouflages used by Röhm and his friends to keep together the disbanded forces. After 5 October, it changed its name to Sturmabteilung (the S.A., or Storm Section of the Party) and was largely composed of ex-Freikorps men, especially from the Ehrhardt Brigade and the Organization Consul which had carried out Erzberger's murder. The first S.A. leader, Johann Ulrich Klintzsch, had been one of Ehrhardt's lieutenants and was for a time in prison in connexion with the Erzberger assassination.

In November 1921, the S.A. went into action in the so-called *Saalschlacht*,[2] a fierce fight with the Reds in a Nazi meeting at the Hofbräuhaus, which was built up into a Party legend. Next year, in August, S.A. formations paraded with swastika flags flying in a demonstration of the Patriotic Associations on the Munich Königsplatz, and a month later eight 'Hundreds' (*Hundertschaften*) were organized. The use Hitler intended to make of the S.A. was shown in October 1922, when he took eight hundred of his storm-troopers to Coburg for a nationalist demonstration, defied the police ban on marching through the town and fought a pitched battle in the streets with the Socialists and Communists.[3] To have been at Coburg was a much-prized distinction in the Nazi Party, and a special medal was later designed for those who had taken part in Coburg Day.

III

By 1921 it was clear that the Party was developing rapidly away from the original conceptions of Harrer and Drexler. Inevitably, Hitler's propaganda methods, his attempt to turn the Party into a mass following for himself and to ride roughshod over the other members of the committee, produced resentment. Harrer resigned from the Party chairmanship in 1920, but this was not the end of

1. Heiden: *History of National Socialism*, p. 73.
2. Literally, 'Hall Battle'.
3. For Hitler's own reminiscences of Coburg, see *Hitler's Table Talk*, pp. 135–7.

the trouble. In the early summer of 1921 Hitler spent some time in Berlin, where he got into touch with certain of the nationalist groups in the north and spoke at the National Club. While he was away from Munich the other members of the Party committee, long since thrust into the shade, revolted against Hitler's dictatorship and tried to recapture the direction of the Party. The occasion was a proposal to unite with certain other small groups, the most important of which was Brunner's and Streicher's German Socialist Party. The merger, it was hoped, would fetter Hitler's freedom of action.

Hitler returned immediately to Munich, and countered the move by offering his own resignation. This put the rest of the committee in an awkward position, for there was no doubt who had brought the Party so far, and who found the Party funds as well as the publicity. The last thing they could afford was to let Hitler resign. Hitler, however, far from making concessions, demanded dictatorial powers if he was to remain, together with the retirement of the committee and a ban on Party negotiations for six years. In a leaflet defending themselves, the members of the committee wrote:

A lust for power and personal ambition have caused Herr Adolf Hitler to return to his post after his six weeks' absence in Berlin, the other purpose of which has not yet been disclosed. He regards the time as ripe for bringing dissension and schism into our ranks by means of shadowy people behind him, and thus furthering the interests of the Jews and their friends. It grows more and more clear that his purpose is simply to use the National Socialist Party as a springboard for his own immoral purposes and to seize the leadership in order to force the Party on to a different track at the psychological moment.[1]

But the committee was no match for Hitler, who received powerful support from Eckart. They had to repudiate the leaflet after Hitler sued the newspaper which printed it for libel and at two meetings on 26 and 29 July they capitulated, making Hitler president and giving him virtually unlimited powers. Drexler was kicked upstairs as Honorary President.

The split between Hitler and the committee went deeper than personal antipathy and mistrust. Drexler and Harrer had always thought of the Party as a workers' and lower-middle-class party, radical and anti-capitalist as well as nationalist. These ideas were expressed in the programme, with its Twenty-five Points (drawn

1. Quoted in Heiden: *History of National Socialism*, pp. 44–5.

up by Drexler, Hitler, and Feder, and adopted in February 1920),
as well as in the name of the German National Socialist Workers'
Party. The programme was nationalist and anti-Semitic in
character. All Germans (including those of Austria and the Sudetenland) were to be united in a Greater Germany. The treaties of
Versailles and St Germain were to be abrogated. Jews were to be
excluded from citizenship and office; those who had arrived since
1914 were to be expelled from Germany.

At the same time the Party programme came out strongly
against Capitalism, the trusts, the big industrialists, and the big
landowners. All unearned income was to be abolished; all war
profits to be confiscated; the State was to take over all trusts and
share in the profits of large industries; the big department stores
were to be communalized and rented to small tradespeople,
while preference in all public supplies was to be given to the small
trader. With this went equally drastic proposals for agrarian
reform: the expropriation without compensation of land needed
for national purposes, the abolition of ground rents, and the
prohibiting of land speculation.

There is no doubt that on Drexler's and Feder's part this
represented a genuine programme to which they always adhered.
Hitler saw it in a different light. Although for immediate tactical
reasons in 1926 he was forced to declare the Party programme
unalterable, all programmes to Hitler were means to an end, to be
taken up or dropped as they were needed. 'Any idea,' he says in
Mein Kampf, 'may be a source of danger if it be looked upon as an
end in itself.'[1] Hitler's own programme was much simpler: power,
power for himself, for the Party, and the nation with which he identified himself. In 1920 the Twenty-five Points were useful, because
they brought support; as soon as the Party had passed that stage,
however, they became an embarrassment. Hitler was as much
interested in the working class and the lower middle class as
Drexler, but he had no more sympathy for them than he had had
in Vienna: he was interested in them as material for political
manipulation. Their grievances and discontents were the raw
stuff of politics, a means, but never an end. Hitler had agreed to
the Socialist clauses of the programme, because in 1920 the
German working class and the lower middle classes were saturated
in a radical anti-capitalism; such phrases were essential for any
politician who wanted to attract their support. But they remained
phrases. What Hitler himself meant by Socialism can be illustrated

1. *Mein Kampf*, p. 184.

by a speech he made on 28 July 1922. 'Whoever is prepared to make the national cause his own to such an extent that he knows no higher ideal than the welfare of his nation; whoever has understood our great national anthem, *Deutschland, Deutschland über Alles*, to mean that nothing in the wide world surpasses in his eyes this Germany, people and land, land and people – that man is a Socialist.'[1]

The situation repeated itself in 1930 when Otto Strasser and his friends left the Party, complaining bitterly that they had been deceived in their belief that it was a radical and socialist movement.

For the same reasons Hitler was not prepared to limit membership of the Party to any one class. All forms of discontent were grist to his mill; there was as much room in his Party for the unemployed ex-officer like Göring and Hess, or the embittered intellectual like Rosenberg and Goebbels, as for the working man who refused to join a trade union or the small shopkeeper who wanted to smash the windows of the big Jewish department stores. Ambition, resentment, envy, avidity for power and wealth – in every class – these were the powerful motive forces Hitler sought to harness. He was prepared to be all things to all men, because to him all men represented only one thing, a means to power. The character of the following Hitler was beginning to collect in Munich, no less than the methods by which he attracted it, shocked the prim, old-fashioned prejudices of Drexler and his friends, but they had no weapons with which to fight against his combination of energy and unscrupulousness, backed by the argument of success. On his side Hitler did not conceal his contempt for those he described in *Mein Kampf* as 'antiquated theorists whose practical success is in inverse proportion to their wisdom'.[2]

The committee which had hitherto controlled the Party was now swept away – Hitler had long since ceased to attend its meetings. The new president put in Max Amann, the ex-sergeant-major of the List Regiment, to run the business side of the Party, and Dietrich Eckart as editor of the *Völkischer Beobachter*. The power of making all big decisions he kept in his own hands. The dismal back room at the Sterneckerbräu which had served as a committee-room was abandoned for new and larger offices at 12 Corneliusstrasse. Bit by bit they accumulated office furniture,

1. *Adolf Hitlers Reden* (Munich, 1934), p. 32.
2. *Mein Kampf*, p. 301.

files, a typewriter, and a telephone. By February 1923, they were able to bring out the *Völkischer Beobachter* as a daily, with editorial offices at 39 Schellingstrasse.

Hitler worked in these early years in Munich as he had never worked before; it was only sheer hard work that could create the illusion of success. But it was work which suited him: his hours were irregular, he was his own master, his life was spent in talking, he lived in a whirl of self-dramatization, and the gap between his private dream-world and his outer life had been narrowed, however slightly.

Until the end of his life Hitler continued to look back and recall these early years of the Nazi movement with pride as the heroic period of the Party's struggle, the *Kampfzeit*. In January 1932 he said:

I cast my eyes back to the time when with six other unknown men I founded this association, when I spoke before eleven, twelve, thirteen, fourteen, twenty, thirty, fifty persons. When I recall how after a year I had won sixty-four members for the movement, I must confess that that which has today been created, when a stream of millions is flowing into our movement, represents something unique in German history. The *bourgeois* parties have had seventy years to work in. Where is the organization which in seventy years has achieved what we have achieved in barely twelve?[1]

This was the 'miracle' of National Socialism. 'And it is truly a miracle to trace this development of our movement. To posterity it will appear like a fairy-tale. A people is shattered and then a small company of men arises and begins an Odyssey of wanderings, which begins in fanaticism, which in fanaticism pursues its course.'[2]

Who were the men with whom Hitler began his 'Odyssey' in Munich? One of the most important was Ernst Röhm, a man for whom soldiering was his whole life and who had little but contempt for anything outside it. 'From my childhood I had only one thought and wish – to be a soldier.' These are the opening words of his Memoirs. Röhm was too independent and had too much the unruly temper of a condottiere to fit easily into the rigid pattern of the Reichswehr: he had finally to resign his commission in 1923. None the less he provided an invaluable link with the

1. Speech at the Industry Club, Düsseldorf, 27 January 1932 (Baynes: vol. I, p. 824).
2. Hitler at Munich, 8 November 1935 (ibid., p. 138).

Army authorities, even after his resignation, and more than any other man it was he who created the S.A.

Two other ex-officers may be mentioned with Röhm. Rudolf Hess, the son of a German merchant, who had been born in Alexandria, was seven years younger than Hitler. He had served for part of the war in the same regiment as Hitler before becoming a pilot in the Air Force. Now a student at the University of Munich, he won a prize for an essay on the theme: 'How Must the Man be Constituted who will Lead Germany back to Her Old Heights?' Hess, a solemn and stupid young man who took politics with great seriousness, conceived a deep admiration for Hitler and became his secretary and devoted follower. It was through Hess that Hitler came into touch with the geopolitical theories of Karl Haushofer, a former general who had become a professor at Munich University.

A very different figure from the humourless Hess was Hermann Göring, the last commander of the crack Richthofen Fighter Squadron and holder of Germany's highest decoration for bravery under fire, the *Pour le Mérite*. Swaggering and loud in his behaviour, Göring and his Swedish wife Karin, who had means of her own, settled in Munich in 1921 and lived in some style. The ex-major dabbled in studies at the University, then in the autumn of 1922 heard Hitler speak and was soon drawn into the movement. Shortly afterwards, he took Klintzsch's place as commander of the S.A.

Like Röhm, Gottfried Feder, and Dietrich Eckart had joined the German Workers' Party before Hitler. Both were men of some education and well known in Munich. Feder was a civil engineer by profession, with unorthodox ideas about economics and the abolition of 'interest slavery' which he preached with the persistence of a crank. Feder made a great impression on Hitler, who writes in admiration of him in *Mein Kampf*;[1] he lost influence, however, and after the Nazis' rise to power remained in obscurity in Munich. Dietrich Eckart was considerably older than Hitler, well known as a journalist, poet, and playwright, a Bavarian character, fond of beer, food, and talk, a great *habitué* of such places as the Brennessel wine-cellar in Schwabing. Eckart was a friend of Röhm, with violent nationalist, anti-democratic, and anti-clerical opinions, a racist with an enthusiasm for Nordic folk-lore and a taste for Jew-baiting. At the end of the war he

1. Hitler is also said to have clipped his long straggling moustache to the famous toothbrush in imitation of Feder.

owned a scurrilous sheet called *Auf gut' Deutsch* and became the editor of the *Völkischer Beobachter*, for which be found the greater part of the purchase price. Eckart was a man who had read widely – he had translated *Peer Gynt* and had a passion for Schopenhauer. He talked well even when he was fuddled with beer, and had a big influence on the younger and still very raw Hitler. He lent him books, corrected his style of expression in speaking and writing, and took him around with him.

It was Eckart who first introduced Hitler to the Obersalzberg, where they frequently stayed at the pension Moritz with Eckart's girl-friend Anna, Hoffmann, Hermann Esser, Drexler, and another friend of Eckart's, Dr Emil Gansser. 'Doctor Gansser deserves eternal gratitude from the Party,' Hitler said later. 'I owe him a whole series of very important relationships. If I hadn't, thanks to him, made the acquaintance of Richard Frank, the wheat man, I wouldn't have been able to keep the *Beobachter* going in 1923. The same's true of Bechstein.'[1]

The Bechsteins, wealthy and famous piano manufacturers, belonged to the wide circle of friends to whom Eckart introduced Hitler. Frau Hélène Bechstein took a great liking to the young man and he was a frequent visitor at her house in Berlin. Frau Bechstein gave parties for people to meet the new prophet, found money for the Party and later visited him in prison. It was through Eckart again, who was a member of the Thule Society – ostensibly interested in Nordic mythology but meddling also in political conspiracy – that Hitler met Hess and Rosenberg.

Alfred Rosenberg was a refugee of German descent from the Baltic town of Reval. He had been trained as an architect in Moscow, but fled to escape the Revolution. Through Rosenberg, who succeeded Eckart as the editor of the *Völkischer Beobachter* in 1923, Hitler came into touch with a group of passionately anti-Bolshevik and anti-Semitic Russian émigrés, the most important of whom was General Skoropadski, the German-appointed Governor of the Ukraine in 1918. Skoropadski, his so-called 'Press-agent', Dr Nemirovitch-Dantchenko, and others of the group used the *Völkischer Beobachter* for their White Russian propaganda. General Biskupski is said to have been one of the paper's principal financial supporters. Another of this group, Scheubner-Richter, a German from the Baltic provinces of Russia, had spent an adventurous war as German consul in Erzerum, stirring up trouble among the Armenians and amongst

1. *Hitler's Table Talk*, p. 218.

the Kurdish tribes. Returning to Munich by way of East Prussia and Danzig, he acted as Ludendorff's liaison man with Hitler and was shot at Hitler's side in the unsuccessful putsch of 1923.

The fact that Rosenberg had been trained as an architect impressed the man who had failed to get into the Vienna Academy, while his pedantic and laborious discussion of questions of race and culture (later published in *Der Mythus des 20. Jahrhunderts*) led Hitler to see in this muddled and stupid 'philosopher' the heir to the mantle of Houston Stewart Chamberlain and the prophet of the new racist *Weltanschauung*.[1] In the summer of 1923, Hitler visited Wahnfried, the home of the Wagner family in Bayreuth. For Hitler this was holy ground. He impressed Winnifried Wagner and captivated the aged Houston Stewart Chamberlain, who had married one of Wagner's daughters and who wrote to him afterwards: 'My faith in the Germans had never wavered for a moment, but my hope, I must own, had sunk to a low ebb. At one stroke you have transformed the state of my soul.'[2]

Friedelind Wagner, the musician's granddaughter, remembers him as a young man 'in Bavarian leather breeches, short, thick woollen socks, a red-blue-checked shirt and a short blue jacket that bagged about his unpadded skeleton. His sharp cheekbones stuck out over hollow, pasty cheeks, and above them was a pair of unnaturally bright-blue eyes. There was a half-starved look about him, but something else too, a sort of fanatical look.'[3] Later, he was to become a frequent visitor to Wahnfried.

Two years after the *Völkischer Beobachter* had been bought for him, Hitler made it into a daily. This required money. Some of it was provided by Frau Gertrud von Seidlitz, a Baltic lady who had shares in Finnish paper mills, while Putzi Hanfstängl, a son of the rich Munich family of art publishers, advanced a loan of a thousand dollars. Hanfstängl, who had been educated at Harvard, not only took Hitler into his own home – where he

1. The tragedy of Rosenberg, pathetically illustrated in the Memoirs he wrote in Nuremberg Prison, was actually to have believed in the Nazi *Weltanschauung*. In his table talk (p. 422) Hitler claimed that he had never done more than glance at Rosenberg's book, but he seems to have felt a certain contemptuous loyalty for him later when he was buffeted about helplessly in the struggle for power in the Party, and he protected him against the malice of his enemies.

2. Quoted in Heiden: *Der Führer*, p. 198.

3. Friedelind Wagner: *The Royal Family of Bayreuth* (London, 1948), p. 8.

delighted him by his piano-playing, especially of Wagner – but introduced him to a number of other well-to-do Munich families, including the Bruckmanns, another firm of Munich publishers.

Like the Bechsteins, the Bruckmanns were charmed and made into friends for life. But Hitler could be highly disconcerting in company. Ill at ease on any formal social occasion, he cleverly exploited his own awkwardness. He deliberately behaved in an exaggerated and eccentric fashion, arriving late and leaving unexpectedly, either sitting in ostentatious silence or forcing everyone to listen to him by shouting and making a speech. A description of him by a fellow guest at a party in 1923 is quoted by Konrad Heiden:

Hitler had sent word to his hostess that he had to attend an important meeting and would not arrive until late: I think it was about eleven o'clock. He came, none the less, in a very decent blue suit and with an extravagantly large bouquet of roses, which he presented to his hostess as he kissed her hand. While he was being introduced, he wore the expression of a public prosecutor at an execution. I remember being struck by his voice when he thanked the lady of the house for tea or cakes, of which, incidentally, he ate an amazing quantity. It was a remarkably emotional voice, and yet it made no impression of conviviality or intimacy but rather of harshness. However, he said hardly anything but sat there in silence for about an hour; apparently he was tired. Not until the hostess was so incautious as to let fall a remark about the Jews, whom she defended in a jesting tone, did he begin to speak and then he spoke without ceasing. After a while he thrust back his chair and stood up, still speaking, or rather yelling, in such a powerful penetrating voice as I have never heard from anyone else. In the next room a child woke up and began to cry. After he had for more than half an hour delivered a quite witty but very one-sided oration on the Jews, he suddenly broke off, went up to his hostess, begged to be excused and kissed her hand as he took his leave. The rest of the company, who apparently had not pleased him, were only vouchsafed a curt bow from the doorway.[1]

As Heiden remarks, no one who was at that party ever forgot Adolf Hitler.

There were other companions who came from the same lower middle class as Hitler himself and with whom he was more at home than with anyone else. Hoffmann, a vulgar, jolly, earthy Bavarian with a weakness for drinking parties and hearty jokes, understood little about politics, but was the one man allowed to photograph Hitler and, long after his friend had become Chancellor and Führer, enjoyed the licence of a court jester. Max

1. Heiden: *Hitler, a Biography* (London, 1936), pp. 102–3.

Amann Hitler's former sergeant-major, tough, rude, but a reliable business man, became the Party's publisher and made a fortune out of *Mein Kampf* and the Party newspapers. Ulrich Graf, Hitler's bodyguard, had been a butcher's apprentice and amateur wrestler, with a great taste for brawling. He was well matched by Christian Weber, a former horse trader of great physical strength who had worked as a 'chucker-out' at various beerhalls and whose social life consisted in drinking endless seidels of Bavarian beer.

Röhm's reputation – his homosexuality was later to become notorious – was none too good; nor was that of Hermann Esser, the only speaker in those early days who for a time rivalled Hitler. Esser was a young man to whom Hitler openly referred as a scoundrel. He boasted of sponging on his numerous mistresses and made a speciality of digging up Jewish scandals, the full stories of which in all their scabrous details were published in the *Völkischer Beobachter*. Esser's only competitor was Julius Streicher, an elementary-school teacher in Nuremberg, who excelled in a violent and crude anti-Semitism. In 1923 Streicher founded *Der Stürmer* (The Stormtrooper), in which he published fantastic accounts of Jewish ritual murders, of the Jewish world conspiracy revealed in the so-called 'Protocols of the Elders of Zion', and of Jewish sexual crimes. Streicher revelled in pornography and was never seen in public without a whip. Hitler's success in persuading him to break away from the German Socialist Party and join the Nazis with his Nuremberg following was a minor triumph, and not only in *Mein Kampf* but as late as December 1941 Hitler went out of his way to express his gratitude to Streicher.[1]

Hitler had no illusions about the type of man his movement attracted in its early days, but he also understood their value. 'Such elements,' he remarked later, 'are unusable in time of peace, but in turbulent periods it's quite different. . . . Fifty bourgeois wouldn't have been worth a single one of them. With what blind confidence they followed me! Fundamentally, they were just overgrown children. . . . During the war they'd fought with the bayonet and thrown hand grenades. They were simple creatures, all of a piece. They couldn't let the country be sold out to the scum who were the product of defeat. From the beginning I knew that one could make a party only with elements like that.

'What a contempt I acquired for the Bourgeoisie! If a bour-

1. *Hitler's Table Talk*, pp. 153–6.

geois gave me a hundred or two hundred marks, he thought he'd given me the whole of Golconda. But these fine chaps, what sacrifices they were willing to make. All day at their jobs, and all night off on a mission for the Party. I specially looked for people of dishevelled appearance. A bourgeois in a stiff collar would have bitched up everything.'[1] Such were the men with whom the 'miracle' of National Socialism was accomplished.

How Hitler managed to make a living at this time is far from clear. In the leaflet which was drawn up by the dissident members of the Committee in July 1921, this was one of the principal points of accusation against Hitler: 'If any member asks him how he lives and what was his former profession, he always becomes angry and excited. Up to now no answer has been supplied to these questions. So his conscience cannot be clear, especially as his excessive intercourse with ladies, to whom he often describes himself as the King of Munich, costs a great deal of money.'

During the libel action to which this led, Hitler was asked to tell the court exactly how he lived. Did he, for instance, receive money for his speeches? 'If I speak for the National Socialist Party,' Hitler replied, 'I take no money for myself. But I also speak for other organizations, such as the German National Defence and Offensive League, and then, of course, I accept a fee. I also have my midday meal with various Party comrades in turn. I am further assisted to a modest extent by a few Party comrades.'[2] Hitler was obviously embarrassed by these inquiries, for Hess was put up to write an open letter to the *Völkischer Beobachter* assuring its readers that the leader, on this side too, was beyond reproach.

The probable answer is that Hitler was as careless about money as he had been in Vienna, that he lived from hand to mouth and bothered very little about who was going to pay for the next meal. At this time his home was at 41 Thierschstrasse, a poorish street near the river Isar. He had a single small room, its floor covered with linoleum and a couple of cheap rugs. His books included a number of popular histories[3] and Clausewitz's great work *On War* which he could quote at length. His other possessions were few. He habitually wore an old trenchcoat or a cheap raincoat

1. *Hitler's Table Talk*, p. 107.   2. Heiden: *Hitler*, pp. 96–7.
3. His historical hero was Frederick the Great; the only two positive figures in English history, he told Hanfstängl, were Cromwell and Henry VIII.

and troubled little about his appearance or comforts. There was more than a touch of Austrian *Schlamperei* about Hitler; in matters of everyday life he was incapable of orderly routine or discipline, able to screw himself up to remarkable exertions, and then as suddenly relapsing into lethargy and a moody indifference.

To begin with, the Party, too, was run in the same casual way. Up to a point this was due to lack of funds and the consequent need to depend upon part-time help. Kurt Ludecke, one of the early Nazis, says in his memoirs:

The organization lived from day to day financially, with no treasury to draw on for lecture-hall rents, printing costs, or the thousand-and-one expenses which threatened to swamp us. The only funds we could count on were membership dues, which were small, merely a drop in the bucket. Collections at mass meetings were sometimes large, but not to be relied on. Once in a while a Nazi sympathizer would make a special contribution, and in a few cases these gifts were really substantial. But we never had money enough. Everything demanded outlays that were, compared to our exchequer, colossal. Many a time, posting the placards for some world-shattering meeting, we lacked money to pay for the poster.[1]

Undoubtedly Hitler received contributions from those who sympathized with the aims of his Party, but their amount and importance have been exaggerated. Hermann Aust, a Munich industrialist who gave evidence at the Court of Inquiry held after the putsch of November 1923, told the judge that he had introduced Hitler to a number of Bavarian business men and industrialists who had asked Hitler to speak to meetings in the Herrenklub and in the Merchants Hall at Munich. As a result several of those present gave Aust donations for the movement, which he passed on to Hitler. Dr Gansser put Hitler in touch with a number of Berlin business men; Dietrich Eckart was generous in settling bills and Frau Seydlitz as well as Frau Bechstein certainly contributed. In 1923, when Hitler and Ludendorff were working together, Fritz Thyssen, the chairman of the big United Steel works (Vereinigte Stahlwerke), gave them a hundred thousand gold marks, but such gifts were very rare in these early days.

There was a persistent rumour at the time, spread by their opponents, that the Nazis were financed by the French, but no concrete evidence has been produced to support this charge. According to other sources, Hitler received some support from

1. Kurt Ludecke: *I Knew Hitler* (London, 1938), p. 78.

Switzerland in 1923. Not until considerably later did be succeed in touching the big political funds of the German industrialists in the Ruhr and the Rhineland. In fact, the Nazi Party was launched on very slender resources.

IV

The situation in Germany failed to improve with the passage of time. Four years after the end of the war Germany was still a sick, distracted and divided nation. A considerable section of the community was irreconcilable in its attitude to the Republican Government and repudiated the idea of loyalty to the existing régime. Only eighteen months after the establishment of the Republic, the parties which supported it lost heavily in the elections of June 1920 to the extremists of both Right and Left. The Social Democrats and the Democrats lost half the votes they had polled in January 1919, and saw the parties to the left and right of them increase their support in the same degree. Even more serious was the undisguised partiality shown by the Law Courts, by many officials and by the Army when it was a question of intimidation, or even murder, practised by the extremists of the Right and directed against the Republic.

In 1921, following the murder of Erzberger on 26 August, the Wirth Government tried to assert its authority. The Kahr Ministry in Bavaria was obliged to give way over the dissolution of the Einwohnerwehr[1] and the para-military organizations, and eventually yielded its place to a ministry formed by Count Lerchenfeld, a man of moderate views who tried to support the government in Berlin. This was in September 1921. The new Bavarian Government forced Hitler to serve at least one of the three months' imprisonment to which he had been sentenced for breaking up Ballerstedt's meeting (24 June–27 July 1922), and showed itself much less friendly to the extremists than its predecessor had been.

But events were on the side of the extremists. In April 1921, the Allies had fixed the figure for reparations to be paid by Germany at 132 thousand million gold marks, or £6,600 million, while in October the League of Nations had overridden the recent plebiscite held in Upper Silesia in order to give the Poles a larger and more valuable share of former German territory. The policy of fulfilling the terms of the Peace Treaty advocated by Wirth and

1. The so-called 'Citizens' Defence' which Röhm had helped to organize and arm.

Rathenau found little support in the face of such bleak facts. Erzberger had been murdered in 1921. In June 1922, an attempt was made on the life of Scheidemann, the man who had proclaimed the Republic, and on 24 June Walther Rathenau, Chancellor Wirth's right-hand man and Foreign Minister, was shot dead in the street. Meanwhile a new and ominous development became more prominent, the fall in the value of the German mark. The mark, which at the end of 1918 had stood at the rate of four to the dollar, had dropped to seventy-five by the summer of 1921. In the summer of 1922 the dollar was worth four hundred marks, by the beginning of 1923 more than seven thousand. The inflation was under way, a further factor undermining stability and adding to the difficulties of the Government, which was forced to ask the Allies for a moratorium on reparation payments.

After the assassination of Rathenau the Wirth Government passed a special Law for the Protection of the Republic prescribing heavy penalties for terrorism. There was a loud outcry from the Right in Bavaria, and the Lerchenfeld Government was put under strong pressure to issue an emergency decree virtually suspending the operation of the new law in Bavaria. This was more than the Reich Government could tolerate, and Lerchenfeld was forced to promise the withdrawal of his decree. Thereupon a new agitation broke out in Bavaria, while Röhm, Pöhner, and Dr Pittinger, head of the Bund Bayern und Reich, the biggest of the anti-republican leagues, planned a *coup d'état* to overthrow the governments in Munich and Berlin, in which Hitler's National Socialists were to march with the rest and to which the Bavarian District Command of the Reichswehr was to give its support.

These plans came to nothing, but the Right-wing parties in Bavaria were unappeased, and on 8 November 1922 Lerchenfeld was obliged to resign in favour of a new Bavarian Minister-President, Eugen von Knilling. Gürtner, a man notorious for his nationalist sympathies, was made Bavarian Minister of Justice, and on 16 November the Bavarian Right-wing organizations united their forces in the Union of Patriotic Societies. At the same time the extremists of the Nationalist Party in the north broke away to form a new German Racial Freedom Party (Deutschvölkische Freiheitspartei). Ludendorff, a rabid nationalist who had been the military dictator of wartime Germany, and who now lived at Ludwigshöhe in Bavaria, provided a link between the Freiheitspartei and the anti-republican forces of the south. The success of Mussolini's March on Rome in October 1922 offered an example and a happy augury for the success of a similar attempt in Germany.

Hitler had taken an active part in the agitation against the Law for Protection of the Republic. Nazi Party formations, including the S.A., had paraded on the Königsplatz on 11 August 1922, in a big mass demonstration organized by the Patriotic Association, at which Hitler himself had been the chief speaker. He had been ready to march in the abortive putsch which Pittinger was to have organized, and the National Socialists had agreed to join the Union of Patriotic Societies founded in November.

At this point, however, a conflict began to develop between Hitler and the Bavarian authorities which supplies the key to the confused events of the twelve months that follow between November 1922 and November 1923. Three issues were involved. The first was the extent to which the quarrel between Bavaria and the Reich Government in Berlin should be pursued. The second was the political use to be made of this quarrel, whether to secure increased autonomy for Bavaria and the restoration of the Bavarian monarchy, even perhaps – as the extreme particularists hoped – separation from North Germany and union with Austria in a Catholic South German State; or, as Hitler demanded, to overthrow the Republican Government in Berlin and establish a nationalist régime in its place without impairing the unity and centralization of power in the Reich. The third was the part to be played by Hitler and the National Socialists in these developments, whether they were to continue in the role of useful auxiliaries for the Bavarian Government and its supporters, the 'respectable' Bavarian Peoples' Party; or to take the lead in a revolutionary movement to sweep out the 'November Criminals' in Berlin, with Hitler as its political director and pacemaker.

The issues were never stated as baldly and simply as this at the time, for obvious reasons. On his side, Hitler had neither the following nor the resources to act on his own. He could only influence events if he could persuade the Bavarian State Government, the other nationalist groups in Bavaria and the Bavarian Command of the Army to go along with him. However much he might rage against all these in private, he was forced to be conciliatory and try to win them over. On their side, the Bavarian authorities, while often embarrassed and irritated by Hitler, especially by his claim to be treated as an equal partner, recognized his usefulness as an agitator, and were anxious to keep control over the small but politically dangerous Nazi Party. The Bavarian Government was in fact divided on the policy to be adopted towards the Nazis. While the Minister of the Interior, Franz Schweyer, was hostile and had already proposed Hitler's deportation to Austria, the new Minister-President, Knilling, and the Minister of Justice, Gürtner, saw in the Nazi movement a force to be put to good use, if it could only be kept in hand. Moreover, the Bavarian authorities, in contrast to Hitler, were themselves uncertain how far they wanted to push their quarrel with Berlin and what was to be made of it, changing course several times and frequently disagreeing among themselves. Indeed, Hitler was one of the few men in Bavaria who saw clearly what he wanted, but he lacked the power to impose his views on those in authority, and so had either to dissemble and compromise, or run the risk of outstripping his own strength.

The latent conflict between Hitler and the men who possessed the power to put his plans into operation began to appear before the end of 1922. On his release from prison at the end of July, Hitler became more and more unrestrained in his speeches. On 18 September he told the audience in the Zirkus Krone:

We want to call to account the November Criminals of 1918. It cannot be that two million Germans should have fallen in vain and that afterwards one should sit down as friends at the same table with traitors. No, we do not pardon, we demand – vengeance! The dishonouring of the nation must cease. For betrayers of the Fatherland and informers, the gallows is the proper place.[1]

In November he was saying:

The Marxists taught – If you will not be my brother, I will bash your skull in. Our motto shall be – If you will not be a German, I will bash your skull in. For we are convinced that we cannot succeed without a struggle. We have to fight with ideas, but, if necessary, also with our fists.[2]

This same month of November, Schweyer, the Minister of the Interior, sent for Hitler and warned him against the consequences of the inflammatory propaganda he was conducting. In particular he sought to dispel any illusion that the police would not fire if he attempted to resort to force. When Hitler, in a state of excite-

1. Hitler at Munich, 18 September 1922 (Baynes: vol. I, p. 107).
2. Hitler at Munich in November 1922, reported in the *V.B.* for 22 November (Prange: p. 122).

ment, shouted, 'Herr Minister, I give you my word of honour, never as long as I live will I make a putsch,' Schweyer replied: 'All respect to your word of honour, but if you go on making such speeches as you have been making, the stream will one day burst loose of its own accord ... and you will swim with it.'[1] At the end of November Hitler's most important link with the Army, Röhm, was removed from his position as adjutant to Major-General Epp, the commander of the infantry forces in Bavaria. He was placed instead on the staff of the G.O.C. in Bavaria, General von Lossow, who had been appointed by the High Command in Berlin to restrain the Munich garrison from the sort of dangerous adventures in which Röhm had been engaging.

In the months that followed neither the Bavarian Government nor the Bavarian Command of the Army showed the least disposition to let this young agitator, who sometimes behaved as if he were half out of his mind, dictate the policy they were to pursue. Yet Hitler persisted in courting one rebuff after another. Why was he so persistent? Partly, no doubt, it was due to his innate ambition and arrogance; partly to an overestimate of his own importance and misjudgement of the political situation in Bavaria. But there was something else which powerfully influenced him: the belief that the circumstances of 1923 presented an opportunity to overthrow the existing régime which might not recur; the suspicion that unless they were hustled and pushed into action the Bavarian authorities might let this opportunity slip, and the fear all the time that the quarrel between Munich and Berlin might be patched up and a deal concluded from which he would be excluded. The mistakes Hitler made in 1923 sprang from the fretting impatience of a man who saw his chance, but lacked the means to take it by himself, and so fell into the trap of over-reaching himself.

Nazism was a phenomenon which throve only in conditions of disorder and insecurity. While these had been endemic in Germany ever since the defeat of 1918, two new factors made their appearance in 1923 which brought the most highly industrialized country of continental Europe to the verge of economic and political disintegration: the occupation of the Ruhr and the collapse of the mark.

By the autumn of 1922 the negotiations on reparation payments between Germany and the allied Powers had reached a

1. Heiden: *Der Führer*, p. 129.

deadlock. In view of the economic difficulties of the country, the German Government professed itself unable to continue paying reparations and requested a moratorium. The French Government of Poincaré refused to make any concession. Convinced that Germany could perfectly well afford to pay, if she wanted to, Poincaré used the technical excuse of a German default in deliveries of timber to move French troops into the industrial district of the Ruhr on 11 January 1923. The occupation of the Ruhr amounted to the application of economic sanctions against Germany, and rapidly turned into a trial of strength between the two countries. The Ruhr was the industrial heart of Germany: after the loss of Upper Silesia it accounted for eighty per cent of Germany's steel and pig-iron production and more than eighty per cent of her coal. To cut off these resources from the rest of Germany, as the French proceeded to do, was to bring the economic life of the whole country to a standstill. Such a prospect in no way deterred Poincaré. By the rigorous application of the letter of the Treaty of Versailles, he appeared to be aiming at a substitute for that policy of breaking up the Reich which France had failed to impose at the end of the war. The support which the French gave to the highly suspect separatist movement for the establishment of an independent Rhineland added colour to this belief.

The result of the French occupation was to unite the German people as they had never been united since the early days of the war. The German Government called for a campaign of passive resistance, which was waged with great bitterness on both sides, and soon extended to the French and Belgian zones of occupation in the Rhineland. Before long, passive resistance became a state of undeclared war in which the weapons on one side were strikes, sabotage, and guerrilla warfare, and on the other arrests, deportations, and economic blockade.

The occupation of the Ruhr gave the final touch to the deterioration of the mark. By 1 July 1923 the rate of exchange with the dollar had risen to a hundred and sixty thousand marks; by 1 August to a million; by 1 November to a hundred and thirty thousand million. The collapse of the currency not only meant the end of trade, bankrupt businesses, food shortage in the big cities and unemployment: it had the effect, which is the unique quality of economic catastrophe, of reaching down to and touching every single member of the community in a way which no political event can. The savings of the middle classes and working classes were wiped out at a single blow with a ruthlessness which no revolution could ever equal; at the same time the purchasing power of wages was reduced to nothing. Even if a man worked till he dropped it was impossible to buy enough clothes for his family – and work, in any case, was not to be found.

Whatever the cause of this phenomenon – and there were sections of the community, among them the big industrialists and landowners, who profited by it and sought to perpetuate its progress in their own interests – the result of the inflation was to undermine the foundations of German society in a way which neither the war, nor the revolution of November 1918, nor the Treaty of Versailles had ever done. The real revolution in Germany was the inflation, for it destroyed not only property and money, but faith in property and the meaning of money. The violence of Hitler's denunciations of the corrupt, Jew-ridden system which had allowed all this to happen, the bitterness of his attacks on the Versailles settlement and on the Republican Government which had accepted it, found an echo in the misery and despair of large classes of the German nation.

Hitler saw the opportunity clearly enough, but it was more difficult to see how to take advantage of it and turn the situation to his own profit. Despite the growth of the Party and the S.A., it was still a provincial South German movement, with neither support nor organization outside Bavaria. The National Socialists had not got the strength to overthrow the Republic on their own. They could do that only if Hitler succeeded in uniting all the nationalist and anti-republican groups in Bavaria, and if he succeeded in securing the patronage of more powerful forces – of which the most obvious was the Bavarian State Government and the Bavarian District Command of the Army – for a march on Berlin. Hitler devoted his energies throughout 1923 to achieving these two objectives.

All the time, however, he was oppressed by anxiety lest events should outstrip him. In the early months of 1923 he was afraid lest the French occupation of the Ruhr might unite Germany behind the Government. Hitler had no use for national unity if he was not in a position to exploit it: the real enemy was not in the Ruhr, but in Berlin. In the *Völkischer Beobachter* he wrote: 'So long as a nation does not do away with the assassins within its borders, no external successes can be possible. While written and spoken protests are directed against France, the real deadly enemy of the German people lurks within the walls of the nation. ... Down with the November criminals, with all their nonsense about a United Front. '

With the tide of national feeling running high against the French, and in support of the Government's call for resistance, this was an unpopular line to take. To make people listen to him, Hitler summoned five thousand of the S.A. Stormtroopers to Munich for a demonstration at the end of January 1923. The authorities promptly banned it. Hitler went on his knees to Nortz, the new Police President who had replaced the sympathetic Pöhner, begging him to get the ban lifted. When Nortz refused, Hitler began to rave: the S.A. would march, even if the police opened fire. The Bavarian Government retorted by issuing an additional ban on twelve meetings which Hitler was to address after the demonstration. Hitler was getting above himself: it was time to take him down a peg.

Even Röhm's intervention with General von Lossow at first failed to secure a reversal of this decision. Only when Lossow had satisfied himself that his officers could be relied on to fire on the National Socialists if necessary – a significant change of attitude – were Röhm and Epp able to secure his promise to inform the Government 'that in the interests of national defence, he would regret any vexation of the national elements'. The ban was thereupon lifted and Hitler held his demonstration.

In his speech at this first Party Day Hitler made no secret of his hope that the Berlin Government would fail to unite the nation in resistance to the French.

Whoever wants this fire [of enthusiasm for the glory of the Fatherland] to consume every single German must realize that first of all the arch-enemies of German freedom, namely, the betrayers of the German Fatherland, must be done away with. . . . Down with the perpetrators of the November crime.[1] And here the great mission of our movement begins. In all this prattle about a 'united front' and the like, we must not forget that between us and those betrayers of the people [i.e. the Republican Government in Berlin] . . . there are two million dead. . . . We must always remember that in any new conflict in the field of foreign affairs the German Siegfried will again be stabbed in the back.[2]

Hitler was interested in the French occupation of the Ruhr only in so far as this might produce a state of affairs in Germany which

1. 'November crime' and 'November criminals' are expressions Hitler habitually used to describe the foundation of the German Republic in November 1918, and the members of the Republican Government.
2. Hitler's speech at Munich, 25 January 1923 (Prange: p. 221).

could be used for the seizure of power. His purpose was revolutionary, and nationalism a means to this end. He had no use for talk of a national uprising and a new war of liberation which could only strengthen the position of the Government and divert attention to the enemy without. The time to deal with the French would come when the Republic had been overthrown. Here Hitler's essentially political outlook differed sharply from that of the Army and ex-Freikorps officers like Röhm, who thought of a war of revenge against France.[1]

This conflict had been present from the beginning in the very different views Hitler and Röhm took of the S.A. Röhm was a soldier first and last. For him, as for the other officers and ex-officers who helped to train the S.A., the first object was to build up in secret the armed forces forbidden by the Treaty of Versailles. The Party's stormtroop formations were a means to this end, just as the Freikorps, the Defence Leagues, and the Einwohnerwehr had been used in their turn as camouflages for an illegal reserve army ready to supplement the small regular Army which was all that Germany was allowed under the Peace Treaty. With the outbreak of a state of undeclared war with France, the Army leaders believed that this might well prove the prelude to a general war. In order to strengthen the Army it was planned to draw on the para-military formations like the S.A. Everything was to be done to bring them up to a high pitch of military efficiency, and Röhm flung himself into the task of expanding and training the S.A. with such effect that by the autumn of 1923 it numbered fifteen thousand men.

For Hitler, on the other hand, the Party, not the Army, came first, and the end was political power. The S.A. was not just a disguised Army reserve; these were to be *political* troops used for political purposes. With shrewder insight than Röhm and his friends, Hitler saw that the way to rebuild Germany's national and military power, and to reverse the decision of the war, was not by playing at soldiers in the Bavarian woods or even by fighting as guerrillas against the French in the Ruhr. This led nowhere, for the French, with their superior forces, were bound to win. It was necessary to begin by capturing political power in the State,

1. Hitler's attitude was not unlike that of another revolutionary leader, Lenin, who in 1918 had insisted on the Bolshevik Government accepting the humiliating terms of the Treaty of Brest-Litovsk, thus placing the political task of carrying out the revolution in Russia before that of driving out the German invader.

and the S.A. were to be used for that purpose. Once that had been secured, the rest would follow – as it did after 1933.[1]

At one time it had looked as if the Army leaders might be prepared to use their own forces for such a purpose, when the unsuccessful Kapp Putsch of 1920 was backed by part of the Army, under the leadership of the Commander in North Germany, General von Luttwitz. If, however, the generals were not prepared to carry out a *coup d'état*, Hitler feared that too great dependence upon the Army might tie his hands.

Hitler's dislike and opposition to the expansion of the S.A. under the patronage of the Reichswehr was thus entirely logical, and when he set to work to rebuild the Party after 1924 there was no point upon which he laid greater stress in *Mein Kampf* than preventing the S.A. from again becoming a defence association in disguise.[2]

In 1923, however, Hitler had to work with those who would work with him. By the beginning of February, largely thanks to Röhm, an alliance had been effected between the Nazis and four other of the Patriotic Leagues in Bavaria – the Reichsflagge (Reich Banner) of Captain Heiss, and Lieutenant Hofmann's Kampfverband Niederbayern (Lower Bavarian Fighting League), both of which had been persuaded to break away from the more cautious Pittinger and join Hitler; Zeller's Vaterländische Vereine München (Patriotic Leagues of Munich); and Mulzer's Bund Oberland (Oberland Defence League). A joint committee was set up, and Lt-Col Kriebel appointed to act as military leader of this Arbeitsgemeinschaft der Vaterländischen Kampfverbände (Working Union of the Patriots Fighting Associations). This had only been accomplished with the greatest difficulty in face of the intrigues and jealousies with which the nationalist organizations were riddled. For the rest of 1923 Hitler and Röhm worked hard to bring in as many of the other groups as they could, and to secure for Hitler a position as political leader on equal terms with Kriebel's as military leader.

1. cf. *Mein Kampf*, pp. 447–8: 'The S.A. must not be either a military defence organization or a secret society. . . . Its training must not be organized from the military standpoint, but from the standpoint of what is most practical for Party purposes.'

2. cf. *Mein Kampf*, pp. 439–53.

V

If the Bavarian Government was not to be won over to the idea of a march on Berlin, what about the Army? When Seeckt, the Commander-in-Chief of the Reichswehr, visited Bavaria on a tour of inspection in March 1923, General von Lossow, the G.O.C. in Bavaria, persuaded him to meet the new political prophet who had arisen in Munich. Hitler launched into a tirade demanding violent action against the French and against the Republican Government which tolerated their occupation of the Ruhr. Seeckt remained cold and unmoved,[1] but Lossow and his staff were clearly impressed, as the General himself later admitted. During April, Hitler called on Lossow almost daily, but the Bavarian Command of the Army was no more prepared than the Bavarian politicians to risk taking action. This is the persistent theme of all Hitler's speeches at this time:

Until the present day the half-hearted and the lukewarm have remained the curse of Germany. . . . For liberation something more is necessary than an economic policy, something more than industry: if a people is to become free, it needs pride and will-power, defiance, hate, hate and once again hate.[2]

We have the duty to speak, since in the near future, when we have gained power, we shall have the further duty of taking these creators of ruin (the November criminals), these clouts, these traitors to their State, and of hanging them to the gallows to which they belong. Let no one think that in them there has come a change of heart.[3]

Hitler's hatred was still directed, not against the French, but against the Republic, which he depicted as a corrupt racket run by the Jews at the expense of the national interests. No accusation against the Jews was too wild for him, but his most bitter scorn was reserved for the 'respectable' parties of the Right who hesitated to act.

You must say farewell to the hope that you can expect action from the parties of the Right on behalf of the freedom of the German people. The

1. According to the account given to Putzi Hanfstängl by Colonel von Selchow (Seeckt's adjutant who was present), Seeckt pointedly asked Hitler what was his attitude to the soldier's oath of allegiance, and ended the interview with the remark: 'You and I, Herr Hitler, have nothing more to say to each other.' Cf. Hanfstaengl, *Hitler, The Missing Years*, pp. 85–7.
2. Hitler in Munich, 10 April 1923 (Baynes: vol. I, pp. 43–4).
3. Hitler in Munich, 13 April 1923 (Baynes: vol. I, p. 53).

most elementary factor is lacking: the will, the courage, the determination.[1]

We are now met by the question: Do we wish to restore Germany to freedom and power? If 'yes', then the first thing to do is to rescue it from the Jew who is ruining our country. . . . We want to stir up a storm. Men must not sleep: they ought to know that a thunderstorm is coming up. We want to prevent our Germany from suffering, as Another did, the death upon the Cross.[2]

But Hitler's speeches were not even reported in the Press.

At the end of April, in an attempt to attract attention, the Nazis and their allies decided to break up the traditional socialist and trade-union demonstrations in Munich on May Day, unless the Bavarian Government acceded to their demand and banned them. This decision was taken at a meeting on 30 April, the minutes of which were later discovered by a Committee of Investigation of the Bavarian Diet.[3]

After the meeting Hitler went to see General von Lossow: he had a cold reception. When he demanded the arms which were stored in the barracks, on the pretext of a Communist putsch, Lossow refused and added that the Army would fire on anyone creating disorder in the streets, regardless of what party he belonged to. Colonel Seisser, the commander of the State police, gave the same answer.

Hitler had now placed himself in a difficult position. Emergency orders had gone out to the S.A. and other formations, and men were moving into Munich from as far away as Landshut and Nuremberg in the expectation that at last they were going to start the long-awaited putsch. It was too late to go back without loss of face. The only thing to do was to go on. The S.A. had considerable quantities of arms – the Landshut detachment led by Gregor Strasser and Himmler brought a hundred and forty rifles and a number of light machine guns with them – and at the last moment Röhm drove up to the barracks with an escort of Storm-troopers in trucks, bluffed his way in and took what he wanted.

But this time Hitler and Röhm had gone too far. On the morning of 1 May, while the Socialists marched peacefully

1. Hitler in Munich, 24 April 1923 (Baynes: vol. I, pp. 61–2).
2. Hitler in Munich, 20 April 1923 (Baynes: vol. I, p. 60).
3. *Hitler und Kahr* – a report on the findings of the Committee of Investigation of the Bavarian Diet, published by the Bavarian Social Democratic Party in Munich, 1928. The report was written by Dr Wilhelm Hoegner, who acted as assistant reporter of the committee.

through the streets of Munich, some twenty thousand Storm-troopers gathered on the Oberwiesenfeld, the big parade-ground on the outskirts of the city, waiting for orders. Hitler, wearing a steel helmet and his Iron Cross, was accompanied by Göring, the commander of the S.A., the two leaders of the Bund Oberland and the Reichsflagge, the veterinary Dr Friedrich Weber and Captain Heiss, Hess, Streicher, Frick, Gregor Strasser, Himmler, and the notorious ex-Freikorps leader, Lieutenant Rossbach, at the head of the Munich S.A. The military command was in the hands of Lt-Col Kriebel.

As the morning wore on, Hitler became more and more anxious: still the agreed signal from Röhm did not come. Röhm in fact was standing to attention before an angry General von Lossow and being reminded of his duty as a soldier. When he reached the Oberwiesenfeld, a little before noon, it was in the company of an armed detachment of troops and police, who drew a cordon round the Stormtroopers. Röhm brought the uncompromising message that the arms must be returned at once, or Hitler must take the consequences. Against the advice of Gregor Strasser and Kriebel, who wanted to use their superior numbers to overpower the troops, Hitler capitulated. The arms were returned to the barracks the same afternoon. Despite his attempt to explain away the 'postponement' of any action, both in his speech on the Oberwiesenfeld, and again that night in the Zirkus Krone, nothing could disguise the fact that Hitler's bluff had been called and that in front of thousands of his followers he had had to accept the public humiliation of defeat. This was the fruit, he must have reflected bitterly, of too great dependence on the Army.

For some time after 1 May Hitler dropped out of the political scene. The early edition of his speeches does not mention a single occasion on which he spoke between 4 May and 1 August: he spent a good deal of the summer at Berchtesgaden and only occasionally visited Munich.[1] Röhm, too, disappeared from Munich in May and did not return until 19 September. None the less the fiasco of May Day had nothing like the consequences that might have been expected. There were two reasons for this: the equivocal attitude of the Bavarian authorities and the mounting state of crisis in Germany.

1. During August Hitler attended a meeting of the Inter-State Bureau of National Socialist Parties, held at Salzburg. He insisted that Munich, not Vienna, must become the centre of the movement, and the Bureau does not appear to have met again. Cf. Ludecke: c. 8.

Hitler's actions on 30 April and 1 May had laid him open to the gravest charges under the law, yet nothing was said or done to limit his freedom of action in the future. Proceedings were actually begun by the State Prosecutor, but the investigation came to an abrupt end on 1 August, and the next entry in the prosecutor's files, dated 22 May 1924, records that the case had been dropped. Hitler himself had written to the State Prosecutor: 'Since for weeks past I have been shamelessly abused in the Press and in the Diet, without being able, by reason of the consideration I owe the Fatherland, to defend myself in public, I am thankful to Fate that it now allows me to conduct my defence before a Court of Justice, where I can speak out openly.'[1]

The hint was taken, and Franz Gürtner, the Bavarian Minister of Justice, intervened to prevent the process of the law continuing. When Röhm was informed that he would be transferred to Bayreuth after the part he had played, he resigned his commission and wrote a letter of complaint against Lossow to the commander of the Munich garrison, General von Danner. Once again matters were patched up. Röhm withdrew his resignation, and Lossow secured the withdrawal of Röhm's dismissal which had been telegraphed from Berlin. Instead, Röhm went on sick leave and retained his position on Lossow's staff.

This compliant attitude on the part of the Bavarian Government and the Army suggested that the worst crimes of which Hitler and Röhm had been guilty were indiscretion and premature action, and that, in more favourable circumstances, another attempt to force the hand of the authorities might succeed. In August and September 1923, the more favourable circumstances appeared to be provided by the sharp deterioration of the political and economic situation in Germany.

The French occupation of the Ruhr still continued, but the initial mood of national unity on the German side had gone. The intensification of the inflation, the desperate economic position of millions of Germans and the growth of extremism both on the Right and on the Left, seemed to have brought the country close to civil war. The Cuno Government in Berlin fumbled with problems which threatened to overwhelm it, and on 11 August the Social Democrats openly demanded the Government's resignation.

Stresemann, who took Cuno's place as Chancellor, at first appeared no more able than his predecessor to master the disintegration of the economy and of the unity of the Reich. The

1. Olden: p. 130.

value of the mark continued to fall. There were widespread strikes and riots under Communist leadership in many working-class districts. Trains and trucks were raided for food by the half-starving population of the cities. The French maintained their support of the Rhenish Separatists, and talk of a break with Berlin was rife in Bavaria as well as in the Rhineland.

Encouraged by the growing disorder, and the increasingly strained relations between Munich and Berlin, Hitler renewed his agitation in August. The fact that Stresemann was known to be anxious to end the exhausting campaign of passive resistance in the Ruhr and Rhineland enabled Hitler to change front. He now adopted the more popular line of attacking the Berlin Government for the betrayal of the national resistance to the French, as well as for allowing the inflation to continue.

On 2 September, the anniversary of the German defeat of France at Sedan in 1870, a huge demonstration, estimated by the police to have involved a hundred thousand people, celebrated German Day at Nuremberg amidst scenes of great enthusiasm. All the Patriotic Associations took part. During the parade Hitler stood at the side of Ludendorff, and afterwards flayed the Government in a characteristically violent speech.

Ludendorff's presence was important. His reputation as the greatest military figure of the war and an unremitting opponent of the Republic made him the hero of the Right-wing extremists, while he still enjoyed considerable prestige in the Army. There was no one better placed to preside over a union of the quarrelsome and jealous patriotic leagues, and Hitler had carefully maintained close relations with the old man for some time past. Ludendorff was no political leader: in matters of politics he was invincibly stupid as well as tactless. He disliked Bavarians, was on the worst possible terms with Crown Prince Rupprecht, the Bavarian Pretender, and constantly attacked the Church in the most Catholic part of Germany. But at least he was reliable on the question of Bavarian separatism, and his political stupidity was an asset from Hitler's point of view, for, skilfully managed, he could bring a great name to Hitler's support without entrenching on the control of policy which Hitler was determined to keep in his own hands.

The demonstration at Nuremberg had immediate practical consequences. The same day a new German Fighting Union (Deutscher Kampfbund) was set up and a manifesto issued over the old signatures of Friedrich Weber (Bund Oberland), Heiss (Reichs-flagge) and Adolf Hitler. The object of this renewed alliance was declared to be the overthrow of the November Republic and of the *Diktat* of Versailles.

VI

The crisis came to a head and entered its final phase at the end of September 1923. On 26 September Stresemann announced the decision of the Reich Government to call off the campaign of passive resistance in the Ruhr unconditionally, and two days later the ban on reparation deliveries to France and Belgium was lifted. This was a courageous and wise decision, intended as the pre-liminary to negotiations for a peaceful settlement. But it was also the signal the Nationalists had been waiting for to stir up a renewed agitation against the Government. 'The Republic, by God,' Hitler had declared on 12 September, 'is worthy of its fathers. . . . The essential character of the November Republic is to be seen in the comings and goings to London, to Spa, to Paris and to Genoa. Subserviency towards the enemy, surrender of the human dignity of the German, pacifist cowardice, tolerance of every indignity, readiness to agree to everything until nothing remains.'[1]

On 25 September the leaders of the Kampfbund – Hitler, Gör-ing, Röhm, Kriebel, Heiss, and Weber – had already met and discussed what they were to do. For two and a half hours Hitler put his point of view and asked for the political leadership of the alliance. So strong was the impression he made that both Heiss and Weber agreed, while Röhm, convinced that they were on the edge of big events, next day resigned his commission and finally threw in his lot with Hitler.

Hitler's first step was to put his own fifteen thousand S.A. men in a state of readiness and announce fourteen immediate mass meetings in Munich alone. Whether he intended to try a *coup d'état* is not clear: probably he looked to the mass meetings and the state of public opinion they would reveal to make the decision for him. But the Bavarian Government was taking no chances. Knilling, the Minister President, was thoroughly alarmed. On 26 September the Bavarian Cabinet proclaimed a state of emerg-ency and appointed Gustav von Kahr, one of the best-known Bavarian Right-wing politicians with strong monarchist and

1. Hitler in Munich, 12 September 1923 (Baynes: vol. I, pp. 80–1).

particularist leanings, as State Commissioner with dictatorial powers. Kahr promptly used his powers to ban Hitler's fourteen meetings and refused to give way when Hitler, beside himself with rage, screamed that he would answer him with bloody revolution.

In the confused events that followed 26 September and led up to the unsuccessful putsch of 8–9 November, the position of two of the three parties is tolerably clear. Hitler consistently demanded a revolutionary course: a move on Berlin to be backed by the political and military authorities in Bavaria, but aiming at the substitution of a new régime for the whole of Germany. As he admitted later: 'I can confess quite calmly that from 1919 to 1923 I thought of nothing else than a *coup d'état*.'[1] The twists and hesitations in Hitler's conduct arose, not from any doubts about his aim, but from recognition of the fact that he could not carry such a plan through with his own resources, and must, somehow or other, persuade Kahr, the State Commissioner, and Lossow, the commanding officer in Bavaria, to join with him.

The attitude of the Central Government in Berlin was equally clearly defined. It had to face the threat of civil war from several directions: from Bavaria, where Hitler was openly calling for revolt, and where Kahr, the State Commissioner, began to pursue an independent course of action which ran counter to the policy of Berlin; from Saxony, where the State Government came increasingly under the influence of the Communists, who were also aiming at a seizure of power; from the industrial centres, like Hamburg and the Ruhr, where Communist influence was strong; from the Rhineland, where the Separatists were still active, and from the nationalist extremists of the north, where the para-military organization known as the Black Reichswehr, under the leadership of Major Buchrucker, attempted to start a revolt at the beginning of October.

The Stresemann Government's chances of mastering this critical situation depended upon the attitude of the Army. The High Command could be relied upon to use force to suppress any attempt at revolution from the Left, but its attitude towards a similar move from the Right might well be uncertain. At the time of the Kapp Putsch in March 1920 part of the Army under General von Luttwitz had openly supported the *coup d'état*, while the Commander-in-Chief, General von Seeckt, although disagreeing with Luttwitz, had declined to allow his troops to be used to support the legal government. In the years since the war

1. Hitler at Munich, 9 November 1936 (Baynes: vol. I, p. 154).

the protection of the Army had been invoked again and again by those like Hitler who were patently disloyal to the Republic and scheming to accomplish its overthrow.

Nothing could more clearly illustrate the unique position of the Army in German politics, a position fully appreciated by Seeckt and the Army High Command. Seeckt, one of the most remarkable men in the long history of the German Army, was equal to the occasion. Ten years later he wrote: 'The error of all those who organize armies is to mistake momentary for the permanent state.'[1] In 1923 he had the insight to see that it was in the long-term interests of Germany, and of the German Army he served, to uphold the authority even of a Republican government, and so to preserve the unity of the Reich, rather than allow the country to be plunged into civil war for the momentary satisfaction of Party rancour and class resentment. In the Order of the Day which he issued on 4 November 1923 Seeckt put his case in half a dozen sentences:

. . . As long as I remain at my post, I shall not cease to repeat that salvation for Germany cannot come from one extreme or the other, neither through help from abroad nor through revolution, whether of the Right or of the Left. It is only by hard work, silently and persistently pursued, that we can survive. This can only be accomplished on the basis of the legal constitution. To abandon this principle is to unleash civil war. In such a civil war none of the parties would succeed in winning; it would be a conflict which would end only in their mutual destruction, a conflict similar to that of which the Thirty Years War provides so terrible an example.[2]

Seeckt's attitude allowed the political and military authorities in Berlin to speak with one voice, and on 26 September President Ebert invoked Clause 48 of the Weimar Constitution to confer emergency powers upon the Minister of Defence, Gessler, and the Commander-in-Chief, Seeckt. Until February 1924, when the state of emergency was brought to an end, this meant that the Army assumed the executive functions of the government and undertook the responsibility of safeguarding both the security of the Reich and the inviolability of the Republican Constitution. An attempt by Hitler – or anyone else – to carry out a march on Berlin would be met by force, with the Army on the side of the Government.

1. General Hans von Seeckt: *Die Reichswehr* (Berlin, 1933), p. 31.
2. General von Rabenau: *Seeckt, Aus Seinem Leben*, vol. II, *1918–36* (Leipzig, 1940), p. 371; Bénoist-Méchin: *Histoire de l'armée allemande*, vol. II, p. 288.

But there was a third party to be taken into account, the civil and military authority in Bavaria represented by Kahr and Lossow. It was the existence of this third factor, and the uncertainty of the policy Kahr and Lossow would adopt, which gave Hitler a chance of success and confuses the development of events for the historian.

Although the Bavarian Government had refused to allow the Nazis a free hand in May, and had now appointed Kahr to keep Hitler in check, relations between Munich and Berlin were strained. It was the action of the Bavarian Government in conferring dictatorial powers on Kahr which had led the Reich Government to declare a state of emergency itself, and Kahr's intentions were regarded with suspicion in Berlin.

Kahr's aims are still far from clear: probably they were never entirely clear to him at the time. Kahr, however, was a Bavarian and a monarchist; he was attracted by the idea of overthrowing the Republican régime in Berlin and putting in a conservative government which would give Bavaria back her old monarchy and a more autonomous position under a new constitution. At other times he played with the possibility of breaking away from the Reich altogether and establishing an independent South German State under a restored Bavarian monarchy. Such ideas were anathema to Hitler. Point I of the Nazi Party's Programme demanded the union of all Germans (including those of Austria as well as Bavaria) in a single German State, while the final point contained an equally clear demand for 'the creation of a strong central authority in the State'. Hitler himself had persistently campaigned against the particularist sympathies of the various Bavarian parties. None the less, he saw that he could use an open quarrel between Munich and Berlin for his own purpose. If Kahr could only be persuaded to help overthrow the Republican régime in Berlin, Hitler had every hope of double-crossing his Bavarian allies once he was in power. It was equally possible for Kahr to use Hitler and the forces of the Kampfbund. Out of this ambiguous situation an uneasy alliance developed between Kahr and the Nazis, each trying to exploit the other's support and subordinate the other's political ends to his own. Once again the critical decision lay with the Army, this time with the local commander in Bavaria, General von Lossow. Like Kahr, however, Lossow never quite succeeded in making up his mind until events decided for him.

In October 1923, the quarrel between Munich and Berlin flared up, under direct provocation from Hitler. When the Nazi *Völkischer Beobachter* printed scurrilous attacks on Seeckt, Stresemann, and Gessler, the Minister of Defence in Berlin used his emergency powers to demand the suppression of the paper, as well as the arrest of Captain Heiss, Captain Ehrhardt, and Lieutenant Rossbach. Kahr refused to take orders from Berlin, and when the Minister of Defence went over his head and ordered General von Lossow to execute the ban, Lossow let himself be persuaded by Kahr into disobeying his orders. The next step was Berlin's removal of Lossow from his post on 20 October and the appointment of General Kress von Kressenstein to take over his command. But again Kahr intervened. He announced that Lossow would remain in command of the Army in Bavaria, and exacted a special oath of allegiance to the Bavarian Government from both officers and men, an open breach of the constitution. On 27 October Kahr rejected an appeal from President Ebert, demanded the resignation of the Reich Government and ordered the armed bands which supported him – not the Kampfbund – to concentrate on the borders of Bavaria and Thuringia.

All this suited Hitler admirably. Power in Bavaria was concentrated in the hands of a triumvirate consisting of Kahr, Lossow, and Colonel Seisser, the head of the State police. An open rupture had occurred between Munich and Berlin. It was now, Hitler argued, only a question of whether Berlin marched on Munich, or Munich on Berlin. The situation in Saxony and Thuringia, on the northern borders of Bavaria, offered a splendid pretext for Kahr and Lossow to act. For there the Social Democratic cabinets of the two State Governments had been broadened to bring the Communists into power as partners of the Social Democrats, thereby providing the Communists with a spring-board for their own seizure of power. Action by the Bavarian Government to suppress this threat of a Left-wing revolution would undoubtedly command wide support, and, once at Dresden, Hitler reckoned, it would not be long before they were in Berlin.

Lossow and Kahr were full of smooth assurances that they would move as soon as the situation was ripe, yet Hitler and Röhm were mistrustful. They suspected that behind the façade of German Nationalism, with its cry of '*Auf nach Berlin*' (On to Berlin!), which Kahr kept up to satisfy the Kampfbund, he was playing with Bavarian separatist ideas under the very different banner of '*Los von Berlin*' (Away from Berlin!). Preparations went forward and discussions continued between Kahr, Lossow, and the Kampfbund leaders, but each side watched the other with growing suspicion.

Meanwhile the Government in Berlin was beginning slowly to master its difficulties. By the end of October the threat of a Communist revolution had been broken. A Communist rising in Hamburg had been suppressed by the police, while General Müller, acting on orders from Berlin, had turned out the offending governments in Saxony and Thuringia, thus depriving the Bavarian conspirators of their best pretext for intervention outside their own frontiers. These developments did not fail to impress Kahr and Lossow, and at the beginning of November Colonel Seisser, the third of the triumvirate, was sent to Berlin to size up the situation.

For Hitler, however, there could be no drawing back. He had committed himself too openly and worked his supporters up to such a pitch of expectation that a failure to act now must mean the collapse of the Nazi Party and the total discredit of its leader. Lieutenant Wilhelm Brückner later gave evidence that he had begged Hitler to strike soon, since 'the day is coming when I won't be able to hold the men back. If nothing happens now, they'll run away from us.' Hitler could not afford to repeat the fiasco of 1 May. Moreover, if the tide of events had really set in Stresemann's favour, Germany might begin to recover from the disorder and insecurity which had haunted her since 1918, and Hitler lose the opportunity which still remained. By November, Röhm says, the preparations for action were complete, and the state of tension in Munich was such that the crisis had to find an immediate solution one way or another; it could not be prolonged.

Seisser's report from Berlin was far from encouraging. He was convinced that there would be no support in Northern Germany for an uprising. Kahr and Lossow, who had no wish to become involved in an enterprise that was bound to fail, insisted at a meeting with the Kampfbund leaders on 6 November that they alone should decide the time to act and that they should not be hustled. It is possible that, left to themselves, they would have continued to sit on the fence until a compromise with the Stresemann Government could be arranged. If Kahr still seriously contemplated action, his inclination was more and more towards independent action by Bavaria, dropping altogether the idea of a march on Berlin and national revolution. Hitler was by now convinced that the only way to get Kahr and Lossow to do what he wanted was to present them with a *fait accompli* and burn their boats for them. Otherwise, he feared, they might carry out their own *coup* without him.

The original plan, proposed by Scheubner-Richter and Rosenberg, was to take advantage of the presence of Kahr, Lossow, and Seisser as well as the Crown Prince Rupprecht, at the parade to be held in Munich on 4 November, *Totengedenktag*, the Day of Homage to the Dead. Armed Stormtroopers were to surround them just before the parade and persuade them at the point of the pistol to lead the national revolution which Hitler would then proclaim. This plan fell through, but its essential features were kept and put into operation on 8 November.

A second plan was now sketched: to concentrate all the forces of the Kampfbund during the night of 10 November on the Fröttmaninger Heath, march into Munich the next day, seize the key points and push Kahr, Lossow, and Seisser into action under the impression of this demonstration of force. At this moment it was announced that a big meeting would be held in the Bürgerbräukeller at which Kahr was to speak on the evening of 8 November. Lossow and Seisser, together with most of the other Bavarian political leaders, were all expected to be present. Kahr refused to see Hitler on the morning of the 8th, and Hitler was soon convinced that this meeting was to be the prelude to the proclamation of Bavarian independence and the restoration of the Wittelsbach monarchy. On the spur of the moment Hitler decided to move forward the date for action to the 8th, and so forestall Kahr.

The meeting on the evening of 8 November was attended by everyone who was well known in Munich politics and society. Hitler took up an inconspicuous position by one of the pillars with Max Amann, Rosenberg, and Ulrich Graf. No one paid any attention to him and the whole assembly was completely taken by surprise when, twenty minutes after Kahr had begun to speak, Göring, with twenty-five armed brownshirts, burst into the hall. In the middle of the uproar Hitler leaped on to a chair and fired a shot at the ceiling, then jumped down and began to push his way on to the platform. 'The National Revolution,' he shouted, 'has begun. This hall is occupied by six hundred heavily armed men. No one may leave the hall. The Bavarian and Reich Governments have been removed and a provisional National Government formed. The Army and police barracks have been occupied, troops and police are marching on the city under the swastika banner.' Many in the hall were angry at the effrontery of this young upstart trying to bluster his way into a political role. But no one could be certain how far Hitler was only bluffing. There were six hundred S.A. men outside, and a machine-gun in the vestibule. Moreover, with the help of Pöhner, the ex-Police President of Munich, Hitler had persuaded Frick, who was still an official in the Police Department, to telephone the police officer at the hall and order him not to intervene, but simply to report if anything happened. Leaving Göring to keep order in the hall, Hitler pushed Kahr, Lossow, and Seisser into a side room. Meanwhile Scheubner-Richter was driving through the night to Ludwigshöhe to fetch General Ludendorff, whom Hitler wanted as the figurehead of his revolution.

Hitler, who was wildly excited, began the interview with Kahr and his companions in melodramatic style: 'No one leaves this room alive without my permission.' He announced that he had formed a new government with Ludendorff. (This, too, was un-true; Ludendorff knew nothing of what was happening.) They had only one choice: to join him. Waving his gun, and looking as if he was half out of his mind, he shouted: 'I have four shots in my pistol. Three for my collaborators if they abandon me. The last is for myself.' Setting the revolver to his head, he declared: 'If I am not victorious by tomorrow afternoon, I shall be a dead man.'

The three men were less impressed than they should have been. They found it difficult to take Hitler's raving at all seriously, despite the gun and the armed guards at the windows. Lossow later claimed that as they went out of the hall he had whispered to Kahr and Seisser: '*Komödie spielen*' (Play a part). Kahr tried to put on a brave front: 'You can arrest me or shoot me. Whether I die or not is no matter.' Seisser reproached Hitler with breaking his word of honour not to carry out a putsch. Hitler was all con-trition: 'Yes, I did. Forgive me. I had to, for the sake of the Fatherland.' But as soon as Kahr began to whisper to the silent Lossow, he flew into a rage and shouted: 'No talking without my permission.'

So far he had made little progress. Now, leaving the room without a word, he dashed into the hall and announced that the three men had agreed to join him in forming a new German government:

The Bavarian Ministry is removed. I propose that a Bavarian govern-ment shall be formed consisting of a Regent and a Prime Minister in-vested with dictatorial powers. I propose Herr von Kahr as Regent and

Herr Pöhner as Prime Minister. The government of the November Criminals and the Reich President are declared to be removed. A new National Government will be nominated this very day, here in Munich. A German National Army will be formed immediately. . . . I propose that, until accounts have been finally settled with the November criminals, the direction of policy in the National Government be taken over by me. Ludendorff will take over the leadership of the German National Army. Lossow will be German Reichswehr Minister, Seisser Reich Police Minister. The task of the provisional German National Government is to organize the march on that sinful Babel, Berlin, and save the German people. . . . Tomorrow will see either a National Government in Germany or us dead.[1]

Hitler's appearance as head of a new national government was far from impressive. He had taken off his trenchcoat and stood in an ill-cut black tailcoat which, as Hanfstängl admitted, made him look like a local collector of taxes in his Sunday best or 'the slightly nervous sort of provincial bridegroom you can see in scores of pictures behind the dusty windows of Bavarian village photographers'.[2]

But Hitler's nerve carried him through. His speech was another piece of bluff, but it worked. The announcement that agreement had been reached completely changed the mood of the crowd in the hall, which shouted its approval: the sound of cheering impressed the three men who were still held under guard in the side room.

No sooner had Hitler returned to them than Ludendorff appeared. He was thoroughly angry with Hitler for springing a surprise on him, and furious at the distribution of offices which made Hitler, not Ludendorff, the dictator of Germany, and left him with the command of an army which did not exist. But he kept himself under control: this was a great national event, he said, and he could only advise the others to collaborate. Hitler added: 'We can no longer turn back; our action is already inscribed on the pages of world history.'

Lossow later denied that he had replied: 'I shall take your Excellency's wishes as an order,' but Ludendorff's intervention turned the scales. When Kahr still made difficulties, Hitler used all his charm: 'If Your Excellency permits, I will drive out to see His Majesty (the Bavarian Crown Prince Rupprecht) at once and

1. The whole of this account, including the text of Hitler's words, is based on the subsequent court proceedings in Munich: *Der Hitler-Prozess* (Deutscher Volksverlag, Munich, 1924).
2. Ernst Hanfstängl: *Hitler, The Missing Years* (London, 1957), p. 100.

inform him that the German people have arisen and made good the injustice done to His Majesty's late lamented father.' At that even Kahr capitulated and agreed to cooperate as the King's deputy.

In apparent unity they all filed back into the hall. While the audience climbed on to the seats and cheered in enthusiasm, each made a brief speech, swore loyalty and shook hands on the platform. Hitler, exultant and relieved, spoke with passion. 'I am going to fulfil the vow I made to myself five years ago when I was a blind cripple in the military hospital: to know neither rest nor peace until the November criminals had been overthrown, until on the ruins of the wretched Germany of today there should have arisen once more a Germany of power and greatness, of freedom and splendour.' No sooner had he finished speaking than the whole assembly broke into *Deutschland über Alles*.

Barely had this touching scene of reconciliation been completed than Hitler was called out to settle a quarrel which had started when Stormtroopers of the Bund Oberland tried to occupy the Engineers' barracks. By a bad error of judgement he left the hall without taking proper precautions. As soon as Hitler had gone, and the audience began to pour out of the exits, Lossow excused himself on the grounds that he must go to his office to issue orders, and left unobtrusively, followed by Kahr and Seisser. It was the last that was seen of General von Lossow or von Kahr that night.

Hitler already had several hundred Stormtroopers of the S.A. and Kampfbund at his command. By morning these had grown to some three thousand men, for considerable forces continued to come in from the countryside during the night – Strasser, for example, bringing a hundred and fifty from Landshut. While his own bodyguard (Stoss Truppe Hitler, the origin of the later black-shirted S.S.) occupied the offices of the Social Democratic *Münchener Post* and smashed the machines, the Reichskriegs-flagge, under Röhm's leadership, seized the War Ministry on Schönfeldstrasse and set up barbed-wire and machine guns. Hitler, whose main forces were kept on the other side of the river, bivouacking in the gardens or sleeping on the floor of the Bürgerbräukeller, came over to Röhm before midnight and held a council of war with Ludendorff, Kriebel and Weber. As time passed, however, they became concerned at the absence of any news from Lossow or Kahr, and were at a loss what to do next.

Messages to Lossow at the 19th Infantry Regiment's barracks produced no answer; nor did the messengers return. The night was allowed to pass without the seizure of a single key position, apart from Röhm's occupation of the Army headquarters. This was partly due to the Kampfbund leaders' ignorance of what was happening and unwillingness to recognize that they had been deceived; even more, however, to the improvised character of the whole affair. Finally, between six and seven o'clock in the morning, Pöhner and Major Hühnlein were dispatched to occupy the police headquarters, but were promptly arrested instead, together with Frick.

As General von Lossow returned from the Bürgerbräukeller he was greeted by Lieutenant-General von Danner, the commander of the Munich garrison, with the cold remark: 'All that of course was bluff, Excellency?' In case Lossow had any doubts, Seeckt telegraphed from Berlin that, if the Army in Bavaria did not suppress the putsch, he would do it himself. There was considerable sympathy with Hitler and Röhm among the junior officers from the rank of major downwards, and the cadets of the Infantry School came over to Hitler's side under the persuasion of the ex-Freikorps leader, Lieutenant Rossbach. But the senior officers were indignant at the insolence of this ex-corporal, and in the end discipline held. Orders were sent out to bring in reinforcements from outlying garrisons. Meanwhile the Bavarian State Government was transferred to Regensburg, and Kahr issued a proclamation denouncing the promises extorted in the Bürgerbräukeller and dissolving the Nazi Party and the Kampfbund. From Crown Prince Rupprecht came a brief but pointed recommendation to crush the putsch at all costs, using force if necessary. Rupprecht had no use for a movement which had Ludendorff as one of its leaders.

By the morning of 9 November it was clear to Hitler, Ludendorff, and the other leaders (although not to the rank and file) that the attempt had miscarried. At dawn Hitler returned with Ludendorff to the Bürgerbräu, leaving Röhm to hold out in the War Ministry. For a time Hitler considered retiring from Munich to Rosenheim and rallying his forces before trying to force his way back into the city. But this was rejected by Ludendorff. Hitler then conceived the idea of getting Crown Prince Rupprecht to intercede and settle matters peacefully. Lieutenant Neunzert, an old friend of the Crown Prince, was sent off to Rupprecht's castle near Berchtesgaden, but failing to find a car had to travel by train and arrived too late for his message to have any effect. For in the meantime, Ludendorff, who was convinced that the Army would never fire on the legendary figure of the First World War, had persuaded Hitler, against his better judgement, that they must take the offensive and try to restore the position by marching on Lossow's headquarters. Once he stood face to face with the officers and men of the Army, Ludendorff was convinced that they would obey him and not Lossow. According to his own account at the subsequent trial, Hitler seems also to have believed that public opinion in Munich might still be won to his side – 'and Messrs Kahr, Lossow, and Seisser could not be so foolish as to turn machine-guns on the aroused people.'

While these anxious discussions were being held in the Bürgerbräu, on the far side of the river, troops of the Regular Army had surrounded Röhm and his men in the centre of the city. Both sides were reluctant to open fire – there were many old comrades among Röhm's Stormtroopers and many among the Army captains and lieutenants who sympathized with his aims. All that Röhm could do was to sit tight and await events.

Shortly after eleven o'clock on the morning of 9 November – the anniversary of Napoleon's *coup d'état* of Brumaire in 1799 – a column of two or three thousand men left the Bürgerbräukeller, on the south bank of the River Isar, and headed for the Ludwig Bridge leading to the centre of the city. Only the leaders knew that this was a last desperate attempt to bluff their way out of a putsch which had already failed. During the night, a number of hostages had been taken, and it was with the threat of shooting these that Göring, the leader of the S.A., persuaded the officer commanding the police at the bridge to let them pass. At the head of the column fluttered the swastika flag and the banner of the Bund Oberland. In the first row marched Hitler, between Ludendorff, Scheubner-Richter, and Ulrich Graf on one side, Dr Weber, Feder, and Kriebel on the other. Most of the men carried arms, and Hitler himself had a pistol in his hand. Crowds thronged the streets and there was an atmosphere of excitement and expectation. Julius Streicher, who had been haranguing the crowd in the Marienplatz, climbed down to take his place in the second rank. Rosenberg and Albrecht von Graefe, the sole representative of the North German Nationalists, who had arrived that morning at Ludendorff's urgent summons, trudged unhappily along with the rest.

From the Marienplatz the column swung down the narrow Residenzstrasse towards the Odeonsplatz, singing as it went. Beyond lay the old War Ministry, where Röhm was besieged. The time was half past twelve.

The police, armed with carbines, were drawn up in a cordon across the end of the street to prevent the column debouching on to the broad Place beyond. The Stormtroopers completely out-numbered the police – there were no troops present – but the narrowness of the street prevented them bringing their superior numbers to bear. Who fired first has never been settled. One of the National Socialists – Ulrich Graf – ran forward and shouted to the police officer: 'Don't fire, Ludendorff and Hitler are coming,' while Hitler cried out: 'Surrender!' At this moment a shot rang out and a hail of bullets swept the street. The first man to fall was Scheubner-Richter, with whom Hitler had been marching arm-in-arm. Hitler fell, either pulled down or seeking cover. The shooting lasted only a minute, but sixteen Nazis and three police already lay dead or dying in the street. Göring was badly wounded, and was carried into a house. Weber, the leader of the Bund Oberland, stood against the wall weeping hysteri-cally. All was confusion, neither side being at all sure what to do next. One man alone kept his head. Erect and unperturbed, General Ludendorff, with his adjutant, Major Streck, by his side, marched steadily on, pushed through the line of police and reached the Place beyond.

The situation might still have been saved, but not a single man followed him. Hitler at the critical moment lost his nerve. Accord-ing to the independent evidence of two eye-witnesses, one of them a National Socialist – Dr Walther Schulz and Dr Karl Gebhard – Hitler was the first to scramble to his feet and, stum-bling back towards the end of the procession, allowed himself to be pushed by Schulz into a yellow motor-car which was waiting on the Max Josef Platz. He was undoubtedly in great pain from a dislocated shoulder, and probably believed himself to have been wounded. But there was no denying that under fire the Nazi leaders had broken and fled, Hitler the first. Only two among them had been killed or badly wounded, Scheubner-Richter and Göring; the other killed and wounded were all in the following ranks, exposed to the fire by the action of their leaders in taking cover.

Two hours later Röhm was persuaded to capitulate and was taken into custody. Göring was smuggled across the Austrian frontier by his wife. On 11 November Hitler was arrested at Uffing, where he had taken refuge in Putzi Hanfstängl's house and was being nursed by his wife.[1]

VII

In many ways the attempt of 8–9 November was a remarkable achievement for a man like Hitler who had started from nothing only a few years before. In less than a couple of hours on the night of 8 November he had transformed the political situation in Bavaria and made a revolution by sheer bluff. However impermanent a triumph, the scene in the Bürgerbräukeller, with Kahr and Hitler shaking hands before the cheering crowd, and Generals Ludendorff and von Lossow agreeing to serve under the dictatorship of the ex-corporal – a scene which would have seemed incredible an hour before – was evidence of political talent of an unusual kind.

But the mistakes had been gross. The Kampfbund disposed of considerable forces – many more than those who took part in the march. They only needed to be concentrated and used to occupy such obvious positions as police headquarters, the central telephone exchange, the railway station and the power station. For all their talk of a putsch, not one of the rebel leaders had thought out the practical problems of making a revolution. Instead, S.A. detachments straggled into Munich all through the night and half the next day, and were left to stand about while the commanders argued what they should do. Finally, when they did decide to march, their leaders, who for years had appealed openly to violence, crumpled up and fled before one volley from a force of armed police whom they outnumbered by thirty to one. Worst of all, from Hitler's point of view, was the contrast between his own behaviour under fire – the first to get to his feet and make his escape by car, leaving the wounded, the dead, and the rest of his followers to fend for themselves – and that of Ludendorff, who, in the sight of all, had marched steadily forward and brushed aside the police carbines with contemptuous ease.

The truth is, however, that Hitler's plans had miscarried long before the column set out for the Odeonsplatz. As he admitted later: 'We went in the conviction that this was the end, in one way or another. I know of one who, on the steps as we set out, said:

1. For a graphic reconstruction of the whole episode, see the novel by Richard Hughes: *The Fox in the Attic* (London, 1961).

"This is now the finish." Everyone in himself carried with him this conviction.'[1] Hitler had never intended to use force; from the beginning his conception had been that of a revolution in agreement with the political and military authorities. 'We never thought to carry through a revolt against the Army: it was *with it* that we believed we should succeed.'[2] This explains why no adequate preparations had been made for a seizure of power by arms. The *coup* was to be limited to forcing Kahr and Lossow into acting with him, in the belief that it was only hesitation, not opposition, that held them back. Again and again Hitler had told his men that when the moment came they need not worry, neither the Army nor the police would fire on them. The shots on the Odeonsplatz represented something more than the resistance any revolutionary party may expect to meet and take in its stride; they represented the final collapse of the premises upon which the whole attempt had been constructed. It was this that accounted for Hitler's despondency on the morning of 9 November and the absence of any plan. From the moment it became certain that Lossow and Kahr had taken sides against him, Hitler knew that the attempt had failed. There was a slender chance that a show of force might still swing the Army back to his side, and so he agreed to march. But it was to be a demonstration, not the beginning of a putsch; the last thing Hitler wanted, or was prepared for, was to shoot it out with the Army.

Never was Hitler's political ability more clearly shown than in the way he recovered from this set-back. For the man who, on 9 November 1923, appeared to be broken and finished as a political leader – and had himself believed this – succeeded by April 1924 in making himself one of the most-talked-of figures in Germany, and turned his trial for treason into a political triumph.

The opportunity for this lay in the equivocal political situation in Bavaria, which had saved him once before after the fiasco of 1 May. This time he had to stand his trial, but the trial was held in Munich, and it was a trial for a conspiracy in which the chief witnesses for the prosecution – Kahr, Lossow, and Seisser – had been almost as deeply involved as the accused. The full story was one which most of the political leaders of Bavaria, the Bavarian People's Party and the Monarchists were only too anxious to

1. Hitler in the Bürgerbräukeller at Munich, 8 November 1935 (Baynes: vol. I, p. 135).
2. Hitler at Munich, 8 November 1933 (Baynes: vol. I, p. 133).

avoid being made public. Hitler exploited this situation to the full.

The trial began before a special court, sitting in the old Munich Infantry School in the Blutenburgstrasse, on 26 February 1924. It lasted for twenty-four days. For the whole of this period it was front-page news in every German newspaper, and a large group of foreign correspondents attended the trial. For the first time Hitler had an audience outside the frontiers of Bavaria. Hitler's old protector and future minister, Franz Gürtner, was still Minister of Justice in the Bavarian Government, and active on his behalf behind the scenes. One of the features of the trial was the leniency with which the judges treated the accused in court, and the mildness of their rebukes to Hitler for his interruptions.

Nine men sat beside Hitler in the dock, all accused of high treason: Ludendorff, Pöhner, and Frick; Röhm, Weber, and Kriebel, the other leaders of the Kampfbund; and Lieutenants Brückner, Wagner, and Pernet, three lesser figures who had been active leaders of the Stormtroopers. Of the ten, Ludendorff was by far the most distinguished and famous, but it was Hitler who took the lead and stood out from all the rest.

From the first day Hitler's object was to recover the political initiative and virtually put the chief witnesses for the prosecution in the dock. He did this by the simple device of assuming full responsibility for the attempt to overthrow the Republic, and, instead of apologizing or trying to belittle the seriousness of this crime, indignantly reproaching Lossow, Kahr, and Seisser with the responsibility for its failure. This was a highly effective way of appealing to nationalist opinion, and turning the tables on the prosecution. In his opening speech[1] Hitler declared: 'One thing was certain, Lossow, Kahr, and Seisser had the same goal that we had – to get rid of the Reich Government with its present international and parliamentary government. If our enterprise was actually high treason, then during this whole period Lossow, Kahr, and Seisser must have been committing high treason along with us, for during all these weeks we talked of nothing but the aims of which we now stand accused.'

This was perfectly true, as everybody in the court knew, and Hitler pressed his advantage. 'I alone bear the responsibility,' he concluded, 'but I am not a criminal because of that. If today I stand here as a revolutionary, it is as a revolutionary against the Revolution. There is no such thing as high treason against the traitors of 1918. It is impossible for me to have committed high

1. *Der Hitler-Prozess*, pp. 18–28.

treason, for the treason would not consist in the events of 8 November, but in all our activities and our state of mind in the preceding months – and then I wonder why those who did exactly the same are not sitting here with me. If we committed high treason, then countless others did the same. I deny all guilt as long as I do not find added to our little company the gentlemen who helped even in the pettiest details of the preparation of the affair. . . . I feel myself the best of Germans who wanted the best for the German people.'

Neither Kahr nor Seisser had the skill to withstand such tactics, while the judges sat placidly through Hitler's mounting attack on the Republic whose authority they represented, only interrupting to reprove those who applauded openly in the court. One man alone stood up to Hitler, and this surprisingly enough was General von Lossow.[1]

Von Lossow was an angry man. His career had ended abruptly as a result of the November affair, and he had to listen in silence while his reputation was torn to shreds in the court, and he was represented as a coward, who had lacked the courage to declare either for or against the conspiracy. Now he had his chance to reply, and he expressed all the contempt of the officer caste for this jumped-up, ill-educated, loud-mouthed agitator who had never risen above the rank of corporal and now tried to dictate to the Army the policy it should pursue. 'I was no unemployed *comitadji*,' he declared; 'at that time I occupied a high position in the State. I should never have dreamed of trying to get myself a better position by means of a putsch.' Lossow dealt bluntly with Hitler's own ambitions: 'He thought himself the German Mussolini or the German Gambetta, and his followers, who had entered on the heritage of the Byzantine monarchy, regarded him as the German Messiah.' For his own part he looked upon Hitler as fitted to play no more than the role of a political drummer. 'The well-known eloquence of Herr Hitler at first made a strong impression on me. But the more I heard him, the fainter this impression became. I realized that his long speeches were almost always about the same thing, that his views were partly a matter-of-course for any German of nationalist views, and partly showed that Hitler lacked a sense of reality and the ability to see what was possible and practicable.' In his closing speech the Public Prosecutor used the same patronizing language: 'At first Hitler

1. *Der Hitler-Prozess*, eleventh day, testimony of Lieutenant-General von Lossow, pp. 109–24.

kept himself free of personal ambition for power. Later on, when he was being idolized by certain circles, he thoughtlessly allowed himself to be carried beyond the position assigned to him.'

But Hitler had the last word. In cross-examination he made Lossow lose his temper, and in his final speech he established a complete mastery over the court. Lossow had said he was fit only to be 'the drummer' and had accused him of ambition.

How petty are the thoughts of small men [Hitler retorted].[1] Believe me, I do not regard the acquisition of a Minister's portfolio as a thing worth striving for. I do not hold it worthy of a great man to endeavour to go down in history just by becoming a Minister. One might be in danger of being buried beside other Ministers. I aimed from the first at something a thousand times higher than a Minister. I wanted to become the destroyer of Marxism. I am going to achieve this task, and if I do, the title of Minister will be an absurdity as far as I am concerned. When I stood for the first time at the grave of Richard Wagner my heart overflowed with pride in a man who had forbidden any such inscription as: Here lies Privy Councillor, Music-Director, His Excellency Baron Richard von Wagner. I was proud that this man and so many others in German history were content to give their names to history without titles. It was not from modesty that I wanted to be a drummer in those days. That was the highest aspiration: the rest is nothing.

The man who is born to be a dictator is not compelled; he wills it. He is not driven forward, but drives himself. There is nothing immodest about this. Is it immodest for a worker to drive himself towards heavy labour? Is it presumptuous of a man with the high forehead of a thinker to ponder through the nights till he gives the world an invention? The man who feels called upon to govern a people has no right to say: If you want me or summon me, I will cooperate. No, it is his duty to step forward.

Looking back on the trial years later, Hitler remarked:

When the Kapp Putsch was at an end, and those who were responsible for it were brought before the Republican courts, then each held up his hand and swore that he knew nothing, had intended nothing, wished nothing. That was what destroyed the bourgeois world – that they had not the courage to stand by their act, that they had not the courage to step before the judge and say: 'Yes, that was what we *wanted* to do; we wanted to destroy the State. . . .' It is not decisive whether one conquers; what is necessary is that one must with heroism and courage make oneself responsible for the consequences.[2]

Hitler not only took the responsibility for what had happened

1. Hitler's closing speech, *Der Hitler-Prozess*, pp. 262–9.
2. Hitler at Munich, 8 November 1934 (Baynes: vol. i, pp. 152–3).

and left to those who had refused to march with him the odium of abandoning the national cause; he deliberately built up the failure of 8 and 9 November into one of the great propaganda legends of the movement. Year after year, even after the outbreak of war, he went back to the Bürgerbräukeller in Munich on 8 November, and to the Feldherrnhalle, the War Memorial on the Odeonsplatz, to renew the memory of what had happened there on that grey November morning in 1923. Regularly each year he spoke to the Nazi Old Guard (the *Alte Kämpfer*) in the Bürgerbräukeller, and the next morning on the Odeonsplatz solemnly recalled the martyrs of the movement who died for their faith.

When the bodies of the sixteen dead of 1923 were re-interred in 1935 in a new memorial, Hitler said: 'They now pass into the German immortality. . . . For us they are not dead. These temples are no crypts: they are an eternal guard post. Here they stand for Germany and keep guard over our people. Here they lie as true witnesses to our movement.'[1] These were the men whom twelve years before Hitler had left dying in the street while he fled. By skilful propaganda he had turned the fiasco of 1923 and his own failure as a leader into retrospective triumph.

But the unsuccessful putsch of 1923 has a still more important place in the history of the Nazi movement for the lessons which Hitler drew from it and by which he shaped his political tactics in the years that followed. In 1936, three years after he became Chancellor, he summed up the lessons of that earlier attempt to seize power: 'We recognized that it is not enough to overthrow the old State, but that the new State must previously have been built up and be practically ready to one's hand. And so only a few days after the collapse I formed a new decision: that now without any haste the conditions must be created which would exclude the possibility of a second failure. Later you lived through another revolution. But what a difference between them! In 1933 it was no longer a question of overthrowing a state by an act of violence; meanwhile the new State had been built up and all that there remained to do was to destroy the last remnants of the old State – and that took but a few hours.'[2]

When Hitler spoke of a 'new decision' he was exaggerating; he had never intended to seize power by force. His revolution – even in 1923 – had been designed as a 'revolution by permission

1. Hitler at Munich, 9 November 1935 (Baynes: vol. I, pp. 158–9).
2. Hitler at Munich, 9 November 1936 (Baynes: vol. I, pp. 155–6).

of the Herr President'. But the failure of 1923 strengthened his hand. 'After the putsch I could say to all those in the Party what otherwise it would never have been possible for me to say. My answer to my critics was: Now the battle will be waged as I wish it and not otherwise.'[1] 'This evening and this day (8–9 November) made it possible for us afterwards to fight a battle for ten years by legal means; for, make no mistake, if we had not acted then I should never have been able to found a revolutionary movement, and yet all the time maintain legality. One could have said to me with justice: You talk like all the others and you will act just as little as all the others.'[2]

Hitler had already laid the foundations of this policy at the trial of 1924. In his closing speech, he went out of his way to avoid recrimination and renew the old offer of alliance with the Army. The failure of 1923 was the failure of individuals, of a Lossow and a Kahr; the most powerful and the most permanent of German institutions, the Army, was not involved. 'I believe that the hour will come when the masses, who today stand in the street with our swastika banner, will unite with those who fired upon them. . . . When I learned that it was the police who fired, I was happy that it was not the Reichswehr which had stained its record; the Reichswehr stands as untarnished as before. One day the hour will come when the Reichswehr will stand at our side, officers and men.'

The President of the Court rebuked Hitler for his slighting reference to the police, but Hitler brushed aside his interruption.

The army we have formed is growing from day to day. . . . I nourish the proud hope that one day the hour will come when these rough companies will grow to battalions, the battalions to regiments, the regiments to divisions, that the old cockade will be taken from the mud, that the old flags will wave again, that there will be a reconciliation at the last great divine judgement which we are prepared to face. . . . For it is not you, gentlemen, who pass judgement on us. That judgement is spoken by the eternal court of history. What judgement you will hand down, I know. But that court will not ask us: 'Did you commit high treason, or did you not?' That court will judge us, the Quartermaster-General of the old Army (Ludendorff), his officers and soldiers, as Germans who wanted only the good of their own people and Fatherland; who wanted to fight and die. You may pronounce us guilty a thousand times over, but the goddess of the eternal court of history will smile and tear to tatters

1. Hitler at Munich, 9 November 1934 (Baynes: vol. i, p. 161).
2. Hitler at Munich, 9 November 1933 (Baynes: vol. i, p. 152).

the brief of the State Prosecutor and the sentence of this court. For she acquits us.[1]

It took Hitler nine years to convince the Army that he was right. Meanwhile, as Konrad Heiden remarks, the verdict of the court was not so far from the judgement of the Goddess of History. Gürtner had seen to that. In face of all the evidence Ludendorff was acquitted, and Hitler was given the minimum sentence of five years' imprisonment. When the lay judges protested at the severity of the sentence, the President of the Court assured them that Hitler would certainly be pardoned and released on probation. Despite the objection of the State Prosecutor and the attempts of the police to get him deported, Hitler was in fact released from prison after serving less than nine months of his sentence – and promptly resumed his agitation against the Republic. Such were the penalties of high treason in a State where disloyalty to the régime was the surest recommendation to mercy.

1. *Der Hitler-Prozess*, p. 269.

CHAPTER THREE

THE YEARS OF WAITING
1924–31

I

FIFTY miles west of Munich in the wooded valley of the Lech
lies the small town of Landsberg. It was here that Hitler served
his term of imprisonment from 11 November 1923 to 20 December 1924, with only the interlude of the trial in Munich to interrupt it. In the early summer of 1924 some forty other National
Socialists were in prison with him, and they had an easy and
comfortable life. They ate well – Hitler became quite fat in prison
– had as many visitors as they wished, and spent much of their
time out of doors in the garden, where, like the rest, Hitler
habitually wore leather shorts with a Tyrolean jacket. Emil
Maurice acted partly as Hitler's batman, partly as his secretary,
a job which he later relinquished to Rudolf Hess, who had
voluntarily returned from Austria to share his leader's imprisonment. Hitler's large and sunny room, No. 7, was on the first floor,
a mark of privilege which he shared with Weber, Kriebel, and
Hess. On his thirty-fifth birthday, which fell shortly after the
trial, the parcels and flowers he received filled several rooms. He
had a large correspondence in addition to his visitors, and as
many newspapers and books as he wished. Hitler presided at the
midday meal, claiming and receiving the respect due to him as
leader of the Party: much of the time, however, from July onwards he shut himself up in his room to dictate *Mein Kampf*,
which was begun in prison and taken down by Emil Maurice
and Hess.

Max Amann, who was to publish the book, had originally
hoped for an account, full of sensational revelations, of the
November putsch. But Hitler was too canny for that; there were
to be no recriminations. His own title for the book was *Four and
a Half Years of Struggle against Lies, Stupidity, and Cowardice*,
reduced by Amann to *Mein Kampf – My Struggle*. Even then
Amann was to be disappointed. For the book contains very little
autobiography, but is filled with page after page of turgid discussion of Hitler's ideas, written in a verbose style which is both
difficult and dull to read.

Hitler took the writing of *Mein Kampf* with great seriousness. Dietrich Eckart, Feder, and Rosenberg had all published books or pamphlets, and Hitler was anxious to establish his own position of intellectual as well as political authority in the Party. He was eager to prove that he too, even though he had never been to a university and had left school without a certificate, had read and thought deeply, acquiring his own *Weltanschauung*. It is this thwarted intellectual ambition, the desire to make people take him seriously as an original thinker, which accounts for the pretentiousness of the style, the use of long words and constant repetitions, all the tricks of a half-educated man seeking to give weight to his words. As a result *Mein Kampf* is a remarkably interesting book for anyone trying to understand Hitler's mind, but as a party tract or a political best-seller it was a failure, which few, even among the party members, had the patience to read.

While Hitler turned his energies to writing *Mein Kampf* the Party fell to pieces; 9 November had been followed by the proscription of the Party and its organizations throughout the Reich, the suppression of the *Völkischer Beobachter* and the arrest or flight of the leaders. Göring remained abroad until 1927, Scheubner-Richter had been killed, and Dietrich Eckart, who had been ill for some time, died at the end of 1923. Quarrels soon broke out among those who remained at liberty or were released from prison.

Before his arrest Hitler had managed to send a pencilled note to Rosenberg with the brief message: 'Dear Rosenberg, from now on you will lead the movement.' As Rosenberg himself admits in his memoirs, this was a surprising choice. Although at one time he had great influence on Hitler, Rosenberg was no man of action and had never been one of the small circle who led the conspiracy. As a leader he was ineffective, finding it difficult either to make up his mind or to assert his authority. It was precisely the lack of these qualities which attracted Hitler: Rosenberg as his deputy would represent no danger to his own position in the Party.

Rosenberg, who was not only an intellectual but respectable and prim as well, was soon on the worst terms with the rougher elements in the Party, notably the two rival Jew-baiters and lechers, Julius Streicher and Hermann Esser, who combined to attack every move made by Rosenberg, Gregor Strasser, Ludendorff, and Pöhner, and accused them of undermining Hitler's position. These in turn retorted by demanding the others' expulsion from the Party and Hitler's repudiation of them. But Hitler declined to take sides: if pushed to decide, he preferred Streicher, Esser, and Amann, however disreputable, because they were loyal to him and dependent on him. Men like Strasser, with ten times the others' abilities, were for that very reason more inclined to follow an independent line.

Political issues of importance were involved in these personal quarrels. What was to be done now that the Party had been dissolved and Hitler was in prison? Hitler's answer, however camouflaged, was simple: Nothing. He had no wish to see the Party revive its fortunes without him. But Gregor Strasser, Röhm, and Rosenberg, supported by Ludendorff, were anxious to take part in the national and State elections of the spring of 1924. Hitler, who was not a German citizen, was automatically excluded, and had from the beginning attacked all parliamentary activity as worthless and dangerous to the independence of the movement. It was true that such tactics were now essential if the Party was to follow the path of legality, but Hitler was concerned with the threat to his personal position as leader of the Party if others were elected to the Reichstag while he remained outside.

Despite Hitler's opposition, loudly echoed by Streicher and Esser, Rosenberg, Strasser, and Ludendorff agreed to cooperate with the other Völkisch[1] groups and won a minor triumph at the April and May elections. The Völkisch bloc became the second largest party in the Bavarian Parliament, while in the Reichstag elections the combined list of the National Socialist German Freedom Movement (N.S. Deutsche Freiheitsbewegung) polled nearly two million votes and captured thirty-two seats. Among those elected were Strasser, Röhm, Ludendorff, Feder, and Frick. Ironically, they owed much of their success to the impression made by Hitler's attitude at the Munich trial, but it was only with great difficulty that Hitler had been persuaded to agree to the election campaign at all.

The combination, under cover of which the proscribed Nazi Party had entered the election campaign, raised another important issue. Ludendorff and Strasser were anxious to consolidate

1. A difficult word to translate: it combines the idea of nationalism with those of race (the *Volk*) and anti-Semitism. The Völkisch groups constituted an extremist wing of the German Nationalists of whose middle-class 'moderation' they were often critical.

and extend the electoral alliance they had concluded with the North German Deutsch-völkische Freiheitspartei led by Albrecht von Graefe and Graf Ernst zu Reventlow, with nationalist, racist, and anti-Semitic views similar to those of the Nazis in the south. In August 1924, a congress of all the Völkisch groups was held at Weimar. In Part I of *Mein Kampf* (written in the years 1924–5) Hitler expressed his dislike of such alliances. 'It is quite erroneous to believe that the strength of a movement must increase if it be combined with other movements of a similar kind. . . . In reality the movement thus admits outside elements which will subsequently weaken its vigour.'[1]

There was some truth in this. The traditional animosity of Prussians and Bavarians; the open hostility of the North Germans to the Roman Catholic Church (whose stronghold was Bavaria), and the opposition of the more bourgeois North German nationalists to the radical and socialist elements in the Nazi programme – all these represented factors which might well weaken the appeal of the Nazis as a Bavarian and South German party. But the root of Hitler's objection was his jealous distrust and fear for his own position. Hitler lacked any ability for cooperation and compromise. The only relationship he understood was that of domination. He preferred a party, however small, over which he could exercise complete and unquestioned control to a combination, however large, in which power must inevitably be shared and his own position reduced to that of equality with other leaders. In Part II of *Mein Kampf* Hitler returns to the question and devotes a whole chapter to it under the title: 'The Strong are Strongest when Alone.'

On the very next page Hitler goes out of his way to praise Julius Streicher, who had magnanimously subordinated his own German Socialists to the Nazi Party, and contrasts his loyalty with the behaviour of those 'ambitious men who at first had no ideas of their own, but felt themselves "called" exactly at that moment in which the success of the N.S.D.A.P. became unquestionable.'[2] There were long and sometimes bitter arguments between Hitler and his visitors at Landsberg on these issues in 1924. Hitler was both suspicious and evasive. He tried by every means to delay decisions until he was released, and once again Streicher and Esser proved their worth to him by founding a rival party, the Grossdeutsche Volksgemeinschaft, in open opposition to Strasser's Völkisch bloc in Bavaria.

1. *Mein Kampf*, p. 293.   2. ibid., p. 243.

A further cause of disagreement was the S.A. Röhm, although found guilty of treason, had been discharged on the day sentence was pronounced. He at once set to work to weld together again the disbanded forces of the Kampfbund. Ludecke was one of those who agreed to help Röhm. 'Many of the men with whom I conferred,' he says, 'were veritable condottieri, such as Captain von Heydebreck and Edmund Heines. Almost without exception they resumed Röhm's work eagerly, only too glad to be busy again at the secret military work without which they found life wearisome.'[1] The Frontbann, as it was now called, grew rapidly, for Röhm was an able organizer and possessed untiring energy: he journeyed from one end of Germany to the other, including Austria and East Prussia, and soon had some thirty thousand men enrolled.

But the greater Röhm's success, the more uneasy Hitler became. His activities threatened Hitler's chances of leaving prison. The Bavarian Government arrested some of the subordinate leaders of the Frontbann, and Hitler's release on parole, which he had expected six months after sentence had been passed, on 1 October 1924, was delayed. 'Hitler, Kriebel, and Weber in their cell,' Röhm wrote later, 'could not realize what was at stake. They felt that their approaching freedom was endangered and laid the blame, not on the enemy, but on the friends who were fighting for them.'[2]

Hitler was no less worried by the character Röhm was giving to the new organization which had replaced and absorbed the old S.A. The two men had never agreed about the function of the Stormtroops. For Hitler the S.A. had first and last a political function: they were to be instruments of political intimidation and propaganda subordinate to the Party. On 15 October, however, Röhm wrote to Ludendorff, as leader of the Völkisch bloc in the Reichstag:

The political and military movements are entirely independent of each other. . . . As the present leader of the military movement I make the demand that the defence organizations should be given appropriate representation in the parliamentary group and that they should not be hindered in their special work. . . . The National Socialist Movement is a fighting movement. Germany's freedom – both at home and abroad – will never be secured by talk and negotiations; it must be fought for.[3]

1. Ludecke: p. 228.
2. Röhm: *Memoiren* (Saarbrücken, 1934), p. 154.
3. ibid., p. 156.

Hitler flatly disagreed with such a view, just as much as he disliked the military organization of the Frontbann, its rapid expansion and growing independence. In December, when new elections for the Reichstag were held, Röhm did not find a place on the Nazi list.

By the end of Hitler's year in prison these quarrels and disagreements had reached such a pitch that it appeared possible to write off the former Nazi Party as a serious force in German or Bavarian politics. The Reichstag elections of December 1924 confirmed this. The votes cast for the Nazi-Völkisch bloc fell by more than half, from 1,918,300 to 907,300; instead of 32 seats they had only 14 in the new Reichstag, less than five per cent of the total. Hitler had already remarked to Hess: 'I shall need five years before the movement is on top again.'

Much of the blame for this state of affairs fell on Hitler – with considerable justice. 'Hitler,' Ludecke writes, 'was the one man with power to set things straight; yet he never so much as lifted his little finger or spoke one word.'[1] Röhm, Strasser, Ludendorff, and Rosenberg all complained in the same exasperated terms. They could never get a firm answer from him. In disgust Rosenberg threw up the job of deputy leader of the Party. Twenty years later, reflecting on what had happened, while waiting to be tried by the International Court of Nuremberg, he wrote: 'Hitler deliberately allowed antagonistic groups to exist within the Party, so that he could play umpire and Führer.'[2]

Ludecke arrived at the same conclusion: 'To suppose that Hitler, behind prison walls, may have been ignorant of conditions outside is to be unjust to his political genius. A more reasonable supposition is that he was deliberately fostering the schism in order to keep the whip-hand over the party.'[3] And he succeeded. The plans for a united Völkisch Front came to nothing. Ludendorff and Röhm left in disgust, and no powerful Nazi group was created in the Reichstag under the leadership of someone else. The price of this disunity was heavy, but for Hitler it was worth paying. By the time he came out of prison the Party had broken up almost completely – but it had not found an alternative

1. Ludecke: p. 214.
2. *Rosenberg's Memoirs*, edited by Serge Lang and Ernst von Scherk (New York, 1949), p. 231.
3. Ludecke: p. 222.

leader, there was no rival to oust. Hitler's tactics of evasion and 'divide and rule' had worked well.

On 8 May 1924, and again on 22 September, the Bavarian State Police submitted a report to the Bavarian Ministry of the Interior recommending Hitler's deportation. Hitler could still be considered an Austrian citizen and put across the frontier. The second of these reports stated: 'The moment he is set free, Hitler will, because of his energy, again become the driving force of new and serious public riots and a menace to the security of the State. Hitler will resume his political activities, and the hope of the nationalists and racists that he will succeed in removing the present dissensions among the para-military troops will be fulfilled.'[1]

Thanks to the intervention of Gürtner, the Bavarian Minister of Justice, this threat of deportation was averted. In July Hitler formally resigned the leadership of the Party as a gesture of appeasement to the authorities. The activities of Röhm and the Frontbann temporarily endangered his release, but the failure of the Nazis in the December elections probably convinced the Bavarian Government that they had nothing more to fear from Hitler. On the afternoon of 20 December a telegram from the Public Prosecutor's office ordered Hitler's and Kriebel's release on parole. Adolf Müller, the Party's printer and Hoffmann at once drove out from Munich to fetch Hitler. Cap in hand and a raincoat belted over his shorts, he paused for his photograph to be taken. An hour or two later he walked up the stairs of 41 Thierschstrasse to the apartment he rented at the top of the house. His room was filled with flowers and laurel wreaths, his dog bounded down the stairs to greet him: he was home for Christmas.

II

Hitler's return from prison by no means meant the end of the quarrels and disunity in the Party. On 12 February 1925, Ludendorff, Strasser, and von Graefe resigned their leadership of the National Sozialistische Freiheitsbewegung, which was thereupon dissolved. After the fiasco of the presidential elections later in the spring the break between Hitler and Ludendorff became irreparable. In April Röhm demanded a decision about the future of the

1. Quoted by R. W. M. Kempner: *Blue Print of the Nazi Underground* (Research Studies of the State College of Washington, vol. XIII, No. 2, June 1945), p. 55.

Frontbann. The independent terms on which Röhm proposed cooperation between the political and military leadership were rejected by Hitler in a conversation on 16 April: rather than agree to these he preferred to let the Frontbann go and build up the S.A. again from scratch. The following day Röhm wrote to resign the leadership of both the S.A. and the Frontbann. Hitler sent no reply. On 30 April Röhm wrote again to Hitler. He ended his letter: 'I take this opportunity, in memory of the fine and difficult hours we have lived through together, to thank you (*Dir*) for your comradeship and to beg you not to exclude me from your personal friendship.'[1] But again Röhm got no reply. The next day a brief notice appeared in the *Völkischer Beobachter* announcing Röhm's resignation of his offices and withdrawal from politics. With Röhm, Brückner too left the Party. Earlier in April Pöhner had been killed in a road accident. Göring was still abroad; Kriebel retired to Carinthia and later went to Shanghai; Scheubner-Richter and Eckart were dead, Rosenberg offended. Not many were left with whom to begin the task of rebuilding.

Hitler's first move on leaving prison had been to consult Pöhner, and on Pöhner's advice he went to call on the Minister-President of Bavaria and leader of the strongly Catholic and particularist Bavarian People's Party, Dr Heinrich Held. The meeting took place on 4 January 1925. Despite Hitler's efforts at conciliation, Dr Held's reception was cold. The putsch, Hitler admitted, had been a mistake; his one object was to assist the Government in fighting Marxism; he had no use for Ludendorff's and the North Germans' attacks on the Catholic Church, and he had every intention of respecting the authority of the State. Held's attitude was one of scepticism tinged with contempt, but he agreed – with a little prompting from Gürtner, still Minister of Justice, and Held's friend as well as Hitler's – to raise the ban on the Party and its newspaper. 'The wild beast is checked,' was Held's comment to Gürtner. 'We can afford to loosen the chain.'[2]

The fact that Hitler had made his peace with the priest-ridden Bavarian Government only increased the scorn and hostility of Ludendorff and the North German Völkisch leaders, Reventlow and Graefe, who were outspoken in their hostility to the Church. Hitler was unrepentant; he even attacked the Völkisch deputies in the Bavarian Parliament for their failure to accept the offer of a

1. Röhm: p. 160.
2. Otto Strasser: *Hitler and I* (London, 1940), p. 71.

seat in Held's Cabinet. When one of the deputies replied that principles were more important than securing Hitler's release, Hitler retorted that his release would have been a thousand times more valuable for the movement than the principles of two dozen nationalist deputies.[1] This uncompromising attack lost him the support of most of the Völkisch bloc: only six of the twenty-four deputies in the Bavarian Landtag remained faithful to him, the rest broke away and gradually drifted into other parties. However compliant Hitler showed himself to Held and the Government, inside the Party he was determined to insist upon unconditional authority and obedience.

On 26 February 1925, the *Völkischer Beobachter* reappeared with a lengthy editorial from Hitler headed 'A New Beginning.' 'I do not consider it to be the task of a political leader,' Hitler wrote, 'to attempt to improve upon, or even to fuse together, the human material lying ready to his hand.'[2] This was his answer to those who still objected to Streicher and Esser. He added 'a special protest against the attempt to bring religious disputes into the movement or even to equate the movement with religious disputes. . . . Religious reformations cannot be made by political children, and in the case of these gentlemen it is very rarely that anything else is in question.'[3] This was his answer to the North German Völkisch movement which put anti-clericalism at the head of its programme.

The next day, 27 February, Hitler gathered the few who remained faithful for a mass meeting in the Bürgerbräukeller. But for the Munich Carnival he would have held it on 24 February, the fifth anniversary of the adoption of the Party's programme. Hitler telephoned to Anton Drexler asking him to take the chair, but Drexler demanded the exclusion of Esser: Hitler told him to go to the devil, and rang off. In Drexler's place, Max Amann conducted the meeting. Strasser, Röhm, and Rosenberg stayed away. Besides Amann, Hitler's only prominent supporters were Streicher and Esser, Gottfried Feder and Frick, and the Bavarian and Thuringian District Leaders, Buttmann and Dintner.

Hitler had not lost his gifts as an orator. When he finished speaking at the end of two hours there was loud cheering from the four thousand who filled the hall. He was perfectly frank in his claims.

1. Heiden: *Hitler*, pp. 196–7.
2. Heiden: *History of National Socialism*, pp. 97–8.
3. Baynes: vol. I, pp. 367–8.

If anyone comes and wants to impose conditions on me, I shall say to him: 'Just wait, my young friend, and see what conditions I impose on you. I am not contending for the favour of the masses. At the end of a year you shall judge, my comrades. If I have acted rightly, well and good. If I have acted wrongly, I shall resign my office into your hands. Until then, however, I alone lead the movement, and no one can impose conditions on me so long as I personally bear the responsibility. And I once more bear the whole responsibility for everything that occurs in the movement. . . . To this struggle of ours there are only two possible issues: either the enemy pass over our bodies or we pass over theirs, and it is my desire that, if in the struggle I should fall, the Swastika banner shall be my winding sheet.'[1]

In the glow of enthusiasm a reconciliation was effected. The leaders shook hands on the platform. Streicher spoke of Hitler's release as a gift from God. Buttmann declared: 'All my scruples vanished when the Führer spoke.'

With the re-founding of the Nazi Party in February 1925, Hitler set himself two objectives. The first was to establish his own absolute control over the Party by driving out those who were not prepared to accept his leadership without question. The second was to build up the Party and make it a force in German politics within the framework of the constitution. Ludecke reports a conversation with Hitler while he was still in Landsberg prison in which he said: 'When I resume active work it will be necessaɪy to pursue a new policy. Instead of working to achieve power by an armed *coup*, we shall have to hold our noses and enter the Reichstag against the Catholic and Marxist deputies. If out-voting them takes longer than out-shooting them, at least the result will be guaranteed by their own Constitution. Any lawful process is slow. . . . Sooner or later we shall have a majority – and after that, Germany.'[2]

The process was to prove even slower than Hitler had expected. Not only had he to begin at the beginning again, but the times were no longer so favourable as they had been in 1920–3. Hitler's speech on 27 February had been too successful, the display of his demagogic power too convincing. He had laid great stress on the need to concentrate opposition against a single enemy – Marxism and the Jew. But he had added, in an aside which delighted his audience: 'If necessary, by one enemy many can be meant.' In

   1. Heiden: *Hitler*, p. 198; and R. T. Clark: *The Fall of the German Republic* (London, 1935), p. 190.
   2. Ludecke: pp. 217–18.

other words, under cover of fighting Marxism and the Jew, the old fight against the State would be resumed. Such phrases as: 'Either the enemy will pass over our bodies or we over theirs,' scarcely suggested that Hitler's new policy of legality was very sincere. The authorities we.e alarmed and immediately afterwards prohibited him from speaking in public in Bavaria. This prohibition was soon extended to other German states as well. It lasted until May 1927 in Bavaria and September 1928 in Prussia, and was a severe handicap for a leader whose greatest asset was his ability as a speaker. Hitler, however, had no option but to obey. He was on parole for some time after leaving prison and he was anxious lest the Bavarian authorities might proceed with the threat to deport him. An interesting correspondence on the question of Hitler's citizenship between Hitler's lawyer, the Austrian Consul-General in Munich, and the Vienna authorities, is to be found in the Austrian police records. It illustrates the anxiety Hitler felt on this score in the mid 1920s.

An even more serious handicap was the improvement in the position of the country, which began while Hitler was in prison and had already been reflected in the reduced Nazi vote at the elections of December 1924. Three days after the unsuccessful putsch, on 12 November 1923, Dr Schacht had been appointed as special commissioner to restore the German currency; by the summer of 1924 he had succeeded and the inflation was at an end. At the end of February 1924, the threat to the stability of the Republic from either the extreme Left or the extreme Right had been mastered and the state of martial law ended. Stresemann's hopes of a settlement with the allied powers had not proved vain. A new reparations agreement – the Dawes Plan – was negotiated, and this was followed in turn by the evacuation of the Ruhr; the Locarno Pact, guaranteeing the inviolability of the Franco-German and Belgian-German frontiers: the withdrawal of allied troops from the first zone of the demilitarized Rhineland, and Germany's entry into the League of Nations by unanimous vote of the League Assembly on 8 September 1926. At each stage the Republican Government had had to meet with violent opposition from both the political extremes, from the Communists and from the Nationalists. The fact that on each occasion it had been able to carry its proposals through the Reichstag, and that in December 1924 the Social Democrat Party increased its vote by thirty per cent on a platform of the defence of the Republic, suggested that at last the period of disturbance which had lasted from 1918 to the beginning of 1924 was at an end.

The presidential elections in the spring of 1925 appeared to mark a turning-point in the history of the Weimar Republic. President Ebert, the former Social Democratic Chancellor, who had held office since the Republic's foundation, died on 28 February 1925. In the election held at the end of March the Nazis put up Ludendorff as their candidate, but won no more than 211,000 votes out of a total of close on 27 millions. As none of the candidates obtained a clear majority, a second election was held in April. This time the Nazis abandoned Ludendorff (this was the cause of the final breach between Hitler and Ludendorff) and supported Field-Marshal von Hindenburg, who had been brought in at the last minute by the Nationalists. Hindenburg won by a narrow margin to the anger and dismay of the democratic and republican forces. But the Nazis had little cause for congratulation. For the election of Hindenburg, the greatest figure of the old Army, a devoted Monarchist, a Conservative, and a Nationalist, had the paradoxical effect, in the short run, of strengthening the Republic. The simple fact that Hindenburg was at the head of the State did more than anything else could have done to reconcile traditionally minded and conservative Germans to the Republican régime. At the same time his scrupulous respect for the democratic constitution during the first five years of his Presidency cut the ground away from under the feet of those who attacked the Republic as the betrayal of the national cause.

Hitler's emphasis on legality was an attempt to adjust the Party's policy to the changed situation in Germany. Legality was a matter of tactics; the ineradicable hostility towards the Republic and all its works, the purpose of overthrowing it, even if by legal means, remained unchanged. In these calmer and more prosperous days, however, Hitler's appeal to hatred, his tirades against 'intolerable burdens' and his prophecies of disaster found less and less response outside the ranks of the converted.

Money, too, was more difficult to find. Until 1929 Hitler had little success in his efforts to tap the political funds of heavy industry and big business. The principal sources of Party revenue remained the members' dues of a mark a month (of which only ten per cent was forwarded to Party headquarters), collections or charges for admission at meetings, such private subscriptions as they could secure, and the income from the Party newspapers and publishing house in the hands of Max Amann.

The ban on his public speaking forced Hitler to turn more to writing between 1925 and 1928. The first volume of *Mein Kampf* was published in the summer of 1925. The style had been pruned and parts of it rewritten by Father Bernhard Stempfle who belonged to the Hieronymite Order and edited a small anti-Semitic paper in Miesbach. Four hundred pages long and costing the high price of twelve marks, the book sold 9,473 copies the year it was published. Sales went down from 6,913 in 1926 to 3,015 in 1928 (by which time the second volume had been published); they more than doubled in 1929 and shot up to 50,000 in 1930 and 1931. By 1940 six million copies had been sold.

No sooner had he finished the first volume of *Mein Kampf* than Hitler set to work on the second part which was published at the end of 1926. He then went on, in the summer of 1928, to dictate a book on foreign policy to his publisher, Max Amann. Amann, who already had *Mein Kampf* on his hands, was not eager to publish another slow-seller, especially as it repeated much that had already been said in *Mein Kampf*. The text soon went out of date and the typescript remained in Amann's office until after the war: it was finally published in 1961 as *Hitlers Zweites Buch*.

From 1925 the royalties from his book and the fees he received for newspaper articles were Hitler's principal source of personal income. After the war his income tax file was discovered, including his correspondence with the tax authorities on the expenses which he claimed.[1] Hitler described himself as a writer and gave his income as 19,843 Reichsmarks in 1925; 15,903 in 1926; 11,494 in 1927; 11,818 in 1928; and 15,448 in 1929. These figures correspond fairly closely to the royalties he received from *Mein Kampf*.

An additional source of income, not mentioned in his tax returns, was the fees which he received for articles published in the Nazi press. The high fees which he was believed to demand for these and which the struggling papers could ill afford to pay, were a cause of much grumbling against Hitler in Party circles.

How much Hitler personally received from the Party's funds or the contributions which he raised remains unknown. To all appearances the years 1925 to 1928 were a lean period for him:

1. cf. O. J. Hale's article 'Adolf Hitler, Taxpayer'. *American Historical Review*, July 1955, pp. 830–42.

he had difficulty in paying his taxes even on the incomplete return which he made, and he ran up considerable debts on which he had to pay interest of 1,706 marks in 1927. Yet he certainly did not live in poverty. He had always shown a particular liking for Berchtesgaden and the mountain scenery of the Bavarian Alps close to the Austrian frontier. After coming out of prison, he spent much of his time there, working on *Mein Kampf* and his newspaper articles. He stayed at first in a boarding house, the pension Moritz, then at the Deutsche Haus in Berchtesgaden. 'I lived there like a fighting cock,' he recalled later. 'Every day I went up to Obersalzberg which took me two and a half hours' walking there and back. That's where I wrote the second volume of my book. I was very fond of visiting the Dreimädlerhaus, where there were always pretty girls. This was a great treat for me. There was one of them, especially, who was a real beauty.'[1]

In 1928 Hitler rented a villa, Haus Wachenfeld, on the Obersalzberg for a hundred marks a month. It had been built by an industrialist from Buxtehude and Hitler later bought it. This was Hitler's home. 'I've spent up there,' he said later, 'the finest hours of my life. . . . It's there that all my great projects were conceived and ripened.' Although he later rebuilt Haus Wachenfeld on a grander scale and re-named it the Berghof, he remained faithful, as he put it, to the original house. As soon as he secured the lease of it, he persuaded his widowed half-sister, Angela Raubal, to come from Vienna and keep house for him, bringing with her her two daughters, with the elder of whom, then a pretty blonde of twenty, Hitler rapidly fell in love.

The following year, 1929, he rented a handsome nine-roomed flat in the fashionable Prinzregentenstrasse of Munich, taking the whole of the second floor of No. 16 and installing Frau Winter, the housekeeper, from the house in which he had lodged in the Thierschstrasse. Geli Raubal was given her own room in the new flat as well as at Obersalzberg.

Another expense which led to animated correspondence with the tax authorities was Hitler's car, a supercharged Mercedes, which he bought shortly after leaving Landsberg prison, at a cost of more than 20,000 marks. When asked to account for this expenditure, Hitler replied that he had raised a bank loan. He had, in fact, long displayed a passion for motoring, and quite apart from this believed that possession of a car was an important stage property for a politician. Before the 1923 putsch he had

1. *Hitler's Table Talk*, p. 215 (16–17 January 1942).

owned an old green Selve tourer, then a Benz which the police seized on his arrest. He did not drive himself but even in 1925 employed a chauffeur. There was another item which aroused the interest of the tax office: a private secretary (Hess), paid 300 marks a month, and an assistant as well as a chauffeur who received 200.

To be driven fast was a great pleasure to Hitler. It fitted the same dramatic picture of himself as the rhinoceros-hide whip which he carried with him wherever he went. But he also delighted to go off on a picnic with a few friends and Geli. This was, in fact, the time in his life when he enjoyed more private life than at any other, and he was later often to refer to it nostalgically.

Many times during the Russian campaign he recalled occasions such as that in 1925 when at the age of thirty-six he stayed with the Bechsteins as their guest at the Bayreuth Festival.

'I used to spend the day in leather shorts. In the evening I would put on a dinner jacket or tails to go to the opera. We made excursions by car into the Fichtelgebirge and the Franconian mountains. . . . My super-charged Mercedes was a joy to all. Afterwards, we would prolong the evening in the company of the actors, either at the theatre restaurant or on a visit to Berneck. . . . From all points of view, those were marvellous days.'[1]

III

Such success as the Nazis had at this time was due less to Hitler than to Gregor Strasser, who was threatening to take Hitler's place as the effective leader of the Party and was breaking new ground in the north of Germany and the Rhineland, where the Party had hitherto failed to penetrate. Gregor Strasser joined the Nazis at the end of 1920 and became the local leader in Lower Bavaria. A Bavarian by birth, and some three years younger than Hitler, he had won the Iron Cross, First Class, in the war and ended his service as a lieutenant. After the war he had married and opened a chemist's shop in Landshut. A powerfully built man with a strong personality, Strasser was an able speaker and an enthusiast of radical views who laid as much stress on the anti-capitalist points in the Nazi programme as on its nationalism. While Hitler was in prison Strasser had been one of the promoters of the attempt to create a united front with the North German Völkisch movement. A man of independent views, he was critical

1. *Hitler's Table Talk*, pp. 283–4; 348–9.

of Hitler's attitude and little disposed to submit to his demands for unlimited authority in the Party. Strasser had not attended the meeting on 27 February, and it was only a fortnight later that Hitler persuaded him to resume work in the Party by offering him the leadership in North Germany.

This suited Strasser very well, and with the help of his brother, Otto Strasser, he rapidly built up a following in the north and an organization which, while nominally acknowledging Hitler as leader, soon began to develop into a separate party. Gregor Strasser, who was a Reichstag deputy with a free pass on the railways and no ban to prevent him speaking in public, spent days and nights in the train, speaking several times in the week at one big town after another in the Rhineland, Hanover, Saxony, and Prussia. He founded a newspaper, the *Berliner Arbeitszeitung*, edited by Otto Strasser, and a fortnightly periodical, *National-sozialistische Briefe*, intended for Party officials. Strasser was particularly active in strengthening the organization of the movement, appointing district leaders and frequently coming down to talk with them. As editor of the *Briefe* and Gregor's private secretary, the Strassers secured a young Rhinelander, then still under thirty, a man of some education who had attended a number of universities, and written novels and film scripts which no one would accept, before taking a job as secretary to a Reichstag deputy. His name was Paul Josef Goebbels, and he soon showed himself to possess considerable talent as a journalist and as a speaker.

The Strasser brothers did not share Hitler's cynical disregard for any programme except as a means to power. Their own programme was vague enough, but it proposed the nationalization of heavy industry and the big estates in the interests of what they called 'State feudalism', together with the decentralization of political power on a federal basis, the break-up of Prussia and the establishment of a chamber of corporations on Fascist lines to replace the Reichstag. Hitler had little sympathy with these ideas, least of all with the Strassers' anti-capitalism and their demand for the breaking up of big estates, which embarrassed him in his search for backers among the industrialists and landowners. But while Hitler spent his time in Berchtesgaden, Gregor and Otto Strasser were actively at work extending their influence in the movement.

On 22 November 1925, the Strassers called together a meeting of the North German district leaders in Hanover. Among the twenty-five present were Karl Kaufmann, from the Ruhr, subsequently Gauleiter of Hamburg; Bernhard Rust, later the Nazi Minister of Education; Kerrl, later Nazi Minister of Ecclesiastical Affairs; Robert Ley, from Cologne, in time the boss of Hitler's Labour Front; Friedrich Hildebrandt, after 1933 the Gauleiter of Mecklenburg; and Erich Koch, who became not only Gauleiter of East Prussia but, after 1941, Reichskommissar for the Ukraine. Hitler was represented by Gottfried Feder, but it was only by a bare majority that Feder was admitted to the meeting at all, after Goebbels had demanded his ejection.

The split between the Strassers and Hitler crystallized round a question which excited much feeling in Germany in 1925-6, whether the former German royal houses should be expropriated and whether their possessions should be regarded as their own private property or as the public property of the different states. On this issue Gregor and Otto Strasser sided with working-class opinion against the princes, while Hitler supported the propertied classes. At this time he was receiving fifteen hundred marks a month (three-quarters of his income) from the divorced Duchess of Sachsen-Anhalt, and he denounced the agitation as a Jewish swindle. The Hanover meeting voted to follow the Strasser line, only Ley and Feder supporting Hitler. When Feder protested in Hitler's name, Goebbels jumped to his feet: 'In these circumstances I demand that the petty bourgeois Adolf Hitler be expelled from the National Socialist Party.' Rust added: 'The National Socialists are free and democratic men. They have no pope who can claim infallibility.'[1] More important still, the Hanover meeting accepted the Strassers' programme and resolved to substitute it for the Twenty-five Points of the official programme adopted in February 1920. This was open revolt.

Hitler took time to meet the challenge, but when he did move he showed his skill in the way he outmanoeuvred Strasser without splitting the Party. On 14 February 1926 he summoned a conference in his turn, this time in the South German town of Bamberg. Hitler deliberately avoided a Sunday, when the North German leaders would have been free to attend in strength. As a result the Strasser wing of the Party was represented only by Gregor Strasser and Goebbels. In the south Hitler had made the position of District Leader (Gauleiter) a salaried office, a step which left the Gauleiters free to attend solely to Party business and

1. Strasser: *Hitler and I*, p. 97.

made them much more dependent upon himself. He could thus be sure of a comfortable majority in the meeting at Bamberg.

The two protagonists fought out their differences in a day-long debate which ranged over half a score of topics: Socialism, the plebiscite on the Princes' property, the policy of legality versus that of revolution, foreign affairs, the role of the working classes, and the organization of the Party. Strasser was outnumbered from the beginning, and Hitler added to his triumph by the capture of Goebbels, hitherto one of the Strassers' strongest supporters. Half-way through the meeting Goebbels stood up and declared that, after listening to Hitler, he was convinced that Strasser and he had been wrong, and that the only course was to admit their mistake and come over to Hitler. Having won his point, Hitler did all he could to keep Strasser in the Party. In the middle of the debate he put his arm round his shoulders and said: 'Listen, Strasser, you really mustn't go on living like a wretched official. Sell your pharmacy, draw on the Party funds and set yourself up properly as a man of your worth should.'[1] Hitler's conciliatory tactics proved successful. The Strasser programme was abandoned, a truce patched up and the unity of the Party preserved. This was not the end of the Strasser episode, but Hitler had handled his most dangerous rival with skill and papered over the breach between himself and the radical wing of the Party.

Hitler had still to face other difficulties in the Party. There was persistent criticism and grumbling at the amount of money the Leader and his friends took out of Party funds for their own expenses, and at the time he spent away from headquarters in Berchtesgaden, or driving around in a large motor-car at the Party's expense. An angry controversy started between Hitler and Gauleiter Munder of Württemberg which led to Munder's eventual dismissal in 1928. Quarrelling, slander, and intrigue over the most petty and squalid issues seemed to be endemic in the Party.

To keep these quarrels within bounds, Hitler set up a Party court in 1926, the Uschla, an abbreviated form of Untersuchungs- und Schlichtungs-Ausschuss (Committee for Investigation and Settlement). Its original chairman, the former General Heine-mann, failed to understand that its primary purpose was to pre-serve Party discipline and the authority of the leader, turning a blind eye to dishonesty, crime, and immorality, except in so far

1. Strasser: op. cit., pp. 100–1.

as these affected the efficiency and unity of the Party. His successor, Major Walther Buch, understood his job better, and with the assistance of Ulrich Graf and a young Munich lawyer, Hans Frank (later Governor-General of Poland), turned the Uschla into an effective instrument for Hitler's tighter control over the Party.

In May 1926, Hitler summoned the Munich members of the Party to a meeting which was a logical consequence of the Bamberg conference of February. At this meeting a resolution was passed to the effect that henceforward the sole 'bearer' of the movement was the National Socialist German Workers' Association in Munich. The Munich group was to choose its own leadership, which would automatically become the leadership of the whole Party. Hitler explained that, although German law required the formal election of the chairman by the members, once elected he would have the right to appoint or dismiss the other Party leaders, including the Gauleiters, at his pleasure. At the same time the Twenty-five Points of the programme adopted in February 1920 were declared to be immutable, not because Hitler attached any importance to them, but as a further prop to his authority over the Party.

In July 1926, Hitler felt strong enough to hold a mass rally of the Party at Weimar, in Thuringia, one of the few States in which he was still allowed to speak. Five thousand men took part in the march past, with Hitler standing in his car and returning their salute, for the first time, with outstretched arm. Hoffman's photographs made it all look highly impressive, and a hundred thousand copies of the *Völkischer Beobachter* were distributed throughout the country. It was the first of the Reichsparteitage later to be staged, year after year, at Nuremberg.

Goebbels was now whole-heartedly Hitler's man. In November Hitler appointed him as Gauleiter of 'Red' Berlin, an assignment which was to stretch to the full his remarkable powers as an agitator. He took over a Party organization so riven with faction that Hitler had to dissolve it, and ordered Goebbels to begin again from the bottom. By moving Goebbels to Berlin Hitler not only strengthened the movement in a key position, but provided another check against the independence of the Strasser group. The Strasser brothers had kept their own press and publishing house in Berlin, and Goebbels, whose desertion to Hitler was regarded as rank treachery by the Strassers, employed every means in his power to reduce their influence and following. In

1927 he founded *Der Angriff* as a rival to the Strassers' paper, and used the S.A. to beat up their most loyal supporters. Appeals to Hitler by Gregor and Otto Strasser produced no effect: he declared he had no control over what Goebbels did. None the less it was Hitler's game that Goebbels was playing for him.

I V

For the next two years the fortunes of Hitler and the Nazi Party changed very little. The old trouble with the S.A. reappeared. In November 1926, Hitler reformed the S.A. and found a new commander in Captain Pfeffer von Salomon, but the ex-officers still thought only in military terms. The S.A. was to be a training ground for the Army and the height of their ambition was to hand it over lock, stock, and barrel to the Army, with jobs for themselves in the higher ranks. Both the Berlin and Munich S.A. leadership had to be purged. The Munich S.A. had become notorious for the homosexual habits of Lieutenant Edmund Heines and his friends: it was not for his morals, however, or his record as a murderer, that Hitler threw him out in May 1927, but for lack of discipline and insubordination. Such was the élite of the new Germany.

Whatever steps Hitler took, however, the S.A. continued to follow its own independent course. Pfeffer held as obstinately as Röhm to the view that the military leadership should be on equal terms with, not subordinate to, the political leadership. He refused to admit Hitler's right to give orders to his Stormtroops. So long as the S.A. was recruited from the ex-service and ex-Freikorps men who had so far provided both its officers and rank and file, Hitler had to tolerate this state of affairs. These men were not interested in politics; what they lived for was precisely this 'playing at soldiers' Hitler condemned – going on manoeuvres, marching in uniform, brawling, sitting up half the night singing camp songs and drinking themselves into a stupor, trying to recapture the lost comradeship and exhilaration of 1914–18. In time Hitler was to find an answer in the black-shirted S.S., a hand-picked corps d'élite (sworn to absolute obedience) very different from the ill-disciplined S.A. mob of camp followers. But it was not until 1929 that Hitler found the right man in Heinrich Himmler, who had been Gregor Strasser's adjutant at Landshut and later his secretary. In 1928 Himmler, who had been trained as an agriculturalist, was running a small poultry farm at the village of Waldtrudering, near Munich. When he took over the S.S. from Erhard Heiden, the troop numbered no more than two hundred men, and it took Himmler some years before he could provide Hitler with what he wanted, an instrument of complete reliability with which to exercise his domination over the Party and eventually over the German nation.

Yet, if the Party still fell far short of Hitler's monolithic ideal, 1927 and 1928 saw a continuation of that slow growth in numbers and activity which had begun in 1926. In May 1927, after giving further assurances for his good behaviour, Hitler was again allowed to speak in Bavaria, and in September 1928 in Prussia. In August 1927, at the first of the Nuremberg Party days, thirty thousand S.A. men are said to have paraded before the Party Leader. From 27,000 in 1925 the number of dues-paying members rose to 49,000 in 1926, 72,000 in 1927, 108,000 in 1928, and 178,000 in 1929. An organization for far bigger numbers was already being built up. The country was divided into *Gaue*, corresponding roughly to the thirty-four Reichstag electoral districts, with a Gauleiter appointed by Hitler at its head. There were seven additional Gaue for Austria, Danzig, the Saar, and the Sudetenland in Czechoslovakia. To the Hitler Youth were added the Nazi Schoolchildren's League (Schülerbund) and Students' League; the Order of German Women; a Nazi Teachers' Association, and unions of Nazi Lawyers and Nazi Physicians. The circulation of the *Völkischer Beobachter* crept up and the *Illustrierter Beobachter* was turned into a weekly.

By 1928 the Party organization was divided into two main branches: one directed by Gregor Strasser and devoted to attacking the existing régime, the other directed by Constantin Hierl and concerned with building up in advance the cadres of the new State. The first section had three divisions: foreign (Nieland), Press (Otto Dietrich), infiltration and the building up of party cells (Schumann). The second section consisted of Walther Darré (Agriculture), Wagener (Economics), Konopath (Race and Culture), Nicolai (work of the Ministry of the Interior), Hans Frank (Legal questions), Gottfried Feder (Technical questions), and Schulz (Labour Service).

Propaganda was a separate department, the director of which worked directly under Hitler. From October 1925 to January 1927, this had been Gregor Strasser's job, but Hitler had then transferred Strasser to build up the organization, and in November 1928 put in Goebbels as his propaganda chief. At the end of 1927 another familiar figure, Hermann Göring, returned to Germany from Sweden. Göring established himself in Berlin, living by his wits and his social connexions. Hitler, looking for just such contacts in upper-class Berlin, soon renewed his association with Göring. In May 1928, as their reward Göring and Goebbels were both elected to the Reichstag on the short Nazi list of twelve deputies, together with Strasser, Frick, and General von Epp, who had resigned from the Army to rejoin the Party. Hitler himself never stood as a candidate for the Reichstag. Since he was not a German citizen he was ineligible. He resigned his Austrian citizenship on 7 April 1925. This left him without a country. Efforts behind the scenes to persuade the Bavarian Government to make him a German national failed and Hitler would ask no favours in public of the Republican régime which he detested. He did not become naturalized until 1932, on the eve of his candidature for the German Presidency, when the Nazis had secured control of the State Government in Brunswick and were in a position to make the change without awkward questions being asked.

But the fact which overshadowed all Hitler's efforts in these years and dwarfed them into insignificance was the continued success of the Republican régime. By 1927 the despised Government of the 'November Criminals', the Jew-ridden 'Republic of Betrayal', had succeeded in restoring order, stabilizing the currency, negotiating a settlement of reparations, ending the occupation of the Ruhr, and securing Germany's entry into the League of Nations. To the Locarno Pact in the west Stresemann had added the settlement with the Soviet Union embodied in the Treaty of Berlin of April 1926, and to the evacuation of the First Zone of the demilitarized Rhineland the withdrawal of the Allied Military Control Commission at the end of January 1927. In August 1928, at the invitation of the French Government, Stresemann visited Paris to sign the Kellogg-Briand Pact renouncing war, on equal terms with the other Great Powers. The visit to Paris and the friendliness of Stresemann's reception symbolized the progress Germany had made, through the policy of 'Fulfilment', in recovering that equality of rights to which Hitler and the Nationalists never tired of appealing.

These successes in the political field, which, it might be argued, affected only that part of the nation which interested itself in politics, were matched by an economic recovery which touched every man and woman in the country. The basis of this recovery was the huge amount of foreign money lent to Germany, especially by American investors, after the Dawes Plan and the re-establishment of the currency seemed to have made her a sound financial risk again. The official estimate of Germany's foreign debts at the end of 1930 was between 28,500 and 30,000 million gold marks, almost all of which had been borrowed between the beginning of 1924 and the beginning of 1929.[1]

Not only the German Government, but the States, the big cities, even the Churches, as well as industry and business, borrowed at high rates and short notice, spending extravagantly without much thought of how the loans were to be repaid except by borrowing more. In this way Germany made her reparation payments promptly, and at the same time financed the rationalization and re-equipment of her industry, great increases in social services of all kinds and a steady rise in the standard of living of all classes. During the inflation (1923) German industrial production had dropped to fifty-five per cent of the 1913 figure, but by 1927 it had recovered to a hundred and twenty-two per cent, a recovery which far outdistanced that of the United Kingdom.[2] Unemployment fell to six hundred and fifty thousand in the summer of 1928. In this same year retail sales showed an increase of twenty per cent over 1925 figures, while by next year, 1929, money wages had risen by eighteen per cent and real wages by ten per cent over the average for 1925.[3]

Against facts like these, translated into the simplest terms of more food, more money, more jobs, and more security, all Hitler's and Goebbels's skill as agitators made little headway. Hitler's instinct was right. The foundations of this sudden prosperity were exceedingly shaky, and Hitler's prophecies of disaster, although he was wrong in predicting a new inflation, were to be proved right. But, in 1927 and 1928, few in Germany wanted to listen to such gloomy threats, any more than they listened to the warnings of the President of the Reichsbank, Dr Schacht, or of the Agent-General for Reparations, Parker Gilbert.

The general mood of confidence and the sense of recovery after the fevers and exhaustion of the post-war years were reflected in

1. C. S. R. Harris: *Germany's Foreign Indebtedness* (Oxford, 1935), c. I.
2. W. Arthur Lewis: *Economic Survey, 1919–29* (London, 1949), p. 91.
3. Harris: Appendix IV, quoting the Report of the Agent-General for Reparations, 21 May 1930.

the results of the Reichstag elections held in May 1928. The Social Democrats, the party most closely identified with the Republic, increased their vote from 7·88 to 9·15 millions, while the Right-wing German National Party, who had been unwavering in their vilification of the Weimar régime, saw their support drop from 6·2 to 4·3 million votes. The Nazis polled only 810,000 votes and secured no more than twelve seats out of a total of 491, ranking as the ninth party in the Chamber.

Thus although Hitler had certainly made some progress in rebuilding the Party when judged by the level to which it had fallen in 1924–5, as soon as it was measured against the standards of national politics his success was seen to be negligible. At the end of 1928 Hitler was still a small-time politician, little known outside the south and even there regarded as part of the lunatic-fringe of Bavarian politics. These were the years of waiting, years in which Hitler had to face the worst of all situations, indifference and half-amused contempt, years in which it would have been all too easy for the movement to disintegrate and founder.

In September 1928, Hitler called a meeting of the Party leaders in Munich and talked to them frankly. Much of his speech was taken up with attempting to belittle Stresemann's achievement in foreign policy.

In the first place our people must be delivered from the hopeless con-fusion of international convictions and educated consciously and syste-matically to fanatical Nationalism. . . . Second, in so far as we educate the people to fight against the delirium of democracy and bring it again to the recognition of the necessity of authority and leadership, we tear it away from the nonsense of parliamentarianism. Third, in so far as we deliver the people from the atmosphere of pitiable belief in possibilities which lie outside the bounds of one's own strength – such as the belief in reconciliation, understanding, world peace, the League of Nations, and international solidarity – we destroy these ideas. There is only one right in the world and that right is one's own strength.[1]

But he did not disguise the difficulties which lay ahead. Above all, they had to strengthen the individual Party comrade's con-fidence in the victory of the movement. 'It does not require much courage to do silent service in an existing organization. It requires more courage to fight against an existing political régime. . . . Attack attracts the personalities which possess more courage. Thus a condition containing danger within itself becomes a

1. Prange: pp. 39–40, quoting from the *Völkischer Beobachter* of 23 September 1928.

magnet for men who seek danger. . . . What remains is a minority of determined, hard men. It is this process which alone makes history explicable: the fact that certain revolutions, emanating from very few men and giving the world a new face, have actually taken place. . . . All parties, public opinion, take a position against us. But therein lies the unconditional, I might say the mathematical, reason for the future success of our movement. As long as we are the radical movement, as long as public opinion shuns us, as long as the existing factors of the State oppose us – we shall continue to assemble the most valuable human material around us, even at times when, as they say, all factors of human reason argue against it.'[1]

It was with such arguments that Hitler held the men around him together. This is the one striking quality of his leadership in these years, the fact that he never let go, never lost faith in himself and was able to communicate this, to keep the faith of others alive, in the belief that some time a crack would come and the tide at last begin to flow in his favour.

V

Hitler's first chance came in 1929, a prelude to the great crisis of 1930–3, and it came in the direction Hitler had foreseen, that of foreign policy.

Although Stresemann's policy had brought solid gains for Germany, nothing would appease the German National Party which continued to attack every item of the Versailles and subsequent settlements. The difficulties of Stresemann's position made him peculiarly vulnerable. Any concession to be secured from a grudging and suspicious France required much patience and circumspection: the policy of 'Fulfilment' could not be hurried. In these circumstances it was the easiest thing in the world for the Nationalists and Nazis to whip up German impatience and decry any success as insufficient and less than Germany was entitled to, attacking the Government for truckling to France and sacrificing national interests. Every outburst of this kind added to Stresemann's difficulties – and was meant to do so – by raising French resistance and casting doubts on his ability to speak for, or control, public opinion in Germany.

Hitler had been unwearying in his attacks on Stresemann. The very idea of reconciliation, of settlement by agreement, roused his

1. Heiden: *Der Führer*, p. 250.

anger. An appeal to nationalist resentment was an essential part of Hitler's stock-in-trade; at all costs that resentment must be kept alive and inflamed. France must be represented as the eternal enemy, and Stresemann's policy of 'Fulfilment' as blind illusion or, better still, deliberate treachery. So far this attack from the Right had failed to destroy the support of the majority for Stresemann's policy, but a better chance of success appeared to offer itself in 1929, and although in the end this, too, failed, the way in which the campaign was organized and the part Hitler was able to secure in it for himself marked a decisive stage in the rise of the Nazi Party.

The occasion was the renewal of negotiations for a final settlement of reparations. The Dawes Plan of 1924 had not attempted to fix the final amount to be paid by Germany or the number of years for which Germany was to continue to pay. In the winter of 1928–9 these questions were submitted to a committee of experts under the chairmanship of the American banker, Owen D. Young. After lengthy negotiations the Young Committee signed a report on 7 June 1929 which required the Germans to pay reparations for a further fifty-nine years. The annual payments were fixed on a graded scale, the average of which was considerably lower then the sum already being paid under the Dawes Plan (2,050 million marks a year as against 2,500 million). The total was substantially less than the 132 milliard gold marks originally claimed by the Allies, while the international controls over Germany's economy established by the Dawes Plan were to be abolished. Whatever doubts he may have entertained, Stresemann proposed to accept these terms, although they were far stiffer than those contained in the German proposals to the Committee, in the hope that thereby he could secure evacuation of the remaining zones of the Occupied Rhineland. In the international conference which met at the Hague in August 1929 he succeeded in linking the two questions of reparations and evacuation, and in persuading the French to agree that the withdrawal of the occupying forces should begin in September, five years ahead of time, and be completed by the end of June 1930.

This was the last of Stresemann's triumphs. He died on 3 October 1929, worn out by the exertions of the past six years. Before he died he had overcome the opposition of the French, but the Germans still remained to be convinced. On 9 July 1929, a national committee had been formed to organize a campaign for a plebiscite rejecting the new reparations settlement and the 'lie' of Germany's war-guilt which represented the legal basis of the Allies' claims. From then until 13 March 1930, when President Hindenburg finally signed the legislation in which the Young Plan was embodied, the Press and parties of the German Right united in a most violent campaign to defeat the Government and to use the issues of foreign policy and reparations for their ultimate purpose of overthrowing, or at least damaging, the hated Republic. It was by means of this campaign that Hitler first made his appearance on the national stage of German politics.

The leader of the agitation was Alfred Hugenberg, a bigoted German nationalist whose aim was to tear up the Versailles Treaty, overthrow the Republic, and smash the organized working-class movement. An ambitious, domineering and unscrupulous man of sixty-three, Hugenberg had large resources at his disposal. At one time a director of Krupps, he made a fortune out of the inflation and with it bought up a propaganda empire, a whole network of newspapers and news agencies, as well as a controlling interest in the big U.F.A. film trust. These he used not so much to make money as to push his own views. In 1928 he took over the leadership of the German National Party and by his extravagant opposition in the next two years caused a secession of more moderate members.

Hugenberg could count on the support of the Stahlhelm, by far the largest of the German ex-servicemen's organizations, under the leadership of Franz Seldte; of the Pan-German League, whose chairman, Heinrich Class, joined Hugenberg's Committee for the Initiative; and of powerful industrial and financial interests, represented by Dr Albert Voegler, General Director of the big United Steel (Vereinigte Stahlwerke), and later by the President of the Reichsbank, Dr Hjalmar Schacht, the two chief German delegates to the Young Committee, both of whom came out violently against the Plan. What they lacked was mass support, someone to go out and rouse the mob. Through Finanzrat Bang, Hitler and Hugenberg were brought together and met at the Deutscher Orden, a nationalist club in Berlin. Hitler was not easily persuaded to come in, partly because of the opposition to such an alliance with the reactionary Hugenberg and the representatives of industry which he could expect to meet from the radical Strasser group. But the advantages of being able to draw on the big political funds at the disposal of Hugenberg, and the offer of an equal position with the National Party in launching the agitation, converted him. He put his price high: complete independence in waging the campaign in his own way, and a large share of the Committee's resources to enable him to do it.[1] For his representative on the Joint Finance Committee Hitler deliberately chose Gregor Strasser: when others in the Party complained, he laughed and told them to wait until he had finished with his allies.

In September 1929, Hugenberg and Hitler published a draft 'Law against the Enslavement of the German People'. After repudiating Germany's responsibility for the war, Section III demanded the end of all reparations and Section IV the punishment of the Chancellor, the Cabinet, and their representatives for high treason if they agreed to new financial commitments. For their bill to be submitted to the Reichstag the sponsors had to secure the support of ten per cent of the electorate; the lists were opened on 16 October and they got the votes of 10·02 per cent, not many over four millions. After all the violent propaganda about turning Germany into a 'Young Colony', crippling national survival for two generations, and enslaving the nation to foreign capitalists, this was a sharp failure. The Committee had even less success in the Reichstag when the Bill was introduced at the end of November and defeated clause by clause, one group of the German National Party under Treviranus refusing to vote for the controversial Section IV and breaking away from Hugenberg. The submission of the motion to a national plebiscite at the end of December, the final stage in the process, underlined the defeat of the extremists. To win, Hugenberg and Hitler needed more than twenty-one million votes; they got less than six million. The bills embodying the legislation for carrying out the Young Plan were passed by the Reichstag on 12 March 1930. The last hope of the Nationalists was that President Hindenburg would refuse to sign them, and pressure was exerted on him by his Nationalist friends. But Hindenburg refused to be diverted from his constitutional duty, and on 13 March put his signature to the Young Plan laws. The fury of the Hugenberg and Nazi Press and their open attacks on the President ('Is Hindenburg still alive?'

1. Fritz Thyssen wrote later that he first financed the National Socialist Party for a single reason: because he wanted to defeat the Young Plan. Cf. Thyssen: *I Paid Hitler*, p. 118.

Goebbels sneered in *Der Angriff*) revealed the bitterness of their defeat.

But the defeat for Hugenberg and his 'Freedom Law' was no defeat for Hitler. In the preceding six months he had succeeded for the first time in breaking into national politics and showing something of his ability as a propagandist. Every speech made by Hitler and the other Nazi leaders had been carried with great prominence by the Hugenberg chain of papers and news agencies. To millions of Germans who had scarcely ever heard of him before Hitler had now become a familiar figure, thanks to a publicity campaign entirely paid for by Hugenberg's rival party. More important still, he had attracted the attention of those who controlled the political funds of heavy industry and big business to his remarkable gifts as an agitator. This, in Hitler's eyes, far outweighed the defeat.

Already, through the agency of Otto Dietrich, Hitler had been brought into touch with Emil Kirdorf. Otto Dietrich, who was soon to become Hitler's Press Chief, was the son-in-law of Reismann-Grone of Essen, the owner of the *Rheinisch-West-fälische Zeitung* (the paper of the Ruhr industrialists), and political adviser to the Mining Union (Bergbaulicher Verein). Kirdorf was one of the biggest names in German industry, the chief share-holder of the Gelsenkirchen Mine Company, the founder of the Ruhr Coal Syndicate, and the man who controlled the political funds of the Mining Union and the North-west Iron Association, the so-called Ruhr Treasury (Ruhrschatz). At the Nuremberg Party Day of August 1929, Kirdorf was a guest of honour and was so impressed by the sixty thousand National Socialists who assembled to cheer their leader that he wrote afterwards to Hitler: 'My wife and I shall never forget how overwhelmed we were in attending the memorial celebration for the World War dead.'[1] From now on Hitler could count upon increasing interest and support from at least some of those who, like Kirdorf, had money to invest in nationalist, anti-democratic and anti-working-class politics.

With this money Hitler began to put the Party on a new footing. He took over the Barlow Palace, an old mansion on the Brienner-strasse in Munich, and had it remodelled as the Brown House. A grand staircase led up to a conference chamber, furnished in red leather, and a large corner room in which Hitler received his visitors beneath a portrait of Frederick the Great. The Brown

1. Heiden: *Der Führer*, p. 271.

House was opened at the beginning of 1931, a very different setting from the dingy rooms in the Corneliusstrasse or the Schellingstrasse. Before that, in 1929, Hitler himself had moved to a large nine-roomed flat covering the entire second floor of No. 16 Prinzregentenstrasse, one of Munich's fashionable streets. Frau Winter, from the Thierschstrasse, came to keep house for him, while Frau Raubal continued to look after Haus Wachenfeld at Berchtesgaden. Hitler himself was now seen more frequently in Munich, occasionally in the company of his favourite niece, Geli Raubal, who had a room in the new flat.

Not only the paymasters, but also the voters of the Right had been impressed by the fact that whatever success had been won in the campaign against the Young Plan was due to Hitler and the Nazis. For years Hitler had been pouring scorn on the bourgeois parties of the Right for their 'respectable' inhibitions and their failure to go to the masses. Now he had been able to demonstrate, on a larger scale than ever before, what he meant. He underlined his criticism by promptly breaking with the National Party once the campaign was over and placing the entire blame for the failure on their half-hearted support. The fact that the Nationalists had split over Hugenberg's tactics added weight to Hitler's criticism, and the lesson was not lost on those who sought more effective means to damage and undermine the democratic Republic. In the provincial elections from October 1929 onwards, the Nazis made considerable gains in Baden, Lübeck, Thuringia, Saxony, and Brunswick, as well as in the communal and municipal elections in Prussia – and they made them very largely at the expense of the National Party. In Thuringia, in December, they won eleven per cent of the votes cast and Frick became the first Nazi to assume office as Thuringian Minister of the Interior. In the summer of 1929 the membership of the Nazi Party had been 120,000; by the end of 1929 it was 178,000; by March 1930 it had grown to 210,000.

At the Party conference which followed the alliance with Hugenberg Hitler had had to meet a good deal of criticism, voiced by Gregor Strasser, of the dangers of being tarred with the reactionary brush and losing support by too close association with the 'old gang', the old ruling class of pre-war Germany, the industrialists, the Junkers, the former generals, and higher officials who were the backbone of the National Party. His critics had underestimated Hitler's unscrupulousness, that characteristic duplicity, now first exhibited on this scale. With considerable skill he turned an episode which in itself was an outright failure to great political advantage for himself and his Party, then not only dropped the alliance with Hugenberg and the Nationalists as unexpectedly as he had made it, but proceeded to attack them. For Hugenberg the campaign against the Young Plan was one more in the disastrous series of mistakes which marked his leadership of the National Party; for Hitler it was a decisive stage, the foundations for the use which he was able to make of the months of opportunity ahead.

VI

In the six years since the ending of 1923 Germany had made an astonishing recovery. This recovery, however, was abruptly ended in 1930 under the impact of the World Depression. The fact that 1930 was also the year in which Hitler and the Nazi Party for the first time became a major factor in national politics is not fortuitous. Ever since he came out of prison at the end of 1924 Hitler had prophesied disaster, only to see the Republic steadily consolidate itself. Those who had ever heard of Adolf Hitler shrugged their shoulders and called him a fool. Now, in 1930, disaster cast its shadow over the land again, and the despised prophet entered into his inheritance. Three years later he told a Munich audience: 'We are the result of the distress for which the others were responsible.'[1] It was the depression which tipped the scales against the Republic and for the first time since 1923 shifted the weight of advantage to Hitler's side.

No country in the world was more susceptible to the depression, which began in the U.S.A. in 1929, intensified and spread in 1930 and 1931, and lasted throughout 1932. Its economic symptoms were manifold: contracting trade and production, cessation of foreign loans and the withdrawal of money already lent, falls in prices and wages, the closing of factories and businesses, unemployment and bankruptcy, the forced sale of property and farms. The foundation of German economic recovery had been the large amounts of money borrowed from abroad. Not only had much of this borrowed money been spent extravagantly; no one had faced the question of how it was to be repaid if the supply of further loans came to an end, and the money already lent,

1. Speech at Munich, 24 February 1933 (Baynes: vol. I, p. 252).

much of it on short-term credit, were to be reclaimed. This began to happen in 1929. At the same time a sharp contraction of world trade made it more difficult than ever for Germany to support herself and pay her way by any increase in exports. Thus, only a few years after the experience of inflation, Germany in 1930–2 again faced a severe economic crisis.

Hitler neither understood nor was interested in economics, but he was alive to the social and political consequences of events which, like the inflation of 1923, affected the life of every family in Germany. The most familiar index of these social consequences is the figure for unemployment. In Germany this rose from 1,320,000 in September 1929 to 3,000,000 in September 1930, 4,350,000 in September 1931, and 5,102,000 in September 1932. The peak figures reached in the first two months of 1932, and again of 1933, were over six millions.[1] These, it should be added, are the figures for only the registered unemployment; they do not give the whole picture of actual unemployment in the country, nor do they take account of short-time working. Translate these figures into terms of men standing hopelessly on the street corners of every industrial town in Germany; of houses without food or warmth; of boys and girls leaving school without any chance of a job, and one may begin to guess something of the incalculable human anxiety and embitterment burned into the minds of millions of ordinary German working men and women. In the history of Great Britain it is no exaggeration to describe the mass unemployment of the early 1930s as the experience which has made the deepest impression on the working class of any in the present century. In Germany the effect was still more marked since it came on top of the defeat and the inflation, through which most of these people had already lived.

The social consequences of the depression were not limited to the working class. In many ways it affected the middle class and the lower middle class just as sharply. For they – the clerks, shopkeepers, small business men, the less successful lawyers and doctors, the retired people living on their savings – were threatened with the loss not only of their livelihood, but of their respectability. The middle classes had no trade unions or unemployment insurance, and poverty carried a stigma of degradation for them that it did not have for the working class. The small property holder, shopkeeper, or business man was forced to sell, only to

1. The figures are those supplied by the I.L.O. and printed in the League of Nations Year Books.

see his property bought up at depreciated values by the big men. As during the inflation, anti-capitalist feeling against the combines, the trusts, and department stores spread widely amongst a class which had once owned, or still owned, property itself.

Nor was the impact of the slump limited to the towns. The fall in agricultural prices was one of the first and most severe symptoms of the crisis. In many parts of Germany the peasants and farmers were in an angry and desperate mood, unable to get a fair return for the work put into raising crops or stock, yet hard pressed to pay the interest on mortgages and loans or be turned out of their homes.

Like men and women in a town stricken by an earthquake, millions of Germans saw the apparently solid framework of their existence cracking and crumbling. In such circumstances men are no longer amenable to the arguments of reason. In such circumstances men entertain fantastic fears, extravagant hatreds, and extravagant hopes. In such circumstances the extravagant demagogy of Hitler began to attract a mass following as it had never done before.

The scale of the depression was not yet evident in the spring and early summer of 1930 and its full force was not to strike Germany until 1931, but it was already clear that economic crisis would produce a political crisis as well – more than a change of government, a crisis of the régime. The greatest weakness of the Weimar Republic from the beginning had been its failure to provide a stable party basis for government. In the Reichstag elections of 1930, for instance, ten parties polled more than a million votes each, a state of division which made it impossible for any of the parties to have a clear majority. Coalition government need not necessarily have meant weak government. In Prussia, where the Social Democrats and the Centre Party commanded a steady majority, the State Government enjoyed a stability which made it the bulwark of democracy in Germany and a particular object of hatred to both the Nazis and the Communists. But in the Reichstag elections, unlike those for the Prussian Diet, the three parties which had been responsible for the adoption of the Weimar Constitution, the so-called Weimar Coalition of the Social-Democrats, the Catholic Centre, and the Democrats, never again obtained a majority after 1919. They could only form a ministry with a majority in the Reichstag if they took in other parties, which meant stretching agreement to disagree to such a point that any firmness of policy was excluded. On the other hand, the chief Opposition parties, the German National Party on the Right, and the Communists on the Left, were never able themselves to construct a coalition which could take the place of the Weimar parties.

The party leaders, absorbed in manoeuvring and bargaining for party advantages – *Kuhhandel*, cattle-trading, is the expressive German word – were not displeased with this situation. Weak governments suited them to this extent that it made those in power more accessible to party pressure and blackmail. But the short-sightedness of this view became evident the moment the country was faced with a major crisis. From March 1930 it no longer proved possible to construct a coalition government which could be sure of a majority of votes in the Reichstag. Each section of the community – industrialists, trade unionists, shopkeepers, landowners, farmers – looked to the State for aid and relief while grudging it to the others. Instead of drawing closer together to establish a government of unity with an agreed programme, the parties insisted on forwarding the sectional economic interests they represented, without regard to the national interests. Differences on the share of sacrifice each class was to bear – whether unemployment pay and wages were to be cut, taxes raised, a capital levy exacted, tariffs increased, and help given to landowners and farmers – were allowed to become so bitter that the methods of parliamentary government, which in Germany meant the construction of a coalition by a process of political bargaining, became more and more difficult to follow. Dr Brüning, who became Chancellor at the end of March 1930, had to rely on precarious majorities in the Reichstag laboriously reassembled for each piece of legislation. Effective government on such a basis was impossible. On 16 July 1930, the Reichstag rejected part of the Government's fiscal programme by 256 votes to 193. Thereupon the President, by virtue of the emergency powers granted to him in Article 48 of the Weimar Constitution, put the Chancellor's programme into effect by decree. The Reichstag challenged the constitutionality of this action and passed a further motion demanding the abrogation of the decrees. Brüning's retort was to dissolve the house and fix new elections.

The responsibility for this deadlock has been much disputed. The case against the Party leaders is that they forced Brüning to act as he did by their refusal to combine; the case against Brüning is that he failed to do all that could have been done to win parliamentary support and that he was too quick to resort to emergency powers. But whoever bore the responsibility, one thing was clear: unless the new elections produced the basis for a stable coalition, which seemed unlikely, parliamentary institutions were in danger of being discredited by their failure to provide the strong government which the country so obviously needed.

Such a situation was much to the advantage of the Nazis, who had been unremitting in their attacks on the parliamentary republic and democratic methods of government. The Nazis had already shown they were alive to the possibilities opening before them by launching a propaganda campaign especially designed to win support among the first class to feel the onset of the depression, the farmers. Through Hess, Hitler had met a German agricultural expert, Walther Darré (like Hess and Rosenberg, born abroad), who had recently written a book on the peasantry as the 'Life Source of the Nordic Race'. Hitler was impressed by Darré and appointed him as the Party's agricultural adviser with the commission to draw up a peasant programme. This was published over Hitler's name on 6 March 1930, and was marked not only by practical proposals to give economic aid to the farming population – State-credits, reduction and remission of taxes, higher tariffs, cheaper artificial manures, cheaper electricity, and the revision of the inheritance laws – but also by its insistence upon the peasantry as the most valuable class in the community. In the years ahead the support which the Nazis received from the rural districts of Germany richly repaid the work of propaganda and organization they began to undertake there during 1930.

In the case of agriculture it was simple to play for the support of both the big landowners and the peasants, since these had a common economic interest in the demand for protection and higher prices, and a common grievance in their neglect by parties which were too preoccupied with the urban population of Germany. But when it came to industry, business, and trade (especially the retail trade), it was not so easy to square the circle, for here there was an open clash of interests and bitter antagonism between the workers and the employers, no less than between the small trader or shopkeeper and the big companies and department stores. Hitler needed the support of both, of the industrialists and big business interests because they controlled the funds to finance his organization and propaganda, of the masses because they had the votes. But in origin the National Socialists had been a radical anti-capitalist party, and this side of the Nazi programme was not only taken seriously by many loyal Party members but was of increasing importance in a period of economic depression.

The question, how seriously Hitler took the socialist character of National Socialism, had already been raised both before and after 1923. It was to remain one of the main causes of disagreement and division within the Nazi Party up to the summer of 1934; this was well illustrated in 1930 by the final breach between Hitler and Otto Strasser.

When Gregor Strasser moved to Munich, his brother Otto remained in Berlin, and through his paper, the *Arbeitsblatt* (which was actually still the official Nazi journal in the north), and his publishing house, the Kampfverlag, maintained an independent radical line which irritated and embarrassed Hitler. In April 1930, the trade unions in Saxony declared a strike, and Otto Strasser came out in full support of their action in the papers which he controlled, notably the *Sächsischer Beobachter*, the Nazi paper in Saxony. It was made perfectly plain to Hitler by the industrialists, on their side, that unless the Party at once repudiated the stand Strasser had taken there would be no more subsidies. With the help of Mutschmann, the Gauleiter of Saxony, Hitler enforced an order that no member of the Party was to take part in the strike, but he was unable to silence Strasser's papers. Following this, on 21 May Hitler suddenly appeared in Berlin and invited Otto Strasser to meet him for a discussion at his hotel. Strasser agreed, and on that day and the next they ranged over the whole field of their differences. The only account we possess of the discussion is Otto Strasser's, but there is little doubt that it can be accepted as accurate in substance. It was published very shortly afterwards, it was never challenged or repudiated by Hitler – although it must have done him considerable damage in some quarters – and all that Hitler is reported to have said is perfectly consistent with his known opinions.[1]

Hitler's tactics were a characteristic mixture of bribery, appeals, and threats. He offered to take over the Kampfverlag on generous terms, and make Otto Strasser his Press Chief for the entire

1. The account that follows is taken from Otto Strasser: *Ministersessel oder Revolution?*, the pamphlet version he published at the time (1930), and from the briefer English version in Otto Strasser: *Hitler and I*, pp. 109–27.

Reich; he appealed to him, with tears in his eyes and in the name of his brother Gregor, as an ex-soldier and a veteran National Socialist; he threatened that if Strasser would not submit to his orders he would drive him and his supporters out of the Party and forbid any Party member to have anything to do with him or his publications.

The discussion began with an argument about race and art, but soon shifted to political topics. Hitler attacked an article Strasser had published on 'Loyalty and Disloyalty', in which the writer, Herbert Blank, had distinguished between the Idea, which is eternal, and the Leader, who is only its servant. 'This is all bombastic nonsense,' Hitler declared, 'it boils down to this, that you would give every Party member the right to decide on the idea – even to decide whether the leader is true to the so-called idea or not. This is democracy at its worst, and there is no place for such a view with us. With us the Leader and the Idea are one, and every Party member has to do what the Leader orders. The Leader incorporates the Idea and alone knows its ultimate goal. Our organization is built up on discipline. I have no wish to see this organization broken up by a few swollen-headed littérateurs. You were a soldier yourself. . . . I ask you: are you prepared to submit to this discipline or not?'

After further discussion, Otto Strasser came to what he regarded as the heart of the matter. 'You want to strangle the social revolution,' he told Hitler, 'for the sake of legality and your new collaboration with the bourgeois parties of the Right.'

Hitler, who was rattled by this suggestion, retorted angrily: 'I am a Socialist, and a very different kind of Socialist from your rich friend, Reventlow. I was once an ordinary working-man. I would not allow my chauffeur to eat worse than I eat myself. What you understand by Socialism is nothing but Marxism. Now look: the great mass of working-men want only bread and circuses. They have no understanding for ideals of any sort whatever, and we can never hope to win the workers to any large extent by an appeal to ideals. We want to make a revolution for the new dominating caste which is not moved, as you are, by the ethic of pity, but is quite clear in its own mind that it has the right to dominate others because it represents a better race: this caste ruthlessly maintains and assures its dominance over the masses.

'What you preach is liberalism, nothing but liberalism,' Hitler continued. 'There are no revolutions except racial revolutions: there cannot be a political, economic, or social revolution – always and only it is the struggle of the lower stratum of inferior race against the dominant higher race, and if this higher race has forgotten the law of its existence, then it loses the day.'

On the next day, 22 May, the conversation was continued in the presence of Gregor Strasser, Max Amann, Hess, and one of Otto Strasser's supporters, Hinkel. Strasser had demanded the nationalization of industry. Hitler regarded such a proposal with scorn: 'Democracy has laid the world in ruins, and nevertheless you want to extend it to the economic sphere. It would be the end of German economy. . . . The capitalists have worked their way to the top through their capacity, and on the basis of this selection, which again only proves their higher race, they have a right to lead. Now you want an incapable Government Council or Works Council, which has no notion of anything, to have a say: no leader in economic life would tolerate it.'

When Strasser asked him what he would do with Krupps if he came to power, Hitler at once replied: 'Of course I should leave it alone. Do you think that I should be so mad as to destroy Germany's economy? Only if people should fail to act in the interests of the nation, then – and only then – would the State intervene. But for that you do not need any expropriation, you do not need to give the workers the right to have a voice in the conduct of the business: you need only a strong State.'

For the moment the conversation was left unfinished. But at the end of June Hitler wrote to Goebbels instructing him to drive Otto Strasser and his supporters from the Party. Goebbels obliged with alacrity. Otto Strasser stuck to his Socialist principles, published his talks with Hitler, broke with his brother Gregor (who stayed with Hitler), and set up a Union of Revolutionary National Socialists, later known as the Black Front. The dispute over the socialist objectives of National Socialism was not yet settled – it was to reappear again and again in the next few years – but Hitler had only gained, not lost, by making clear his own attitude. Even in the provincial elections in Saxony, held in June, 1930, the Nazi representation rose from five to fourteen, making them the second strongest party in Saxony, despite Hitler's open repudiation of the strike earlier in the year. In September the Nazi success at the National elections astonished the world. It was Hitler, not Strasser, who captured the mass vote, while the Black Front dwindled into insignificance and its founder sought refuge over the frontier.

VII

In the election campaign, which followed the dissolution in July and led up to polling day on 14 September, the Nazis used every trick of propaganda to attract attention and win votes. In the big towns there was a marked increase in public disorder in which the S.A. took a prominent part. Slogans painted on walls, posters, demonstrations, rallies, mass meetings, crude and unrestrained demagogy, anything that would help to create an impression of energy, determination and success was pressed into use. Hitler's appeal in the towns was especially to the middle class hit by the depression, and was aimed to take votes from the more moderate and respectable bourgeois parties like the Democrats, the People's Party, and the Economic Party – as well as from the rival parties of the Right, Hugenberg's Nationalists and the break-away Conservatives of Treviranus. He had advantages over both. He was prepared to be much more extreme than the middle-class parties at a time when extremism was the growing mood, and he was able to exploit German nationalism and xenophobia without rousing the dislike many people felt for the Nationalists and Conservatives as 'class' parties, preoccupied with putting the old ruling class back in power. What Hitler offered them was their own lower middle-class brand of extremism – radical, anti-Semitic, against the trusts and the big capitalists, but at the same time (unlike the Communists and the Social Democrats) socially respectable; nationalist, pan-German, against Versailles and reparations, without looking back all the time (as the Nationalists did) to the lost glories and social prestige of the past and the old Imperial Germany.

At the same time the Nazis devoted much time and attention to the rural voter, and in both town and countryside swept in the new generation. Many who were voting for the first time responded eagerly to attacks on the 'System' which left them without jobs, and to the display of energy, the demand for discipline, sacrifice, action and not talk, which was the theme of Nazi propaganda.

In 1930 the mood of a large section of the German nation was one of resentment. Hitler, with an almost inexhaustible fund of resentment in his own character to draw from, offered them a series of objects on which to lavish all the blame for their misfortunes. It was the Allies, especially the French, who were to blame, with their determination to enslave the German people; the Republic, with its corrupt and self-seeking politicians; the money barons, the bosses of big business, the speculators and the monopolists; the Reds and the Marxists, who fostered class hatred and kept the nation divided; above all, the Jews, who fattened and grew rich on the degradation and weakness of the German people. The old parties and politicians offered no redress; they were themselves contaminated with the evils of the system they supported. Germany must look to new men, to a new movement to raise her up again, to make her strong and feared, to restore to her people the dignity, security and prosperity which were their birthright, to recover the old German virtues of discipline, industry, self-reliance, and self-respect.

To audiences weighed down with anxiety and a sense of helplessness Hitler cried: If the economic experts say this or that is impossible, to hell with economics. What counts is will, and if our will is hard and ruthless enough we can do anything. The Germans are the greatest people on earth. It is not your fault that you were defeated in the war and have suffered so much since. It is because you were betrayed in 1918 and have been exploited ever since by those who are envious of you and hate you; because you have been too honest and too patient. Let Germany awake and renew her strength, let her remember her greatness and recover her old position in the world, and for a start let's clear out the old gang in Berlin.

This is a fair summary of the sort of speech Hitler and his lieutenants made in hundreds of meetings in the summer of 1930. Their opponents scorned such methods as being demagogy of the most blatant kind, but it showed a psychological perception of the mood of a large section of the German people which was wholly lacking from the campaigns of the other parties. Hitler never forgot the principle he had underlined in *Mein Kampf*: go for the masses. Their neglect of this accounted, in Hitler's eyes, for the failure of the other principal Right-wing Party, the Nationalists, to recover its old position in the country. Only the Communists could rival Hitler in this sort of agitation, but the Communists deliberately limited their appeal to one class, while Hitler aimed to unite the discontented of all classes; the Communists were hampered by rigid doctrinaire beliefs, while Hitler was prepared to adapt or abandon his programme to suit his audience; and the Communists, while they could outbid the Nazis in radicalism, could not hope to match the skill with which Hitler played on the nationalist drum as well, potentially the most powerful appeal in German politics.

In the middle of September thirty million Germans went to the polls, four millions more than in 1928. The results surprised even Hitler, who had hoped at most for fifty or sixty seats. The Nazi vote leaped from the 1928 figure of 810,000 to 6,409,600, and their numbers in the Reichstag from 12 to 107. From ninth the Nazis had become the second Party in the State. Little less spectacular were the Communists' gains, 4,592,000 votes as against 3,265,000 in 1928, and 77 in place of 54 deputies in the Reichstag. The two parties which had openly campaigned for the overthrow of the existing régime and had deliberately framed their appeal in extremist terms had together won close on a third of the votes and of the seats in the new House. The three bourgeois parties, the Democrats, the People's Party, and the Economic Party, had lost a million and a quarter of their 1928 votes between them, and had completely failed to capture the new votes of those who went to the polls for the first time. Still more interesting from Hitler's point of view was the fact that the biggest set-back in the elections had been suffered by his chief rivals on the Right, the Nationalists, whose vote fell from 4,381,600 in 1928 to 2,458,300 in 1930. Although Hugenberg succeeded in reuniting some of the factions into which the German National Party had been split, with only 41 deputies against Hitler's 107 he was now in a position of inferiority in any combination of the Right that might be proposed.

Overnight, therefore, Hitler had become a politician of European importance. The foreign correspondents flocked to interview him. *The Times* printed his assurances of goodwill at length, while in the *Daily Mail* Lord Rothermere welcomed Hitler's success as a reinforcement of the defences against Bolshevism.

Now that the Nazis had won this great electoral success the question arose, what use were they going to make of it. Hitler gave part of an answer in a speech he made at Munich ten days after the election: 'If today our action employs among its different weapons that of Parliament, that is not to say that parliamentary parties exist only for parliamentary ends. For us Parliament is not an end in itself, but merely a means to an end. ... We are not on principle a parliamentary Party – that would be a contradiction of our whole outlook – we are a parliamentary Party by compulsion, under constraint, and that compulsion is the

Constitution. The Constitution compels us to use this means. . . . And so this victory that we have just won is nothing else than the winning of a new weapon for our fight. . . . It is not for seats in Parliament that we fight, but we win seats in Parliament in order that one day we may be able to liberate the German people.'[1]

This was quite in accord with what Hitler had said before the elections: 'It is not parliamentary majorities that mould the fate of nations. We know, however, that in this election democracy must be defeated with the weapons of democracy.'[2] What Hitler's speech failed to make clear was how far he meant to go with these tactics of legality; whether he meant to use the Nazi faction in the Reichstag to discredit democratic institutions and bring government to a standstill, following this with a seizure of power by force; or whether he intended to come to power legally as a result of success in the elections and postpone any revolutionary action until after he had secured control of the machinery of the State.

Almost certainly it was the second of these alternatives which Hitler had in mind. Hitler meant to have his revolution, but he meant to have it after, not before, he came to power. He was too impressed by the power of the State to risk defeat in the streets, as he had, against his better judgement, in November 1923. The revolutionary romanticism of the barricades was out of date; it had ceased to be plausible since the invention of the machine-gun. Hitler's aim now – as it had been in 1923 – was a revolution with the power of the State on his side. But revolution was not the means of securing such power; that had to be obtained legally.

There were several reasons, however, why Hitler was unwilling to say this too openly. He had to consider the effect such a declaration might have on his own Party. For many were attracted to the Party by the promise of violence. They thought in terms of a March on Berlin and the seizure of power by an act of force, and they only tolerated Hitler's talk of legality because they thought it was a camouflage behind which the real plans for a putsch could be prepared with great immunity. At the same time, his greatest asset in persuading those who controlled access to power – the Army commanders, for instance, and the President's advisers – to bring him in, was their fear that he would seize power by force if his terms were not met peacefully. To repudiate revolution altogether was to throw away his best chance of coming to

1. Baynes: vol. I, pp. 188–90, quoting the *Frankfurter Zeitung* for 26 September 1930.
2. Hitler at Munich, 18 July 1930. (Prange: p. 42).

power legally. Finally, Hitler had always to reckon with the possibility that, if the tactics of legality failed, he might be faced with the alternatives of political decline or making a putsch in earnest. It was a gamble which Hitler would always be reluctant to make, but one which, in desperation, he might be forced to take. Meanwhile the attitude of the average Party member was probably best summed up by Göring when he said: 'We are fighting against this State and the present System because we wish to destroy it utterly, but in a legal manner – for the long-eared plain-clothes men. Before we had the Law for the Protection of the Republic we said we hated this State; under this law we say we love it – and still everyone knows what we mean.'[1]

Two particular problems were bound up with the question of legality which recur throughout the history of the National Socialist movement up to 1934, the relations of the Nazi Party and the Army, and the role to be played by the brown-shirted S.A. The two questions are in fact only different sides of the same penny, but it will be easier to deal with them separately.

Since Röhm's resignation the relations between the Nazis and the Army had been bad. In an effort to keep control over the S.A., Hitler had forbidden them to have any connexion with the Army, and the Ministry of Defence had retorted by forbidding the Army to accept National Socialists as recruits or to employ them in arsenals and supply depots, 'since the Party has set itself the aim of overthrowing the constitutional State form of the German Reich'. This was in 1927.

Yet Hitler was very much aware that the support, or at least the neutrality, of the Army was the essential key to his success – as it had been in 1923. In March 1929, he delivered a speech at Munich on the subject of National Socialism and the Armed Forces which was in the nature both of a challenge to the Army and of a bid for its favour. Hitler began by attacking the idea which General von Seeckt had made the guiding principle of the new Army – that the Army must stand apart from politics. This, Hitler declared, was simply to put the Army at the service of the Republican régime, which had stabbed the old Army in the back in 1918 and betrayed Germany to her enemies.

There is another State in which the Army had a different conception of these needs. That was in the State where, in October 1922, a group made

1. Kempner: p. 121.

ready to take the reins of the State out of the hands of the gangsters, and the Italian Army did not say: 'Our only job is to protect peace and order.' Instead they said: 'It is our task to preserve the future for the Italian people.' And the future does not lie with the parties of destruction, but rather with the parties who carry in themselves the strength of the people, who are prepared and who wish to bind themselves to this Army, in order to aid the Army some day in defending the interests of the people. In contrast we still see the officers of our Army belatedly tormenting themselves with the question as to how far one can go along with Social-Democracy. But, my dear sirs, do you really believe that you have anything in common with an ideology which stipulates the dissolution of all that which is the basis of the existence of an army? . . .

The victory of one course or the other lies partially in the hands of the Army – that is, the victory of the Marxists or of our side. Should the Leftists win out through your wonderful un-political attitude, you may write over the German Army: 'The end of the German Army.' For then, gentlemen, you must definitely become political, then the red cap of the Jacobins will be drawn over your heads. . . . You may then become hangmen of the régime and political commissars, and, if you do not behave, your wife and child will be put behind locked doors. And if you still do not behave, you will be thrown out and perhaps stood up against a wall, for a human life counts little to those who are out to destroy a people.[1]

Hitler's speech was published verbatim in a special Army issue of the *Völkischer Beobachter*, and Hitler followed it up by articles in a new Nazi monthly, the *Deutscher Wehrgeist* (The German Military Spirit), in which he argued that by its attitude of hostility towards nationalist movements like the Nazis the Army was betraying its own traditions and cutting the ground away from under its own feet. Hitler's arguments, which showed again his uncanny skill in penetrating the minds of those he sought to influence, were not without effect, especially among the younger officers, who saw little prospect of promotion in an army limited by the Treaty to a hundred thousand men, and who were attracted by Hitler's promises that he would at once expand and restore the Army to its old position in the State if he came to power.

The success of this Nazi campaign to win over opinion in the Army was shown in 1930 at the trial of Lieutenants Scheringer, Ludin, and Wendt before the Supreme Tribunal at Leipzig. In November 1929, Scheringer and Ludin, who were officers of the Ulm garrison, had gone to Munich and there got into touch with a number of Nazi leaders, including Captain von Pfeffer, the

1. Hitler's speech, delivered on 15 March 1929, is quoted at length in Kempner: pp. 99–105.

chief of the S.A. They had undertaken to bring as many other officers as they could into sympathy with the Nazi point of view and had subsequently travelled to Hanover and Berlin on this business. To Lieutenants Wintzer and Lorenz, whom he met at Hanover, Ludin declared that the Army must be prevented from running into a conflict with Hitler like that of 1923. The Nazis would not enter into anything if they knew the Army would oppose them, and the Army must be prevented from taking up such an attitude of opposition. The important thing was to find a few officers in each military district who could be relied on.

Shortly afterwards, in February 1930, Scheringer, Ludin, and Wendt were arrested and charged with spreading Nazi propaganda in the Army. General Groener, the Minister of Defence, tried to treat the matter as a simple breach of discipline, but was compelled by the attitude of the accused to let the case go before the Supreme Court at Leipzig. Groener was criticized for this by General von Seeckt himself and by other senior officers; Seeckt accused him of weakening the spirit of comradeship and solidarity within the Officer Corps, a revealing comment.

By the time the trial opened, on 23 September, Hitler had become the leader of the second most powerful Party in the country, and the Army leaders were extremely interested to discover what his attitude towards the Army would be. On 25 September Hans Frank, the Nazi defence lawyer, introduced Hitler as a witness. Hitler did not miss his opportunity, and every one of his statements was made with an eye to its effect, not on the Court, but on the Army. He went out of his way to reassure them about the S.A. Stormtroops. 'They were set up exclusively for the purpose of protecting the Party in its propaganda, not to fight against the State. I have been a soldier long enough to know that it is impossible for a Party Organization to fight against the disciplined forces of the Army. ... I did everything I could to prevent the S.A. from assuming any kind of military character. I have always expressed the opinion that any attempt to replace the Army would be senseless. We are none of us interested in replacing the Army; my only wish is that the German State and the German people should be imbued with a new spirit.'[1]

For the same reason, he insisted, 'I have always held the view that every attempt to disintegrate the Army was madness. None of us have any interest in such disintegration.' In view of the

1. *Frankfurter Zeitung*, 26 September 1930.

evidence before the Court this was a barefaced lie, but Hitler carried it off with assurance: 'We will see to it that, when we have come to power, out of the present Reichswehr a great German People's Army shall arise. There are thousands of young men in the Army of the same opinion.'

The President of the Court here interrupted to remark that the Nazis could scarcely hope to realize these ideals by legal means. Hitler indignantly denied this. There were no secret directives. 'On questions of this kind only my orders are valid and my basic principle is that if a Party regulation conflicts with the law it is not to be carried out. I am even now punishing failure to comply with my orders. Many Party members have been expelled for this reason; among them Otto Strasser, who toyed with the idea of revolution.'

All this was meant for the generals, but there was also the Party to be considered, and Hitler added, with sinister ambiguity: 'I can assure you that, when the Nazi movement's struggle is successful, then there will be a Nazi Court of Justice too, the November 1918 revolution will be avenged, and heads will roll.' At this there were loud cheers from the gallery.

What then, asked the President, did Hitler mean by the expression, the German National Revolution?

It should always be considered [Hitler blandly replied] in a purely political sense. For the Nazis it means simply an uprising of the oppressed German people. . . . Our movement represents such an uprising, but it does not need to prepare it by illegal means. . . . Our propaganda is the spiritual revolutionizing of the German people. Our movement has no need of force. The time will come when the German nation will get to know of our ideas; then thirty-five million Germans will stand behind me. . . . We will enter the legal organizations and will make our Party a decisive factor in this way. But when we do possess constitutional rights, then we will form the State in the manner which we consider to be the right one.
THE PRESIDENT: This, too, by constitutional means.
HITLER: Yes.[1]

When General Jodl was examined at Nuremberg after the war he told the Tribunal that he had not been reassured until Hitler, during the Leipzig Trial, gave the assurance that he was opposed to any disorganization of the Reichswehr.[2] There is, indeed, little

1. *Frankfurter Zeitung.*
2. *Proceedings of the International Military Tribunal at Nuremberg*, part xv, pp. 276–7.

doubt that it was Hitler's explicit statement at Leipzig, coming immediately after his success in the elections, which provided the basis for his subsequent negotiations with the Army leaders and their eventual agreement to his assumption of power.

Hitler's talk of legality, however, was only a half-truth, a trick to get power on the cheap, to persuade the generals and the other guardians of the State to hand over power without forcing him to seize it. They were only tactics of legality, for everything about the movement proclaimed its brazen contempt for law. Hitler had therefore to take care that in his preoccupation with tactics he did not so far compromise the revolutionary character of his movement as to rob it of its attractive power. The possibility of such a danger was illustrated by the subsequent history of Lieutenant Scheringer, who, after being condemned to eighteen months' imprisonment, went over to the Communists while still in prison. When Goebbels telegraphed to ask if the letter which a Communist deputy had read in the Reichstag was genuine, Scheringer wired back: 'Declaration authentic. Hitler revolution betrayed.' If many others were to follow Scheringer – or Otto Strasser – Hitler would be in a difficult position.

The danger point was the S.A., which was to become, between 1930 and the summer of 1934, the expression of the Party's revolutionary purpose. One of the favourite S.A. slogans was: 'Possession of the streets is the key to power in the State,' and from the beginning of 1930 the political struggle in the Reichstag and at elections was supplemented – in part replaced – by the street fights of the Party armies in Berlin and the other big cities of Germany.

In the course of one of these gang feuds in February 1930, a young Berlin S.A. leader, Horst Wessel, was shot by the Communists, and was skilfully built up by Goebbels into the prototype of the martyred Nazi idealist, whose verses provided the S.A. with their marching song, the famous *Horst Wessel Lied*. In the first six months of 1930 the authorities issued a number of prohibitions to check this growth of public disorder. Outdoor meetings and parades were forbidden in Prussia (16 January); a new Law for the Protection of the Republic and for the suppression of political disturbances was passed by the Reichstag in March; in June the Prussian Minister of the Interior prohibited the Nazis from wearing uniforms and emblems. But these measures proved ineffective; forbidden to wear their brown shirts, the

Nazis paraded in white. Night after night they and the Communists marched in formation singing down the streets, broke up rival political meetings, beat up opponents, and raided each other's 'territory'. As the unemployment figures rose, the number of recruits mounted. Anything was better than loafing on the street corners, and the S.A. offered a meal and a uniform, companionship and something exciting to do.

In July 1930, one of the Nazi deputies, Wagner, summed up the character of the Nazi campaign in one sentence, when he said: 'The N.S.D.A.P. will not let the people rest in peace until they have obtained power.' The key to this campaign was incessant activity, a sustained effort of propaganda and agitation not limited to elections, but kept up all the year round. In this the S.A. had an essential part to play, for violence and the display of force had always formed a central part of Nazi propaganda. But it was propaganda that Hitler had in mind; the S.A. were to be the shock troops of a revolution that was never to be made. Hitler's problem was to keep the spirit of the S.A. alive without allowing it to find an outlet in revolutionary action; to use them as a threat of civil war, yet never to let them get so far out of hand as to compromise his plan of coming to power without a head-on collision with the forces of the State, above all with the Army.

Just before the elections of September 1930 the Berlin S.A. mutinied and smashed up the Berlin headquarters of the Party. Their real grievance was their pay, but undercurrents of discontent against the Party leadership also came to the surface. Goebbels proved incapable of handling the situation – he had actually to ask for police protection to get the Brown Shirts out of headquarters – and Hitler had to intervene personally. He levied a special tax for the S.A. on the whole Party, came at once to Berlin and drove round one beer-hall after another, appealing to the Stormtroopers, promising them better pay, telling them the Party was on the eve of great victories, and assuring them that in future bad leaders (on whom he threw the blame) would not be allowed to come between him and the faithful rank-and-file. At the end of an exhausting night Hitler had restored his authority; he promptly took the opportunity to retire Captain von Pfeffer, and on 2 September himself assumed the position of Oberster S.A. Führer – Supreme S.A. Leader.

In the electoral successes that followed, the incident was soon forgotten – not, however, by Hitler. The following month,

October, he persuaded Ernst Röhm, then serving as an officer in the Bolivian Army, to leave South America and return to Germany, to take over the reorganization of the S.A. as its Chief of Staff. In Röhm, he hoped, he had found the man to pull the S.A. together and keep it in hand.

Despite these troubles, as the year 1930 came to an end Hitler had considerable cause for satisfaction. Party membership was rising towards the four hundred thousand figure; a vote of more than six millions at the elections had raised the Nazi strength in the Reichstag to 107. When the swastika flag was hoisted over the Brown House on 1 January 1931 he could feel he had already covered the most difficult part of the road; there was no danger now that people would not pay attention to the unknown man of the 1920s. In the Reichstag the Nazis – every man in brown uniform – had already shown their strength and their contempt for Parliament by creating such disorder that the sittings had to be frequently suspended. In the streets the S.A. had scored another triumph by forcing the Government to ban the further showing of the anti-militarist film, *All Quiet on the Western Front*, by calculated hooliganism.

Hitler was in no danger of underestimating the opposition to his leadership which still existed in the Party. Failure or setbacks would bring it quickly to the surface; success alone would silence criticism. Yet success no longer seemed impossible. This was the measure of his achievement in 1930. He had reached the threshold of power.

VIII

At the beginning of January 1931, Röhm took over his new duties as Chief of Staff of the S.A. He immediately set to work to make the S.A. by far the most efficient of the Party armies. The whole of Germany was divided into twenty-one districts, with an S.A. Group in each under the command of an Obergruppenführer. The organization was closely modelled on that of the Army, with its own headquarters and General Staff quite separate from the organization of the Party, and its own training college for S.A. and S.S. leaders opened at Munich in June 1931.

Since 1929 Himmler had been Reichsführer of the S.S., but he too was now brought under Röhm, although the S.S. with its distinctive black uniform and death's head badge retained its separate identity. Another of Röhm's auxiliaries was the N.S.K.K. – the Nazi Motor Corps – a flying squad under the command of Major Hühnlein. At the time Röhm took over, in January 1931, the S.A. numbered roughly a hundred thousand men; a year later Hitler could claim three hundred thousand.

The Party Organization itself, designed by Gregor Strasser, also followed a highly centralized pattern, subject to the will of the Party chairman and leader, Hitler. The basis of this organization was the Gau and the Gauleiter, each Gau in turn being divided and subdivided down to the lowest unit, the Cell, corresponding to the S.A. squad. The central directorate of the Party was still in Munich, where special departments sprang up and multiplied rapidly, among them the Factory Cell Organization (N.S. Betriebszellen-Organisation), under Walther Schumann; the Economic Policy Department, run by Otto Wagener; and the pension fund (*Hilfskasse*), administered by Martin Bormann, to aid the families of those killed or disabled in the Party's fight.[1]

The direction of the Party in the years 1931 and 1932 was for all practical purposes in the hands of six men – Hitler himself, Röhm, Gregor Strasser, Göring, Goebbels, and Frick. Röhm's importance consisted not only in his talents as an organizer and his office as Chief of Staff of the S.A., but also in his contacts with the Army. Göring, with his wide range of acquaintances, his good-humoured charm and ease of manner, became in the course of 1931 Hitler's chief political 'contact-man' in the capital, with a general commission to negotiate with other parties and groups.[2] The following year he was Hitler's choice for the Presidency of the Reichstag when this office fell to the Nazis as the strongest Party. From the end of August 1932, when he was elected, to Hitler's appointment as Chancellor, the Reichstag President's palace opposite the Reichstag was the centre from which the Party's manoeuvres and intrigues were directed.

The leader of the Nazi Party in the Reichstag – and the first Nazi Minister to hold office (in Thuringia) – was Dr Wilhelm Frick, by profession a civil servant, and in 1919–23 one of Hitler's protectors in the Munich police. An early and convinced National Socialist, although one of the less colourful of the Nazi leaders, he was useful to Hitler as a good administrator and a man who knew thoroughly the machinery and the mentality of the German civil service.

1. For the departments already established, cf. above, p. 141.
2. cf. Göring's evidence at Nuremberg, N.P. ix, p. 68.

The remaining two had been enemies ever since Goebbels's desertion of Strasser after the Bamberg meeting in 1926. Both were able speakers, and both held high office in the Party, Goebbels as Propaganda Director and Gauleiter of Berlin, Strasser at the head of the Political Organization, with powerful influence among the Gauleiters and local branches. How far Hitler trusted Strasser may well be questioned, but Strasser was undoubtedly the most powerful of Hitler's lieutenants, the only man in the Party who, if he had had more of Hitler's power of will and ambition, and less good-natured easy-going Bavarian indulgence in his nature, might have challenged Hitler's leadership. Strasser possessed the personality to be a leader in his own right if he bestirred himself; Goebbels, undersized, lame and much disliked for his malicious tongue, could rise only under the aegis of someone like Hitler, to whom he was useful for his abounding energy and fertility of ideas, apt at times to be too clever and to over-reach himself, but exploiting with brassy impudence every trick of propaganda.

There were others – Darré, the agricultural and peasant expert; Baldur von Schirach, the leader of the Hitler Youth; Hess, the Führer's inseparable secretary; Wilhelm Brückner, his personal adjutant; Max Amann, the Party's publisher; Franz Xavier Schwarz, the fat, bald Party treasurer; Philipp Bouhler, the Party's young business manager; Hans Frank, the Party's legal expert; and Otto Dietrich, its Press chief. But none of these held anything like the position of Röhm and Strasser, Göring and Goebbels, or even Frick, the five men with whom Hitler captured power.

It is obvious that so highly organized a machine must have cost large sums of money to run. 'When I visited Berlin before we came to power,' Hitler recalled later, 'I used to stay at the Kaiserhof; and as I was always accompanied by a complete general staff, I generally had to book a whole floor and our bill for food and lodging usually came to about 10,000 marks a week. I earned enough to defray these costs mostly by means of interviews and articles for the foreign press. Towards the end of the *Kampfzeit*, I was being paid as much as two or three thousand dollars a time for such work.'[1] This was Hanfstängl's job as Foreign Press Chief, to place Hitler's articles and arrange interviews with him.

A good deal of money, of course, came from the Party itself –

1. *Hitler's Table Talk*, 6 July 1942, p. 564.

from membership dues; from the sale of Party newspapers and literature, which members were always being pressed to buy; from the admission charges and collections at the big meetings. There is no doubt that the Party made heavy demands on its members – even the unemployed S.A. men had to hand over their unemployment-benefit money in return for their food and shelter. Almost certainly the proportion of revenue which was raised by the Party itself has been underestimated. But there were also subsidies from interested supporters.

Some light on the means by which these subsidies were obtained is thrown by the interrogation of Walther Funk at Nuremberg after the war. Funk, a shifty, unimpressive little man who was later to succeed Schacht as President of the Reichsbank and Minister of economics, had been editor-in-chief of the *Berliner Börsen-Zeitung*, a leading financial newspaper, in the 1920s. In 1931 he gave up his post as editor and began to act as a 'contact-man' between the Nazi Party and certain industrial and business interests. For a time he ran the *Wirtschaftspolitischer Pressedienst*, an economic Press and Information Service controlled by Dr Wagener, the head of the Nazi Party's Economic Policy Department. There were no more than sixty subscribers to this agency, but according to Funk 'they paid very well'. In return Funk was expected to influence the Party's economic policy and to persuade Hitler to repudiate the anti-capitalist views of men like Gottfried Feder. 'At that time,' Funk says, 'the leadership of the Party held completely contradictory and confused views on economic policy. I tried to accomplish my mission by impressing on the Führer and the Party as a whole that private initiative, the self-reliance of the business man, and the creative powers of free enterprise should be recognized as the basic economic policy of the Party. The Führer personally stressed time and again, during talks with me and industrial leaders to whom I had introduced him, that he was an enemy of state-economy and of so-called "planned economy", and that he considered free enterprise and competition as absolutely necessary in order to gain the highest possible production.'[1]

An illustration of the consequences of the new contacts which Hitler was now making is given by an incident which took place in the autumn of 1930. On 14 October the Nazi Party in the Reichstag introduced a bill to limit rates of interest to four per cent; to expropriate the entire property of 'the bank and stock-exchange

1. Nuremberg Document (N.D.) EC-440: Statement by Walther Funk.

magnates', and of all Eastern Jews without compensation; and to nationalize the big banks. This was the work of Gregor Strasser, Feder, and Frick. Hitler at once intervened and forced them to withdraw the motion. When the Communists reintroduced the Bill in the exact wording the Nazis had used, he compelled the Party to vote against it. If Hitler intended to impress Funk's friends, there was no room for such bills in the Party's programme. On the other hand, Funk found Hitler very reserved about the policy he would himself adopt once in power. 'I cannot', Hitler told him, 'commit myself to an economic policy at present; the views expressed by my economic theorists, such as Gottfried Feder, are not necessarily mine.'[1] Hitler, in short, while anxious to keep the industrialists friendly, declined to tie his own hands, and he very largely succeeded. As Funk admits: 'My industrial friends and I were convinced in those days that the N.S.D.A.P. would come to power in the not too distant future and that this *had* to be, if Communism and civil war were to be avoided.'[2]

Only a section of German industry and big business was willing to support Hitler and the Nazis at this time. Funk says specifically that the greater part of industry's political funds still went to the German National Party, the Democrats, and the People's Party. The main support for the Nazis came from a powerful group of coal and steel producers in the Rhineland and Westphalia. In addition to Emil Kirdorf, the biggest figure in the Ruhr coal industry, Fritz Thyssen and Albert Voegler of the United Steel Works, Funk mentions Friedrich Springorum and Tengelmann, Ernest Buskühl and H. G. Knepper of the Gelsenkirchen Mine Company. Among bankers and financiers who, according to Funk, met Hitler in 1931–2 and, in some cases at least, helped him, were Stein and Schröder of the Stein Bank in Cologne; E. G. von Stauss, of the Deutsche Bank; Hilgard, of the Allianz Insurance Corporation; and two more bankers, Otto Christian Fischer and Fr. Reinhart.

Funk's list is haphazard and is obviously not comprehensive. None the less, it gives some interesting clues to the sort of men Hitler was beginning to meet and who were now interested to meet him, even if these encounters did not always lead to such direct financial aid as in the case of Thyssen. Besides the names already mentioned, Funk adds the potash industry led by August Rosterg of Kassel, and August Diehn; shipping circles in Ham-

1. N.P., XIII, p. 100 (Funk's evidence).
2. N.D. EC-440.

burg, of whom the most important was Cuno, of the Hamburg-Amerika Line; Otto Wolf, a big Cologne industrialist and business man who was friendly with Robert Ley, the local Gauleiter; the brown coal industry of Central Germany – Deutsches Erdöl, Brabag, and the Anhaltische Kohlenwerke; and Dr Erich Lubbert of the A.G. für Verkehrswesen and the Baugesellschaft Lenz.

There were, of course, others besides Funk who were interested in bringing together Hitler and the men with money and influence. When Dr Schacht, the ex-President of the Reichsbank, first met Hitler in January, 1931, it was at Göring's flat, where he and Fritz Thyssen spent an evening listening to Hitler talking. Göring was particularly active in arranging such meetings; so was the Graf von Helldorf, who became the S.A. leader in Berlin. Grauert, an influential figure in Düsseldorf as manager of the Employers' Association in the Rhineland and Westphalia, with its large funds for strike-breaking, used his position to help the Nazi cause, and was later rewarded with the post of Göring's Under-Secretary in the Prussian Ministry of the Interior. Wilhelm Keppler, another who aspired to be Hitler's economic adviser, had wide connexions, was friendly with Schröder, the Cologne banker, and founded Himmler's private circle known by the pleasing name of *Freundeskreis der Wirtschaft*, literally 'Friends of the Economy'. Otto Dietrich, the young journalist who introduced Hitler to Kirdorf and who became the Party's Press chief, writes in his memoirs 'In the summer of 1931 our Führer suddenly decided to concentrate systematically on cultivating the influential economic magnates. . . . In the following months he traversed Germany from end to end, holding private interviews with prominent personalities. Any rendezvous was chosen, either in Berlin or in the provinces, in the Hotel Kaiserhof or in some lonely forest-glade. Privacy was absolutely imperative, the Press must have no chance of doing mischief. Success was the consequence.'[1]

How much all this produced in hard cash it is impossible to say. Funk mentions three figures. In his interrogation at Nuremberg[2] he said that during the elections of 1932, when the Party was short of money, he asked directly for money: 'in three or four cases where direct intervention was sought, the total was approximately

1. Otto Dietrich: *Mit Hitler in die Macht*; English translation, *With Hitler on the Road to Power* (London, 1934), pp. 12–13.
2. Dated 4 June and 26 June 1945: N.D. 2828-PS.

half a million marks.' The second figure he gives is for the contributions of the important Rhenish-Westphalian group in 1931–32: during that period, he states in his affidavit, they did not amount to one million marks.[1] Finally, when he was asked to give a global figure for the support Hitler received from industry in the period before he became Chancellor, Funk answered: 'In contrast to other parties, I don't think that it was much more than a couple of million marks.'[2]

Thyssen's memoirs, despite their title – *I Paid Hitler*[3] – are disappointing, and add little to Funk's evidence. Thyssen joined the Party openly in December 1931, and was responsible for the best-known of all Hitler's meetings with industrialists, when he spoke to the Industry Club at Düsseldorf in January 1932.[4] 'I have,' he writes, 'personally given altogether one million marks to the Nazi Party. . . . It was during the last years preceding the Nazi seizure of power that the big industrial corporations began to make their contributions. But they did not give directly to Hitler; they gave them direct to Dr Alfred Hugenberg, the leader of the Nationalists, who placed at the disposal of the Nazi Party about one-fifth of the amounts given. All in all, the amounts given by heavy industry to the Nazis may be estimated at two million marks a year.'[5] Unfortunately, it is not clear to what period Thyssen is referring.

Beyond such tantalizing and imprecise figures it is not yet possible to go. But it is easy to exaggerate the importance of these outside subventions, for the most important point of all is that Hitler, however much he received from Kirdorf, Thyssen, and the rest, was neither a political puppet created by the capitalists, nor a mere agent of the big industrialists who had lost his independence. Thyssen's and Schacht's accounts are there as records of the disillusionment of those who thought they had bought Hitler and would henceforward call the tune he was to play. They were to discover, like the conservative politicians and the generals, that, contrary to the popular belief, bankers and business men are too innocent for politics when the game is played by a man like Hitler.

1. N.D. EC-440.   2. N.D. 2828-PS.
3. Fritz Thyssen: *I Paid Hitler* (London, 1941).
4. See below, pp. 196–9.   5. Thyssen: pp. 133–4.

IX

In speaking of the Nazi movement as a 'party' there is a danger of mistaking its true character. For the Nazi Party was no more a party, in the normal democratic sense of that word, than the Communist Party is today; it was an organized conspiracy against the State. The Party's programme was important to win support, and, for psychological reasons which Hitler discussed quite frankly in *Mein Kampf,* the programme had to be kept unalterable and never allowed to become a subject for discussion. But the attitude of the leaders towards the programme was entirely opportunist. For them, as for most of the old Party members, the real object was to get their hands on the State. They were the Catilines of a new revolution, the gutter élite, avid for power, position, and wealth; the sole object of the Party was to secure power by one means or another.

The existence of such an organization was in fact incompatible with the safety of the Republic. No State could tolerate the threat which it implied, if it was resolved to remain master in its own house. Why then were no effective steps taken by the German Government to arrest the leaders of the Nazi Party and break up their organization? As Dr Kempner has shown, recommendations to this effect, with legal grounds for the action proposed, were submitted by the police authorities to the Reich Attorney-General even before the Nazis' electoral triumph of September 1930.[1] Yet no action was tak

In the case of Dr Kempner s police report, the Reich Attorney-General was a crypto-Nazi who used his office to prevent any action being taken. This in itself is a significant enough sidelight on the state of affairs in Germany in 1930–3, but it is not a sufficient answer to the more general question. If the people in authority in Germany at this time had been really determined to smash the Nazi movement they would have found the means. The question to be asked is, why they lacked the will and the determination. To this there are not one, but several, answers.

In the first place, Hitler's tactics of legality were designed to

1. The full text of the Police Report prepared by Dr Kempner in the Police Division of the Prussian Ministry of the Interior in 1930 has been reprinted by him in *Research Studies of the State College of Washington* (vol. XIII, No. 2, June 1945), pp. 56–130. It is accompanied by his correspondence with the Reich Attorney-General, pp. 131–4.

enable him to win the maximum advantage from the democratic constitution of the Weimar Republic. Thereby he avoided giving his opponents the chance of shifting the fight for power on to a level where the Army would be the decisive factor. As Hitler was shrewd enough to realize, he would be the loser, not the gainer, in any attempt to resort to force, whereas so long as he kept within the letter of the law he could fetter the authorities with their own slow-moving legal processes.

In May 1931, four National Socialists were brought for trial after a shooting affair with some Communists. Hitler was called upon to give evidence. 'I have never left any doubt,' he declared, 'that I demanded from the S.A. men the strict observance of the path of legality, and, if this veto on illegality was anywhere violated, then the leaders concerned have always been brought to account. ... Acts of violence have never been contemplated by our Party, nor has the individual S.A. man ever wished for them. ... We stand absolutely as hard as granite on the ground of legality.'[1] In December 1931, Hitler again underlined the importance he attached to keeping within the law by a proclamation to the S.A. and S.S. in which he assured them that victory was certain, if they remained true to the policy of legality. They were not to allow themselves to be provoked. 'He who fails in the last days of his test is not worthy to witness victory.'[2]

In the second place, so long as the challenge to the authority of the State remained latent and was camouflaged by fair words, there was a strong temptation for any government in Germany in 1931 and 1932 not to add to its difficulties. For throughout the winter of 1930–1 the economic crisis, far from lifting, bore down more heavily upon the German people. The figures for registered unemployment, which, in September 1930 had stood at three millions, mounted to four and three-quarter millions at the end of March 1931. The financial crisis reached its peak in July 1931, when, following the failure of Austria's greatest banking institution the Kreditanstalt, and an unprecedented flight of capital from Germany, the Darmstadt and National Bank (the Danat), one of the big three joint-stock banks in Germany, had to close its doors and suspend payment. When the British Ambassador returned to Berlin on 16 July he wrote: 'I was much struck by the emptiness of the streets and the unnatural silence hanging

1. 8 May 1931, (Baynes: vol. I, pp. 163–4).
2. ibid.: vol. I, p. 178, quoting the *Frankfurter Zeitung* for 3 December 1931.

over the city, and particularly by an atmosphere of extreme tension similar in many respects to that which I observed in Berlin in the critical days immediately preceding the war.'[1]

With help from abroad the threat of financial collapse was staved off, but the measures taken by the Brüning Government – heavy additional taxation, cuts in official salaries and wage rates, the reduction of unemployment benefits – while imposing considerable sacrifices on the people, were insufficient to enable the Government to master the crisis. In such circumstances Hitler found no difficulty in laying the blame for all the economic distress of the country on the Government's policy, particularly as Germany was still saddled with reparation payments, and the worsening of the crisis in the summer of 1931 had been partly occasioned by a stinging rebuff in foreign policy.

In March 1931, the German Foreign Minister, in an effort to alleviate the effects of the slump in Central Europe, put forward the proposal of an Austro-German Customs Union. Whatever the economic arguments in favour of such a step, France, supported by Italy and Czechoslovakia, had taken this to be a move towards the political and territorial union of Austria with Germany which was expressly forbidden by the Treaties of Versailles and St Germain. She had promptly mobilized her financial as well as her diplomatic resources to prevent it. The measures taken by the French proved effective: they not only helped to precipitate the failure of the Austrian Kreditanstalt and the German financial crisis of the summer but forced the German Foreign Minister to announce on 3 September that the project was being abandoned. The result was to inflict a sharp humiliation on the Brüning Government and to inflame national resentment in Germany.

Hitler was not slow to point the lesson: so long as Germany continued to be ruled by the present system she would continue to suffer economic misery at home and contemptuous insults abroad. Two years before Gregor Strasser had written in the *Nationalsozialistische Briefe:* 'Everything that is detrimental to the existing order has our support. . . . We are promoting catastrophic policies – for only catastrophe, that is, the collapse of the liberal system, will clear the way for the new order. . . . All that serves to precipitate the catastrophe of the ruling system – every strike, every governmental crisis, every disturbance of the State power, every weakening of the System – is good, very good for us

1. *Documents on British Foreign Policy*, 2nd series, vol. II, No. 225.

and our German revolution.'[1] The Nazis were now beginning to garner the harvest of their policy of catastrophe.

Faced with such difficulties, both in domestic and foreign policy, any government was likely to hesitate before adding to its problems by the uproar which the suppression of the Nazi Party, the second largest in the Reichstag, would inevitably have entailed, so long as Hitler was clever enough to avoid any flagrant act of illegality. For the Brüning Ministry lacked the support to play the role of a strong government. The Chancellor's appeal for national unity had failed, and the elections of September 1930, far from producing a stable parliamentary basis for Brüning's policy, had only multiplied the strength of the two extremist parties, the Nazis and the Communists. Brüning was only able to continue governing Germany after the elections because the Social Democrats, alarmed at the growing political and economic crisis, gave him unofficial support in the Reichstag, and the President of the Republic continued to use his emergency powers under Article 48 to sign the necessary decrees. The refusal of the German parties to sink their differences, unite in face of the emergency, and jointly assume responsibility for the unpopular measures which had to be taken, drove Brüning into a dangerous dependence on support outside the Reichstag, upon the support of the President and the support of the Army. The attitude of both towards the Nazis was equivocal. Here was the third reason for the reluctance to take action against the Nazis.

From the beginning of 1930, General Groener, the Minister of Defence, a man of integrity and experience, had been uneasily conscious that a good many members of the Officer Corps were becoming sympathetic to the Nazis. The Leipzig Trial of Lieutenants Ludin and Scheringer, and the storm of criticism to which he had been subjected for allowing the trial to take place at all, showed that Hitler's propaganda directed at the Army had been far from unsuccessful. After the elections of September 1930, the British Military Attaché reported that the officers he had met on the autumn manoeuvres were deeply impressed by the growth of National Socialism. 'It is the *Jugendbewegung* (Youth Movement),' they said; 'it can't be stopped.'[2] Professor Meinecke records that the attitude of Army officers was summed up in the

1. *N.S. Briefe*, No. 23, June 1929, quoted in the Police Report of 1930, Kempner: pp. 97–8.
2. *Brit. Doc.*, 2nd series, vol. I, p. 512, note.

phrase: 'What a pity it would be to have to fire on these splendid youths in the S.A.'[1] The nationalist appeal of Nazi propaganda and its promise of a powerful Germany with an expanded Army were beginning to have their effect.

The Army could still be relied on to support Brüning if Hitler attempted to make a putsch. 'It is a complete mistake to ask where the Army stands,' Groener told his friend, Meinecke. 'The army will do what it is ordered to do, *und damit Basta* – and that's that.'[2] To General von Gleich, Groener wrote that, if Hitler resorted to force, he would meet 'the unqualified employment of the resources of the State. The Army is so completely in our hands that it will never hesitate in this eventuality'.[3] In an article published since the war Dr Brüning confirms this. In the autumn of 1931 he writes: 'the two generals (von Schleicher and von Hammerstein) and myself were fully agreed that, if the Nazis imitated Mussolini's March on Rome the Army would make short work of them. ... We also expected that we would finally get Hindenburg's consent to the immediate suppression of the Nazi Party, if they resorted to open revolt.'[4]

But it was not at all certain that the Government would be able to count on the support of the Army if it was a question of suppressing the Nazi Party without the pretext of revolt. Once again the cleverness of Hitler's tactics of legality was demonstrated. Groener, who never wavered in his dislike and contempt for Nazism, hesitated to take action against the Party, even after he had become Minister of the Interior as well as Minister of Defence (October 1931). Later he admitted to Meinecke: 'We ought to have suppressed them by force.'[5] But at the time Groener was too unsure of feeling in the Army to risk action, at least until Brüning should have secured the agreement of the other Powers to the creation of a German conscript militia, which would reassure those officers who looked to the S.A. as an Army reserve in

1. Friedrich Meinecke: *Die deutsche Katastrophe* (Wiesbaden, 1947), p. 71.
2. Meinecke: pp. 68–9.
3. Groener Correspondence, 26 January 1932, quoted by Gordon A. Craig: 'The Reichswehr and National Socialism', *Political Science Quarterly*, vol. LXIII, No. 2 (June 1948), p. 210.
4. Heinrich Brüning: 'Ein Brief', in *Deutsche Rundschau*, July 1947. This post-war account by Dr Brüning should be compared with the version of events given in J. W. Wheeler-Bennett: *Hindenburg, The Wooden Titan* (London, 1936), which is partly based on the author's conversations with Brüning at that time.
5. Meinecke: p. 74.

case of war, and draw away the young men attracted by the militarist propaganda of the Nazis.

The President, Field-Marshal von Hindenburg, was now a very old man, eighty-four in October 1931, and such political judgement as he had ever had was failing. What he cared about most of all was the German Army in which he had spent his life. Between the President and the Army there existed, as Professor Meinecke says, 'relations of mutual dependence. The Reichswehr obeyed him, but he listened to it. He absorbed into his mind and spirit everything to which it was sensitive. He was flesh and blood of its flesh and blood, an off-shoot of that Prusso-German militarism which had produced so many first-rate technical and so few politically far-sighted heads.'[1] Faithfully reflecting opinion in the Army, Hindenburg too was opposed to the use of force against the Nazis. He would only agree to it if there was some unequivocal act of rebellion on their part or if at the same time action were taken against the other extremist party, the Communists.[2]

More important still than the opinion of either General Groener or President Hindenburg was that of Major-General Kurt von Schleicher, who, by 1930–2, had made himself virtually the authoritative voice of the Army in politics. General Schleicher was a General Staff Officer – able, charming, and ambitious – who was far more interested in politics and intrigue than in war. Fifteen years younger than Groener, he had risen rapidly from one Staff appointment to another until Groener became Minister of Defence in 1928 – partly thanks to Schleicher's efforts on his behalf – and made Schleicher the head of a new department in his Ministry, the Ministeramt. This was to handle all matters common to both the Army and Navy and to act as liaison between the armed services and other ministries. Schleicher used the key position created for him to make himself one of the most powerful political figures in Germany. Both Groener and the C.-in-C. of the Army, General von Hammerstein, were under his influence. Through the fortunate chance of an old friendship with the President's son, Colonel Oskar von Hindenburg, he had an entrée to the old man, who listened and was impressed by what he said. Indeed it was Schleicher who had first proposed Brüning's name to the President in 1930 and had overcome Brüning's own objections to serving as Chancellor. In dealing with his

1. Meinecke: p. 73.
2. cf. Brüning's letter, already cited.

brother officers Schleicher had the advantage of quickness and self-confidence in political matters, where they were hesitant and diffident. In dealing with politicians he had the indefinable advantage in German politics of being a general, not a civilian, and of being able to claim that he represented the views of the Army in a country where the Army took precedence over every other institution as the supreme embodiment of the national tradition.

Schleicher's object was to secure a strong government which, in place of coalitions spending their energy in political horse-dealing and compromise, would master the economic and political crisis and prevent the Army being forced to intervene to put down revolution. He believed he had found the answer in Brüning, whose cabinet was made up of men from several parties, without being based upon a coalition, and who, with the promise of the President's emergency powers at his disposal, could follow a firm policy without having to truckle too much to the parties in the Reichstag. But the appeal Brüning made over the heads of the parties to the German people at the elections of September 1930 had failed. It was not Brüning but the two extremist parties which had won the votes, and Schleicher's anxieties revived. 'The load which constantly weighed on General Schleicher's mind', Brüning writes, 'was the fear, based on the experience of 1923, that Nazi and Communist uprisings might break out simultaneously and thus give foreign powers an opportunity to extend their borders still further at Germany's expense.'[1] In particular he feared an attack by Poland, if the German Army should be fully occupied in dealing with simultaneous Nazi and Communist risings.

Schleicher, therefore, shared fully – and was partly responsible for – the reluctance of Groener and Hindenburg to take any initiative against the Nazis. But Schleicher went further: impressed by the Nazi success at the elections and by their nationalist programme, Schleicher began to play with the idea of, somehow or other, winning Hitler's support for Brüning and converting the Nazi movement with its mass following into a prop of the existing government, instead of a battering ram directed against it. Here was an attractive alternative to that of using the Army to suppress the Nazis; it might even be possible to bring them into a coalition government in which they would be forced to share the responsibility for the unpopular measures which would have to be taken.

1. Brüning: 'Ein Brief', already cited.

It was in this direction that Schleicher began to look during 1931 for a way out of the political deadlock. It took time for his ideas to mature, but he made a beginning by removing the old causes of quarrel between the Army and the Nazi Party. The ban on the Army's employment of National Socialists in arsenals and supply depots and the prohibition of Nazi enlistment in the Army were removed in January 1931. In return Hitler reaffirmed his adherence to the policy of legality by an order (dated 20 February 1931) forbidding the S.A. to take part in street-fighting. During the succeeding months Schleicher had several talks with Röhm, eager as always to work with the Army, as well as with Gregor Strasser. By the latter half of 1931 he was ready to try to secure Hitler's agreement to Hindenburg's re-election – his seven-year term of office expired in 1932 – as a first step to drawing the Nazis into support of the Government and taming their revolutionary ardour.

Nothing could have suited Hitler better. For, a year after the great success he had won at the September elections of 1930, Hitler was still no nearer attaining office. He had built up a remarkable organization, the strength of which grew steadily, but the question remained how was he to change the success he had won into the hard coin of political power.

The two most obvious ways by which men come to supreme power in the State – apart from conquest in war – are by force, i.e. by revolution, or by consent, i.e. by an electoral majority. The first of these Hitler himself ruled out, but the second never became a practical alternative. At the height of their success in the elections of July 1932, when they won 230 out of 608 seats in the Reichstag, the Nazis were never in sight of a clear majority. Even in the elections held after Hitler had come to power, the elections of March 1933, they obtained no more than 288 out of 647 seats.

One way of adding to the Nazi vote was to combine with Hugenberg's German National Party. On 9 July 1931, Hitler and Hugenberg met in Berlin and issued a statement to the effect that they would henceforward cooperate for the overthrow of the existing 'System'. The first fruit of this alliance, which had produced the plebiscite against the Young Plan in 1929, was another plebiscite in August 1931, this time demanding a dissolution of the Diet in Prussia, by far the most important of the German states, in which power was exercised by a coalition of the hated Social Democrats and the Catholic Centre Party. Even with the support of the Communist vote, which was flung against the rival working-class party of the Social Democrats, the two Right-wing parties, however, secured no more than thirty-seven per cent of the votes and promptly proceeded to blame each other for the failure. Alliance with the Nationalists, with their strongly upper-class character, was in fact a dubious policy for the Nazis, bound to lead to much discontent in the radical wing of the Party. Although Hitler continued to make intermittent use of the Nationalist alliance, it was with reluctance and misgivings, for limited purposes only, when no other course presented itself.

Yet the only justification of the course of legality was success. It would not be possible to hold the precarious balance between legality and illegality indefinitely. As General Groener remarked: 'Despite all the declarations of legality . . . such an organization has its dynamic in itself and cannot simply be declared now legal and now illegal.'[1] The grumbling in the S.A. at Hitler's policy again found a focus in Berlin and a revolt, which had contacts with Otto Strasser's revolutionary Black Front, was planned by Walter Stennes, a former police captain and the leader of the S.A. for the whole of Eastern Germany. An immediate grievance was Hitler's order of 20 February, ordering the S.A. to refrain from street-fights. Hitler intervened at the beginning of April 1931, before the revolt had got under way, threw out Stennes, and replaced him by one of the most notorious of Rossbach's former Freikorps men, Edmund Heines, who had already served a term of imprisonment for murder and whom Hitler himself had expelled from the Party in 1927. This was, however, the second S.A. mutiny in Berlin in seven months, and it was noticeable that Stennes, instead of making his peace with Hitler, denounced him and joined forces with Otto Strasser.

If Hitler was to carry his policy of legality to success it could only be done in one way, a possibility created by the peculiar system under which Germany was now governed. From the breakdown of the coalition headed by Herman Müller in 1930, Brüning, his successor as Chancellor, and Brüning's own successor, Papen, had both to govern without being able to find a stable parliamentary majority or to win an election. The use of the President's emergency powers, upon which they relied to issue decrees, placed great power in the hands of the President and his advisers; in effect, political power in Germany was transferred from the nation to the little group of men round the President. The most

1. Groener, in the Reichstag, 10 May 1932; Craig: op. cit., p. 212.

important members of this group were General von Schleicher; Oskar von Hindenburg; Otto Meissner, the head of the Presidential Chancery; Brüning and, after his loss of favour, Papen, Brüning's successor as Chancellor. If Hitler could persuade these men to take him into partnership and make him Chancellor, with the right to use the President's emergency powers – a presidential, as opposed to a parliamentary, government – then he could dispense with the clear electoral majority which still eluded him and with the risky experiment of a putsch.

At first sight nothing appeared more improbable than such a deal. Yet neither Schleicher nor the President was at all satisfied with the existing situation. They did not believe that the President's emergency powers could be made into a permanent basis for governing the country. They were looking for a government which, while prepared to take resolute action to deal with the crisis, would also be able to win mass support in the country, and, if possible, secure a majority in the Reichstag. Brüning had failed to win such a majority at the elections. Schleicher, therefore, began to look elsewhere for the mass support which he felt to be necessary for the presidential government.

With six million votes Hitler was a possibility worth considering. For Hitler had two assets, both of which counted with the General. The Nazi success at the elections was a promise of the support Hitler would be able to provide, if he was bought in. The organized violence of the S.A. was a threat of the revolution he might make if he were left out. Hitler's game, therefore, from 1931 to 1933 was to use the revolution he was unwilling to make and the mass support he was unable to turn into a majority, the first as a threat, the second as a promise, to persuade the President and his advisers to take him into partnership and give him power.

This is the key to the complicated and tortuous political moves of the period between the autumn of 1931 and 30 January 1933, when the game succeeded and Hindenburg appointed Adolf Hitler as Chancellor legally. The milestones on the path of the Nazi Party to power between these two dates are the successive negotiations between the little group of men who bore the responsibility for the experiment of presidential government and the Nazi leaders. Hitler did not at the time see this as the only means by which he could come to power legally. He continued to speculate on the possibility of a coalition with the Nationalists – even at one time with the Centre – or, better still, on the chances

of winning an outright majority at the next elections. Each time
the negotiations broke down he turned again to these alternatives. Yet each time he gives the impression that his eye is
always on a resumption of negotiations, and that the measures he
takes are designed primarily to put pressure on the other side to
begin talks again rather than to bring him into office by other
means.

Years ago, in Vienna, Hitler had admired the tactics of Karl
Lueger and had summed them up in two sentences in *Mein Kampf*:
'In his political activity, Lueger attached the main importance to
winning over those classes whose threatened existence tended to
stimulate rather than paralyse their will to fight. At the same time
he took care to avail himself of all the instruments of authority at
his disposal, and to bring powerful existing institutions over to
his side, in order to gain from these well-tried sources of power
the greatest possible advantage for his own movement.'[1] Hitler
was well on the way to 'winning over those classes whose existence was threatened'; now he faced the task of 'bringing the
powerful existing institutions over to his side', above all the
Army and the President. The years of waiting were at an end.

1. *Mein Kampf*, p. 95.

CHAPTER FOUR

THE MONTHS OF OPPORTUNITY

October 1931–30 January 1933

I

THE first contacts between Hitler and the men who disposed of power in Germany were scarcely auspicious. At the beginning of the autumn of 1931 Schleicher had a meeting with Hitler, arranged with Röhm's help, and subsequently persuaded both the Chancellor and the President to see him. Brüning received the Nazi leader, accompanied by Göring, at the home of one of his Ministers, Treviranus.

What Brüning asked for was Hitler's support until the reparations question was settled and Hindenburg re-elected as President. After this had been accomplished he was willing to retire and allow someone else more acceptable to the parties of the Right to take his place. Instead of giving a direct answer, Hitler launched into a monologue, the main point of which was that when he came to power he would not only get rid of Germany's debts but would re-arm and, with England and Italy as his allies, force France to her knees. He failed to impress either the Chancellor or Treviranus, and the meeting ended inconclusively, neither Hitler nor Hugenberg (whom Brüning saw about the same time) being willing to bind themselves.

The interview with the President on 10 October was the first occasion on which the two men had met. Hitler was nervous and ill-at-ease; his niece, Geli Raubal, with whom he was in love, had committed suicide three weeks before,[1] and he had wired to Göring, who was at the bedside of his dying wife in Sweden, to return and accompany him. Nazi accounts of the meeting are singularly reticent,[2] but Hitler obviously made the mistake of talking too much and trying to impress the old man with his demagogic arts; instead he bored him. Hindenburg is said to have grumbled to Schleicher afterwards that he was a queer fellow who would never make a Chancellor, but, at most, a Minister of Posts.

Altogether it was a bad week for Hitler. The day after his

1. See below, c. 7.
2. cf., e.g. Gerhard Schultze-Pfälzer: *Hindenburg und Hitler zur Führung vereint* (Berlin, 1933), pp. 115–15.

interview with the President he took part in a great demonstration of the Right-wing 'National' opposition at Harzburg, a little watering-place in the Hartz Mountains. Hugenberg, representing the Nationalists; Seldte and Düsterberg, the leaders of the Stahlhelm; Dr Schacht and General von Seeckt; Graf Kalkreuth, the president of the Junkers' Land League, and half a score of figures from the Ruhr and Rhineland industries, all joined in passing a solemn resolution uniting the parties of the Right. They demanded the immediate resignation of Brüning's Government and of the Braun Ministry in Prussia, followed by new elections in both the Reich and Prussia. Hitler only agreed to take part in the Rally with great reluctance, and Frick felt obliged to defend the decision to the Nazi contingent with a speech in which he said openly that they were only using the Nationalists as a convenient ladder to office, just as Mussolini had begun with a coalition and later got rid of his allies. The whole atmosphere irritated Hitler. He felt oppressed by his old lack of self-confidence in face of all these frock-coats, top-hats, Army uniforms, and formal titles. This was the *Reaktion* on parade, and the great radical Tribune was out of place. To add to his irritation, the Stahlhelm arrived in much greater numbers than the S.A., and Hugenberg and Seldte stole the limelight. Hitler declined to take part in the official procession, read his speech in a perfunctory fashion, and left before the Stahlhelm marched past. The united front of the National Opposition had virtually collapsed before it was established. The fight between the rival Right-wing parties, and the rival party armies, Stahlhelm and S.A., continued unabated, despite the bitter complaints of the Nationalist and Stahlhelm leaders at the Nazis' uncomradely conduct.[1]

Two days later, on 13 October, Brüning presented to the Reichstag a reconstituted government in which General Groener, the Minister of Defence – at Schleicher's suggestion – took over the Ministry of the Interior, and the Chancellor himself became Foreign Minister. In face of the Nationalists' and Nazis' demands for his resignation, Brüning appeared to be taking on a new lease of political life, with renewed proofs of the support of the Army and the President.

Hitler expressed his frustration and fury at the course of events

1. See the collection of acrimonious letters between Hitler, Röhm, and the Stahlhelm leaders, dating from October–December 1931, and printed verbatim in Th. Düsterberg: *Der Stahlhelm und Hitler* (Wolfenbüttel, 1949), pp. 15–33.

in an open letter to the Chancellor (published on 14 October) in which he attacked the policy of the Government as a disastrous betrayal of German interests, adding a stinging postscript for the benefit of Generals Groener and von Schleicher:

The most regrettable feature of all is that the last instrument which is still sound in its general outlook – the instrument on which you alone can still today rely for support – the Army – is now involved through its representatives in the Government directly and indirectly in these struggles. . . . For us the Army is the expression of the strength of the nation for the defence of its national interests abroad. For you, Herr Chancellor Brüning, it is in the last resort an institution for the defence of the Government at home. The triumph of our ideas will give the entire nation a political and philosophical outlook which will bring the Army in spirit into a truly close relationship to the whole people and will thus free it from the painful circumstance of being an alien body within its own people. The consequence of your view, Herr Chancellor, will be an obligation on the part of the Army to uphold a political system which in its traditions and inmost views is the deadly opponent of the spirit of an army. And so finally, whether deliberately or not, the Army will be stamped with the character of a police-troop designed more or less for internal purposes.[1]

Having delivered this broadside, Hitler went off on 17 October to Brunswick, where more than a hundred thousand S.A. and S.S men tramped past the saluting base for six hours, and the thundering cheers mollified his wounded vanity. Thirty-eight special trains and five thousand lorries brought the Brown Shirts pouring into Brunswick. Hitler presented twenty-four new standards, and at night a great torchlight parade lighted up the countryside. This was a show the like of which neither Hugenberg and the Stahlhelm nor the Government could put on: while they continued to talk of the need for popular support, Hitler already had it.

The first attempt to initiate negotiations had broken down, but the failure was not irremediable. Events continued to flow in Hitler's favour. In December 1931, the figure of registered unemployment passed the five-million mark. On 8 December the President signed new emergency decrees making further reductions in wages, prices, and interest rates, together with an increase in taxation. It was a grim winter in Germany. Brüning described

1. Hitler's open letter, published together with other letters exchanged with Dr Brüning, in a Nazi pamphlet: *Hitlers Auseinandersetzung mit Brüning* (Munich, 1932), pp. 35–6.

his measures as unequalled in the demands they made on the German people, yet all he could do was to hold on in the hope that, with the spring, the Depression might begin to lessen in severity. Then he might be able to negotiate the end of reparations (which were already suspended) and secure some satisfaction of Germany's demands from the Disarmament Conference due to meet in the coming year. This was poor comfort, however, to a people suffering from the primitive misery of hunger, cold, lack of work, and lack of hope. Nor was Brüning, with his aloof and reserved manner, the man to put across a programme of sacrifice and austerity.

By contrast, the Nazis gained steadily in strength. Their membership of 389,000 at the beginning of 1931 rose to more than 800,000 at the end of the year. Following their success in the Oldenburg provincial elections in May (over thirty-seven per cent of the votes), and at Hamburg in September, the Nazis swept the board at the Hessian elections in November.[1] They more than doubled the votes they had won in Hesse during the Reichstag elections of September 1930, and pushed up their numbers in the Diet from one to twenty-seven deputies. Their average vote for the eight most recent provincial elections was thirty-five per cent, compared with the eighteen per cent which had given them over six million votes in the national elections of September 1930. The threat and the promise were gaining in weight.

These facts were not lost on General von Schleicher, who continued his talks with Hitler in November and December. Schleicher was more and more impressed with the need to bring Hitler into the game and make use of him. The French Military Attaché in Berlin, Colonel Chapouilly, reported on 4 November 1931: 'In Schleicher's view, Hitler knows very well how to distinguish between the demagogy suitable to a young Party, and the needs of national and international life. He has already moderated the actions of his troops on more than one occasion, and one can secure more from him. Faced with the forces he controls, there is only one policy to adopt – to use him and win him over,

1. There were seventeen states in Germany, of the most remarkable diversity in size and power: Prussia (thirty-eight millions); Bavaria (seven millions); Saxony (five millions); Württemberg and Baden (each over two millions); Thuringia, Hesse, and Hamburg (a million to a million and a half each); Mecklenburg-Schwerin, Oldenburg, and Brunswick (over half a million); Anhalt and Bremen (a third of a million); Mecklenburg-Strelitz, Lippe, Lübeck (ranging from 110,000 to 163,000); and Schaumburg-Lippe (48,000).

foreseeing with some reason the loss of the revolutionary wing of his party.'[1] Under the influence of Schleicher, even Groener – so Professor Meinecke records[2] – resigned himself during the winter to the idea of compromising with the Nazis and bringing individual National Socialists into the Government.

Hitler meanwhile kept up the attack on Brüning as the embodiment of all the evils of the 'System' by which Germany had been governed since 1918. He answered Brüning's broadcast of 8 December, in which the Chancellor explained and defended his new decrees, with another open letter (published 13 December 1931). Brüning's appeal for national unity and an end of factious criticism he met with the retort that there was still freedom of speech in Germany. 'You yourself, Herr Chancellor, jealously see to it that only the Government is permitted liberty of action in Germany; and thus there arises of necessity the limitation of the opposition to the sphere of criticism, of speech. ... The Government, Herr Chancellor, can act. It can prove the rightness of its views by deeds. And it takes jealous care that no one else shall enjoy such possibilities. What then, Herr Chancellor, remains for us but speech, to bring to the knowledge of the German nation our views on the ruinous character of your plans, or the errors which underlie them, and the disasters which must ensue?'[3]

This letter is interesting for a frank statement by Hitler of what he meant by legality. In his broadcast Brüning had said: 'When a man declares that once he has achieved power by legal means he will break through the barriers, he is not really adhering to legality.'[4] Hitler replied: 'You refuse, as a "statesman", to admit that if we come to power legally we could then break through legality. Herr Chancellor, the fundamental thesis of democracy runs: "All power issues from the People." The constitution lays down the way by which a conception, an idea, and therefore an organization, must gain from the people the legitimation for the realization of its aims. But in the last resort it is the People itself which determines its Constitution.

'Herr Chancellor, if the German nation once empowers the

1. Quoted by G. Castellan: 'Von Schleicher, von Papen et l'avènement de Hitler' in *Cahiers d'Histoire de la Guerre*, Publication du Comité d'Histoire de la Guerre (Paris No. 1, January 1949), p. 18.
2. Meinecke: p. 74.
3. *Hitlers Auseinandersetzung mit Brüning*, pp. 49–51. I have used the translation of this passage in Baynes: vol. 1, pp. 496–7.
4. ibid., p. 45. Brüning's broadcast of 8 December 1931.

National Socialist Movement to introduce a Constitution other than that which we have today, then you cannot stop it. . . . When a Constitution proves itself to be useless for its life, the nation does not die – the Constitution is altered.'[1]

Here was a plain enough warning of what Hitler meant to do when he got power, yet Schleicher, Papen, and the rest were so sure of their own ability to manage this ignorant agitator that they only smiled and took no notice.

Brüning had fewer illusions, but all his plans depended upon being able to hold out until economic conditions improved, or he could secure some success in foreign policy. His ability to do this depended in turn upon the re-election of Hindenburg as President at the end of his term of office. This was a considerable risk to take, as Hindenburg was eighty-four and failing in health, yet Brüning believed that he could rely on Hindenburg to support him and continue to sign the decrees he laid before him. The old man was reluctant to go on, and only agreed when the Chancellor promised to try to secure an agreement with the Party leaders in the Reichstag which would provide the two-thirds majority necessary to prolong the presidential term of office without re-election. In any case, a bitter electoral contest for the Presidency at such a time was something to be avoided. And so Brüning, too, agreed to further negotiations with Hitler in order to win him over to his plan.

Hitler was in Munich, in the offices of the *Völkischer Beobachter*, when the summons came. A telegram was brought in to him as he stood talking to Hess, Rosenberg, and Wilhelm Weiss, one of the editors. When he read it he is reported to have purred with satisfaction and crashed his fist down on the telegram in exultation: 'Now I have them in my pocket. They have recognized me as a partner in their negotiations.'[2]

The talks took place early in the New Year, 1932. Hitler saw General Groener on 6 January, Brüning and Schleicher on the 7th. Further conferences followed on the 10th, at which Hitler was accompanied, as before, by Röhm. Brüning's proposal was substantially the same as in the previous autumn: Hitler was asked to agree to a prolongation of Hindenburg's presidency for a year or two, until the country had begun its economic recovery and the issues of reparations and the German claim to equality of

1. *Hitlers Auseinandersetzung mit Brüning*, p. 56.
2. Heiden: *Der Führer*, p. 342.

rights in armaments had been settled. In return, Brüning renewed his offer to resign as soon as he had settled the question of reparations. According to some accounts,[1] although this is omitted by others and neither confirmed nor denied by Dr Brüning himself, the Chancellor added that he would then suggest Hitler's name to the President as Chancellor.

Hitler asked for time to consider his reply and withdrew to the Kaiserhof, the big hotel in the Wilhelmstrasse, opposite the Reich Chancellery and the Presidential Palace, where he had made his headquarters. Hugenberg, who was also consulted by the Chancellor, as leader of the Nationalists, was strongly opposed to prolonging Hindenburg's term of office, arguing that it could only strengthen Brüning's position. Goebbels took the same view. In his diary he wrote: 'The Presidency is not really in question. Brüning only wants to stabilize his own position indefinitely. ... The contest for power, the game of chess, has begun. It may last throughout the year. It will be a fast game, played with intelligence and skill. The main point is that we hold fast, and waive all compromise.'[2] Two opposing arguments had to be weighed against each other. Gregor Strasser's view was that Hindenburg would be unbeatable in any election the Nazis might force on the Government, and that it was in the Party's interests to accept a temporary truce. But Röhm as well as Goebbels argued that it would be a fatal mistake for the Party to appear to avoid a chance to go to the nation, especially after the recent successes in the provincial elections. Long and anxious debates followed among the Nazi leaders. In the end Röhm's point of view was accepted.

Hugenberg's reply to Brüning's proposal, on behalf of the Nationalists, was delivered on 12 January 1932, and contained a blank refusal. Hitler also rejected it, but tried to drive a wedge between Chancellor and President. He did this by writing direct to the President over Brüning's head, warning him that the Chancellor's plan was an infringement of the Constitution; adding, however, that he himself was willing to support Hindenburg's re-election if the President would repudiate Brüning's proposal. To Meissner, whom he invited to a conference at the Kaiserhof as the President's

1. e.g., Heiden: *History of National Socialism*, p. 151; Bénoist-Méchin: *Histoire de l'armée allemande*, vol. II, p. 426.

2. Goebbels: *Vom Kaiserhof zur Reichskanzlei*. English translation: *My Part in Germany's Fight* (London, 1935), pp. 16–17 (hereafter referred to as Goebbels).

representative, Hitler offered to make Hindenburg the joint presidential candidate of the Nazis and the Nationalists, if the old man would agree to dismiss Brüning, form a Right-wing 'National' government, and hold new elections for the Reichstag and the Prussian Diet.[1] The newly elected Reichstag, in which Hitler was confident of a majority for the Nazi and Nationalist parties, would then proceed to prolong his term of office.

When this manoeuvre broke down on Hindenburg's refusal, Hitler launched a violent attack on Brüning in two more open letters, dated 15 and 25 January, the second being in answer to Brüning's reply. Hitler repeated the charge that Brüning was proposing to violate the Constitution in order to keep himself in power, and declared that the Reichstag elected in 1930 was not competent to prolong Hindenburg's term of office, since it no longer represented the German people. When Brüning in turn accused Hitler of playing party politics at the expense of Germany's chances of improving her international position, Hitler retorted that nothing could be more beneficial to German foreign policy then the overthrow of the 'System' by which Germany had been governed since 1918. 'It would never have come to a Treaty of Versailles, if the parties which support you – the Centre, the Social Democrats, and the Democrats – had not undermined, destroyed, and betrayed the old Reich, if they had not prepared and carried through the Revolution (of 1918) or at least accepted and defended it.'[2]

After this exchange any hopes of avoiding an election for the presidency were at an end. For a second time the attempt to do a deal with Hitler had failed. Brüning, who had never had much hope of its success, threw all his energy into the campaign. Schleicher, who had counted on Röhm to get the other Nazi leaders to accept the proposal made to them, was equally set on securing the President's re-election, since the position and powers of the Presidency were the basis of his plans. Until that had been accomplished he could not develop these plans further. For that reason he was willing to support Brüning's continuance in office so that he could manage the election campaign. After that, General von Schleicher considered, a lot of things might happen. The President himself was nettled by the refusal of the Right-wing parties to support the prolongation of his office, and finally

1. Otto Meissner: *Staatssekretär* (Hamburg, 1950), pp. 216–17.
2. *Hitlers Auseinandersetzung mit Brüning* (in which Hitler's first letter, Brüning's reply and Hitler's second letter are printed in full), p. 92.

agreed to offer himself for re-election. On the Government side of the fence, therefore, the breakdown of the negotiations had been followed by at least a temporary consolidation of forces in Brüning's favour.

II

This was far from being the case in the Nazi camp. Now that his attempt to split Hindenburg and Brüning had failed, Hitler had to face an awkward decision. Was he to risk an open contest with Hindenburg? The President's reputation as the most famous figure of the old Army would inevitably attract many votes from the Right, while his position as the defender of the Republic against the extremists would win the support of the moderate and democratic parties. Hindenburg, or rather the Hindenburg legend, was a formidable opponent. Failure might destroy the growing belief in Nazi invincibility: on the other hand, dare they risk evading the contest?

For a month Hitler hesitated, and Goebbels's diary is eloquent on the indecision and anxiety of the Nazi leaders. By 2 February Hitler had tentatively decided to stand, but to delay the announcement. Goebbels adds: 'The whole thing teems with worry.' The next days he records: 'Late at night many old members of the Party come to see me. They are discouraged at not yet having heard anything decisive. They fear the Leader may wait too long.' A week after the first decision, on 9 February, Goebbels writes: 'The Leader is back in Berlin. More discussions at the Kaiserhof. Everything is in suspense.' 12 February: 'Publication of the decision is put off a few days longer.' 21 February: 'This everlasting waiting is almost demoralizing.' Not until 22 February would Hitler allow Goebbels to announce his candidature to a packed Nazi meeting at the big Berlin Sportpalast. 'When, after about an hour's preparation, I publicly proclaim that the Leader will come forward as a candidate, a storm of deafening applause rages for nearly ten minutes. Wild ovations for the Leader. The audience rises with shouts of joy. They nearly raise the roof. . . . People laugh and cry at the same time.'[1]

Shortly before Goebbels spoke the Nationalists and the Stahlhelm announced that they would put up their own candidate. The Harzburg front of the Nationalists and Nazis was thus finally broken; or, as Goebbels put it: 'We have come to grips now for the first time with the Reaction.' With little confidence in the

1. Goebbels: pp. 33–47.

result, the Nationalists chose as their candidate, not Hugenberg, nor even Seldte, the leader of the Stahlhelm, but Seldte's second-in-command, Duesterberg. This was as good as saying that they expected to lose in advance. Characteristically, Hitler, after hesitating for a month, now staked everything on winning, and flung himself into the campaign with a whole-hearted conviction of success. Once he had embarked on a course of action, Hitler was not a man to look back.

The period of waiting had not been wasted. Even before Hitler finally broke off the negotiations with Brüning, Goebbels was already at work preparing for the election campaign. On 24 January he noted in his diary: 'The elections are prepared down to the minutest detail. It will be a struggle such as the world has never before witnessed.' On 4 February he writes: 'The lines of the election campaign are all laid down. We now need only to press the button to set the machine going.'

One of Goebbel's greatest anxieties had been the financing of the election campaign. On 5 January he wrote despairingly: 'Money is wanting everywhere. It is very difficult to obtain. Nobody will give us credit. Once you get the power you can get the cash galore, but then you need it no longer. Without the power you need the money, but then you can't get it.' A month later (8 February) he was much more cheerful: 'Money affairs improve daily. The financing of the electoral campaign is practically assured.' One of the reasons for this sudden change of tone in Goebbels's references to finance was a visit Hitler had paid to Düsseldorf, the capital of the German steel industry, on 27 January.

The meeting, arranged by Fritz Thyssen, was held in the Park Hotel, where Hitler spoke to the Industry Club. It was the first time that many of the West German industrialists present had met Hitler, and their reception of him was cool and reserved. Yet Hitler, far from being nervous, spoke for two and a half hours without pause, and made one of the best speeches of his life. In it is to be found every one of the stock ideas out of which he built his propaganda, brilliantly dressed up for the audience of businessmen he was addressing. For this reason it is worth quoting at some length as an example of his technique as a speaker.

With his mind still full of the last exchange of letters with the Chancellor, Hitler began by attacking |Brüning's view that the dominant consideration in German politics at this time ought to be the country's foreign relations. 'I regard it as of the first importance to break down the view that our destiny is conditioned by world events. . . . Assertions that a people's fate is solely determined by foreign powers have always formed the shifts of bad governments.' The determining factor in national life was the inner worth of a people and its spirit. In Germany, however, this inner worth had been undermined by setting up the false values of democracy and the supremacy of mere numbers in opposition to the creative principle of individual personality.

Hitler chose his illustrations with skill. Private property, he pointed out, could only be justified on the ground that men's achievements in the economic field were unequal. 'But it is absurd to build up economic life on the conceptions of achievement, of the value of personality and on the authority of personality, while in the political sphere you deny this authority and thrust in its place the law of the greatest number – democracy.' Not only was it inconsistent, it was dangerous, for the philosophy of egalitarianism would in time be extended from politics to economics, as it already had been in Bolshevik Russia: 'In the economic sphere Communism is analogous to democracy in the political sphere.'

Hitler dwelt at length on the threat of Communism, for it was something more, he said, than 'a mob storming about in some of our streets in Germany, it a conception of the world which is in the act of subjecting to itself the entire Asiatic continent'. Unless it were halted it would 'gradually shatter the whole world . . . and transform it as completely as did Christianity'. Already, thanks to the economic crisis, Communism had gained a foothold in Germany. Unemployment was driving millions of Germans to look on Communism as the 'logical theoretical counterpart of their actual economic situation'. This was the heart of the German problem – not the result of foreign conditions, 'but of our internal aberration, our internal division, our internal collapse'. And this state of affairs was not to be cured by the economic expedients embodied in emergency decrees, but by the exercise of political power. It was not economics but politics that formed the prime factor in national life.

For it was not German business that conquered the world, followed by the development of German power, but the power-State which created for the business world the general conditions for its subsequent prosperity [*Very true!*]. In my view it is to put the cart before the horse when today people believe that by business methods they can recover Germany's power-position, instead of realizing that the power-position is also the condition for the improvement of the economic situation. . . . There is only one fundamental solution – the realization that there can be no flourishing economic life which has not before it and behind it a flourishing, powerful State as its protection. . . . There can be no economic life unless behind this economic life there stands the determined political will of the nation absolutely ready to strike – and to strike hard. . . . The essential thing is the formation of the political will of the nation: that is the starting point for political action.

The same, Hitler went on, was true of foreign policy.

The Treaty of Versailles in itself is only the consequence of our own slow inner confusion and aberration of mind. . . . In the life of peoples the strength which can be turned outwards depends upon the strength of a nation's internal organization, and that in turn upon the stability of views held in common on certain fundamental questions.

It was no good appealing for national unity and sacrifice for the State when

fifty per cent of the people wish only to smash the State in pieces and feel themselves to be the vanguard not only of an alien attitude towards the State . . . but of a will which is hostile to the State . . . when only fifty per cent of a people are ready to fight for the national colours, while fifty per cent have hoisted another flag which stands for a State which is to be found only outside the bounds of their own State.

Unless Germany can master this internal division in *Weltanschauungen* no measures of the legislature can stop the decline of the German nation. [*Very true!*]

Recognizing this fact, the Nazi movement had set out to create a new outlook which would re-unite and re-vitalize the German people.

Here is an organization which is filled with an indomitable, aggressive spirit, an organization which, when a political opponent says 'Your behaviour we regard as a provocation,' does not see fit immediately to retire from the scene, but brutally enforces its own will and hurls against the opponent the retort: 'We fight today! We fight tomorrow! And if you regard our meeting today as a provocation we shall hold yet another next week – until you have learned that it is no provocation when *German* Germany also professes its belief. . . .' And when people cast in our teeth our intolerance, we proudly acknowledge it – yes, we have formed the inexorable decision to destroy Marxism in Germany down to its very last root. . . . Today we stand at the turning-point of Germany's destiny. . . . Either we shall succeed in working out a body-politic hard as iron from this conglomeration of parties, associations, unions, and *Weltanschauungen*, from this pride of rank and madness of class, or else, lacking this internal consolidation, Germany will fall in final ruin. . . .

Remember that it means sacrifice when today many hundreds of thousands of S.A. and S.S. men every day have to mount on their lorries, protect meetings, undertake marches, sacrifice themselves night after night and then come back in the grey dawn to workshop and factory, or as unemployed to take the pittance of the dole; it means sacrifice when from the little they possess they have to buy their uniforms, their shirts, their badges, yes, and even pay their own fares. But there is already in all this the force of an ideal – a great ideal! And if the whole German nation today had the same faith in its vocation as these hundred thousands, if the whole nation possessed this idealism, Germany would stand in the eyes of the world otherwise than she stands now![1]

When Hitler sat down the audience, whose reserve had long since thawed, rose and cheered him wildly. 'The effect upon the industrialists,' wrote Otto Dietrich, who was present, 'was great, and very evident during the next hard months of struggle.'[2] Thyssen adds that, as a result of the impression Hitler made, large contributions from the resources of heavy industry flowed into the Nazi treasury. With an astuteness which matched that of his appeal to the Army, Hitler had won an important victory. As the Army officers saw in Hitler the man who promised to restore Germany's military power, so the industrialists came to see in him the man who would defend their interests against the threat of Communism and the claims of the trade unions, giving a free hand to private enterprise and economic exploitation in the name of the principle of 'creative individuality'.

III

The election campaign for the Presidency was the first of five major electoral contests in Germany in less than nine months. It was notable for a number of reasons. First, because of the bitterness with which it was fought. Goebbels set the tone by his reference to Hindenburg in the Reichstag as 'the candidate of the party of deserters', and the Nazis, who knew they were fighting against heavy odds, spared neither the President nor anyone else in their attacks on the 'System'. Their violence aroused the Republican parties to great efforts in their turn: nearly eighty-five

1. Baynes: vol. I, pp. 777–829, a verbatim translation of the speech.
2. Otto Dietrich: (English translation) p. 14.

per cent of the total electorate voted, and in many urban areas the vote was as high as ninety-five per cent. Second, because of the extraordinary confusion of parties. Hindenburg, a Protestant, a Prussian, and a monarchist, received his most solid support from the Social Democrats and the trade unions, the Catholic Centre (Brüning's own party), and the other smaller democratic parties, to whom the old man had become a symbol of the Constitution. The conservative upper classes of the Protestant north voted either for Düsterberg, the candidate of the Nationalist Party (to which Hindenburg himself belonged by rights), or for the Austrian demagogue, Hitler, who was hurriedly made a German citizen only on the eve of the election by the Nazi-controlled state of Brunswick. Industry and big business divided its support between all three candidates, while the working-class vote was split by the Communists, whose bitterest attack was directed against the rival Social Democrats and the trade unions.

The third factor which made the election notable was the character of the Nazi campaign, a masterpiece of organized agitation which attempted to take Germany by storm. Every constituency down to the most remote village was canvassed. In the little Bavarian hamlet of Dietramszell, where the President spent his summer holidays, the Nazis brought in some of their best speakers to capture 228 votes against the Field-Marshal's 157 – a typical piece of Nazi spite. The walls of the towns were plastered with screaming Nazi posters; films of Hitler and Goebbels were made and shown everywhere (an innovation in 1932); gramophone records were produced which could be sent through the post, two hundred thousand marks spent on propaganda in one week alone. But, true to Hitler's belief in the superiority of the spoken word, the main Nazi effort went into organizing a chain of mass meetings at which the principal Nazi orators, Hitler, Goebbels, Gregor Strasser, worked their audiences up to hysterical enthusiasm by mob oratory of the most unrestrained kind. Goebbels's own programme, which can be reconstructed from his diary, is impressive enough. Between 22 February and 12 March he made nineteen speeches in Berlin (including four in the huge Sportpalast) and addressed mass meetings in nine other towns as widely separated as Breslau, Dresden, Cologne, Hamburg, and Nuremberg, dashing back to Berlin by the night train to supervise the work of the central propaganda organization. At Breslau Hitler spoke to sixty thousand people; in other places to crowds estimated at one hundred thousand.

The result was baffling. When the polls were closed on the evening of 13 March the Nazi vote had been pushed up from just under six and a half millions in September 1930 to just under eleven and a half millions, an increase of eighty-six per cent, giving Hitler nearly one-third of the total votes in Germany. But all the Nazi efforts left them more than seven million votes behind Hindenburg's figure of 18,661,736. In Berlin alone Hindenburg had polled 45 per cent of the votes and the Communists 28·7 as against Hitler's 23 per cent. This was outright defeat, and Goebbels was in despair.

By a quirk of chance, however, Hindenburg's vote was 0·4 per cent – less than two hundred thousand votes – short of the absolute majority required. A second election had therefore to be held. While Goebbels in Berlin threw up his hands, Hitler in Munich immediately announced that he would stand again, and before morning on 14 March special editions of the *Völkischer Beobachter* were on the streets carrying a new election manifesto: 'The first election campaign is over, the second has begun today. I shall lead it.'

It was an uphill fight, with Hitler driving a tired and dispirited Party, but the ingenious mind of Goebbels, once he had recovered his nerve, hit on a novel electioneering device. The leader should cover Germany by plane – 'Hitler over Germany'. On 3 April the flight began with four mass meetings in Saxony, at which Hitler addressed a quarter of a million people. After Dresden, Leipzig, Chemnitz, and Plauen came more meetings at Berlin, Königsberg, Nuremberg, Frankfurt, Essen, Stuttgart, and Munich – in all. twenty different towns in a week from East Prussia to Westphalia, from the Baltic to Bavaria. On 8 April, when a violent storm raged over Western Germany and all other air traffic was grounded, the leader flew to Düsseldorf and kept his engagement, with the whole Nazi Press blaring away that here at last was the man with the courage Germany needed.

Defeat was certain, but by his exacting performance Hitler pushed up his vote again on 10 April by more than two millions to 13,417,460. The President was safely home with a comfortable 53 per cent – over nineteen and a quarter million votes – yet by tenacity and boldness Hitler had avoided disaster, capturing votes not only from the Nationalist candidate, who had failed to stay the course in the second election, but also from the Communists, whose vote fell by over a million. The day after the election Goebbels wrote in his diary: 'The campaign for the Prussian

State elections is prepared. We go on without a breathing space.'

Once again, however, the awkward question presented itself: how was electoral success, which, however remarkable, still fell far short of a clear majority, to be turned to political advantage? On 11 March Goebbels noted: 'Talked over instructions with the S.A. and S.S. commanders. Deep uneasiness is rife everywhere. The notion of an uprising haunts the air.' And again, on 2 April: 'The S.A. getting impatient. It is understandable enough that the soldiers begin to lose morale through these long-drawn-out political contests. It has to be stopped though, at all costs. A premature putsch would nullify our whole future.' On the other side, Gregor Strasser, who had opposed fighting the presidential campaign from the beginning, now renewed his argument that the chances of success for the policy of legality were being thrown away by Hitler's 'all-or-nothing' attitude and his refusal to make a deal, except on his own exaggerated terms. What was the point of Hitler's virtuoso performance as an agitator, Strasser asked, if it led the Party, not to power, but into a political cul-de-sac?

For the moment Hitler had no answer to either side, either to the impatient S.A. or to the critical Strasser. It was the Government which, strengthened by the elections, now took the initiative and used its advantage to move at last against the S.A.

At the end of November 1931 the State authorities of Hesse had secured certain documents drawn up by the legal adviser to the Nazi Party in Hesse, Dr Werner Best, after secret discussions among a small group of local Nazi leaders at the house of a Dr Wagner, Boxheimer Hof – from which they became known as the Boxheim Papers. These papers contained a draft of the proclamation to be issued by the S.A. in the event of a Communist rising, and suggestions for emergency decrees to be issued by a provisional Nazi government after the Communists had been defeated. Such an emergency, according to the documents captured, would justify drastic measures, and arrangements were to be made for the immediate execution of those who resisted the Nazi authorities, who refused to cooperate or who were found in possession of arms. Amongst the measures proposed was the abolition of the right to private property, of the obligation to pay debts of interest on savings, and of all private incomes. The S.A. was to be given the right to administer the property of the State and of all private citizens; all work was to be compulsory, without reward, and people were to be fed by a system of food cards and public kitchens. Provision was added for the erection of courts-martial under Nazi presidents.

The discovery of these plans caused a sensation, and seriously embarrassed Hitler, who declared (probably with justice) that he had known nothing of them and, had he known, would have disavowed them. Despite pressure from the Prussian State Government, however, the Reich Government declined to take action against the Nazis, and General Groener, the Reich Minister of the Interior, expressed his confidence in Hitler's adherence to a policy of legality.[1]

Evidence of Nazi plans for a seizure of power continued to accumulate. However much Hitler underlined his insistence upon legal methods, the character of the S.A. organization was such that the idea of a putsch was bound to come naturally to men whose politics were conducted in an atmosphere of violence and semi-legality. On the day of the first presidential election Röhm had ordered his S.A. and S.S. troops to stand by in their barracks, while a ring of Nazi forces was drawn round the capital. Prussian police, raiding Nazi headquarters, found copies of Röhm's orders and marked maps which confirmed the report that the S.A. had been prepared to carry out a *coup d'état* if Hitler secured a majority. Near the Polish frontier other orders were captured instructing the local S.A. in Pomerania not to take part in the defence of Germany in the event of a surprise Polish attack.

As a result of these discoveries the State governments, led by Prussia and Bavaria, presented Groener with an ultimatum. Either the Reich Government must act against the S.A. or, they hinted, they would take independent action themselves. In his letter of 1947 Brüning expresses the view that such action was premature[2] although he gives no reasons for this. Groener, however, felt obliged to act, partly to avoid a situation which would undermine the authority of the Reich Government, partly to avoid the loss of the Social Democratic support on which Brüning depended, and which was likely to be withdrawn if the demands of the Prussian State Government were not met. On 10 April, the day of the second election, a meeting presided over by the Chancellor confirmed Groener's view, and on the 14th a decree was promulgated dissolving the S.A., the S.S., and all their

1. Conference at the Ministry of the Interior, 14 December 1931. Craig: op. cit., p. 216.
2. Brüning: 'Ein Brief', p. 4.

affiliated organizations. The decree added, as the grounds for this belated action: 'These organizations form a private army whose very existence constitutes a state within the State, and represent a permanent source of trouble for the civil population. . . . It is exclusively the business of the State to maintain organized forces. The toleration of such a partisan organization . . . inevitably leads to clashes and to conditions comparable to civil war.'

Röhm for a moment thought of resistance; after all, the S.A. now numbered four hundred thousand men, four times the size of the Army allowed to Germany by the Treaty of Versailles. But Hitler was insistent: the S.A. must obey. His authority held, and overnight the Brown Shirts disappeared from the streets. But the S.A. organization was left intact; the S.A. troops were merely dismissed from parade, to reappear as ordinary Party members; Brüning and Groener would get their answer, Hitler declared, at the Prussian elections.

Prussia was by far the largest of the German states, embracing nearly two-thirds of the whole territory of the Reich, with a population of forty out of a total of sixty-five millions. Throughout the period of the Weimar Republic the Prussian Diet and the Prussian State Government, based on a coalition of the Social Democratic and Centre parties, had been the stronghold of German democracy. The Prussian Ministry of the Interior, which controlled by far the biggest administration and police force in Germany and was held by a Social Democrat, Karl Severing, had been more active than any other official agency in trying to check Nazi excesses, and was the object of venomous Nazi attacks. To capture a majority in Prussia, therefore, would be a political victory for the Nazis second only in importance to securing a majority in the Reichstag.

The date of the Prussian elections had been fixed for 24 April, at the same time as State elections in Bavaria, Anhalt, Württemberg and Hamburg. Altogether some four-fifths of Germany would go to the polls. The Nazi propaganda machine was switched immediately from the Presidential to the State elections. In a second series of highly publicized flights over Germany, Hitler spoke in twenty-six towns between 15 and 23 April. His attack this time was directed against the Social Democrats, and in the working-class quarters of the big towns the Nazis got rough handling. In Prussia they won the same thirty-six per cent of votes they had secured in the second presidential election, and, with eight million votes, became the strongest party in the Prussian Diet. The coalition of the Social Democrats and the Centre lost its majority, and the Government of Prussia without Nazi cooperation became an impossibility. Yet once again the Nazis fell short of the majority for which they had hoped.

Even with the support of the Nationalists, the Nazis were not strong enough to form an administration in Prussia. Elsewhere – in Württemberg, Bavaria, and Hamburg – their gains in the number of deputies were offset by the fact that they had failed to reach the national percentage of votes they had won in the second presidential election. By comparison with the thirty-six per cent they secured on 10 April, their votes now stood at 26·4 per cent in Württemberg, 32·5 in Bavaria, and 31 per cent in Hamburg. In all three they were well short of a majority. The deadlock therefore continued. Three times the trumpet had sounded and still the walls refused to fall. At the end of a list of their triumphs Goebbels added to his diary the despondent comment: 'Something must happen now. We *must* shortly come to power, otherwise our victory will be a Pyrrhic one.'[1]

At this moment there appeared a *deus ex machina* in the shape of General von Schleicher, prepared to discuss once again the admission of the Nazis by the back door.

IV

General Schleicher had resumed his relations with Röhm and with the Chief of the Berlin S.A., Helldorf, before the presidential elections. He appears at this time to have been playing with the idea of detaching the S.A. from Hitler, and bringing them under the jurisdiction of the State as the militia Röhm had always wanted to make them.[2] Unknown to Hitler, it had already been agreed between Röhm and Schleicher that, in the event of a war-emergency, the S.A. would come under the command of the Army. Schleicher, however, was still attracted by the alternative idea of bringing Hitler himself into the Government camp. In either case, the prohibition of the S.A. was bound to embarrass his plans.

1. Goebbels: p. 82.
2. cf. Heiden: *Der Führer*, pp. 355–6; also Gordon Craig: p. 227, where he says that Groener inclined to the view that Schleicher hoped to seduce the S.A. from its allegiance to the Führer through his own close liaison with Röhm.

Although he agreed to Groener's action on 8 April, when it was first discussed, the next day Schleicher began to make objections and propose changes of plan – such as a last warning to Hitler. This was rejected at the meeting in the Chancellery on the 10th, but Schleicher persisted in stirring up opposition in the Army and went behind Groener's back to the President. He let Hitler know that he did not agree with the ban, and persuaded Hindenburg to write an irritable letter to Groener complaining about the activities of the Social Democratic organization, the Reichsbanner, with the implication that the prohibition of the S.A. had been one-sided. The material for this letter, Groener discovered, had been provided from a section in his own Ministry of Defence which was under Schleicher's direction, and the letter had been made public almost before he had received it. A malicious whispering campaign against Groener himself now began, and on 10 May Göring delivered a violent attack on him in the Reichstag. When Groener, a sick man, attempted to reply, he met a storm of abuse and obstruction from the Nazi benches. Scarcely had he sat down, exhausted by the effort, when he was blandly informed by Schleicher, the man he regarded almost as his own son, and by Hammerstein, the Commander-in-Chief, that the Army no longer had confidence in him, and that it would be best for him to resign. Brüning loyally defended Groener, but on 12 May there were such scenes of uproar in the Reichstag that the Chamber had to be cleared by the police. The next day Groener resigned. The Nazis were jubilant.

Groener's fall, treacherously engineered by Schleicher, was a grave blow to German democracy. One of the greatest weaknesses of the Weimar Republic was the equivocal attitude of the Army towards the republican régime. Groener was the only man amongst the Army's leaders who had served it with whole-hearted loyalty, and there was no one to replace him.

But Groener's departure was only a beginning. Schleicher had now made up his mind that the chief obstacle to the success of his plan for the deal with the Nazis was Brüning, who was reluctant to make concessions to the Nazis to win their support, and who had become the butt of Nazi attacks on the 'System'. The man he had himself proposed as Chancellor in March 1930 had outlived his usefulness. With the same cynical disloyalty with which he had stabbed Groener in the back, Schleicher now set about unseating Brüning.

Brüning was not in a strong position to defend himself.

Although he had striven honestly and dourly to master the crisis in Germany for two years, success still eluded him. He had failed to secure a stable majority in the Reichstag, and had so far failed to restore prosperity to Germany, even though he believed that the next few months would see a gradual easing of the depression. His great hope of redressing the humiliation of the Austro-German Customs Union plan and of offsetting domestic failure by a big success in foreign policy – the cancellation of reparations and the recognition of Germany's right to equality in armaments – had been frustrated, the first by the postponement of the Reparations Conference at Lausanne until June 1932, the second by the long-draw-out opposition of the French at the Disarmament Conference. He was to enjoy the bitter consolation of seeing his successors secure the fruits of his own labours in foreign policy, but his efforts for Germany abroad were to contribute nothing to alleviate his own difficulties. Ironically, his one great success, the re-election of the President, weakened rather than strengthened his position. For, with that safely accomplished, Brüning no longer appeared indispensable, and, under the careful coaching of Schleicher and other candid friends, the old man had come to feel resentment against the Chancellor as the man whose obstinacy had forced him to endure an election campaign, and to stand as the candidate of the Left against his own friends on the Right.

Moreover, Brüning had made powerful enemies who enjoyed great influence with the President, the man on whose willingness to continue signing emergency decrees the Chancellor ultimately depended. The industrialists complained of his attempts to keep prices down and of the social policies initiated by Stegerwald, Brüning's Labour Minister, the leader of the Catholic trade unions. A proposal for taking over insolvent properties in Eastern Germany and using these for land-colonization roused the passionate hostility of the powerful Junker class, who used the opportunity of Hindenburg's visit to his estate of Neudeck at Whitsuntide to press their demand for Brüning's dismissal as the sponsor of 'Agrarian Bolshevism'. Finally, Schleicher, claiming to speak with the legendary authority of the Army, announced that the Army no longer had confidence in the Chancellor. A stronger man was needed to deal with the situation, and he already had a suitable candidate ready in Papen. He added the all-important assurance that the Nazis had agreed to support the new Government. With Papen the President would be sure of a

Ministry which would be acceptable to his friends of the Right and to the Army, and at the same time command popular support – that elusive combination which Brüning had failed to provide.

Ostensibly Hitler played no part in the manoeuvres which led to Brüning's dismissal. On the surface, the Nazi leaders were occupied with negotiations for a possible coalition in Prussia and with the provincial elections in Mecklenburg. The possibility of a combination between the Nazis and the Catholic Centre to form a government in Prussia interested Brüning, who hoped in this way to force the Nazis to accept a share of responsibility. Safeguards could be provided by combining the premiership of Prussia with his own office of Chancellor, as Bismarck had done, and by placing control of the police in Prussia and the other federal states in the hands of the Reich Minister of the Interior. On the Nazi side, Brüning's offer was supported by Gregor Strasser, still seeking to effect a compromise solution. Even Goebbels, who hated Strasser, was impressed. On 26 April he wrote in his diary: 'We have a difficult decision to make. Coalition with the Centre and power, or opposition to the Centre minus power. From a parliamentary point of view, nothing can be achieved without the Centre – either in Prussia or the Reich. This has to be thoroughly thought over.' But Schleicher, who was in touch with the Nazi leaders through Röhm and Helldorf, and who was bent on frustrating Brüning's plans, offered more tempting possibilities. The negotiations with the Centre suddenly ceased to make progress.

On 28 April Hitler himself had a talk with Schleicher, and Goebbels, after noting that the conference went off well, added: 'The Leader has decided to do nothing at the moment, but mark time. Things are not to be precipitated.' On 8 May another meeting took place. In order to lull Brüning's suspicion, it was decided that Hitler should keep away from Berlin. Until the end of the month Hitler spent most of his time in Mecklenburg and Oldenburg – two states in which provincial elections were impending – or down in Bavaria. Röhm and Göring acted as his representatives in Berlin, but they had little more to do than to keep in touch with Schleicher and wait for news of developments.

What Schleicher offered was the overthrow of the Brüning Cabinet, the removal of the ban on the S.A. and S.S., and new elections for the Reichstag. In return for these solid advantages he asked only for tacit support, the 'neutrality' of the Nazis towards the new presidential cabinet which Papen was to form. Such a promise cost Hitler nothing to give. Time would show who was to do the double-crossing, Schleicher or the Nazis. Meanwhile Hitler's agreement provided Schleicher with a winning argument for Hindenburg. Papen would be able to secure what Brüning had failed to get, Hitler's support, without taking him into the Cabinet. If necessary, Schleicher too reflected, alliances could always be repudiated; the important thing was to get Brüning out and Papen in.

Groener's fall on 13 May raised the hopes of the Nazi leaders high. On the 18th Goebbels wrote in his diary: 'Back in Berlin' – he had been to Munich to report to Hitler – 'For Brüning alone winter seems to have arrived. He is being secretly undermined and is already completely isolated. He is anxiously looking for collaborators – "My kingdom for a Cabinet Minister!" General Schleicher has declined the Ministry of Defence.[1] . . . Our mice are busily at work gnawing through the last supports of Brüning's position.' 'Rat' would perhaps have been a better word to describe the part played by General von Schleicher. Goebbels added some venomous comments on the activities of Gregor Strasser, who was still trying to revive the idea of a coalition with the Centre and a compromise with Brüning as an alternative to the deal with Schleicher. But Strasser's manoeuvres came to nothing. On the 24th Goebbels wrote: 'Saturday [28 May] will see the end of Brüning. The list of Ministers is more or less settled. The main point as far as we are concerned is that the Reichstag is dissolved.'

Once Brüning had secured the passage of the Finance Bill through the Reichstag there was no further need to delay. At the end of May Schleicher's and the Junkers' intrigues were crowned by the President's abrupt request for the Chancellor's resignation. On 30 May Brüning resigned. That fatal reliance on the President which he had been forced to accept as the only way out of the political deadlock had produced a situation in which governments could be made and unmade by the simple grant or withdrawal of the President's confidence. Who bore the responsibility for allowing such a situation to arise will long be a matter of

1. When Brüning, after taxing Schleicher with the intrigue against Groener, demanded that Schleicher should take his place as Minister of Defence, Schleicher retorted: 'I will, but not in your government.' cf. Wheeler-Bennett: *Hindenburg, the Wooden Titan*, p. 385.

controversy, but the result was plain enough: it was the end of democratic government in Germany. The key to power over a nation of sixty-five million people was now openly admitted to lie in the hands of an aged soldier of eighty-five and the little group of men who determined his views.

Hitler was at Horumersiel, on the North Sea, taking part in the Oldenburg elections which on 29 May provided the Nazis with a well-timed success, over forty-eight per cent of the votes and a clear majority of seats in the Diet. Over the week-end he moved to Mecklenburg. Hardly had he begun work there when the news came that Brüning was out. Goebbels rang up from Berlin just after noon and motored out to meet Hitler at Nauen. As they drove back they discussed the situation. There was little time to talk, for Hitler had to see the President at four o'clock. Göring accompanied him and the interview lasted only a few minutes. Hindenburg informed them briefly that he intended to appoint von Papen as Chancellor and understood that Hitler had agreed to support him. Was this correct? Hitler answered: 'Yes.' Back in Berlin, Goebbels commented in his diary: 'Von Papen is, it seems, to be appointed Chancellor, but that is neither here nor there. The Poll! The Poll! It's the people we want. We are all entirely satisfied.'

V

The new Chancellor, Franz von Papen, a man in his fifties, came from a Catholic family of the Westphalian nobility. He had belonged to the right cavalry regiment (he was a celebrated gentleman-rider) and now to the right clubs, the Herrenklub and the Union. He had great charm, a wide acquaintance in the social world, connexions with both German and French industry (he had married the daughter of a wealthy Saar industrialist), and considerable political ambitions. So far these ambitions had not been taken seriously by anyone else. He owned a big block of shares in *Germania*, the Centre Party's paper, and was nominally a member of the Centre Party. He only sat in the Prussian Diet, however, not in the Reichstag, and there he was in single-handed opposition to the Centre's combination with the Social Democrats by which Prussia had been governed until the April elections. Papen was no democrat; he talked vaguely of a Christian Conservatism, which in practice meant a restoration of the privileges and power of the old ruling class of Imperial days in an authoritarian state with a veneer of respectability. If Schleicher did not go as far as Clemenceau, who is reported to have urged the election of Sadi Carnot to the French Presidency with the recommendation 'Vote for the stupidest', he was certainly attracted to the improbable choice of Papen as Chancellor by the belief that he would prove a pliant instrument in his hands. This was to prove a serious underestimate of Papen's ambition and tenacity, no less than of his unscrupulousness. It was a choice which startled everyone and pleased few, with the important exception of the President, who was delighted with the company of a Chancellor who knew how to charm and flatter so well that he soon established relations with him such as no other minister had ever had.

If Schleicher believed that Papen would be able to rally a coalition of the Centre and the Right he was soon disillusioned. The Centre Party, furious at the arbitrary way in which Brüning had been dismissed, went into determined opposition. Hugenberg, the leader of the Nationalists, was indignant at the failure to consider his own claims, while Hitler had bound himself to no more than a vague promise of support, and no Nazis were included in the Ministry. The character of the new Government was in fact so blatantly out of keeping with feeling in the country that it aroused a universal storm of abuse. Only with great difficulty, and by the exercise of the President's personal authority, had it been possible to collect a Cabinet of men willing to serve under Papen. Of its ten members, none of whom was a political figure of the front rank, seven belonged to the nobility with known Right-wing views. Of the remainder, Professor Warmbold, the Minister of Economics, was connected with the great Dye Trust, I.G. Farben; Schaeffer, the Minister of Labour, was a director of Krupps; while the Minister of Justice, Franz Gürtner, was the Bavarian Minister who had most persistently protected Hitler in the 1920s.

Brüning, although driven to rely on the President's emergency power, had none the less been a parliamentary Chancellor in the sense that he had only once been actually defeated in the Reichstag and had then gone to the country. But from the beginning there was not the least chance of Papen avoiding an overwhelming defeat if he met parliament; the power of the 'Cabinet of Barons' was openly and unashamedly based upon the support of the President and the Army. The Social Democratic paper, *Vorwärts*, could be excused a justifiable exaggeration when it wrote of 'this little clique of feudal monarchists, come to power by backstairs methods with Hitler's support, which now announces the class-war from above'.

Of the four parties in Germany which commanded mass support, two, the Communists and the Social Democrats, were bound to oppose Papen's government; the third, the Centre, had excommunicated him; only the fourth, the Nazis, remained as a possible ally. A temporary tolerance had been secured from the Nazis at the price of two concessions: the dissolution of the Reichstag and the lifting of the ban on the S.A. The question which dominated German politics from the end of May 1932 to the end of January 1933 was whether this temporary arrangement could be turned into a permanent coalition.

Both sides were willing to consider such a proposal – Hitler because this was the only way in which he could come to power if he failed to win an outright majority, and turned his back on a putsch; and the group around the President, Papen and Schleicher, because this offered the only prospect of recruiting popular support for their rule and the best chance, as they believed, of taking the wind out of the Nazi sails. The elements of a deal were present all the time; the question was, on whose terms – Hitler's or Papen's? Hitler was even less content than in 1923 to be the drummer and leave the decisions to the gentlemen and the generals. On the other side, Papen and Schleicher persisted in believing that they could get Nazi support for less than Hitler demanded. Each side therefore tried to blockade the other. When Papen could not get Nazi support on his terms, he left them to cool their heels, calculating that the strain on the Party of continued frustration would force Hitler to reduce his demands. Hitler, on his side, tried to stick it out without capitulating. This is the underlying pattern of events in the latter half of 1932. Superimposed on it is a second pattern created by the fact that both sides, the group around the President and the Nazi leaders, became divided on the right tactics to pursue; on one side this is represented by a split between Papen and Schleicher, on the other side by the quarrel between Hitler and Gregor Strasser.

With this in mind, the period from Papen's Chancellorship to Hitler's can be divided into four sections.

The first, from Brüning's resignation on 30 May 1932 to the Reichstag elections on 31 July.

The second, from the Reichstag election of July to those of 6 November 1932.

The third, from the Reichstag elections of November to the

beginning of Schleicher's Chancellorship on 2 December 1932.

The fourth, from Schleicher's Chancellorship to Hitler's, which began on 30 January 1933.

The first of these periods was inconclusive, indeed was bound to be so. For, until the elections had been held, neither side was able to gauge its own or the other's strength. Hitler was still hopeful that the elections, the first elections for the Reichstag since September 1930, might bring him an outright majority. At the Mecklenburg provincial elections on 5 June the Nazis polled forty-nine per cent of the votes, and in Hesse, later in the month, forty-four per cent. The tide still appeared to be running in their favour.

Papen dissolved the Reichstag on 4 June, and fixed the new elections for the last day of July. Even this brief delay aroused Nazi suspicions; and when the lifting of the S.A. ban was postponed until the middle of the month, relations between Hitler and the new Government became strained. On 5 June Goebbels wrote in his diary: 'We must disassociate ourselves at the earliest possible moment from the temporary bourgeois Cabinet.' When Hitler saw Papen on the 9th, he made no pretence of his attitude. 'I regard your Cabinet,' he told the Chancellor,' only as a temporary solution and will continue my efforts to make my party the strongest in the country. The Chancellorship will then devolve on me.'[1] There was considerable grumbling in the Party at a 'compromise with Reaction'. Unless the Nazis were to be tarred with the same brush, and to leave to the parties of the Left a monopoly of attacking the 'Cabinet of Barons', they had to assert their independence.

When the ban on the S.A. was lifted, Thaelmann, the Communist leader, described it as an open provocation to murder. This proved to be literally true, for, in the weeks which followed, murder and violence became everyday occurrences in the streets of the big German cities. According to Grzesinski, the Police President of Berlin at the time, there were 461 political riots in Prussia alone between 1 June and 20 July 1932, in which eighty-two people were killed and four hundred seriously wounded.[2] The fiercest fighting was between the Nazis and the Communists; of eighty-six people killed in July 1932, thirty were Communists and thirty-eight Nazis. Provocation was certainly not confined to

1. Franz von Papen: *Memoirs* (London, 1952), p. 162.
2. Albert Grzesinski: *Inside Germany* (N.Y., 1939), c. 10.

one side: on an election visit to the Ruhr in July, Goebbels was given a rough reception, and the funerals of S.A. men became the occasion of big Nazi demonstrations. Pitched battles took place on Sunday 10 July in which eighteen people were killed. The next Sunday, the 17th, saw the worst riot of the summer, at Altona, near 'Red' Hamburg, where the Nazis under police escort staged a march through the working-class districts of the town, and were met by a fusillade of shots from the roofs and windows, which they immediately returned. Nineteen people were reported to have been killed and two hundred and eighty-five wounded on that day alone.

The Altona riots gave Papen the excuse he needed to end the political deadlock in Prussia, where the Social-Democratic and Centre coalition remained in office without a majority in the Diet. On the flimsy pretext that the Prussian Government could not be relied on to deal firmly with the Communists, Papen used the President's emergency powers on 20 July to depose the Prussian Ministers, appointing himself as Reich Commissioner for Prussia, and Bracht, the Burgomaster of Essen, as his Deputy and Prussian Minister of the Interior. By this action Papen hoped partly to conciliate the Nazis, partly to steal some of the Nazi thunder against 'Marxism'. To carry out his plan Papen had stretched the constitutional powers of the President to the limit, and Karl Severing, the Social Democratic Minister of the Interior in Prussia, required a show of force before he was prepared to yield. But it was only a show. The trade unions and the Social Democratic Party, which had defeated the Kapp Putsch in 1920 by a general strike, discussed the possibility of another such strike, only to reject it. Whether they were right to yield or should have resisted, and what would have been their chances of success, has been much debated since.[1] Whatever view one takes of the Labour leaders' action, however, the fact that the two largest working-class organizations in Germany, the Social Democratic Party and the trade unions, had not put up even a token resistance in face of Papen's *coup d'état*, was a significant pointer to the opposition (or lack of it) which Hitler might expect to meet if he came to power.

The removal of the Prussian Government, even if it was only the logical sequel to the defeat of the Government parties at the Prussian elections of April 1932, was a heavy blow to those who

1. The writer found Herr Severing still ready to defend his course of action when he talked to him at Bielefeld in July 1945. Cf. also his memoirs *Mein Lebensweg* (Köln, 1950), vol. II.

still remained loyal to the Weimar Republic. The republican parties were shown to be on the defensive and lacking the conviction to offer more than a passive resistance. However much Papen and Schleicher might claim the credit of this show of energy for the new government, in fact any blow which discredited democratic and constitutional government must bring advantage to the Nazis and the Communists, the two extremist parties. The impression that events favoured the triumph of one or other form of extremism was strengthened, and helped both parties to win votes at the coming elections.

The elections were held on the last day of July. Goebbels had been making his preparations since the beginning of May and the fourth election compaign in five months found the Nazi organization at the top of its form. The argument that things must change, and the promise that, if the Nazis came to power, they would, proved a powerful attraction in a country driven to the limit of endurance by two years of economic depression and mass unemployment, made worse by the inability of the Government to relieve the nation's ills. It was the spirit of revolt engendered by these conditions to which Nazism gave expression, unhampered by the doctrinaire teaching and class exclusiveness of Communism.

'The rise of National Socialism,' Gregor Strasser said in the Reichstag on 10 May, 'is the protest of a people against a State that denies the right to work and the revival of natural intercourse. If the machinery for distribution in the present economic system of the world is incapable of properly distributing the productive wealth of nations, then that system is false and must be altered. The important part of the present development is the anti-capitalist sentiment that is permeating our people; it is the protest of the people against a degenerate economic system. It demands from the State that, in order to secure its own right to live, it shall break with the Demons Gold, World Economy, Materialism, and with the habit of thinking in export statistics and the bank rate, and shall be capable of restoring honest payment for honest labour. This anti-capitalist sentiment is a proof that we are on the eve of a great change – the conquest of Liberalism and the rise of new ways of economic thought and of a new conception of the State.'[1]

It may well be asked how Strasser's speech was to be reconciled

1. Quoted in Heiden: *History of National Socialism*, p. 188.

with Hitler's talk to the industrialists at Düsseldorf a few months before, or what precisely the Nazis meant by 'new ways of economic thought and a new conception of the State'. In 1932, however, large sections of the German people were in no mood to criticize the contradictions of the Nazi programme, but were attracted by the radicalism of its appeal and the violence of its protest against a system which – whatever was to be put in its place – they passionately desired to see overthrown.

This sentiment was exploited by skilful electioneering. 'Once more eternally on the move,' Goebbels complained on 1 July. 'Work has to be done standing, walking, driving, flying. The most urgent conferences are held on the stairs, in the hall, at the door, or on the way to the station. It nearly drives one out of one's senses. One is carried by train, motor-car, and aeroplane criss-cross through Germany. . . . The audience generally has no idea of what the speaker has already gone through during the day before he makes his speech in the evening. . . . And in the meantime he is struggling with the heat, to find the right word, with the sequence of a thought, with a voice that is growing hoarse, with unfortunate acoustics and with the bad air that reaches him from the tightly packed audience of thousands of people.'[1]

The whole familiar apparatus of Nazi ballyhoo was brought into play – placards, Press, sensational charges and counter-charges, mass meetings, demonstrations, S.A. parades. As a simple feat of physical endurance, the speaking programme of men like Hitler and Goebbels was remarkable. Again Hitler took to the skies, and in the third 'Flight over Germany' visited and spoke in close on fifty towns in the second half of July. Delayed by bad weather, Hitler reached one of his meetings, near Stralsund, at half past two in the morning. A crowd of thousands waited patiently for him in drenching rain. When he finished speaking they saluted the dawn with the mass-singing of *Deutschland über Alles*. This was more than clever electioneering. The Nazi campaign could not have succeeded as it did by the ingenuity of its methods alone, if it had not at the same time corresponded and appealed to the mood of a considerable proportion of the German people.

When the results were announced on the night of 31 July the Nazis had outstripped all their competitors, and with 13,745,000 votes and 230 seats in the Reichstag had more than doubled the support they had won at the elections of September 1930. They

1. Goebbels: pp. 116–17.

were now by far the largest party in Germany, their nearest rivals, the Social Democrats, polling just under eight million votes, the Communists five and a quarter million, and the Centre four and a half. Taking 1928 as the measuring rod, the gains made by Hitler – close on thirteen million votes in four years – are still more striking. If he had done little to shake the solid bloc of Social Democratic and Centre votes, he had taken away some six million votes from the parties to the Right of them and captured the greater part of the six million new voters. The mass support of the Nazis in 1932 came from those who had voted in 1928 for the middle-class parties, like the People's Party, the Democrats, and the Economic Party, whose combined vote of 5,582,500 in 1928 had sunk to 954,700 in 1932; from the Nationalist Party, which had lost a million and a half votes; from young people, many without jobs, voting for the first time; and from those who had not voted before, but had been stirred by events and by propaganda to come to the polls this time.

The second period began therefore with a resounding success for the Nazis, but a success which remained inconclusive, and left Papen and Hitler free to put very different interpretations on the situation. For the Nazi vote (37·3 per cent) still fell short of the clear majority for which they had hoped. Moreover, although the Nazis' figures showed an increase in votes, the rate of increase was dropping:

September 1930 (Reichstag)	18·3 per cent of votes cast
March 1932 (1st presidential election)	30 ,, ,, ,, ,, ,,
April 1932 (2nd presidential election)	36·7 ,, ,, ,, ,, ,,
April 1932 (Prussian Diet)	36·3 ,, ,, ,, ,, ,,
July 1932 (Reichstag)	37·3 ,, ,, ,, ,, ,,

As the British Ambassador remarked in a dispatch to the Foreign Secretary: 'Hitler seems now to have exhausted his reserves. He has swallowed up the small bourgeois parties of the Middle and the Right, and there is no indication that he will be able to effect a breach in the Centre, Communist, and Socialist parties. . . . All the other parties are naturally gratified by Hitler's failure to reach anything like a majority on this occasion, especially as they are convinced that he has now reached his zenith.'[1]

From the point of view, however, of a deal with Papen and Schleicher, Hitler felt himself to be in a very strong position. The

1. Sir H. Rumbold to Sir J. Simon, 3 August 1932: *Brit. Doc.*, 2nd series, vol. IV, No. 8.

Nationalist and People's parties, to which alone the Government could look for support apart from the Nazis, had again lost votes, and together held no more than 44 out of a total of 608 seats. The combined strength of the two extremist parties, the Nazi and the Communists (230 and 89), added up to more than fifty per cent of the Reichstag, sufficient to make government with parliament impossible, unless the Nazis could be brought to support the Government. With a voting strength of 13,700,000 electors, a party membership of over a million and a private army of 400,000 S.A. and S.S., Hitler was the most powerful political leader in Germany, knocking on the doors of the Chancellery at the head of the most powerful political party Germany had ever seen.

Inflamed by the election campaign, and believing that the long-awaited day was within sight, the S.A. threatened to get out of hand. On 8 August, Goebbels wrote in his diary: 'The air is full of presage. . . . The whole party is ready to take over power. The S.A. down everyday tools to prepare for this. If things go well, everything is all right. If they do not, it will be an awful setback.' Two days later: 'The S.A. is in readiness for an alarm and is standing to. . . . The S.A. are closely concentrated round Berlin; the manoeuvre is carried out with imposing precision and discipline.' The outbreaks of street-shooting and bomb-throwing flared up, especially in the eastern provinces of Silesia, and East Prussia. In the first nine days of August a score of incidents was reported every day, culminating on 9 August in the murder at Potempa, a village in Silesia, of a Communist called Pietrzuch, who was brutally kicked to death by five Nazis in front of his mother. The same day Papen's Government announced the death penalty for clashes which led to people being killed. The Nazis at once protested indignantly.

Aware of the highly charged feeling in the Party, Hitler took time before he moved. He held a conference of his leaders at Tegernsee, in Bavaria, on 2 August, but arrived at no final decision. A coalition with the Centre Party would provide a majority in the Reichstag, but Hitler was in a mood for 'all-or-nothing'. He must have the whole power, not a share of it. On 5 August he saw General von Schleicher at Fürstenberg, north of Berlin, and put his demands before him: the Chancellorship for himself, and other Nazis at the head of the Prussian State Government, the Reich, and Prussian Ministries of the Interior (which controlled the police). With these were to go the Ministry of Justice and a new Ministry of Popular Enlightenment and Propaganda, which was reserved for Goebbels. An Enabling Bill, giving Hitler full power to govern by decree, would be presented to the Reichstag; if the Chamber refused to pass it, it would be dissolved. Whatever Schleicher said, Hitler came away in high hopes that the General would use all his influence to secure the Chancellorship for him. He was so pleased that he suggested to Schleicher a tablet should be affixed to the walls of the house to commemorate their historic meeting. He then returned to Berchtesgaden to await events.

On 9 August, Strasser and Frick joined him there with disquieting news. The violent behaviour of the S.A. and some of the wilder election and post-election statements were making people ask if the Nazis were fit to have power. Funk, who arrived with a message from Schacht, confirmed this. Business and industrial circles were becoming worried lest a Hitler Chancellorship should lead to radical economic experiments on the lines Gottfried Feder and Gregor Strasser had often threatened. Still no word came from Berlin.

On 11 August Hitler decided to bring matters to a head.[1] Sending messengers ahead to arrange for him to see the Chancellor and the President, he left the mountains, and, after a further conference with his lieutenants on the shores of the Chiemsee, motored north to Berlin. Goebbels summed up the results of the conference: 'If they do not afford us the opportunity to square accounts with Marxism, our taking over power is absolutely useless.'[2] This assurance was Hitler's sop to the impatient S.A.

Late in the evening of the 12th Hitler reached Berlin and drove out to Goebbels's house at Caputh, to avoid being seen. Röhm had already visited Papen and Schleicher and had asked bluntly who was to be Chancellor. Had Hitler misunderstood Schleicher? The answer Röhm had been given was none too satisfactory. After Goebbels told him the news, Hitler paced up and down for a long time, uneasily calculating his chances. A hundred times he must have asked himself whether he was pitching his claims too high. On the other hand, to pitch them lower, to agree to

1. Other accounts say that Hitler was summoned to Berlin by telegram, but Meissner states in his affidavit (Nuremberg Document 3309-PS) that the interview with the President was at the personal request of Hitler, transmitted to Meissner by Hitler's adjutant, Brückner.
2. Goebbels: p. 136.

anything less than full power, was to court trouble with the Party and the S.A. Hitler went to bed late, after listening to some music; the decisive meeting with Papen and Schleicher was fixed for the next day at noon.

What had been happening on the Government side of the fence since the elections is more difficult to follow. Despite the failure of the two parties he had counted on for support – the Nationalists and the People's Party – Papen was less impressed by Hitler's success than might have been expected. Hitler had failed to win the majority he hoped for, and Papen could argue that the results of the elections and the divisions in the Reichstag were such as to justify the continuation of a presidential cabinet, independent of the incoherent Party groupings. Indeed, Papen saw no reason at all why he should resign in Hitler's favour. He enjoyed the favour of the President as no one ever had before, and the President certainly had no wish to exchange the urbane and charming Papen for a man whom he disliked and regarded as 'queer'. Nazi violence during and after the election had hardened opinion against them, not only in the circle round the President, but among the propertied classes generally, and, most important of all, in the Army. Reports from abroad of the possible repercussions of Hitler's advent to power had impressed the Cabinet and the Army, while for the President it was quite enough that Hitler had broken his promise and attacked a government he had undertaken to support. Finally, Papen, like most other political observers, was convinced that the Nazis had reached their peak and from now on would begin to lose votes. If he was still prepared to do a deal with Hitler it must be on his, and not Hitler's, terms.

Schleicher's attitude too had changed since the meeting at Fürstenberg on the 5th. When Hitler met the General and Papen together on the 13th, the most they were prepared to offer him was the Vice-Chancellorship, together with the Prussian Ministry of the Interior for one of his lieutenants. Hitler's claim to power as the leader of the largest party in the Reichstag was politely set aside. The President, Papen told him, insisted on maintaining a presidential cabinet in power and this could not be headed by a Party leader like Hitler. Hitler rejected Papen's offer out of hand, lost his temper and began to shout. He must have the whole power, nothing less. He talked wildly of mowing down the Marxists, of a St Bartholomew's Night, and of three days' freedom of the streets for the S.A. Both Papen and Schleicher were shocked by the raging uncontrolled figure who now confronted them. They were scarcely reassured by his declaration that he wanted neither the Foreign Ministry nor the Ministry of Defence, but only as much power as Mussolini had claimed in 1922. While Hitler meant by this a coalition government, including non-Fascists, such as Mussolini had originally formed, they understood him to be claiming a dictatorship in which he would govern alone without them – and, as the history of Hitler's Chancellorship in 1933 was later to show, they were fundamentally right.

After prolonged and heated argument, Hitler left in a rage of disappointment, and drove back to Goebbels's flat on the Reichskanzlerplatz. When a telephone call came from the President's Palace at three o'clock, Frick or Goebbels answered that there was no point in Hitler coming, as a decision had already been arrived at. But the President insisted. Nothing, it was said, would be finally decided till he had seen Hitler – and Hitler, angry and shaken, went.

The President received him standing up and leaning on his stick. His manner was cold. Hitler's argument that he sought power by legal means, but to obtain his ends must be given full control over government policy, made no impression on the old man. According to Meissner, who was one of those present at the interview, the President retorted that in the present tense situation he could not take the risk of transferring power to a new Party which did not command a majority and which was intolerant, noisy, and undisciplined.

At this point Hindenburg, with a certain show of excitement, referred to several recent occurrences – clashes between the Nazis and the police, acts of violence committed by Hitler's followers against those of different opinions, excesses against Jews and other illegal acts. All these incidents had strengthened him in his conviction that there were numerous wild elements in the Party beyond effective control. Conflicts with other states had also to be avoided under all circumstances. Hindenburg proposed to Hitler that he should cooperate with the other parties, in particular with the Right and the Centre, and that he should give up the one-sided idea that he must have complete power. In cooperating with other parties he would be able to show what he could achieve and improve upon. If he could show positive results, he would acquire increasing influence even in a coalition government. This would also be the best way to eliminate the widespread fear that a National Socialist government would make ill use of its power. Hindenburg added that he was ready to accept Hitler and his movement in a coalition government, the precise composition of which could be a subject of negotiation, but that he could not take the responsibility of giving exclusive power to Hitler alone. . . . Hitler, however, was adamant in his refusal to put himself in the position of bargaining with the leaders of the other parties and of facing a coalition government.[1]

Before the interview was over Hindenburg took the chance to remind Hitler of the promise, which he had now broken, to support Papen's Government. In the words of the communiqué, 'he gravely exhorted Herr Hitler to conduct the opposition on the part of the N.S. Party in a chivalrous manner, and to bear in mind his responsibility to the Fatherland and to the German people.' For once, the Nazi propaganda machine was caught off its guard, and the Government's damaging version of the meeting was on the streets and half-way round the world before the Nazis realized what was happening. It spoke of Hitler's 'demand for entire and complete control of the State'; described the President's refusal to hand over power to 'a movement which had the intention of using it in a one-sided manner'; referred explicitly to Hitler's disregard of the promises of support he had given before the election, and repeated Hindenburg's warning to him on the way to conduct opposition. Hitler's humiliation in the eyes of the world, and of his own Party, was complete.

VI

If ever Hitler needed confidence in his own judgement, it was now. A false move could have destroyed his chances of success, and it was easy to make such a move. The policy of legality appeared discredited and bankrupt. Hitler had won such electoral support as no other party had had in Germany since the First World War, he had kept strictly to the letter of the Constitution and knocked on the door of the Chancellery, only to have the door publicly slammed in his face. The way in which his demands had been refused touched Hitler on a raw spot; once again he had been treated as not quite good enough, an uneducated, rough sort of fellow whom one could scarcely make Chancellor. This was Lossow, Kahr, and Munich all over again, and his old hatred and contempt for the bourgeoisie and their respectable politicians – top-hat, frock-coat, the *Herr Doktor* with his diploma – flared up.

1. Affidavit of Otto Meissner, Chief of the Presidential Chancery, 1920–45, at Nuremberg, 28 November 1945. N.D. 3309-PS. Cf. also Otto Meissner: *Staatssekretär*, pp. 239–41.

He was angry and resentful, feeling he had walked into a trap and was being laughed at by the superior people who had made a fool of him. He had made the mistake of playing his cards too high; now his bluff had been called and, instead of sweeping into power, he had had to stand and listen to the President giving him a dressing-down for bad manners and behaviour not becoming a gentleman. In such a mood there was a great temptation to show them he was not bluffing, to give the S.A. their head, and let the smug bourgeois politicians see whether he was just a 'revolutionary of the big mouth', as Goebbels had once called Strasser.

There was strong pressure from the Party in the same direction. A considerable section, strongly represented in the S.A., had always disliked the policy of legality, and had only been constrained to submit to it with difficulty. Now that legality had led to an open set-back and humiliation they were even more restive and critical. The difficulties with which Hitler was confronted are vividly illustrated by the case of the Potempa murderers. The five Nazis responsible for the murder of the Communist miner, Pietrzuch, were sentenced to death on 22 August. All five men were members of the S.A., and the case had attracted the widest publicity. The S.A. were furious: this was to place the nationally-minded Nazis and the anti-national Communists on the same footing, the very reverse of what Hitler and the Nazis meant by justice. Hitler had therefore to choose between offending public opinion and travestying his own policy of legality if he came out on the side of the murderers, or risking a serious loss of confidence on the part of the S.A. if he failed to intervene on their behalf, thus publicly admitting his inability to defend his own followers. Hitler's answer was to send a telegram to the five murderers: 'My comrades: in the face of this most monstrous and bloody sentence I feel myself bound to you in limitless loyalty. From this moment, your liberation is a question of our honour. To fight against a government which could allow this is our duty.' He followed this with a violent manifesto in which he attacked Papen for deliberately setting on foot a persecution of the 'nationally minded' elements in Germany: 'German fellow countrymen: whoever among you agrees with our struggle for the honour and liberty of the nation will understand why I refused to take office in this Cabinet. . . . Herr von Papen, I understand your bloody "objectivity" now. I wish that victory may come to nationalist Germany and destruction upon its Marxist destroyers and spoilers, but I am certainly not fitted to be the executioner of nationalist fighters for the liberty of the German people.'[1] Röhm visited the condemned men and assured them they would not be executed. Nor was this an idle boast: a few days after Hitler's telegram their sentences were commuted to imprisonment for life.

There is no doubt that Hitler's action shocked German public opinion, for the justice of the sentence scarcely admitted dispute. Yet this was the price which Hitler had to pay if he meant to keep his movement together and preserve his own authority. Nor is there any reason to suppose that he felt the least compunction about the murder at Potempa; the publicity it had received was inconvenient, but kicking a political opponent to death was well within the bounds of what Hitler meant by legality.

Nevertheless, although the Nazi Press and Nazi speeches show an increasing radicalism from August up to the second Reichstag elections in November, and although Hitler came out in uncompromising opposition to Papen's Government, he still refused to depart from his tactics of legality, or to let himself be provoked into the risk of attempting a seizure of power by force. The very day of his humiliating interview with the President he called in Röhm and the other S.A. leaders to insist that they must give up any idea of a putsch. Goebbels, recording the meeting, adds: 'Their task is the most difficult. Who knows if their units will be able to hold together. . . . The S.A. Chief of Staff (Röhm) stays with us for a long time. He is extremely worried about the S.A.'[2] To this line of policy Hitler remained faithful throughout; he was determined to avoid open conflict with the Army and to come to power legally. The situation was not yet ripe, he told Goebbels; Papen and the President were not yet convinced that they would have to take him on his own terms, but it was still to a deal, and not to revolution, that he looked as the means to power.

Shortly after the Potempa incident Hermann Rauschning, one of the leaders of the Danzig Senate, visited Hitler at Haus Wachenfeld on the Obersalzberg. The little party from Danzig found him moody and preoccupied, sitting on the veranda and staring out over the mountain landscape. His silence was interspersed with excited and violent comments, many of them on the character of the next war. Much of it was prophetic; he laid great stress upon the psychological and subversive preparations for war – if these were carried out with care, peace would be signed before

1. Heiden: *History of National Socialism*, p. 182.
2. Goebbels: pp. 139–40.

the war had begun. 'The place of artillery preparation for frontal attack will in future be taken by revolutionary propaganda, to break down the enemy psychologically before the armies begin to function at all. . . . How to achieve the moral break-down of the enemy before the war has started – that is the problem that interests me. . . . We shall provoke a revolution in France as certainly as we shall *not* have one in Germany. The French will hail me as their deliverer. The little man of the middle class will acclaim us as the bearers of a just social order and eternal peace. None of these people any longer want war or greatness.'[1] Rauschning could get little out of Hitler about the current political situation. He was angry and uncertain, 'divided', Rauschning thought, 'between his own revolutionary temperament which impelled him to passionate action, and his political astuteness which warned him to take the safe road of political combination and postpone his revenge till later.'[2] Hitler talked much of ruthlessness and was inclined to lash out at anyone who irritated him. He was scornful and impatient of economic problems on which Rauschning tried to draw him: if the will were there the problems would solve themselves, he retorted. Only when they came to discuss Danzig did Hitler show any interest in the actual position in Germany. His first question was whether Danzig had an extradition agreement with Germany, and it was soon clear that his mind was occupied with the possibility of having to go underground, if the Government should move against the Party and ban it. In that case Danzig, with its independent status under the League of Nations, might well offer a useful asylum.

As they left to drive to Munich Goebbels came stumping up the path to the house, summoned from Berlin for more anxious consultations on the policy to be pursued if the Party was to get out of the political cul-de-sac into which it had been manoeuvred.

Desultory contacts with the Government continued through the rest of the summer and into the autumn, but they led nowhere. Papen was still confident that by a process of 'wearing-down' the Nazis, by keeping them waiting on the threshold of power, he could force Hitler to accept his terms. It was a question of who would crack first.

In August and September the Nazis made an approach to the Centre Party: together they could command a majority in the

1. Hermann Rauschning: *Hitler Speaks* (London, 1939), pp. 19–21.
2. ibid., p. 27.

Reichstag, and Hitler, amongst other proposals, suggested that they should put through a joint motion deposing the President and providing for a new election. On 25 August Goebbels noted: 'We have got into touch with the Centre Party, if merely by way of bringing pressure to bear upon our adversaries. . . . There are three possibilities. Firstly: Presidential Cabinet. Secondly: Coalition. Thirdly: Opposition. . . . In Berlin I ascertain that Schleicher already knows of our feelers in the direction of the Centre. That is a way of bringing pressure to bear on him. I endorse and further it. Perhaps we shall succeed thus in expediting the first of these solutions.'[1] One practical result of these talks was the election of Göring to the presidency of the Reichstag by the combined votes of the Nazis, the Centre, and the Nationalists on 30 August.

Papen refused to be impressed by the threat of a Nazi–Centre combination against him. He was firmly convinced that the prolongation of the deadlock was working to the disadvantage of the Nazis, and that in any new elections they were bound to lose votes. He believed that, in the threat to dissolve the Reichstag and force a further appeal to the country, he held the ace of trumps, and, if necessary, he was resolved to play it.

The climax of these weeks of intrigue and manoeuvring came on 12 September. After the election of Göring to its presidency on 30 August the Reichstag had adjourned until the 12th, the first full session since the elections at the end of July. Foreseeing trouble, the Chancellor procured a decree for the Chamber's dissolution from the President in advance. With this up his sleeve, he felt in complete command of the situation. The actual course of events on 12 September, however, took both sides by surprise. When the session opened, before a crowded audience in the diplomatic and public galleries, the Communist deputy Torgler moved a vote of censure on the Government as an amendment to the Order of the Day. It had been agreed amongst the other parties that there was nothing to be gained by such a move, and that one of the Nationalist deputies should formally oppose it, the objection of one member being sufficient to prevent an amendment to the Order of the Day without due notice. When the moment came, however, the Nationalists made no move, and amid a puzzled and embarrassed silence Frick rose to his feet to ask for half an hour's delay. In the excited crowd which filled the lobbies and corridors it was said that Papen had decided to

1. Goebbels: pp. 142–3.

dissolve, and that it was in agreement with him that the Nationalists had gone back on the original plan. At a hurried meeting in
the palace of the Reichstag President, Göring, Hitler, Strasser,
and Frick decided to out-smart the Chancellor, vote with the
Communists, and defeat the Government before the Chamber
could be dissolved.

Immediately the deputies had taken their seats again Göring,
as President, announced that a vote would be taken at once on the
Communist motion of no-confidence. Papen, rising in protest,
requested the floor. But Göring, studiously affecting not to see
the Chancellor, looked in the other direction, and the voting
began. White with anger, Papen produced the traditional red
portfolio which contained the decree of dissolution, thrust it on
Göring's table, then ostentatiously marched out of the Chamber
accompanied by the other members of his cabinet. Still Göring
had no eyes for anything but the voting. The Communist vote of
no-confidence was carried by 513 votes to 32, and Göring
promptly declared the Government overthrown. As for the scrap
of paper laid on his desk, which he now found time to read, it
was, he declared, obviously worthless since it had been counter-
signed by a Chancellor who had now been deposed.

Whether – as the Nazis affected to believe – the elaborate farce
in the Reichstag, and the almost unanimous vote against him, had
really damaged Papen or not, for the moment the Chancellor had
the advantage. For Papen insisted that, as the decree of dissolution had already been signed and placed on the table before
the vote took place, the result of the motion was invalid. The
Reichstag was dissolved, after sitting for less than a day, and the
Nazis faced the fifth major electoral contest of the year.

Privately they were only too well aware that Papen was right
and that they must count on a reduced vote. Hitler refused to
consider a compromise, and accepted von Papen's challenge, but
there was no disguising the fact that this would be the toughest
fight of all. On 16 September Goebbels wrote with a heavy heart:
'Now we are in for elections again! One sometimes feels this sort
of thing is going on for ever. . . . Our adversaries count on our
losing morale, and getting fagged out. But we know this and will
not oblige them. We would be lost and all our work would have
been in vain if we gave in now . . . , even if the struggle should
seem hopeless.'[1] A month later he admitted: 'The organization

1. Goebbels: p. 157.

has naturally become a bit on edge through these everlasting elections. It is as jaded as a battalion which has been too long in the trenches, and just as nervy. The numerous difficulties are wearing me out.'[1]

One of the worst difficulties was lack of money. Four elections since March had eaten deep into the Party's resources, and the invaluable contributions from outside had lately begun to dwindle. Hitler's refusal to come to terms, his arrogant claim for the whole power, his condonation of violence at Potempa, the swing towards Radicalism in the campaign against the 'Government of Reaction' – all these factors, combined, no doubt, with strong hints from von Papen to industrial and business circles not to ease the blockade, had placed the Party in a tight spot. In the middle of October Goebbels complained: 'Money is extraordinarily difficult to obtain. All gentlemen of "Property and Education" are standing by the Government.'[2]

In these circumstances it was only Hitler's determination and leadership that kept the Party going. His confidence in himself never wavered. When the Gauleiters assembled at Munich early in October he used all his arts to put new life and energy into them. 'He is great and surpasses us all,' Goebbels wrote enthusiastically. 'He raises the Party's spirits out of the blackest depression. With him as leader the movement must succeed.'

Another picture of the Nazi leader at this time is given by Kurt Ludecke.[3] Ludecke had gone to visit Hitler in Munich at the end of September, and, after an evening spent in Hitler's company at his Munich flat listening to him denounce the influence of Christianity, he accompanied him by car to a mass Hitler Youth demonstration at Potsdam.

Ludecke found Hitler imperturbable and confident, already talking of what he would do when he became Chancellor. They started out from Munich in the late afternoon in three powerful Mercedes, one of them filled with Hitler's bodyguard of eight, armed with revolvers and hippopotamus whips, under the command of Sepp Dietrich, later to achieve fame as an S.S. general. Hitler, although he never took the wheel himself, had a passion for speed, and they drove fast across Bavaria towards the frontiers of Saxony. Ludecke talked about America, and Hitler, who had never been out of Germany, questioned him eagerly. As a boy

1. Goebbels, pp. 171–2.   2. ibid., p. 172.
3. Kurt Ludecke: *I Knew Hitler*, c. 27–8.

he had read Karl May's stories about the Red Indians, and they found a common interest in the adventures of Old Shatterhand and Winnetou. Every time Hitler dozed he would rouse himself again: 'Go on, go on – I mustn't fall asleep. I'm listening.' At Nuremberg Julius Streicher was waiting, while at Berneck, where they paused for a brief sleep in an inn, Göring met them and stayed talking with Hitler until 4 a.m. Soon after nine they were on the road again, a road of which Hitler knew every bend and dip, halting for a picnic lunch and then driving through the Communist districts of Saxony. At one point they passed a line of trucks filled with Communist demonstrators. 'We slowed down. It was apparent that because of the state of the road we were going to have to pass them at low speed. I could see Sepp Dietrich whistling through his teeth. Everybody stopped talking, and I noticed that the right hand of each of the men in the car in front disappeared at his side. We crept by. Everyone, the Führer included, looked straight into the faces of the Communists.' He was recognized and hissed at, but nobody dared to interfere with the bodyguard.

At Potsdam more than a hundred thousand boys and girls of the Hitler Youth had gathered in the torch-lit stadium. After a brief address Hitler spent the rest of the night trying to find accommodation for the thousands who had arrived unexpectedly. In the morning the review began at eleven o'clock on a sunny October day. From then until six o'clock in the evening, for seven hours, Hitler stood to take the salute as the steady columns of brown-shirted Hitler Youth marched past him. Once he came over to Ludecke and said: 'You see? No fear – the German race is on the march.' Later that night, after Hitler had dined with Prince Auwi, one of the Kaiser's sons who had joined the S.A., Ludecke saw him again in the train for Munich. 'As we stepped into the railway carriage, Brückner, Hitler's adjutant, blocked the way: "Leave him alone," he said. "The man's played out." He was sitting in the corner of the compartment, utterly spent. Hitler motioned weakly to us to come in. He looked for a second into my eyes, clasped my hand feebly, and I left.

'When next I saw him he was Chancellor.'[1]

The genuineness of the Nazis' radical campaign against the 'caste government of Reaction' was put to the test a few days before the election by the outbreak of a transport strike in Berlin. The strike was caused by a cut in wages as part of Papen's policy

1. Ludecke: pp. 478–9.

of meeting the crisis. It was disavowed by the Social Democrats and the Trade Unions, but was backed by the Communists. To many people's surprise the Nazis joined the Communists in supporting the strikers. Goebbels, in his diary, is quite frank about the reasons: 'The entire Press is furious with us and calls it Bolshevism; but as a matter of fact we had no option. If we had held ourselves aloof from this strike our position among the working classes would have been shaken. Here a great occasion offers once again of demonstrating to the public that the line we have taken up in politics is dictated by a true sympathy with the people, and for this reason the N.S. party purposely eschews the old bourgeois methods.'[1]

The Nazi move, however, had other consequences as well. The next day Goebbels wrote: 'Scarcity of money has become chronic. . . . The strike is grist to the mill of the bourgeois Press. They are exploiting it against us unconscionably. Many of our staunch partisans, even, are beginning to have their doubts. . . . The consequences of the strike are daily putting us into new predicaments.'[2]

The election campaign came to an end on the evening of 5 November. 'Last attack,' Goebbels commented. 'Desperate drive of the Party against defeat. We succeed in obtaining ten thousand marks at the very last moment. These are to be thrown into the campaign on Saturday afternoon. We have done all possible. Now let Fate decide.'[3]

VII

The Nazi leaders were under no illusions about the election results. The fifth election of the year found a mood of stubborn apathy growing among the German people, a feeling of indifference and disbelief, against which propaganda and agitation beat in vain. It was precisely on this that Papen had calculated and his calculation was not far wrong. For the first time since 1930 the Nazis lost votes, two millions of the 13,745,000 they had polled in July 1932, cutting their percentage from 37·3 to 33·1. Their seats in the Reichstag were reduced from 230 out of 608 to 196 out of 584, although they still remained by far the largest party in the Chamber.

1. Goebbels: 2 November, p. 181.   2. ibid., p. 182.
3. ibid., p. 184.

This set-back was thrown into sharper relief by the success of two other parties. The Nationalists, who had been steadily losing votes since 1924, suddenly raised the number of their seats from 37 to 52, and the Communists, who polled close on six million votes, secured a hundred seats in the Reichstag. The Communist success was particularly striking for it showed that the Nazis were beginning to lose their hold on that current of revolt which had so far carried them forward. It was no secret that the bulk of the Communists' new voters were disillusioned supporters of the Nazis and the Social Democrats, looking for a genuinely revolutionary party.

Papen was delighted with the results, which he regarded as a moral victory for his government and a heavier defeat for Hitler than the figures actually showed. The Nazi movement had always claimed to be different from the other parties, to be a movement of national resurgence. Now its spell was broken, the emptiness of its claims exposed and Hitler himself reduced to the proportions of any other politician scrambling for power. Its fall, Papen was convinced, would be as rapid as its rise. If Hitler wanted power he had better come to terms before his electoral assets dwindled still further.

At first, therefore, it looked as if the November elections would be followed by a repetition of what had happened after 31 July, with the odds against Hitler lengthened, and a much greater likelihood of his being forced to accept von Papen's terms. In this third period, however, it was Papen who overplayed his hand, with unexpected results.

Determined, in spite of the electoral set-back, not to walk into another trap like that of 13 August, Hitler sat tight and refused to be drawn by Papen's first indirect approaches. On 9 November Goebbels recorded in his diary: 'The Wilhelmstrasse has sent an emissary to the Leader. The same conditions are proposed as those suggested on 13 August (i.e. the Vice-Chancellorship), but he remains inexorable.' Three days later he wrote: 'The Leader is keeping away from Berlin. The Wilhelmstrasse waits for him in vain; and that is well. We must not give in as we did on 13 August.'[1]

On 13 November Papen wrote officially to Hitler suggesting that they should bury their differences and renew negotiations for a concentration of all the nationally minded parties.[2] Hitler let a couple of days pass, and replied at length on the 16th with a

1. Goebbels: pp. 188 and 190.   2. N.D. D.-633.

letter which was an open rebuff. He laid down four conditions for any negotiations: that they should be conducted in writing, so that there could be no disagreement this time about what was said; that the Chancellor should take full responsibility for his actions, and not try to dodge behind the figure of the President as he had in August; that he, Hitler, should be told in advance what policy he was being asked to support, 'since, in spite of the closest consideration, I have never quite understood the present Government's programme'; and, finally, that the Chancellor should assure him that Hugenberg, the leader of the Nationalists, was prepared to enter a national bloc.[1] Hitler's reply ruled out the possibility of any further negotiations between himself and Papen at this stage. Indeed, he had already issued a manifesto immediately after the elections in which, underlining the fact that ninety per cent of the nation were ranged against the Government, he had charged Papen with the responsibility for the increase in the Communist vote. By this reactionary policy, Hitler declared, Papen was driving the masses to Bolshevism. There could be no compromise with such a régime.

While this exchange was taking place, Papen, who was perfectly prepared to plunge the country into still another election in order to force the Nazis to their knees, unexpectedly encountered opposition in his own Cabinet, notably from Schleicher. Not only was Schleicher irritated by Papen's increasing independence and the close relationship he had established with the President, but he began to see in Papen's personal quarrel with Hitler, and his determination to prosecute it to the limit, an obstacle to securing that concentration of the 'national' forces which was, in Schleicher's view, the only reason for ever having made Papen Chancellor. Papen was now beginning to talk confidently of governing the country by a dictatorship, if Hitler would not come to his senses. Schleicher, on the other hand, had not failed to notice the ominous increase in the Communist vote, the growing radicalism of the Nazis and their cooperation with the Communists in the Berlin transport strike. He was more than ever alarmed at the prospect of a civil war in which both the Communists and the Nazis might be on the other side of the barricade. It did not take long for him to reach the conclusion that Papen was becoming more of a hindrance than an asset to the policy of a deal with the Nazis which was still his own objective.

Schleicher found support for his views in the Cabinet, and

1. N.D. D.-634.

Papen was urged to resign, in order to allow the President to consult the Party leaders and try to find a way out of the deadlock, which appeared to be impossible so long as he remained in office. With considerable shrewdness Papen swallowed his anger and agreed; he was confident that, in any case, negotiations with Hitler and the other Party leaders would not remove the deadlock, and that after their failure he would return to office with his hand strengthened. He would then be able to insist on whatever course he saw fit to recommend. His own influence over the President, and the fact that Hindenburg was obviously irritated by the whole affair, saw no reason at all why he should part with Papen, and had become increasingly suspicious of Schleicher, augured well for the success of these calculations. Accordingly, on 17 November, Papen tendered the resignation of his Cabinet, and the President, on his advice, requested Hitler to call on him.

Events followed the course Papen had foreseen. On 18 November Hitler arrived in Berlin and spent some hours in discussion with Goebbels, Frick, and Strasser; Göring was hastily summoned from Rome, where he had been engaged in talks with Mussolini. The next day, cheered by the crowds, Hitler drove to the Palace. The conversation was at least more friendly than the chilly interview of 13 August. He was invited to sit down and stayed for over an hour. A second conference followed on the 21st. The gist of Hindenburg's offer was contained in three sentences from the official record of the discussion on the 21st. 'You have declared,' the President said, 'that you will only place your movement at the disposal of a government of which you, the leader of the Party, are the head. If I consider your proposal, I must demand that such a Cabinet should have a majority in the Reichstag. Accordingly, I ask you, as the leader of the largest party, to ascertain, if and on what conditions, you could obtain a secure workable majority in the Reichstag on a definite programme.'

On the face of it this was a fair offer, but it was so designed as to make it impossible for Hitler to succeed. For Hitler could not secure a majority in the Reichstag. The Centre Party, in view of their vendetta with Papen, might be willing to join a coalition with Hitler – Göring was already engaged in negotiating with the Centre leaders – but Hugenberg and the Nationalists would never come in. In any case, what Hitler wanted was to be made, not a parliamentary Chancellor, shackled by a coalition, but a presidential Chancellor, with the same sweeping powers as the President had given to Papen. To this the old man sternly refused to agree. If Germany had to be governed by the emergency powers of a presidential Chancellor, then there was no point in replacing Papen; the only argument in favour of his resignation was that Hitler would be able to provide something which Papen had failed to secure, namely, a parliamentary majority.

A lengthy correspondence between Hitler and the President's State Secretary, Meissner, failed to alter the terms of the offer. Papen's presidential Cabinet, Meissner pointed out, had resigned 'because it could not find a majority in parliament to tolerate its measures. Consequently a new presidential Cabinet would be an improvement only if it could eliminate this deficiency.'[1] In his final letter on the 24th Meissner said that the President was unable to give the powers of a presidential Chancellor to a Party leader 'because such a Cabinet is bound to develop into a party dictatorship and increase the state of tension prevailing among the German people.' For this the President could not take the responsibility before his oath and his conscience. Hitler could only retort that the negotiations had been foredoomed to fail in view of Hindenburg's resolve to keep Papen, whatever the cost. There was nothing left but to admit defeat and break off the negotiations. Once again the policy of legality had led to public humiliation; once again the Leader returned from the President's palace empty-handed and out-manoeuvred.

Discussions between the President and other Party leaders produced no better result. But at this point Papen's calculations began to go wrong. For Schleicher, too, had not been idle, and through Gregor Strasser he was now sounding out the possibility of the Nazis joining a Cabinet in which, not Papen, but Schleicher himself would take the Chancellorship. The offer was communicated to Hitler in Munich, and on the evening of 29 November Hitler left by train for the north. According to one version, Hitler was inclined to accept and was already on his way to Berlin when he was intercepted by Göring at Jena, persuaded to go no farther and taken off to Weimar for a conference with the other Nazi leaders. For once the Nazi version, as it is given by Otto Dietrich and Goebbels, seems more probable: according to this, Hitler declined to be drawn by Schleicher's move and called

1. The correspondence is printed in full in *Jahrbuch des öffentlichen Rechts*, vol. 21 (1933–4).

a conference of his chief lieutenants at Weimar, where he was already due to take part in the election campaign for the forth-coming Thuringian elections. At this Weimar conference, on 1 December, Strasser came out strongly in favour of joining a Schleicher Cabinet and found some support from Frick. Göring and Goebbels, however, were opposed to such a course, and Hitler accepted their point of view. A long talk with an officer, Major Ott, whom Schleicher had sent to see Hitler at Weimar, failed to change this decision; Hitler still held out and was only prepared to make a deal on his own terms. Goebbels wrote in his diary: 'Anyone can see that the "System" is breathing its last, and that it would be a crime to form an alliance with it at the present moment.'[1]

Meanwhile, on the evening of 1 December, Schleicher and Papen saw Hindenburg together. Papen's plan was perfectly clear: the attempt to find an alternative government had failed, and he proposed that he should resume office, prorogue the Reichstag indefinitely, and prepare a reform of the constitution to provide for a new electoral law and the establishment of a second Chamber. Until that could be carried out he would proclaim a state of emergency, govern by decree, and use force to smash any opposition. Schleicher's objections were threefold: such a course was unconstitutional; it involved a danger of civil war, since the vast majority of the nation had declared themselves emphatically opposed to Papen in two elections; and it was unnecessary. He announced that he was convinced he himself could obtain a parliamentary majority in the Reichstag.

If Hitler would not join him, he was confident that he could detach Gregor Strasser and as many as sixty Nazi deputies from the Party. To these, Schleicher believed, he could add the middle-class parties and the Social Democrats, and might even win the support of the trade unions.

From the discussion that followed Papen emerged triumphant. The old President was shocked at Schleicher's suggestion and turning to Papen entrusted him, not Schleicher, with the task of forming a new government.[2] But Schleicher had the last word. As he and Papen parted, he used the phrase addressed to Luther on

1. Goebbels: p. 200.
2. Papen's Interrogation at Nuremberg, 3 September 1945; Papen's examination in court, Nuremberg Proceedings, Part xvi, pp. 269–72; and Papen's letter of 10 April 1948, to M. François-Poncet, quoted by Castellan, pp. 20–2.

the eve of his journey to the Diet of Worms: 'Little Monk, you have chosen a difficult path.'

The next day, 2 December, Schleicher played his trump card once again. At a cabinet meeting held at nine o'clock in the evening, he announced that the Army no longer had confidence in Papen and was not prepared to take the risk of civil war – with both the Nazis and the Communists in opposition – which Papen's policy would entail. Developing his argument, Schleicher produced one of his officers, Major Ott (later Hitler's ambassador in Tokyo), to provide detailed evidence in its support. In November Schleicher had ordered the Ministry of Defence to discuss with the police and Army authorities what steps would have to be taken in the event of civil war. Their conclusion was that, in view of the possibility of a surprise attack by Poland at the same time as risings by the Communists and the Nazis and a general strike, the State did not possess sufficient forces to guarantee order. They must therefore recommend the Government not to declare a state of emergency.[1] Whether this was a just appreciation of the situation or not – Schleicher's production of the report at this moment was too pat not to arouse suspicion – his authority as the representative of the Army was incontestable.

Once again the Army had shown itself to be the supreme arbiter in German politics, and Papen was left without a reply. 'I went to Hindenburg,' Papen told the Court at Nuremberg, 'and reported to him. Herr von Hindenburg, deeply stirred by my report, said to me: "I am an old man, and I cannot face a civil war of any sort in my country. If General von Schleicher is of this opinion, then I must – much as I regret it – withdraw the task with which I charged you last night."'[2]

Von Papen had only two consolations, but they were to prove substantial. At last Schleicher, the man who had used his influence behind the scenes to unseat Müller, Groener, Brüning, and now Papen, was forced to come out into the open and assume personal responsibility for the success or failure of his plans. On 2 December General von Schleicher became the last Chancellor of pre-Hitler Germany, and – Papen's second consolation – he took office at a time when his credit with the President, on which he

1. See in addition to the sources already cited, Castellan, pp. 23–5, in which Colonel Ott's account of his report, in a letter of November 1946, is reproduced in full; Meissner's Affidavit, 28 November 1945 (3309-PS), and the report of the British Ambassador, 7 December 1932, in *Brit. Doc.*, Second Series, vol. IV, No. 44.

2. Nuremberg Proceedings, Part XVI, p. 272.

had drawn so lavishly in the past year, was destroyed. The old man, who had tolerated the intrigues which had led to the dismissal of Groener and Brüning, neither forgot nor forgave the methods by which Schleicher turned out Papen. Let von Schleicher succeed if he could; but if he failed, and turned to the President for support, he need expect no more loyalty or mercy than he had shown his own victims.

VIII

With the opening of the fourth and final period, from Schleicher's Chancellorship which began on 2 December 1932, to Hitler's which began on 30 January 1933, this tortuous story of political intrigue draws to its close. Yet the most surprising twists of all were reserved for the last chapter.

Schleicher had now to make good his claim that he could succeed where Papen had failed, and produce that national front, including the Nazis, which had been his consistent aim for two years. For all his love of intrigue and lack of scruple, Schleicher was an intelligent man. Without Papen's class prejudices he had a far clearer conception than any of the men around the President of the depth and seriousness of the crisis through which German society had been passing since the end of 1929. He had never fallen into the error of supposing that 'strong' government by itself was a remedy for the crisis, nor did he underestimate the force which lay behind such extremist movements as the Nazis and the Communists. His aim, stated again and again in these years, was to harness one of these movements, the Nazis, to the service of the State.

Schleicher's closest contact in the Nazi Party at this time was Gregor Strasser. If Hitler represented the will to power in the Party, and Röhm its preference for violence, Gregor Strasser represented its idealism – a brutalized idealism certainly, but a genuine desire to make a clean sweep. To Strasser National Socialism was a real political movement, not, as it was to Hitler, the instrument of his ambition. He took its programme seriously, as Hitler never had, and he was the leader of the Nazi Left-wing which, to the annoyance of Hitler's industrialist friends, still dreamed of a German Socialism and still won votes for the Party by its anti-capitalist radicalism. But Strasser, if he was much more to the Left than the other Party leaders, was also the head of the Party Organization, more in touch with feeling throughout the local branches than anyone else, and more impressed than any of the other leaders by the set-backs of the autumn, culminating in the loss of two million votes at the November elections. Strasser was particularly impressed by the disillusionment of the more radical elements in the Party and their tendency to drift towards the Communists. He became convinced that the only course to save the Party from going to pieces was to make a compromise and get into power at once, even as part of a coalition. Hitler's attitude he regarded as illogical. The Nazi leader's insistence on legality offended and roused the suspicions of those who wanted a revolution, while his uncompromising demand for 'all or nothing' defeated his own policy when he was offered a share in power. Strasser was a convert to the tactics of legality, but saw the Party's chance to influence government policy and carry out at least a part of its programme being sacrificed to Hitler's ambition and his refusal to accept anything less than 'the whole power'.

This division of opinion in the Party leadership, and the strains to which it gave rise, had been present for some time. Goebbels, who was Strasser's sworn enemy, records Hitler's first open mention of the conflict on 31 August. Thereafter there are a dozen references to Strasser's 'intrigues' between the beginning of September and the beginning of December.

The day after Schleicher became Chancellor he sent for Gregor Strasser and made an offer to the Nazis. Having failed to get Hitler to discuss a deal, Schleicher suggested that Strasser himself should enter his Cabinet as Vice-Chancellor and Minister-President of the Prussian State Government. If he accepted, Strasser could take over Schleicher's plans for dealing with unemployment and help to establish cooperation with the trade unions. Schleicher's programme was a broad front extending from the reasonable Nazis to the reasonable Socialists, with an energetic programme to reduce unemployment. The offer to Strasser was a clever move on Schleicher's part. Not only was it attractive to Strasser as a way out of the Party's difficulties, but it would almost certainly split the Party leadership. In that case, if Hitler stood out Strasser might agree to come into the Cabinet on his own responsibility, and carry his following out of the Party. The same day, 3 December, elections in Thuringia showed nearly a forty per cent drop in the Nazi vote since July. This added force to Strasser's arguments for accepting Schleicher's offer in order at all costs to avoid further national elections.

On 5 December a conference of the Party leaders was held in

the Kaiserhof. Strasser found support from Frick, the leader of the Nazi group in the Reichstag, whose members were powerfully impressed by the Thuringian results and the threat that they might lose their seats and salaries in a new election. Göring and Goebbels, however, were hotly opposed, and carried Hitler with them. Hitler laid down terms for discussion with Schleicher, but placed the negotiations with the Chancellor in the hands of Göring and Frick – according to another version, of Göring and Röhm – deliberately excluding Strasser. On 7 December Hitler and Strasser had a further conversation in the Kaiserhof, in the course of which Hitler bitterly accused Strasser of bad faith, of trying to go behind his back and oust him from the leadership of the Party. Strasser angrily retorted that he had been entirely loyal, and had only thought of the interests of the Party. Going back to his room in the Hotel Excelsior, he sat down and wrote Hitler a long letter in which he resigned from his position in the Party. He reviewed the whole course of their relationship since 1925, attacked the irresponsibility and inconsistency of Hitler's tactics, and prophesied disaster if he persisted in them.

It is possible that if Strasser had stayed to fight out his quarrel with Hitler he could have carried a majority of the Party with him, although it would be unwise to underestimate Hitler's wiliness when in a corner. There is no doubt that Hitler was shaken by Strasser's revolt, as he had never been by any electoral defeat. The threat to his own authority in the Party touched him more closely than the loss of votes or the failure of negotiations had ever done. Goebbels wrote in his diary: 'In the evening the Leader comes to us. It is difficult to be cheerful. We are all rather downcast, in view of the danger of the whole Party falling to pieces and all our work being in vain. We are confronted with the great test. . . . Phone call from Ley. The situation in the Party is getting worse from hour to hour. The Leader must immediately return to the Kaiserhof. . . . Treachery, treachery, treachery! For hours the Leader paces up and down the room in the hotel. Suddenly he stops and says: "If the Party once falls to pieces, I shall shoot myself without more ado!"'[1]

But Strasser had always lacked the toughness to challenge Hitler outright, as his earlier capitulations had shown. When his brother, Otto, had defied Hitler and been cast off, Gregor Strasser had made his peace and remained. He had never planned a revolt such as Hitler suspected, and now, instead of rallying the latent

1. Goebbels: p. 206.

opposition to Hitler in the Party, he cursed the whole business and vanished without a word. While Frick searched anxiously for him in Berlin, he caught the train to Munich, and took his family off for a holiday in Italy.

Strasser's disappearance gave Hitler time to recover his confidence and quell any signs of mutiny. The Party's Political Organization department was broken up, Ley taking over part of its duties under Hitler's direct supervision, the rest being transferred to Goebbels and Darré. A declaration condemning Strasser in the sharpest terms was submitted to a full meeting of the Party leaders and Gauleiters in the Palace of the President of the Reichstag on 9 December. When Feder, who shared Strasser's Socialist ideals, refused to accept it, he was told to sign or get out. He signed. Hitler used all his skill to appeal to the loyalty of his old comrades and brought tears to their eyes. With a sob in his voice he declared that he would never have believed Strasser guilty of such treachery. Julius Streicher blubbered: 'Maddening that Strasser could do this to our leader.' At the end of this emotional *tour de force* 'the Gauleiters and Deputies,' Goebbels records, 'burst into a spontaneous ovation for the leader. All shake hands with him, promising to carry on until the very end and not to renounce the great Idea, come what may. Strasser now is completely isolated, a dead man. A small circle of us remain with the Leader, who is quite cheerful and elated again. The feeling that the whole Party is standing by him with a loyalty never hitherto displayed has raised his spirits and invigorated him.'[1] A few days later, on 15 December, a Central Party Commission was set up under Hess to supervise and coordinate the policy of the Party throughout Germany.

While Hitler worked to restore the threatened unity of his Party, Schleicher continued his talks with the other Party leaders, including representatives of the trade unions. The failure to bring in the Nazis at this stage did not unduly depress him. On 15 December he expounded his plans in a broadcast to the nation. He asked his listeners to forget that he was a soldier, and to think of him as 'the impartial trustee of the interests of all in an emergency'. He supported neither Capitalism nor Socialism, he declared: his aim was to provide work. A Reich Commissioner had been appointed to draw up plans for reducing unemployment; meanwhile there would be no new taxes or further wage

1. Goebbels: p. 209.

cuts. The system of agricultural quotas which Papen had introduced for the benefit of the big landowners would be ended; a huge programme of subsidized land settlement in the eastern provinces would be undertaken; and the Government would control prices, in the first place those of meat and coal. The Chancellor followed his speech by the restoration of recent wage and relief cuts, and the grant of greater freedom of the Press and of assembly.

In the event, Schleicher fell between two stools. He failed to overcome the distrust and hostility of the Social Democrats and the trade unions, or even of the Centre, which, remembering his part in the overthrow of Brüning, was not converted to his support by his advocacy of a policy not unlike Brüning's own. At the same time he stirred up the violent opposition of powerful interests in industry and agriculture. The industrialists disliked his conciliatory attitude towards labour; the farmers were furious at his reduction of agricultural protection; the East Elbian landowners denounced his plans for land settlement as 'agrarian Bolshevism' with the same uncompromising class spirit they had shown towards Brüning.

Schleicher made the great mistake of underestimating the forces opposed to him. In January 1933, Kurt von Schuschnigg, at that time Austrian Minister of Justice, paid a call on the Chancellor while visiting Berlin. 'General von Schleicher,' he wrote later, 'showed himself to be exceptionally optimistic with regard to the state of affairs in the Reich, of which he talked in very lively terms, particularly as regards its economic and political prospects. I remember clearly the words he used in this connexion: he was endeavouring, he said, to establish contacts throughout the trade-union organizations, and hoped in this way to build up a sound political platform, which would ensure a peaceful and prosperous development of the political situation. Herr Hitler was no longer a problem, his movement had ceased to be a political danger, and the whole problem had been solved, it was a thing of the past.'[1] Schuschnigg was so surprised by Schleicher's optimism, which no one else in Berlin shared, that he made a note of the conversation and its date: it was 15 January. A fortnight later Schleicher was to be sadly disillusioned.

The basis of the Chancellor's confidence was his belief that his enemies were unable to combine against him. So far as the Nazis

1. Kurt von Schuschnigg: *Dreimal Österreich*; English translation, *Farewell Austria* (London, 1938), pp. 165–6.

were concerned there were good grounds for believing them to be a declining force. The last three months before Hitler came to power – November and December 1932, January 1933 – marked the lowest point of Hitler's fortunes since he had broken into national politics in 1930. The most immediate problem was shortage of funds. The Nazi organization – an embryonic State within the framework of the old State, as Hitler claimed – was highly expensive to run. The Party was filled with thousands of officials who kept their places on the Party pay-roll often without clearly defined functions, often with duties that were either unnecessary or duplicated by someone else. The S.A., the hard core of which consisted of unemployed men who lived in S.A. messes and barracks, must have cost immense sums, however limited the amount spent on each man. Even at the rate of one mark a day, which is probably too low, that would mean an expenditure of the order of two million eight hundred thousand marks a week. Goebbels's own comments on party finances are despondent:

11 November – Receive a report on the financial situation of the Berlin organization. It is hopeless. Nothing but debts and obligations, together with the complete impossibility of obtaining any reasonable sum of money after this defeat.
10 December – The financial situation of Gau Berlin is hopeless. We must institute strict measures of economy, and make it self-supporting.
22 December – We must cut down the salaries of our Gauleiters, as otherwise we cannot manage to make shift with our finances.[1]

This was the time when S.A. men were sent into the streets to beg for money, rattling their boxes and asking passers-by to spare something 'for the wicked Nazis'. Konrad Heiden speaks of debts of twelve million marks, others of twenty million.

More serious was the sense of defeatism and demoralization in the Party. The very day after the loyal demonstration in Göring's palace, Goebbels noted: 'The feeling in the Party is still divided. All are waiting for something to happen.'[2] Every week-end after the Strasser crisis, Hitler, Göring, Ley, and Goebbels visited the different Gaue to talk to Party officials, and restore their confidence in the leadership. On 12 December, for instance, Goebbels reports that Hitler returned from a tour of Saxony where he spoke three times a day. The same evening he spoke again in Breslau. On the 18th, after speaking in Hagen and Münster, Goebbels joined Ley for a visit to the Ruhr. Together they addressed eight thousand local officials, Amtswalter, at Essen, and another ten

1. Goebbels: pp. 189, 209, 214.   2. ibid., p. 209.

thousand at Düsseldorf. Despite Goebbels's efforts at whistling in the dark to keep his spirits up, at the end of 1932, two and a half years after the first great election campaign, he wrote in his diary: 'This year has brought us eternal ill-luck. . . . The past was sad, and the future looks dark and gloomy; all chances and hopes have quite disappeared.'[1]

Suddenly, at the turn of the year, Hitler's luck changed, and a chance offered itself. The varied antagonisms which Schleicher had aroused found a common broker in the unexpected figure of Franz von Papen, and on 4 January Papen and Hitler met quietly in the house of the Cologne banker, Kurt von Schröder. The circumstances and purpose of this meeting have been much disputed: the account followed here is in the main that given by Schröder himself in a statement made at Nuremberg on 5 December 1945.[2] The meeting was arranged through Wilhelm Keppler, one of the Nazi 'contact-men' with the world of business and industry. The idea was broached to Schröder by Papen about 10 December 1932. About the same time Keppler got in touch with Schröder with a similar proposal from Hitler. The beginning of January was fixed upon, when Papen would be staying in the Saar, and Hitler would be going to conduct an election campaign in Lippe-Detmold. Considerable precautions were taken to keep the meeting secret. Hitler took a night train to Bonn, drove to Godesberg, changed cars, and, giving the rest of his party a rendezvous outside Cologne, disappeared in a closed car for an unknown destination.

Hitler took with him Hess, Himmler, and Keppler, but the talk with Papen, which lasted for two hours, was held in Schröder's study with only the banker present besides the two principals. First, misunderstandings had to be removed: the sentence on the Potempa murderers and Papen's behaviour on 13 August. Papen slipped out of the responsibility for Hitler's humiliation by putting all the blame on Schleicher for Hindenburg's refusal to consider Hitler as Chancellor. The change of attitude on the President's part, he said, had come as a great surprise to him. But what Papen had really come to talk about was the prospect of replacing Schleicher's Government: he suggested the establishment of a Nationalist and Nazi coalition in which he and Hitler would be joint Chancellors. 'Then Hitler made a long speech in

1. Goebbels: p. 215.
2. Text in *Nazi Conspiracy and Aggression*, vol. II, pp. 922–4.

which he said, if he were made Chancellor, it would be necessary for him to be the head of the Government, but that supporters of Papen's could go into his Government as ministers, if they were willing to go along with him in his policy of changing many things. The changes he outlined at this time included elimination of the Social Democrats, Communists, and Jews from leading positions in Germany, and the restoration of order in public life. Papen and Hitler reached agreement in principle so that many of the points which had brought them in conflict could be eliminated and they could find a way to get together.' After lunch Schröder's guests stayed chatting together and left about 4 p.m.

Next day, to the embarrassment of both the participants, the meeting was headline news in the Berlin papers, and awkward explanations had to be given. Papen denied that the meeting was in any way directed against Schleicher, and, at his trial in Nuremberg,[1] he not only repudiated Schröder's account as entirely false, but claimed that his main purpose had been to persuade Hitler to enter the Schleicher Cabinet. There seems no reason to suppose, however, that Schröder gave an inaccurate report; perhaps Papen's memory played him a trick for once.

It is certainly wrong to suppose that the Hitler–Papen Government, which was to replace Schleicher, was agreed upon at Cologne; much hard bargaining lay ahead, and Schleicher's position had still to be more thoroughly undermined. But the first contact had been made; the two men had found common ground in their dislike of Schleicher and their desire to be revenged on him, each had sounded out the other's willingness for a deal. Hitler, moreover, received the valuable information that Schleicher had not been given the power to dissolve the Reichstag by the President, and – a point about which Schröder is modestly silent – arrangements were made to relieve the financial straits of the Nazi Party. Schröder was one of a group of industrialists and bankers who, in November 1932, sent a joint letter to Hindenburg urging him to give Hitler the powers to form a presidential cabinet.[2] Among those who had been active in collecting signatures was Dr Schacht,[3] and those who signed included many of the leaders of West German industry. At that

1. Nuremberg Proceedings, Part XVI, especially pp. 329–35.
2. N.D. 3901-PS.
3. cf. his letter to Hitler of 12 November 1932, N.D. EC-456, and also Dr Schacht's testimony at the Nuremberg trial, N.P., Part XIII, p. 29.

time Papen had intervened to cut off financial supplies from the Nazis, but now, with his blessing and Schröder's help, arrangements were made to pay the Nazis' debts. Hitler's break with Gregor Strasser, the acknowledged leader of the radical, anti-capitalist wing of the Party, may well have helped to make the agreement more easy. A few days later Goebbels noted: 'The financial situation has improved all of a sudden.'[1] The political hopes of the Nazis rose at the same time. On 5 January, commenting on the news of the meeting, Goebbels remarked: 'The present Government knows that this is the end for them. If we are successful, we cannot be far from power.'[2]

The Nazis could do little to help forward the intrigue against Schleicher; that had to be left to von Papen, who was still by chance living next door to the President in Berlin, and was a welcome and frequent visitor in his house.[3] It was important, however, to remove the impression of their declining strength. For this purpose Hitler decided to concentrate all the Party's resources on winning the elections in the tiny state of Lippe. The total vote at stake was only ninety thousand, but Hitler and Goebbels made their headquarters at Baron von Öynhausen's castle, Schloss Vinsebeck, and spent days haranguing meetings in the villages and small towns of the district. At Schwalenberg Hitler declared: 'Power comes at last in Germany only to him who has anchored this power most deeply in the people.'[4] On 15 January the Nazis were rewarded by an electoral victory in which they secured 39·6 per cent of the votes, a rise of 17 per cent. The Nazi Press brought out banner headlines, claiming that the Party was on the march again. 'Signal Lippe' was the title of Goebbels's own leader, and so loud was the noise made by the Nazi propaganda band that, even against their own better judgement, the group round the President were impressed.

The Nazis then proceeded to follow their success at Lippe by staging a mass demonstration in front of the Communist headquarters in Berlin, the Karl Liebknecht Haus. 'We shall stake everything on one throw to win back the streets of Berlin,' Goebbels wrote. The Government, after some hesitation, banned the Communists' counter-demonstration, and on 22 January, with a full escort of armed police, ten thousand S.A. men paraded

1. Goebbels: p. 228.   2. ibid., p. 221, cf. also p. 223.
3. Meissner's Affidavit. This too was denied by von Papen at Nuremberg.
4. Baynes: vol. I, p. 194.

on the Bülowplatz and listened to a ranting speech by Hitler. 'The Bülow Platz is ours,' Goebbels exulted. 'The Communists have suffered a great defeat. . . . This day is a proud and heroic victory for the S.A. and the Party.'[1]

By 20 January it was clear that Schleicher's attempt to construct a broad front representing all but the extremist parties had failed. The possibility of Gregor Strasser entering Schleicher's Cabinet was revived at the beginning of January, when Strasser returned to Berlin; and on 4 January, the day Hitler was meeting Papen in Cologne, Schleicher arranged for Strasser to talk to Hindenburg. As late as 14 January Goebbels was speculating anxiously on Strasser's entry into the Government. By the 16th, however, Goebbels writes that the papers are dropping Strasser and that he is finished; by the 19th Strasser was asking to see Hitler, and was refused.

One after another all the German Party leaders turned down Schleicher's approaches. The Nationalists had been alienated by the Chancellor's schemes for land colonization and by the threat to publish a secret Reichstag report on the scandals of the *Osthilfe*, the 'loans' which successive governments had made available to distressed landowners in the eastern provinces. They finally broke with Schleicher on 21 January and turned to the Nazis. Hitler had already seen Hugenberg, the Nationalist leader, on the 17th, and the final stage of negotiations for a Nazi–Nationalist Coalition opened on the evening of the 22nd in Ribbentrop's house at Dahlem.

Up to the very evening before the announcement of Hitler's Chancellorship, Papen continued to balance two possible plans. Either he could become Chancellor himself, with the support of Hugenberg and the Nationalists, in a presidential cabinet and dissolve the Reichstag for an indefinite period; or he could take the office of Vice-Chancellor in a Hitler Ministry, which would aim at a parliamentary majority with the help of the Nationalists and possibly of the Centre, dissolving the Reichstag if necessary in order to win a majority at fresh elections. In the second case, guarantees of various sorts would have to be obtained against the Nazis' abuse of power, they would have to be tied down by their partners in the coalition and the President's dislike of having Hitler as Chancellor would have to be overcome. Though he still insisted on the Chancellorship for himself, Hitler was now pre-

1. Goebbels: p. 231.

pared to enter a coalition and to search for a parliamentary majority, but there was room for a great deal of manoeuvring and bargaining on the composition of the Cabinet and the reservation of certain posts – the Foreign Minister and the Minister President of Prussia, the Ministers of Defence and Finance – for the President's own nominees.

On the Nazi side the principal negotiator was Göring, who was hastily summoned back from Dresden on 22 January for a meeting that evening, at which Papen, Meissner, and the President's son, Oskar von Hindenburg, met Hitler, Göring, and Frick.[1] One important gain Hitler made that night was to win over Oskar von Hindenburg, with whom he had a private conversation of an hour. It is believed that Hitler secured his support by a mixture of bribes and blackmail, possibly threatening to start proceedings to impeach the President and to disclose Oskar's part in the *Osthilfe* scandals and tax evasion on the presidential estate at Neudeck. It is not perhaps irrelevant to note that in August 1933 five thousand acres tax free were added to the Hindenburg estate, and that a year later Oskar was promoted from colonel to major-general. 'In the taxi on the way back,' Meissner recorded, 'Oskar von Hindenburg was extremely silent, and the only remark he made was that it could not be helped – the Nazis had to be taken into the Government.'[2]

The negotiations continued for another week. On the 23rd, the day after Hitler's meeting with Papen and Oskar von Hindenburg, Schleicher went to see the President. His hopes of splitting the Nazi Party had been frustrated; he admitted that he could not find a parliamentary majority and he asked for power to dissolve the Reichstag and govern by emergency decree. Hindenburg refused, using the same argument Schleicher himself had employed against Papen on 2 December: that such a course would lead to civil war. Ironically, Schleicher had reached the same position as Papen at the beginning of December, when he had forced Papen out because the latter wanted to fight Hitler, and had himself urged the need to form a government which would have the support of the National Socialists. The positions were exactly reversed, for it was now Papen who was able to offer the President

1. The meeting took place in the Dahlem home of a hitherto unknown Nazi, Ribbentrop, who was a friend of Papen's.

2. Meissner's Affidavit. For Oskar von Hindenburg's denials, cf. the record of his trial before the De-Nazification Court at Ülzen in March 1949: *Protokoll der mündlichen Verhandlung in dem Entnazifizierungsverfahren gegen den Generalleutnant a. D. Oskar von Hindenburg.*

the alternative which Schleicher had advocated in December, the formation of a government with a parliamentary majority in which the Nazi leader would himself take a responsible position. With the knowledge that this alternative was now being prepared behind Schleicher's back (Hitler and Papen had met again on the 24th), the President again refused his request on 28 January for power to dissolve the Reichstag, and left the Chancellor with no option but to resign. At noon the same day, Hindenburg officially entrusted Papen with the negotiations to provide a new government.

It was still uncertain whether it would be possible to bring Hitler and Hugenberg into the same coalition, and Papen had not yet put out of his mind the possibility of a presidential chancellorship with the support of Hugenberg and the Nationalists alone. Eager at any cost to prevent a Papen Chancellorship, and still convinced that the only practical course was to bring Hitler into the Government, Schleicher sent the Commander-in-Chief of the Army, General von Hammerstein, to see Hitler at the Bechsteins' house in Charlottenburg on the afternoon of Sunday, 29 January, and to warn him that they might still both be left out in the cold by Papen. In that case Schleicher put forward the suggestion of a Hitler–Schleicher coalition to rule with the united support of the Army and the Nazis. Hitler, however, who was still hoping to hear that agreement had been reached for a full coalition between Papen, Hugenberg, and himself, returned a non-committal reply.

Much more alarming to Hitler was the possibility that the Army, under the leadership of Schleicher and Hammerstein, might intervene at the last moment to prevent the formation of the proposed coalition. On the evening of the 29th a rumour spread that Schleicher was preparing a putsch with the support of the Potsdam garrison. According to Hitler's own later account, he feared that Schleicher might carry off the President to East Prussia, and proclaim martial law.[1]

How much truth there may have been in this it is difficult to say.[2] If they ever seriously considered such a plan, Schleicher and Hammerstein took no steps to put it into effect. But Hitler could

1. Hitler's version of the final negotiations leading up to 30 January, given after dinner on 21 May 1942, is recorded in *Hitler's Table Talk* (London, 1953), pp. 495–9.
2. For the detailed story of the so-called Potsdam Putsch, see J. W. Wheeler Bennett: *The Nemesis of Power*, pp. 281–6.

not afford to take chances. On the night of 29 January he placed the Berlin S.A. under Helldorf in a state of alert and arranged with a Nazi police major, Wecke, to have six battalions of police ready to occupy the Wilhelmstrasse. Warning messages were sent to Papen and Hindenburg. Finally, arrangements were made for General von Blomberg, who had been recalled from Geneva to act as the new Minister of Defence, to be taken to the President the moment he reached Berlin the following morning.

The keys to the attitude of the Army were held by the President, the old Field-Marshal who was the embodiment of the military tradition, and thus in a position to suppress any possible attempt at a *coup*, and by General von Blomberg. Hindenburg had agreed to the formation of a Ministry in which Hitler was to be Chancellor and had nominated Blomberg to serve as Minister of Defence under Hitler. If Blomberg accepted the President's commission, Hitler could be virtually sure of the Army. It would be interesting to know how far Blomberg had been courted by the Nazis in advance. Both Blomberg and Colonel von Reichenau, his Chief of Staff while he was in command in East Prussia, had been in touch with Hitler,[1] and Blomberg, who had recently been serving as chief military adviser to the German delegation at the Disarmament Conference, had been hurriedly recalled without Schleicher's or Hammerstein's knowledge. Hammerstein's adjutant, Major von Kuntzen, was at the station when Blomberg arrived early on the morning of 30 January and ordered the general to report at once to the Commander-in-Chief. But beside von Kuntzen, another officer, Oskar von Hindenburg, adjutant to his father, was also present and ordered Blomberg to report at once to the President of the Republic. Fortunately for Hitler, it was the latter summons which the general obeyed. He accepted his new commission from the President, and the threat of a last-minute repudiation by the Army was thereby avoided. In September 1933, Hitler declared: 'On this day we would particularly remember the part played by our Army, for we all know well that if, in the days of our revolution, the Army had not stood on our side, then we should not be standing here today.'[2] For once he spoke no more than the truth.

1. A letter from Hitler to Colonel von Reichenau, dated 4 December 1932, and setting out his policy at length, is among the captured German documents. Blomberg and Reichenau were brought into contact with Hitler by Müller, the Protestant Chaplain to the Forces in East Prussia, who was an enthusiastic Nazi and later became Reich Bishop.

2. Hitler, on 23 September 1933. (Baynes: vol. I, p. 556).

It is possible that fear of what Schleicher might do helped Papen and Hugenberg to make up their minds and hastily compose their remaining differences with the Nazis. At any rate, on the morning of Monday the 30th, after a sleepless night during which he sat up with Göring and Goebbels to be ready for any eventuality, Hitler received the long-awaited summons to the President. The deal which Schleicher had made the object of his policy, and for which Strasser had worked, was accomplished at last, with Schleicher and Strasser left out.

During the morning a silent crowd filled the street between the Kaiserhof and the Chancellery. Already the members of the new coalition had begun to quarrel. While they were waiting in Meissner's office to go into the President, Hitler started to complain that he had not been appointed Commissioner for Prussia. If his powers were to be limited, he would insist on new Reichstag elections. This at once set Hugenberg off and a heated argument began which was only ended by Meissner insisting that the President would wait no longer and ushering them into his presence.[1]

In the meantime, at a window of the Kaiserhof, Röhm was keeping an anxious watch on the door from which Hitler must emerge. Shortly after noon a roar went up from the crowd: the Leader was coming. He ran down the steps to his car and in a couple of minutes was back in the Kaiserhof. As he entered the room his lieutenants crowded to greet him. The improbable had happened: Adolf Hitler, the petty official's son from Austria, the down-and-out of the Home for Men, the *Meldegänger* of the List Regiment, had become Chancellor of the German Reich.

1. Papen, *Memoirs*, pp. 243–4.

BOOK II

CHANCELLOR
1933–9

CHAPTER FIVE

REVOLUTION AFTER POWER

30 January 1933–August 1934

I

NAZI propaganda later built up a legend which represented Hitler's coming to power as the upsurge of a great national revival. The truth is more prosaic. Despite the mass support he had won, Hitler came to office in 1933 as the result, not of any irresistible revolutionary or national movement sweeping him into power, nor even of a popular victory at the polls, but as part of a shoddy political deal with the 'Old Gang' whom he had been attacking for months past. Hitler did not seize power; he was jobbed into office by a backstairs intrigue.

Far from being inevitable, Hitler's success owed much to luck and even more to the bad judgement of his political opponents and rivals. While the curve of Communist success at the elections continued to rise, the Nazis had suffered their sharpest set-back in November 1932, when they lost two million votes. As Hitler freely admitted afterwards, the Party's fortunes were at their lowest ebb when the unexpected intervention of Papen offered them a chance they could scarcely have foreseen.

Before he came to power Hitler never succeeded in winning more than thirty-seven per cent of the votes in a free election. Had the remaining sixty-three per cent of the German people been united in their opposition he could never have hoped to become Chancellor by legal means; he would have been forced to choose between taking the risks of a seizure of power by force or the continued frustration of his ambitions. He was saved from this awkward dilemma by two factors: the divisions and ineffectiveness of those who opposed him, and the willingness of the German Right to accept him as a partner in government.

The inability of the German parties to combine in support of the Republic had bedevilled German politics since 1930, when Brüning had found it no longer possible to secure a stable majority in the Reichstag or at the elections. The Communists openly announced that they would prefer to see the Nazis in power rather than lift a finger to save the Republic. Despite the violence of the clashes on the streets, the Communist leaders followed a policy approved by Moscow which gave priority to the elimination of the Social Democrats as the rival working-class party.

Once the organization of the Social Democratic Party and the trade unions had been destroyed and the Nazis were in power the Communists believed that they would be within sight of establishing the dictatorship of the proletariat. Sectarian bitterness and dogmatic miscalculation continued to govern their actions even after Hitler became Chancellor, and they rejected any suggestion of a common front with the Social Democrats up to the dissolution of the Party by the new Government. The Social Democrats themselves, though more alive to the Nazi threat, had long since become a conservative trade-union party without a single leader capable of organizing a successful opposition to the Nazis. Though loyal to the Republic, since 1930 they had been on the defensive, had been badly shaken by the Depression and were hamstrung by the Communists' attacks.

The Catholic Centre, like the Social Democrats, maintained its voting strength to the end, but it was notoriously a Party which had never taken a strong independent line, a Party whose first concern was to make an accommodation with any government in power in order to secure the protection of its particular interests. In 1932–3 the Centre Party was so far from recognizing the danger of a Nazi dictatorship that it continued negotiations for a coalition with the Nazis and voted for the Enabling Law which conferred overriding powers on Hitler after he had become Chancellor.

In the 1930s there was no strong middle-class liberal Party in Germany – the lack of such a Party has more than once been one of the disasters of German political development. The middle-class parties which might have played such a role – the People's Party and the Democrats – had suffered a more severe loss of votes to the Nazis than any other German parties, and this is sufficient comment on the opposition they were likely to offer.

But the heaviest responsibility of all rests on the German Right, who not only failed to combine with the other parties in defence of the Republic but made Hitler their partner in a coalition government. The old ruling class of Imperial Germany had never reconciled itself to the loss of the war or to the overthrow of the monarchy in 1918. They were remarkably well treated by the Republican régime which followed. Many of them were left in positions of power and influence; their wealth and estates remained untouched by expropriation or nationalization; the Army leaders were allowed to maintain their independent position; the industrialists and business men made big profits out of a weak and complaisant government, while the help given to the Junkers' estates was one of the financial scandals of the century. All this won neither their gratitude nor their loyalty. Whatever may be said of individuals, as a class they remained irreconcilable, contemptuous of and hostile to the régime they continued to exploit. The word 'Nationalist', which was the pride of the biggest Party of the Right, became synonymous with disloyalty to the Republic.

There was certainly a period after Hindenburg was elected President in 1925 when this attitude was modified, but it hardened again from 1929 onwards, and both Papen and Hugenberg shared it to the full. What the German Right wanted was to regain its old position in Germany as the ruling class; to destroy the hated Republic and restore the monarchy; to put the working classes 'in their places'; to rebuild the military power of Germany; to reverse the decision of 1918 and to restore Germany – their Germany – to a dominant position in Europe. Blinded by interest and prejudice, the Right forsook the role of a true conservatism, abandoned its own traditions and made the gross mistake of supposing that in Hitler they had found a man who would enable them to achieve their ends. A large section of the German middle class, powerfully attracted by Hitler's nationalism, and many of the German Officer Corps followed their lead.

This was the policy put into effect by the formation of the coalition between the Nazis and the Right at the end of January 1933. The assumption on which it was based was the belief that Hitler and the Nazis, once they had been brought into the government, could be held in check and tamed. At first sight the terms to which Hitler had agreed appeared to confirm this belief.

He was not even a presidential chancellor; Hindenburg had been persuaded to accept 'the Bohemian corporal' on the grounds that this time Hitler would be able to provide – what he had been unable to provide in November 1932 – a parliamentary majority. No sooner was the Cabinet formed than Hitler started negotiations to bring the Centre Party into the coalition. Their 70 seats added to the 247 held by the Nazis and the Nationalists would give the new government a majority in the Reichstag. For this purpose the Ministry of Justice had been kept vacant, and when these negotiations did not lead to agreement it was Hitler who insisted, against Hugenberg's opposition, that new elections must be held in order to provide a parliamentary basis for the coalition in the form of an electoral majority.

Papen might well feel scepticism about Hitler's sincerity in looking so assiduously for a parliamentary majority; but he still saw nothing but cause for self-congratulation on his own astuteness. He had levelled scores with General von Schleicher, yet at the same time realized Schleicher's dream, the harnessing of the Nazis to the support of the State – and this, not on Hitler's, but on his own terms. For Hitler, Papen assured his friends, was his prisoner, tied hand and foot by the conditions he had accepted. True, Hitler had the Chancellorship, but the real power, in Papen's view, rested with the Vice-Chancellor, himself.

It was the Vice-Chancellor, not the Chancellor, who enjoyed the special confidence of the President; it was the Vice-Chancellor who held the key post of Minister-President of Prussia, with control of the Prussian administration and police; and the Vice-Chancellor who had the right, newly established, to be present on all occasions when the Chancellor made his report to the President.

Only three of the eleven Cabinet posts were held by Nazis, and apart from the Chancellorship both were second-rate positions. The Foreign Ministry and the Ministry of Defence – with control of the Army – had been reserved for men of the President's own choice – the first for Freiherr von Neurath, a career diplomat of conservative views, the second for General von Blomberg. The key economic ministries – the Ministry of Economy and the Ministry of Food and Agriculture, both in the Reich and in Prussia – were in the hands of Hugenberg, while the Ministry of Labour had been given to Seldte, the leader of the Stahlhelm. This was highly reassuring to the industrialists and landowners. All that was left for Hitler's own Party was the Reich Ministry of the Interior (which did not control the State's police forces) for Frick, and a Ministry without Portfolio for Göring. In addition, Göring was made Prussian Minister of the Interior, but, with Papen as head of the Prussian Government, Göring too would be pinned down.

It was with these arguments that Papen overcame Hindenburg's reluctance to make Hitler Chancellor. In this way they would obtain that mass support which the 'Cabinet of Barons' had so notoriously lacked. Hitler was to play his old role of 'Drummer', the barker for a circus-show in which he was now to have a place as partner and his name at the top of the bill, but in which the real decisions would be taken by those who outnumbered him by eight to three in the Cabinet. This was *Realpolitik* as practised by Papen, a man who – as he prided himself – knew how to distinguish between the reality and the shows of power.

Rarely has disillusionment been so complete or so swift to follow. Those who, like Papen, believed they had seen through Hitler were to find they had badly underestimated both the leader and the movement. For Hitler's originality lay in his realization that effective revolutions, in modern conditions, are carried out with, and not against, the power of the State: the correct order of events was first to secure access to that power and then begin his revolution. Hitler never abandoned the cloak of legality; he recognized the enormous psychological value of having the law on his side. Instead he turned the law inside out and made illegality legal.

In the six months that followed the formation of the coalition government, Hitler and his supporters were to demonstrate a cynicism and lack of scruple – qualities on which his partners particularly prided themselves – which left Papen and Hugenberg gasping for breath. At the end of those six months they were to discover, like the young lady of Riga, the dangers of going for a ride on a tiger.[1] The first part of this chapter is the history of how the Nazis took their partners for a ride.

At five o'clock on the afternoon of Monday 30 January, Hitler presided over his first Cabinet meeting, the minutes of which are among the German documents captured after the war.[2] The Cabinet was still committed to seeking a parliamentary majority by securing the support of the Centre Party, and Göring duly reported on the progress of his talks with the leader of the Centre, Monsignor Kaas. If these failed, then, Hitler suggested, it would be necessary to dissolve the Reichstag and hold new elections. One at least of Hitler's partners, Hugenberg, saw the danger of letting Hitler conduct an election campaign with the power of the

1. 'There was a young lady of Riga,' it will be recalled,
   'Who smiled as she rode on a tiger.
   They returned from the ride
   With the lady inside,
   And a smile on the face of the tiger.'
2. N.D., 351-PS.

State at his command. On the other hand, it was Hugenberg who, more than anyone else, objected to the inclusion of the Centre in the coalition. Hugenberg's own solution was frankly to dispense with the Reichstag and set up an authoritarian régime. This, however, conflicted with the promise to Hindenburg that, if he agreed to Hitler as Chancellor, the new Ministry would relieve him of the heavy responsibility of governing by the use of the President's emergency powers and would provide the constitutional support of a majority in the Reichstag. Reluctantly, Hugenberg allowed himself to be manoeuvred into agreeing that, if the talks with the Centre Party broke down, the Cabinet should dissolve the Reichstag and hold new elections. In return he [had Hitler's solemn promise – reaffirmed at the Cabinet meeting of 30 January – that the composition of the coalition government would not be altered, whatever the results of the elections.

The next day, when Hitler saw Monsignor Kaas, he took good care that the negotiations with the Centre should fail. When Kaas submitted a list of questions and guarantees on which the Centre would first require satisfaction – a list simply intended to serve as a basis for discussion – Hitler declared to his colleagues that his soundings had shown there was no possibility of agreement and that the only course was to dissolve at once. He gave the most convincing assurances of loyalty to his partners, and, on the advice of Papen, Hindenburg agreed once more to sign a decree dissolving the Reichstag 'since the formation of a working majority has proved impossible'. The Centre Party protested to the President that this was not true, that the questions they had submitted to Hitler had only been intended as preliminaries to further discussion and that the negotiations had been allowed to lapse by the Chancellor himself. But by then it was too late: the decree had been signed, the date for the new elections fixed and the first and most difficult of the obstacles to Hitler's success removed. Papen and Hugenberg had allowed themselves to be gently guided into the trap. For the last time the German nation was to go to the polls: this time, Goebbels wrote confidently in his diary, there would be no mistake. 'The struggle is a light one now, since we are able to employ all the means of the State. Radio and Press are at our disposal. We shall achieve a masterpiece of propaganda. Even money is not lacking this time.'[1]

In order to leave no doubts of the expectations they had, Gör-

1. Goebbels: p. 240 (3 February).

ing summoned a number of Germany's leading industrialists to his palace on the evening of 20 February. Among those present were Krupp von Bohlen; Voegler, of the United Steel Works; Schnitzler and Basch, of I.G. Farben, Walter Funk – in all some twenty to twenty-five people, with Dr Schacht to act as host.[1] Hitler spoke to them on much the same lines as at Düsseldorf a year before. 'Now,' he told his audience, 'we stand before the last election. Whatever the outcome, there will be no retreat. One way or another, if the election does not decide, the decision must be brought about by other means.' Göring, who followed, was blunter. 'Other circles not taking part in this political battle should at least make the financial sacrifices so necessary at this time. . . . The sacrifice asked for is easier to bear if it is realized that the elections will certainly be the last for the next ten years, probably even for the next hundred years.'[2] After a short speech of thanks by Krupp von Bohlen, at Schacht's suggestion it was agreed to raise an election fund of three million Reichsmarks from leading German firms. The fund was to be divided between the partners in the coalition, but there was little doubt that the Nazis would claim – and get – the lion's share.

Throughout the election campaign Hitler refused to outline any programme for his Government. At Munich he said: 'If, today, we are asked for the programme of this movement, then we can summarize this in a few quite general sentences: programmes are of no avail, it is the human purpose which is decisive. . . . Therefore the first point in our programme is: Away with all illusions!'[3]

At Kassel he retorted on his opponents: 'They have had no programme. Now it is too late for their plans, the time for their ideas is past. . . . The period of international phrases, of promises of international solidarity, is over and its place will be taken by the solidarity of the German people. No one in the world will help us – only ourselves.'[4]

The Nazi campaign was directed against the record of the fourteen years of party government in Germany; above all, against the Social Democratic and Centre Parties. 'In fourteen years the System which has now been overthrown has piled

1. Affidavit of Georg von Schnitzler, 10 November 1945, N.D. E C-439; Schacht's Interrogation, 20 July 1945, N.D. 3725-PS; Schacht's testimony in Court, Nuremberg Proceedings, Part XII, pp. 398–9; Funk's Interrogation, 26 June 1945; N.D. 2828-PS.
2. Report of Hitler's and Göring's speeches, N.D. D-203.
3. Hitler at Munich, 24 February 1933 (Baynes: vol. I, p. 252).
4. At Kassel, 11 February 1933 (ibid., p. 238).

mistake upon mistake, illusion upon illusion.'[1] What had the Nazis to put in its place? He was no democratic politician, Hitler virtuously replied, to trick the people into voting for him by a few empty promises. 'I ask of you, German people, that after you have given the others fourteen years you should give us four.'[2] 'What I claim is fair and just: only four years for us and then others shall form their judgement and pass sentence. I will not flee abroad, I will not seek to escape sentence.'[3]

Hitler did not rely on the spoken word alone. Although the other parties were still allowed to function, their meetings were broken up, their speakers assaulted and beaten, their posters torn down and their papers continually suppressed. Even the official figures admitted fifty-one people killed during the election campaign and several hundreds injured. This time the Nazis were inside the gate, and they did not mean to be robbed of power by any scruples about fair play or free speech.

Papen believed he had tied Hitler down by restricting the number of Cabinet posts held by the Nazis to a bare minimum, but while Hugenberg shut himself up with his economic plans and the Foreign Office was kept in safe hands the real key to power in the State – control of the Prussian police force and of the Prussian State Administration – lay with Göring. By the curious system of dual government which existed in Germany, the Prussian Ministry of the Interior carried out the work of administering two-thirds of Germany, and was of much greater importance than the Reich Ministry of the Interior, a head without a body. In the critical period of 1933–4, no man after Hitler played so important a role in the Nazi revolution as Göring. His energy and ruthlessness, together with his control of Prussia, were indispensable to Hitler's success. The belief that Göring at the Prussian Ministry of the Interior would be restrained by Papen as Minister President of Prussia proved ill-founded. Goering showed no intention of being restrained by anybody: he issued orders and enforced his will, as if he were already in possession of absolute power.

The moment Göring entered office he began a drastic purge of the Prussian State service, in which hundreds of officials were dismissed and replaced by men who could be relied on by the Nazis. Göring paid particular attention to the senior police

1. At Stuttgart, 15 February 1933 (Baynes: vol. I, p. 239).
2. At Cologne, 19 February (ibid., p. 250).
3. At Dortmund, 17 February (ibid., p. 243).

officers, where he made a clean sweep in favour of his own appointments, many of them active S.A. or S.S. leaders. In the middle of February Göring issued an order to the Prussian police to the effect that 'the police have at all costs to avoid anything suggestive of hostility to the S.A., S.S., and Stahlhelm, as these organizations contain the most important constructive national elements. . . . It is the business of the police to abet every form of national propaganda.' After urging the police to show no mercy to the activities of 'organizations hostile to the State' – that is to say, the Communists, and Marxists in general – Göring continued: 'Police officers who make use of fire-arms in the execution of their duties will, without regard to the consequences of such use, benefit by my protection; those who, out of a misplaced regard for such consequences, fail in their duty will be punished in accordance with the regulations.' In other words, when in doubt shoot. To make his intentions quite clear, Göring added: 'Every official must bear in mind that failure to act will be regarded more seriously than an error due to taking action.'[1]

On 22 February Göring went a step further. He published an order establishing an auxiliary police force on the grounds that the resources of the regular police were stretched to the limit and must be reinforced. Fifty thousand men were called up, among them twenty-five thousand from the S.A. and fifteen thousand from the S.S. All they had to do was to put a white arm-band over their brown shirts or black shirts: they then represented the authority of the State. It was the equivalent of handing over police powers to the razor and cosh gangs. For the citizen to appeal to the police for protection became more dangerous than to suffer assault and robbery in silence. At best, the police turned their backs and looked the other way; more often the auxiliaries helped their S.A. comrades to beat up their victims. This was 'legality' in practice. In one of his dispatches the British Ambassador remarked that the daily Press now contained three regular lists:

1. A list of Government and police officials who have either been suspended or sent away altogether;
2. a list of papers suppressed or suspended; and
3. a list of persons who have lost their lives or been injured in political disturbances.[2]

The day after Hitler became Chancellor, Goebbels noted in his

1. Heiden: *History of National Socialism*, p. 216.
2. Sir H. Rumbold to Sir J. Simon, 1 March 1933, *Brit. Doc.*, 2nd Series, vol. iv, No. 246.

diary: 'In a conference with the Leader we arrange measures for combating the Red terror. For the present we shall abstain from direct action. First the Bolshevik attempt at a revolution must burst into flame. At the given moment we shall strike.'[1] Goebbels's requirement was to be literally fulfilled. On 24 February the police raided Communist H.Q. in Berlin at the Karl Liebknecht Haus. An official communiqué reported the discovery of plans for a Communist revolution. The publication of the captured documents was promised in the immediate future. They never appeared, but the search for the counter-revolution was intensified, and on the night of 27 February the Reichstag building mysteriously went up in flames.

While the fire was still spreading, the police arrested a young Dutch Communist, van der Lubbe, who was found in the deserted building in circumstances which left little doubt that he was responsible.

Göring had been looking for a pretext to smash the Communist Party and at once declared that van der Lubbe was only a pawn in a major Communist plot to launch a campaign of terrorism for which the burning of the Reichstag was to be the signal. The arrest of Communist leaders, including the Bulgarian Dimitroff, followed at once, and the Reichstag Fire Trial was held in Leipzig with all the publicity the Nazis could contrive. The publicity, however, badly misfired. Not only did Dimitroff defend himself with skill, but the prosecution failed completely to prove any connexion between van der Lubbe and the other defendants. The trial ended in a fiasco with the acquittal and release of the Communist leaders, leaving the unhappy van der Lubbe to be hurriedly executed.

The convenience of the pretext which Göring found for attacking the Communists led many (including the present author) to believe that the burning of the Reichstag was, in fact, planned and carried out by the Nazis themselves. A circumstantial version described how a band of Berlin S.A. men led by Karl Ernst penetrated into the deserted building by an underground tunnel and set the place ablaze. Van der Lubbe, who had been picked up by the S.A. after attempting to set fire to other buildings as a protest against the way society had treated him, was used as a dupe and allowed to climb into the Reichstag and start a fire on his own in another part.

Whichever version is accepted, the part played by van der

1. Goebbels: p. 238 (31 January).

Lubbe remains a mystery, and it was this which led Herr Fritz Tobias to start an independent investigation of the evidence in 1955. Herr Tobias's conclusion (published in *Der Spiegel* in 1959) rejects both the Nazi and the anti-Nazi account in favour of van der Lubbe's own declaration, from which he never wavered, that he alone was reponsible for the fire and that he carried it out as a single-handed act of protest. Herr Tobias may well be right in arguing that this, the simplest explanation of all, is the true one.[1]

The question, Who started the fire? remains open, but there is no doubt about the answer to the question, Who profited by it? Hitler needed no prompting.

During the Reichstag Fire [he recalled later] I went in the middle of the night to the offices of the *Völkischer Beobachter*. It took half an hour before I could find anyone to let me in. Inside there were a few compositors sitting around, and eventually some sub-editor appeared heavy with sleep. . . . 'There's no one here at this time of night; I must ask you to come back during business hours.' 'Are you mad!' I cried. 'Don't you realize that an event of incalculable importance is actually now taking place.' In the end I got hold of Goebbels, and we worked till dawn preparing the next day's edition.[2]

The day after the fire, on 28 February, Hitler promulgated a decree signed by the President 'for the protection of the People and the State'. The decree was described 'as a defensive measure against Communist acts of violence'. It began by suspending the guarantees of individual liberty under the Weimar Constitution:

Thus, restrictions on personal liberty, on the right of free expression of opinion, including freedom of the Press; on the rights of assembly and association; violations of the privacy of postal, telegraphic and telephonic communications; warrants for house searches; orders for confiscation as well as restrictions on property, are permissible beyond the legal limits otherwise prescribed.

Article 2 authorized the Reich Government if necessary to take over full powers in any federal State. Article 5 increased the penalty for the crimes of high treason, poisoning, arson, and sabotage to one of death, and instituted the death penalty, or hard labour for life, in the case of conspiracy to assassinate members of the Government, or grave breaches of the peace.[3]

Armed with these all-embracing powers, Hitler and Göring were in a position to take any action they pleased against their

1. cf. Fritz Tobias: *Der Reichstagsbrand*, Rastadt, 1962.
2. *Hitler's Table Talk*, p. 649.   3. N.D. 1390-PS.

opponents. They cleverly postponed the formal proscription of the Communist Party until after the elections, so that the working-class vote should continue to be divided between the rival parties of the Communists and the Social Democrats. But acts of terrorism against the leaders, the Press, and organizations of the Left-wing parties were now intensified. When a British correspondent, Sefton Delmer of the *Daily Express*, asked Hitler what truth there was in rumours of a projected massacre of his political opponents, Hitler replied: 'My dear Delmer, I need no St Bartholomew's Night. By the decrees issued legally we have appointed tribunals which will try enemies of the State legally, and deal with them legally in a way which will put an end to these conspiracies.'[1]

Meanwhile, in the last week of the election campaign, the Nazi propaganda machine redoubled the force of its attack on the 'Marxists', producing the most hair-raising accounts of Communist preparations for insurrection and a 'blood-bath', for which the Reichstag Fire and the arrest of van der Lubbe were used to provide substantiation. Even those who regarded the official version of the Fire with scepticism were impressed and intimidated by the ruthlessness of the Nazi tactics. Hitler stormed the country in a last hurricane campaign, declaring his determination to stamp out Marxism and the parties of the Left without mercy. For the first time the radio carried his words into every corner of the country.

To leave no doubt of what they meant, Göring assured an audience at Frankfurt on 3 March:

Fellow Germans, my measures will not be crippled by any judicial thinking. My measures will not be crippled by any bureaucracy. Here I don't have to worry about Justice, my mission is only to destroy and exterminate, nothing more. This struggle will be a struggle against chaos, and such a struggle I shall not conduct with the power of the police. A bourgeois State might have done that. Certainly, I shall use the power of the State and the police to the utmost, my dear Communists, so don't draw any false conclusions; but the struggle to the death, in which my fist will grasp your necks, I shall lead with those down there – the Brown Shirts.[2]

The campaign reached its climax on Saturday 4 March, the 'Day of the Awakening Nation', when Hitler spoke in Königsberg, the ancient coronation town and capital of the separated

1. Hitler's interview with Sefton Delmer, *Daily Express*, 3 March 1933.
2. Göring's speech at Frankfurt-on-Main, 3 March 1933, N.D. 1856-PS.

province of East Prussia. Attacking the 'November politicians', Hitler declared:

We have been asked today to define our programme. For the moment we can only say one thing: You began with a lie, and we want to make a fresh beginning with the truth. . . . And the first thought contained in this truth is this: a people must understand that its future lies only in its own strength, in its capacity, its industry, its courage. . . .

One must be able to say once again: German People, hold your heads high and proudly once more! You are no longer enslaved and in bondage, but you are free again and can justly say: We are all proud that through God's powerful aid we have once more become true Germans.[1]

As Hitler finished speaking bonfires blazed out on the hill-tops, all along the 'threatened frontier' of the east. It was the culmination of a month in which the tramping columns of S.A. troops, the torchlight parades, the monster demonstrations, cheering crowds, blaring loudspeakers, and mob-oratory, the streets hung with swastika flags, the open display of brutality and violence, with the police standing by in silence – all had been used to build up the impression of an irresistible force which would sweep away every obstacle in its path.

In face of all this it is a remarkable fact that still the German people refused to give Hitler the majority he sought. With close on ninety per cent of the electorate voting, the Nazis increased their own share of votes by five and a half millions, polling 17,277,200 out of a total of 39,343,300, a percentage of 43·9. Despite the Nazi hammering, the Centre Party increased their votes from 4,230,600 to 4,424,900; the Social Democrats held steady at 7,181,600, a drop of only 66,400; while even the Communists lost little more than a million votes, still returning a figure of 4,848,100. With the help of his Nationalist allies, who polled 3,136,800 votes (a meagre gain of 180,000), Hitler had a bare majority in the new Reichstag, 288 plus 52 seats in a house of 647 deputies. Disappointing though the results were, this was just enough, and it did not escape the attention of the Nazi leaders that with the proscription of the Communist deputies they would have a clear parliamentary majority themselves, without the need of the Nationalist votes. After the experience of the past few weeks, the chances of Papen, Hugenberg, and the Nationalists acting as an effective brake on their partners in the coalition appeared slight.

1. Hitler at Königsberg, 4 March 1933 (Baynes: vol. I, pp. 116 and 409).

II

Hitler's dictatorship rested on the constitutional foundation of a single law. No National or Constitutional Assembly was called and the Weimar Constitution was never formally abrogated. Fresh laws were simply promulgated as they appeared necessary. What Hitler aimed at was arbitrary power. It took time to achieve this, but from the first he had no intention of having his hands tied by any constitution; there was no equivalent of the Fascist Grand Council which in the end was used to overthrow Mussolini. Long before the Second World War, even the Cabinet had ceased to meet in Germany.

The fundamental law of the Hitler régime was the so-called Enabling Law, *Gesetz zur Behebung der Not von Volk und Reich* (Law for Removing the Distress of People and Reich). As it represented an alteration of the Constitution, a majority of two-thirds of the Reichstag was necessary to pass it, and Hitler's first preoccupation after the elections was to secure this. One step was simple: the eighty-one Communist deputies could be left out of account, those who had not been arrested so far would certainly be arrested if they put in an appearance in the Reichstag. Negotiations with the Centre were resumed and, in the meantime, Hitler showed himself in his most conciliatory mood towards his Nationalist partners. Both the discussions in the Cabinet,[1] and the negotiations with the Centre,[2] revealed the same uneasiness at the prospect of the powers the Government was claiming. But the Nazis held the whip-hand with the decree of 28 February. If necessary, they threatened to make sufficient arrests to provide them with their majority without bothering about the votes of the Centre. The Nationalists comforted themselves with the clause in the new law which declared that the rights of the President remained unaffected. The Centre, after receiving lavish promises from Hitler, succeeded also in getting a letter from the President in which he wrote that 'the Chancellor has given me his assurance that, even without being forcibly obliged by the Constitution, he will not use the power conferred on him by the Enabling Act without having first consulted me.'[3] These were

1. The Cabinet Minutes of 15 March and 20 March have been published: N.D. 2962-3-PS.
2. cf. the account by Dr Brüning in 'Ein Brief', pp. 15–20.
3. Quoted in full in J. W. Wheeler Bennett: *Hindenburg* (London, 1936), p. 448.

more paper-dykes to hold out the flood-tide, but Hitler was prepared to promise anything at this stage to get his bill through, with the appearances of legality preserved intact.

Hitler's master-stroke of conciliation towards the President, the Army, and the Nationalists was the ceremony in the Potsdam Garrison Church on 21 March, to mark the opening of the Reichstag, two days before it met to consider the Enabling Bill. At the same time Hitler established the claim of the new régime to be the heir of the military traditions of old Prussia and its Hohenzollern kings.

Potsdam, the royal town of the Hohenzollerns, and the Garrison Church, which had been founded by Frederick William I and contained the grave of Frederick the Great, stood in deliberate contrast to Weimar, the city of Goethe and Schiller, where the National Assembly of the 'November Republic' had met in 1919. The date, 21 March, was that on which Bismarck had opened the first Reichstag of the German Empire in 1871, and on which Hitler was now to open the first Reichstag of the Third Reich. The guard of honour of the Army drawn up on one side, and the S.A. on the other, were the symbols of the two Germanies, the old and the new, united by the handshake of President and Chancellor.

It was a brilliant spring day in Potsdam, and the houses were hung with huge swastika banners, side by side with the black-white-red flags of the old Empire. In the church itself one whole gallery was filled with the marshals, generals, and admirals of the Imperial régime, all wearing their pre-war uniforms, and headed by Field-Marshal von Mackensen in the uniform of the Death's Head Hussars. The chair reserved for the Kaiser was left empty, and immediately behind sat the former Crown Prince, in full-dress uniform. On the floor of the church were ranged the Nazi deputies, in brown shirts, flanked by the Nationalists and the Centre; not a single Social Democrat was present.

When the door was thrown open, the audience rose to its feet. The members of the Government entered the church. All eyes were on two men: the Austrian, Adolf Hitler, clad in formal morning-dress with a cut-away coat, awkward but respectful, and beside him the massive figure of the aged President, the Prussian Field-Marshal, who had first stood in this church in 1866 when, as a young lieutenant of the Guards, he had returned from the Austro-Prussian War in which German unity had been forged.

Slowly the old man advanced down the aisle, leaning on his cane. As he reached the centre, he turned and solemnly saluted with his Field-Marshal's baton the empty throne of the Kaiser and the Crown Prince.

The President's address, which he read, was brief. 'May the old spirit of this celebrated shrine,' he ended, 'permeate the generation of today, may it liberate us from selfishness and Party strife and bring us together in national self-consciousness to bless a proud and free Germany, united in herself.'

Hitler's speech was framed with an eye to the representatives of the old régime who sat before him:

The revolution of November 1918 ended a conflict into which the German nation had been drawn in the most sacred conviction that it was but protecting its liberty and its right to live. Neither the Kaiser, nor the Government nor the Nation wanted the war. It was only the collapse of our nation which compelled a weakened race to take upon itself, against its most sacred convictions, the guilt for this war. . . . By a unique upheaval, in the last few weeks our national honour has been restored and, thanks to your understanding, *Herr General-Feldmarschall*, the union between the symbols of the old greatness and the new strength has been celebrated. We pay you homage. A protective Providence places you over the new forces of our Nation.[1]

With these words the Chancellor crossed to the old Marshal's chair and, bending low, grasped his hand: the apostolic succession had been established.

Alone, the old man descended stiffly into the crypt to the tomb of Frederick the Great. Outside, in the March sunshine, the guns roared in salute and, to the crash of trumpets and drums, the German Army, followed by the S.A. and the Stahlhelm, paraded before the President, the Chancellor and the Crown Prince. As night fell a torchlight procession of ten thousand S.S. troops swept through the Brandenburger Tor to the cheers of a huge crowd, while at the Opera Furtwängler conducted a brilliant performance of Wagner's *Die Meistersinger*.

As the French Ambassador later wrote: 'After the dazzling pledge made by Hitler at Potsdam, how could Hindenburg and his friends fail to dismiss the apprehension with which they had begun to view the excesses and abuses of his party? Could they now hesitate to grant him their entire confidence, to concede the full powers he claimed?'[2]

1. *Dokumente der deutschen Politik*, i (1935), pp. 20–4.
2. A. François-Poncet: *The Fateful Years, Memoirs of a French Ambassador in Berlin* (London, 1949), p. 61.

It was the other face of Nazism that was to be seen when the Reichstag assembled in the temporary quarters of the Kroll Opera House two days later. The Enabling Bill which was laid before the House contained five clauses. The first and fifth gave the Government the power for four years to enact laws without the cooperation of the Reichstag. The second and fourth specifically stated that this power should include the right to deviate from the Constitution and to conclude treaties with foreign States, the only subject reserved being the institutions of the Reichstag and Reichsrat. The third provided that laws to be enacted by the Government should be drafted by the Chancellor, and should come into effect on the day after publication.[1]

As the deputies pushed their way in they could see behind the tribune occupied by the Cabinet and the President of the Reichstag, a huge swastika banner filling the wall. Outside, they had had to pass through a solid rank of black-shirted S.S. men encircling the building; inside, the corridors and walls were lined with brown-shirted S.A. troops.

Hitler's opening speech was restrained. He spoke of the disciplined and bloodless fashion in which the revolution had been carried out, and of the spirit of national unity which had replaced the party and class divisions of the Republic.

The Government [he declared] will only make use of these powers in so far as they are essential for carrying out vitally necessary measures. Neither the existence of the Reichstag nor that of the Reichsrat is menaced. The position and rights of the President remain unaffected. It will always be the foremost task of the Government to act in harmony with his aims. The separate existence of the federal States will not be done away with. The rights of the Churches will not be diminished, and their relationship to the State will not be modified. The number of cases in which an internal necessity exists for having recourse to such a law is in itself a limited one. All the more, however, the Government insist upon the passing of the law. They prefer a clear decision.

The Government [he concluded] offers to the parties of the Reichstag the opportunity for friendly cooperation. But it is equally prepared to go ahead in face of their refusal and of the hostilities which will result from that refusal. It is for you, gentlemen of the Reichstag, to decide between war and peace.[2]

After a recess it was the turn of the leader of the Social Democrats, Otto Wels, to speak. There was silence as he walked to the

1. Text in Baynes: vol. I, pp. 420–1.
2. ibid., p. 246.

tribune, but from outside came the baying of the Stormtroopers chanting: 'We want the Bill – or fire and murder.' It needed courage to stand up before this packed assembly – most of the Communists and about a dozen of the Social Democrat deputies had already been thrown into prison – and to tell Hitler and the Nazis to their faces that the Social Democratic Party would vote against the Bill. Wels spoke with moderation; to be defenceless, he added, was not to be without honour. But the very suggestion of opposition had been enough to rouse Hitler to a fury; there was not a scrap of generosity in him for a defeated opponent. Brushing aside Papen's attempt to restrain him, he mounted the tribune a second time and gave the Reichstag, the Cabinet, and the Diplomatic Corps a taste of his real temper, savage, mocking, and brutal. 'I do not want your votes,' he spat at the Social Democrats. 'Germany will be free, but not through you. Do not mistake us for bourgeois. The star of Germany is in the ascendant, yours is about to disappear, your death-knell has sounded.'

The rest of the speeches were an anti-climax. Monsignor Kaas, still clinging to his belief in Hitler's promises, rose to announce that the Centre Party, which had once humbled Bismarck in the *Kulturkampf*, would vote for the Bill, a fitting close to the shabby policy of compromise with the Nazis which the Centre had followed since the summer of 1932. Then came the vote, and excitement mounted. When Göring declared the figures – for the Bill, 441; against, 94 – the Nazis leaped to their feet and with arms outstretched in salute sang the Horst Wessel song.

Outside in the square the huge crowd roared its approval. The Nazis had every reason to be delighted: with the passage of the Enabling Act, Hitler secured his independence, not only from the Reichstag but also from the President. The earlier Chancellors, Brüning, Papen, and Schleicher, had all been dependent on the President's power to issue emergency decrees under Article 48 of the Constitution: now Hitler had that right for himself, with full power to set aside the Constitution. The street gangs had seized control of the resources of a great modern State, the gutter had come to power.

III

In March 1933, however, Hitler was still not the dictator of Germany. The process of *Gleichschaltung* – 'coordination' – by which the whole of the organized life of the nation was to be brought under the single control of the Nazi Party, had still to be carried out. To illustrate what *Gleichschaltung* meant in practice it will be best to take the three most important examples: the federal States, the trade unions, and the political parties. Hitler and Frick had not waited for the passage of the Enabling Act to take steps to bring the governments of the States firmly under their control. Hitler had no intention of allowing such a conflict between Bavaria and the Reich as he had exploited in 1923 to develop again, and he knew that since 30 January there had been renewed talk of restoring the monarchy, and even of secession, in Bavaria. On the evening of 9 March von Epp, with full authority from Berlin, carried out a *coup d'état* in Munich. The Held Government was turned out, and Nazis appointed to all the principal posts. Hitler knew all the moves in the Bavarian political game. When the Prime Minister, Held, applied to the local Army C.-in-C., General von Leeb, for help against the Nazis, von Leeb telephoned to Berlin. He immediately received orders from Colonel von Reichenau at the Defence Ministry to avoid taking any part in internal politics and keep the Army off the streets. The ghost of Lossow had been laid.

Similar action was taken in the other States. Frick intervened, by virtue of the decree of 28 February, to appoint Reich Police Commissars in Baden, Württemberg, and Saxony. In each case they were Nazis, and in each case they used their powers to turn out the Government and put in Nazi-controlled ministries. Prussia was already under the control of Göring's rough hand, and the State elections held there on 5 March produced much the same results as those for the Reichstag. On 31 March Hitler and Frick issued a law dissolving the Diets of all the other States and ordered them to be re-constituted without fresh elections, 'according to the number of votes which in the election to the German Reichstag were given to the electoral lists within each federal State. In this connexion seats falling to the Communist Party will not be given out.'[1] A week later Hitler nominated Reich Governors (Reichsstatthälter in every State, and gave them the power to appoint and remove State Governments, to dissolve the Diets, to prepare and publish State laws, and to appoint and dismiss State officials.[2] All eighteen of the new Reich Governors were Nazis, usually the local Gauleiters. In Prussia the new law afforded an opportunity to turn out Papen, who had

1. Law of 31 March 1933, Article 4, N.D. 2004-PS.
2. Law of 7 April 1933, N.D. 2005-PS.

hitherto united the offices of Vice-Chancellor and Reich Com-missioner for Prussia, with Göring as his subordinate. Hitler now appointed himself Reichsstatthälter for Prussia and promptly delegated his powers to Göring as Prussian Minister-President. Papen 'asked to be relieved of his post', and the office of Reich Commissioner for Prussia, which had been instituted at the time of Papen's *coup d'état* in July 1932, was abolished.

On the first anniversary of Hitler's accession to power, 30 January 1934, a Law for the Reconstruction of the Reich rounded off this work of subordinating the federal States to the authority of the central Government. The State Diets were abolished; the sovereign powers of the States transferred to the Reich; and the Reichsstatthälter and State Governments placed under the Reich Government.[1] This was the culmination of a year of *Gleichschaltung*, in which all representative self-government from the level of the States downwards through the whole system of local government had been stamped out. Although formally the individual States were not abolished, in fact the dual system of government, divided between the Reich and the States, which both the Bismarckian and the Weimar Constitutions had had to tolerate, was swept away. In March 1934, Hitler defined the position of the Reichsstatthälter in terms that left no doubt of his intentions. 'They are not,' he said, 'the administrators of the separate States, they execute the Will of the supreme leadership of the Reich; their commission comes, not from the States, but from the Reich. They do not represent the States over against the Reich, but the Reich over against the States. . . . National Social-ism has as its historic task to create the new Reich and not to preserve the German States.'[2]

The process of *Gleichschaltung* did not stop with the institutions of government. If Hitler meant to destroy Marxism in Germany he had obviously to break the independent power of the huge German trade-union movement, the foundation on which the Social Democratic Party rested. In March and April the S.A. broke into and looted the offices of many local trade-union branches, but the trade-union leadership still hoped that they might obtain recognition from the Government: after all, no previous German Government had ever gone so far as to touch the unions. They, too, were soon disillusioned. The Nazis cleverly camouflaged their intentions by declaring May Day a national

1. Law of 30 January 1934, N.D. 2006-PS.
2. Speech of 22 March 1934 (Baynes: vol. I, pp. 275–6).

holiday, and holding an immense workers' rally in Berlin which was addressed by Hitler. On the morning of the next day the trade-union offices all over the country were occupied by S.A. and S.S. troopers. Many union officials were arrested, beaten, and thrown into concentration camps. All the unions were then merged into a new German Labour Front. 'Once the trade unions are in our hands,' Goebbels commented, 'the other parties and organizations will not be able to hold out long. . . . In a year's time Germany will be entirely in our hands.'[1]

Hitler deliberately avoided placing the trade unions under the existing N.S.B.O. (National Socialist Factory Cell Organization), which was tainted with Socialist ideas and Strasserism. He gave control of the Labour Front to Robert Ley, who had been an opponent of Gregor Strasser's as long ago as 1925, and had replaced him as head of the Political Organization in December 1932. In his initial proclamation Ley declared: 'Workers! Your institutions are sacred to us National Socialists. I myself am a poor peasant's son and understand poverty, I myself was seven years in one of the biggest industries in Germany and I know the exploitation of anonymous capitalism. Workers! I swear to you we will not only keep everything which exists, we will build up the protection and rights of the worker even further.'[2]

Hitler gave similar assurances when he addressed the First Congress of German Workers on 10 May. This speech[3] is well worth comparison with his address to the Industry Club at Düsseldorf a year before, as an example of Hitler's skill in adapting himself to the audience he was facing. But the intentions behind Hitler's talk of honouring labour and abolishing the class war were not long concealed. Before the month was out a new law ended collective bargaining and appointed Labour Trustees, under the Government's orders, to settle conditions of work.[4]

Just as Leipart and Grassmann, the trade-union leaders, had hoped to preserve their organization intact by doing everything possible to avoid provoking the country's new rulers, the Social Democrats too attempted to carry on loyally for a time, even after the Enabling Act had been passed. Their efforts proved

1. Goebbels: p. 280.
2. Proclamation of the Action Committee for the Protection of German Labour, 2 May 1933, N.D. 614-PS.
3. A translation is to be found in Baynes: vol. I, pp. 839–64.
4. Law of 19 May 1933, N.D. 405-PS.

equally futile. On 10 May Göring ordered the occupation of the Party's buildings and newspaper offices, and the confiscation of the Party's funds. Some of the Social Democratic leaders, like Otto Wels, moved to Prague and set up a centre of opposition there; others, like Karl Severing, simply retired into the obscurity of private life. As late as 19 June a new Party committee of four was elected in Berlin, but three days later Frick put an end to their uncertainty by banning the Social Democratic Party as an enemy of people and State. Social Democratic representation on any elected or other public body, like that of the Communists, was annulled.[1] The Communists, of course, had been virtually proscribed since the Reichstag Fire, although for tactical reasons they had been allowed to put forward a list at the Reichstag election. None of their deputies, however, had ever been allowed to take his seat, and on 26 May Hitler and Frick promulgated a law confiscating the entire assets and property of the Party.

The remaining parties represented a more delicate problem, but this did not long delay their disappearance. After the Bavarian People's Party, the ally of the Centre, had seen their offices occupied and their leaders arrested on 22 June – on the pretext of a conspiracy with the Austrian Christian Socialists – the Party announced its own dissolution on 4 July, and was followed by the Centre Party on 5 July. The fact that a Catholic Party no longer existed in Germany was accepted by the Vatican in the Concordat which it concluded with Hitler's Government this same summer. The Democrats (Staatspartei) and the People's Party, which Stresemann had once led, reduced to mere shadows by the success of the Nazis in capturing the middle-class vote, had already immolated themselves.[2] Not even Hitler's partners in the coalition, the Nationalists, were spared. Hugenberg's resistance in the Cabinet and an angry appeal to the President proved ineffectual. On 21 June the police and S.A. occupied the Party's offices in a number of German towns, and a week later the leaders, bowing to the inevitable, dissolved the Party.

On 14 July the Official Gazette contained the brief announcement:

The German Government has enacted the following law, which is herewith promulgated:

1. Law of 7 July 1933, N.D. 2058-PS.
2. The Democrats announced their dissolution on 28 June 1933; the People's Party on 4 July.

Article I: The National Socialist German Workers' Party constitutes the only political Party in Germany.

Article II: Whoever undertakes to maintain the organizational structure of another political Party or to form a new political Party will be punished with penal servitude up to three years or with imprisonment up to three years, if the action is not subject to a greater penalty according to other regulations.

The Reich Chancellor,
Adolf Hitler.
The Reich Minister of the Interior,
Frick.
The Reich Minister of Justice,
Dr Gürtner.[1]

The Stahlhelm took a little longer to absorb. A first step was Hitler's success in persuading Seldte, the Stahlhelm leader and its representative in the Cabinet, to dismiss his second-in-command, Düsterberg, and to join the National Socialist Party himself. A succession of uneasy compromises with the S.A., punctuated by fights between the rival private armies, raids and arrests of Stahlhelm leaders, led to the incorporation of the Stahlhelm in the S.A. by the end of 1933, and to its formal dissolution in November 1935.

The remnants of the old Freikorps were ceremonially dissolved at Munich on the tenth anniversary of the unsuccessful putsch of 9 November 1923. The agitator who had then fled before the shots of the Bavarian police, now the Chancellor of Germany, laid a wreath on the tomb of the martyrs of the movement with the inscription: 'Despite all, you have conquered.' The roll-call of the Freikorps was called one by one – the Freikorps of the Baltic, of Silesia, and the Ruhr, the Ehrhardt Brigade, Oberland, Rossbach, the Hitler Shock Troop and the rest. As each answered 'Present', their stained and tattered flags were borne forward for the last time, and solemnly laid up in the hall of the Brown House under an S.A. guard of honour. It was the closing of a strange and sinister page in the post-war history of Germany. Just as the ceremony at Potsdam in March had marked the claim of the Nazis to be the heirs of the old Prussia, so by the Munich ceremony in November they made good their claim to embody the traditions of the Freikorps.

With the suppression of the parties, the basis of the coalition which had brought Hitler into power disappeared. With the

1. N.D. 1388-A-PS.

passage of the Enabling Law the need for it had gone. Hitler had never been under any illusion about the intention of Papen and Hindenburg to tie him down; but equally, he had never had any doubts of his own ability to sweep away the restrictions with which they attempted to hedge him round. 'The reactionary forces,' Rauschning reports Hitler saying after the Reichstag Fire, 'believe they have me on the lead. I know that they hope I will achieve my own ruin by mismanagement. But we shall not wait for them to act. Our great opportunity lies in acting before they do. We have no scruples, no bourgeois hesitations. . . . They regard me as an uneducated barbarian. Yes, we are barbarians. We want to be barbarians. It is an honourable title.'[1]

As so often later in his foreign policy, Hitler resorted to his favourite tactic of surprise, of doing just the things no one believed he would dare to do, with a bland contempt for convention or tradition. In a few weeks he had banned the Communist and Social Democratic Parties, dissolved the Catholic Centre and the Right-wing Nationalists, and taken over the Stahlhelm and the trade unions, six of the most powerful organizations in Germany – and, contrary to all expectations, nothing had happened. The strength of these organizations, even of a revolutionary party like the Communists, was shown to be a sham. Hitler had scoffed at the tradition of making concessions to Bavarian particularist feeling, and with equal success had ridden rough-shod over the rights of the federal States. The methods of gangsterism applied to politics, the crude and uninhibited use of force in the first, not in the last, resort, produced startling results.

Any opposition in the Cabinet crumpled up before the wave of violence which was eliminating all the political landmarks in the German scene. Papen, shorn of his power as Reich Commissioner in Prussia, was a shrunken figure. Hitler no longer paid attention to the rule that the Vice-Chancellor must always be present when he saw the President; indeed, he rarely bothered to see the President at all, now that he had the power to issue decrees himself. Seldte, the Stahlhelm leader and Minister of Labour, was soon persuaded to hand over his organization to Hitler and surrender his independence. Hugenberg held out till the end of June, but lost his fight to preserve the Nationalist Party, and was forced to resign on 29 June. His place as Minister of Economy was taken by Dr Schmitt. As Minister of Food and Agriculture his successor was Darré, who had already forced the once powerful Land

1. Hermann Rauschning: *Hitler Speaks*, pp. 86–7.

League into a union with his own Nazi *Agrarpolitischer Apparat*, and turned out its Junker president, Graf Kalkreuth, on a framed charge of corruption. Immediately after the elections, Goebbels had been brought into the Cabinet as head of a new Ministry of Public Enlightenment and Propaganda.[1] Three days later, after a short conversation with Hitler, the President of the Reichsbank, Dr Luther, suddenly resigned. His place was taken by Dr Schacht, a former President who had written to Hitler in August 1932, 'to assure you of my unchanging sympathy – you can always count on me as your reliable assistant'.[2]

Thus by the summer of 1933 Hitler was complete master of a Government in which Papen only remained on sufferance, and which was independent alike of Reichstag, President, and political allies. All Papen's calculations of January, his assurance that once the Nazi Party was harnessed to the State it would be tamed, had proved worthless. For Hitler had grasped a truth which eluded Papen, the political dilettante, that the key to power no longer lay in the parliamentary and presidential intrigues by means of which he had got his foot inside the door – and by means of which Papen still hoped to bind him – but, outside, in the masses of the German people. Papen, deceived by Hitler's tactics of legality, had never grasped that the revolutionary character of the Nazi movement would only be revealed after Hitler had come to power, and was now astonished and intimidated by the forces he had released.

For it is a mistake to suppose, as Papen did, that because Hitler came to power by the backstairs there was no genuine revolutionary force in the Nazi Party. The S.A. regarded Hitler's Chancellorship and the election victory of 5 March as the signal for that settling of accounts which they had been promised for so long. In the circumstances of Germany between 1930 and 1933, with the long-drawn-out economic depression and the accompanying political uncertainty and bitterness, the revolutionary impulse of the S.A. was bound to strike echoes in a large section of the German people. This wave of revolutionary excitement which passed across Germany in 1933 took several forms.

Its first and most obvious expression was violence. Violence had been common enough in Germany for many months before 1933, but the violence of the period between the Reichstag Fire and the end of the year was on a different scale from anything that had

1. Decree of 13 March 1933, N.D. 2029-PS.
2. Schacht to Hitler, 29 August 1932, N.D. EC-457.

happened before. The Government itself deliberately employed violence and intimidation as a method of governing, using such agencies as the Gestapo (the Prussian Secret State Police established by Göring), and the concentration camps opened at Oranienburg, Dachau, and other places. At the same time, the open contempt for justice and order shown by the State encouraged those impulses of cruelty, envy, and revenge which are normally suppressed or driven underground in society. Men were arrested, beaten, and murdered for no more substantial reason than to satisfy a private grudge, to secure a man's job or his apartment, and to gratify a taste for sadism. In Berlin and other big cities local S.A. gangs established 'bunkers' in disused warehouses or cellars, to which they carried off anyone to whom they took a dislike, either to maltreat them or hold them to ransom. The normal sanctions of the police and the courts were withdrawn, and common crime from robbery to murder brazenly disguised as 'politics'. The only measure taken by the Government was to issue amnesties for 'penal acts committed in the national revolution'.

This breakdown of law and order, of the ordinary security of everyday life, not from any weakness or collapse of authority, but with the connivance of the State, was a profound shock to the stability of a society already shaken by the years of depression and mass unemployment. Yet violence, if it repelled, also attracted many, especially among the younger generation. It was indeed a characteristic part of revolutionary idealism. For 1933, like other revolutionary years, produced great hopes, a sense of new possibilities, the end of frustration, the beginning of action, a feeling of exhilaration and anticipation after years of hopelessness. Hitler recognized this mood when he told the German people to hold up their heads and rediscover their old pride and self-confidence. Germany, united and strong, would end the crippling divisions which had held her back, and recover the place that was her due in the world. Many people believed this in 1933 and thought that a new era had begun. Hitler succeeded in releasing pent-up energies in the nation, and in re-creating a belief in the future of the German people. It is wrong to lay stress only on the element of coercion, and to ignore the degree to which Hitler commanded a genuine popular support in Germany – so much less, as Mill once remarked, do the majority of the people prefer liberty to power. The law introducing the plebiscite[1] is evidence of the

1. Law of 14 July 1933.

confidence Hitler felt that he could carry a majority of the German people with him, once he had come to power and broken all organized resistance. To suppose that the huge votes which he secured in these plebiscites were solely, or even principally, due to the Gestapo and the concentration camps is to miss what Hitler knew so well, the immense attraction to the masses of force plus success.

Side by side with this – and yet another expression of the mood of 1933 in Germany – went the familiar and seamy accompaniment of all revolutionary upheavals, the rush to clamber on the band wagon and the scramble for jobs and advantages. The Germans invented a word, the *Märzgefallene*, for those opportunists who first joined the Party in March 1933 and were eager to secure the favour of the new bosses. The purge of the civil service, the closing of the professions to Jews,[1] the creation of new posts in government and local government service, in industry and business, whetted the appetites of the unsuccessful, the ambitious, and the envious. Most of the men who now held power in Germany, Hitler himself, Göring, Goebbels, and the thousands of Nazis who had become mayors of cities, Reichstag or Landtag deputies, government officials, heads of departments, chairmen of committees, and directors on company boards belonged to one or other of these classes. The *Altkämpfer*, the Old Fighters, and many who claimed without justification to be Party members of long standing, now crowded their antechambers, clamouring for jobs. Rauschning relates how one man, who asked him for a job in Danzig, shouted at him: 'I won't get down again. Perhaps you can wait. You're not sitting on a bed of glowing coals. No job, man, no job! I'll stay on top no matter what it costs me. We can't get on top twice running.'[2] The six million unemployed in Germany, who had not disappeared overnight when Hitler came to power, represented a revolutionary pressure that was not easily to be dammed.

It was by harnessing these forces of discontent and revolt that

1. Laws purging the civil service were promulgated on 7 April, 30 June, and 20 July 1933, removing any official of Jewish descent and any who had ever shown Left-wing, or even staunchly Republican, sympathies. Admission to the Bar was regulated by a law of 7 April. All journalistic, musical, theatrical, and radio work was brought under the control of Goebbels by the establishment of a Reich Chamber of Culture (22 September), and the journalistic profession was purged by a special law of 4 October.
2. Hermann Rauschning: *Hitler Speaks*, p. 103.

Hitler had created the Nazi movement, and as late as the middle of June 1933 he was still prepared to tell a gathering of Nazi leaders in Berlin: 'The law of the National Socialist Revolution has not yet run its course. Its dynamic force still dominates development in Germany today, a development which presses forward irresistibly to a complete remodelling of German life.' A new political leadership had to be established; it was the job of the National Socialist movement to provide this new ruling class. 'Just as a magnet draws from a composite mass only the steel chips, so should a movement directed exclusively towards political struggle draw to itself only those natures which are called to political leadership. . . . The German Revolution will not be complete until the whole German people has been fashioned anew, until it has been organized anew, and has been reconstructed.'[1]

Hitler used the same language to the S.A. At Kiel on 7 May he told them: 'You have been till now the Guard of the National Revolution; you have carried this Revolution to victory; with your name it will be associated for all time. You must be the guarantors of the victorious completion of this Revolution, and it will be victoriously completed only if through your school a new German people is educated.'[2]

In the early summer of 1933 it seemed probable that this revolutionary wave, with its curious compound of genuine radicalism and job-seeking, would not exhaust itself until every single institution in Germany had been remodelled and brought under Nazi control.

But there was a point beyond which this process could not go without seriously endangering the efficiency of the State and of the German economy. This was a threat to which Hitler, who was now the head of the Government as well as the leader of a Party, could not remain indifferent. The two dangers to which he had to pay particular attention were the disruption of the economic organization of the country, and attempts to interfere with the inviolability of the Army.

Hitler's arrival in power had been accompanied by a recrudescence of Nazi attacks upon the big capitalists. Otto Wagener, the head of the Party's Economic Section in the Brown House, attempted to secure control of the employers' associations which

1. Speech of 14 June, to the *Führertagung* (Baynes: vol. I, pp. 223 and 481–3).
2. Speech of 7 May, at Kiel (Baynes: vol. I, p. 181).

had combined to form the Reich Corporation (Reichstand) of German Industry. Dr Adrian von Renteln, the leader of the Combat League of Middle-Class Tradespeople, established himself as president of the German Industrial and Trade Committee (the union of German Chambers of Commerce), and declared that the Chambers of Commerce would be the cornerstone in the new Nazi edifice of Reich Corporations. The hostility of the small shopkeepers, whom Renteln represented, was especially directed against the department stores and cooperatives. Walther Darré, the new Minister of Agriculture, demanded a drastic cut in the capital value of agrarian debts and the reduction of the rate of interest to two per cent. Men like Gottfried Feder believed that the time had come to put into practice the economic clauses of the Party's original programme, with its sweeping proposals for nationalization, profit-sharing, the abolition of unearned incomes and 'the abolition of the thraldom of interest'. (Points 13, 14, and 11.)

Hitler had never been a Socialist; he was indifferent to economic questions. What he saw, however, was that radical economic experiments at such a time would throw the German economy into a state of confusion, and would prejudice, if not destroy, the chances of cooperation with industry and business to end the Depression and bring down the unemployment figures. Such an argument, an argument which directly touched his own power, took precedence over the economic panaceas peddled by Feder, or the importunate desires of those who believed, as Hitler told Rauschning, that Socialism meant their chance to share in the spoils. Hitler made his changed attitude perfectly clear in the course of July.

To the Reichsstatthälter, gathered in the Reich Chancellery on 6 July, Hitler now said bluntly:

The revolution is not a permanent state of affairs, and it must not be allowed to develop into such a state. The stream of revolution released must be guided into the safe channel of evolution. . . . We must therefore not dismiss a business man if he is a good business man, even if he is not yet a National Socialist; and especially not if the National Socialist who is to take his place knows nothing about business. In business, ability must be the only authoritative standard. . . .

History will not judge us [Hitler continued] according to whether we have removed and imprisoned the largest number of economists, but according to whether we have succeeded in providing work. . . . The ideas of the programme do not oblige us to act like fools and upset everything, but to realize our trains of thought wisely and carefully. In the long run our political power will be all the more secure, the more we succeed in underpinning it economically. The Reichsstatthälter, must therefore see to it that no organizations or Party offices assume the functions of government, dismiss individuals and make appointments to offices, to do which the Reich Government alone – and in regard to business the Reich Minister of Economics – is competent.[1]

A week later Hitler summoned the Gauleiters to Berlin and made the same point to them: 'Political power we had to conquer rapidly and with one blow; in the economic sphere other principles of development must determine our action. Here progress must be made step by step without any radical breaking up of existing conditions which would endanger the foundations of our own life. . . .'[2]

At the end of June when Hitler replaced Hugenberg as Minister of Economy and Trade he chose as his successor Dr Schmitt, director-general of the largest insurance company in Germany, the Allianz. Schmitt, like Schacht at the Reichsbank, was wholly opposed to the plans of economic cranks like Feder, who was only made an Under-Secretary. Wagener was dismissed and his place taken by the 'reliable' Wilhelm Keppler, who now became the Führer's Deputy for Economic Questions. Krupp von Bohlen remained as president of the Reich Corporation of German Industry, and Thyssen became chairman of the two powerful Rhineland groups, the Langnamverein[3] and the North-western Employers' Association. The Combat League of Middle-class Tradespeople was dissolved in August: on 7 July, Hess, the deputy leader of the Party, had issued a statement forbidding members of the Party to take any action against department stores and similar undertakings. Darré, it is true, remained as Minister of Agriculture, but no more was heard of his demand to reduce the rate of interest on rural debts to two per cent. Finally, Schmitt let it be known that there would be no further experiments in the corporate development of the national economy, and Hess banned such talk in the Party on pain of disciplinary measures.

1. Hitler's speech to the Reichsstatthälter, 6 July 1933 (Baynes: vol. I, pp. 865–6).
2. Hitler's speech to the Gauleiters, 13 July 1933 (Baynes: vol. I, pp. 484–5 and 867–8).
3. Literally, The Long Name Union, a popular abbreviation of the Association for the Preservation of Economic Interests in the Rhineland and Westphalia.

July 1933 in fact marked a turning point in the development of the revolution. At the end of June, about the time that the crisis over economic policy came to a head, Hitler had been summoned to Neudeck to receive a remonstrance from the President on the turmoil caused by the Nazi 'German Christians' in the Protestant Churches. On his return to Berlin he knocked the Church leaders' heads together and enforced a compromise for the sake of ecclesiastical peace. In a speech which he delivered a few days later at Leipzig he spoke of the ending of the second phase of the battle for Germany: 'We could with a single revolutionary on-rush frame our attack to win power in the State; now before us lies the next phase of our struggle. . . . The great fighting movement of the German people enters on a new stage.'[1] The task of this new phase Hitler described as 'educating the millions who do not yet in their hearts belong to us'.

Hitler's own wish to bring the revolution to an end, for the time being at least, and to consolidate its gains, is plain enough. To quote another sentence of his speech to the Reichsstatthälter on 6 July: 'Many more revolutions have been successful at the outset than have, when once successful, been arrested and brought to a standstill at the right moment.'[2]

Hitler, however, was far from convincing all his followers of the necessity of his new policy. Once again opposition found its strongest expression in the S.A. Its leader was Ernst Röhm, the S.A. Chief of Staff, who spoke in the name of the hundreds of thousands of embittered Nazis who had been left out in the cold, and wanted no end to the revolution until they too had been provided for. At the beginning of August Göring, in line with the change of policy, announced the dismissal of the S.A. and S.S. auxiliary police; they were no longer needed. On 6 August, before a parade of eighty thousand S.A. men on the Tempelhof Field outside Berlin, Röhm gave his answer: 'Anyone who thinks that the tasks of the S.A. have been accomplished will have to get used to the idea that we are here and intend to stay here, come what may.'[3]

From the summer of 1933 to the summer of 1934 this quarrel over the Second Revolution was to form the dominant issue in German politics.

1. Hitler's speech at Leipzig, 16 July 1933 (Baynes: vol. I, p. 638).
2. ibid., vol. I, p. 865.
3. Quoted by Bénoist-Méchin: p. 549; and by Konrad Heiden: *Der Führer*, p. 564.

IV

Throughout the autumn of 1933 and the spring of 1934 for the next nine months demands to renew and extend the Revolution grew louder and more menacing. Röhm, Goebbels, and many of the S.A. leaders made open attacks on *Reaktion*, that comprehensive word which covered everyone the S.A. disliked, from capitalists and Junkers, Conservative politicians and stiff-necked generals, to the respectable bourgeois citizen with a job and the civil service bureaucrats. The S.A. looked back nostalgically to the spring of the previous year, when the gates to the Promised Land had been flung open, and Germany had appeared to be theirs to loot and lord it over as they pleased. Then an official job, a Mercedes, and an expenses account had appeared to be within the reach of every S.A. sub-leader. Now, they grumbled, the Nazis had gone respectable, and many who had secured a Party card only the day before were allowed to continue with their jobs, while deserving *Alte Kämpfer* were left out on the streets. In characteristically elegant language the S.A. began to talk of clearing out the pig-sty, and driving a few of the greedy swine away from the troughs.

While the S.A., which was a genuine mass movement with strong radical and anti-capitalist leanings, became restive, and attracted to it all those dissatisfied elements who sought to perpetuate the revolution, Röhm and the S.A. leadership became involved in a quarrel with the Army. It was the old issue which Röhm had fought over with Hitler in the 1920s. On this subject Hitler's views had never wavered: he was as strongly opposed as ever to Röhm's inveterate desire to turn the S.A. into soldiers and to remodel the Army.

There were particularly strong reasons why Hitler wished to avoid alienating the Army leaders at this time. The willingness of the Army to see Hitler become Chancellor, the benevolent neutrality of the Army during the months following 30 January, in which he successfully crushed all resistance and arrogated more and more power to himself – these were decisive factors in the establishment of the Nazi régime, just as the Army's repudiation of Hitler in 1923 had been decisive for his failure. The key figure in guaranteeing the friendly attitude of the Army was General von Blomberg who took the office of Minister of Defence in Hitler's cabinet. On 2 February, three days after he became Chancellor,

Hitler visited the house of Hammerstein, the Army Commander-in-Chief, and spoke for two hours to the leading generals and admirals.[1] He laid stress on two points which made a powerful appeal to his audience. The first was his promise to restore German military strength by rearmament, the second his assurance that the Army would not be called upon to intervene in a civil war. As an earnest of his willingness to preserve the unique position of the German Army in the state, Hitler promulgated a new Army Law on 20 July which ended the jurisdiction of the civil courts over the military and abolished the republican practice of electing representatives of the rank and file.

The Army remained loyal to its bargain, and Hitler's relations with Blomberg became closer as he began to take the first steps in rebuilding the military power of Germany. Hitler was dependent upon the generals for the technical skill necessary to plan and carry out German rearmament. Looking ahead to the time when the aged President must die, he recognized the importance of having the Army again on his side, if he was to secure the succession to Hindenburg for himself. For both reasons, Hitler was anxious that nothing should disturb the confidence of the Army leaders in the new régime.

Röhm took a different view. By the end of 1933 the S.A. numbered between two and three million men, and Röhm stood at the head of an army more than ten or twenty times the size of the regular Reichswehr. The S.A. leaders, ambitious and hungry for power, saw in their organization the revolutionary army which should provide the military power of the New Germany. Most of the S.A. leaders had come through the rough school of the Freikorps; they were contemptuous of the rigid military hierarchy of the professional Army, and resentful at the way they were treated by the Officer Corps. Like the gangsters they were, they were envious and avid for the prestige, the power and the pickings they would acquire by supplanting the generals. Their motives were as crude as their manners, but undeniably men like Röhm and Heines were tough, possessed ability, and commanded powerful forces. To Rauschning, Röhm grumbled: 'The basis (of the new army) must be revolutionary. You can't inflate it afterwards. You only get the opportunity once to make something big that'll help us to lift the world off its hinges. But Hitler puts me off with fair words. . . . He wants to inherit an

1. A brief account of this meeting was given later by Admiral Raeder, who was present: N.C.A. viii, p. 707.

army all ready and complete. He's going to let the "experts" file away at it. When I hear that word, I'm ready to explode. Afterwards he'll make National Socialists of them, he says. But first he leaves them to the Prussian generals. I don't know where he's going to get his revolutionary spirit from. They're the same old clods, and they'll certainly lose the next war.'[1]

In the long run Hitler was to treat the German generals just as roughly as Röhm would have done, but in 1933–4 he needed their support, and was not prepared to let Röhm and the S.A. spoil his plans. On their side, the generals were adamant in their refusal to accept the S.A. on an equal footing with the Army, and determined to maintain the Army's privileged position in the State. Here was one institution which they were resolved should not be Nazified, and Röhm's pretensions were rejected with contempt.

In a number of speeches in the latter half of 1933, Hitler went out of his way to reassure the generals that he remained loyal to his compact with them. On 1 July, addressing his S.A. leaders at Bad Reichenhall, he declared: 'This army of the political soldiers of the German Revolution has no wish to take the place of our Army or to enter into competition with it.'

On 19 August at Bad Godesberg he repeated: 'The relation of the S.A. to the Army must be the same as that of the political leadership to the Army.'[2] On 23 September, after recognizing the debt the movement owed to the Army at the time he became Chancellor he added: 'We can assure the Army that we shall never forget this, that we see in them the bearers of the tradition of our glorious old Army, and that with all our heart and all our powers we will support the spirit of this Army.'[3]

But the problem of the S.A. remained. If it was not to be incorporated into the Army, as Röhm wanted, what was to become of it? The S.A. was the embarrassing legacy of the years of struggle. In it were collected the 'old fighters' who had been useful enough for street brawling, but for whom the Party had no further use when it came to power and took over the State; the disillusioned radicals, resentful at Hitler's compromise with exist-

1. A conversation with Röhm at Kempinski's in Berlin, in 1933; Rauschning: *Hitler Speaks*, pp. 154–6.
2. Both quotations from Baynes: vol. I, p. 554.
3. Hitler's speech on Stahlhelm Day, 23 September 1933 (Baynes: vol. I, p. 556).

ing institutions; the ambitious, who had failed to get the jobs they
wanted, and the unsuccessful, who had no jobs at all. As the
revolutionary impetus slackened and more normal conditions
began to return, the S.A., conscious of the unpopularity which
their excesses had won for them, began to feel themselves no
longer wanted. In a speech to fifteen thousand S.A. officials in the
Berlin Sportpalast in November 1933, Röhm gave expression to
this mood of frustration in a violent attack on the 'reactionaries',
the respectable civil servants, the business men and the army
officers, on whom Hitler now relied for cooperation. 'One often
hears voices from the bourgeois camp to the effect that the S.A.
have lost any reason for existence,' he declared. But he would
tell these gentlemen that the old bureaucratic spirit must still be
changed 'in a gentle, or if need be, in an ungentle manner'.[1]
Röhm's attack was greeted with loud applause.

Thus the particular issue of the relations between the S.A. and
the Army became part of a much bigger problem. It became a test
case involving the whole question of the so-called Second
Revolution – the point at which the revolution was to be halted –
and the classic problem of all revolutionary leaders once they
have come to power, the liquidation of the Party's disreputable
past.

Hitler first attempted to solve this problem by conciliation and
compromise, a policy to which he clung in the face of growing
difficulties, up to June 1934. A Law to Secure the Unity of Party
and State, promulgated on 1 December, made both Röhm as
Chief of Staff of the S.A., and Hess, the deputy leader of the
Party, members of the Reich Cabinet. So far as Röhm was concerned, this repaired an omission which had long been a grievance
with the S.A.

At the beginning of the New Year Hitler addressed a letter to
Röhm of unusual friendliness, employing throughout the intimate form of the second person singular:

My dear Chief of Staff,
The fight of the National Socialist movement and the National
Socialist Revolution were rendered possible for me by the consistent
suppression of the Red Terror by the S.A. If the Army has to guarantee
the protection of the nation against the world beyond our frontiers, the
task of the S.A. is to secure the victory of the National Socialist Revolution and the existence of the National Socialist State and the community

1. Quoted by Heiden: *Der Führer*, p. 573.

of our people in the domestic sphere. When I summoned you to your present position, my dear Chief of Staff, the S.A. was passing through a serious crisis. It is primarily due to your services if after a few years this political instrument could develop that force which enabled me to face the final struggle for power and to succeed in laying low the Marxist opponent.

At the close of the year of the National Socialist Revolution, therefore, I feel compelled to thank you, my dear Ernst Röhm, for the imperishable services which you have rendered to the National Socialist movement and the German people, and to assure you how very grateful I am to Fate that I am able to call such men as you my friends and fellow combatants.

In true friendship and grateful regard,

Your Adolf Hitler[1]

With Röhm and Hess in the Cabinet more attention was now paid to the needs and grievances of the 'old fighters', and the end of the first year of Hitler's Chancellorship was signalized by a law passed in February 1934, 'Concerning Provision for the Fighters of the National Movement'. Members of the Party or S.A. who had suffered sickness or injury in the political struggle for the national movement were to receive pensions or payments from the State in the same way as those injured in the First World War.

Röhm, however, was not to be silenced by such sops. In February he proposed in the Cabinet that the S.A. should be used as the basis for the expansion of the Army, and that a single Minister should be appointed to take charge of the Armed Forces of the State, together with all para-military and veterans' organizations. The obvious candidate for such a post was Röhm himself. This was to touch the Army on its most tender spot. Hindenburg had only agreed to Hitler's Chancellorship on the express condition that he, and not Hitler, should appoint the Minister of Defence, and the Army would never agree to a Nazi, least of all to Röhm, in such a position. The Army High Command, presented a unanimous opposition to such a proposal and appealed to the President, as the guardian of the Army's traditions, to put a stop to Röhm's attempted interference.

Hitler declined to take Röhm's side in the dispute, and the plan was allowed to drop for the moment. When Mr Eden, then Lord Privy Seal, visited Berlin on 21 February, Hitler was prepared privately to offer a reduction of the S.A. by two-thirds, and

1. Published in the *Völkischer Beobachter* on 2 January 1934, and translated in Baynes: vol. I, p. 289.

to permit a scheme of supervision to see that the remainder neither possessed arms nor were given military training. These proposals were renewed in April. Not only were they a clever piece of diplomatic bargaining on Hitler's part, but they provide an illuminating sidelight on the direction in which he was moving. For, although temporarily checked, Röhm kept up his pressure on the Army, and relations between himself and General von Blomberg, the Minister of Defence, grew strained. Among the captured German documents is a letter of Blomberg's dated 2 March 1934, in which he drew Hitler's attention to the recruitment and arming of special S.A. Staff Guards. 'This would amount to six to eight thousand S.A. men permanently armed with rifles and machine-guns in the area of the VI Military District H.Q. alone.'[1] It is evident that each side in the dispute was taking every opportunity to score off the other.

At the end of March, Hitler indignantly – almost too indignantly – repudiated the suggestion of an Associated Press Correspondent that there were divisions in the Party leadership. A few days later, however, the situation was transformed for Hitler when he and von Blomberg were secretly informed that President Hindenburg could not be expected to live very much longer. Within a matter of months, perhaps of weeks, the question of the succession would have to be settled.

V

It had long been the hope of conservative circles that Hindenburg's death would be followed by a restoration of the monarchy, and this was the President's own wish, expressed in the Political Testament which he signed secretly on 11 May 1934. Although he had at one time found it politic to talk in vague terms of an ultimate restoration, Hitler never seriously entertained the project, and in his Reichstag speech of 30 January 1934 he declared the times to be inopportune for such a proposal. He was equally opposed to a perpetuation of the existing situation. So long as the independent position of the President existed alongside his own, so long as the President was Commander-in-Chief of the Armed Forces, and so long as the oath of allegiance was taken to the President and not to himself, Hitler's power was something less than absolute. While the old Field-Marshal remained alive Hitler had to accept this limitation, but he was determined that when

1. N.D. D-951, with Röhm's reply.

Hindenburg died he and no one else should succeed to the President's position. It was to Adolf Hitler, and not to a possible rival, that the Armed Forces should take the new oath of allegiance. The first and most important step was to make sure of the Army, whose leaders, in the tradition of General von Seeckt, claimed to represent the permanent interests of the nation independently of the rise and fall of governments and parties. This was a claim which it was virtually certain Hitler would sooner or later challenge; but he was content to bide his time and negotiate for the Army's support on the generals' own terms.

In the second week of April an opportunity presented itself. On 11 April Hitler left Kiel on the cruiser *Deutschland* to take part in naval manoeuvres. He was accompanied by General von Blomberg, the Minister of Defence; Colonel General Freiherr von Fritsch, the Commander-in-Chief of the German Army, and Admiral Raeder, the Commander-in-Chief of the German Navy. It is believed to have been during the course of this short voyage that Hitler came to terms with the generals: the succession for himself, in return for the suppression of Röhm's plans and the continued inviolability of the Army's position as the sole armed force in the State. On his return from East Prussia Hitler quietly renewed his offer to the British and French Governments to reduce the S.A. On the Army side, a conference of senior officers under Fritsch's chairmanship which met at Bad Nauheim on 16 May, to discuss the question of the succession, endorsed Blomberg's decision in favour of Hitler after – but only after – the terms of the *Deutschland* Pact had been communicated to them.

The news of Hitler's offer to cut down the numbers of the S.A., which leaked out and was published in Prague, sharpened the conflict between Röhm and the Army. Röhm had powerful enemies inside the Party as well as in the Army. Göring, who had been made a general by Hindenburg to his great delight at the end of August 1933, once in power gravitated naturally towards the side of privilege and authority, and was on the worst of terms with the Chief of Staff of the S.A. He began to collect a powerful police force 'for special service', which he kept ready under his own hand at the Lichterfelde Cadet School near Berlin. On 1 April 1934, Himmler, already head of the Bavarian police and Reichsführer of the black-shirted S.S., was unexpectedly appointed by Göring as head of the Prussian Gestapo. With the help of Reinhard Heydrich, Himmler was engaged in building up a police empire within the Nazi State, and it appears likely that Göring surrendered his authority over the Gestapo with an ill grace. But Göring found in Himmler an ally against a common enemy, for the first obstacle Himmler sought to remove from his path was Ernst Röhm. Himmler and his S.S. were still a part of the S.A. and subordinate to Röhm's command, although the rivalry between the S.A. and S.S. was bitter, and Röhm's relationship with Himmler could hardly have been less cordial. When the time came, the S.S. corps d'élite provided the firing-squads for the liquidation of the S.A. leaders, while Himmler – far more than the generals – was the ultimate beneficiary of the humbling of the rival S.A. Hess, Bormann, and Major Buch (the chairman of the Uschla) were meanwhile diligent in collecting complaints and scandals – and there were plenty – about Röhm and the other S.A. leaders.

Röhm's only friends in the Party leadership were Goebbels and – paradoxically enough – the man who had him murdered, Hitler. Goebbels was by temperament a radical and more attracted by the talk of a Second Revolution than by the idea of any compromise with the *Reaktion*, which he continued to attack in his speeches and articles. It was Goebbels who still kept in touch with Röhm and maintained a link between the Chief of Staff and Hitler until the middle of June. Only at the last moment did the Minister of Propaganda come over to the other side and turn against Röhm, in the same way that he had betrayed Strasser in 1926. As for Hitler, whatever view is taken of the conflict which was going on in his mind it is clear that it was not until the latter part of June that he was persuaded to move against Röhm and the S.A., as Göring and Himmler had been urging him to do for some time past.

Röhm's strength lay in the S.A. troops, and his closest associates were all prominent S.A. leaders. But Röhm himself and other S.A. leaders, like the brutal and corrupt Heines, had acquired a bad reputation for the disorder, luxury, and per-version of their way of living. Although it suited Hitler and Röhm's enemies to play this up after his murder,[1] there is no doubt that it had seriously weakened Röhm's position, even if

---

1. In Hitler's Order of the Day to the S.A. after Röhm's execution he made great play with such charges as luxurious staff-headquarters, costly banquets, expensive limousines, the misuse of official funds, sexual per-version, and moral corruption. Cf. also his apologia before the Reichstag, 13 July 1934, printed in Baynes: vol. I, pp. 290–328.

there were few among the other Nazi leaders who were well placed to cast reproaches. By the middle of May, Röhm so far recognized that the S.A. were on the defensive as to send out an order dated 16 May, instructing his local leaders to keep a record of all complaints and attacks directed against the S.A.[1]

The history of the following weeks can only be reconstructed with difficulty. The outlines of the situation are clear enough, but the parts played by individuals, by Goebbels and by Strasser, for instance; the intentions of the two principal actors, Hitler and Röhm; whether there ever was a conspiracy, and if so who was involved in it – all these represent questions to which more than one answer can be given. The official accounts fail to cover all the known facts and involve obvious contradictions, while the accounts compiled from the evidence of men who survived and from hearsay necessarily contain much that is unverifiable, even where it rings true. Unfortunately, the documentary material captured in Germany at the end of the Second World War and so far published has yielded virtually nothing: perhaps this was one of the episodes in the history of the Third Reich of which no records were allowed to remain.

The situation with which Hitler had to deal was produced by the intersection of three problems, the problems of the Second Revolution, of the S.A. and the Army, and of the succession to President von Hindenburg. Neither the first nor the second of these was new, and Hitler's instinct was to attempt to ride out the crisis and avoid making an outright decision in favour of either side. It was the third problem, that of the succession, which introduced a note of urgency by making Hitler's own position vulnerable.

If Hitler was to secure their support for his succession to the Presidency, the Army and the conservative interests with which the Army leadership was identified were determined to exact in return the removal of the S.A. threat to take over the Army and renew the revolution. The only alternative to accepting their terms was that urged by Röhm – for Hitler himself to take the lead in renewing the revolution and, relying on the S.A., to destroy any opposition by force. But this was a course which would create more problems than it would remove. It would

1. Printed in *Weissbuch über die Erschiessungen des 30. Juni 1934* (Carrefour, Paris, 1934), pp. 57–8. This is a report produced by German émigrés, including a number who escaped at the time of the purge.

mean the risk of open conflict with the Army, avoidance of which had been a guiding principle with Hitler ever since the fiasco of 1923; it would divide and weaken the nation, wreck the chances of economic recovery and possibly produce international complications, even the threat of foreign intervention.

For weeks these were the considerations which Hitler weighed in his mind. Driven at last to decide, he chose to stand by his agreement with the Army and repudiate the Revolution, but for as long as possible he sought to avoid a decision. When he had made it, he disguised it as action forced on him not by pressure from the Right, but by disloyalty and conspiracy on the Left.

On 4 June Hitler sent for Röhm and had a conversation with him which lasted for five hours. According to Hitler's later account of this talk, he warned Röhm against any attempt to start a Second Revolution – 'I implored him for the last time to oppose this madness of his own accord, to use his authority to stop a development which in any event could only end in a catastrophe.'[1] At the same time as he assured Röhm that he had no intention of dissolving the S.A., Hitler reproached him with the scandal created by his own behaviour and that of his closest associates in the S.A. leadership. What else was said is not known, but it would be surprising if Hitler did not mention the succession to Hindenburg and the difficulties which Röhm was creating for him by antagonizing the Army. It would be equally surprising if Röhm did not attempt to win Hitler over to his view of the future of the S.A. as the core of a new army. Whatever was said between the two men, a day or two later Hitler ordered the S.A. to go on leave for the month of July, returning to duty on 1 August, while Röhm announced on 7 June that he himself was about to take a period of sick leave. During their leave the S.A. were forbidden to wear their uniforms or to take part in any demonstrations or exercises. This was evidently Hitler's way of relieving the tension and freeing himself temporarily of the embarrassment of his more impetuous followers. Lest there should be any misunderstanding, however, Röhm issued his own communiqué to the S.A.

I expect, then, on 1 August that the S.A., fully rested and strengthened, will stand ready to serve the honourable tasks which People and Fatherland may expect from them. If the foes of the S.A. are nursing the hope that the S.A. will not return from their leave, or that a part only will

1. Hitler's speech to the Reichstag, 13 July 1934 (Baynes: vol. I, p. 316).

return, we are ready to let them enjoy this hope for a short time. At the hour and in the form which appears to be necessary they will receive the fitting answer. The S.A. is, and remains, Germany's destiny.[1]

Röhm's statement certainly suggests that Hitler had failed to persuade him to moderate his attitude, but Röhm left Berlin in the belief that no decision would be taken in the near future. Hitler indeed agreed to attend a conference of S.A. leaders to discuss the future of the movement at Wiessee, near Munich, on 30 June. It was a rendezvous which Hitler did not fail to keep.

What then happened between 8 June and 30 June?

Hitler gave his version in his speech of 13 July. According to this, Röhm through the agency of a certain Herr von A. (identified as Werner von Alvensleben) had renewed his old relations with General von Schleicher. The two men, according to Hitler, agreed on a concrete programme:

1. The present régime in Germany could not be supported.
2. Above all the Army and all national associations must be united in a single band.
3. The only man who could be considered for such a position was the Chief of Staff, Röhm.
4. Herr von Papen must be removed, and Schleicher himself would be ready to take the position of Vice-Chancellor, and in addition further important changes must be made in the Reich Cabinet.[2]

Since Röhm was not sure that Hitler would agree to such a programme – and it appears that it was still proposed to retain Hitler as Chancellor – he made preparations to carry out his plan by a *coup*, the main role in which was to be played by the S.A. Staff Guards, to which, as we have already seen, Blomberg had drawn Hitler's attention. To complete the conspiracy, Hitler continued, Schleicher and General von Bredow got in touch with 'a foreign Power' (later identified as France). At the same time Gregor Strasser, who had retired into private life after Hitler's Chancellorship, was brought into the plot.

After his talk with Hitler on 4 June, Röhm – still according to Hitler's version – pressed on with plans to capture the Government quarter in Berlin and take Hitler captive, hoping to use his authority to call out the S.A. and paralyse the other forces in the State. The action taken at the end of June was directed, Hitler claimed, to forestalling Röhm's putsch which was about to be staged in a matter of hours.

1. *Frankfurter Zeitung*, 10 June 1934; translated by Baynes: vol. I, p. 287.
2. ibid., p. 311.

Part of this story can with some certainty be rejected as untrue from the beginning. If Röhm was preparing to make a putsch, his plans were certainly not ready to be put into operation at the end of June. All the evidence shows that the S.A. leaders were taken completely by surprise. On the very day he was supposed to be storming the Chancellery in Berlin, Röhm was seized in bed at the hotel in Wiessee where he was taking a cure and awaiting Hitler's arrival for the conference they had arranged. Most of the other S.A. leaders were either on their way to Wiessee or had actually arrived. Karl Ernst, the S.A. leader in Berlin (whom Hitler represented as one of the most important figures in the plot), was taken prisoner at Bremen, where he was about to leave by boat for a honeymoon in Madeira. The whole story of an imminent *coup d'état* was a lie, either invented later by Hitler as a pretext for his own action, or possibly made use of at the time by Göring and Himmler to deceive Hitler and force him to move against Röhm. Frick, the Minister of the Interior, testified after the war that it was Himmler who convinced Hitler that Röhm meant to start a putsch.[1] Indeed, the view that Hitler genuinely, although mistakenly, believed that he had to deal with a conspiracy would fit very well with his own behaviour at the time. So great was Hitler's capacity for self-dramatization and duplicity, however, and so convenient the pretext, that it would be wiser, on the evidence we have, to keep an open mind.

By the time he came to make his Reichstag speech even Hitler seems to have realized that there was precious little substance in his accusation of intrigues with a foreign Power.[2] Whatever contacts Schleicher or Röhm had with the French Ambassador, or any other foreign representative, appear to have been entirely casual, and the German Foreign Ministry later presented a note to the Quai d'Orsay in Paris officially stating that any suspicions directed against the French Ambassador in Berlin were wholly without foundation.[3]

Stripped of its mysterious foreign complications and its melodramatic denouement in an S.A. march on Berlin at the end of June, there remains the double charge that Röhm discussed with

1. Frick's Affidavit, 19 November 1945. N.D. 2950-PS.
2. cf. the remark in his speech that the meeting of Schleicher and Röhm with a foreign diplomat under suspicious circumstances deserved punishment with death 'even if it should prove that at a consultation which was thus kept secret from me they talked of nothing save the weather, old coins, and like topics' (Baynes: vol. I, pp. 323-4).
3. François-Poncet, pp. 138-41.

Schleicher – possibly also with Strasser – the programme outlined by Hitler, and that there was talk in the S.A. leadership of forcing Hitler to take the lead in a revolutionary settlement which would include the establishment of the S.A. as the nucleus of the new German Army. Neither charge is implausible. Röhm certainly had such ambitions for his S.A. and made no secret of them. He had been in close relations with Schleicher before 30 January 1933 – so had Gregor Strasser, who was to have been Schleicher's Vice-Chancellor. Schleicher was an able, ambitious and unscrupulous intriguer. At one time he had thought of incorporating the S.A. as a reserve for the Army; and he had plenty of reason for seeking to revenge himself on Papen, as well as on Blomberg and the other generals who had accepted his dismissal in January 1933 without protest. But this remains speculation, and the one fact that is established, namely, that Schleicher and Strasser were both shot in the same purge as Röhm, is open to a very different interpretation. For, if there were two men in Germany who might well have felt insecure in the event of any purge, two men whom Hitler was certain to regard as dangerous, whatever they did, they were Gregor Strasser and Kurt von Schleicher. There were many old scores levelled on the week-end of 30 June 1934, and the murder of Schleicher and Strasser may well fall into this category.

As to the second charge, it is very likely that Röhm and those who shared his views discussed how to win Hitler over and force his hand, but there is no proof at all that such discussions had gone so far as to merit the name of a conspiracy. The conspirators of June 1934 were not Röhm and the S.A., but Göring and Himmler, the enemies of Röhm; the treachery and disloyalty were not on Röhm's side, but on theirs and Hitler's; and if ever men died convinced – not without reason – that they had been 'framed', it was the men who were shot on 30 June 1934.

Without being dogmatic, therefore, there is good reason to regard the account which Hitler gave of these events with suspicion, as the awkward apologia of a murderer seeking to justify his crime by defaming his victims.

VI

Throughout June 1934 there was an ominous tension in Berlin, heightened by rumours and much speculation. At the end of May both Brüning and Schleicher were warned that, in the event of a purge, their lives were in danger. The possibility of such a purge was now widely canvassed, although there were the most divergent accounts of who was to make the purge and who was to be purged. Brüning took the advice seriously and left for Switzerland; Schleicher went no farther than the Starnbergersee, and returned in time to be shot.

On 14 June Hitler made his first foreign visit since becoming Chancellor, and flew to Venice for the first of many celebrated conversations with Mussolini. The first, as it happened, was among the least auspicious of all. Mussolini, at the height of his reputation and resplendent with uniform and dagger, patronized the worried Hitler, who appeared in a raincoat and a soft hat. Mussolini was not only pressing on the subject of Austria, where Nazi intrigues were to lead to trouble before the summer was out, but frank in his comments on the internal situation in Germany. He advised Hitler to put the Left wing of the Party under restraint, and Hitler returned from Venice depressed and irritable.

No part is more difficult to trace in this confused story than that played by Gregor Strasser – if indeed he played any part at all other than that of victim. Hitler had apparently renewed touch with Strasser earlier in the year, and, according to Gregor's brother Otto, saw him the day before he left for Venice, in order to offer him the Ministry of National Economy. Strasser, always a poor politician, made the mistake of imposing too many conditions, demanding the dismissal of both Göring and Goebbels. This was more than Hitler could agree to, and he let Strasser go.

About the same time, again according to Otto Strasser, Goebbels had been seeing Röhm secretly in a back room of the Bratwurst-Glöckle tavern[1] in Munich. Immediately on Hitler's return from Venice Goebbels reported to him on his conversations with the S.A. Chief of Staff.

These attempts to keep in touch with Strasser, the one-time leader of the Left wing of the Party, and with Röhm, the leader of the S.A., in which radicalism was endemic, were evidently related to a conflict still going on in Hitler's mind. What were the terms of this conflict? Two explanations seem possible. The first is the explanation usually given, that Hitler was weighing the advantages of going with the radicals against the *Reaktion*, or with the Army and the Right against the radicals. On this view he kept in touch with Röhm and allowed Goebbels to go on with his talks,

1. The victims of the purge are reported to have included the landlord and headwaiter of the Bratwurst-Glöckle, who had seen too much.

because he had still not made up his mind. The second explanation is that given by Hitler himself. In his speech of 13 July he
said: 'I still cherished the secret hope that I might be able to spare
the movement and my S.A. the shame of such a disagreement and
that it might be possible to remove the mischief without severe
conflicts.'[1]

On this view Hitler was preoccupied not with the choice
between the radicals and the *Reaktion*, between the S.A. and the
Army, but with the possibility of postponing such a choice and
patching up a compromise, at least until the question of the succession had been decided. On *a priori* grounds this seems a more
plausible explanation of Hitler's hesitation than that of vacillation
between the reactionary and the revolutionary course. For it is
difficult to believe that Hitler ever contemplated the risk of an
open clash with the Army, whereas it is very easy to believe that
he was eager to avoid dealing a heavy blow to the Party, by
delaying action in the hope that Hindenburg might die suddenly,
or that in some other way the crisis could be solved without
irrevocable decisions. At present there is not sufficient evidence
to decide in favour of one view or the other.

At this stage Hitler was given a sharp reminder of the realities
of the situation from an unexpected quarter. Papen had dropped
into the background since the spring of 1933, but he remained
Vice-Chancellor and still enjoyed the special confidence of the old
President. The divisions within the Party offered him a chance of
re-asserting his influence, and for the last time he made use of
his credit with the President to stage a public protest against the
recent course, and, even more, against the prospective course, of
events in Germany. If Hitler refused to listen, or if his protest led
to trouble, then Papen hoped and believed that he would have
the support of Hindenburg, who was equally unhappy about the
state of affairs in Germany. In case of need Papen counted on the
President's ordering the Army to intervene.

Papen's protest was drafted for him by Edgar Jung, with the
cooperation of a number of others who belonged to the Catholic
Action group and hoped to use Papen as the mouthpiece of their
ideas. Amongst them were Papen's secretaries, von Bose and von
Detten, and Erich Klausener, the leader of Catholic Action. The
protest was made in the course of a speech at the University of
Marburg on 17 June and crystallized the anxieties and uncertain-

1. Baynes: vol. I, p. 309.

ties of the whole nation. It was studded with references to Catholic and Conservative principles, but its outstanding passages were those which dealt with the talk of a Second Revolution and the shortcomings of Nazi propaganda.

It goes without saying [Papen declared] that the supporters of the revolutionary principle will first of all occupy the positions of power. But when the revolution is completed, then the government can represent only the totality of the nation. . . . We cannot think of repeating the division of the people, on the ancient Greek model, into Spartans and Helots. . . . Selection indeed is necessary, but the principle of natural selection must not be replaced by the criterion of adherence to a special political doctrine.

The Vice-Chancellor then turned specifically to the talk of a Second Revolution.

Whoever toys irresponsibly with such ideas should not forget that a second wave of revolution might be followed by a third, and that he who threatens to employ the guillotine may be its first victim.

Nor is it clear where such a second wave is to lead. There is much talk of the coming socialization. Have we gone through the anti-Marxist revolution in order to carry out a Marxist programme? . . . Would the German people be the better for it, except perhaps those who scent booty in such a pillaging raid? . . . No people can afford to indulge in a permanent revolt from below if it would endure in history. At some time the movement must come to a stop and a solid social structure arise. . . . Germany must not embark on an adventure without a known destination, nobody knowing where it will end. History has its own clock. It is not necessary continually to urge it on.

No less outspoken were the references to the mishandling of propaganda:

Great men [Papen remarked] are not created by propaganda, but grow until their deeds are acknowledged by history. Nor can Byzantinism cheat these laws of Nature. Whoever speaks of Prussians should first of all think of quiet, selfless service, and of reward and recognition only at the very last, or best, not at all.

In his concluding passage Papen returned to the place and purpose of propaganda:

If one desires close contact and unity with the people, one must not underestimate their understanding. One must return their confidence and not everlastingly keep them in leading strings. . . . No organization, no propaganda, however excellent, can alone maintain confidence in the long run. It is not by incitement, especially the incitement of youth, and not by threats against the helpless part of the nation, but only by talking things over with people that confidence and devotion can be maintained. ... It is time to join together in fraternal friendship and respect for all our fellow countrymen, to avoid disturbing the labours of serious men and to silence fanatics.[1]

The same day that Papen made his speech at Marburg, Hitler spoke at Gera and was scathing in his references to 'the pygmy who imagines he can stop with a few phrases the gigantic renewal of a people's life'.[2] But Papen's protest was not so easily brushed aside. Goebbels took immediate steps to ban its publication, seizing a pamphlet version and the edition of the *Frankfurter Zeitung* in which the text had been printed, but copies were smuggled out of Germany and published abroad, creating a sensation which did not fail to penetrate to Germany. When Papen appeared in public at Hamburg on 24 June he was loudly cheered. It was evident that he had spoken for a great part of the nation.

On 20 June Papen went to see Hitler and demand the removal of the ban on publishing his speech. In a stormy interview Papen threatened his own and the resignation of the other conservative ministers in the Cabinet – von Neurath, the Foreign Minister, and Schwerin von Krosigk, the Minister of Finance. Goebbels continued to make speeches attacking the upper classes and the *Reaktion* as the enemies of National Socialism,[3] but Hitler saw quite clearly that he was face to face with a major crisis and that action could not be deferred much longer. If he had any doubts, they were removed by his reception when he flew to Neudeck on 21 June to see the ailing President. He was met by the Minister of Defence, General von Blomberg, with an uncompromising message: either the Government must bring about a relaxation of the state of tension or the President would declare martial law and hand over power to the Army. Hitler was allowed to see the President only for a few minutes, but the interview, brief though it was, sufficed to confirm von Blomberg's message. The Army was claiming the fulfilment of its bargain, and by now Hitler must have realized that more was at stake than the succession to the Presidency: the future of the whole régime was involved.

1. I have used with slight modifications the English translation printed by Oswald Dutch in his life of von Papen, *The Errant Diplomat* (London, 1941), pp. 191–209.
2. Baynes: vol. I, 231–2.
3. e.g. at Essen on 24 June.

It is impossible to penetrate Hitler's state of mind in the last week of June. Obviously he must have been aware of the preparations which were now rapidly put in hand and have agreed to them at least tacitly, yet to the very last day he seems to have hesitated to take the final step. At this stage it was not Hitler but Göring and Himmler who gave the orders and prepared to eliminate their rivals in the Party leadership. In the background the Army made its own arrangements. On 25 June the Commander-in-Chief, General von Fritsch, placed the Army in a state of alert, ordering all leave to be cancelled and the troops to be confined to barracks. On 28 June the German Officers' League expelled Röhm, and on 29 June the *Völkischer Beobachter* carried a signed article by General von Blomberg, the Minister of Defence, which was a plain statement of the Army's position.

The Army's role [Blomberg wrote] is clearly determined; it must serve the National Socialist State, which it affirms with the deepest conviction. Equally it must support those leaders who have given it back its noblest right to be not only the bearer of arms, but also the bearer, recognized by State and people, of their unlimited confidence. ... In the closest harmony with the entire nation ... the Army stands, loyal and disciplined, behind the rulers of the State, behind the President, Field-Marshal von Hindenburg, its Supreme Commander, and behind the leader of the Reich, Adolf Hitler, who came from its ranks and remains one of ours.[1]

The Army leaders were quite content to leave it to Göring and Himmler to carry out the purge, but after Blomberg's article there could be no doubt that whatever was done would be done with their blessing.

On Thursday, 28 June, Hitler, who had only just returned from Bavaria, left Berlin for Essen to attend the marriage of the local Gauleiter, Terboven. It is possible, as some accounts report, that he also went to see Krupp and Thyssen; even so, his absence from the capital at so critical a time is curious and suggests that he was either deliberately trying to lull the suspicions of the watchful, or else refusing to take part in preparations to which he was only half reconciled. While he was away, on the 28th, Göring and Himmler ordered their police commandos and S.S. to hold themselves in readiness.

Far away from the tension and rumours of Berlin, on the shores of the Tegernsee, Röhm continued to enjoy his sick leave with his usual circle of young men, and to prepare lazily for the S.A.

1. *Weissbuch*, p. 70.

conference at the week-end, at which Hitler was expected. So little was he aware of what was being planned that he had left his Staff Guards in Munich. His carelessness and confidence are astonishing. Yet, even in Berlin, the local S.A. leader, Karl Ernst, who was uneasily aware of something in the wind and alerted the Berlin S.A. on the afternoon of 29 June, was so far misled as to believe the danger was a putsch by the Right directed against Hitler. Ernst never understood what had happened, even after his arrest, and died shouting: '*Heil Hitler.*'

On the 29th Hitler, still keeping away from Berlin, made a tour of labour camps in Westphalia, and in the afternoon stopped at Godesberg on the Rhine, where in 1938 he was to receive Neville Chamberlain. At Godesberg he brought himself to take the final decision. Goebbels, who in the past few days had hurriedly dropped his radical sympathies and his contacts with Röhm, brought the news that the Berlin S.A., although due to go on leave the next day, had been suddenly ordered to report to their posts. Other alarming news of S.A. restlessness is said to have come from Munich. Whether Hitler really believed that this was the prelude to an S.A. mutiny, as he later claimed, it is impossible to say. He may have been influenced by the news that Dr Sauerbruch, an eminent German specialist, had been suddenly summoned to the bedside of President Hindenburg. During the evening of the 29th, Viktor Lutze, one of the reliable S.A. leaders (he was later appointed to succeed Röhm as Chief of Staff), was brought hurriedly from Hanover to Godesberg to join Hitler, Goebbels, and Otto Dietrich. At two o'clock in the morning Hitler took off from the Hangelar airfield, near Bonn, to fly to Munich. Before leaving he had telegraphed to Röhm to expect him at Wiessee the next day. 'It was at last clear to me that only one man could oppose and must oppose the Chief of Staff.'[1]

The purge had already begun in Munich when Hitler landed at the Oberwiesenfeld airfield at four o'clock on the Saturday morning. On the evening of the 29th Major Buch, the chairman of the Uschla, and the Bavarian Minister of the Interior, Adolf Wagner, formed a group of men including Christian Weber, Emil Maurice, and Joseph Berchthold, dim figures from Hitler's old days in Munich, and arrested the local S.A. leaders on the pretext that they were about to carry out a *coup d'état*. At the Ministry of the Interior, where the S.A. Obergruppenführer, Schneidhuber and

1. Speech of 13 July; Baynes: vol. I, p. 321.

his deputy were held under guard, a Hitler who had now worked himself up into a fury tore off their insignia with his own hand and cursed them for their treachery.

In the early morning of the 30th a fast-moving column of cars tore down the road from Munich to Wiessee where Röhm and Heines were still asleep in their beds at the Hanselbauer Hotel. The accounts of what happened at Wiessee are contradictory. Heines, the S.A. Obergruppenführer for Silesia, a convicted murderer who was found sleeping with one of Röhm's young men, is said to have been dragged out and shot on the road. Other accounts say he was taken to Munich with Röhm and shot there.

Back in Munich, seven to eight hundred men of Sepp Dietrich's S.S. Leibstandarte Adolf Hitler had been brought in from their barracks – the Army providing the transport – and ordered to provide a shooting squad at the Stadelheim Prison. It was there that Röhm had been imprisoned on 9 November 1923, after the unsuccessful Munich putsch; it was there that he was now shot by order of the man whom he had launched on his political career and who seven months before had written to thank him for his imperishable services. Hitler ordered a revolver to be left in his cell, but Röhm refused to use it: 'If I am to be killed, let Adolf do it himself.' According to an eyewitness at the 1957 Munich trial of those involved, he was shot by two S.S. officers who emptied their revolvers into him at point blank range. 'Röhm wanted to say something, but the S.S. officer told him to shut up. Then Röhm stood at attention – he was stripped to the waist – with his face full of contempt.'

In Berlin the executions, directed by Göring and Himmler, began on the night of 29–30 June and continued throughout the Saturday and Sunday. The chief place of execution was the Lichterfelde Cadet School, and once again the principal victims were the leaders of the S.A. But in Berlin the net was cast more widely. When the bell rang at General von Schleicher's villa and the general went to the door, he was shot down where he stood and his wife with him. His friend, General von Bredow, was shot on his doorstep the same evening. Gregor Strasser, arrested at noon on the Saturday, was executed in the Prinz Albrechtstrasse Prison. Göring would certainly have removed Papen too, if he had not been Vice-Chancellor and under the special protection of the President. Despite this, Papen's office was wrecked, he himself was kept under house arrest for four days, two of his advisers, Bose and Edgar Jung, were shot, and two others arrested.

Late on the Saturday, Hitler returned from Munich. Among those who waited at the Tempelhof was H. B. Gisevius, who has described the scene. Göring, Himmler, Frick, and a group of police officers stood watching for the plane. As it dived out of the sky and rolled across the field a guard of honour presented arms. The first to step out was Hitler. 'A brown shirt, black bow-tie, dark-brown leather jacket, high black army boots. He wore no hat; his face was pale, unshaven, sleepless, at once gaunt and puffed. Under the forelock pasted against his forehead his eyes stared dully.' Without saying a word, Hitler shook hands with the group on the airfield; the silence was broken only by the repeated click of heels. He walked slowly past the guard of honour, and not until he had started to walk towards his car did he begin to talk to Göring and Himmler. 'From one of his pockets Himmler took a long, tattered list. Hitler read it through, while Göring and Himmler whispered incessantly into his ear. We could see Hitler's finger moving slowly down the sheet of paper. Now and then it paused for a moment at one of the names. At such times the two conspirators whispered even more excitedly. Suddenly Hitler tossed his head. There was so much violent emotion, so much anger in the gesture, that everyone noticed it. ... Undoubtedly, we thought, they were now informing him of Strasser's "suicide". ... The bathos of the scene, the woebegone expressions, the combination of violent fantasy and grim reality, the gratuitously blood-red sky, 'ike a scene out of Wagner – it was really too much for me.'[1]

The executions went on all day Sunday – while Hitler gave a tea-party in the Chancellery garden – and were not confined to Berlin. A considerable number of people, as many as fifty-four according to the *White Book* later published in Paris, were shot at Breslau, and another thirty-two in the whole of the rest of Silesia. Only on Monday morning did the shooting cease, when the German people, shaken and shocked, returned to work, and Hindenburg addressed his thanks to the Chancellor for his 'determined action and gallant personal intervention, which have nipped treason in the bud'. On Tuesday General von Blomberg conveyed the congratulations of the Cabinet to the Chancellor. The General had already expressed the devotion and fidelity of the Army in an Order of the Day: 'The Führer asks us to establish

1. H. B. Gisevius: *To the Bitter End* (London, 1948), pp. 167–9.

cordial relations with the new S.A. This we shall joyfully endeavour to do in the belief that we serve a common ideal.'[1] The Army was very well satisfied with the events of the week-end.

VII

How many were killed has never been settled. According to Gisevius, Göring ordered all the documents relating to the purge to be burned. Little by little, a list of names was pieced together. Hitler in his speech to the Reichstag admitted fifty-eight executed and another nineteen who had lost their lives. In addition, he mentioned a number of acts of violence unconnected with the plot, which were to be brought before the ordinary courts. The *White Book* published in Paris gave a total of four hundred and one, and listed one hundred and sixteen of them by name.

The largest group of victims belonged to the S.A., and included, besides Röhm, three S.A. Obergruppenführer – Heines, von Krausser, and Schneidhuber; Hans Hayn and Peter von Haydebreck, the Gruppenführer for Saxony and Pomerania, and Karl Ernst, the ex-hotel porter who was S.A. Gruppenführer for Berlin and who was stopped by S.S. gunmen on his honeymoon journey to Bremen, his wife and chauffeur wounded, and he himself brought back unconscious for execution in Berlin. Another group was formed by Schleicher and his wife; his former assistant in the Defence Ministry, General von Bredow; Gregor Strasser; and Papen's two assistants, who served as substitutes for Papen himself, von Bose and Edgar Jung. Bose was talking to two industrialists from the Rhineland in the Vice-Chancellery when he was asked to step into the next room and see three S.S. men who had just arrived: shots rang out, and when the door was opened the S.S. men had gone and Bose was lying dead on the floor. A number of other Catholic leaders were shot, the most important being Erich Klausener, the German leader of Catholic Action.

Many of those murdered had little, if any, connexion with Röhm or the S.A., and fell victims to private quarrels. Kahr, who had played a big role in 1923, but had since retired – he was now seventy-three – was found in a swamp near Dachau; his body was hacked to pieces. Father Bernhard Stempfle, who had once revised the proofs of *Mein Kampf*, was discovered in the woods outside Munich; he had been shot 'while trying to escape'. In Hirschberg, Silesia, a group of Jews was murdered, for no other

---

1. Quoted by Bénoist-Méchin, op. cit.: vol. II, p. 578.

apparent reason than to amuse the local S.S. In Munich, on the evening of 30 June, Dr Willi Schmidt, the music critic of the *Münchener Neueste Nachrichten*, was playing the cello in his flat while his wife made supper and their three children were playing. Suddenly the door bell rang and four armed S.S. men came to take him away without explanation. There never was any explanation, except that the S.S. men were looking for someone else with the same name and shot the wrong man. When Frau Schmidt got her husband's body back, she was warned under no circumstances to open the coffin: the S.S. sent her a sum of money in recognition of her loss and their mistake. When she refused to accept it, Himmler rang up and told her to take the money and keep quiet. When she still refused, Hess called and eventually, through his help, Frau Schmidt secured a pension: she should think of her husband's death, Hess told her, as the death of a martyr for a great cause.[1]

In an effort to prevent too much becoming known, Goebbels forbade German newspapers to carry obituary notices of those who had been executed or 'had committed suicide'. The ban on any mention of what had happened only led to exaggerated rumours and to the intensification of the feeling of horror and fear Not until 13 July did Hitler appear before the Reichstag and reveal a part of the story.

Hitler was very much on the defensive, at least until the end of his speech. He began with a lengthy recital of the achievements of National Socialism, in defence of his policy as Chancellor. When he came to describe the events leading up to 30 June he threw the whole blame on Röhm, who had forced him to act against his own wishes. Hitler gave great prominence to the charges of corruption, favouritism, and homosexuality against Röhm's group, and went out of his way to represent them as betraying the ordinary, decent S.A. man who had been exploited by a depraved and unscrupulous leadership. Hitler did not attempt, however, to conceal the real charges against Röhm. He spoke of those who had become 'uprooted and had thereby lost altogether any sympathy with any ordered human society. They became revolutionaries who favoured revolution for its own sake and desired to see revolution established as a permanent condition.' But, Hitler replied, 'for us the Revolution is no permanent condition. When some mortal check is imposed with violence upon the

1. Deposition of Kate Eva Hörlin, the former wife of Willi Schmidt, 7 July 1945, N.D. L-135.

natural development of a people, then the artificially interrupted evolution can rightly by a deed of violence open up the way for itself in order to regain liberty to pursue its natural development. But there can be no such thing as a state of permanent revolution; neither can any beneficent development be secured by means of periodically recurrent revolts.'

Hitler's references to the quarrel between Röhm and the Army were still clearer. After outlining Röhm's plan for a single organization to incorporate the Army and the S.A., with himself as Minister of Defence, Hitler spoke of his unalterable opposition to Röhm's ideas. 'For fourteen years I have stated consistently that the fighting organizations of the Party are *political* institutions and that they have nothing to do with the Army.' He recalled his promise to Hindenburg that he would keep the Army out of politics, and spoke in glowing terms of his debt to General von Blomberg, the Minister of Defence, 'who reconciled the Army with those who were once revolutionaries and has linked it up with their Government today'. Finally he repeated the promise, which to the Army leaders was the covenant in which they placed their faith: 'In the State there is only one bearer of arms, and that is the Army; there is only one bearer of the political will, and that is the National Socialist Party.'

The Officer Corps, intent only on preserving the privileged position of the Army, and indifferent to what happened in Germany so long as Nazification stopped short of the military institutions of the country, could see no further than the ends of their own noses. The menace of the S.A. was broken for good on the week-end of 30 June. Under Viktor Lutze, its new Chief of Staff, it never again played an independent, or even a prominent, role in the Third Reich. But already a new and far more dangerous challenge to the autonomy of the Army was taking shape. As a reward for their service in the Röhm purge, Himmler's S.S. were now given their independence of the S.A., and placed directly under Hitler's orders with Himmler as Reichsführer S.S. At last the long dispute between Hitler and Röhm was ended, and Hitler had got what he had always wanted, an absolutely dependable and unquestioning instrument of political action. When, in 1936, Himmler acquired control of all German police forces as well, the framework of Hitler's police state was complete. What the Army leaders did not foresee was that, within less than ten years of Röhm's murder, the S.S. would have succeeded, where the S.A. had failed, in establishing a Party army in open rivalry with the generals' army, daily encroaching still further on their once proud but now sadly reduced position. No group of men was to suffer so sharp a reversal of their calculations as the Army officers, who, in the summer of 1934, ostentatiously held aloof from what happened in Germany and expressed an arrogant satisfaction at the Chancellor's quickness in seeing where the real power in Germany lay.

For anyone less blind than the generals, the way in which Hitler dealt with the threat of a second revolution must have brought consternation rather than satisfaction. Never had Hitler made so patent his total indifference to any respect for law or humanity, and his determination to preserve his power at any cost. Never had he illustrated so clearly the revolutionary character of his régime as in disowning the Revolution. At the close of his Reichstag speech Hitler brushed aside the suggestion that the guilty men should have been tried before execution. 'If anyone reproaches me and asks why I did not resort to the regular courts of justice, then all I can say to him is this: in this hour I was responsible for the fate of the German people, and thereby I became the supreme Justiciar (oberster Gerichtsherr) of the German people.' . . . Lest there should be any doubt of the moral to be drawn, Hitler added: 'And everyone must know for all future time that if he raises his hand to strike the State, then certain death is his lot.'[1]

If Hitler's hesitations in the last ten days of June had led people to say that he had virtually abdicated, he triumphantly re-asserted and increased his authority in the week-end that followed. Papen's Marburg speech had its answer, but it was Hitler, not Papen and the *Reaktion*, the peddlers of Christian Conservatism, who emerged triumphant from the test of June 1934.

When Rauschning called on Hitler shortly after the purge, Hitler remarked: 'They underestimate me because I've risen from below; because I haven't had an education, because I haven't the manners that their sparrow brains think right. . . . But I have spoiled their plans. They thought I wouldn't dare; they thought I was afraid. They saw me already wriggling in their net. They thought I was their tool, and behind my back they laughed at me and said I had no power now, that I had lost my Party. I saw through all that long ago. I've given them a cuff on the ear that

1. Baynes: vol. I, pp. 290–328.

they'll long remember. What I have lost in the trial of the S.A., I shall regain by the verdict on these feudal gamblers and professional card-sharpers. . . . I stand here stronger than ever before. Forward, *meine Herren* Papen and Hugenberg! I am ready for the next round.'[1]

The easy assurances of Neurath, who had told Rauschning in the spring of 1934: 'Let it run its course, in five years no one will remember it,'[2] were shown to be as worthless as Papen's confident declarations of January 1933. Papen was glad enough to escape with his life and hurriedly accepted the offer to go to Vienna as Hitler's special envoy. A little late in the day the ex-Vice-Chancellor was beginning to learn that he who sups with the Devil needs a very long spoon.

Now that Hitler had with one blow removed the pressure on him from both the Left and the Right, he could proceed to deal with the problem of the Succession at his leisure. Having honoured his own share of the pact with the Army, he could claim the fulfilment of the Army's promise, and in General von Blomberg he had found a man he could rely on. When President von Hindenburg died on the morning of 2 August, all had been arranged. There was neither hitch nor delay. Within an hour came the announcement that the office of President would henceforward be merged with that of the Chancellor, and that Hitler would become the Head of the State – as well as Supreme Commander-in-Chief of the Armed Forces of the Reich. Among the signatures at the foot of the law announcing these changes were those of von Papen, von Neurath, Graf Schwerin von Krosigk, General von Blomberg, and Schacht: the representatives of Conservatism acquiesced in their own defeat.

The same day the officers and men of the German Army took the oath of allegiance to their new Commander-in-Chief. The form of the oath was significant. The Army was called on to swear allegiance not to the Constitution, or to the Fatherland, but to Hitler personally: 'I swear by God this holy oath: I will render unconditional obedience to the Führer of the German Reich and People, Adolf Hitler, the Supreme Commander of the Armed Forces, and will be ready, as a brave soldier, to stake my life at any time for this oath.' On 6 August, when the Reichstag assembled in the Kroll Opera House to hear Hitler's funeral

1. Rauschning: *Hitler Speaks*, pp. 172–3.
2. ibid., p. 152.

oration, and on 7 August, when the old Field-Marshal was buried with the full honours of State in the monument of his victory at Tannenberg, Hitler renewed the symbolic gesture of Potsdam – but with a difference. Between March 1933 and August 1934 the balance of power in Germany had shifted decisively in Hitler's favour. In that year and a half he had mastered the machine of State, suppressed the opposition, dispensed with his allies, asserted his authority over the Party and S.A., and secured for himself the prerogatives of the Head of the State and Commander-in-Chief of the Armed Forces. The Nazi revolution was complete: Hitler had become the dictator of Germany.

On 19 August the German people was invited to express by a plebiscite its approval of Hitler's assumption of Hindenburg's office as Führer and Reich Chancellor, the official title by which Hitler was now to be known. The Political Testament of President Hindenburg, much discussed but so far not discovered, was now conveniently produced. According to Papen, Hindenburg had decided to omit any reference to the restoration of the monarchy from his testament but to embody a strong recommendation of such a course in a separate letter to Hitler. Both documents were delivered to Hitler, but the letter was never seen again and no more was heard of a restoration. To remove any doubt, Colonel Oskar von Hindenburg was put up to broadcast on the eve of the plebiscite. 'My father,' he told the German people, 'had himself seen in Adolf Hitler his own direct successor as Head of the German State, and I am acting according to my father's intention when I call on all German men and women to vote for the handing over of my father's office to the Führer and Reich Chancellor.'[1]

On the day of the plebiscite 95·7 per cent of the forty-five and a half million voters went to the polls, and more than thirty-eight million voted 'Yes', 89·93 per cent of the votes cast. Four and a quarter millions had the courage to vote 'No'; another eight hundred and seventy thousand spoiled their papers.

It was an impressive majority, and when the Party Rally was held at Nuremberg in September Hitler was in benign mood. In his proclamation he spoke a good deal about the Nazi revolution which had now, he announced, achieved its object and come to an end. 'Just as the world cannot live on wars, so peoples cannot live on revolutions. . . . Revolutions,' he added, 'have always been rare in Germany. The Age of Nerves of the nineteenth century has

1. cf. Papen, *Memoirs*, c. 18.

found its close with us. In the next thousand years there will be no other revolution in Germany.'[1]

It was an ambitious epitaph.

1. Hitler's Proclamation to the Parteitag, 5 September 1934 (Baynes: vol. I, pp. 328–9).

CHAPTER SIX

THE COUNTERFEIT PEACE
1933–7

I

IT does not lie within the scope of this study to present a picture of the totalitarian system in Germany, or of its manifold activities in economic and social policy, the elaboration of the police State, control of the courts, the régime's attitude towards the Churches and the strait-jacketing of education.[1] Hitler bore the final responsibility for whatever was done by the régime, but he hated the routine work of government, and, once he had stabilized his power, he showed comparatively little interest in what was done by his departmental Ministers except to lay down general lines of policy. In the Third Reich each of the Party bosses, Göring, Goebbels, Himmler, and Ley, created a private empire for himself, while the Gauleiters on a lower level enjoyed the control of their own local pashaliks. Hitler deliberately allowed this to happen; the rivalries which resulted only increased his power as supreme arbiter. Nobody ever had any doubt where the final authority lay – the examples of Röhm and Gregor Strasser were there, if anyone needed reminding – and Hitler admitted no equals. But so long as his suspicions were not stirred, he left the business of running the country very much in the hands of his lieutenants. Not until his own position, or special interests, were affected did he rouse himself to intervene actively. An illustration of this is the case of Dr Schacht. 'As long as I remained in office,' Schacht wrote later, 'whether at the Reichsbank or the Ministry of Economics, Hitler never interfered with my work. He never attempted to give me any instructions, but let me carry out my own ideas in my own way and without criticism. . . . However, when he realized that the moderation of my financial policy was a stumbling block to his reckless plans (in foreign policy), he began, with Göring's connivance, to go behind my back and counter my arrangements.'[2]

1. For an excellent summary of the most important facts, the reader should turn to c. 8 of *The Rise and Fall of the Third Reich*, by William L. Shirer (London, 1960).
2. Schacht, pp. 55–6.

Certain subjects, even in internal affairs, always interested Hitler – building plans, and anti-Semitic legislation, for instance – but he rapidly became absorbed in the two fields of foreign policy and preparation for war. At Nuremberg Göring told the Court: 'Foreign policy above all was the Führer's very own realm. By that I mean to say that foreign policy on the one hand, and the leadership of the Armed Forces on the other, enlisted the Führer's greatest interest and were his main activity. He busied himself exceptionally with the details in both these spheres.'[1]

This was not accidental. Hitler was not interested in administration, or carrying out a programme of reform – he was interested in power. The Party had been the instrument by which he acquired power in Germany; the State was now to be the instrument by which he meant to acquire power in Europe. From his schooldays at Linz Hitler had been a violent German nationalist; he felt the defeat of Germany as a personal disaster, and from the beginning of his political career had identified his own ambition with the re-establishment and extension of German power. The reversal of the verdict of 1918, the overthrow of the Peace Settlement of 1919, and the realization of the Pan-German dream of a German-dominated Europe were the hard core of his political programme.

The aggressive – or, to use the favourite Nazi word, dynamic – foreign policy which Germany began to follow under Hitler's leadership corresponded to the most powerful force in modern German history, German nationalism and the exaltation of the *Machtstaat*, the Power State. It gave expression to the long-smouldering rebellion of the German people against the defeat of 1918 and the humiliation of the Peace Settlement. Through the sense of national unity which it fostered, it served to strengthen the political foundations of the régime in popular support. Through the revived industrial activity which it stimulated by the rearmament programme, it helped to overcome the economic crisis in which the Republic had foundered. The recovery and re-assertion of German power abroad were substitute satisfactions for the frustrated social revolution at home; the revolutionary impulse in Nazism was diverted into challenging the existing order outside Germany's frontiers and the creation of a European New Order, in which the big jobs and the privileges would go to the *Herrenvolk*. Above all, such a foreign policy was the logical projection of that unappeased will to power, both in Hitler

1. N.P., Part IX, p. 174.

himself and in the Nazi Party, which, having conquered power in Germany, was now eager to extend its mastery further.

At the time of the French occupation of the Ruhr, in 1923, Hitler had insisted that the first task was to overthrow the Republic, rather than to waste German strength in a fight with the French which the Germans were bound to lose. It ought to have been recognized, he repeats in *Mein Kampf*, 'that the strength of a nation lies, first of all, not in its arms, but in its will, and that before conquering the external enemy the enemy at home would have to be eliminated'.[1] Hitler never wavered in this view. At Düsseldorf in 1932 he argued that Germany's misfortunes were due, not so much to the Treaty of Versailles, as to the internal weaknesses and divisions which allowed the Treaty to be imposed on her. 'We are not the victims of the treaties, but the treaties are the consequences of our own mistakes; and if I wish in any way to better the situation, I must first change the value of the nation; I must above all recognize that it is not the primacy of foreign politics which can determine our action in the domestic sphere – rather, the character of our action in the domestic sphere is decisive for the character of the success of our foreign policy.'[2]

The first prerequisite of a foreign policy was, therefore, to replace the Republic by a strong, authoritarian government in Berlin. That had been done; by now the way was clear for the second stage, the removal of the limitations which had been placed on Germany's freedom of action as the result of her defeat in 1918 and – as Hitler believed – as a consequence of the weakness of the Republican Governments and their betrayal of national interests.

II

In the 1920s Hitler wrote in *Mein Kampf*: 'What a use could be made of the Treaty of Versailles! . . . How each one of the points of that Treaty could be branded in the minds and hearts of the German people until sixty million men and women find their souls aflame with a feeling of rage and shame; and a torrent of fire bursts forth as from a furnace, and a will of steel is forged from it, with the common cry: "*Wir wollen wieder Waffen!* – We will have arms again!"'[3]

1. *Mein Kampf*, p. 555.
2. Speech to the Industry Club at Düsseldorf, 27 January 1932 (Baynes: vol. i, p. 814).
3. *Mein Kampf*, p. 515.

If Hitler ever came to power there was little doubt that his first objective in foreign policy would be to annul the Treaty of Versailles, and in January 1941 he himself said, with considerable justification: 'My programme was to abolish the Treaty of Versailles. It is nonsense for the rest of the world to pretend to-day that I did not reveal this programme until 1933, or 1935, or 1937. Instead of listening to the foolish chatter of émigrés, these gentlemen would have been wiser to read what I have written and rewritten thousands of times. No human being has declared or recorded what he wanted more often than I. Again and again I wrote these words – the Abolition of the Treaty of Versailles.'[1]

In practice, now that reparations had been ended, this could only mean Germany's right to rearm on terms of full equality with other nations, and the recovery of at least part of the territories lost in 1918–19: the Saar, Alsace-Lorraine, the German colonies, above all Danzig, and the lands incorporated in the new state of Poland.

But this was only a part of Hitler's programme in foreign policy, as Hitler had said quite plainly in *Mein Kampf*: 'To demand that the 1914 frontiers of Germany should be restored,' he wrote, 'is a political absurdity. . . . The confines of the Reich as they existed in 1914 were thoroughly illogical; because they were not really complete, in the sense of including all the members of the German nation. . . . They were temporary frontiers established in virtue of a political struggle that had not been brought to a finish.'[2]

It is not difficult to see what Hitler meant by this. His aim was to extend the frontiers of Germany to include those people of German race and speech who, even in 1914, had lived outside the Reich, the Germans of Austria, and the Sudeten Germans of Czechoslovakia, who, before 1914, had formed part, not of the German Empire, but of the Hapsburg Monarchy.

Hitler was an Austrian. This is a fact of the greatest importance in understanding his foreign policy. For, in the 1860s, when Bismarck carried out the unification of Germany and founded the German Empire, he deliberately excluded from it the Germans of the Hapsburg Monarchy. After the collapse of the Hapsburg Monarchy these Germans still remained outside the German Reich: they became citizens either of the Austrian Republic or, like the Germans of Bohemia and Moravia, of Czechoslovakia.

1. Speech in Berlin, 30 January 1941 (Prange: p. 216).
2. *Mein Kampf*, p. 529.

It was amongst these Germans of the old Hapsburg Monarchy that there had sprung up before the war an extreme Pan-German nationalism which sought to re-establish a union of all Germans in a single Greater Germany, and which was now violently opposed to the claims of the Czechs and the other former subject peoples of the Monarchy to nationhood and equality with the Germans. The one exception, already made in *Mein Kampf*, was the German population of the South Tyrol, which was to be sacrificed to the needs of the alliance with Fascist Italy.

Hitler was the heir to the ambitions and animosities of the Pan-German nationalists of the old Monarchy. He saw himself as the man destined to reverse the decision, not only of 1918, but of 1866. Born on the frontier between Germany and Austria, he felt – as he says on the opening page of *Mein Kampf* – called upon to reunite the two German states which had been left divided by Bismarck's solution of the German problem.[1] This is the background to the annexation of Austria, and to the wresting of the Sudetenland from Czechoslovakia. His hatred for the Czechs was the product of his early life in an empire where the Germans felt themselves on the defensive against the rising tide of Slav nationalism, most strongly represented in Hitler's experience by the Czech working men whom he met in Vienna. Here, too, is to be found one of the roots of the distinction Hitler made between the *Volk*, all those of German race and speech, and the State, which need not be co-extensive with the first, or might – as in the case of the old Hapsburg Monarchy and Czechoslovakia – include peoples of different races.

Even this does not exhaust the meaning of Hitler's remark about the inadequacy of Germany's 1914 frontiers. For in the Nazi Party programme, adopted as early as 1920, after the first two points – the union of all Germans to form a Greater Germany, the abolition of the Peace Treaties of Versailles and St Germain – there appears a third: 'We demand land and territory for the nourishment of our people and for settling our surplus population.' The culmination of Hitler's foreign policy is to be found in the demand for *Lebensraum*, living room for the future of the *Volk*, which formed the basis for his programme of expansion.

Ever since the great increase in Germany's population and her

1. Bismarck's solution of the problem of German unity, which excluded the Germans of the Hapsburg Monarchy, was known by the formula of *Kleindeutschland* (Little Germany). The alternative, eventually realized by Hitler with the annexation of Austria and the Sudetenland, was *Grossdeutschland*, Greater Germany.

rapid economic expansion in the second half of the nineteenth century this had been a familiar subject of discussion in Germany. Hitler's criticism of the policy followed up to 1914 is interesting and acute. There are, he says in *Mein Kampf*, four possible answers to the problem of Germany's need to expand. The first two he dismisses as defeatist: these are the limitation of population, and what he calls internal colonization, the intensified development of the territory she already possessed. To adopt either of these alternatives was to give up the struggle, and, since struggle is the law of life, a nation which ceases to struggle ceases to be great.

A third answer was to be found in commercial expansion overseas on the model of England. This was the policy pursued by the Kaiser's Germany, and led inevitably to a disastrous clash with England. It was not a policy suited to the genius or traditions of the German people. These could only find expression in the fourth policy, the one which Hitler advocated, a continental policy of territorial expansion eastwards, seeking *Lebensraum* for Germany in Eastern Europe, in the rich plains of Poland, the Ukraine, and Russia. Such a policy would mean the resumption of that ancient struggle against the Slavs which had founded Austria, the old Ostmark, and had carried the Order of the Teutonic Knights along the southern shores of the Baltic into East Prussia and beyond.

In all this, no doubt, one can discern the influence of Rosenberg, the Baltic German who had fled from Russia after the Revolution. But the belief in the civilizing mission of Germany in Eastern Europe based on her cultural superiority was an old German dream. General Ludendorff, for instance, the least imaginative of men, describes in his memoirs how he felt on taking up his quarters at Kovno:[1]

Kovno is a typical Russian town, with low, mean, wooden houses and wide streets. From the hills which closely encircle the town there is an interesting view of the town and the confluence of the Niemen and the Vilia. On the further bank of the Niemen there stands the tower of an old German castle of the Teutonic Knights, a symbol of German civilization in the East. ... My mind was flooded with overwhelming historical memories: I determined to renew in the occupied territories that work of civilization at which the Germans had laboured in these lands for many centuries. The population, made up as it is of such a mixture of races, has never produced a culture of its own, and, left to itself, would succumb to Polish domination.[2]

1. Later known as Kaunas, the capital of Lithuania.
2. General Erich Ludendorff: *My War Memories* (London, 1919), vol. I, pp. 178–9.

In 1918, when he dictated the Treaty of Brest-Litovsk, which virtually dismembered European Russia, and when a German Army of Occupation proceeded to strip the Ukraine, Ludendorff must have felt well on the way to realizing his historical dreams. Just over twenty years later Hitler was to entertain even more grandiose schemes as a German Army again occupied the Ukraine and German guns shelled Leningrad. The continuity of Germany's eastern policy is impressive.

The logical consequence of such a policy was, of course, war with Russia. Hitler faced and accepted this as early as the 1920s when he was writing *Mein Kampf*.

We put an end to the perpetual Germanic march towards the south and west of Europe [he wrote] and turn our eyes towards the lands of the east. We finally put a stop to the colonial and commercial policy of pre-war times and pass over to the territorial policy of the future. But when we speak of new territory in Europe today, we must principally think of Russia and the border states subject to her. Destiny itself seems to wish to point out the way for us here. . . . This colossal empire in the east is ripe for dissolution.[1]

Bismarck had followed a different policy towards Russia, laying great stress on the need to preserve close relations between Berlin and St Petersburg. After 1918 this conception of foreign policy reappeared in the argument that Germany and Russia should make common cause as the two dissatisfied Powers with an interest in overthrowing the Peace Settlement of 1919. Such a view had advocates in the Army as well as the German Foreign Office, and found a temporary, but sensational, expression in the Treaty of Rapallo of 1922. Hitler was an out-and-out opponent of any such plan. Post-war Russia, he argued, was no longer the Russia with which Bismarck had dealt. Moscow had become the home not only of Bolshevism, but of the Jewish world-conspiracy, the two implacable enemies of Germany. This conflict over the policy to be pursued towards Russia has never been wholly absent from German foreign policy, and it was reflected inside the leadership of the Nazi Party.[2] The pro-Russian school seemed to come into its own at the time of the Nazi-Soviet Pact. But Hitler's

1. *Mein Kampf*, p. 553.
2. General Haushofer, for instance, the founder of the Munich school of geopolitics, and a close friend of Hess, was one of those who favoured a pro-Russian alignment in foreign policy. So, at one time, according to Rauschning, was Erich Koch, the influential Gauleiter of East Prussia. Cf. *Hitler Speaks*, p. 133.

own views altered remarkably little. The Pact was a temporary expedient, no more; and when the German armies invaded the Soviet Union in 1941 it was in execution of a policy the outlines of which are already to be found in *Mein Kampf*.

It was to the conquest of Eastern Europe and Russia that Hitler looked for the opportunity to build his New Order, the empire of the *Herrenvolk* based upon the slave-labour of the inferior races. The year before he came to power, in the summer of 1932, Hitler told a gathering of the Party élite in the Brown House: 'Our great experimental field is in the East. There the new European social order will arise, and this is the great significance of our Eastern policy. Certainly we shall admit to our new ruling class members of other nations who have been worthy in our cause. . . . In fact, we shall very soon have overstepped the bounds of the narrow nationalism of today. World empires arise on a national basis, but very quickly they leave it far behind.'[1] Such plans involved the movement of populations, the deliberate depression of whole races to a lower standard of life and civilization, the denial of any chance of education or medical facilities, even, in the case of the Jews, their systematic extermination.

In these schemes for redrawing the map of the world and remodelling the distribution of power upon biological principles the authentic flavour of Nazi geopolitics is to be discovered. Hitler's over-inflamed imagination set no bounds to the expansion of Nazi power. As Papen remarked after the war: 'It was on the limitless character of Nazi aims that we ran aground.'[2] In the early 1930s these appeared no more than the fantasies with which Hitler beguiled the early morning hours round the fire in the Berghof; by the early 1940s, however, the fantastic was on the verge of being translated into reality.[3]

III

These ideas did not depend upon the triumphs of 1938–41 for their conception. They can be traced from the pages of *Mein Kampf*, through the conversations recorded by Rauschning in 1932–4, up to the talks in the Führer's H.Q. in 1941–2 and Himmler's wartime addresses to the S.S. But in 1933–4, in the first year or two after Hitler had come to power, the prospects of

1. Rauschning: *Hitler Speaks*, p. 50.
2. Papen's Affidavit. N.D. 3300-PS.
3. For a discussion of the Nazi New Order, see below, pp. 692–713.

accomplishing even the annexation of Austria, still less of over-running Russia, appeared remote. Germany was politically isolated. Economically, she was only beginning to recover from the worst slump in her history. Her army, limited to the hundred thousand men permitted by the Treaty, was easily outnumbered by that of France alone. A move in any direction – in the west, against Austria, Czechoslovakia, or Poland – appeared certain to run into the network of alliances with which France sought to strengthen her security. So impressed were the German diplomats and the German generals with the strength of the obstacles in Germany's way that up to 1938, and indeed up to the Battle of France in 1940, their advice was always on the side of caution.

Hitler, on the other hand, became more and more sure of himself, more and more contemptuous of the professionals' advice. He was convinced that he had a far keener appreciation of political – or military – factors than the High Command or the Foreign Office, and he dazzled them by the brilliant success of the bold tactics he adopted. Hitler took office as Chancellor without any previous experience of government. He had never even been a Reichstag deputy, leave alone a minister. He had no knowledge of any country outside Germany and Austria, and spoke no foreign language. His sole experience of politics had been as a Party leader and agitator. He knew nothing and cared less for official views and traditions; he was suspicious of anyone who might try to instruct him. In the short run, these were assets. He refused to be impressed by the strength of the opposition his schemes were likely to meet, or to be restricted to the conventional methods of diplomacy. He displayed a skill in propaganda and a mastery of deceit, a finesse in exploring the weaknesses of his opponents and a crudeness in exploiting the strength of his own position which he had learned in the struggle for power in Germany and which he now applied to international relations with even more remarkable results.

This is not to suggest that Hitler, any more than Bismarck in the 1860s, foresaw in 1933 exactly how events would develop in the course of the next decade. No man was more of an opportunist, as the Nazi-Soviet Pact shows. No man had more luck. But Hitler knew how to turn events to his advantage. He knew what he wanted and he held the initiative. His principal opponents, Great Britain and France, knew only what they did not want – war – and were always on the defensive. The fact that Hitler was ready to risk war, and started preparing for it from the day he came to power, gave him a still greater advantage. Disinclined to bestir themselves, the British and the French were eager to snatch at any hope of avoiding a conflict and only too ready to go on believing in Hitler's pacific assurances.

The first and indispensable step was to rearm. Until he had the backing of military power for his diplomacy, Hitler's foreign policy was bound to be restricted in its scope. This period during which the German Armed Forces were being expanded and re-equipped, was one of considerable danger. Until rearmament reached a certain stage Germany was highly vulnerable to any preventive action which France or the other Powers might take, and the provisions of the Treaty of Versailles could be used to provide grounds for such intervention. The overriding objective of German foreign policy, therefore, for the first years of Hitler's régime was to avoid such action, and thus to secure the time and the freedom to rebuild Germany's military power.

Hitler's speeches from this period are masterpieces of the art of propaganda. He chose his ground with care. Well aware of the fact that there were many abroad – especially in Great Britain – who had long felt uneasy about the shortcomings of the Peace Settlement, he hinged all arguments upon the unequal treatment of Germany after the war and the perpetuation of the distinction between victors and vanquished. This had three great advantages. It invoked sympathy for Germany, the defeated nation unfairly treated. It allowed Hitler to appear as the representative of reason and justice, protesting against the unreasonableness and injustice of Germany's former opponents. It enabled him to turn round and use with great effect against the supporters of the League of Nations all the slogans of Wilsonian idealism, from self-determination to a peace founded upon justice.

Hitler struck this note in the famous *Friedensrede*, or Peace Speech, which he delivered before the Reichstag on 17 May 1933.[1] With an eye to the Disarmament Conference meeting in Geneva, he presented Germany as the one nation which had so far disarmed and now demanded the fulfilment of their promises by the other Powers. If they refused to carry out these promises and disarm themselves, he argued, it could only mean that they sought, under cover of the Peace Settlement and the League of Nations, to degrade the German people permanently to the status of a second-class nation unable to defend itself.

1. Text in Baynes: vol. II, pp. 1,041–58.

Hitler spoke with deep feeling of his dislike of war:

It is in the interests of all that present-day problems should be solved in a reasonable and peaceful manner. . . . The application of violence of any kind in Europe could have no favourable effect upon the political and economic position. . . . The outbreak of such unlimited madness would necessarily cause the collapse of the present social and political order. . . .

On the other hand, the disqualification of a great people cannot be permanently maintained, but must at some time be brought to an end. How long is it thought that such an injustice can be imposed on a great nation? . . . Germany, in demanding equality of rights such as can only be achieved by the disarmament of other nations, has a moral right to do so, since she has herself carried out the provisions of the treaties.

Germany, Hitler continued, was perfectly ready to disband her entire military establishment, to renounce all offensive weapons, to agree to any solemn pact of non-aggression – on one condition only, that the other Powers did the same. She was the only nation which had any cause to fear invasion, yet she asked not for rearmament, but for the disarmament of the other states. 'We have,' he concluded, 'no more earnest desire than to contribute to the final healing of the wounds caused by the war and the Treaty of Versailles.'

In October 1933, when it became clear that the French – uneasily conscious of the inferiority of their manpower and industrial resources to those of Germany – were not prepared to disarm, Hitler pushed his argument a stage further. On 14 October he announced that Germany was driven, by the denial of equal rights, to withdraw from the Disarmament Conference and the League of Nations. Germany had tried to cooperate, but had suffered a bitter disillusionment and humiliation. In sorrow, rather than in anger, he had decided to take this step, which was demanded by the self-respect of the German people.

Former German Governments [he declared in a wireless address to the nation on that same day] entered the League of Nations in the hope and confidence that in the League they would find a forum for a just settlement of the interests of peoples, above all for a sincere reconciliation with their former foes. But this presupposes the recognition of the ultimate restoration of the German people to equality of rights. . . . To be written down as a member of such an institution possessing no such equality of rights is, for an honour-loving nation of sixty-five million folk and for a government which loves honour no less, an intolerable humiliation! . . .

No war can become humanity's permanent state; no peace can be the perpetuation of war. One day Conquerors and Conquered must find their way back into the community of mutual understanding and confidence. For a decade and a half the German people has hoped and waited for the time when at last the end of the war should also become the end of hate and enmity. But the aim of the Treaty of Versailles seems not to be to give peace to humanity at last, but rather to keep humanity in a state of everlasting hatred.[1]

The withdrawal from the League was not without risks, in view of Germany's military inferiority, and a secret directive to the Armed Forces, in case the League should apply sanctions, was issued by General von Blomberg.[2] It was the first of Hitler's gambles in foreign policy – and it succeeded. Events wholly justified his diagnosis of the state of mind of his opponents – their embarrassment in face of a case which they felt was not without justice; the divided public opinion of Great Britain and France; the eagerness to be reassured and to patch up a compromise, all those elements on which Hitler was to play with such skill time and again. With this in mind he issued a proclamation in which he declared force to be useless in removing international differences, affirmed the German people's hopes in disarmament and renewed his offer to conclude pacts of non-aggression at any time.

Four days later, in an interview with Ward Price, the *Daily Mail* Correspondent, Hitler was at his most convincing.

Nobody here [he told them] desires a repetition of war. Almost all the leaders of the National Socialist movement were actual combatants. I have yet to meet the combatant who desires a renewal of the horrors of those four and a half years. . . . Our youth constitutes our sole hope for the future. Do you imagine that we are bringing it up only to be shot down on the battlefield?

We are manly enough to recognize that when one has lost a war, whether one was responsible for it or not, one has to bear the consequences. We have borne them, but it is intolerable for us as a nation of sixty-five millions that we should repeatedly be dishonoured and humiliated. We will put up with no more of this persistent discrimination against Germany. So long as I live I will never put my signature as a statesman to any contract which I could not sign with self-respect in private life. I will maintain this resolution, even if it means my ruin! For I will sign no document with a mental reservation not to fulfil it. What I sign, I will stand by. What I cannot stand by, I will not sign.[3]

1. Speech of 14 October 1933 (Baynes: vol. II, pp. 1,092–104).
2. N.D. C-140.
3. Interview published in the *Daily Mail*, 19 October 1933 (Baynes: vol. II, pp. 1,105–8).

In another interview, published by the Paris paper, *Le Matin*, on 22 November, Hitler declared categorically that, once the question of the Saar had been settled, there were no further issues between Germany and France. He had renounced Alsace-Lorraine for good, and had told the German people so.

Hitler's cleverest stroke was to announce, on the same day as the withdrawal from the League, that he would submit his decision at once to a plebiscite. This was to invoke the sanctions of democracy against the democratic nations. The day chosen was 12 November, the day after the anniversary of the Armistice of 1918. 'See to it,' he told a packed meeting at Breslau, 'that this day shall later be recorded in the history of our people as a day of salvation – that the record shall run: on an eleventh of November, the German people formally lost its honour; fifteen years later came a twelfth of November and then the German people restored its honour to itself.'[1] All the long-pent-up resentment of the German people against the loss of the war and the Treaty of Versailles was expressed in the vote: ninety-six per cent of those entitled to vote went to the polls, and ninety-five per cent voted in approval of Hitler's policy. On the same day, single-list elections for the Reichstag gave the Nazi Party a solid majority of ninety-two per cent.

To Rauschning, who had returned from Geneva just after Germany's withdrawal from the League, Hitler remarked that, now he had left Geneva, he would more than ever speak the language of the League. 'And my party comrades,' he added, 'will not fail to understand me when they hear me speak of universal peace, disarmament, and mutual security pacts!'[2] These were the tactics of legality applied to international relations with even greater success than in the fight for power in Germany.

Hitler had now manoeuvred himself into the strongest possible position in which to begin German rearmament. When the other Great Powers sought to renew negotiations, Hitler replied that disarmament was clearly out of the question. All that could be hoped for was a convention for the limitation of armaments, and Germany's terms for cooperation would be the recognition of her right to raise an army of three hundred thousand men, based on conscription and short-term enlistment. A prolonged exchange of notes throughout the winter and spring of 1933–4 failed to produce agreement, but Hitler was well content. Rearmament had

1. Speech at Breslau, 4 November 1933 (Baynes: vol. II, pp. 1,131–3).
2. Rauschning: *Hitler Speaks*, p. 116.

already begun,[1] while Great Britain and France had placed themselves in the disadvantageous position, from which they were never to recover until the war, of asking the German dictator what concessions he would accept to reduce his price.

While these negotiations continued, and brought Mr Eden to Berlin, in April 1934, on the first of many fruitless journeys undertaken by British statesmen in these years, Hitler strengthened his hand in an unexpected direction. No feature of the Treaty of Versailles stirred more bitter feelings in Germany than the loss of territory to the new State of Poland. Relations between Poland and Germany continued to be strained throughout the history of the Weimar Republic, and Stresemann refused to supplement the Locarno Pact by an eastern Locarno, which would have meant Germany's renunciation of her claims to the return of Danzig, Silesia, Posen, and the other surrendered lands. Nowhere was the rise to power of the Nazis viewed with more alarm than in Warsaw.

It caused a diplomatic sensation, therefore, when, on 26 January 1934, Hitler announced that the first country with which Nazi Germany had concluded a Non-Aggression Pact was Poland. The Pact was never popular in Germany, but it was an astute move for Hitler to make. Ultimately, there was no place for an independent Poland in Hitler's Europe; the most she could hope for was the position of a vassal state. But Hitler could not move against Poland for years to come. Instead of accepting this situation with a bad grace, as the more sentimental nationalists would have done, he turned it to his advantage, and made an ostentatious parade of his enforced virtue.

Hitler was thus able to substantiate his claim to peaceful intentions by pointing to the fact that his first diplomatic action, after leaving the League, had been to initiate an entirely new course in one of the most dangerous and intractable problems of Europe, Polish–German relations. In the same common-sense language as before, he told the Reichstag: 'Germans and Poles will have to learn to accept the fact of each other's existence. Hence it is more sensible to regulate this state of affairs, which the last thousand years has not been able to remove, and the next thousand will not be able to remove either, in such a way that the highest possible profit will accrue from it for both nations.'[2] The

1. Large increases in the German military budget were made public in March 1934.
2. Speech to the Reichstag, 30 January 1934 (Baynes: vol. II, pp. 1,151–71).

Pact with Poland was constantly used in the 'peace' speeches which Hitler continued to make throughout 1934, 1935, and 1936.

But the importance of the Pact was greater than its value as propaganda. Poland, which had been the ally of France since 1921, was one of the bastions of the French security system in Eastern Europe. It was no secret that the Poles were becoming restive at the casual way in which they felt they were treated by France. The Polish Government was beginning to turn away from the policy of collective security, supported by France, towards an independent neutrality, in which it was hoped that Poland would be able to balance between her two great neighbours, Germany and Russia. The Nazi offer of a Ten-Year Pact fitted admirably into this new policy, and Hitler was thereby able to weaken any possible united front against Germany. Here was the first breach in the French alliance system and the first display of those tactics of 'one-by-one' with which he was to achieve so much.

This was a good beginning, but there were reminders during 1934 of the dangers of the situation, notably in the case of Austria. Hitler's electoral successes between 1930 and 1933, followed by the Nazis' capture of power, had revived National Socialism in Austria. The Party was reorganized by Alfred Eduard Frauenfeld, a thirty-year-old clerk in the Vienna Bodenkreditanstalt, who lost his job when the bank failed and took up full-time Party work. In three years the Vienna Nazi Party's membership grew from three hundred to forty thousand.

The incorporation of Austria into a Greater Germany occupied the first place both in the Party programme of 1920 and in the opening pages of *Mein Kampf*. The Austrian Nazis, who formed a part of the German Party under Hitler's leadership, lived and worked for the day when the *Anschluss* should take place. With the help of Habicht, a member of the German Reichstag and the man Hitler had appointed as Inspector of the Austrian Party, Frauenfeld, Prokosch, and the other local leaders kept up a violent propaganda campaign, backed by intimidation and acts of terrorism. There was no doubt where the funds came from: anyone in Austria had only to tune in to the Munich radio station across the frontier to get confirmation of the support the Austrian Nazis were receiving from Germany. It appeared to be no more than a matter of months, possibly of weeks, before the local Nazis would try to capture power by a rising.

German relations with Austria, however, were not simply a family affair, as Hitler tried to insist. France, the ally of Czechoslovakia, and Italy, the patron of Dollfuss's fascist régime in Austria and of Hungary, were bound to be disturbed by the prospect of an *Anschluss* and a consequent Nazi advance to the threshold of the Balkans. The increased Nazi agitation in Austria, the information the Dollfuss Government succeeded in collecting of Nazi plans for a putsch, and the unfriendly references Hitler made to Austria in his speech of 30 January 1934 combined to produce a sense of urgency. No doubt Hitler was sincere in disclaiming any intention of attacking Austria: if all went well there would be no need of overt German intervention. But at this stage the Powers, with Mussolini to prompt their sense of realism, were not so credulous as they later became. On 17 February the governments of France, Great Britain, and Italy published a joint declaration to the effect that they took 'a common view of the necessity of maintaining Austria's independence and integrity in accordance with the relevant treaties'. Exactly a month later Mussolini underlined Italy's interest in Central Europe by signing the Rome Protocols with Austria and Hungary. Although primarily concerned with economic relations, the Protocols strengthened the ties of political dependence between Italy and her two client states on the Danube.

The Nazi agitation in Austria, however, continued, and Mussolini's suspicions were not removed by Hitler's assurances at their meeting at Venice in June. At last, on 25 July, while Madame Dollfuss and her family were actually staying with Mussolini, the Austrian Nazis made their attempt, breaking into the Vienna Chancellery and shooting Dollfuss, while others occupied the radio station and announced the appointment of Rintelen as Chancellor. Hitler was at Bayreuth when he received the news. As he sat in his box listening to Wagner's *Rheingold*, his adjutants Schaub and Brückner kept coming in to whisper further news to him. 'After the performance,' Friedelind Wagner recalls, 'the Führer was most excited. . . . It was terrible to witness. Although he could scarcely wipe the delight from his face, Hitler carefully ordered dinner in the restaurant as usual. "I must go across for an hour and show myself," he said, "or people will think I had something to do with this." '[1]

This was precisely what people did think, for the German

1. Friedelind Wagner: *The Royal Family of Bayreuth* (London, 1948), pp. 98–9.

Legation in Vienna had been heavily implicated in the plot, and rumours of an attempt had been rife in Munich and Berlin twenty-four hours before the action began. It is unlikely, in fact, that Hitler knew what was planned. This was no time for foreign adventures, so soon after the events of 30 June and with the succession to Hindenburg still in the balance. Moreover – and this was decisive for Hitler – although Dollfuss died of his wounds, the putsch failed. The rebels in Vienna were quickly overpowered, and after some days' fighting in Styria and Carinthia order was restored. The leaders, followed by several thousand Austrian Nazis, only escaped by getting across the German frontier. Even more important was the news that Mussolini, furious at what he regarded as Hitler's bad faith, had ordered Italian divisions to the Austrian frontier and sent the Austrian Government an immediate telegram promising Italian support in the defence of their country's independence.

The Nazis had over-reached themselves, and Hitler had promptly to repudiate all connexion with the conspiracy. The initial announcement of the official German News Agency, couched in enthusiastic terms, was hurriedly suppressed; the murderers of Dollfuss were surrendered to the Austrian Government; Habicht, the Party Inspector for Austria, was dismissed; the German Minister in Vienna was recalled in disgrace; and Hitler appointed Papen to go to Vienna as Minister-Extraordinary in order to repair the damage. The choice of Papen, a Catholic, a Conservative, and Vice-Chancellor in Hitler's Cabinet, was intended to conciliate the Austrians; at the same time it was a convenient way of getting rid of the man who had made the Marburg speech and who had been lucky to escape with his life on the week-end of 30 June. These hasty measures tided over the crisis and preserved appearances. But it had been made plain enough to Hitler that he was not yet in a position where he could afford to use high-handed methods, and that the opposition to his schemes would have to be divided before it could be overcome.

For the rest of 1934 the unanimity of the other Powers in face of further German adventures was strengthened, rather than weakened. In the summer Louis Barthou, the French Foreign Minister, made a tour of eastern European capitals to put new life into the French alliances with Czechoslovakia, Rumania, Yugoslavia, and Poland. In May France sharply rejected Sir John Simon's proposals to concede equality of armaments to Hitler, and Barthou became active in advocating an Eastern Locarno (which should include Russia as well as Germany), with the object of tying Hitler's hands in Eastern Europe as well as in the west. The fact that the Soviet Union, hitherto one of the most out-spoken critics of Geneva, was now willing to join the League of Nations, and was elected to a permanent seat on the Council in September, lent colour to the belief that the Great Powers were awake to the danger of a resurgent German nationalism.

Hitler could only continue to protest the innocence of his intentions. 'If it rests with Germany,' he told Ward Price in an-other interview in August, 'war will not come again. This country has a more profound impression than any other of the evil that war causes. . . . In our belief Germany's present-day problems cannot be settled by war.'[1] When M. Jean Goy, a deputy for the Seine, visited him in November, he made much of the experiences which the ex-servicemen of Germany and France had in common; they had been through too much in the last war ever to allow war to break out again. 'We know too well, you and I, the uselessness and horror of war.' His one object was to build a new social order in Germany; he had no time or energy to spare for war, and in his social plans he was erecting a more enduring monument to fame than any great captain after the most glorious victories. The interview was duly published by *Le Matin*;[2] indeed, the word 'peace' was never out of Hitler's mouth at this time.

So the year ended quietly, but not without some cause for con-gratulation on Hitler's part. On 9 October Louis Barthou, the energetic French Foreign Minister, who stood for a policy of firmness in face of Nazi demands, was assassinated while welcom-ing King Alexander of Yugoslavia at Marseille. His successor at the Quai d'Orsay was Pierre Laval, as unscrupulous as he was clever, a master of *combinazioni* and shady political deals. Despite appearances, Hitler held to his belief that behind the façade of unity the Powers lacked the will to oppose him or to combine together for long. In 1927 Hitler said to Otto Strasser: 'There is no solidarity in Europe; there is only submission.'[3] It was the essential premise on which all his plans depended; the next year, 1935, was to show how just was his diagnosis.

1. *Daily Mail*, 6 August 1934 (Baynes: vol. II, pp. 1,181–4).
2. *Le Matin*, 18 November 1934 (ibid., pp. 1,190–3).
3. Otto Strasser: *Hitler and I*, p. 225.

I V

From the summer of 1934 the principal object of the Western Powers' diplomacy was to persuade Germany to sign a pact of mutual assistance covering Eastern Europe. Just as the Locarno Pact included France, Germany, Belgium, Great Britain, and Italy, each undertaking to come to the immediate aid of France and Belgium, or Germany, if either side were attacked by the other, so this Eastern Locarno would include Russia, Germany, Poland, Czechoslovakia, and the other states of Eastern Europe and would involve the same obligation of automatic assistance in the case of an attack.

Hitler had no intention of entering into any such scheme: it was not aggression that he feared, but checks upon his freedom of action. His preference – for obvious reasons – was for bilateral agreements, and if he were to sign a multilateral pact of non-aggression it would only be one from which all provisions for mutual aid had been removed, a statement of good intentions unsupported by any guarantees to enforce them. German opposition, which had already been made clear in 1934, was powerfully assisted by that of Poland. Pilsudski was highly suspicious of Russia and anxious that Poland should not be pushed into the front line of an anti-German combination – which could only mean that Poland would be either the battleground of a new clash between her two neighbours or the victim of a deal concluded between them at her expense, as happened in 1939. Polish quarrels with Lithuania and dislike of Czechoslovakia added further reasons to his reluctance to enter any such all-embracing project. Pilsudski, and his successor Beck, saw the only way out of Poland's difficulties as a policy of balancing between Moscow and Berlin, a policy which fatally overestimated Poland's strength, and fatally underestimated the danger from Germany.

Hitler courted the Poles assiduously, constantly urging on them the common interest Poland and Germany had in opposing Russia. 'Poland,' he told the Polish Ambassador in November 1933, 'is an outpost against Asia. . . . The other States should recognize this role of Poland's.'[1]

Göring, who was used by Hitler in the role of a candid friend of the Poles, spoke even more plainly when he visited Warsaw at the end of January 1935. He began his conversations in the

1. *The Polish White Book* (English translation, London, 1939), p. 17.

Polish Foreign Ministry by mentioning the possibility of a new partition of Poland by agreement between Germany and Russia. But he did this only to dismiss it as a practical impossibility: in fact, he continued, Hitler's policy needed a strong Poland, to form a common barrier with Germany against the Soviet Union. In his talks with Polish generals and with Marshal Pilsudski, Göring 'outlined far-reaching plans, almost suggesting an anti-Russian alliance and a joint attack on Russia. He gave it to be understood that the Ukraine would become a Polish sphere of influence and North-western Russia would be Germany's'.[1] The Poles were wary of such seductive propositions, but they were impressed by the friendliness of the German leaders, and in the course of 1935 relations between the two governments became steadily closer. Göring visited Cracow for Pilsudski's funeral in May. The same month Hitler himself had a long conversation with the Ambassador, and after a visit of the Polish Foreign Minister, Colonel Beck, to Berlin in July the communiqué spoke of 'a far-reaching agreement of views'. The attention Hitler paid to Polish–German relations was to repay him handsomely.

Meanwhile, the British and French Governments renewed their attempts to reach a settlement with Germany. The Saar plebiscite in January 1935 had produced a ninety per cent vote for the return of the territory to Germany. The result had scarcely been in doubt, although the Nazis cried it up inside Germany as a great victory and the destruction of the first of the Versailles fetters. The removal of this issue between France and Germany, which Hitler had constantly described as the one territorial issue dividing them, seemed to offer a better chance of finding the Führer in a more reasonable mood.

The proposals which the British and French Ambassadors presented to Hitler at the beginning of February 1935 sketched the outline of a general settlement which would cover the whole of Europe. The existing Locarno Pact of mutual assistance, which applied to Western Europe, was to be strengthened by the conclusion of an agreement to cover unprovoked aggression from the air. At the same time it was to be supplemented by two similar pacts of mutual assistance, one dealing with Eastern Europe, the other with Central Europe.

1. *The Polish White Book*, op. cit., pp. 25–6: Count Szembek's reports on Göring's conversations in Poland.

Hitler faced a difficult decision. German rearmament had reached a stage where further concealment would prove a hindrance. It seemed clear from their proposals that the Western Powers would be prepared to waive their objections to German rearmament in return for Germany's accession to their proposals for strengthening and extending collective security. Against that Hitler had to set his anxiety to avoid tying his hands, and his need of some dramatic stroke of foreign policy to gratify the mood of nationalist expectation in Germany which had so far received little satisfaction. On both these grounds a bold unilateral repudiation of the disarmament clauses of the Treaty of Versailles would suit him very much better than negotiations with the Western Powers, in which he would be bound to make concessions in return for French and British agreement. Could he afford to take the risk?

Hitler's first reply showed uncertainty. He welcomed the idea of extending the original Locarno Pact to include attack from the air, while remaining evasive on the question of the proposed Eastern and Danubian Pacts. The German Government invited the British to continue discussions, and a visit to Berlin by the British Foreign Minister, Sir John Simon, was arranged for 7 March. Before the visit could take place, however, on 4 March the British Government published its own plans for increased armaments, basing this on 'the fact that Germany was . . . rearming openly on a large scale, despite the provisions of Part V of the Treaty of Versailles'.[1] The British White Paper went on to remark 'that not only the forces, but the spirit in which the population, and especially the youth of the country, are being organized, lend colour to, and substantiate, the general feeling of insecurity which has already been incontestably generated'. Great indignation was at once expressed in Germany, and Hitler contracted a 'chill' which made it necessary to postpone Sir John Simon's visit. On the 9th the German Government officially notified foreign governments that a German Air Force was already in existence. This seems to have been a kite with which to test the Western Powers' reaction. As Sir John Simon told the House of Commons that he and Mr Eden were still proposing to go to Berlin and nothing else happened, it appeared safe to risk a more sensational announcement the next week-end. On 16 March 1935, the German Government proclaimed its intention of re-introducing conscription and building up a peacetime army of

1. British White Paper, Cmd 4827 of 1935.

thirty-six divisions, with a numerical strength of five hundred and fifty thousand men.[1]

Four days before, the French Government had doubled the period of service and reduced the age of enlistment in the French Army, in order to make good the fall in the number of conscripts due to the reduced birth-rate of the years 1914–18. This served Hitler as a pretext for his own action. He was able to represent Germany as driven reluctantly to take this step, purely in order to defend herself against the warlike threats of her neighbours. From the time when the German people, trusting in the assurances of Wilson's Fourteen Points, and believing they were rendering a great service to mankind, had laid down their arms, they had been deceived again and again in their hopes of justice and their faith in the good intentions of others. Germany, Hitler declared, was the one Power which had disarmed; now that the other Powers, far from disarming themselves, were actually beginning to increase their armaments, she had no option but to follow suit.[2]

The announcement was received with enthusiasm in Germany, and on 17 March, Heroes Memorial Day (*Heldengedenktag*), a brilliant military ceremony in the State Opera House celebrated the rebirth of the German Army. At Hitler's side sat von Mackensen, the only surviving field-marshal of the old Army. Afterwards, amid cheering crowds, Hitler held a review of the new Army, including a detachment of the Air Force. So widespread was German feeling against the Treaty of Versailles, and so strong the pride in the German military tradition, that German satisfaction at the announcement could be taken for granted. Everything turned on the reaction abroad to this first open breach of the Treaty's provisions. Hitler had anticipated protests, and was prepared to discount them; what mattered was the action with which the other signatories of the Treaty proposed to support their protests.

The result more than justified the risks he had taken. The British Government, after making a solemn protest, proceeded to ask whether the Führer was still ready to receive Sir John Simon. The French appealed to the League, and an extraordinary session of the Council was at once summoned, to be preceded by a

1. According to General Manstein, this figure was fixed by Hitler: if the General Staff had been asked, they would have proposed a figure of 21 divisions.
2. cf. Hitler's Proclamation to the German People, 16 March 1935.

conference between Great Britain, France, and Italy at Stresa. But the French Note, too, spoke of searching for means of conciliation and of the need to dispel the tension which had arisen. This was not the language of men who intended to enforce their protests. When Sir John Simon and Mr Eden at last visited Berlin at the end of March they found Hitler polite, even charming, but perfectly sure of himself and firm in his refusal to consider any pact of mutual assistance which included the Soviet Union. He made a good deal of the service Germany was performing in safeguarding Europe against Communism, and, when the discussion moved to German rearmament, asked: 'Did Wellington, when Blücher came to his assistance at Waterloo, first ask the legal experts of the Foreign Office whether the strength of the Prussian forces exceeded the limits fixed by treaty?'[1] It was the Englishmen who had come to ask for cooperation and Hitler who was in the advantageous position of being able to say 'no', without having anything to ask in return. The very presence of the British representatives in Berlin, after the announcement of 16 March, was a triumph for his diplomacy.

In the weeks that followed, the Western Powers continued to make a display of European unity which, formally at least, was more impressive. At Stresa, on 11 April, the British, French, and Italian Governments condemned Germany's action, reaffirmed their loyalty to the Locarno Treaty and repeated their declaration on Austrian independence. At Geneva the Council of the League duly censured Germany and appointed a committee to consider what steps should be taken the next time any State endangered peace by repudiating its obligations. Finally, in May, the French Government, having failed to make headway with its plan for a general treaty of mutual assistance in Eastern Europe, signed a pact with the Soviet Union by which each party undertook to come to the aid of the other in case of an unprovoked attack. This treaty was flanked by a similar pact, concluded at the same time, between Russia and France's most reliable ally, Czechoslovakia.

Yet, even if Hitler was taken aback by the strength of this belated reaction, and if the Franco–Russian and Czech–Russian treaties in particular faced him with awkward new possibilities, his confidence in his own tactics was never shaken. He proceeded

1. Paul Schmidt: *Statist auf diplomatischer Bühne*, p. 300; and François-Poncet, p. 175.

to test the strength of this new-found unity; it did not take long to show its weaknesses.

On 21 May Hitler promulgated in secret the Reich Defence Law which placed Schacht in charge of economic preparations for war and reorganized the commands of the armed forces under himself as Supreme Commander of the Wehrmacht. But this was not the face that Hitler showed in public. On the evening of the same day, he appeared before the Reichstag to deliver a long and carefully prepared speech on foreign policy. It is a speech worth studying, for in it are to be found most of the tricks with which Hitler lulled the suspicions and raised the hopes of the gullible. His answer to the censure of the Powers was not defiance, but redoubled assurances of peace, an appeal to reason, justice and conscience. The new Germany, he protested, was misunderstood, and his own attitude misrepresented.

No man ever spoke with greater feeling of the horror and stupidity of war than Adolf Hitler.

The blood shed on the European continent in the course of the last three hundred years bears no proportion to the national result of the events. In the end France has remained France, Germany Germany, Poland Poland and Italy Italy. What dynastic egoism, political passion and patriotic blindness have attained in the way of apparently far-reaching political changes by shedding rivers of blood has, as regards national feeling, done no more than touched the skin of the nations. It has not substantially altered their fundamental characters. If these States had applied merely a fraction of their sacrifices to wiser purposes the success would certainly have been greater and more permanent. . . . If the nations attach so much importance to an increase in the number of the inhabitants of a country they can achieve it without tears in a simpler and more natural way. A sound social policy, by increasing the readiness of a nation to have children, can give its own people more children in a few years than the number of aliens that could be conquered and made subject to that nation by war.[1]

Collective security, Hitler pointed out, was a Wilsonian idea, but Germany's faith in Wilsonian ideas, at least as practised by the former Allies, had been destroyed by her treatment after the war. Germany had been denied equality, had been treated as a nation with second-class rights, and driven to rearm by the failure of the other Powers to carry out their obligation to disarm. Despite this experience, Germany was still prepared to cooperate

1. Text of the speech in Baynes: vol. II, pp. 1,218–47.

in the search for security. But she had rooted objections to the proposal of multilateral pacts, for this was the way to spread, not to localize, war. Moreover, in the east of Europe, Hitler declared, there was a special case, the existence of a State, Bolshevik Russia, pledged to destroy the independence of Europe, a State with which a National Socialist Germany could never come to terms.

What Hitler offered in place of the 'unrealistic' proposal of multilateral treaties was the signature of non-aggression pacts with all Germany's neighbours. The only exception he made was Lithuania, since Lithuania's continued possession of the German Memelland was a wrong which the German people could never accept, and a plain denial of that right of self-determination proclaimed by Wilson. Germany's improved relations with Poland, he did not fail to add, showed how great a contribution such pacts could make to the cause of peace: this was the practical way in which Germany set about removing international misunderstandings.

Hitler supported his offer with the most convincing display of goodwill. The fact that Germany had repudiated the disarmament clauses of the Treaty of Versailles did not mean that she had anything but the strictest regard for the Treaty's other provisions – including the demilitarization of the Rhineland – or for her other obligations under the Locarno Treaty. She had no intention of annexing Austria and was perfectly ready to strengthen the Locarno Pact by an agreement on air attack, such as Great Britain and France had suggested. She was ready to agree to the abolition of heavy arms, such as the heaviest tanks and artillery; to limit the use of other weapons – such as the bomber and poison gas – by international convention; indeed, to accept an over-all limitation of armaments provided that it was to apply to all the Powers. Hitler laid particular stress on his willingness to limit German naval power to thirty-five per cent of the strength of the British Navy. He understood very well, he declared, the special needs of the British Empire, and had no intention of starting a new naval rivalry with Great Britain. He ended with a confession of his faith in peace. 'Whoever lights the torch of war in Europe can wish for nothing but chaos. We, however, live in the firm conviction that in our time will be fulfilled, not the decline, but the renaissance of the West. That Germany may make an imperishable contribution to this great work is our proud hope and our unshakable belief.'

Hitler's mastery of the language of Geneva was unequalled.

His grasp of the mood of public opinion in the Western democracies was startling, considering that he had never visited any of them and spoke no foreign language. He understood intuitively their longing for peace, the idealism of the pacifists, the uneasy conscience of the liberals, the reluctance of the great mass of their peoples to look beyond their own private affairs. At this stage in the game these were greater assets than the uncompleted panzer divisions and bomber fleets he was still building, and Hitler used them with the same skill he had shown in playing on German grievances and illusions.

In *Mein Kampf* Hitler had written: 'For a long time to come there will be only two Powers in Europe with which it may be possible for Germany to conclude an alliance. These Powers are Great Britain and Italy.'[1] The greatest blunder of the Kaiser's Government – prophetic words – had been to quarrel with Britain and Russia at the same time: Germany's future lay in the east, a continental future, and her natural ally was Great Britain, whose power was colonial, commercial, and naval, with no territorial interests on the continent of Europe. 'Only by alliance with England was it possible (before 1914) to safeguard the rear of the German crusade. . . . No sacrifice should have been considered too great, if it was a necessary means of gaining England's friendship. Colonial and naval ambitions should have been abandoned.'[2]

Although Hitler's attitude towards Britain was modified later by growing contempt for the weakness of her policy and the credulity of her governments, the idea of an alliance with her attracted him throughout his life. It was an alliance which could only, in Hitler's view, be made on condition that Britain abandoned her old balance-of-power policy in Europe, accepted the prospect of a German hegemony on the Continent and left Germany a free hand in attaining it. Even during the war Hitler persisted in believing that an alliance with Germany on these terms was in Britain's own interests, continually expressed his regret that the British had been so stupid as not to see this, and never quite gave up the hope that he would be able to overcome their obstinacy and persuade them to accept his view.[3] No British Government, even before the war, was prepared to go as far as an alliance on these terms, yet there was a section of British opinion

1. *Mein Kampf*, p. 509.   2. ibid., p. 128.
3. cf. *Hitler's Table Talk*, pp. 11–14; 23; 26; 46; 50; 92–3; 264–5.

which was sufficiently impressed by Hitler's arguments to be attracted to the idea of a settlement which would have left him virtually a free hand in Central and Eastern Europe, and Hitler, if he never succeeded in his main objective, was remarkably successful for a time in weakening the opposition of Great Britain to the realization of his aims. The policy of appeasement is not to be understood unless it is realized that it represented the acceptance by the British Government, at least in part, of Hitler's view of what British policy should be.

The speech of 21 May had been intended to influence opinion in Great Britain in Hitler's favour. The quickness of the British reaction was surprising. During his visit to Berlin in March Sir John Simon had been sufficiently impressed by a hint thrown out by the Führer to suggest that German representatives should come to London to discuss the possibility of a naval agreement between the two countries. Hitler must have been delighted to see the speed with which the British Foreign Minister responded to his bait, and in his speech of 21 May he again underlined his willingness to arrive at such an understanding. Even Hitler, however, can scarcely have calculated that the British Government would be so maladroit as to say nothing of their intentions to the Powers with whom they had been so closely associated in censuring Germany's repudiation of the Versailles disarmament clauses in the previous weeks.

Early in June Ribbentrop, whom Hitler now began to use for special missions, flew to London. Despite the brusque and tactless way in which he refused to permit discussion of the Führer's offer, he returned with the British signature of a naval pact. This bound the Germans not to build beyond thirty-five per cent of Britain's naval strength, but it tacitly recognized Germany's right to begin naval rearmament and specifically agreed by an escape-clause that, in the construction of U-boats, Germany should have the right to build up to one hundred per cent of the submarine strength of the British Commonwealth. The affront to Britain's partners, France and Italy, both of whom were also naval powers, but neither of whom had been consulted, was open and much resented. The solidarity of the Stresa Front, the unanimity of the Powers' condemnation of German rearmament, was destroyed. The British Government, in its eagerness to secure a private advantage, had given a disastrous impression of bad faith. Like Poland, but without the excuse of Poland's difficult position between Germany and Russia, Great Britain had accepted Hitler's carefully calculated offer without a thought of its ultimate consequences.

In September the Führer attended the Party's rally at Nuremberg. For the first time detachments of the new German Army took part in the parade and Hitler glorified the German military tradition: 'in war the nation's great defiance, in peace the splendid school of our people. It is the Army which has made men of us all, and when we looked upon the Army our faith in the future of our people was always reinforced. This old glorious Army is not dead; it only slept, and now it has arisen again in you.'[1]

Hitler's speeches throughout the rally were marked by the confidence of a man sure of his hold over the people he led. The Reichstag was summoned to Nuremberg for a special session, and Hitler presented for its unanimous approval the Nuremberg Laws directed against the Jews, the first depriving Germans of Jewish blood of their citizenship, the second – the Law for the Protection of German Blood and German Honour – forbidding marriages between Germans and Jews and the employment of German servants by Jews. These laws, Hitler declared, 'repay the debt of gratitude to the movement under whose symbol [the swastika, now adopted as the national emblem] Germany has recovered her freedom'.[2]

The same month, while Hitler at Nuremberg was making use of the power he held in Germany to gratify his hatred of the Jews, a quarrel began at Geneva which was to provide him with the opportunity to extend his power outside the German frontiers of 1914.

The alliance with Mussolini's Italy to which Hitler already looked at the time he wrote *Mein Kampf* had hitherto been prevented by Mussolini's Danubian ambitions, and the Duce's self-appointed role as the patron of Austrian independence. After the murder of Dollfuss, Mussolini had been outspoken in his dislike and contempt for the 'barbarians' north of the Alps, and he had cooperated with the other Powers in their condemnation of Germany's unilateral decision to rearm. Mussolini, however, had long been contemplating a showy success for his régime in Abyssinia. It may be that he was prompted by uneasy fears that his chances of expansion in Europe would soon be reduced by the growth of German power; it may be that he was stimulated by a

1. Speech on 16 September 1935 (Baynes: vol. I, p. 561).
2. Speech of 15 September 1935 (ibid., p. 732).

sense of rivalry with the German dictator; it is almost certain that he hoped to profit by French and British preoccupation with German rearmament to carry out his adventure on the cheap.

Abyssinia had appealed to the League under Article 15 of the Covenant in March. So far the dispute had been discreetly kept in the background, but in September the British Government, having just made a sensational gesture of appeasement to Germany by the Naval Treaty of June, astonished the world for the second time by taking the lead at Geneva in demanding the imposition of sanctions against Italy. She supported this by reinforcing the British Fleet in the Mediterranean. To the French, who judged that Germany, not Italy, was the greater danger to the security of Europe, the British appeared to be standing on their heads and looking at events upside down.

There was only one assumption on which British policy could be defended. If the British were prepared to support sanctions against Italy to the point of war, thereby giving to the authority of the League the backing of force which it had hitherto lacked, their action might so strengthen the machinery of collective security as to put a check to any aggression, whether by Italy or Germany. The outbreak of hostilities between Italy and Abyssinia in October soon put the British intentions to the test. The course pursued by the Baldwin Government made the worst of both worlds. By insisting on the imposition of sanctions Great Britain made an enemy of Mussolini and destroyed all hope of a united front against German aggression. By her refusal to drive home the policy of sanctions, in face of Mussolini's bluster, she dealt the authority of the League as well as her own prestige a fatal blow, and destroyed any hope of finding in collective security an effective alternative to the united front of the Great Powers against German aggression.

If the British Government never meant to do more than make a show of imposing sanctions it would have done better to have followed the more cynical but more realistic policy of Laval and made a deal with Italy at the beginning. Even the Hoare–Laval Pact of December 1935 would have been a better alternative than allowing the farce of sanctions to drag on to its inconclusive and discreditable end. For the consequences of these blunders extended much farther than Abyssinia and the Mediterranean: their ultimate beneficiary was, not Mussolini, but Hitler.

Germany at first confined herself to a policy of strict neutrality in the Abyssinian affair, but the advantages to be derived from the quarrel between Italy and the Western Powers did not escape Hitler. If Italy lost the war, that would mean the weakening of the principal barrier to German ambitions in Central and South-eastern Europe. On the other hand, if Italy proved to be successful, the prospects for Hitler were still good. His one fear was that the quarrel might be patched up by some such compromise as the Hoare–Laval Pact, and when the Polish Ambassador in Berlin saw him two days after the announcement of the terms of the Hoare–Laval Agreement he found him highly excited and alarmed at this prospect.[1] The further development of the dispute, however, only gave him greater cause for satisfaction. Not only was the Stresa front ended and Italy driven into a position of isolation, in which Mussolini was bound to look more favourably on German offers of support, but the League of Nations suffered a fatal blow to its authority from which, after its previous failure to halt Japanese aggression, it never recovered. French confidence in England was further shaken, and the belief that Great Britain was a spent force in international politics received the most damning confirmation.

The events of 1935 thus provided an unexpected opportunity for Hitler to realize his Italian plans: as Mussolini later acknowledged, it was in the autumn of 1935 that the idea of the Rome–Berlin Axis was born. No less important was the encouragement which the feebleness of the opposition to aggression gave Hitler to pursue his policy without regard to the risks. 'There was now, as it turned out,' writes Mr Churchill, 'little hope of averting war or of postponing it by a trial of strength equivalent to war. Almost all that remained open to France and Britain was to await the moment of the challenge and do the best they could.'[2]

V

Throughout the autumn and winter of 1935–6 Hitler watched and waited. By March 1936 he judged the moment opportune for another *coup* in foreign policy. There had been ample warning of where his next move would be. In his speech of 21 May 1935 he had put forward the view that the alliance concluded between France and Russia 'brought an element of legal insecurity into

1. Elizabeth Wiskemann: *The Rome–Berlin Axis* (Oxford, 1949), p. 51–2.
2. Winston S. Churchill: *The Second World War*, vol. I, *The Gathering Storm* (London, 1948), p. 148.

the Locarno Pact', with the obligations of which, he argued, it was incompatible. The German Foreign Office repeated this in a note to the French Government, and, although their view was rejected by both the French and the other signatories of the Locarno Pact, Hitler refused to give up his grievance. After an interview with Hitler on 21 November the French Ambassador, M. François-Poncet, reported to Paris that Hitler had made up his mind to use the pretext of the Franco-Soviet treaty to denounce Locarno and reoccupy the demilitarized zone of the Rhineland. He was only waiting for an appropriate moment to act.

The treaty between France and Russia had still not been ratified. It had become a subject of bitter controversy in French politics, and ever since the beginning of July 1935 the French Right-wing Press and parties had been conducting a campaign against it. This had little to do with foreign affairs; it was an extension of the class and party conflicts inside France to her external policy. Hitler was thus deliberately choosing as his pretext an issue which divided France; nor was he ignorant of the fact that in London, too, there was no enthusiasm for France's latest commitment.

On 11 February 1936, the Franco-Soviet treaty finally came before the French Chamber of Deputies, and on the 27th it was ratified by 353 votes to 164. The French Government seems to have been nervous about the reception of the news in Berlin. When, on the morning after the ratification, *Paris-Midi* published a delayed interview with Hitler, in which he spoke in friendly terms of his desire for an agreement with France, the French Ambassador was instructed to ask the Führer how he conceived this *rapprochement* could be achieved. But when François-Poncet saw Hitler on 2 March his reception was far from friendly. Hitler declared angrily that he had been made a fool of, that the interview with *Paris-Midi* had been given on 21 February and deliberately held up in Paris until after the ratification of the Treaty. He was, however, still willing to answer the French Government's inquiry and he promised the Ambassador detailed proposals in the near future.

Hitler's reply, as François-Poncet had foreseen, was to march German troops into the demilitarized Rhineland. Blomberg's first directive to the unorganized armed forces in May 1935 had ordered the preparation of plans for such a step. None the less, it was a proposal which thoroughly alarmed Hitler's generals. German rearmament was only beginning and the first conscripts had only been taken into the Army a few months before. France, together with her Polish and Czech allies, could immediately mobilize ninety divisions, with a further hundred in reserve – and this took no account of Russian forces. If the French and their allies marched, the Germans would be heavily outnumbered, and it is to be remembered that the reoccupation of the Rhineland represented not only a breach of the Treaty of Versailles but a *casus foederis* under the Locarno Pact. Hitler did not dispute these facts; he based his decision on the belief that the French would not march – and he was right. According to General Jodl, the German occupation forces which moved into the Rhineland consisted of approximately one division,[1] and only three battalions moved across the Rhine, to Aachen, Trier, and Saarbrücken, The General Staff, worried by the first reports from Paris and London, wanted to move these three battalions back across the Rhine, and General Beck, the Chief of Staff, suggested that Germany should undertake not to build fortifications west of the Rhine.[2] Hitler turned down both proposals without a moment's hesitation. The German generals could not believe that the French would not march this time, but Hitler remained confident in his diagnosis of the state of public opinion in France and Great Britain.

Years later, reminiscing over the dinner table, Hitler asked: 'What would have happened if anybody other than myself had been at the head of the Reich! Anyone you care to mention would have lost his nerve. I was obliged to lie and what saved me was my unshakable obstinacy and my amazing aplomb. I threatened unless the situation eased to send six extra divisions into the Rhineland. The truth was, I only had four brigades. Next day, the English papers wrote that there had been an easing of the situation.'[3]

Blomberg's directive for the operation was issued on 2 March, the day on which Hitler saw François-Poncet.[4] On the morning of 7 March, as the German soldiers were marching into the Rhineland, greeted with flowers flung by wildly enthusiastic crowds, Neurath, German Foreign Minister, summoned the British, French, and Italian Ambassadors to the Wilhelmstrasse and presented them with a document which contained, in addition to

1. Sir Winston Churchill (op. cit., vol. I, p. 150) puts the forces a good deal higher, at thirty-five thousand.
2. Examination of General Jodl. N.P., Part xv, pp. 320–1.
3. *Hitler's Table Talk*, pp. 258–9 (27 January 1942).
4. Text of the Directive. N.D., C-159.

Germany's grounds for denouncing the **Locarno Pact** (the incompatibility of its obligations with the Franco-Soviet treaty), new and far-reaching peace proposals. As M. François-Poncet, the French Ambassador, described it, 'Hitler struck his adversary in the face, and as he did so declared: "I bring you proposals for peace!"'[1] In place of the discarded Locarno Treaty, Hitler offered a pact of non-aggression to France and Belgium, valid for twenty-five years and supplemented by the air pact to which Britain attached so much importance. The whole agreement was to be guaranteed by Great Britain and Italy, with Holland included if she so wished. A new demilitarized zone was to be drawn on both sides of the western frontier, treating France and Germany on terms of equality, while in the east Germany offered non-aggression pacts to her neighbours on the model of the agreement she had concluded with Poland. Finally, now that equality of rights had been restored, Germany was prepared to re-enter the League of Nations and to discuss the colonial problem and the reform of the League Covenant.

At noon Hitler addressed the Reichstag. His speech was another masterpiece of reasonableness.

You know, fellow-members of the Reichstag, how hard was the road that I nave had to travel since 30 January 1933 in order to free the German people from the dishonourable position in which it found itself and to secure equality of rights, without thereby alienating Germany from the political and economic commonwealth of European nations, and particularly without creating new ill-feeling from the aftermath of old enmities. . . . At no moment of my struggle on behalf of the German people have I ever forgotten the duty incumbent on me and on us all firmly to uphold European culture and European civilization. . . .

Why should it not be possible to put an end to this useless strife (between France and Germany) which has lasted for centuries and which has never been and never will be finally decided by either of the two nations concerned? Why not replace it by the rule of reason? The German people have no interest in seeing the French people suffer. And what advantage can come to France when Germany is in misery? . . . Why should it not be possible to lift the general problem of conflicting interests between the European states above the sphere of passion and unreason and consider it in the calm light of a higher vision?

It was France, Hitler declared, who had betrayed Europe by her alliance with the Asiatic power of Bolshevism, pledged to destroy all the values of European civilization – just as it was

1. François-Poncet, p. 193.

France who, by the same action, had invalidated the Locarno Pact. Once again, reluctantly but without flinching, he must bow to the inevitable and take the necessary steps to defend Germany's national interests. He ended with the sacred vow to work now more than ever to further the cause of mutual understanding between the nations of Europe, but the roar of enthusiasm with which the packed Reichstag welcomed the announcement of the reoccupation of the Rhineland belied the words of peace.[1] As Hitler had told Rauschning: 'My Party comrades will not fail to understand me when they hear me speak of universal peace, disarmament and mutual security pacts!'[2] It was the assertion of German power, not the offer of peace, that brought the Reichstag to their feet, stamping and shouting in their delight.

Hitler later admitted: 'The forty-eight hours after the march into the Rhineland were the most nerve-racking in my life. If the French had then marched into the Rhineland we would have had to withdraw with our tails between our legs, for the military resources at our disposal would have been wholly inadequate for even a moderate resistance.'[3] Events, however, followed exactly the same pattern as the year before. There were anxious consultations between Paris and London; appeals for reason and calm – after all, people said, the Rhineland is part of Germany; much talk of the new opportunities for peace offered by Hitler's proposals – 'A Chance to Rebuild' was the title of *The Times* leading article. The Locarno Powers conferred; the Council of the League conferred; the International Court at The Hague was ready to confer, if Hitler would agree to submit his argument that the Franco-Soviet Treaty and the Locarno Pact were incompatible. Germany's action was again solemnly condemned and the censure again rejected by Hitler. But no one marched – except the Germans; no one spoke openly of sanctions or of enforcing the Locarno Treaty. The Polish Government, believing that France could never tolerate the German action in the Rhineland, suddenly offered, on 9 March, to bring their military alliance with France into operation; when they found that France was not going to move, the Poles had some embarrassment in explaining away their gesture, which had become known in Berlin.

Meanwhile Hitler dissolved the Reichstag and invited the German people to pass judgement on his policy. He came before them as the Peacemaker. 'All of us and all peoples,' he said at

1. Text in Baynes: vol. II, pp. 1,271–93.
2. See above, p. 324.   3. Paul Schmidt, p. 320.

Breslau, 'have the feeling that we are at the turning-point of an age. . . . Not we alone, the conquered of yesterday, but also the victors have the inner conviction that something was not as it should be, that reason seemed to have deserted men. . . . Peoples must find a new relation to each other, some new form must be created. . . . But over this new order which must be set up stand the words: Reason and Logic, Understanding and Mutual Consideration. They make a mistake who think that over the entrance to this new order there can stand the word "Versailles". That would be, not the foundation stone of the new order, but its gravestone.'[1]

When the election was held on 29 March the results were announced as:

Total of qualified voters	45,453,691
Total of votes cast	45,001,489 (99 per cent)
Votes cast against or invalid	540,211
Votes cast for the list	44,461,278 (98·8 per cent).

If the election figures showed a suspicious unanimity, there can be little doubt that a substantial majority of the German people approved Hitler's action, or that it raised the Führer to a new peak of popularity in Germany.

No event marks a clearer stage in the success of Hitler's diplomatic game than the reoccupation of the Rhineland. The demilitarized Rhineland was all that was left to France of the guarantees against a renewed German attack which she had sought to obtain after 1918. She had still a clear military superiority over the German Army; the terms of the Locarno Pact specifically recognized the German action as a *casus foederis*; ample warning had been given by the French Ambassador in Berlin. The French could certainly expect little support from the Baldwin Government in London, but to allow Hitler's action to pass unchallenged was tantamount to confessing that France was no longer prepared to defend the elaborate security system she had built up since 1918. This was a political fact which was bound to have major consequences in Central and Eastern Europe. While the Western Powers continued a futile exchange of notes with Berlin, the other European governments began to accommodate themselves to the new balance of power.

1. Speech of 22 March 1936 (Baynes: vol. ii, pp. 1,313–15).

VI

The first government to feel the effect of the change was the Austrian. The premise upon which Austrian independence was based, the unity of Italy, France, and Great Britain in face of Germany, and their superiority over Germany in power, was being destroyed. Sooner or later Mussolini would be bound to draw nearer to Germany; sooner or later the 1934 guarantee of Italian divisions on the Brenner frontier would be withdrawn.

In a letter to Hitler, dated 18 October 1935, Papen, now German Minister in Vienna, wrote: 'We can confidently leave further developments to sort themselves out in the near future. I am convinced that the shifting of Powers on the European chessboard will permit us in the not too distant future to take up actively the question of influencing the south-eastern area.'[1] In 1936 Papen, whose aim was to undermine Austrian independence from within and to bring about the *Anschluss* peacefully, gained his first successes. On 13 May, Prince Starhemberg, the Austrian Vice-Chancellor and an outspoken opponent of the Austrian Nazis, was forced to resign. Starhemberg was a particular friend of Mussolini, but the Duce was content simply to intercede for his personal safety. According to one well-informed Austrian, Guido Zernatto, it was actually from Mussolini that Schuschnigg, the Austrian Chancellor, received the hint to get rid of Starhemberg in order to placate Hitler.

Already in the spring of 1936, when he visited Rome, Starhemberg had found the Duce preoccupied with the threat of German power and with the way in which his own quarrel with Britain and France was working to Hitler's advantage. When, three weeks after Starhemberg had gone, the Austrian Chancellor, Schuschnigg, informed Mussolini that the Austrian Government was about to sign an agreement with Germany, the Duce, though repeating his assurances of support for Austrian independence, gave his approval.

The Austro-German Agreement of 11 July 1936 was designed on the surface to ease and improve relations between the two countries. Although Hitler had given his approval in advance, he was angry with Papen when he learned that the agreement had been signed. 'Instead of expressing his gratification, he broke into

1. Von Papen to Hitler, 18 October 1935 (N.D. D-692).

a flood of abuse. I had misled him into making exaggerated concessions. The whole thing was a trap.'[1] This was to prove far from the truth.

The three published clauses reaffirmed Hitler's recognition of Austria's full sovereignty; promised non-intervention in each other's internal affairs; and agreed that, although Austria would 'maintain a foreign policy based always on the principle that Austria acknowledges herself to be a German State', this should not affect her special relationship with Italy and Hungary established by the Rome Protocols of 1934. The secret clauses covered a relaxation of the Press war between the two countries, an amnesty for political prisoners in Austria, measures for dealing with the Austrian Nazi refugees in Germany, resumption of normal economic relations and German removal of the restrictions on tourist traffic between the two States. Most important of all, the Austrian Government agreed to give representatives of the so-called National Opposition in Austria, 'respectable' crypto-Nazis like Glaise-Horstenau and later Seyss-Inquart, a share in political responsibility.[2]

Ostensibly, Austro-German relations were now placed on a level satisfactory to both sides. But, in fact, for the next eighteen months the Germans used the Agreement as a lever with which to exert increasing pressure on the Austrian Government and to extort further concessions, a process of whittling down Austrian independence which culminated in the famous interview between Hitler and Schuschnigg in February 1938. The Agreement, as it was exploited by the Germans, thus marked a big step forward in that policy of capturing Austria by peaceful methods to which Hitler resorted after the failure of the putsch in July 1934.

The importance of the Agreement was not limited to the relations between Austria and Germany. Its signature materially improved Hitler's prospects of a *rapprochement* with Italy. Here again he had extraordinary luck. On 4 July 1936, the League Powers tacitly admitted defeat and withdrew the sanctions they had tried to impose on Italy. Less than a fortnight later, on 17 July, civil war broke out in Spain and created a situation from which Hitler was able to draw no fewer advantages than from Mussolini's Abyssinian adventure.

1. Papen, *Memoirs*, p. 370.
2. Text in *Documents on German Foreign Policy: From the Archives of the German Foreign Ministry* (hereafter referred to as G.D.), Series D. vol. I No. 152.

There is no evidence that Hitler had any hand in the events leading up to the civil war. He was at Bayreuth on 22 July when a German business man from Morocco and the local Nazi leader there arrived with a personal letter from General Franco. After Hitler's return from the theatre he sent for Göring and his War Minister, Blomberg. That night he decided to give active help to Franco. In the course of the next three years Germany sent men and military supplies, including experts and technicians of all kinds and the famous Condor Air Legion. German aid to Franco was never on a major scale, never sufficient to win the war for him or even to equal the forces sent by Mussolini, which in March 1937 reached the figure of sixty to seventy thousand men.[1] Hitler's policy, unlike Mussolini's, was not to secure Franco's victory, but to prolong the war. In April 1939, an official of the German Economic Policy Department, trying to reckon what Germany had spent on help to Franco up to that date, gave a round figure of five hundred million Reichsmarks,[2] not a large sum by comparison with the amounts spent on rearmament. But the advantages Germany secured in return were disproportionate – economic advantages (valuable sources of raw materials in Spanish mines); useful experience in training her airmen and testing equipment such as tanks in battle conditions; above all, strategic and political advantages.

It only needed a glance at the map to show how seriously France's position was affected by events across the Pyrenees. A victory for Franco would mean a third Fascist State on her frontiers, three instead of two frontiers to be guarded in the event of war. France, for geographical reasons alone, was more deeply interested in what happened in Spain than any other of the Great Powers, yet the ideological character of the Spanish Civil War divided, instead of uniting, French opinion. The French elections shortly before the outbreak of the troubles in Spain had produced the Left-wing Popular Front Government of Léon Blum. So bitter had class and political conflicts grown in France that – as in the case of the Franco-Soviet Treaty – foreign affairs were again subordinated to internal faction, and many Frenchmen were prepared to support Franco as a way of hitting at their own Government. The Spanish Civil War exacerbated all those factors of disunity in France upon which Hitler had always hoped to play,

1. Figure given by Grandi to the German Chargé d'Affaires in London in February 1938; G.D., D. III No. 519.
2. ibid., No. 783.

and so long as the Civil War lasted French foreign policy was bound to be weakened.

From the first Mussolini intervened openly in Spain, giving all the aid he could spare to bring about a victory for Franco. Thus at the very moment when the withdrawal of sanctions might have made it possible for the Western Powers to establish better relations with Italy, the Spanish War and the continual clash between Italian intervention and British and French attempts to enforce non-intervention kept the quarrel between them alive. As von Hassell, the German Ambassador in Rome, pointed out: 'The role played by the Spanish conflict as regards Italy's relations with France and England could be similar to that of the Abyssinian conflict, bringing out clearly the opposing interests of the Powers and thus preventing Italy from being drawn into the net of the Western Powers. . . . The struggle for dominant political influence in Spain lays bare the natural opposition between Italy and France; at the same time the position of Italy as a power in the Western Mediterranean comes into competition with that of Britain.'[1]

As the published diplomatic documents now make clear, the quarrel over Spain, added to the legacy of suspicion from the episode of sanctions, wrecked all the efforts of London and Paris to draw Mussolini closer to their side in the years between 1936 and 1939. Indeed, the common policy of Italy and Germany towards Spain created one of the main foundations on which the Rome–Berlin Axis was built, and the Spanish Civil War provided much greater scope for such cooperation than the Abyssinian War from which Germany had held aloof.

In September 1936, Hitler judged circumstances favourable for creating a closer relationship between Germany and Italy in order to exploit a situation in which the two countries had begun to follow parallel courses. In the year that had passed since the outbreak of the Abyssinian War events had produced great changes in the relations of the Great Powers. Hitherto Hitler had been content to watch; now the time had come to make use of the advantages these changes offered him. The July Agreement between Germany and Austria removed the biggest obstacle to an understanding between Rome and Berlin, and on 29 June the German Ambassador conveyed to Ciano, the Italian Foreign

1. Dispatch from von Hassell to the German Foreign Ministry, 18 December 1936; G.D., D. III, No. 157.

Minister, an offer from Hitler to consider the recognition of the new Italian Empire – a point on which the Duce was notoriously touchy – whenever Mussolini wished. In September Hitler sent Hans Frank, his Minister of Justice, who happened to speak Italian fluently, on an exploratory mission to Rome.

Frank saw Mussolini in the Palazzo Venezia on 23 September. He brought a cordial invitation from the Führer for both Mussolini and Ciano to visit Germany. In Spain, he said, Germany was assisting the Nationalists from motives of ideological solidarity, but she had neither interests nor aims of her own in the Mediterranean. 'The Führer is anxious,' Ciano noted, 'that we should know that he regards the Mediterranean as a purely Italian sea. Italy has a right to positions of privilege and control in the Mediterranean. The interests of the Germans are turned towards the Baltic, which is their Mediterranean.' In Germany, Frank declared, the Austrian question was now considered to have been settled, and after suggesting a common policy in presenting their colonial demands, and renewing the offer to recognize the Italian Empire, Frank concluded by expressing Hitler's belief in the need for increasingly close collaboration between Germany and Italy.[1] Throughout the interview Mussolini was careful not to be too forthcoming and affected a certain disinterestedness, but a month later Ciano set out for Germany.

After a talk with the German Foreign Minister, Neurath, in Berlin on 21 October, Ciano visited Hitler himself at Berchtesgaden on the 24th. Hitler laid himself out to be charming and was greatly touched by the cordial greetings from 'the leading statesman in the world, to whom none may even remotely compare himself'. Twice he telephoned to Munich to make sure of the details of Ciano's reception, and although he monopolized the conversation he was obviously at pains to impress Ciano with his friendliness.

The gist of Hitler's remarks was the need for Italy and Germany to create a common front against Bolshevism and against the Western Powers. The possibilities of Poland, Yugoslavia, Hungary, and Japan were passed in rapid review. Towards England Hitler still showed uncertainty. If England faced the formation of a strong German–Italian bloc, she might well seek to come to terms with it. If she still continued to work against them, then Germany and Italy would have the power to defeat her.

1. Ciano's Minutes in *Ciano's Diplomatic Papers*, edited by Malcolm Muggeridge (London, 1948), pp. 43–8.

German and Italian rearmament [Hitler declared] is proceeding much more rapidly than rearmament can in Great Britain, where it is not only a case of producing ships, guns, and aeroplanes, but also of undertaking psychological rearmament, which is much longer and more difficult. In three years Germany will be ready, in four years more than ready; if five years are given, better still. . . . According to the English there are two countries in the world today which are led by adventurers: Germany and Italy. But England too, was led by adventurers when she built her Empire. Today she is governed merely by incompetents.[1]

A protocol had been prepared by the Italian and German Foreign Offices before Ciano's visit, and was signed by the two Foreign Ministers in Berlin. It covered in some detail German–Italian cooperation on a number of issues – the proposals for a new Locarno Pact; policy towards the League; Spain; Austria; the Danubian States (the Germans were eager to bring Yugoslavia and Italy closer together); Abyssinia, and the recognition of the Japanese puppet state of Manchukuo. Nothing was said of this document (known as the October Protocols) in the communiqué issued at the end of Ciano's visit, but when Mussolini went to Milan on 1 November 1936 he spoke of an agreement between the two countries and for the first time used the famous simile of an axis, 'round which all those European states which are animated by a desire for collaboration and peace may work together.'

VII

By the end of 1936 Hitler had succeeded in establishing one of the two conditions, an alliance with Italy, on which he had counted in *Mein Kampf.* For the initiative in forging the Axis unquestionably came from Hitler, who exploited with great skill the situation in which Mussolini was placed. But the second condition, an understanding with Britain, still eluded him.

In August, Hitler had determined on a new approach to London and appointed Ribbentrop as the German Ambassador to the Court of St James. Ribbentrop was four years younger than the Führer whom he slavishly admired and copied, had served in the First World War and had later become a business man dealing in wines. In 1920 he married Anna Henkel, the daughter of a big champagne dealer, and after, as before, the war spent a good deal of time travelling abroad. He joined the Party in the early 1930s, when Hitler had already become prominent as a political leader,

1. Ciano's Minutes, *Ciano's Diplomatic Papers*, pp. 56–60.

and it was at his villa in Dahlem that the decisive conversation leading to the formation of the coalition government took place on 22 January 1933. An ambitious man, Ribbentrop succeeded in persuading the new Chancellor that he could provide him with more reliable information about what was happening abroad than reached him through the official channels of the Foreign Office. With Party funds he set up a Ribbentrop Bureau on the Wilhelmstrasse, facing the Foreign Office; it was staffed by journalists, business men out of a job, and by those members of the Party who were eager for a diplomatic career. After serving as Special Commissioner for Disarmament in 1934, Ribbentrop's big chance came in 1935, when he succeeded in negotiating the Anglo-German Naval Treaty behind the back of the German Foreign Office, and made his reputation.

Arrogant, vain, humourless, and spiteful, Ribbentrop was one of the worst choices Hitler ever made for high office. But he shared many of Hitler's own social resentments (especially against the regular Foreign Service), he was prepared to prostrate himself before the Führer's genius, and his appointment enabled Hitler to take the conduct of relations with Great Britain much more closely into his own hands. Ribbentrop's ambition was to replace Neurath as Foreign Minister, and he accepted the London post with a bad grace, believing with some justification that Neurath was trying to get him out of the way. None the less, further success along the lines of the Anglo-German Naval Treaty would be a big feather in his cap, and both Ribbentrop and Hitler had considerable hopes of the new appointment.

What puzzled Hitler and Ribbentrop was the fact that although the British were disinclined to take any forceful action on the Continent and only too prepared to put off awkward decisions, they found them wary of committing themselves to cooperate with Germany. At the time of Ciano's visit Hitler was still in two minds about the British: he was reluctant to take open action which would alienate them, in the hope that he might still win them over, yet he was tempted at times to regard Britain as 'finished' and her value either as an ally or an opponent as negligible. This alternation of moods persisted in varying degree until the war, and never wholly disappeared from Hitler's ambivalent attitude towards Britain.

Hitler's best argument with the Conservative Government in Britain, an argument which commanded attention not only in

London, but in many other capitals, was one which he used more frequently after the outbreak of the Spanish Civil War: the common interest of the European States in face of Communism. Hitler had been talking of Germany as a 'bulwark against Bolshevism' since 1919. But the Spanish Civil War sharpened the sense of ideological conflict in Western Europe. This was the era of Popular Fronts, attempts to unite all 'progressive' parties and organizations in common opposition to Fascism; it was also the period in which the extremists of the French Right coined the slogan, 'Better Hitler than Blum'. Many people in England as well as in France, who would have looked askance at a blatant German nationalism, were impressed by Hitler's anti-Communism; it served the same purpose as Russia's own peace campaign and similar moves after the Second World War. Again and again Hitler used the example of Spain as a land ravaged by Bolshevism, and pointed to the Popular Front Government in France as the equivalent of the Girondins who were replaced by the more extreme Jacobins, or of Kerensky's Provisional Government in Russia swept away by the Bolsheviks in the second October Revolution of 1917. 'Perhaps the time is coming more quickly than we think,' he declared in November 1936, 'when the rest of Europe will see in our Germany the strongest safeguard of a truly European, a truly human, culture and civilization. Perhaps the time is coming more quickly than we think when the rest of Europe will no longer regard with resentment the founding of a National Socialist German Reich, but will rejoice that this dam was raised against the Bolshevik flood. . . .'[1]

Anti-Communism could also be used to provide the basis for the power-bloc of which Hitler had spoken to Ciano. For months Ribbentrop had been working – quite independently of the German Foreign Office – to reach agreement with Japan. In November he succeeded, and flew to Berlin from London for the signature of the Anti-Comintern Pact. The ideological objectives of the pact – the defeat of the Communist 'world-conspiracy' – gave it a universal character which a straightforward agreement aimed against Russia could not have had. It was expressly designed to secure the adherence of other States, and it was not long before Hitler began to collect new signatories. The public provisions of the pact dealt with no more than the exchange of information on Comintern activity, cooperation in preventive measures, and severity in dealing with Comintern agents. There

1. Speech at Munich, 9 November 1936 (Baynes: vol. ii, pp. 1, 331–2).

was also a secret Protocol which dealt specifically with Russia and bound both parties to sign no political treaties with the U.S.S.R. In the event of an unprovoked attack or threat of attack by Russia on either Power, the Protocol added, each agreed to 'take no measures which would tend to ease the situation of the U.S.S.R'.[1] This was still vague, but the statement made by Ribbentrop on the day the treaty was signed left little doubt that Germany hoped to make more of this new political grouping. 'Japan,' Ribbentrop declared, 'will never permit any dissemination of Bolshevism in the Far East. Germany is creating a bulwark against this pestilence in Central Europe. Finally, Italy, as the Duce informs the world, will hoist the anti-Bolshevist banner in the south.'[2] In Hitler's eyes the October Protocols signed with Italy, and the Anti-Comintern Pact concluded with Japan, were to become the foundations of a new military alliance.

From every point of view, therefore, Hitler could feel satisfaction with his fourth year of power. The remilitarization of the Rhineland, German rearmament, and the contrast between his own self-confident leadership and the weakness of the Western Powers had greatly increased his prestige both abroad and at home. Distinguished visitors were eager to meet him – among them Lloyd George, who left the unfortunate impression of confirming Hitler in his belief that if Germany had only held out in 1918 she would have won the war. Most of those who went to stare returned half-convinced by the claims of Europe's new Man of Destiny, and swept away by their impressions of the dynamic new Germany he had called into being. When the Olympic Games were held in Berlin in August 1936, thousands of foreigners crowded the capital, and the opportunity was used with great skill to put the Third Reich on show. Germany's new masters entertained with a splendour that rivalled the displays of *le Roi Soleil* and the Tsars of Russia. At Nuremberg, in September, the Party Rally, which lasted a week, was on a scale which even Nazi pageantry had never before equalled.

Hitler rounded off his first four years of office by a long speech to the Reichstag on 30 January 1937, in which he formally withdrew Germany's signature from those clauses of the Treaty of Versailles which had denied her equality of rights and laid on her the responsibility for the war. 'Today,' Hitler added, 'I must humbly thank Providence, whose grace has enabled me, once an

1. G.D.I, D., No. 734.
2. *Documents on International Affairs, 1936* (London, 1937), pp. 299–300.

unknown soldier in the war, to bring to a successful issue the struggle for our honour and rights as a nation.'[1]

It was an impressive record to which Hitler was able to point, not only in the raising of German prestige abroad, but in economic improvement and the recovery of national confidence at home. It is pointless to deny that Hitler succeeded in releasing in the German people a great store of energy and faith in themselves, which had been frustrated during the years of the Depression. The Germans responded to the lead of an authoritarian government which was not afraid to take both risks and responsibility. Thus, to quote only one instance, between January 1933 and December 1934 the number of registered unemployed fell from six millions to two million six hundred thousand, while the number of insured workers employed rose from eleven and a half to fourteen and a half millions.[2] Granted that some measure of economic recovery was general at this time, none the less in Germany it was more rapid and went further than elsewhere, largely as a result of heavy Government expenditure on improving the resources of the country and on public works.

It is natural, therefore, to ask, as many Germans still ask, whether there was not some point up to which the Nazi movement was a force for good, but after which its original idealism became corrupted. Whatever truth there may be in this, so far as it is a question of the rank and file of the movement, so far as Hitler and the Nazi leadership are concerned, this is a view contradicted by the evidence. For all the evidence points to the opposite view, namely, that from the first Hitler and the other Nazi leaders thought in terms solely of power, their own power, and the power of the nation over which they ruled.

In a secret memorandum of 3 May 1935, Dr Schacht, the man who had the greatest responsibility for Germany's economic recovery, wrote: 'The accomplishment of the armament programme with speed and in quantity is *the* problem of German politics, and everything else should be subordinated to this purpose, as long as the main purpose is not imperilled by neglecting all other questions.'[3] This view is repeated again and again through all the discussions on economic policy in these years. The basis of Schacht's later opposition to Hitler's policy, which came to a head

1. Speech of 30 January 1937 (Baynes: vol. II, pp. 1,334–47).
2. Figures quoted from C. W. Guillebaud, *The Economic Recovery of Germany, 1933–38* (London, 1939), p. 46.
3. Memorandum from Schacht to Hitler, 3 May 1935 (N.D. 1168-PS).

in 1937 and led to his resignation, was Hitler's persistent refusal to take into account any other economic or social objective besides the overriding need to provide him with the most efficient military machine possible in the shortest possible time.

The driving force behind German rearmament was Hitler. Looking back on earlier days during the Russian campaign he told Jodl:

As for the Navy they never once made any demands on their own behalf; it was always I who had to do it for them and then, if you please, the Navy would whittle down the programme I proposed for them! The army were no better; here again it was I who had to urge the adoption of a programme of real expansion, and it was the Army which countered with hesitancy and evasions. I was so frustrated that in the end I was compelled to withdraw their prerogatives from the Army and assume them myself.[1]

In August 1936, the period of conscription was extended to two years, while at Nuremberg, in September, impatient with the difficulties raised by the economic experts, Hitler proclaimed a Four-Year Plan and put Göring in charge fully armed with the powers to secure results whatever the cost. German economy was henceforward subordinated to one purpose, preparation for war. It is this fact that explains why, although Germany made so remarkable an economic recovery, and by the end of this period was one of the best-equipped industrial nations in the world, this was reflected, not in the standard of living of her people, but in her growing military strength.

Moreover, it is necessary to add to this, that the biggest single factor in the recovery of confidence and faith in Germany was the sense of this power, a renewed confidence and faith in 'the German mission', expressed in an increasingly aggressive nationalism which had little use for the rights of other, less powerful nations. The psychology of Nazism, no less than Nazi economics, was one of preparation for war. Both depended for their continued success upon the maintenance of a national spirit and a national effort which in the end must find expression in aggressive action. War, the belief in violence and the right of the stronger, were not corruptions of Nazism, they were its essence. Anyone who visited Germany in 1936–7 needed to be singularly blind not to see the ends to which all this vast activity was directed. Recognition of the benefits which Hitler's rule brought to Germany in the first four years of his régime needs to be tempered therefore by the

1. *Hitler's Table Talk*, p. 634.

realization that for the Führer – and for a considerable section of the German people – these were the by-products of his true purpose, the creation of an instrument of power with which to realize a policy of expansion that in the end was to admit no limits.

VIII

Throughout 1937 Hitler pursued the lines of policy he had established in the previous year. It was a year of preparation – and of growing confidence in German strength. For, although Hitler was still at pains to protest his love of peace, there was a new note of impatience in his voice. In his speech of 30 January he dealt at some length with Germany's demand for the return of the colonies taken from her at the end of the war. In the same speech he spoke of 'the justified feeling of national honour existing among those nationalities who are forced to live as a minority within other nations.'[1] The demand for colonies was raised with increasing frequency in 1937, and at the end of the year, speaking in Augsburg, Hitler declared: 'What the world shuts its ears to today it will not be able to ignore in a year's time. What it will not listen to now it will have to think about in three years' time, and in five or six it will have to take into practical consideration. We shall voice our demand for living-room in colonies more and more loudly till the world cannot but recognize our claim.'[2]

There were two particular grounds for Hitler's confidence: the progress of German rearmament, and the consolidation of the Axis. Göring, now the economic dictator of Germany, had as little respect for economics as Hitler. His methods were crude, but not ineffective.

In December 1936, Göring told a meeting of industrialists that it was no longer a question of producing economically, but simply of producing. So far as securing foreign exchange was concerned it was quite immaterial whether the provisions of the law were complied with or not, provided only that foreign exchange was brought in somehow. 'No limit on rearmament can be visualized. The only alternatives are victory or destruction. . . . We live in a time when the battle is in sight. We are already on the threshold of mobilization and we are already at war. All that is lacking is the actual shooting.'[3]

1. Text of the speech in Baynes: vol. ii, pp. 1,334–47.
2. Speech at Augsburg, 21 November 1937 (Baynes: vol. ii, pp. 1,370–2).
3. Speech of 17 December 1936 (N.D., NI-051).

Hitler's and Göring's programme of autarky and the search for *ersatz* raw materials were criticized by Dr Schacht at the time, but his economic arguments fell on deaf ears. They were men in a hurry, indifferent to the cost or to the long-term economic consequences, provided they got the arms they wanted quickly. When Schacht persisted in his protests his resignation was accepted,[1] and Göring continued to ride rough-shod over economic theories and economic facts alike. By the spring of 1939 Hitler had carried out an expansion of German military power unequalled in German history.

The consolidation of the Rome–Berlin Axis was marked by increased consultation between the two parties and frequent exchanges of visits culminating in Mussolini's State reception in Germany in September, and Italy's signature of the Anti-Comintern Pact in November. Among those whom Hitler sent to Rome were Göring (January); Neurath, the Foreign Minister (May); Blomberg, the War Minister (June); and Ribbentrop (October). The initiative still came from Berlin, and – as the captured diplomatic documents show – Hitler watched with some anxiety the attempts of the British and French to renew friendly relations with the Duce.

On 2 January 1937, Ciano signed a 'gentlemen's agreement' with England in which each country recognized the other's vital interests in the freedom of the Mediterranean, and agreed that there should be no alteration in the *status quo* in that region. (The British were particularly anxious about the possibility of Italy's acquiring the Balearic Islands, off Spain.) Shortly afterwards Hitler sent Göring to Rome on an exploratory mission. Göring had two talks with Mussolini, on 15 January and 23 January, in which he clumsily tried to sound out the Duce's opinions on a number of issues. It is evident from the record of the two conversations that each side regarded with some suspicion the other's attempts to reach an understanding with England. Above all, Austria was still a danger-point in German–Italian relations, and Mussolini did not relish Göring's obvious assumption of the inevitability of the *Anschluss*. Paul Schmidt, who was present as the interpreter, says that Mussolini shook his head vehemently, and Hassell, the German Ambassador, reported to Berlin: 'I got the impression that General Göring's statement regarding Austria had met with a cool reception, and that he himself,

1. See below, pp. 412–13.

realizing this fact, had by no means said all that he had planned to say.'[1]

At his second conversation with the Duce a week later (23 January), Göring was more circumspect. He confined himself to urging Mussolini to bring pressure to bear on the Austrian Government to observe the terms of the Austro-German Agreement, and although he made plain Germany's dislike of the Schuschnigg Government, and her refusal to tolerate a Hapsburg restoration in Austria, he added the assurance that for Hitler's part there would be no surprises as far as Austria was concerned.[2] According to Hassell, who subsequently had a conversation with Ciano, Göring's more tactful behaviour on the second occasion reassured the Italians. 'Of special importance,' Hassell wrote to Göring, 'was the fact that you clearly stated that, within the framework of German–Italian friendship, any German action on the Austrian question aiming at a change in the present situation would take place only in consultation with Rome. I added that we, for our part, assumed we were safe from a repetition of Italy's previous partnership with other Powers ("The Watch on the Brenner"). Ciano agreed to that as a matter of course.'[3]

These suspicions and difficulties were not easily removed. The Italians quickly took offence at any slighting reference, such as the Germans were only too prone to make, to their martial qualities. General von Blomberg's visit to Italy in June was far from being an unqualified success, and Ciano's suspicions in turn were roused by the news that the German Foreign Minister, Neurath, was preparing to visit London. Göring's talks with Mussolini showed that, over Austria, Hitler still needed to proceed with care, and when Neurath saw the Duce in May he assured him 'that the Führer intends to keep as the basis of his policy towards Austria the Pact of 11 July. Although the question is the subject of lively interest, it is not considered by the Germans to be acute.'[4] The only exception would be in the event of a Hapsburg restoration.

None the less, the pull of events was too strong for Mussolini. His Mediterranean ambitions, his intervention in Spain, his anxiety to be on the winning side and to share in the plucking of

1. Memorandum by von Hassell (G.D., D. I, No. 199).
2. Schmidt's Minute, *Ciano's Diplomatic Papers*, pp. 80–1.
3. Hassell to Göring, 30 January 1937 (G.D., D. I, No. 208).
4. Conversation of 3 May 1937, *Ciano's Diplomatic Papers*, pp. 115–17.

the decadent democracies, not least his resentment over British and French policy in the past, were added to the vanity of a dictator with a bad inferiority complex in international relations, and pointed to the advantages of the partnership which Hitler persistently pressed on him. On 4 September it was announced that the two leaders would meet in Germany, and on the 23rd the Duce set out for Germany in a new uniform specially designed for the occasion. It was a fatal step for Mussolini; the beginning of that surrender of independence which led his régime to disaster and himself to the gibbet in the Piazzale Loreto in Milan.

Hitler received the Duce at Munich, where the Nazi Party put on a superbly organized show, including a ceremonial parade of S.S. troops. Mussolini had hardly recovered his breath when he was whisked away to a display of Germany's military power at the Army manoeuvres in Mecklenburg, and of her industrial resources in the Krupp factories at Essen. The visit reached its climax in Berlin, where the capital was put *en fête* to receive the impressionable Duce, and the two dictators stood side by side to address a crowd of eight hundred thousand on the Maifeld. Before the speeches were over, a terrific thunderstorm scattered the audience in pandemonium, and in the confusion Mussolini was left to find his way back to Berlin alone, soaked to the skin and in a state of collapse. But even this unfortunate contretemps could not destroy the spell which his visit cast over him. He returned from Germany bewitched by the display of power which had been carefully staged for him. There had been no time for diplomatic conversations between the two Heads of State, but Hitler had achieved something more valuable than a dozen protocols: he had stamped on Mussolini's mind an indelible impression of German might from which the Duce was never able to set himself free.

Hitler laid himself out to charm as well as to impress, and publicly acclaimed the Duce as 'one of those lonely men of the ages on whom history is not tested, but who themselves are the makers of history'.[1] Hitler's admiration for Mussolini was unfeigned. Mussolini, like himself – and like Stalin, whom Hitler also admired – was a man of the people; Hitler felt at ease with him as he never felt when with members of the traditional ruling classes, and, despite his later disillusionment with the Italian performance in the war, he never betrayed or discarded him. All trace of the

1. Speech on the Maifeld, 28 September 1937 (Baynes: vol. II, pp. 1,361–4).

unhappy meeting at Venice in 1934 was wiped out by the German visit and Hitler presented the Axis to the world as a solid bloc of a hundred and fifteen million people.

'From the consciousness of that which the Fascist and National Socialist relations have in common,' Hitler proclaimed, 'there has today arisen not merely a community of views, but also a community of action.

'Fascist Italy through the creative activity of a man of constructive power has become a new Imperium. And you, Benito Mussolini, in these days will have been assured with your own eyes of one fact concerning the National Socialist State – that Germany, too, in her political attitude and her military strength is once more a World Power.

'The forces of these two empires form today the strongest guarantee for the preservation of a Europe which still possesses a perception of its cultural mission and is not willing through the action of destructive elements to fall into disintegration.'[1]

Three weeks later Ribbentrop appeared in Rome to urge the Duce to put Italy's signature to the year-old Anti-Comintern Pact between Germany and Japan. Ribbentrop was disarmingly frank. He had failed in his mission to London, he told Mussolini, and had to recognize that the interests of Germany and Great Britain were irreconcilable. This was excellent hearing for the Duce, and he made little difficulty about signing the Pact. After the ceremony, which took place on 6 November, Mussolini declared that this represented 'the first gesture which will lead to a much closer understanding of a political and military nature between the three Powers'. Ribbentrop, still smarting from his failure in London, added with some satisfaction that the British reaction would be lively 'since the Pact will be interpreted as the alliance of the aggressive nations against the satisfied countries'.[2]

Ribbentrop's report on Mussolini's discussion of Austria can only have delighted Hitler. During the State visit he paid to Venice in April 1937, Schuschnigg, the Austrian Chancellor, had already sensed a change in the Italian attitude. Although Mussolini still assured him of his loyalty to Austrian independence, he laid stress on the need for Austria to meet Germany's demands under the July Agreement, and spoke of maintaining Austria's

1. Speech on the Maifeld, 28 Septemper 1937 (Baynes; vol. II, pp. 1,361–4).
2. Ciano's Minutes of Ribbentrop's conversations, 22 October–6 November 1937, *Ciano's Diplomatic Papers*, pp. 139–46.

integrity, within the framework of the Rome–Berlin Axis.[1] Now, in his November conversation, Mussolini told Ribbentrop that he was tired of mounting guard over Austrian independence, especially if the Austrians no longer wanted their independence.

Austria is German State No. 2. It will never be able to do anything without Germany, far less against Germany. Italian interest today is no longer as lively as it was some years ago, for one thing because of Italy's imperialist development, which was now concentrating her interest on the Mediterranean and the Colonies. . . . The best method is to let events take their natural course. One must not aggravate the situation, so as to avoid crises of an international nature. On the other hand, France knows that if a crisis should arise in Austria, Italy would do nothing. This was said to Schuschnigg, too, on the occasion of the Venice conversation. We cannot impose independence on Austria. . . . It is necessary, therefore, to abide by the formula: nothing will be done without previous exchange of information.[2]

Mussolini's embarrassment is obvious in every line of Ciano's minute, and was certainly not lost on Hitler. His exploitation of the quarrel between Italy and the Western Powers was beginning to yield dividends; in his cultivation of Mussolini's friendship Hitler had found the key to unlock the gate to Central Europe. Four months later the gate was swung back without effort, and German troops stood on the old Austro-Italian frontier of the Brenner Pass.

Hitler's interest in Italy did not lead him to neglect Poland. In 1936 the Poles, worried by the growth of Nazi influence in Danzig and still distrustful of Germany's fair words, tried to strengthen their ties with France. Friendship with France as well as with Germany would help to reinforce that independent position which was the object of Colonel Beck's policy. The reoccupation of the Rhineland gave a jolt to Beck's complacency, and under the immediate shock the Poles renewed their offer to the French to march if France decided to make an issue of it.

Well aware of the stiffening in the Polish attitude, Hitler and Ribbentrop gave the most convincing assurances to Count Szembek, the Polish Under-Secretary for Foreign Affairs, when they received him in Berlin during August 1936. In Danzig, Hitler

1. Ciano's Minute of the Venice Talks, 22 April 1937, *Ciano's Diplomatic Papers*, pp. 108–15; Kurt von Schuschnigg: *Austrian Requiem* pp. 109–11.
2. Ciano's Minute, *Ciano's Diplomatic Papers*, p. 146.

declared, Germany would act entirely by way of an understanding with Poland, and with respect for all her rights. Ribbentrop, dismissing Danzig as a question of secondary importance, laid heavy emphasis on the common interests of Poland and Germany in face of the menace of Bolshevism.

In his speech of 30 January 1937, Hitler now coupled Poland with Germany and Italy. 'True statesmanship must face realities and not shirk them. The Italian nation and the new Italian State are realities. The German nation and the German State are likewise realities. And for my own fellow citizens I should like to state that the Polish nation and the Polish State have also become realities.'[1] Shortly after Göring's return from Rome at the end of January Hitler sent him to Warsaw, where he used that bluff hypocrisy which was his diplomatic stock-in-trade, to disarm Polish suspicions.

'Germany (Göring told Marshal Smigly-Rydz) was completely reconciled to her present territorial status. Germany would not attack Poland and had no intention of seizing the Polish Corridor. "We do not want the Corridor. I say that sincerely and categorically; we do not need the Corridor." He could not give proof of this; it was a question of whether his word was believed or not.'[2]

Indeed, Göring excelled himself on this occasion. He told the Poles in confidence that there had been many advocates of a *rapprochement* with Russia and of the Rapallo policy in the old Germany Army, but Hitler had changed that. Germany needed a strong Poland; a weak Poland would be a standing invitation to Russian aggression, and for that reason Germany had no quarrel with the Franco-Polish alliance.

Hitler followed these reassurances by offering to negotiate a minorities treaty with Poland, which was signed in Berlin on 5 November – the date, as we shall see, is worth noting. When Hitler received the Polish Ambassador, Lipski, he not only expressed his satisfaction at settling the minorities question, but added, with great precision, that there would be no change in the position of Danzig, and that Poland's rights in the Free State would be fully respected. Twice he repeated to Lipski: '*Danzig ist mit Polen verbunden* – Danzig is bound up with Poland.'[3]

1. Baynes: vol. ii, p. 1,342.
2. Minute of Göring's conversation with Marshal Smigly-Rydz, 16 February 1937, *Polish White Book*, pp. 36–8.
3. ibid., pp. 40–3.

Further visits of Colonel Beck to Berlin (January 1938) and of Göring to Warsaw (in February) only served to re-emphasize Hitler's friendly intentions. The Polish neutrality, which Hitler thereby ensured throughout his operations in 1938, was of the greatest value to him. So long as Poland stood out, and refused to cooperate against Germany, it was impossible to build up effective resistance to Hitler's eastern ambitions. If Italy's friendship was the key to Austria, Poland's was one of the keys to Czechoslovakia.

Meanwhile, the Western Powers continued to be preoccupied with Spain. Their efforts to enforce non-intervention with the cooperation of the blatantly interventionist Italian and German Governments, though well-intentioned, only lowered their prestige. The world, however shocked, was a good deal more impressed by the German bombardment of the port of Almeria as reprisal for a bombing attack on the cruiser *Deutschland*. Hitler was much less interested in Franco's victory than in prolonging the war. Thereby he kept open the breach between Italy and the Western Powers, made Britain and France look foolish by pursuing obstructionist tactics on the Non-Intervention Committee, and provided himself with an unequalled text for preaching his crusade against Bolshevism. His closing speech to the Nuremberg Rally in September 1937 was notable for the violence of his attack on Communism, in the course of which he compared the clash between the rival *Weltanschauungen* of National Socialism and Bolshevism to that between Christianity and Mohammedanism. He produced the identification of Communism with the Jewish world conspiracy directed from Moscow as 'a fact proved by irrefutable evidence'. The Jews had established a brutal dictatorship over the Russian people, and now sought to extend it to the rest of Europe and the rest of the world. This, he declared in a frenzied peroration, was the struggle being fought out on Spanish soil, this was the historical issue to which the dilettante statesmen of London and Paris were blind.[1]

IX

The German denunciation of the Locarno Pact had been followed by the reversion of Belgium to a professed policy of neutrality, a policy, in King Leopold's words, which 'should aim resolutely at

1. Speech of 13 September 1937. Text in Baynes: vol. I, pp. 688–712.

placing us outside any dispute of our neighbours'.[1] The with-drawal of Belgium, accepted by France and Britain in April 1937, was a further stage in the disintegration of the European Security system which had been created after Germany's defeat in 1918. Yet London and Paris still did not give up their attempts to reach some form of general agreement with Hitler, and a desultory ex-change of notes, inquiries and diplomatic approaches continued.

A new impetus was given to these dragging negotiations with the replacement of Mr Baldwin by Mr Neville Chamberlain as Prime Minister at the end of May 1937. Baldwin has been characterized by Mr Churchill as possessing a genius for waiting upon events, knowing little of Europe, and disliking what he knew. 'Neville Chamberlain, on the other hand, was alert, business-like, opinionated and self-confident in a very high degree. Unlike Baldwin, he conceived himself able to comprehend the whole field of Europe and indeed the world. . . . His all-pervading hope was to go down in history as the great Peacemaker; and for this he was prepared to strive continually in the teeth of facts, and face great risks for himself and his country.'[2] Above all, Chamber-lain was determined to make a new attempt to arrive at a com-prehensive settlement with the two dictators.

The first fruits of Chamberlain's policy were the visit of Lord Halifax, then Lord President of the Council, to Germany in November 1937. The ostensible pretext was an invitation from Göring to visit a Hunting Exhibition in Berlin, but Lord Halifax was authorized by the British Prime Minister to see Hitler as well, and to discover what was in the Führer's mind.

Hitler declined to come to Berlin but was willing to receive Lord Halifax at Berchtesgaden. When Halifax arrived, Hitler showed himself both wilful and evasive. It was impossible, he declared, to make agreements with countries where political decisions were dictated by party considerations and were at the mercy of the Press. The British could not get used to the fact that Germany was no longer weak and divided; any proposal he made was automatically suspected, and so on. He brought up the question of colonies – 'the sole remaining issue between Germany and England' – only to declare that the British were not prepared to discuss it reasonably; at the same time, he was careful to avoid defining Germany's colonial claims.

The German account of the interview gives the impression that

1. Speech of 14 October 1936.
2. Churchill: *The Second World War*, vol. I, pp. 173–4.

Hitler deliberately exaggerated the difficulties in the way of negotiations. He threw doubt on the value of attempting to reach a comprehensive settlement, insisting that discussions would need the most careful preparation, that it was better not to be in a hurry, and that diplomatic exchanges would be preferable to the direct negotiations proposed by the British.[1] Whether these were deliberate tactics or an expression of temperament it is impossible to say.

Later, after Halifax had reported, Chamberlain wrote in his private journal: 'The German visit was from my point of view a great success because it achieved its object, that of creating an atmosphere in which it is possible to discuss with Germany the practical questions involved in a European settlement.'[2] Halifax had already indicated these to Hitler. Speaking of questions which 'fell into the category of possible alterations in the European order which might be destined to come about with the passage of time', Halifax mentioned specifically Danzig, Austria, and Czechoslovakia. It was not, he told Hitler, the English attitude that the *status quo* must be maintained under all circumstances. 'It was recognized that one might have to contemplate an adjustment to new conditions.' The one point on which Halifax insisted was that these 'adjustments' should be carried out peacefully.[3]

However sincere Chamberlain's desire to reach a settlement with Germany, in practice it amounted to an invitation to diplomatic blackmail which Hitler was not slow to exploit.

Exactly a fortnight before he listened to Mr Chamberlain's well-meant messages, on 5 November, Hitler disclosed something of his own thoughts to a small group of men in a secret meeting at the Reich Chancellery. Only five others were present besides himself and Colonel Hossbach, the adjutant whose minutes are the source of our information.[4] They were Field-Marshal von Blomberg, the German War Minister; Colonel-General von Fritsch, Commander-in-Chief of the Army; Admiral Raeder, Commander-in-Chief of the Navy; Göring, Commander-in-Chief

1. Memorandum on Halifax–Hitler Conversations, 19 November 1937 (G.D., D.I, No. 31).
2. Keith Feiling: *The Life of Neville Chamberlain* (London, 1946), p. 332.
3. G.D., D.I, No. 31.
4. G.D., D.I, No. 19, usually referred to as the Hossbach Minutes.

of the Air Force, and Neurath, the German Foreign Minister.

Hitler began by explaining that what he had to say was the fruit of his deliberation and experiences during the past four and a half years. Then he put the problem in the simplest terms: 'The aim of German policy was to make secure and to preserve the racial community and to enlarge it. It was therefore a question of space.' Two possible solutions were mentioned only to be dismissed: autarky, and an increased participation in world economy. Germany could never be more than partially self-sufficient in raw materials; she could never supply her growing population with sufficient food from her own resources. Yet to look to increased trade offered no alternative; there Germany had to face limitations, in the form of competition, which it was not in her power to remove.

Germany's future, Hitler declared, could only be safeguarded by acquiring additional *Lebensraum*. Such living space was to be sought, not overseas, but in Europe, and it could be found only at the risk of conflict. 'The history of all ages had proved that expansion could only be carried out by breaking down resistance and taking risks; set backs were inevitable. There had never been spaces without a master, and there were none today: the attacker always comes up against a possessor. The question for Germany ran: where could she achieve the greatest gain at the lowest cost.'

Germany had to reckon with two 'hate-inspired antagonists' – not Russia despite all Hitler's talk of the Bolshevik menace, but Britain and France. Neither country was so strong as appeared. There were signs of disintegration in the British Empire – Ireland, India, the threat of Japanese power in the Far East and of Italian in the Mediterranean. In the long run, the Empire could not maintain its position. France's situation was more favourable than that of Britain, but she was confronted with internal political difficulties. None the less, Britain, France, Russia, and their satellites must be included as factors of power in Germany's political calculations.

'Germany's problem,' Hitler therefore concluded, 'could only be solved by means of force, and this was never without attendant risk.' Granted the resort to force, there remained to be answered the questions 'when?' and 'how?' In considering these questions, Hitler distinguished three cases.

First, the peak of German power would be reached by 1943–5. After that, equipment would become obsolete, and the rearmament of the other Powers would reduce the German lead.

'It was while the rest of the world was preparing its defences that we were obliged to take the offensive. ... One thing only was certain, that we could not wait longer. If he was still living, it was his unalterable resolve to solve Germany's problem of space at the latest by 1943–5.'

In the second and third cases, the necessity for action would arise before that date. The second case was one in which internal strife in France might reach such a pitch as to disable the French Army. This must be used at once for a blow against the Czechs, whenever it occurred. The third case would arise if France became involved in war with another state and so could not take action against Germany. 'The Führer saw case 3 coming definitely nearer; it might emerge from the present tensions in the Mediterranean, and he was resolved to take advantage of it, whatever happened, even as early as 1938.' It was in Germany's interest to prolong the war in Spain. Possibly a *casus belli* might arise out of the Italian occupation of the Balearic Islands. In such a war, the crucial point would be North Africa. Should such a conflict develop, Germany must take advantage of French and British preoccupation to attack the Czechs.

In all three cases, the first objective must be to overrun Czechoslovakia and Austria and so secure Germany's eastern and southern flanks. Hitler went on to discuss the probable attitude of the other Powers to such action. 'Actually, the Führer believed that almost certainly Britain, and probably France as well, had already tacitly written off the Czechs and were reconciled to the fact that this question would be cleared up in due course by Germany.' In any case, France would be very unlikely to make an attack without British support, and the most that would be necessary would be to hold the western defences in strength. Once Austria and Czechoslovakia had been overrun, this would greatly increase Germany's economic resources and add twelve divisions to her army. Italy's neutrality would depend upon Mussolini; that of Poland and Russia, upon the swiftness of the military decision.

The significance of this meeting in November 1937 has been a subject of considerable controversy. It is surely wrong to suggest that this was the occasion when 'the die was cast. Hitler had communicated his irrevocable decision to go to war.'[1] Hitler was far too skilful a politician to make an irrevocable decision on a series of hypothetical assumptions. Far from working to a time-

1. William L. Shirer: *The Rise and Fall of the Third Reich*, p. 307.

table, he was an opportunist, prepared to profit by whatever turned up, to wait for the mistakes made by others. For the best part of two years after November 1937, Hitler used all his skill to draw the maximum advantage from diplomacy backed by the threat of force without actual resort to the means of war.

It is far more probable, therefore, that the reason for the meeting which Hossbach recorded was to override the doubts about the pace of rearmament expressed by General Fritsch, and earlier by Schacht, than to announce some newly conceived decision to commit Germany to a course deliberately aimed at war.

But to look for such a decision is to misunderstand the character of Hitler's foreign policy and his responsibility for the war which followed. For while Hitler's tactics were always those of an opportunist, the aim of his foreign policy never changed from its first definition in *Mein Kampf* in the 1920s to the attack on Russia in 1941: German expansion towards the East. Such a policy, as Hitler explicitly recognized in *Mein Kampf*, involved the use of force and the risk of war. He repeated this in November 1937: 'Germany's problem could only be solved by force and this was never without attendant risk.' What changed was not the objective or the means, but Hitler's judgement of the risks he could afford to run.

In his first four years of power, Hitler was cautious. He relied upon his skill as a politician to exploit the divisions, feebleness of purpose and bad conscience of the other Powers to win a series of diplomatic successes without even the display of force. In 1938–9, with German rearmament under way and his confidence fortified by success, he was prepared to take bigger risks and to invoke the threat of force if his claims were refused. By September 1939 he was ready actually to use force against Poland, and run the risk of a general European war; by 1940 to start such a general European conflict himself by his attack in the West and by 1941 to go to the limit and extend it to a world war by his invasion of the Soviet Union and his declaration of war on the United States. To repeat: what changed was not the objective or the means, but Hitler's judgement of the risks he could afford to run.

It is in this context that the meeting of November 1937 is to be seen. The harangue which Hitler delivered reflects the change of mood at the end of the first period and the opening of the second, a new phase in which Hitler was ready to increase the pressure and enlarge the risks of his foreign policy.

The picture he had formed of the immediate future was

inaccurate. Events did not follow the course he predicted; war came at a date and as a result of a situation he had not foreseen. But the inaccuracy of the details matters little, for Hitler was an opportunist ready to take advantage of any situation that emerged. The importance of the occasion lies in the changed tone in which Hitler spoke, in his readiness to run the risk of war and to annex Czechoslovakia and Austria whenever circumstances offered a favourable opportunity, 'even as early as 1938'. His remarks that autumn evening in the Chancellery summed up, as he himself said, the experience of four and a half years and opened the window on what was to follow. At Augsburg on 21 November Hitler told the Nazi Old Guard: 'I am convinced that the most difficult part of the preparatory work has already been achieved. . . . Today we are faced with new tasks, for the *Lebensraum* of our people is too narrow'.[1]

The years of preparation and concealment were at an end: the Man of Peace was to give way to the Man of Destiny, a new role in which, by March 1939, Hitler was to achieve both the objectives of November 1937, the annexation of Austria and the conquest of Czechoslovakia.

1. Speech at Augsburg, 21 November 1937 (Baynes: vol. ii, pp. 1,370–2).

CHAPTER SEVEN

THE DICTATOR

I

IN the spring of 1938, on the eve of his greatest triumphs, Adolf Hitler entered his fiftieth year. His physical appearance was unimpressive, his bearing still awkward. The falling lock of hair and the smudge of his moustache added nothing to a coarse and curiously undistinguished face, in which the eyes alone attracted attention. In appearance at least Hitler could claim to be a man of the people, a plebeian through and through, with none of the physical characteristics of the racial superiority he was always invoking. The quality which his face possessed was that of mobility, an ability to express the most rapidly changing moods, at one moment smiling and charming, at another cold and imperious, cynical and sarcastic, or swollen and livid with rage.

Speech was the essential medium of his power, not only over his audiences but over his own temperament. Hitler talked incessantly, often using words less to communicate his thoughts than to release the hidden spring of his own and others' emotions, whipping himself and his audience into anger or exaltation by the sound of his voice. Talk had another function, too. 'Words,' he once said, 'build bridges into unexplored regions.'[1] As he talked, conviction would grow until certainty came and the problem was solved.

Hitler always showed a distrust of argument and criticism. Unable to argue coolly himself, since his early days in Vienna his one resort had been to shout his opponent down. The questioning of his assumptions or of his facts rattled him and threw him out of his stride, less because of any intellectual inferiority than because words, and even facts, were to him not a means of rational communication and logical analysis, but devices for

1. '*Das Wort baut Brücken in unerforschte Gebiete.*' Zoller: *Hitler Privat*, p. 45. This book is a valuable source for Hitler's personal life. Edited by an Interrogation Officer of the U.S. 7th Army, it is the reminiscences of one of Hitler's secretaries taken down in 1945. Although her name is not given, from internal evidence the secretary in question appears to be Frl. Schröder. She first began to work for Hitler in 1933 and continued to be a member of his household until April 1945. Much of what she told Zoller has been confirmed by the *Table Talk*.

manipulating emotion. The introduction of intellectual processes of criticism and analysis marked the intrusion of hostile elements which disturbed the exercise of this power. Hence Hitler's hatred of the intellectual: in the masses 'instinct is supreme and from instinct comes faith. ... While the healthy common folk instinctively close their ranks to form a community of the people, the intellectuals run this way and that, like hens in a poultry-yard. With them it is impossible to make history; they cannot be used as elements supporting a community.'[1]

For the same reason Hitler rated the spoken above the written word: 'False ideas and ignorance may be set aside by means of instruction, but emotional resistance never can. Nothing but an appeal to hidden forces will be effective here. And that appeal can scarcely be made by any writer. Only the orator can hope to make it.'[2]

As an orator Hitler had obvious faults. The timbre of his voice was harsh, very different from the beautiful quality of Goebbels's. He spoke at too great length; was often repetitive and verbose; lacked lucidity and frequently lost himself in cloudy phrases. These shortcomings, however, mattered little beside the extraordinary impression of force, the immediacy of passion, the intensity of hatred, fury, and menace conveyed by the sound of the voice alone without regard to what he said.

One of the secrets of his mastery over a great audience was his instinctive sensitivity to the mood of a crowd, a flair for divining the hidden passions, resentments and longings in their minds. In *Mein Kampf* he says of the orator: 'He will always follow the lead of the great mass in such a way that from the living emotion of his hearers the apt word which he needs will be suggested to him and in its turn this will go straight to the hearts of his hearers.'[3]

One of his most bitter critics, Otto Strasser, wrote:

Hitler responds to the vibration of the human heart with the delicacy of a seismograph, or perhaps of a wireless receiving set, enabling him, with a certainty with which no conscious gift could endow him, to act as a loudspeaker proclaiming the most secret desires, the least admissible instincts, the sufferings, and personal revolts of a whole nation. ... I have been asked many times what is the secret of Hitler's extraordinary power as a speaker. I can only attribute it to his uncanny intuition, which infallibly diagnoses the ills from which his audience is suffering. If he tries to bolster up his argument with theories or quotations from

1. Hitler's speech at Munich, 8 November 1938 (Baynes: vol. II, p. 1,551).
2. *Mein Kampf*, p. 392.   3. ibid., pp. 391–2.

books he has only imperfectly understood, he scarcely rises above a very poor mediocrity. But let him throw away his crutches and step out boldly, speaking as the spirit moves him, and he is promptly transformed into one of the greatest speakers of the century. . . . Adolf Hitler enters a hall. He sniffs the air. For a minute he gropes, feels his way, senses the atmosphere. Suddenly he bursts forth. His words go like an arrow to their target, he touches each private wound on the raw, liberating the mass unconscious, expressing its innermost aspirations, telling it what it most wants to hear.[1]

Hitler's power to bewitch an audience has been likened to the occult arts of the African medicine-man or the Asiatic Shaman; others have compared it to the sensitivity of a medium, and the magnetism of a hypnotist.

The conversations recorded by Hermann Rauschning for the period 1932–4, and by the table talk at the Führer's H.Q. for the period 1941–2,[2] reveal Hitler in another favourite role, that of visionary and prophet. This was the mood in which Hitler indulged, talking far into the night, in his house on the Obersalzberg, surrounded by the remote peaks and silent forests of the Bavarian Alps; or in the Eyrie he had built six thousand feet up on the Kehlstein, above the Berghof, approached only by a mountain road blasted through the rock and a lift guarded by doors of bronze.[3] There he would elaborate his fabulous schemes for a vast empire embracing the Eurasian Heartland of the geopoliticians; his plans for breeding a new élite biologically preselected; his design for reducing whole nations to slavery in the foundation of his new empire. Such dreams had fascinated Hitler since he wrote *Mein Kampf*. It was easy in the late 1920s and early 1930s to dismiss them as the product of a disordered and overheated imagination soaked in the political romanticism of Wagner and Houston Stewart Chamberlain. But these were still the themes of Hitler's table talk in 1941–2 and by then, master of the greater part of Europe and on the eve (as he believed) of conquering Russia and the Ukraine, Hitler had shown that he was capable of translating his fantasies into a terrible reality. The invasion of Russia, the S.S. extermination squads, the planned elimination of the Jewish race; the treatment of the Poles and

1. Otto Strasser: *Hitler and I*, pp. 74–7.
2. *Hitler's Table Talk* (London, 1953); see below, pp. 655–7 and 670–3.
3. It is typical of Hitler that, according to the secretary whose account has already been quoted, he rarely visited the pavilion on the Kehlstein, except to impress foreign visitors like M. François-Poncet.

Russians, the Slav *Untermenschen* – these, too, were the fruits of Hitler's imagination.

All this combines to create a picture of which the best description is Hitler's own famous sentence: 'I go the way that Providence dictates with the assurance of a sleepwalker.'[1] The former French Ambassador speaks of him as 'a man possessed'; Hermann Rauschning writes: 'Dostoevsky might well have invented him, with the morbid derangement and the pseudo-creativeness of his hysteria';[2] one of the Defence Counsel at the Nuremberg Trials, Dr Dix, quoted a passage from Goethe's *Dichtung und Wahrheit* describing the Demoniac and applied this very aptly to Hitler.[3] With Hitler, indeed, one is uncomfortably aware of never being far from the realm of the irrational.

But this is only half the truth about Hitler, for the baffling problem about this strange figure is to determine the degree to which he was swept along by a genuine belief in his own inspiration and the degree to which he deliberately exploited the irrational side of human nature, both in himself and others, with a shrewd calculation. For it is salutary to recall, before accepting the Hitler Myth at anything like its face value, that it was Hitler who invented the myth, assiduously cultivating and manipulating it for his own ends. So long as he did this he was brilliantly successful; it was when he began to believe in his own magic, and accept the myth of himself as true, that his flair faltered.

So much has been made of the charismatic[4] nature of Hitler's leadership that it is easy to forget the astute and cynical politician in him. It is this mixture of calculation and fanaticism, with the difficulty of telling where one ends and the other begins, which is the peculiar characteristic of Hitler's personality: to ignore or underestimate either element is to present a distorted picture.

II

The link between the different sides of Hitler's character was his extraordinary capacity for self-dramatization. 'This so-called

1. In a speech at Munich on 15 March 1936, just after the successful re-occupation of the Rhineland, against the experts' advice, had triumphantly vindicated his power of intuition.
2. Hermann Rauschning: *Hitler Speaks*, pp. 253–4.
3. N.P., Part xviii, p. 372.
4. The word is used by Max Weber to describe the authority of those who claim to be divinely inspired and endowed by Providence with a special mission.

Wahnsystem, or capacity for self-delusion,' Sir Nevile Henderson, the British Ambassador, wrote, 'was a regular part of his technique. It helped him both to work up his own passions and to make his people believe anything that he might think good for them.'[1] Again and again one is struck by the way in which, having once decided rationally on a course of action, Hitler would whip himself into a passion which enabled him to bear down all opposition, and provided him with the motive power to enforce his will on others. An obvious instance of this is the synthetic fury, which he could assume or discard at will, over the treatment of German minorities abroad. When it was a question of refusing to listen to the bitter complaints of the Germans in the South Tyrol, or of uprooting the German inhabitants of the Baltic States, he sacrificed them to the needs of his Italian and Russian alliances with indifference. So long as good relations with Poland were necessary to his foreign policy he showed little interest in Poland's German minority. But when it suited his purpose to make the 'intolerable wrongs' of the Austrian Nazis, or the Germans in Czechoslovakia and Poland, a ground for action against these states, he worked himself into a frenzy of indignation, with the immediate – and calculated – result that London and Paris, in their anxiety for peace, exerted increased pressure on Prague or Warsaw to show restraint and make further concessions to the German demands.

One of Hitler's most habitual devices was to place himself on the defensive, to accuse those who opposed or obstructed him of aggression and malice, and to pass rapidly from a tone of outraged innocence to the full thunders of moral indignation. It was always the other side who were to blame, and in turn he denounced the Communists, the Jews, the Republican Government, or the Czechs, the Poles, and the Bolsheviks for their 'intolerable' behaviour which forced him to take drastic action in self-defence.

Hitler in a rage appeared to lose all control of himself. His face became mottled and swollen with fury, he screamed at the top of his voice, spitting out a stream of abuse, waving his arms wildly and drumming on the table or the wall with his fists. As suddenly as he had begun he would stop, smooth down his hair, straighten his collar and resume a more normal voice.

This skilful and deliberate exploitation of his own temperament extended to other moods than anger. When he wanted to

1. Sir N. Henderson: *Failure of a Mission* (London, 1940), p. 229.

persuade or win someone over he could display great charm. Until the last days of his life he retained an uncanny gift of personal magnetism which defies analysis, but which many who met him have described. This was connected with the curious power of his eyes, which are persistently said to have had some sort of hypnotic quality. Similarly, when he wanted to frighten or shock, he showed himself a master of brutal and threatening language, as in the celebrated interviews with Schuschnigg and President Hacha.[1]

Yet another variation in his roles was the impression of concentrated will-power and intelligence, the leader in complete command of the situation and with a knowledge of the facts which dazzled the generals or ministers summoned to receive his orders. To sustain this part he drew on his remarkable memory, which enabled him to reel off complicated orders of battle, technical specifications and long lists of names and dates without a moment's hesitation. Hitler cultivated this gift of memory assiduously. The fact that subsequently the details and figures which he cited were often found to contain inaccuracies did not matter: it was the immediate effect at which he aimed. The swiftness of the transition from one mood to another was startling: one moment his eyes would be filled with tears and pleading, the next blazing with fury, or glazed with the faraway look of the visionary.

Hitler, in fact, was a consummate actor, with the actor's and orator's facility for absorbing himself in a role and convincing himself of the truth of what he was saying at the time he said it. In his early years he was often awkward and unconvincing, but with practice the part became second nature to him, and with the immense prestige of success behind him, and the resources of a powerful state at his command, there were few who could resist the impression of the piercing eyes, the Napoleonic pose, and the 'historic' personality.

Hitler had the gift of all great politicians for grasping the possibilities of a situation more swiftly than his opponents. He saw, as no other politician did, how to play on the grievances and resentments of the German people, as later he was to play on French and British fear of war and fear of Communism. His insistence upon preserving the forms of legality in the struggle for power showed a brilliant understanding of the way to disarm

1. See below, c. 8.

opposition, just as the way in which he undermined the independence of the German Army showed his grasp of the weaknesses
of the German Officer Corps.

A German word, *Fingerspitzengefühl* – 'finger-tip feeling' –
which was often applied to Hitler, well describes his sense of
opportunity and timing.

No matter what you attempt [Hitler told Rauschning on one occasion],
if an idea is not yet mature you will not be able to realize it. Then there
is only one thing to do: have patience, wait, try again, wait again. In the
subconscious, the work goes on. It matures, sometimes it dies. Unless I
have the inner, incorruptible conviction: *this is the solution*, I do nothing.
Not even if the whole Party tries to drive me into action.[1]

Hitler knew how to wait in 1932, when his insistence on holding
out until he could secure the Chancellorship appeared to court
disaster. Foreign policy provides another instance. In 1939 he
showed great patience while waiting for the situation to develop
after direct negotiations with Poland had broken down and while
the Western Powers were seeking to reach a settlement with
Soviet Russia. Clear enough about his objectives, he contrived to
keep his plans flexible. In the case of the annexation of Austria
and of the occupation of Prague, he made the final decision on the
spur of the moment.

Until he was convinced that the right moment had come Hitler
would find a hundred excuses for procrastination. His hesitation
in such cases was notorious: his refusal to make up his mind to
stand as a Presidential candidate in 1932, and his attempt to defer
taking action against Röhm and the S.A. in 1934, are two
obvious examples. Once he had made up his mind to move, however, he would act boldly, taking considerable risks, as in the
reoccupation of the Rhineland in 1936, or the invasion of Norway
and Denmark just before the major campaign in the west.

Surprise was a favourite gambit of Hitler's, in politics, diplomacy, and war: he gauged the psychological effect of sudden,
unexpected hammer-blows in paralysing opposition. An illustration of his appreciation of the value of surprise and quick
decision, even when on the defensive, is the second presidential
campaign of 1932. It had taken Goebbels weeks to persuade

1. Hermann Rauschning: *Hitler Speaks*, p. 181. The present author
shares the view of Professor Trevor-Roper that Rauschning's account of his
conversations with Hitler in this book has been vindicated by the evidence
of Hitler's views which has been discovered since its publication and that it
is an important source for any biography of Hitler.

Hitler to stand for the Presidency at all. The defeat in the first ballot brought Goebbels to despair; but Hitler, now that he had committed himself, with great presence of mind dictated the announcement that he would stand a second time and got it on to the streets almost before the country had learned of his defeat. In war the psychological effect of the *Blitzkrieg* was just as important in Hitler's eyes as the strategic: it gave the impression that the German military machine was more than life-size, that it possessed some virtue of invincibility against which ordinary men could not defend themselves.

No régime in history has ever paid such careful attention to psychological factors in politics. Hitler was a master of mass emotion. To attend one of his big meetings was to go through an emotional experience, not to listen to an argument or a pro-gramme. Yet nothing was left to chance on these occasions. Every device for heightening the emotional intensity, every trick of the theatre was used. The Nuremberg rallies held every year in September were masterpieces of theatrical art, with the most carefully devised effects. 'I had spent six years in St Petersburg before the war in the best days of the old Russian ballet,' wrote Sir Nevile Henderson, 'but for grandiose beauty I have never seen a ballet to compare with it.'[1] To see the films of the Nuremberg rallies even today is to be recaptured by the hypnotic effect of thousands of men marching in perfect order, the music of the massed bands, the forest of standards and flags, the vast perspectives of the stadium, the smoking torches, the dome of searchlights. The sense of power, of force and unity was irresistible, and all converged with a mounting crescendo of excitement on the supreme moment when the Führer himself made his entry. Paradoxically, the man who was most affected by such spectacles was their originator, Hitler himself, and, as Rosenberg remarks in his memoirs, they played an indispensable part in the process of self-intoxication.

Hitler had grasped as no one before him what could be done with a combination of propaganda and terrorism. For the com-plement to the attractive power of the great spectacles was the compulsive power of the Gestapo, the S.S., and the concentration camp, heightened once again by skilful propaganda. Hitler was helped in this not only by his own perception of the sources of power in a modern urbanized mass-society, but also by possession of the technical means to manipulate them. This was a point well

1. Henderson, p. 71.

made by Albert Speer, Hitler's highly intelligent Minister for Armaments and War Production, in the final speech he made at his trial after the war.

Hitler's dictatorship [Speer told the court] differed in one fundamental point from all its predecessors in history. His was the first dictatorship in the present period of modern technical development, a dictatorship which made complete use of all technical means for the domination of its own country.

Through technical devices like the radio and the loud-speaker, eighty million people were deprived of independent thought. It was thereby possible to subject them to the will of one man. . . .

Earlier dictators needed highly qualified assistants, even at the lowest level, men who could think and act independently. The totalitarian system in the period of modern technical development can dispense with them; the means of communication alone make it possible to mechanize the lower leadership. As a result of this there arises the new type of the uncritical recipient of orders. . . . Another result was the far-reaching supervision of the citizens of the State and the maintenance of a high degree of secrecy for criminal acts.

The nightmare of many a man that one day nations could be dominated by technical means was all but realized in Hitler's totalitarian system.[1]

In making use of the formidable power which was thus placed in his hands Hitler had one supreme, and fortunately rare, advantage: he had neither scruples nor inhibitions. He was a man without roots, with neither home nor family; a man who admitted no loyalties, was bound by no traditions, and felt respect neither for God nor man. Throughout his career Hitler showed himself prepared to seize any advantage that was to be gained by lying, cunning, treachery, and unscrupulousness. He demanded the sacrifice of millions of German lives for the sacred cause of Germany, but in the last year of the war was ready to destroy Germany rather than surrender his power or admit defeat.

Wary and secretive, he entertained a universal distrust. He admitted no one to his counsels. He never let down his guard, or gave himself away. 'He never', Schacht wrote, 'let slip an unconsidered word. He never said what he did not intend to say and he never blurted out a secret. Everything was the result of cold calculation.'[2]

While he was in Landsberg gaol, as long ago as 1924, Hitler had

1. Final statement by Speer (N.P., Part XXII, pp. 406–7).
2. Schacht, p. 219.

preserved his position in the Party by allowing rivalries to develop among the other leaders, and he continued to apply the same principle of 'divide and rule' after he became Chancellor. There was always more than one office operating in any field. A dozen different agencies quarrelled over the direction of propaganda, of economic policy, and the intelligence services. Before 1938 Hitler continually went behind the back of the Foreign Office to make use of Ribbentrop's special bureau or to get information through Party channels. The dualism of Party and State organizations, each with one or more divisions for the same function, was deliberate. In the end this reduced efficiency, but it strengthened Hitler's position by allowing him to play off one department against another. For the same reason Hitler put an end to regular cabinet meetings and insisted on dealing with ministers singly, so that they could not combine against him. 'I have an old principle,' he told Ludecke: 'only to say what must be said to him who must know it, and only when he must know it.' Only the Führer kept all the threads in his hand and saw the whole design. If ever a man exercised absolute power it was Adolf Hitler.

He had a particular and inveterate distrust of experts. He refused to be impressed by the complexity of problems, insisting until it became monotonous that if only the will was there any problem could be solved. Schacht, to whose advice he refused to listen and whose admiration was reluctant, says of him: 'Hitler often did find astonishingly simple solutions for problems which had seemed to others insoluble. He had a genius for invention. . . . His solutions were often brutal, but almost always effective.'[1] In an interview with a French correspondent early in 1936 Hitler himself claimed this power of simplification as his greatest gift:

It has been said that I owe my success to the fact that I have created a *mystique* . . . or more simply that I have been lucky. Well, I will tell you what has carried me to the position I have reached. Our political problems appeared complicated. The German people could make nothing of them. In these circumstances they preferred to leave it to the professional politicians to get them out of this confused mess. I, on the other hand, simplified the problems and reduced them to the simplest terms. The masses realized this and followed me.[2]

The crudest of Hitler's simplifications was the most effective: in

1. Schacht, p. 220.
2. Interview with Bertrand de Jouvenel, of the *Paris-Midi*, on 21 February 1936 (Baynes: vol. II, pp. 1,266–8).

almost any situation, he believed, force or the threat of force would settle matters – and in an astonishingly large number of cases he proved right.

III

In his Munich days Hitler always carried a heavy riding-whip, made of hippopotamus hide. The impression he wanted to convey – and every phrase and gesture in his speeches reflected the same purpose – was one of force, decision, will. Yet Hitler had nothing of the easy, assured toughness of a condottiere like Göring. His strength of personality, far from being natural to him, was the product of an exertion of will: from this sprang a harsh, jerky and over-emphatic manner which was very noticeable in his early days as a politician. No word was more frequently on Hitler's lips than 'will', and his whole career from 1919 to 1945 is a remarkable achievement of will-power.

To say that Hitler was ambitious scarcely describes the intensity of the lust for power and the craving to dominate which consumed him. It was the will to power in its crudest and purest form, not identifying itself with the triumph of a principle as with Lenin or Robespierre – for the only principle of Nazism was power and domination for its own sake – nor finding satisfaction in the fruits of power, for, by comparison with other Nazi leaders like Göring, Hitler lived an ascetic life. For a long time Hitler succeeded in identifying his own power with the recovery of Germany's old position in the world, and there were many in the 1930s who spoke of him as a fanatical patriot. But as soon as the interests of Germany began to diverge from his own, from the beginning of 1943 onwards, his patriotism was seen at its true value – Germany, like everything else in the world, was only a means, a vehicle for his own power, which he would sacrifice with the same indifference as the lives of those he sent to the Eastern Front. By its nature this was an insatiable appetite, securing only a temporary gratification by the exercise of power, then restlessly demanding an ever further extension of it.

Although, looking backwards, it is possible to detect anticipations of this monstrous will to power in Hitler's early years, it remained latent until the end of the First World War and only began to appear noticeably when he reached his thirties. From the account in *Mein Kampf* it appears that the shock of defeat and the Revolution of November 1918 produced a crisis in which hitherto dormant faculties were awakened and directed towards the goal of becoming a politician and founding a new movement. Resentment is so marked in Hitler's attitude as to suggest that it was from the earlier experiences of his Vienna and Munich days, before the war, that there sprang a compelling urge to revenge himself upon a world which had slighted and ignored him. Hatred, touchiness, vanity are characteristics upon which those who spent any time in his company constantly remark. Hatred intoxicated Hitler. Many of his speeches are long diatribes of hate – against the Jews, against the Marxists, against the Czechs, the Poles, and the French. He had a particularly venomous contempt for the intellectuals and the educated middle-classes, 'the gentlemen with diplomas', who belonged to that comfortable bourgeois world which had once rejected him and which he was determined to shake out of its complacency and destroy in revenge.

No less striking was his constant need of praise. His vanity was inappeasable, and the most fulsome flattery was received as no more than his due. The atmosphere of adulation in which he lived seems to have deadened the critical faculties of all who came into it. The most banal platitudes and the most grotesque errors of taste and judgement, if uttered by the Führer, were accepted as the words of inspired genius. It is to the credit of Röhm and Gregor Strasser, who had known Hitler for a long time, that they were irritated and totally unimpressed by this Byzantine attitude towards the Führer, to which even the normally cynical Goebbels capitulated: no doubt, this was among the reasons why they were murdered.

A hundred years before Hitler became Chancellor, Hegel, in a famous course of lectures at the University of Berlin, had pointed to the role of 'World-historical individuals' as the agents by which 'the Will of the World Spirit', the plan of Providence, is carried out.

They may all be called Heroes, in as much as they have derived their purposes and their vocation, not from the calm regular course of things, sanctioned by the existing order; but from a concealed fount, from that inner Spirit, still hidden beneath the surface, which impinges on the outer world as on a shell and bursts it into pieces. (Such were Alexander, Caesar, Napoleon.) They were practical, political men. But at the same time they were thinking men, who had an insight into the requirements of the time – what was ripe for development. This was the very Truth for their age, for their world. . . . It was theirs to know this nascent principle, the necessary, directly sequent step in progress, which their world was to take; to make this their aim, and to expend their energy in promoting it. World-historical men – the Heroes of an epoch – must therefore be recognized as its clear-sighted ones: *their* deeds, *their* words are the best of their time.[1]

To the objection that the activity of such individuals frequently flies in the face of morality, and involves great sufferings for others, Hegel replied:

World History occupies a higher ground than that on which morality has properly its position, which is personal character and the conscience of individuals. ... Moral claims which are irrelevant must not be brought into collision with world-historical deeds and their accomplishment. The litany of private virtues – modesty, humility, philanthropy, and forbearance – must not be raised against them.[2] So mighty a form [he adds elsewhere] must trample down many an innocent flower – crush to pieces many an object in its path.[3]

Whether Hitler ever read Hegel or not, like so many other passages in nineteenth-century German literature – in Nietzsche, in Schopenhauer, in Wagner – it finds an echo in Hitler's belief about himself. Cynical though he was, Hitler's cynicism stopped short of his own person: he came to believe that he was a man with a mission, marked out by Providence, and therefore exempt from the ordinary canons of human conduct.

Hitler probably held some such belief about himself from an early period. It was clear enough in the speech he made at his trial in 1924,[4] and after he came out of prison those near him noticed that he began to hold aloof, to set a barrier between himself and his followers. After he came to power it became more noticeable. It was in March 1936, that he made the famous assertion already quoted: 'I go the way that Providence dictates with the assurance of a sleep-walker.'[5] In 1937 he told an audience at Würzburg:

However weak the individual may be when compared with the omnipotence and will of Providence, yet at the moment when he acts as Providence would have him act he becomes immeasurably strong. Then there streams down upon him that force which has marked all greatness in the world's history. And when I look back only on the five years which lie

1. Hegel: *Lectures on the Philosophy of History*, translated by J. Sibree (London, 1902), pp. 31–2.
2. Hegel, p. 70.   3. ibid., p. 34.
4. See above, p. 117.
5. Hitler's speech at Munich, 15 March 1936.

behind us, then I feel that I am justified in saying: That has not been the work of man alone.[1]

Just before the occupation of Austria, in February 1938, he declared in the Reichstag:

Above all, a man who feels it his duty at such an hour to assume the leadership of his people is not responsible to the laws of parliamentary usage or to a particular democratic conception, but solely to the mission placed upon him. And anyone who interferes with this mission is an enemy of the people.[2]

It was in this sense of mission that Hitler, a man who believed neither in God nor in conscience ('a Jewish invention, a blemish like circumcision'), found both justification and absolution. He was the Siegfried come to reawaken Germany to greatness, for whom morality, suffering and 'the litany of private virtues' were irrelevant. It was by such dreams that he sustained the ruthlessness and determination of his will. So long as this sense of mission was balanced by the cynical calculations of the politician, it represented a source of strength, but success was fatal. When half Europe lay at his feet and all need of restraint was removed, Hitler abandoned himself entirely to megalomania. He became convinced of his own infallibility. But when he began to look to the image he had created to work miracles of its own accord – instead of exploiting it – his gifts deteriorated and his intuition deluded him. Ironically, failure sprang from the same capacity which brought him success, his power of self-dramatization, his ability to convince himself. His belief in his power to work miracles kept him going when the more sceptical Mussolini faltered. Hitler played out his 'world-historical' role to the bitter end. But it was this same belief which curtained him in illusion and blinded him to what was actually happening, leading him into that arrogant overestimate of his own genius which brought him to defeat. The sin which Hitler committed was that which the ancient Greeks called *hybris*, the sin of overweening pride, of believing himself to be more than a man. No man was ever more surely destroyed by the image he had created than Adolf Hitler.

IV

After he became Chancellor Hitler had to submit to a certain

1. Hitler at Würzburg, 27 June 1937 (Baynes: vol. I, p. 411).
2. Hitler before the Reichstag, 20 February 1938 (Baynes: vol. II, pp. 1,381–2).

degree of routine. This was against his natural inclination. He hated systematic work, hated to submit to any discipline, even self-imposed. Administration bored him and he habitually left as much as he could to others, an important fact in explaining the power of men like Hess and Martin Bormann, who relieved him of much of his paper-work.

When he had a big speech to prepare he would put off beginning work on it until the last moment. Once he could bring himself to begin dictating he worked himself into a passion, rehearsing the whole performance and shouting so loudly that his voice echoed through the neighbouring rooms. The speech composed, he was a man with a load off his mind. He would invite his secretaries to lunch, praising and flattering them, and often using his gifts as a mimic to amuse them. He fussed about corrections, however, especially about his ability to read them when delivering his speech, for Hitler wore spectacles in his office, but refused to be seen wearing them in public. To overcome this difficulty his speeches were typed on a special machine with characters twelve millimetres high. Although his secretaries, like his personal servants, tended to stay with him, he was not an easy man to work for, incalculable in his moods and exacting in his demands.

Most North Germans regarded such *Schlamperei*, slovenliness, and lack of discipline as a typical Austrian trait. In Hitler's eyes it was part of his artist nature: he should have been a great painter or architect, he complained, and not a statesman at all. On art he held the most opinionated views and would tolerate no dissent. He passionately hated all forms of modern art, a term in which he included most painting since the Impressionists. When the House of German Art was to be opened in 1937, Hitler dismissed the pictures chosen by the jury and threatened to cancel the exhibition, finally agreeing to let Hoffmann, his photographer, make a fresh choice subject to his own final approval. Hoffmann filled one room with more modern paintings, in the hope of winning Hitler over, only to see the lot swept away with an angry gesture. Hitler's taste was for the Classical models of Greece and Rome, and for the Romantic: Gothic and Renaissance art were too Christian for his liking. He had a particular fondness for nineteenth-century painting of the more sentimental type, which he collected for a great museum to be built in Linz, the town he regarded as his home. He admired painstaking craftsmanship, and habitually kept a pile of paper on his desk for sketching in idle moments.

Architecture appealed strongly to him – especially Baroque – and he had grandiose plans for the rebuilding of Berlin, Munich, and Nuremberg and the other big German cities. The qualities which attracted him were the monumental and the massive as in the new Reich Chancellery: the architecture of the Third Reich, like the Pyramids, was to reflect the power of its rulers. In Munich Hitler spent many hours in the studio of Professor Troost, his favourite architect. After Troost's death Albert Speer succeeded to his position. To the last days of his life Hitler never tired of playing with architectural models and drawings of the great cities that would one day rise from the bombed shells of the old, especially Linz.

Hitler looked upon himself not only as a connoisseur of painting and an authority on architecture, but as highly musical. In fact, his liking for music did not extend very much further than Wagner, some of Beethoven, and Bruckner, light opera like *Die Fledermaus* and such operettas as Lehar's *The Merry Widow* and *La Fille du Régiment*. Hitler never missed a Wagner festival at Bayreuth and he claimed to have seen such operas as *Die Meistersinger* and *Götterdämmerung* more than a hundred times. He was equally fond of the cinema, and at the height of the political struggle in 1932 he and Goebbels would slip into a picture-house to see *Mädchen in Uniform*, or Greta Garbo. When the Chancellery was rebuilt he had projectors and a screen installed on which he frequently watched films in the evening, including many of the foreign films he had forbidden in Germany.

Hitler rebuilt both the Chancellery and his house on the Obersalzberg after he came to power, the original Haus Wachenfeld becoming the famous Berghof. He had a passion for big rooms, thick carpets, and tapestries. A sense of space pleased him, and at the Berghof the Great Hall and the Loggia had magnificent views over the mountains. Apart from this delight in building and interior decoration, Hitler's tastes were simple and altered little after he came to power. Rauschning, who was frequently in Hitler's company in 1933, speaks of 'the familiar blend of *petit bourgeois* pleasures and revolutionary talk'. He liked to be driven fast in a powerful car; he liked cream cakes and sweets (specially supplied by a Berlin firm); he liked flowers in his rooms, and dogs; he liked the company of pretty – but not clever – women; he liked to be at home up in the Bavarian mountains.

It was in the evenings that Hitler's vitality rose. He hated to go to bed – for he found it hard to sleep – and after dinner he would gather his guests and his household, including the secretaries, round the big fireplace in the Great Hall at the Berghof, or in the drawing-room of the Chancellery. There he sat and talked about every subject under the sun until two or three o'clock in the morning, often later. For long periods the conversation would lapse into a monologue, but to yawn or whisper was to incur immediate disfavour. Next morning Hitler would not rise until eleven.

There was little ceremony about life at the Berghof. Hitler had no fondness for formality or for big social occasions, where he rarely felt at ease and which he avoided as far as possible. Although he lived in considerable luxury, he had few needs. He was indifferent to the clothes he wore, ate very little, never touched meat, and neither smoked nor drank. Hitler not only kept a special vegetarian cook to prepare his meals for him, but held strongly that eating meat or any cooked food was a pernicious habit which had led to the decay of past civilizations. 'There's one thing I can predict to eaters of meat, that the world of the future will be vegetarian.'[1]

The chief reason for Hitler's abstinence seems to have been anxiety about his health. He lived an unhealthy life, with little exercise or fresh air; he took part in no sport, never rode or swam, and he suffered a good deal from stomach disorders as well as from insomnia. With this went a horror of catching a cold or any form of infection. He was depressed at the thought of dying early, before he had had time to complete his schemes, and he hoped to add years to his life by careful dieting and avoiding alcohol, coffee, tea, and tobacco. In the late-night sessions round the fireplace Hitler never touched stimulants, not even real tea. Instead he sipped peppermint-tea or some other herbal drink. He became a crank as well as a hypochondriac, and preached the virtues of vegetarianism to his guests at table with the same insistence as he showed in talking politics.

Hitler had been brought up as a Catholic and was impressed by the organization and power of the Church. Its hierarchical structure, its skill in dealing with human nature and the unalterable character of its Creed, were all features from which he claimed to have learned. For the Protestant clergy he felt only contempt: 'They are insignificant little people, submissive as dogs, and they sweat with embarrassment when you talk to them.

1. *Hitler's Table Talk*, p. 125 (11 November 1941).

They have neither a religion they can take seriously nor a great position to defend like Rome.'[1] It was 'the great position' of the Church that he respected, the fact that it had lasted for so many centuries; towards its teaching he showed the sharpest hostility. In Hitler's eyes Christianity was a religion fit only for slaves; he detested its ethics in particular. Its teaching, he declared, was a rebellion against the natural law of selection by struggle and the survival of the fittest. 'Taken to its logical extreme, Christianity would mean the systematic cultivation of the human failure.'[2] From political considerations he restrained his anti-clericalism, seeing clearly the dangers of strengthening the Church by persecution. For this reason he was more circumspect than some of his followers, like Rosenberg and Bormann, in attacking the Church publicly. But, once the war was over, he promised himself, he would root out and destroy the influence of the Christian Churches. 'The evil that is gnawing our vitals,' he remarked in February 1942, 'is our priests, of both creeds. I can't at present give them the answer they've been asking for but ... it's all written down in my big book. The time will come when I'll settle my account with them. . . . They'll hear from me all right. I shan't let myself be hampered with judicial samples.'[3]

Earnest efforts to establish self-conscious pagan rites roused Hitler's scorn: 'Nothing would be more foolish', he declared, 'than to re-establish the worship of Wotan. Our old mythology had ceased to be viable when Christianity implanted itself. . . . I especially wouldn't want our movement to acquire a religious character and institute a form of worship. It would be appalling for me, if I were to end up in the skin of a Buddha.'[4]

Nor is there any evidence to substantiate the once popular belief that he resorted to astrology. His secretary says categorically that he had nothing but contempt for such practices, although faith in the stars was certainly common among some of his followers like Himmler.

The truth is that, in matters of religion at least, Hitler was a rationalist and a materialist. 'The dogma of Christianity,' he declared in one of his wartime conversations,

gets worn away before the advances of science. . . . Gradually the myths crumble. All that is left is to prove that in nature there is no frontier

1. Conversation with Rauschning on 7 April 1933; *Hitler Speaks*, p. 62.
2. *Hitler's Table Talk*, p. 57.   3. ibid., p. 304.
4. ibid., p. 61 (14 October 1941).

between the organic and the inorganic. When understanding of the universe has become widespread, when the majority of men know that the stars are not sources of light, but worlds, perhaps inhabited worlds like ours, then the Christian doctrine will be convicted of absurdity. . . . The man who lives in communion with nature necessarily finds himself in opposition to the Churches, and that's why they're heading for ruin – for science is bound to win.[1]

It was in keeping with this nineteenth-century faith in science replacing the superstitions of religion that Hitler's plans for the rebuilding of Linz included a great observatory and planetarium as its centrepiece.

Thousands of excursionists will make a pilgrimage there every Sunday. They'll have access to the greatness of our universe. The pediment will bear this motto: 'The heavens proclaim the glory of the everlasting.' It will be our way of giving men a religious spirit, of teaching them humility – but without the priests. For Ptolemy the earth was the centre of the world. That changed with Copernicus. Today we know that our solar system is merely a solar system amongst many others. What could we do better than allow the greatest possible number of people like us to become aware of these marvels? . . . Put a small telescope in a village and you destroy a world of superstitions.[2]

Hitler's belief in his own destiny held him back from a thorough-going atheism. 'The Russians,' he remarked on one occasion, 'were entitled to attack their priests, but they had no right to assail the idea of a supreme force. It's a fact that we're feeble creatures and that a creative force exists.'[3] On another occasion he answered his own question:

By what would you have me replace the Christians' picture of the Beyond? What comes naturally to mankind is the sense of eternity and that sense is at the bottom of every man. The soul and the mind migrate, just as the body returns to nature. Thus life is eternally reborn from life. As for the 'why' of all that, I feel no need to rack my brains on the subject. The soul is unplumbable.[4]

What interested Hitler was power, and his belief in Providence or Destiny was only a projection of his own sense of power. He had no feeling or understanding for either the spiritual side of human life or its emotional, affective side. Emotion to him was the raw material of power. The pursuit of power cast its harsh shadow like a blight over the whole of his life. Everything was

1. *Hitler's Table Talk*, pp. 59–61.   2. ibid., pp. 322–2.
3. ibid., p. 87.   4. ibid., p. 144.

sacrificed to the 'world historical' image; hence the poverty of his private life and of his human relationships.

After his early days in Munich, Hitler made few, if any, friends. In a nostalgic mood he would talk regretfully of the *Kampfzeit*, the Years of the Struggle, and of the comradeship he had shared with the *Alte Kämpfer*, the Old Fighters. With almost no exceptions, Hitler's familiars belonged to the Nazi Old Guard: Goebbels, Ley, Hess, Martin Bormann; his two adjutants, Julius Schaub and Wilhelm Bruckner; his chauffeur, Julius Schreck; Max Amann, the Party publisher; Franz Xavier Schwarz, the Party treasurer; Hoffmann, the court photographer. It was in this intimate circle, talking over the old days, in the Berghof or in his flat in Munich, that Hitler was most at his ease. Even towards those like Julius Streicher or Christian Weber, who were too disreputable to be promoted to high office, Hitler showed considerable loyalty; when Streicher's notorious behaviour finally led to his removal from the position of Gauleiter of Franconia, he was still protected by Hitler and allowed to live in peace on his farm.

Apart from a handful of men like Ribbentrop and Speer, Hitler never lost his distrust of those who came from the bourgeois world. It was on the Old Guard alone that he believed he could rely, for they were dependent on him. More than that, he found such company, however rough, more congenial than that of the Schachts and Neuraths, the bankers and generals, high officials and diplomats, who were eager to serve the new régime once it had come to power. Their stiff manners and 'educated' talk roused all his old class resentment and the suspicion that they sneered at him behind his back – as they did. Dictatorship knows no equals, and with the Old Guard Hitler was sure of his ascendancy. Even Göring and Goebbels, who stood on more equal terms with Hitler than any other of the Nazi leaders, knew very well that there were limits beyond which they dared not go. 'When a decision has to be taken,' Göring once told Sir Nevile Henderson, 'none of us count more than the stones on which we are standing. It is the Führer alone who decides.'[1]

Hitler enjoyed and was at home in the company of women. At the beginning of his political career he owed much to the encouragement of women like Frau Hélène Bechstein, Frau Carola Hoffmann, and Frau Winnifried Wagner. Many women were

1. Henderson, p. 282.

fascinated by his hypnotic powers; there are well-attested accounts of the hysteria which affected women at his big meetings, and Hitler himself attached much importance to the women's vote. If ladies were present at table he knew how to be attentive and charming, as long as they had no intellectual pretensions and did not try to argue with him. Gossip connected his name with that of a number of women in whose company he had been frequently seen, and speculated eagerly on his relations with them, from Henny Hoffmann, the daughter of his photographer, and Leni Riefenstahl, the director of the films of the Nuremberg Rallies, to Unity Mitford, the sister-in-law of Sir Oswald Mosley, who attempted to commit suicide at Munich.

Much has been written, on the flimsiest evidence, about Hitler's sex life. Amongst the mass of conjecture, two hypotheses are worth serious consideration. The first is that Hitler was affected by syphilis.

There are several passages in *Mein Kampf*[1] in which Hitler speaks with surprising emphasis of 'the scourge of venereal disease' and its effects. 'The problem of fighting venereal disease', he declared, 'should be placed before the public – not as a task for the nation but as *the* main task.' According to reports which Hanfstängl, for example, repeats, Hitler contracted syphilis while he was a young man in Vienna. This may well be malicious gossip but it is worth adding that more than one medical specialist has suggested that Hitler's later symptoms – psychological as well as physical – could be those of a man suffering from the tertiary stage of syphilis. Unless, however, a medical report on Hitler should some day come to light this must remain an open question.

A second hypothesis, which is not of course inconsistent with the first, is that Hitler was incapable of normal sexual intercourse. Putzi Hanfstängl, who knew Hitler well in his Bavarian days and later, says plainly that he was impotent. He adds:

The abounding nervous energy which found no normal release sought compensation first in the subjection of his entourage, then of his country, then of Europe. . . . In the sexual no man's land in which he lived, he only once nearly found the woman, and never even the man, who might have brought him relief.[2]

The gallantry, the hand-kissing and flowers, were an expression

1. pp. 209–16 of the English edition.
2. Hanfstängl: *The Missing Years*, p. 22.

of admiration but led to nothing more. 'We used to think that Jenny Haugg, his driver's sister, was his girl-friend. . . . Jenny would often be sitting in the back-seat waiting for him. They would drive off together, but I knew he was only going to a café to stay up talking half the night. A bit of petting may have gone on, but that, it became clear to me, was all that Hitler was capable of. My wife summed him up very quickly: "Putzi," she said, "I tell you he is a neuter." '[1]

This too must remain a hypothesis, but Hanfstängl's belief (which others shared) is not inconsistent with what is known of Hitler's relations with the only two women in whom he showed more than a passing interest – his niece, Geli Raubal, and the woman he married on the day before he took his life, Eva Braun.

Geli and Friedl Raubal, the daughters of Hitler's widowed half-sister, Angela Raubal, accompanied their mother when she came to keep house for Hitler on the Obersalzberg in 1925. Geli was then seventeen, simple and attractive, with a pleasant voice which she wanted to have trained for singing. During the next six years she became Hitler's constant companion, and when her uncle acquired his flat on the Prinz-Regentenstrasse she spent much time with him in Munich as well as up at the Obersalzberg. This period in Munich Hitler later described as the happiest in his life; he idolized this girl, who was twenty years younger than himself, took her with him whenever he could – in short, he fell in love with her. Whether Geli was ever in love with him is uncertain. She was flattered and impressed by her now famous uncle, she enjoyed going about with him, but she suffered from his hyper-sensitive jealousy. Hitler refused to let her have any life of her own; he refused to let her go to Vienna to have her voice trained; he was beside himself with fury when he discovered that she had allowed Emil Maurice, his chauffeur, to make love to her, and forbade her to have anything to do with any other man. Geli resented and was made unhappy by Hitler's possessiveness and domestic tyranny.

On the morning of 17 September 1931, Hitler left Munich with Hoffmann, his photographer and friend, after saying good-bye to Geli. He was bound for Hamburg, but had only got beyond Nuremberg when he was called to the telephone by Hess and told that Geli was dead. She had shot herself in his flat shortly after his departure. Why?

1. Hanfstängl: *The Missing Years*, p. 52.

Hoffmann, who knew both Hitler and the girl well, believed that she was in love with someone else and committed suicide because she could not endure her uncle's despotic treatment of her. Frau Winter, the housekeeper, believed that she was in love with Hitler, and that her suicide followed from disappointment or frustration.[1]

Whatever the reason, Geli's death dealt Hitler a greater blow than any other event in his life. For days he was inconsolable and his friends feared that he would take his own life. According to some accounts, his refusal to touch meat dates from the crisis through which he passed at this time. For the rest of his life he never spoke of Geli without tears coming into his eyes; according to his own statement to a number of witnesses, she was the only woman he ever loved, and there is no reason to doubt this statement. Whether he would ever have married her is another matter. Her room at the Berghof was kept exactly as she had left it, and remained untouched when the original Haus Wachenfeld was rebuilt. Her photograph hung in his room in Munich and Berlin, and flowers were always placed before it on the anniversary of her birth and death. There are mysteries in everyone's personality, not least in that strange, contradictory, and distorted character which was Adolf Hitler, and it is best to leave it as a mystery.

Hitler's relations with Eva Braun were on a different level. As Speer later remarked, 'For all writers of history, Eva Braun is going to be a disappointment.'

Eva was the middle of the three daughters of Fritz Braun, a master craftsman from Simbach on the Inn. She was a pretty, empty-headed blonde, with a round face and blue eyes, who worked as a shop girl in Hoffmann's photographer's shop. Hitler met her there, paid her a few casual compliments, gave her flowers, and occasionally invited her to be one of his party on an outing. The initiative was all on Eva's side: she told her friends that Hitler was in love with her and that she would make him marry her.

In the summer of 1932 (less than a year after Geli's death) Eva Braun, then twenty-one, attempted to commit suicide. Hitler was understandably sensitive to such a threat at a time when he was anxious to avoid any scandal and, according to Hoffmann, 'it

1. See the first-hand account in Heinrich Hoffmann: *Hitler was My Friend* (London, 1955), pp. 148–59.

was in this manner that Eva Braun got her way and became Hitler's *chère amie*'.

Hoffmann's further comment is worth quoting in full:

At that time there was established no liaison between them in the accepted sense of the word. Eva moved into his house, became the constant companion of his leisure hours and, to the best of my knowledge, that was all there was to it. Indeed, I can think of no more apt simile than once more to liken Hitler to some ardent collector, who preferred to gloat over his latest treasure in the privacy of his own collection. . . .

That Eva became his mistress some time or other before the end is certain, but when – neither I nor anyone else can say. Not at any time was there any perceptible change in his attitude towards her which might have pointed to the assumption of more intimate relations between them; and the secrecy which surrounded the whole affair is emphasized by the profound astonishment of all of us in his most intimate circle when, at the bitter end, the marriage was announced.[1]

Eva was kept very much in the background. She stayed at Hitler's Munich flat, where Hitler saw her as occasion offered, or went to the Berghof when he was in residence there. This led to strained relations with Hitler's half-sister, Frau Raubal, who still kept house at the Berghof after Geli's death and hated the upstart Eva. After a series of rows, Frau Raubal left for good in 1936, and thereafter Eva took her place as *Hausfrau* and sat on Hitler's left hand when he presided at lunch.

Hitler rarely allowed Eva Braun to come to Berlin or appear in public with him. When big receptions or dinners were given she had to stay upstairs in her room. Only after her sister, Gretl, married Fegelein, Himmler's personal representative with the Führer, during the war, was she allowed to appear more freely in public. She could then be introduced as Frau Fegelein's sister and the Führer's reputation preserved untarnished.

Eva made no pretensions to intellectual gifts or to any understanding of politics. Her interests in life were sport – she was an excellent skier and swimmer – animals, the cinema, sex, and clothes. Such ideas as she had were drawn from cheap novelettes and trashy films, the sole subject of which was 'love'. In return for her privileged position she had to submit to the same petty tyranny that Hitler had attempted to establish over Geli. She only dared to dance or smoke in secret, because the Führer disapproved of both; she lived in constant terror lest a chance photograph or remark should rouse Hitler's anger at her being in the company of other men, yet herself suffered agonies of

1. Hoffmann, op. cit., pp. 162–3.

jealousy at Hitler's interest in the women he met. Sometimes he did not come to see her for weeks at a time, and fear that he would leave her for someone else made her life a misery. Dissatisfied with her ambiguous status, she longed for the respectability of marriage.

After the beginning of the war Eva's position became more secure. Hitler cut himself off from all social life and was wholly absorbed in the war. She had no more rivals to fear, and the liaison had now lasted so long that Hitler accepted her as a matter of course. On the other hand, she saw much less of him. In the latter part of the war Hitler paid few visits to the Berghof and she was not allowed to move to the Führer's headquarters. At no time was she in a position to influence even the most trivial discussions.

None the less, in time, Hitler became genuinely fond of Eva. Her empty-headedness did not disturb him; on the contrary, he detested women with views of their own. It was her loyalty which won his affection and it was as a reward for her loyalty that, after more than twelve years of a relationship which was more domestic than erotic in character, Hitler finally gave way and on the last day of his life married her. Before that he had always refused to discuss marriage on the grounds that it would be a hindrance to his career. Explaining his action in his will, he spoke of 'many years of true friendship', and there is little reason to doubt that he was sincere in saying this. In Eva's company he was at ease and could cease to play a part. The nearest he came to being either human or happy in normal terms was during the hours he spent sprawling back in his chair beside her at tea-time, walking with her on the terrace at the Berghof, or going for a picnic with a few friends.

Egotism is a malignant as well as an ugly vice, and it may well be doubted whether Hitler, absorbed in the dream of his own greatness, ever had the capacity to love anyone deeply. At the best of times he was never an easy man to live with: his moods were too incalculable, his distrust too easily aroused. He was quick to imagine and slow to forget a slight; there was a strong strain of vindictiveness in him which often found expression in a mean and petty spite. Generosity was a virtue he did not recognize: he pursued his enmities unremittingly.

There is no doubt that Hitler, if he was in the right mood, could be an attractive, indeed a fascinating companion. On the outings in which he delighted he not only showed great capacity for enjoyment himself, but put others at their ease. He could talk well and he had the actor's gift of mimicry to amuse his companions. On the other hand, his sense of humour was strongly tinged with *Schadenfreude*, a malicious pleasure in other people's misfortunes or stupidities. The treatment of the Jews only roused his amusement, and he would laugh delightedly at the description by Goebbels of the indignities the Jews had suffered at the hands of the Berlin S.A. Indifferent towards the sufferings of others, he lacked any feeling of sympathy, was intolerant and callous, and filled with contempt for the common run of humanity. Pity and mercy he regarded as humanitarian clap-trap and signs of weakness. The only virtue was to be hard, and ruthlessness was the distinctive mark of superiority. The more absorbed he became by the arrogant belief in his mission and infallibility the more complete became his loneliness, until in the last years of his life he was cut off from all human contact and lost in a world of inhuman fantasy where the only thing that was real or mattered was his own will.

V

'A man who has no sense of history,' Hitler declared, 'is like a man who has no ears or eyes.' He himself claimed to have had a passionate interest in history since his schooldays and he displayed considerable familiarity with the course of European history. His conversation was studded with historical references and historical parallels. More than that: Hitler's whole cast of thought was historical, and his sense of mission derived from his sense of history.

Like his contemporary Spengler, Hitler was fascinated by the rise and fall of civilizations. 'I often wonder,' he remarks in his table talk, 'why the Ancient World collapsed.' Nor was this idle speculation. He saw himself born at a similar critical moment in European history when the liberal bourgeois world of the nineteenth century was disintegrating. What would take its place? The future lay with the 'Jewish–Bolshevik' ideology of the masses unless Europe could be saved by the Nazi racist ideology of the élite. This was his mission and he drew upon history to fortify him in it. Hence his interest in the Roman Empire in which Christianity – the invention of the Jew, Saul of Tarsus – had played the same disintegrative role as Bolshevism – the invention of the Jew, Marx – in the Europe of his own time.

To this view of history, this *Weltanschauung*, however repellent, Hitler remained remarkably consistent. Once formed, it was rigid and inflexible. Hitler's was a closed mind, violently rejecting any alternative view, refusing to criticize or allow others to criticize his assumptions. He read and listened, not to learn, but to acquire information and find additional support for prejudices and opinions already fixed in his mind. Of historical study as a critical discipline, or of the rich fields of human history beside the quest for power, war, and the construction of empires, he was invincibly ignorant.

The hostility Hitler showed towards freedom of thought or discussion represented a personal dislike quite as much as a political expedient. On occasion he could be a good listener but he was intolerant of disagreement or even interruption once he had begun to speak himself. The habits of despotism extended from political to personal life, and he became accustomed to have his opinions on any subject accepted as the *ex cathedra* pronouncements of an oracle, no matter how ignorant and ill-founded they might be.

In fact, Hitler's views on every other topic besides politics were as dogmatic and intolerant – with this difference that in this case they were banal, narrow-minded, and totally unoriginal as well as harsh and brutal. What he had to say about marriage, women, education, religion, bore the indelible stamp of an innate vulgarity and coarseness of spirit. He was not only cut off from the richest experiences of ordinary human life – love, marriage, family, human sympathy, friendship – but the whole imaginative and speculative world of European literature was closed to him. His secretary recalls that his library contained not a single classic of literature, not a single book reflecting humane tastes. Everything that spoke of the human spirit and of the thousand forms in which it has flowered, from mysticism to science, was alien to him.

The basis of Hitler's political beliefs was a crude Darwinism. 'Man has become great through struggle. . . . Whatever goal man has reached is due to his originality plus his brutality. . . . All life is bound up in three theses: Struggle is the father of all things, virtue lies in blood, leadership is primary and decisive.'[1] On another occasion he declared: 'The whole work of Nature is a mighty struggle between strength and weakness – an eternal

1. Speech at Chemnitz, 2 April 1938 (Prange: pp. 8–9).

victory of the strong over the weak. There would be nothing but decay in the whole of Nature if this were not so. States which offend against this elementary law fall into decay.'[1] It followed from this that 'through all the centuries force and power are the determining factors. . . . Only force rules. Force is the first law.'[2] Force was more than the decisive factor in any situation; it was force which alone created right. 'Always before God and the world, the stronger has the right to carry through what he wills. History proves: He who has not the strength – him the "right in itself" profits not a whit.'[3]

The ability to seize and hold a decisive superiority in the struggle for existence Hitler expressed in the idea of race, the role of which is as central in Nazi mythology as that of class in Marxist. All that mankind has achieved, Hitler declared in *Mein Kampf*, has been the work of the Aryan race: 'It was the Aryan who laid the groundwork and erected the walls of every great structure in human culture.'[4] But who were the Aryans?

Although Hitler frequently talked as if he regarded the whole German nation as of pure Aryan stock (whatever that may mean) his real view was rather different. It was only a part of any nation (even of the German nation) which could be regarded as Aryan. These constituted an élite within the nation (represented by the Nazi Party and especially by the S.S.) which stamped its ideas upon the development of the whole people, and by its leadership gave this racial agglomeration an Aryan character which in origin belonged only to a section.[5] Thus Hitler's belief in race could be used to justify both the right of the German people to ride roughshod over such inferior peoples as the uncouth Slavs and the degenerate French, and the right of the Nazis, representing an élite, sifted and tested by the struggle for power, to rule over the German people. This explains why Hitler often referred to the Nazi capture of power in Germany as a racial revolution, since it represented the replacement of one ruling caste by another. As Hitler told Otto Strasser in May 1930: 'We want to make a selection from the new dominating caste which is not moved, as you are, by any ethic of pity, but is quite clear in its own mind

1. Speech at Munich, 13 April 1923; *Adolf Hitlers Reden*, pp. 43–4.
2. Speech at Essen, 22 November 1936 (Prange: p. 4).
3. Speech at Munich, 13 April 1923, already cited.
4. *Mein Kampf*, p. 243.
5. cf., e.g. Hitler's closing speech at the Nuremberg Parteitag, 3 September 1933 (Baynes: vol. I, pp. 464–6).

that it has the right to dominate others because it represents a better race.'[1]

In Hitler's and Himmler's plans for the S.S. – a racial élite selected with the most careful eye to Nazi eugenics – recruitment was to be open not only to Germans, but to Aryans of other nations as well.

The conception of the nation [Rauschning records Hitler saying] has become meaningless. We have to get rid of this false conception and set in its place the conception of race. The New Order cannot be conceived in terms of the national boundaries of the peoples with an historic past, but in terms of race that transcend these boundaries. . . . I know perfectly well that in the scientific sense there is no such thing as race. But you, as a farmer, cannot get your breeding right without the conception of race. And I, as a politician, need a conception which enables the order that has hitherto existed on an historic basis to be abolished, and an entirely new and anti-historic order enforced and given an intellectual basis. . . . And for this purpose the conception of race serves me well. . . . France carried her great Revolution beyond her borders with the conception of the nation. With the conception of race, National Socialism will carry its revolution abroad and recast the world.

I shall bring into operation throughout all Europe and the whole world this process of selection which we have carried out through National Socialism in Germany. . . . The active sections in nations, the militant, Nordic section, will rise again and become the ruling element over these shopkeepers and pacifists, these puritans and speculators and busybodies. . . . There will not be much left then of the clichés of nationalism, and precious little among us Germans. Instead there will be an understanding between the various language elements of the one good ruling race.[2]

This is Hitler at his most flamboyant, and it is not to be taken too literally. Hitler was a master of nationalist appeal, and old-fashioned nationalism was very far from being played out in Europe. Hitler's foreign policy was nationalist in character, and nationalism, both that of the Occupied Countries and that of the Germans, cut across and wrecked the attempt to turn the Quislings and the S.S. into an international Nazi élite, just as it proved too strong for the Jacobins outside France in the 1790s. But it is also a passage characteristic of Hitler's way of talking: a straightforward claim to unlimited power was dressed up in the myth of a 'pure' race, just as on other occasions Hitler gave it a Wag-

1. Otto Strasser: *Ministersessel oder Revolution?* reporting their discussion of 21 May 1930, pp. 12–14.
2. Rauschning: *Hitler Speaks*, pp. 229–30.

nerian colouring and talked of founding a new Order of Knights.

What Hitler was seeking to express in his use of the word 'race' was his belief in inequality – both between peoples and individuals – as another of the iron laws of Nature. He had a passionate dislike of the egalitarian doctrines of democracy in every field, economic, political and international.

There are [he said in this speech to the Düsseldorf Industry Club] two closely related factors which we can time and time again trace in periods of national decline: one is that for the conception of the value of personality there is substituted a levelling idea of the supremacy of mere numbers – democracy – and the other is the negation of the value of a people, the denial of any difference in the inborn capacity, the achievement of individual peoples. . . . Internationalism and democracy are inseparable conceptions.[1]

Hitler rejected both in favour of the superior rights of the *Herrenvolk* in international affairs and of the Nazi élite in the government of the state.

Just as he opposed the concept of 'race' to the democratic belief in equality, so to the idea of personal liberty Hitler opposed the superior claims of the *Volk*.[2]

National Socialism [Hitler declared] takes as the starting point of its views and its decisions neither the individual nor humanity. It puts consciously into the central point of its whole thinking the *Volk*. This *Volk* is for it a blood-conditioned entity in which it sees the God-willed building-stone of human society. The individual is transitory, the *Volk* is permanent. If the Liberal *Weltanschauung* in its deification of the single individual must lead to the destruction of the *Volk*, National Socialism, on the other hand, desires to safeguard the *Volk*, if necessary even at the expense of the individual. It is essential that the individual should slowly come to realize that his own ego is unimportant when compared with the existence of the whole people . . . above all he must realize that the freedom of the mind and will of a nation are to be valued more highly than the individual's freedom of mind and will.[3]

In an interview with the *New York Times* Hitler summed up his

1. Speech at Düsseldorf, 27 January 1932 (Baynes: vol. I, p. 783).
2. I have used the original German word instead of translating it into its usual English equivalent of 'people' or 'nation', in order to keep the suggestion of the primitive, instinctive tribal community of blood and soil – by contrast with such modern and artificial constructions as the State.
3. Speech at the Nazi Harvest Thanksgiving Celebrations at Bückeburg, 7 October 1933 (Baynes: vol. I, pp. 871–2).

view in the sentence: 'The underlying idea is to do away with egoism and to lead people into the sacred collective egoism which is the nation.'[1]

The *Volk* not only gave meaning and purpose to the individual's life, it provided the standard by which all other institutions and claims were to be judged.

Party, State, Army, the economic structure, the administration of justice are of secondary importance, they are but a means to the preservation of the *Volk*. In so far as they fulfil this task, they are right and useful. When they prove unequal to this task they are harmful and must either be reformed or set aside or replaced by better means.[2]

Here was the justification for the campaign of the Nazis and other Völkisch groups against the Weimar Republic: their loyalty had been, not to the Republican State, but to the *Volk*, for betraying the interests of which men like Rathenau and Erzberger had been assassinated. Justice, truth and the freedom to criticize must all be subordinated to the overriding claims of the *Volk* and its preservation.

The Strassers and the radical wing of the Party argued that if the same criterion were applied to the economic system it meant the socialist organization of the national economy in the interests of the *Volk*. Hitler's views about economics, however, were entirely opportunist. The truth is that he was not at all interested in economics. He preached the true doctrine of the totalitarian State – which the rulers of Soviet Russia also practised, but found it embarrassing to admit – the supremacy of politics over economics. It is not economics but power that is decisive. As early as 1923, at the time of the occupation of the Ruhr and the post-war inflation, Hitler kept on saying that Germany would not solve her problems 'until the German people understands that one can conduct politics only when one has the support of power – and again power. Only so is reconstruction possible. . . . It is not an economic question which now faces the German people, it is a political question – how shall the nation's determination be recovered?'[3] During the Inflation and the Depression this was clever propaganda. He was able to cut through the technicalities of the economists, declaring that all that was needed was the united will of the German people to end their troubles – given

1. Interview with Anne O'Hara McCormick, published in the *New York Times*, of 10 July 1933 (Baynes: vol. I, p. 866).
2. Speech to the Reichstag, 30 January 1937 (Baynes: vol. I, p. 525).
3. Speech in Munich, 4 May 1923; *Adolf Hitlers Reden*, pp. 64–7.

that, the rest would follow. It also corresponded to Hitler's own practice when he came to power: faced with economic problems, you gave orders that they were to be solved; if the orders were not carried out, you shot people. It was on this basis that Hitler and Göring conducted the economic policy of the Third Reich, and left it to Dr Schacht and his successors to find the answers.

VI

As soon as Hitler began to think and talk about the organization of the State it is clear that the metaphor which dominated his mind was that of an army. He saw the State as an instrument of power in which the qualities to be valued were discipline, unity and sacrifice. It was from the Army that he took the *Führerprinzip*, the leadership principle, upon which first the Nazi Party, and later the National Socialist State, were built.

In Hitler's eyes the weakness of democracy was that it bred irresponsibility by leaving decisions always to anonymous majorities, and so putting a premium on the avoidance of difficult and unpopular decisions. At the same time, the Party system, freedom of discussion and freedom of the Press sapped the unity of the nation – he habitually described discussion as 'corrosive'. From this, he told the Hitler Youth, 'we have to learn our lesson: one will must dominate us, we must form a single unity; one discipline must weld us together; one obedience, one subordination must fill us all, for above us stands the nation.'[1]

'Our Constitution,' wrote Nazi Germany's leading lawyer, Dr Hans Frank, 'is the will of the Führer.'[2] This was in fact literally true. The Weimar Constitution was never replaced, it was simply suspended by the Enabling Law, which was renewed periodically and placed all power in Hitler's hands. Hitler thus enjoyed a more complete measure of power than Napoleon or Stalin or Mussolini, since he had been careful not to allow the growth of any institution which might in an emergency be used as a check on him.

Yet Hitler was equally careful to insist that his power was rooted in the people; his was a plebiscitary and popular dictatorship, a democratic Caesarism. This distinguished the Third Reich from Imperial Germany: 'Then the leaders had no roots in the

1. Speech to the Hitler Youth at Nuremberg, 2 September 1933 (Baynes: vol. I, p. 538).
2. In the *Völkischer Beobachter*, 20 May 1936.

people: it was a class state.'[1] After each of his early *coups* in foreign policy Hitler duly submitted his action to the people for confirmation in a plebiscite. In the election campaign which followed the denunciation of the Locarno Pact and the reoccupation of the Rhineland, Hitler publicly declared:

In Germany bayonets do not terrorize a people. Here a government is supported by the confidence of the entire people. I care for the people. In fifteen years I have slowly worked my way up together with this movement. I have not been imposed by anyone upon this people. From the people I have grown up, in the people I have remained, to the people I return. My pride is that I know no statesman in the world who with greater right than I can say that he is the representative of his people.[2]

Such statements may be taken for what they are worth, yet it is obvious that Hitler felt – and not without justification – that his power, despite the Gestapo and the concentration camps, was founded on popular support to a degree which few people cared, or still care, to admit.

If the *Führerprinzip* corresponded to Hitler's belief in the role played in history by personality, the Nazi Party and particularly the S.S. exemplified the aristocratic principle, the role played by élites. The first function of the Party was to recruit such an élite and from it to provide the leadership of the State. 'With the German Army as its model, the Party must see as its task the collection and advancement in its organization of those elements in the nation which are most capable of political leadership.'[3]

Like all revolutionary movements, Nazism drew much of its strength from a new *carrière ouverte aux talents*, the formation of a new leadership drawn from other than the traditional classes.

The fundamental conception of this work [Hitler told the Party Rally in 1937] was to break with all traditional privileges, and in all spheres of life, especially in the political sphere, to place the leadership of the nation in the hands of hand-picked men, who should be sought and found without regard to descent, to birth, or to social and religious association – men chosen solely on the basis of their personal gifts and of their character.[4]

The Party's fourteen years of struggle served as a process of

1. Speech at Munich, 8 November 1944.
2. Speech at Hamburg, 20 March 1936 (Baynes: vol. II, pp. 1,312–13).
3. Speech at the Nuremberg Parteitag, 16 September 1935 (Baynes: vol. I, p. 442).
4. Proclamation to the Nuremberg Parteitag, 7 September 1937 (ibid., pp. 684–5).

natural selection – 'just as the magnet draws to itself the steel splinters, so did our movement gather together from all classes and callings and walks of life the forces in the German people which can form and also maintain states.'[1] In this way, even before coming to power, the Party created the cadres of leadership to take over the State. The difference between promise and practice will appear in the subsequent course of this history.

Once in power the Party remained the guarantor of the National Socialist character of the State. 'Our Government is supported by two organizations: politically by the community of the *Volk* organized in the National Socialist movement, and in the military sphere by the Army.'[2] These, to use another phrase of Hitler's, were the two pillars of the State. The Party was a power held in reserve to act, if the State should fail to safeguard the interests of the *Volk*; it was the link between the Führer and his *Volk*; finally it was the agent for the education of the people in the Nazi *Weltanschauung*. Education is an ambiguous word in this context; on another occasion Hitler spoke of 'stamping the Nazi *Weltanschauung* on the German people'.[3] For its highest duty was intolerance: 'it is only the harshest principles and an iron resolution which can unite the nation into a single body capable of resistance – and thereby able to be led successfully in politics.'[4] 'The main plank in the Nationalist Socialist programme,' Hitler declared in 1937, 'is to abolish the liberalistic concept of the individual and the Marxist concept of humanity and to substitute for them the *Volk* community, rooted in the soil and bound together by the bond of its common blood.'[5]

While Hitler's attitude towards liberalism was one of contempt, towards Marxism he showed an implacable hostility. The difference is significant. Liberalism he no longer regarded as a serious threat; its values had lost their attraction in the age of mass-politics, especially in Germany, where liberalism had never had deep roots. Marxism, however, whether represented by revisionist Social Democracy or revolutionary Communism, was a rival *Weltanschauung* able to exert a powerful attractive force over the masses comparable with that of Nazism. Ignoring the profound

1. Speech to the Nuremberg Parteitag, 3 September 1933 (ibid., pp. 478–80).
2. Speech at Hamburg, 17 August 1934 (ibid., p. 566).
3. Speech at Godesberg, 19 August 1933 (ibid., p. 485).
4. Speech at Nuremberg, 16 September 1935 (ibid., p. 445).
5. Hitler to the Reichstag, 30 January 1937 (Prange, p. 80).

differences between Communism and Social Democracy in practice and the bitter hostility between the rival working-class parties, he saw in their common ideology the embodiment of all that he detested – mass democracy and a levelling egalitarianism as opposed to the authoritarian state and the rule of an élite; equality and friendship among peoples as opposed to racial inequality and the domination of the strong; class solidarity versus national unity; internationalism versus nationalism.

With Marxism there could be no compromise. 'When people cast in our teeth our intolerance we proudly acknowledge it – yes, we have formed the inexorable decision to destroy Marxism in Germany down to its very last root.'[1] This was said in 1932, at a time when Hitler saw in the unbroken organization of the Social Democratic Party and the trade unions the most solid obstacle to his ambitions, and in the rival extremists of the German Communist Party, the only other German party whose votes mounted with his own.

Hitler regarded the Marxist conception of class war and of class solidarity cutting across frontiers as a particular threat to his own exaltation of national unity founded on the community of the *Volk*. The object of National Socialist policy was to create a truly classless society. 'The slogan, "The dictatorship of the bourgeoisie must make way for the dictatorship of the proletariat", is simply a question of a change from the dictatorship of one class to that of another, while we wish for the dictatorship of the nation, that is, the dictatorship of the whole community. Only then shall we be able to restore to the millions of our people the conviction that the State does not represent the interests of a single group or class, and that the Government is there to manage the concerns of the entire community.'[2] This single-minded concept of the national interest was to be embodied in, and guaranteed by, the absolutism of the State, as it had been in the time of Frederick the Great and in the Prussian tradition of the State glorified by Hegel.

Just as Hitler ascribed to the 'Aryan' all the qualities and achievements which he admired, so all that he hated is embodied in another mythological figure, that of the Jew. There can be little doubt that Hitler believed what he said about the Jews; from

1. Hitler at Düsseldorf, 27 January 1932 (Baynes: vol. i, p. 823).
2. Hitler to the Labour Front, in Berlin, 10 May 1933 (ibid. p. 433).

first to last his anti-Semitism is one of the most consistent themes in his career, the master idea which embraces the whole span of his thought. In whatever direction one follows Hitler's train of thought, sooner or later one encounters the satanic figure of the Jew. The Jew is made the universal scapegoat. Democracy is Jewish – the secret domination of the Jew. Bolshevism and Social Democracy; capitalism and the 'interest-slavery' of the money-lender; parliamentarianism and the freedom of the Press; liberalism and internationalism; anti-militarism and the class war; Christianity; modernism in art (*Kultur-Bolschewismus*), prostitution and miscegenation – all are instruments devised by the Jew to subdue the Aryan peoples to his rule. One of Hitler's favourite phrases, which he claimed – very unfairly – to have taken from Mommsen, was: 'The Jew is the ferment of decomposition in peoples.' This points to the fundamental fact about the Jew in Hitler's eyes; unlike the Aryan, the Jew is incapable of founding a State and so incapable of anything creative. He can only imitate and steal – or destroy in the spirit of envy.

The Jew has never founded any civilization, though he has destroyed hundreds. He possesses nothing of his own creation to which he can point. Everything he has is stolen. Foreign peoples, foreign workmen build him his temples; it is foreigners who create and work for him; it is foreigners who shed their blood for him. He has no art of his own; bit by bit he has stolen it all from other peoples. He does not even know how to preserve the precious things others have created. . . . In the last resort it is the Aryan alone who can form States and set them on their path to future greatness. All this the Jew cannot do. And because he cannot do it, therefore all his revolutions must be international. They must spread as a pestilence spreads. Already he has destroyed Russia; now it is the turn of Germany, and with his envious instinct for destruction he seeks to disintegrate the national spirit of the Germans and to pollute their blood.[1]

From this early speech of 1922, through the Nuremberg Laws of 1935 and the pogrom of November 1938 to the destruction of the Warsaw Ghetto and the death camps of Mauthausen and Auschwitz, Hitler's purpose was plain and unwavering. He meant to carry out the extermination of the Jewish race in Europe, using the word 'extermination' not in a metaphorical but in a precise and literal sense as the deliberate policy of the German State – and he very largely succeeded. On a conservative estimate,[2]

1. Speech at Munich, 28 July 1922 (ibid., pp. 21–41).
2. Gerald Reitlinger: *The Final Solution*, Appendix I, where the figures are examined in detail.

between four and four and a half million Jews perished in Europe under Hitler's rule – apart from the number driven from their homes who succeeded in finding refuge abroad. History records few, if any, crimes of such magnitude and of so cold-blooded a purpose.

VII

Stripped of their romantic trimmings, all Hitler's ideas can be reduced to a simple claim for power which recognizes only one relationship, that of domination, and only one argument, that of force. 'Civilization,' the Spanish philosopher, Ortega y Gasset, once wrote, 'consists in the attempt to reduce violence to the *ultima ratio*, the final argument. This is now becoming all too clear to us, for direct action reverses the order and proclaims violence as the *prima ratio*, or rather the *unica ratio*, the sole argument. It is the standard that dispenses with all others.'

Hitler was not original in this view. Every single one of his ideas – from the exaltation of the heroic leader, the racial myth, anti-Semitism, the community of the *Volk*, and the attack on the intellect, to the idea of a ruling élite, the subordination of the individual and the doctrine that might is right – is to be found in anti-rational and racist writers (not only in Germany but also in France and other European countries) during the hundred years which separate the Romantic movement from the foundation of the Third Reich. By 1914 they had become the commonplaces of radical, anti-Semitic and pan-German journalism in every city in Central Europe, including Vienna and Munich, where Hitler picked them up.

Hitler's originality lay not in his ideas, but in the terrifying literal way in which he set to work to translate these ideas into reality, and his unequalled grasp of the means by which to do this. To read Hitler's speeches and table talk is to be struck again and again by the lack of magnanimity or of any trace of moral greatness. His comments on everything except politics display a cocksure ignorance and an ineradicable vulgarity. Yet this vulgarity of mind, like the insignificance of his appearance, the badly fitting raincoat and the lock of hair plastered over his forehead of the early Hitler, was perfectly compatible with brilliant political gifts. Accustomed to associate such gifts with the qualities of intellect which Napoleon possessed, or with the strength of character of a Cromwell or a Lincoln, we are astonished and offended by this combination. Yet to underestimate Hitler as a politician, to dismiss him as an ignorant demagogue, is to make precisely the mistake that so many Germans made in the early 1930s.

It was not a mistake which those who worked closely with him made. Whatever they felt about the man, however much they disagreed with the rightness of this or that decision, they never underrated the ascendancy which he was able to establish over all who came into frequent contact with him. At Nuremberg, Admiral Dönitz, the Commander-in-Chief of the German Navy, admitted:

I purposely went very seldom to his headquarters, for I had the feeling that I would thus best preserve my power of initiative, and also because, after several days at headquarters, I always had the feeling that I had to disengage myself from his power of suggestion. I am telling you this because in this connexion I was doubtless more fortunate than his Staff, who were constantly exposed to his power and his personality.[1]

Dönitz's experience can be matched a hundred times over. Generals who arrived at his headquarters determined to insist on the hopelessness of the situation not only failed to make any protest when they stood face to face with the Führer, but returned shaken in their judgement and half convinced that he was right after all.

On one occasion [Schacht records] I managed to persuade Göring to exercise his influence on Hitler to put on the brake in some economic matter or other only to learn afterwards that he had not dared raise the question after all. When I reproached him he replied: 'I often make up my mind to say something to him, but then when I come face to face with him my heart sinks into my boots.'[2]

On another occasion when Schacht had demonstrated to the Minister of Defence, General von Blomberg, the hopelessness of finding any solution to a certain problem, Blomberg answered: 'I know you are right, but I have confidence in Hitler. He will be able to find some solution.'[3]

The final test of this ascendancy belongs to the later stages of this history when, with the prestige of success destroyed, the German cities reduced to ruins, and the greater part of the country occupied, this figure, whom his people no longer saw or heard,

1. N.P., Part XIII, p. 245.
2. Schacht, p. 216.
3. ibid., p. 220.

was still able to prolong the war long past the stage of hopelessness until the enemy was in the streets of Berlin and he himself decided to break the spell. But the events of these earlier years cannot be understood unless it is recognized that, however much in retrospect Hitler may seem to fall short of the stature of greatness, in the years 1938 to 1941, at the height of his success, he had succeeded in persuading a great part of the German nation that in him they had found a ruler of more than human qualities, a man of genius raised up by Providence to lead them into the Promised Land.

CHAPTER EIGHT

FROM VIENNA TO PRAGUE

1938–9

I

THE winter of 1937–8 marks the turning-point in Hitler's policy from the restricted purpose of removing the limitations imposed on Germany by the Treaty of Versailles to the bolder course which brought the spectacular triumphs of the years 1938–41. It was not so much a change in the direction or character of his foreign policy – which altered little from the time he wrote *Mein Kampf* – as the opening of a new phase in its development. The time was ripe, he judged, for the realization of aims he had long nurtured.

Hitler had no cut-and-dried views about how he was to proceed, but, as Hossbach's minutes of the meeting of 5 November 1937 show, he was revolving certain possibilities in his mind and, granted favourable circumstances, he was prepared to move against Austria and Czechoslovakia as early as the new year, 1938.

The prospects Hitler had unfolded at that meeting, however, alarmed at least some of those who were present. The brief report of the discussion which followed Hitler's exposition shows clearly enough the doubts of the Army's leaders, Blomberg and Fritsch, about the risk of war with Great Britain and France, and their anxiety about such material points as the incomplete state of Germany's western fortifications, France's military power and the strength of the Czech defences. Neurath, the Foreign Minister, supported them so far as to remind Hitler that a conflict between Great Britain, France, and Italy was neither so close nor so certain as he appeared to assume.

These doubts were not removed by Hitler's irritable assurances that he was convinced Britain would never fight and that he did not believe France would go to war on her own. On 9 November, Fritsch requested a further interview with Hitler and renewed his objections: Germany, he argued, was not in a position to court the danger of war. Neurath, too, attempted to see Hitler and dissuade him from the course he proposed to follow. By this time, however, Hitler was so irritated that he left Berlin abruptly for Berchtesgaden and refused to receive the Foreign Minister until his return in the middle of January.

Reasoned criticism of any kind always roused Hitler's anger: he hated to have his intuition subjected to analysis. It is possible that he had already made up his mind to get rid of the last of those in positions of authority who were not National Socialists and might have doubts about forcing the pace in foreign policy. At any rate, within less than three months of the meeting of 5 November, three of the men who had listened to him – Blomberg, Fritsch, and Neurath – were removed from office, while those who remained were the two who had silenced whatever doubts they felt – Göring and Raeder.

Schacht had already gone at the end of 1937. He did not oppose German rearmament: on the contrary, as the Army journal *Militär-Wochenblatt* said on his sixtieth birthday, Schacht was 'the man who made the reconstruction of the Wehrmacht possible', and he had carried out his work as Plenipotentiary for War Economy as well as Minister of Economics with enthusiasm. It was Schacht who, by his device of the Mefo-bills, enabled Hitler to finance his big programme of rearmament and public works without an excessive inflation. It was Schacht again who set up the elaborate network of control over German imports, exports, and foreign exchange transactions, and who provided a new basis for Germany's foreign trade by his barter trading, blocked-mark accounts, and clearing agreements, manipulating these with such skill as to secure great advantages for Germany in trade negotiations.

There were limits, however, beyond which Schacht as an economist felt it dangerous to make increasing demands on the economy for rearmament, and in 1935–6 he several times warned Hitler that these limits were being approached. Hitler was irritated. He did not think in economic terms at all. In the long run, if he got the arms, he believed that he would be able to solve Germany's economic problems by other than economic means. On the other hand, he needed Schacht, with his unrivalled grasp of finance and foreign trade to steer Germany through the first difficult years until she was strong enough to take what she wanted.

The situation was complicated by Göring's invasion of the economic field. Ironically, it was Schacht who persuaded Hitler, in April 1936, to appoint Göring as Commissioner for Raw Materials and Foreign Exchange, in the hope that this would put a stop to the extravagant waste of Germany's foreign exchange assets and her limited supplies of raw materials by Party agencies, such as the Ministry of Propaganda. Göring, having once entered the field of economic policy, began to take an interest in what was going on and to amass power. In September 1936 Hitler named him Plenipotentiary for the Four-Year Plan, a scheme to make Germany self-sufficient which Schacht regarded as impossible. To Schacht's contempt for Göring's ignorance of economics was added the pique of a vain and ambitious man at the rise of a rival power. After months of quarrelling in which he attacked Göring's policies as economically unsound, Schacht travelled to the Obersalzberg in August 1937 and insisted on resigning.

Hitler was extremely reluctant to let Schacht go. A stormy meeting at the Berghof in August, in which Hitler did everything he could to persuade him to stay, led to no conclusion, although Hitler came out on to the terrace afterwards and excitedly declared that he could not go on working with him any longer. On 5 September Schacht went on leave of absence from the Ministry of Economics, and after further protests his resignation was accepted on 8 December 1937. In order to preserve appearances he remained Minister without Portfolio, and for the time being President of the Reichsbank as well, but from now on Göring was able to carry out Hitler's economic plans in preparation for war without hindrance.

Schacht's successor as Minister of Economics was Walther Funk, once one of Hitler's 'contact men' with business and industrial circles. But the post was shorn of the greater part of its powers, being wholly subordinated to Göring as Plenipotentiary for the Four-Year Plan. The casual way in which Funk's appointment was made shows clearly enough how slight was the authority the new Minister could expect to enjoy. Meeting Funk one night at the Opera, Hitler took him aside during the interval, told him he was to succeed Schacht and sent him to Göring for instructions. It was only after Göring had carried out a thorough reorganization of the Ministry that it was finally transferred to Funk in February 1938.

After replacing Schacht by Göring, Hitler turned to the two principal institutions of the State which had so far escaped the process of *Gleichschaltung* – the Foreign Service and the Army. Both were strongholds of that upper-class conservatism which roused all Hitler's suspicion and dislike. Hitler had at first accepted the view that the cooperation of the professional diplomats and the generals was indispensable to him, but he rapidly came to feel contempt for the advice he received from the Foreign Office, whose political as well as social traditions he regarded as too respectable and too limited for the novel, half-revolutionary, half-gangster tactics with which he meant to conduct his foreign policy. It was not so much the moral scruples of the Wilhelmstrasse – these, he had little doubt, could be overcome – as the social pretensions, squeamishness and lack of imagination which irritated him. They still thought in terms of the old diplomacy, not of the revolutionary propaganda fifth-column technique, corruption, and incitement with which he proposed to conquer opposition. Neurath, the Foreign Minister, was one of President Hindenburg's appointments, and still retained some independence of position. Now in the subservient Ribbentrop Hitler had found the man he wanted to replace him, and by the beginning of 1938 he judged that this situation too was ripe for settlement.

But the critical relationship was that with the Army. So far the bargain of 1934 had worked well, but not without signs of trouble, which were ominous for the future. The generals, although delighted with the rearmament of Germany, were critical of the speed with which it had been rushed through. The flood of conscripts which began to pour into the depots was more than the four thousand officers of the small Regular Army could train satisfactorily. The figure of thirty-six divisions for the peacetime force which Hitler announced in 1935 had been arbitrarily fixed without the agreement of the General Staff, who would have preferred a figure of twenty-one divisions. They regarded twenty-four divisions, which represented a trebling of the existing force of eight divisions, as the maximum with which they could deal. According to Manstein, who was at that time Chief of Staff at the headquarters of the important Military Area III (in Berlin), he and his commanding officer learned of Hitler's decision for the first time over the radio.

In 1936, again, Hitler had sprung his decision to reoccupy the Rhineland on the Army High Command with the least possible notice. Manstein, who had to draft the orders for the occupation, was given one afternoon in which to draw them up before the generals came to receive their instructions the following morning. On this occasion Blomberg and the Army C.-in-C., Fritsch, protested to Hitler at the risks he was running. Hitler did not forget their opposition, more especially as events justified his judgement and not theirs.

If Hitler found it difficult to get on with the stiff, buttoned-up hierarchy of the Army, the generals had their grievances as well. They knew little of what was discussed in the circle round the Führer, and the one representative of the Army who was on friendly terms with Hitler – General, later Field-Marshal, von Blomberg, the Minister of War – was regarded as so much under Hitler's influence and so compliant with his wishes that he was given the scornful nicknames of the 'Rubber-Lion' (*Gummi-Löwe*), and 'Hitler Youth Quex', after a highly enthusiastic Nazi film. The Army had lost the old independent position which it had enjoyed under the Empire and – thanks to Seeckt and Schleicher – under the Republic as well. There was a new master in Germany, and one with whose foreign and internal politics the generals were far from being in agreement. They disliked the Pact with Poland; they were inclined – following the Seeckt tradition – to be friendly with Russia and China, while they had little use for an alliance with Japan and nothing but scorn for Italy. They were alarmed at the prospect of a two-front war after the Franco–Russian Pact, and felt a traditional respect for France as a great military Power, which was at variance with Hitler's contemptuous dismissal of the French as a divided nation. The Party's attitude towards the Churches – in particular the arrest of Pastor Niemoeller in July 1937 – roused considerable opposition in the Officer Corps. This was reinforced by dislike of the S.S. and S.A., whose ideas began to penetrate the Army as the inevitable result of conscription. The S.S. leader, Himmler, and his chief lieutenant, Heydrich – who had been expelled from the Naval Officer Corps for scandalous conduct in 1930 – had secured complete control of the police in Germany in 1936. They now entertained the ambition of humbling the proud independence of the Officer Corps, which treated the S.S. and its 'officers' with icy contempt.

The man to whom the Army looked to defend its interests was not Blomberg, but its Commander-in-Chief, Colonel-General von Fritsch. Fritsch had so far kept the Party at arm's length, but he lacked any quality of greatness such as Seeckt had possessed, and he was to prove unequal to the hopes placed in him.

The key to the relationship between the Army and the Nazi régime was Hitler's own attitude. Closer acquaintance had reduced the exaggerated respect he originally felt for the generals. After 1935–6 he saw them as no more than a group of men who, with few exceptions, lacked understanding of anything outside their own highly important but narrow field of specialization, a caste whose pretensions were unsupported by political ability or, when put to the test, by solidarity in face of an appeal to their self-interest. Hitler indeed was one of the few Germans to emancipate himself from the legendary spell of German militarism. By the beginning of 1938, with his power securely established and with the foundations of German military rearmament solidly laid, he no longer felt the same need to buy the Army's support on its own terms as he had in 1933 and 1934, when its tacit support had been a decisive factor in his securing and retaining power. Thus when Blomberg and Fritsch, on the grounds of Germany's unpreparedness, attempted to apply a brake to the development of his foreign policy, he paid no heed either to their judgement or to the need of appeasing their doubts.

II

Hitler was still smarting with irritation at the opposition Fritsch had expressed in November 1937, when an apparently unconnected series of events provided him with the chance to end once and for all the pretensions of the High Command to independent views. The trap was sprung by Himmler and Göring, and it is possible that Hitler was unaware of what was being planned by these two. But Hitler was nobody's dupe, and the use which he made of the opportunity thrust into his hands displayed his political gifts to sinister advantage.

The trouble began with Blomberg's eagerness to get married (for the second time) to a certain Fräulein Erna Grühn, whose origins were obscure and who, Blomberg admitted, was a lady with a 'past'. Aware of the shock this would give to the rigid views of the Officer Corps on the social suitability of the wife of a Field-Marshal and a Minister of War, Blomberg consulted Göring as a brother-officer. Göring not only encouraged him, but helped to ship an inconvenient rival off to South America. When the marriage took place – very quietly – on 12 January, Hitler and Göring were the two principal witnesses.

At this stage, however, complications arose. A police dossier was discovered which disclosed that the wife of the Field-Marshal had a police record as a prostitute and had at one time been convicted of posing for indecent photographs. Blomberg had dishonoured the Officer Corps, and the generals saw no reason to spare a man whom they had long disliked for his attitude towards Hitler. Supported by Göring, and urged on by the Chief of Staff, General Beck, the Commander-in-Chief, von Fritsch, requested an interview with Hitler and presented the Army's protest: Blomberg must go. Hitler, who appears to have felt that he too had been made to look a fool, eventually agreed. The question then arose who was to succeed Blomberg as Minister of War and Commander-in-Chief of the Armed Forces.[1]

Fritsch was the obvious candidate, but there were powerful forces opposed to his appointment. Himmler regarded him as the man responsible for defeating his attempts to extend the power of the S.S. to the Army. For a long time he had been watching for an opportunity to get rid of Fritsch. Göring, already Commander-in-Chief of the Air Force, was ambitious to get Blomberg's place for himself. Indeed, the part played by Göring throughout the whole affair – his encouragement of Blomberg, and the fact that it was he who informed Hitler of the information which had come to light about Erna Grühn after the marriage – invites suspicion.[2] Finally, Hitler too must have hesitated to appoint a man who had shown himself so lukewarm and unconvinced by the Führer's genius at the secret conference on 5 November.

Whatever Hitler's doubts, Himmler and Göring settled the matter by again producing a police dossier, this time to show that General von Fritsch had been guilty of homosexual practices. They went further: when Hitler summoned Fritsch to the Chancellery at noon on 26 January and faced him with the charges in the dossier, they arranged for the Commander-in-Chief to be confronted with Hans Schmidt, a young man who made his living by spying on and blackmailing well-to-do homosexuals.

Schmidt identified Fritsch as one of those from whom he had extorted money. In view of Schmidt's police record this was the flimsiest piece of evidence, and was later torn to shreds at the court of inquiry. The officer in question, it then emerged, was not Fritsch at all, but a retired cavalry officer of the name of Frisch. This fact was perfectly well known to the Gestapo, who later

1. i.e. Commander-in-Chief of the Wehrmacht, which included all the Armed Forces of the State. Fritsch was the Commander-in-Chief of the Army (Reichswehr), which formed a part of the Wehrmacht.
2. At the Nuremberg Trials in 1946 Göring sent a threatening message to Gisevius that, if he said too much in the witness-box about the Blomberg case, he would tell all that he knew about Schacht, Gisevius's patron. Cf. N.P., Part xii, pp. 214–16.

arrested Frisch in order to prevent the defence getting his evidence. Eventually Schmidt confessed in court that he had been threatened by the Gestapo if he did not agree to their demands and incriminate Fritsch, as Himmler ordered. Schmidt paid for this indiscretion with his life. But by then the trick had served its purpose. In face of Hitler's angry charges, General von Fritsch maintained an indignant silence, and when Hitler, either genuinely deceived or feigning conviction, sent him on indefinite leave, he refused to take any action to defend himself.[1]

For a few days it looked as if the affair might lead to a major crisis comparable with that of 30 June 1934. Hitler postponed his customary speech to the Reichstag on 30 January, and a furious battle developed behind the scenes round the question whether there should be a court of inquiry into the charges against Fritsch and, if so, who should conduct it, the Army or the Party. Behind this loomed the far bigger question of who was to be given command of the Army, for now not only Blomberg's office of Minister of War and Commander-in-Chief of the Armed Forces, but also Fritsch's as Commander-in-Chief of the Army, had to be filled.

On 31 January Beck accompanied Rundstedt, the senior general of the Army, to an interview in which Hitler raged against all generals. The one concession they got from him was a reluctant agreement to an inquiry into the Fritsch case. Hitler, however, had already seen how to turn the situation to his own advantage, without giving in to the demands of Göring and Himmler on the one hand, or of the Army represented by Beck and Rundstedt on the other.

His solution to the problem was presented to the German Cabinet, when it met for the last time during the Third Reich on Monday, 4 February. After announcing Blomberg's resignation, Hitler added that von Fritsch, too, had asked to be relieved of his duties as Commander-in-Chief of the Army on the grounds of ill-health. Blomberg's successor was to be neither Fritsch nor Göring, but Hitler himself. Hitler had been, since Hindenburg's death, the Supreme Commander of the Armed Forces, an office which went with that of Head of the State. Now he assumed in addition Blomberg's office of Commander-in-Chief of the Armed Forces and abolished the old post of War Minister which Blomberg had held as well. He wanted no successor to a position which in the hands of an independent man might have been used to

1. cf. Graf Kielmansegg: *Der Fritsch Prozess* (Hamburg, 1949).

represent the views of the Army in opposition to his own. The work of the War Ministry was henceforward to be done by a separate High Command of the Armed Forces (Oberkommando der Wehrmacht, the familiar O.K.W. of the War Communiqués), which in fact became Hitler's personal staff. To the head of the O.K.W. he appointed a man who was to prove quite incapable of withstanding him, even if he had wanted to – General Wilhelm Keitel.

In General von Brauchitsch Hitler found a man acceptable to the Officer Corps of Fritsch's post of Commander-in-Chief of the Army, and he eventually agreed that the case against Fritsch should be investigated by a military court. At the same time, however, he took the chance to retire sixteen of the senior generals and to transfer forty-four others to different commands. To console Göring, Hitler promoted him to the rank of Field-Marshal, a step which gave him precedence over the other Commanders-in-Chief and made him the senior German officer.

The purge extended further than the Army. Neurath was relieved of his office as Foreign Minister, appointed as President of a newly created Cabinet Privy Council (which never met), and replaced at the Wilhelmstrasse by Ribbentrop. The three ambassadors in the key posts of Vienna (Papen), Rome (Hassell), and Tokyo (Herbert von Dirksen) were simultaneously replaced. Finally, the insignificant Walter Funk assumed office at the Ministry of Economics after it had been stripped of the powers which Schacht had exercised.

Thus at a single blow Hitler succeeded in removing the few checks which remained upon his freedom of action by using a situation not of his making to establish a still firmer grip upon the control of policy and the machinery of the State. He had replaced Blomberg and Fritsch, Neurath and Schacht, with creatures of his own will – Keitel, Ribbentrop, and Funk – and added to the power in his own hands by assuming direct control of the Armed Forces. When put to the test, the claim of the Army to stand apart from the process of *Gleichschaltung* in the totalitarian state had proved to be hollow. Nor had the solidarity of the Officer Corps prevented Hitler finding men who were eager enough to serve him. The concern of the generals for the honour of their caste had been limited to securing Blomberg's dismissal for a *mésalliance* and a court of inquiry to vindicate Fritsch. After long delays the Court met on 11 March, only to be adjourned because of the Austrian crisis. When it reassembled on the 17th, the régime, covered with the glory of the *Anschluss*, was un-assailable. Once again Hitler showed his ability to make use of unexpected opportunities. Fritsch's reputation was vindicated, but the verdict had no further consequences: he was not reinstated in office, but retired into private life with the simple distinction of Colonel-in-Chief of his old regiment. With that the generals were content, and Fritsch himself acquiesced. As he remarked to the ex-Ambassador von Hassell in an illuminating comment: 'This man, Hitler, is Germany's destiny for good and for evil. If he now goes over the abyss (which Fritsch believes he will) he will drag us all down with him. There is nothing we can do'.[1]

In the triumphs that followed the Fritsch Affair was forgotten. It marked none the less the last stage in the revolution after power; the end of the Conservatives' hopes that in Schacht, Neurath, and Fritsch they still preserved some slender guarantees against the recklessness of the Nazis, and the prelude to the new era in foreign policy.

III

About nine o'clock on the evening of 4 February (the day of the Cabinet Meeting in Berlin) Franz von Papen, the Führer's special representative in Vienna, was sitting in his study at the Legation when the telephone bell rang. It was the State Secretary, Lammers, speaking from the Reich Chancellery, with the brief announcement that Papen's mission in Vienna was at an end and he had been recalled. Lammers regretted that he could give no explanation.

Papen's surprise was considerable, for he had seen Hitler personally only the week before and nothing had then been said about his recall or transfer. The question everyone asked in Vienna was whether Papen's recall would be followed by a change in German policy towards Austria.

For the past eighteen months, Austro-German relations had been governed by the Agreement of July 1936. The interpretation of that Agreement by the two parties, however, showed wide differences of opinion which are reflected in the diplomatic ex-changes.[2] The Austrian Government had originally, though not

1. *The Von Hassell Diaries* (London, 1948), p. 28.
2. cf. G.D., D. I, chapter II: Germany and Austria, July 1936–July 1938.

very strongly, hoped that the Agreement might serve as a final settlement of the differences between Germany and themselves. The Germans, on the other hand, clearly regarded it as a lever with which to exercise pressure on the Austrians in such a way that, in the end, Austrian independence would be undermined and the *Anschluss* carried out peacefully, on the initiative of a Nazi-controlled government in Vienna. Schuschnigg's[1] room for manoeuvre in resisting such pressure was limited. For there was a strong underground Nazi party in Austria which bitterly resented the policy of peaceful penetration represented by Papen and itched to seize power by a putsch. Hitler had so far refused to give the Austrian Nazis a free hand, but this was an alternative which he could use to bring additional pressure on the Austrian Government if Schuschnigg proved too obstinate or evasive in meeting German demands.

On 25 January 1938 a police raid on the Austrian Nazis' headquarters in Vienna brought to light plans for a rising in the spring of 1938 and for an appeal to Hitler to intervene. There was no proof that Hitler knew or approved of these plans, but Schuschnigg was uneasy and only too well aware of Austria's increased isolation with the establishment of the Rome–Berlin Axis. At the time of Papen's sudden recall, the Austrian Chancellor was already revolving in his mind the advantage of a personal meeting with Hitler to put German–Austrian relations on a clearer footing.

Papen now had very good reasons of his own for advocating such a meeting. Here might be a chance to reinstate himself and the day after his dismissal he hurried to Berchtesgaden to put the proposal to Hitler personally. He found him 'exhausted and *distrait*' but the suggestion that Schuschnigg might come to see him aroused Hitler's interest. Ignoring the fact that he had just recalled Papen from his post, he ordered him to return at once to Vienna and make the necessary arrangements.

Neither at this stage nor in the subsequent interview with Schuschnigg is there any evidence that Hitler was yet thinking of marching an army into Austria and carrying out the *Anschluss* by force. At most this was a threat to be used in the same way as the other threat of a putsch by the Austrian Nazis, as a means of bringing pressure to bear on the Austrian Government. Hitler had not abandoned the 'peaceful solution of the Austrian prob-

1. Kurt von Schuschnigg became Federal Chancellor of Austria after Dollfuss's murder in 1934, and held the office until the *Anschluss*.

lem': the new factor was his decision to force the pace and end the Austrian tactics of evasion by pinning Schuschnigg down to pursue political conditions which he would have to accept under the threat of direct action if he refused.

Looking back from later events, it is easy to conclude (as many did at the time) that Papen's recall from Vienna was the first sign of Hitler's decision to bring relations with Austria to a head. It is more probable, however, that Papen, like Neurath, was pushed out of office as part of the clean sweep which Hitler made after the Fritsch affair. His recall may have had nothing to do with Austria and it my well be – as Papen himself suggests[1] – that Hitler took up his proposal of a meeting with Schuschnigg in order to distract attention from the Fritsch affair and its aftermath by a new success in foreign affairs. A sudden decision of this sort, especially after the strain of the crisis which had just ended, appealed strongly to Hitler. But it was only the opportunity which Papen suggested: the purpose to which he would put it was formed in Hitler's mind.

Returning to Vienna, Papen urged Schuschnigg to take what might well be the last opportunity to reach a satisfactory agreement with the Führer. Schuschnigg tried to safeguard himself by asking for assurances that the 1936 Agreement should remain the basis of Austro-German relations in the future. Papen – and Hitler – were perfectly ready to give such assurances, and on the evening of 11 February Schuschnigg and his Secretary of State for Foreign Affairs, Guido Schmidt, quietly left Vienna by train on their way to the Obersalzberg.

It was a cold winter morning when the two Austrians, motoring up from Salzburg, reached the frontier. Papen, who was there to meet them, was in the best of tempers, and only remarked casually that he hoped Schuschnigg would not mind the presence of one or two German generals who happened to be staying with Hitler at the Berghof. Hitler was waiting on the steps when they arrived and at once conducted the Austrian Chancellor into his study for a private talk before lunch.

Scarcely had they sat down than Hitler, brushing aside Schuschnigg's polite remarks about the view from his window, launched into an angry tirade against the whole course of Austrian policy. Schuschnigg's attempts to interrupt and defend himself were shouted down.

1. Papen, *Memoirs*, p. 406.

The whole history of Austria [Hitler declared] is just one uninterrupted act of high treason. That was so in the past, and it is no better today. This historical paradox must now reach its long-overdue end. And I can tell you, here and now, Herr Schuschnigg, that I am absolutely determined to make an end of all this. The German Reich is one of the Great Powers, and nobody will raise his voice if it settles its border problems.[1]

Hitler rapidly worked himself into a towering rage. He talked excitedly of his mission: 'I have achieved everything that I set out to do, and have thus become perhaps the greatest German in history.' Characteristically, he began to abuse Schuschnigg for ordering defence works to be constructed on the border. This was an open affront to Germany:

Listen. You don't really think that you can move a single stone in Austria without my hearing about it the very next day, do you? You don't seriously believe that you can stop me, or even delay me for half an hour, do you? . . . After the Army, my S.A., and the Austrian Legion would move in, and nobody can stop their just revenge – not even I. Do you want to make another Spain of Austria? I would like to avoid all that, if possible.

Austria, Hitler sneered, was alone: neither France, nor Britain, nor Italy would lift a finger to save her. And now his patience was exhausted. Unless Schuschnigg was prepared to agree, at once, to all that he demanded, he would settle matters by force.

Think it over, Herr Schuschnigg, think it over well. I can only wait until this afternoon. If I tell you that, you will do well to take my words literally. I don't believe in bluffing. All my past is proof of that.

For the moment, however, Hitler said nothing of what his demands were. After this tirade, which lasted for two hours, he suddenly broke off and led his guest in to lunch. Throughout the meal he was charm itself, but the presence of the generals at the table did not escape the Austrians' notice.

After lunch Hitler excused himself and left Schuschnigg and Schmidt to a desultory conversation with the other guests, while he went off to talk to one of the Austrian Nazi leaders, Mühlmann, and Keppler (Hitler's agent in Austria), whose visit had been well timed to coincide with that of the Austrian Chancellor.

1. The following account is taken from Kurt von Schuschnigg: *Austrian Requiem* (London, 1947) pp. 19–32. Although Schuschnigg's account of the conversation was written down later from memory, and does not claim to be an exact record of Hitler's words, all the other evidence confirms that it gives a substantially accurate picture of what was said at the Berghof on 12 February.

In the middle of the afternoon Schuschnigg was taken to see Ribbentrop and Papen. They presented him with a draft of Hitler's demands. These were far-reaching in their scope. The Austrian Government was to lift the ban on the Nazi Party and to recognize that National Socialism was perfectly compatible with loyalty to Austria. Seyss-Inquart, a 'respectable' crypto-Nazi, was to be appointed Minister of the Interior, with control of the police and the right to see that Nazi activity was allowed to develop along the lines indicated. An amnesty for all imprisoned Nazis was to be proclaimed within three days, and Nazi officials and officers who had been dismissed were to be reinstated in their posts. Another pro-Nazi, Glaise-Horstenau, was to be appointed Minister of War, and to assure close relations between the German and Austrian Armies there was to be a systematic exchange of officers. Finally, the Austrian economic system was to be assimilated to that of Germany, and a third Nazi nominee, Fischbök, appointed Minister of Finance.[1]

Schuschnigg's efforts to secure alterations in the draft, other than minor changes, were unavailing. It was, Ribbentrop warned him, Hitler's last word; he must accept all the clauses or take the consequences. When the Austrian Chancellor saw Hitler a little later he found him in the same intransigent mood: there was nothing to be discussed, not a word could be changed. 'You will either sign as it is and fulfil my demands within three days, or I will order the march into Austria.' When Schuschnigg explained that, although willing to sign, he could not, by the Austrian Constitution, guarantee ratification, or the observance of the time limit for the amnesty. Hitler lost his temper, flung open the door, and, turning Schuschnigg out, shouted for General Keitel.

According to Papen,[2] when Keitel hurried up and asked for Hitler's orders, 'Hitler grinned and said, "There are no orders. I just wanted you here."' The effect of the summons to Keitel however was well calculated, and Schmidt remarked to the Chancellor that he would not be surprised if they were arrested in the next five minutes. Half an hour later, however, Hitler again sent for Schuschnigg. 'I have decided to change my mind,' he told him. 'For the first time in my life. But I warn you – this is your very last chance. I have given you three more days before the Agreement goes into effect.'

1. Draft protocol in G.D., D.I, No. 294.
2. *Memoirs*, p. 417.

This was the limit of Hitler's concessions, and the Austrian Chancellor had little option but to sign.[1] With that Hitler began to calm down and talk more normally. But he was giving nothing away. When they discussed the communiqué to be issued to the Press, Schuschnigg asked for the promised confirmation of the 1936 Agreement. 'Oh, no!' Hitler retorted. 'First you have to fulfil the conditions of our Agreement. This is what is going to the Press: "Today the Führer and Reich Chancellor conferred with the Austrian Chancellor at the Berghof." That's all.'

To this, too, Schuschnigg had perforce to agree. His one anxiety now was to get away. He declined Hitler's invitation to stay to a late supper. The Austrians were silent as they drove down towards Salzburg, but Papen was still in the best of tempers. 'Well, now,' he remarked to Schuschnigg, 'you have seen what the Führer can be like at times. But the next time I am sure it will be different. You know, the Führer can be absolutely charming.'

Just twenty-four hours after they had arrived at Salzburg the Austrian Chancellor's train set out again for Vienna. Up at the Berghof the Führer relaxed: it had been a highly successful day.

IV

Mussolini described the interval between the Berchtesgaden interview and the *Anschluss* as that between the fourth and fifth acts of the Austrian tragedy. Hitler had not altered his course. On Saturday 26 February he saw the five leading Austrian Nazis, who were ordered to remain in Germany.

The Führer stated that in the Austrian problem he had to indicate a different course for the Party, *as the Austrian question could never be solved by a revolution.* There remained only two possibilities: force, or evolutionary means. He wanted the evolutionary course to be taken, whether or not the possibility of success could today be foreseen. The Protocol signed by Schuschnigg was so far-reaching that, if completely carried out, the Austrian problem would be automatically solved. He did not now desire a solution by violent means, if it could at all be avoided, since the danger for us in the field of foreign policy became less each year and our military power greater.[2]

But if Hitler had not changed his mind about the character of the policy to be pursued he certainly expected the Berchtesgaden

1. Text of final protocol in G.D., D.I, No. 295.
2. Memorandum by Wilhelm Keppler, who was present. G.D., D.I, No. 328.

meeting to hasten events. On 13 February General Jodl recorded a meeting with Keitel: 'He tells us that the Führer's order is that military pressure by shamming military action should be kept up until the 15th.' The next day Jodl added: 'The effect is quick and strong. In Austria the impression is created that Germany is undertaking serious military preparations.'[1] On the 16th, the Austrian Government announced a general amnesty for Nazis (including those convicted of the murder of Dolfuss) and the reorganization of the cabinet, with Seyss-Inquart as Minister of the Interior. The new minister at once left for Berlin to get his orders, and when Schuschnigg attempted to rally Austrian opinion by a speech on 24 February the Nazis in Styria stormed Graz Town Hall and hoisted the swastika flag.

Seyss-Inquart was beginning to act more and more independently of the Chancellor, and the Austrian Nazis were already boasting that within a matter of weeks, if not of days, they would be in the saddle and give Austria a taste of the whip.

At the end of the first week of March Schuschnigg reached a point where he felt that, if he stood aside inactive any longer, the Austrian Government would cease to be master in its own house. He resolved upon a desperate expedient which, he hoped, would destroy the strongest argument Hitler had so far used – that a majority of the Austrian people were in favour of an *Anschluss* with Germany. On the evening of 8 March he determined to hold a plebiscite on Sunday 13 March, in which the Austrian people should be invited to declare whether they were in favour of an Austria which was free and independent, German and Christian.

Schuschnigg had been revolving such a step in his mind since the end of February. Mussolini, who had been sounded out the day before (7 March) by Colonel Liebitzky, the Austrian military attaché in Rome, had returned the answer '*C'è un errore*' (That's a mistake). Schuschnigg, however, once he had made up his mind, persisted with an obstinate, if blind, courage.

The news of the plebiscite was slow in reaching Hitler, who does not appear to have been informed until the afternoon of 9 March. That same evening Schuschnigg made the official announcement to a meeting of the Patriotic Front at Innsbruck. While Schuschnigg was speaking in the Tyrol urgent summons were sent out from Berlin. Hitler was furious that Schuschnigg

1. Jodl's diary, N.D. 1780-PS. Jodl was chief of the Operations Staff in the O.K.W.

should try to obstruct him in this way, but he had been taken by surprise and nothing was prepared for such an eventuality. Göring and Keitel were at once called to the Chancellery, General von Reichenau was summoned back from a meeting of the Olympic Games Committee in Cairo, and Glaise-Horstenau, one of the crypto-Nazi Ministers in Schuschnigg's Government, who happened to be in the Palatinate, was rushed to Berlin. Ribbentrop was in London, and Neurath had to be brought back to deputize for him at the Foreign Office.

The only plan which existed for military action against Austria had been drawn up to prevent Otto of Hapsburg reclaiming the throne. This had to be made the basis for the improvised orders which the General Staff hurriedly drew up. Hitler approved the military plans on the evening of the 10th, but his directive still left the decision open: it was his intention to invade Austria, but only 'if other measures proved unsuccessful'.

The question that most preoccupied Hitler was Mussolini's reaction to the news that the German Army was preparing to march over the Austrian frontier. Ciano had not disguised Italian annoyance at the fact that the Berchtesgaden meeting of 12 February had been sprung on Italy without any notice, and there were signs of an Anglo–Italian *rapprochement* which worried Hitler. At noon, therefore, Hitler sent off Prince Philip of Hesse to the Duce with a letter which he had instructions to deliver personally.

The letter began with an argument which was so unconvincing that the Germans later secured its omission when the text was published – the argument that Austria had been conspiring with the Czechs, in order to restore the Hapsburgs and 'to throw the weight of a mass of at least twenty million men against Germany if necessary'. Hitler then continued on more familiar ground, the oppression of the Germans in Austria by their own government. Both complaints, he said – Austria's designs against Germany and the maltreatment of the national-minded majority in Austria – he had presented forcefully to Schuschnigg at Berchtesgaden. Schuschnigg had then promised changes. With these assurances Hitler had been content, but Schuschnigg had broken his promise. Now, at last, the Austrian people were rising against their oppressors, and Austria was being brought to a state of anarchy. He could no longer remain passive in face of his responsibilities as Führer of the German Reich and as a son of Austrian soil.

I am now determined to restore law and order in my homeland, and enable the people to decide their own fate according to their judgement in an unmistakable, clear and open manner. . . .
I now wish solemnly to assure Your Excellency, as the Duce of Fascist Italy:

1. Consider this step only as one of national self-defence. . . . You too, Excellency, could not act differently if the fate of Italians were at stake. . . .

2. In a critical hour for Italy I proved to you the steadfastness of my sympathy. Do not doubt that in the future there will be no change in this respect.

3. Whatever the consequences of the coming events may be, I have drawn a definite boundary between Germany and France and now draw one just as definite between Italy and us. It is the Brenner. This decision will never be questioned or changed.[1]

In the course of the night 10–11 March Hitler gave his orders to Glaise-Horstenau, the Austrian Cabinet Minister who was still waiting in Berlin, and packed him off to Vienna by plane. At two o'clock in the morning Directive No. 1 for Operation Otto was issued.

1. If other measures prove unsuccessful, I intend to invade Austria with armed forces in order to establish constitutional conditions and to prevent further outrages against the pro-German population.

2. The whole operation will be directed by myself. . . .
The forces detailed must be ready on 12 March (Saturday) at the latest from 1200 hours. I reserve the right to decide the actual moment for invasion. The behaviour of the troops must give the impression that we do not want to wage war against our Austrian brothers. . . .
On the remaining German frontiers no security measures are to be taken for the time being.[2]

By the time Hitler went to bed early on the morning of 11 March the Army trucks and tanks were already beginning to roll south towards the frontier.

The same morning, in the Chancellor's flat in Vienna, the telephone woke Schuschnigg from his sleep at half past five. The Chief of Police, Skubl, was on the line: the German border at Salzburg had been closed an hour before, and all rail traffic between the two countries stopped. The Chancellor dressed and drove through the still dark streets to early Mass at St Stephen's Cathedral. At the Chancellery the offices were deserted, and as

1. G.D., D.I, No. 352.　　　　2. N.D., C-102.

Schuschnigg looked out of the window he watched people in the streets hurrying to their jobs unconscious of what was already in train on the far side of the frontier.

There were other early risers in Vienna that morning. At dawn Papen left by air for Berlin, and not long afterwards the Austrian Minister of the Interior, Seyss-Inquart, was to be seen walking up and down at the airport waiting for the promised message from Hitler. It was brought by Glaise-Horstenau, and at half past nine the two Ministers called on the Chancellor to present Hitler's demands: the original plebiscite must be cancelled and replaced by another to be held in three weeks' time. For two hours the three men argued to and fro, but reached no conclusion. At half past eleven Seyss-Inquart and Glaise-Horstenau went off to a meeting with the leaders of the Austrian Nazi Party. After lunch they returned to the Chancellery and again saw Schuschnigg. The Chancellor, who had in the meantime been with President Miklas, told them he agreed to the postponement of the plebiscite. But by now the German demands were being raised. At 2.45 p.m. Göring began a series of telephone calls from Berlin to Vienna which continued until late in the evening, and the transcripts of which, prepared by Göring's own Forschungsamt (Research Department), are among the most dramatic of the documents captured after the war.[1]

Having secured the abandonment of the plebiscite, Göring on Hitler's instructions now called for the resignation of Schuschnigg. When that was agreed to in the middle of the afternoon, he demanded the appointment of Seyss-Inquart. But here the Nazis encountered an unexpected obstacle in the Austrian President, Miklas, who stubbornly refused to make Seyss-Inquart Chancellor, and kept up his resistance until shortly before midnight. Keppler, who had arrived from Berlin in the afternoon, and promptly set up an improvised office in the Chancellery, went to see the President, accompanied by the German Military Attaché, General Muff. Keppler had brought the list of Seyss-Inquart's Ministers with him from Berlin; he threatened invasion if the President would not agree, but still Miklas held out.

At half past five an angry Göring, roaring down the wire from Berlin, demanded to speak to Seyss-Inquart:

Look here, you go immediately together with Lieutenant-General Muff and tell the Federal President that, if the conditions which are known to

1. N.D. 2949-PS.

you are not accepted immediately, the troops already stationed at the frontier will move in tonight along the whole line, and Austria will cease to exist. . . . Tell him there is no time now for any joke. . . . The invasion will be stopped and the troops held at the border only if we are informed by 7.30 that Miklas has entrusted you with the Federal Chancellorship. . . . Then call out the National Socialists all over the country. They should now be in the streets. So, remember, we must have a report by 7.30. If Miklas could not understand in four hours, we shall make him understand now in four minutes.

As the evening drew on, an excited mob filled the Inner City and surged round the Chancellery. On the stairs and in the corridors Schuschnigg noticed unfamiliar figures with swastika armbands, saluting each other with outstretched arms and pushing their way unceremoniously in and out of the offices. Shortly after half past seven Schuschnigg broadcast to the nation the news that Germany had delivered an ultimatum, and rebutted the lie that civil war had broken out in Austria. The President still refused to appoint Seyss-Inquart as Chancellor, and neither Keppler nor Muff could shake him.

Some time after eight o'clock Göring rang up again. If Schuschnigg had resigned, he told Muff, Seyss-Inquart should regard himself as still in office and entitled to carry out necessary measures in the name of the Government. If anyone objected or attempted to resist they would have to face a German court-martial by the invading troops. With Seyss-Inquart technically in office the façade of legality could be preserved. This was all that was needed. When Keppler telephoned to Berlin shortly before 9 p.m. to report that Seyss-Inquart was acting as instructed, Göring replied:

Listen. You are the Government now. Listen carefully and take notes. The following telegram should be sent here to Berlin by Seyss-Inquart:
'The provisional Austrian Government, which, after the dismissal of the Schuschnigg Government, considers it its task to establish peace and order in Austria, sends to the German Government the urgent request to support it in its task and to help it prevent bloodshed. For this purpose it asks the German Government to send German troops as soon as possible.'

Göring added a few more instructions. Seyss-Inquart was to form a government from the names on the list sent from Berlin; Göring's own brother-in-law was to get the Ministry of Justice. The frontiers were to be watched, to prevent people getting away. As to the telegram:

Well, he does not even have to send the telegram – all he needs to do is to say: Agreed.

An hour later Keppler telephoned Berlin again: 'Tell the General Field-Marshal that Seyss-Inquart agrees.'

Throughout the country the local Nazis were already seizing town halls and government offices. To their anger they had been largely excluded from the decisive events in the Chancellery, where the principal parts were played by Hitler's agent, Keppler, by the German military attaché, General Muff, and by Seyss-Inquart, a fellow-traveller long regarded with dislike by the true-blue Nazis of the illegal Party. None the less, by the threat of a seizure of power by force, which was implicit in the noisy mob filling the street outside the Chancellery, they contributed to the atmosphere of compulsion before which in the end the President had to yield.

A little before midnight President Miklas capitulated: to avoid bloodshed and in the hope of securing at least the shadow of Austrian independence, he nominated Seyss-Inquart as Federal Chancellor of Austria. At two o'clock in the morning General Muff rang up Berlin and, at Seyss-Inquart's request, asked that the German troops should be halted at the frontier. It was too late. An appeal to Hitler was turned down: the occupation must go on.

The time marked on Hitler's order to march is 2045 hours, 11 March, which suggests that Hitler had already signed it before Göring finished dictating the faked telegram to Vienna between 8.48 and 8.54 p.m. The hour for crossing the frontier was fixed at daybreak on Saturday, the 12th. Before then Hitler had received the message he had been waiting for all day – news from Rome. When Prince Philip rang up at 10.25 p.m. on the night of 11 March, it was Hitler, not Göring, who came to the telephone.

HESSE: I have just come back from the Palazzo Venezia. The Duce accepted the whole thing in a very friendly manner. He sends you his regards. . . .
HITLER: Then please tell Mussolini I will never forget him for this.
HESSE: Yes.
HITLER: Never, never, never, whatever happens. . . . As soon as the Austrian affair is settled, I shall be ready to go with him, through thick and thin, no matter what happens.
HESSE: Yes, my Führer.
HITLER: Listen, I shall make any agreement – I am no longer in fear of

the terrible position which would have existed militarily in case we had got into a conflict. You may tell him that I thank him ever so much; never, never shall I forget.

HESSE: Yes, my Führer.

HITLER: I will never forget, whatever may happen. If he should ever need any help or be in any danger, he can be convinced that I shall stick to him, whatever may happen, even if the whole world were against him.

HESSE: Yes, my Führer.[1]

With that load off his mind Hitler was content to leave Göring to take over the direction of affairs in Berlin. The Field-Marshal had kept a thousand distinguished guests waiting for an hour at a sumptuous reception in the Haus der Flieger, where the State Opera ballet was to dance. No sooner had he arrived and taken his seat than he scribbled on his programme: 'Immediately the music is over I should like to talk to you, and *will explain everything to you.*' The note was passed to the British Ambassador.[2] A little later Henderson saw Göring in his room and delivered a protest 'in the strongest terms'. The protest produced no effect and it is hard to believe that the British Government ever supposed it would.

Hitler was not much worried about the risk of British or French intervention, but the Czechs were a different matter. They had a well-equipped army and they were close at hand. If the German operation was to retain its peaceful character, it was of great importance that the Czechs should not clash with German troops. As soon as the Czech Minister, Dr Mastny, arrived at the reception he was shown straight to Göring's room. The Field-Marshal was only too eager to reassure him: what was happening in Austria would have no effect at all on Germany's relations with Czechoslovakia. 'I give you my word of honour that Czechoslovakia has nothing to fear from the Reich.' In return he asked for assurances that Czechoslovakia would not mobilize. Mastny left at once to ring up Prague, and Göring went in to join his guests. After he had finished talking to Henderson, the Czech Minister returned. He had spoken to the Czech Foreign Minister himself: in Prague they were appreciative of the German goodwill and gave a definite promise that the Czech Army would not be mobilized. Göring was delighted and reiterated the undertaking he had already given, this time in the name of the German Government.

1. N.D., 2949-PS.
2. Sir N. Henderson: *Failure of a Mission*, pp. 124–5.

By noon on the 12th Hitler was with General Keitel at the H.Q. of the 8th Army. A proclamation broadcast to the German nation contained a long indictment of the oppressive misgovernment of Austria and an eloquent account of Hitler's restraint in trying to reach a settlement with Vienna. The plan to hold a plebiscite, under conditions in which there could be no security for freedom or impartiality, was the last straw. The Führer had decided to liberate Austria and to come to the help of these brother Germans in distress.[1]

Shortly after lunch Hitler himself crossed the frontier, and drove through decorated villages into the crowded, cheering streets of Linz. There, in the town in which he had once gone to school, he was met by the two Austrian Ministers, Seyss-Inquart and Glaise-Horstenau. In the background was Himmler, who had already visited Vienna the night before to put the machinery of the Gestapo and S.S. into operation and begin the arrests.

Hitler was in an excited mood: he had come home at last. The next day he went out to lay a wreath on his parents' grave at Leonding. To Mussolini he sent a telegram: 'I shall never forget this. Adolf Hitler.' To the crowds he declared:

When years ago I went forth from this town I bore within me precisely the same profession of faith which today fills my heart. Judge of the depth of my emotion when, after so many years, I have been able to bring that profession of faith to its fulfilment. If Providence once called me forth from this town to be the leader of the Reich, it must, in so doing, have charged me with a mission, and that mission could be only to restore my dear homeland to the German Reich. I have believed in this mission, I have lived and fought for it, and I believe I have now fulfilled it.[2]

That night Hitler spent in Linz, while Seyss-Inquart returned by car to Vienna. It was here, perhaps under the influence of the enthusiastic reception he had met in his homeland, that he decided not to set up a satellite government under Seyss-Inquart but to incorporate Austria directly into the Reich.

Next morning, the Sunday on which the ill-fated plebiscite was to have been held, one of Hitler's State Secretaries, Stuckart, flew to Vienna to place Hitler's plan before the new Austrian Government. The terms in which the suggestion was framed

1. Text in Baynes: vol. II, pp. 1,416–21.
2. Speech at Linz, 12 March 1938 (Baynes: vol. II, pp. 1,422–3).

admitted of only one answer. A Cabinet meeting was hurriedly summoned, and when Seyss-Inquart reached Linz again late on the night of the 13th he was able to present the Führer with the text of a law already promulgated, the first article of which read: 'Austria is a province of the German Reich.'[1] Hitler was deeply moved. Tears ran down his cheeks, and he turned to his companions with the remark: 'Yes, a good political action saves blood.'[2] The same night the arrests began: in Vienna alone they were to total seventy-six thousand.[3]

All day on the 13th crowds waited in Vienna for the Führer to make his triumphant entry into the capital. It was not until the afternoon of Monday, the 14th, that he finally arrived. Among the reasons for the delay were Himmler's dissatisfaction with the security arrangements and, to Hitler's fury, the breakdown of a great part of the German mechanized and motorized troops on the road.[4] When Hitler reached Vienna he was not in the best of tempers; he stayed only one night and then flew back to Munich. Yet the huge crowds filling the Heldenplatz and the Ring, the reception in the Hapsburgs' palace of the Hofburg, the element of personal triumph in his return to the city which had rejected him – all this must have given him deep satisfaction. Once he had cursed his generals and recovered his temper this sense of satisfaction, even of exaltation, is to be found in the speeches of the election campaign which followed. For Austria was to have its plebiscite after all, a plebiscite in which not only Austria but the whole of Greater Germany was to take part, this time under Nazi auspices.

When he presented his report to the Reichstag on 18 March Hitler announced the dissolution of the Reichstag and new elections for 10 April, appealing for another four years of power to consolidate the gains of the new Grossdeutschland.

In the course of the electoral campaign Hitler travelled from end to end of Germany. In the first ten days of April he moved to Austria and visited Graz, Klagenfurt, Innsbruck, Salzburg, and

1. Full text in G.D., D.I, No. 374.
2. Memorandum by Seyss-Inquart, 9 September 1945 (N.D. 3254-PS).
3. Figures given by Seyss-Inquart's Counsel at Nuremberg (N.P., Part XIX, p. 165).
4. At Nuremberg General Jodl stated that seventy per cent of all armoured vehicles and cars were stranded on the roads from Salzburg and Passau to Vienna (N.P., Part XV, p. 323). General Guderian, who commanded the armoured troops, denies this; cf. Heinz Guderian: *Panzer Leader* (London, 1952), pp. 53–6.

Linz, with a closing demonstration at Vienna on the 9th. To the Burgomaster of Vienna he said: 'Be assured that this city is in my eyes a pearl. I will bring it into that setting which is worthy of it and I will entrust it to the care of the whole German nation.'[1]

As he stood there, master of this city in which he had starved in obscurity, heir to the Hapsburgs his father had served as a customs officer, the belief in his mission, and in himself as the Man of Destiny, swelled within him.

I believe that it was God's will to send a youth from here into the Reich, to let him grow up, to raise him to be the leader of the nation so as to enable him to lead back his homeland into the Reich. . . .

In three days the Lord has smitten them. . . . And to me the grace was given on the day of the betrayal to be able to unite my homeland with the Reich. . . . I would now give thanks to Him who let me return to my homeland in order that I might now lead it into my German Reich. Tomorrow, may every German recognize the hour, and measure its import and bow in humility before the Almighty who in a few weeks has wrought a miracle upon us.[2]

Under the Nazi system of voting there was no room for surprises – 99·08 per cent voted their approval of his actions; in Austria the figure was higher still: 99·75. 'For me,' Hitler told the Press, 'this is the proudest hour of my life.'[3]

V

The union of Austria with Germany was the fulfilment of a German dream older than the Treaty of Versailles, which had specifically forbidden it, or even than the unification of Germany, from which Bismarck had deliberately excluded Austria. With the dissolution of the Hapsburg Monarchy at the end of the war many Austrians saw in such a union with Germany the only future for a State which, shorn of the non-German provinces of the old Empire, appeared to be left hanging in the air. Austria's none too happy experience in the post-war world, including grave economic problems like unemployment, added force to this argument. If the rise of Nazism in Germany diminished Austrian enthusiasm for an *Anschluss*, yet the pull of sentiment, language and history, reinforced by the material advantages offered by

1. Baynes: vol. II, p. 1,457.
2. Closing speech of the campaign at Vienna, 9 April 1938 (Baynes: vol. II, pp. 1,457–8).
3. *Reichspost*, 11 April 1938.

becoming part of a big nation, was strong enough to awaken genuine welcome when the frontier barriers went down and the German troops marched in, garlanded with flowers. For months, even years, Austria had been living in a state of insecurity; no one could see where Schushnigg's policy of independence was to lead, and there was a widespread sense of relief, even among those who were far from being Nazis, that the tension was at an end, and that what had appeared inevitable had happened at last, peacefully. Moreover, the Austrian Nazi Party had attracted a considerable following before 1938. Vienna, where the Jews had played a more brilliant part than in almost any other European city, was an old centre of anti-Semitism, and in provinces like Styria Nazism made a powerful appeal.

Disillusionment was not slow to come. The Austrian Legion returned from Germany with the two ideas of grabbing jobs and taking their revenge; some of the worst anti-Semitic excesses took place in Vienna, and many who had welcomed the *Anschluss* were shocked by the characteristic Nazi mixture of arrogance and ignorance, and of terrorism tempered by corruption. Even Austrian Nazis were soon to complain at the shameless way in which the new province was plundered. Vienna was relegated to the position of a provincial town and the historical traditions of Austria obliterated.[1] For most Austrians the gilt had worn off the gingerbread long before the Russian campaign began to take its toll of Austrian regiments.

None the less, in 1938 Hitler had a plausible case to argue when he claimed that the *Anschluss* was only the application of the Wilsonian principle of self-determination. Those outside Austria who wanted to lull their anxieties to sleep again could shrug their shoulders and say it was inevitable – after all, the Austrians were Germans, and Hitler himself an Austrian. 'The hard fact is,' Chamberlain told the House of Commons on 14 March, 'that nothing could have arrested what actually has happened – unless this country and other countries had been prepared to use force.' The Left found additional consolation in the thought that Schuschnigg, like Dollfuss before him, represented a Clerical-Fascist régime which had fired on the Vienna workers in February

---

1. Among those who descended on Vienna was the President of the Reichsbank, Dr Schacht, arriving to take over the Austrian National Bank. 'Thank God', he told its employees, 'Adolf Hitler has created a communion of German will and German thought. ... Not a single person will find a future with us who is not wholeheartedly for Adolf Hitler.' N.D. EC-297-A.

1934. The German Government strongly denied the story of an ultimatum, and played up the argument that Hitler's action alone had saved Austria from becoming another Spain in the heart of Europe.

In Rome Mussolini made the best of a bad job and shouted down Italian doubts by loudly proclaiming the value and strength of the Axis. In Warsaw Göring had been the guest of Colonel Beck only a fortnight before: as they walked into dinner they passed an engraving of John Sobieski, the Polish king coming to the relief of the besieged city of Vienna in 1683. Beck drew Göring's attention to the title: 'Don't worry,' he remarked, 'that incident will not recur.'[1] In London and Paris there was uneasiness, but reluctance to draw too harsh conclusions. The French reaffirmed their obligations to the Czechs, but Mr Chamberlain, in the same speech of 14 March, refused to consider giving a British guarantee to Czechoslovakia, or to France in support of her obligations under the Franco-Czech Alliance. When Russia proposed a Four-Power Conference to discuss means of preventing further aggression, the British Prime Minister declined. Such action, he told the House of Commons on 24 March, would aggravate the divisions of Europe into two blocs. He strongly deprecated the talk of force being used; it could only increase the feeling of insecurity. Mr Chamberlain had not yet abandoned that hope of a settlement with the Dictators which had led him to sacrifice Mr Eden a month before.

Yet those who, like Mr Churchill, saw in the annexation of Austria a decisive change in the European balance of power were to be proven right. The acquisition of Vienna, for centuries regarded as the gateway to South-eastern Europe, placed the German Army on the edge of the Hungarian plain and at the threshold of the Balkans. To the south Germany now had a common frontier with Italy and Yugoslavia, no more than fifty miles from the Adriatic. To the north Hitler was in a position to outflank Czechoslovakia's defences and press her from three directions at once. Germany's strategic position had been immeasurably improved. Nor was the contribution of Austria's economic resources in iron, steel, and magnesite to be disregarded.

1. The incident was recounted by Göring to one of the American interrogation team after the war, De Witt C. Poole, who records it in 'Light on Nazi Foreign Policy', *Foreign Affairs*, October 1946, vol. 25, No. 1, pp. 130–54.

The execution of the *Anschluss*, it is true, had been hastily improvised, in answer to a situation Hitler had not foreseen, but such a step had always been one of his first objectives in foreign policy, and the ease with which it had been accomplished was bound to tempt him to move on more rapidly to the achievement of the next. Every step Hitler had taken in foreign policy since 1933 had borne an increased risk, and every time he had been successful in his gamble. The telephone conversation with Philip of Hesse on the night of 11 March is sufficient evidence of the anxiety he felt at the possibility of foreign intervention. To his astonishment and delight this time there had not even been a special session of the League of Nations to rebuke him. The door to further successful adventures appeared to be already half-open, needing only a vigorous kick to swing it right back.

His experience in the Austrian affair, therefore, confirmed Hitler in the conclusions he had already reached at the end of 1937. German armaments were now increasing at a much more rapid rate. On 1 April 1938, according to General Jodl's testimony at Nuremberg, twenty-seven or twenty-eight divisions were ready; by the late autumn of 1938, including reserve divisions, this figure had grown to fifty-five divisions.[1] Expenditure on rearmament was mounting by leaps and bounds. In the fiscal year 1935–6 Germany had spent 6·2 milliard marks; in 1936–7 ten milliard; in 1937–8 14·6 milliard. In the year 1938–9 the figure rose to sixteen milliard.[2]

This increase in German military strength could be foreseen. It did not yet amount to military supremacy in Europe, but taken with the fears, disunity and weakness of the opposition – those psychological factors to which he always attached the greatest importance – Hitler calculated that by the autumn of 1938 he would be in a position to press home his next demands with an even greater chance of success. Certainly such a course involved risks, as his generals continued to urge, but his whole career so far encouraged him to take such risks, and since the reorganization of 4 February he was in a stronger position to override the doubts of the Army. Ten days after the result of the plebiscite on Austria had been announced, therefore, on 21 April, Hitler sent

1. N.P., Part xv, pp. 368–9.
2. Figures given in *The World in March 1939*, edited by Arnold Toynbee and Frank Ashton-Gwatkin (London, 1952), Appendix ii: German Expenditure on Armaments.

for General Keitel and set his Staff to work out new plans for aggression.

There was no doubt where Hitler would turn next. He had hated the Czechs since his Vienna days, when they had appeared to him as the very type of those Slav *Untermenschen* – 'sub-humans' – who were challenging the supremacy of the Germans in the Hapsburg Monarchy. The Czechoslovak State, created by the Peace Settlement, was the symbol of Versailles – democratic in character, a strong supporter of the League of Nations, the ally of France and of Russia. The Czech Army, a first-class force, backed by the famous Skoda armaments works and provided with defences comparable with the Maginot Line in strength, was a factor which had to be eliminated before he could move east-wards. For the Bohemian quadrilateral is a natural defensive position of almost unequalled strategic value in the heart of Central Europe, within less than an hour's flying time from Berlin, and a base from which, in the event of war, heavy blows could be dealt at some of the most important German industrial centres. As he had already insisted at the conference of November 1937, the annexation of Czechoslovakia, after that of Austria, was the second necessary step in the development of his pro-gramme for securing Germany's future.

The Czechs had few illusions about their German neighbours. They had done their best to build up their own defences and to buttress their independence by alliances with France and Russia. On paper this meant that any attack on Czechoslovakia must inevitably lead to general war. Paradoxically, however, this was a fact in Hitler's favour: it meant that France and Great Britain, in their anxiety to avoid war, were prepared to go to great lengths to prevent the Czechs invoking the guarantees they had been given.

The value of these alliances had steadily depreciated. Russia could not come to the support of Czechoslovakia (except by air) unless she could secure passage through either Poland or Rumania. Both countries were bitterly anti-Russian, both had moved out of the French orbit towards the German, and neither was likely to incur the enmity of Germany by allowing the Russians to march through. In any case the Russians were wary of being drawn into a single-handed conflict with Germany, and their alliance only came into operation if the French moved first to the Czechs' support. France, however, was no longer to be relied upon. Although the French Government had immediately

DENMARK

SWEDE

NORTH SEA

● Hamburg

HOLLAND

BELGIUM

GERMANY

■ Ber

Leipzig ●

Dresden ●

● Cologne

LUXEMBURG

FRANCE

Nuremberg ●

P

Z

GERMAN ANNEXATIONS 1938 - 1939

Frontiers of January 1938

Territory annexed March 1938

Territory ceded to Germany as a result of the Munich Conference 80 September 1938

Memelland, annexed March 1939

Protectorate of Bohemia - Moravia, annexed March 1939

The Puppet State of Slovakia, established March 1939

Territory annexed from Poland and Lithuania after the beginning of the war

● Munich

Linz

Salzburg

Berchtesgade

AUSTR

BRENNER PASS

ITALY

BALTIC SEA

Memel

LITHUANIA

Kaunas

Koenigsberg

Danzig

Elbing

EAST
PRUSSIA

THE
SUWALKI
TRIANGLE

ANNEXED BY
U.S.S.R., 1939

Posen

Warsaw

Brest
Litovsk

P O L A N D

Breslau

Lublin

Lwow

Cracow

ANNEXED BY
U.S.S.R., 1939

C H O S L O V A K I A

Brünn

nna

BRATISLAVA

ANNEXED BY
HUNGARY, 1938-9

Budapest

RUMANIA

az

N

HUNGARY

0   50   100
miles

reaffirmed its obligations to Czechoslovakia after the annexation of Austria, their retreat for the past three years in face of Hitler's demands had undermined the system of security they had built up in Central and Eastern Europe. As Neurath had predicted, the reoccupation of the Rhineland and German rearmament had been followed by a marked change of attitude in the countries to the east of Germany. No one was going to risk quarrelling with the new Reich, and there was already a rush to reinsure in Berlin. In 1938 the Czechs were, therefore, likely to be isolated, unless the French should at last decide to call a halt to Hitler and prepare to fight. While his generals continued to be impressed by the number of French divisions, however, Hitler, with a shrewder eye for the psychological and social sources of military strength, was convinced that the French lacked the will to risk war, if they could possibly avoid it.

As for the British, all reports from London showed Chamberlain determined to press the Czechs to meet the German demands in order to avoid the danger of war and open up the way to the general European settlement to which he was convinced Hitler could be persuaded to agree once the Czech problem was out of the way.

VI

The lever with which Hitler planned to undermine the Czech Republic was the existence inside the Czech frontiers of a German minority of some three and a quarter millions, former subjects of the old Hapsburg Empire. The grievances of the Sudeten Germans had been a persistent source of trouble in Czech politics since the foundation of the Republic. The rise of the Nazis to power across the frontier and the growing strength of Germany had been followed by sharpened demands from the Sudeten Germans for a greater measure of autonomy from Prague and by the spread of Nazi ideas and Nazi organization among the German minority. From 1935 the German Foreign Office secretly subsidized the Nazi Sudeten German Party under the leadership of Konrad Henlein at the rate of fifteen thousand marks a month, and during 1938 Henlein succeeded in ousting the rival parties among the German minority from the field.

Aware of the dangers represented by this Trojan Horse within their walls, the Czech Government made a renewed effort to-

wards the end of 1937 to reach a satisfactory settlement with the
Sudeten German leaders. Ostensibly this remained the issue
throughout the whole crisis – a square deal for the German
minority in Czechoslovakia, not the relations between the
sovereign states of Germany and Czechoslovakia, except in so far
as Hitler insisted that satisfaction for the Sudeten Germans'
demands was indispensable to the improvement of German–
Czech relations. By presenting the issue in this way Hitler succeeded in confusing public opinion in the rest of the world, and
mobilizing sympathy for the wrongs of an oppressed minority,
which would have been denied to the aggressive demands of a
Great Power on one of its smaller neighbours.

After the annexation of Austria, however, the rights or wrongs
of the German minority ceased to be anything more than the
excuse with which Hitler was pushing his foot into the door. For,
on 28 March 1938, Konrad Henlein, the Sudeten German leader,
had a talk of three hours with Hitler, Ribbentrop, and Hess in
Berlin at which he was told that he must henceforth consider himself as the representative of the Führer and was given instructions
to put forward demands which would be unacceptable to the
Czech Government. 'Henlein summarized his view,' says the
German report, 'as follows: We must always demand so much
that we can never be satisfied. The Führer approved this view.'[1]
In this way Hitler planned to create a situation of permanent
unrest in Czechoslovakia which could be progressively intensified
until it reached a pitch where he could plausibly represent himself
as forced, once again, to intervene in order to prevent civil war
and the continued oppression of a minority of the German race.

The events in Austria had already led to big demonstrations in
the Sudetenland, much wild talk of 'going home to the Reich'
and the intimidation of Czechs living near the frontier. At Saaz,
the day before Henlein saw Hitler, fifteen thousand Germans
marched through the streets shouting the slogan: *Ein Volk, Ein
Reich, Ein Führer*. At Eger the demonstrators numbered twenty-
five thousand, and the church bells were pealed in celebration.
Rumours were current of troop movements on the German side
of the frontier and an imminent invasion. But events must not
outstrip Germany's preparations. Hitler wanted no repetition of
the improvisation of March, with German tanks and trucks
stranded by the wayside. So Henlein was told to keep his supporters in hand, and when Hitler saw Keitel on 21 April he laid it

1. G.D., D.II, No. 107.

down that plans to breach the Czech fortifications must be prepared down to the smallest detail.

The first four days of military action are, politically speaking, decisive. In the absence of outstanding military successes, a European crisis is certain to rise. *Faits accomplis* must convince foreign powers of the hopelessness of military intervention.[1]

The objective in Hitler's mind was, from the first, the destruction of the Czechoslovak State. This was only recognized in the west with the occupation of Prague a year later. Throughout 1938 the Czech crisis continued to be discussed in terms of the Sudetenland, of Home Rule for the Sudeten Germans, or at the most the cession of these frontier districts (in which the Czech fortifications were situated) to Germany. On 24 April Henlein announced his Eight Points in a speech at Karlsbad, and these provided a programme with which to rally the Sudeten Germans, keep the Czech Government in play, and bamboozle public opinion abroad.

Having put this in train, Hitler set out for Rome on 2 May on a State visit, the invitation for which had been given when Mussolini was in Germany the autumn before. Every Party boss and Nazi hanger-on tried to squeeze into the four special trains which were needed to carry the German delegation and its cumbrous equipment of special uniforms. The competition to share, at Italian expense, in the endless galas, receptions and banquets, the expensive presents and imposing decorations, was intense. Nothing appealed to the gutter-élite of Germany so much as a free trip south of the Alps.

Hitler was delighted with Italy. No cities in the world, he declared later,[2] could compare with Florence and Rome, nothing could equal the beauty of Tuscany and Umbria. The frustrated artist in him warmed to the incomparable buildings and their setting under a southern sky. He was less pleased by the fact that protocol required him, as Head of the State, to stay with the King in the Quirinal. The formality of his reception at the Palace irked him and left him with a permanent dislike of the Italian Royal House.

Since the two dictators had last met in September the Axis had been subjected to considerable strain. For the first time they met

1. From the summary of the Hitler–Keitel conversations by Major Schmundt, N.D. 388-PS, to be found in G.D., DII., pp. 239–40.
2. cf. *Hitler's Table Talk*, p. 10 (21–2 July 1941).

as neighbours. The *Anschluss* was not forgotten in Italy, where anxiety about the South Tyrol had revived, while the Anglo-Italian Agreement of April had been noted without enthusiasm in Berlin. When Ribbentrop produced a draft German–Italian treaty of alliance, Mussolini and Ciano were evasive. After such a display of friendship, Ciano replied, a formal treaty was superfluous. In the closely packed round of visits, which included Naples and Florence as well as Rome, there was little time for political conversations, but at the State banquet in the Palazzo Venezia on 7 May Hitler underlined the solidarity of the Axis Powers and reassured his hosts that he had no intention of reclaiming the South Tyrol. 'It is my unalterable will and my bequest to the German people that it shall regard the frontier of the Alps, raised by nature between us both, as for ever inviolable.'[1]

Hitler's references to the new Italy were in a generous vein, and by the time he left he had succeeded in restoring cordiality to the relations between the two régimes. It seems probable from later references that Hitler informed Mussolini in general terms of his intention to deal next with the Czechs. Mussolini, who disliked the Czechs, made no objections, although by the end of the summer he was to show considerable alarm at the danger of a general war as a result of Hitler's demands.

The reports which Hitler found on his return to Germany were highly satisfactory: the diplomatic situation was developing even more favourably than he had expected. At the end of April 1938 the French Prime Minister and Foreign Minister had conferred with Mr Chamberlain and Lord Halifax in London, but both sides had been at pains, separately, to convey reassurances to Hitler. Indeed, the first fruits of the Anglo–French conference were a joint *démarche* in Prague, urging the Czechs to make the utmost concessions possible to the Sudeten Germans. Not content with this, Lord Halifax then instructed the British Ambassador in Berlin to call on Ribbentrop, to tell him that Britain was pressing the Czechs to reach a settlement with Henlein, and to ask for German cooperation. Ribbentrop's reply was that the British and French action was warmly welcomed by the Führer, who must have been delighted at the way in which the other Powers were doing his work for him. A day or two later the Führer's Adjutant, Schmundt, inquired of the General Staff how many German divisions were stationed on the Czech frontiers ready to

1. Baynes: vol. II, pp. 1,460–3.

march at twelve hours' notice (the answer was twelve) and what was the precise strength of the Czech fortifications.

On 20 May Keitel sent Hitler a draft of the military directive for Operation Green (the code name for Czechoslovakia) based on the Führer's instructions:

It is not my intention to smash Czechoslovakia by military action in the immediate future without provocation, unless an unavoidable development of political conditions inside Czechoslovakia forces the issue, or political events in Europe create a particularly favourable opportunity which may never recur.

Operations will be launched, either:

(*a*) after a period of increasing diplomatic controversies and tension linked with military preparations which will be exploited so as to shift the war guilt on the enemy;

(*b*) by lightning action as the result of a serious incident which will subject Germany to unbearable provocation and which, in the eyes of at least a part of world opinion, affords the moral justification for military measure.

Case (*b*) is more favourable ooth from a military and political point of view.[1]

The directive clearly foresaw action by Hungary and Poland against Czechoslovakia, and the hesitation of France 'to unleash a European war by intervening against Germany'. Russian military support for the Czechs was accepted as likely, but everything, Hitler insisted, turned on the speed with which the operation could be carried through before intervention could be organized. For this reason, only minimum forces were to be kept in the West and the rest concentrated on the main task: 'to smash the Czechoslovak Army and to occupy Bohemia and Moravia as quickly as possible'.

At this juncture, however, there was a sudden and unexpected turn to events. On 20 May the Czech Government, alarmed by reports of German troop concentrations near the frontier and by persistent rumours of preparations for a German attack, ordered a partial mobilization of its forces. The Czechs may have been genuinely misled by these reports, or they may have decided to halt the gradual development of the situation in Germany's favour by forcing the issue. Whatever the explanation, their move produced a prompt reaction. The British and French Governments at once made representations in Berlin warning of the grave

1. G.D., D.II, pp. 299–303.

danger of general war if the Germans made any aggressive move against the Czechs. At the same time the French, supported by the Russians, reaffirmed their promise of immediate aid to Czechoslovakia. A council of war hastily summoned to the Berghof on Sunday 22 May, and attended by Henlein, was faced with a display of solidarity on the part of the European Powers which, in the unanimous opinion of Hitler's military advisers, left him with no option but to call a retreat. Hitler was furious – the more so because his preparations were not yet complete, and the rumours on which the Czech Government had acted were exaggerated and premature. He had now, however, to calm the storm that had been aroused.

On 23 May the Czech Ambassador in Berlin was assured that Germany had no aggressive intentions towards his country; Henlein was packed off to Czechoslovakia to resume negotiations with Prague, while indignant denials were made by the German Foreign Office of the reports of troop concentrations.

The alarm felt in London and Paris at the prospect of German military action, however, rapidly turned into irritation with the Czechs. The advocates of appeasement described the May crisis as a grave blunder and blamed President Benes for his 'provocative' action, while Chamberlain determined never to run so grave a risk of war again.

Hitler's reaction was different. For a week he remained at the Berghof in a black rage, which was not softened by the crowing of the foreign Press at the way in which he had been forced to climb down. Then, on 28 May, he suddenly appeared in Berlin and summoned another conference at the Reich Chancellery. Among those who attended were Göring, Ribbentrop, Neurath, Generals Beck, Keitel, Brauchitsch, and the Commander-in-Chief of the Navy, Raeder. Spread out on the table in the winter garden was a map, and on it Hitler sketched with angry gestures exactly how he meant to eliminate the State which had dared to inflict this humiliation on him.

Two days later he revised the opening sentence of the draft for Operation Green to read: 'It is my unalterable decision to smash Czechoslovakia by military action in the near future. It is the business of the political leadership to await or bring about the suitable moment from a political and military point of view.'[1] The details of the military action proposed remained unchanged

1. G.D., D.II, No. 221.

from the original draft, but with the directive Keitel sent a covering letter containing the instruction: 'The execution of this Directive must be assured by 1 October 1938 at the latest.'

VII

The German and British diplomatic documents illustrate clearly enough Hitler's tactics for the next three months, June, July, and August of 1938. Ostensibly the dispute was still one between the Sudeten German Party and the Czech Government: the German Government was careful to decline any responsibility. Hitler himself remained silent, spending the greater part of the summer at the Berghof, letting the tension slowly build up towards the deadline which, according to reports from Berlin, was fixed for the Party rally at Nuremberg in September. So impressed was the British Government with the danger of the situation that at the end of July Chamberlain announced the dispatch of Lord Runciman to Czechoslovakia on a mission of investigation and mediation. In their anxiety to avoid war London and Paris urged the Czechs to make more and more concessions to the Sudeten Germans. None of this was missed by Hitler, who noted with satisfaction the strain to which the Czechs were being subjected by the intervention of the British and the French, by the feeling of being pushed and hurried by their friends, and by their sense of isolation.

To the east Hitler pressed the Rumanians not to make transit facilities available to the Russians and kept a watchful eye on Poland. The reports from Moltke, the German Ambassador in Warsaw, were highly satisfactory. Polish opinion was inflexible in its opposition to any idea of Soviet troops marching across its territory to come to the aid of the Czechs. The Polish Government – especially Colonel Beck – was unfriendly towards the Czechs, and preoccupied with the possibility of taking advantage of their difficult position to secure the valuable district of Teschen in Czech Silesia.

The Poles were not the only people whose appetite for territory might be encouraged at the expense of Czechoslovakia. At the end of the war Hungary had lost the whole of Slovakia to the new Czechoslovak State. Budapest's demand for the return at least of the districts inhabited by Magyars, better still of the whole province, had never wavered. To safeguard Slovakia against the claims of the Hungarian revisionists, Benes had concluded the

Little Entente with Rumania and Yugoslavia, who were affected by similar Hungarian claims. The Hungarians were eager enough to take advantage of the Czechs' difficulties, but were worried lest in doing so they should provide a *casus foederis* for the Little Entente and commit themselves too completely to the German side. The tortuous efforts of the Hungarians to find a way out of this dilemma and to sit on the fence to the last moment met with little appreciation in Berlin. When the Hungarian Regent, Horthy, accompanied by the Prime Minister and Foreign Minister, visited Germany towards the end of August, Ribbentrop angrily reproached them. Hitler remarked contemptuously that he had nothing to ask of Hungary, but 'that he who wanted to sit at table must at least help in the kitchen'.[1] The Hungarians' caution was a disappointment to Hitler throughout the crisis; it was, none the less, a serious anxiety to the Czechs.

With Russia Hitler could do little. He confined himself to putting obstacles in the way of her giving aid to the Czechs, and played heavily on British and French dislike of inviting Russian cooperation in order to keep any United Front from coming into existence. No attempt was made by London or Paris to establish a common policy with Moscow, despite the Franco-Russian and Russo-Czech pacts of 1935. So successful had been Hitler's anti-Bolshevik propaganda that these Pacts were regarded by the British and French Governments as liabilities rather than as assets. On the Russian side there was equal distrust of the Western Powers, and a determination not to go one step ahead of France and Britain in risking war with Germany. Hitler's remark to Otto Strasser – 'There is no solidarity in Europe' – was still true: it was the major premise of his diplomacy.

Meanwhile Henlein and his Party continued the negotiations with the Czech Government in a desultory way, taking care always to find fresh objections to the successive Czech offers of a greater measure of Home Rule for the Sudeten Districts. The Sudeten German Party made a particular point of capturing Lord Runciman's sympathy. Their other task was to keep feeling against the Czechs in the frontier districts at fever-pitch: by the end of the summer the tension between the Sudeten population and the Czech officials was reaching snapping-point.

On the German side of the frontier the military preparations were systematically continued. Hitler, however, now began to

1. Report on the German–Hungarian conversations at Kiel, 23 August 1938 (G.D., D.II, No. 383).

encounter some resistance to his plans in the Army High Command. The risk of a general war alarmed his staff officers, and not all were convinced by Hitler's declaration that intervention by France and Britain could be discounted. The opposition was led by General Ludwig Beck, Chief of Staff of the Army. Although the grounds of Beck's opposition to the Nazi régime broadened later, at this stage his objections were professional in character, the dangers of a war with the Western Powers over Czechoslovakia, and Germany's inadequate preparations for such a conflict in 1938. These views Beck expressed in a series of memoranda (May–July 1938) with which he tried to persuade the Commander-in-Chief of the Army, General von Brauchitsch, to make a stand against Hitler.[1] In his diary for 30 May General Jodl wrote:

The whole contrast becomes once more acute between the Führer's intuition that we *must* do it this year, and the opinion of the Army that we cannot do it yet, as most certainly the Western Powers will interfere, and we are not as yet equal to them.[2]

Brauchitsch, although he agreed with Beck's argument, temporized and tried to avoid taking action. In the first week of August, however, at Beck's insistence, a meeting of the leading commanders was held in Berlin under the chairmanship of Brauchitsch. There was almost universal support for Beck's views, only two generals expressing dissent. This time Brauchitsch went so far as to submit Beck's memorandum to Hitler.

News of the generals' conference and of Beck's memorandum had already reached Hitler. After a stormy argument with Brauchitsch, on 10 August Hitler summoned another conference, this time to the Berghof. The senior generals were excluded; Hitler appealed to the younger generation of the Army and Air Force leaders, and for three hours he used all his skill to set before them the political and military assumptions on which his plans were based. Then, for the first – and last – time at a meeting of this sort, he invited discussion. The result was disconcerting. General von Wietersheim, Chief of Staff to the Army Group Commander at Wiesbaden, General Adam, got up and said bluntly that it was his own, and General Adam's, view that the

1. The memoranda are printed in Wolfgang Foerster: *Ein General kämpft gegen den Krieg: Aus nachgelassenen Papieren des Generalstabchefs Ludwig Beck* (Munich, 1949).
2. N.D. 1780-PS.

western fortifications against France could be held for only three weeks. A furious scene followed, Hitler cursing the Army as good-for-nothing and shouting: 'I assure you, General, the position will not only be held for three weeks, but for three years.'[1] Jodl added the comment: 'The vigour of the soul is lacking, because in the end they [the Staff Officers] do not believe in the genius of the Führer. And one does perhaps compare him with Charles XII of Sweden.'

The result of this clash was inconclusive. Brauchitsch declined to go further. When Beck thereupon resigned, and demanded that the Commander-in-Chief resign with him, Brauchitsch refused. As Hassell noted in his diary, 'Brauchitsch hitches his collar a notch higher and says: "I am a soldier; it is my duty to obey".'[2] Beck's resignation was kept secret until 31 October, after Munich. In the meantime General Halder took over his duties as Chief of Staff from 1 September. Hitler rejected any alteration in his policy, yet he was conscious of the fact that the opposition, if it had been silenced, had not been convinced.

On 3 September Hitler summoned Keitel, Chief of the O.K.W., and Brauchitsch, the Commander-in-Chief of the Army, to the Berghof to go over the final arrangements. Field units were to be moved up on 28 September and X-day fixed by noon on 27 September.[3] The next day President Benes put an end to the Sudeten leaders' game by asking them to visit him in the Hradschin Palace and inviting them to set down on paper their full demands, with the promise to grant them immediately whatever they might be. Caught off their guard, the Sudeten Party found to their horror that the Czechs' fourth offer, virtually dictated by themselves, fulfilled the Eight Points demanded in Henlein's Karlsbad speech. In their embarrassment the Sudeten leaders used the pretext of incidents at Moravska-Ostrava to break off the negotiations with Prague and send an ultimatum demanding the punishment of those responsible before they could be resumed. Benes had knocked the bottom out of the argument that the issue was Sudeten grievances and immediately afterwards, Henlein left for Germany.

For some time past the foreign embassies in Berlin had been

1. Jodl's diary for 10 August. Cf. also the accounts of Field-Marshal von Brauchitsch and Field-Marshal von Manstein; N.P., Part XXI, pp. 24 and 48.
2. *The Von Hassell Diaries*, p. 6.
3. Notes of the Conference by Hitler's Adjutant, Schmundt (G.D., D.II, No. 424).

reporting that the opening of the final stage of the Czech crisis would coincide with the Nuremberg Party Rally, due to begin on 6 September. Hitler's closing speech on 12 September, it was said, would show which way the wind was blowing and perhaps decide the issue of peace or war.

Meanwhile a small group of conspirators was discussing the possibility of seizing Hitler by force as soon as he gave the order to attack the Czechs, and putting him on trial before the People's Court. Amongst those involved were Beck; Karl Goerdeler, a former Oberbürgermeister of Leipzig and for three years Reich Price Controller; Ulrich von Hassell, Ambassador in Rome until February 1938; General von Witzleben, commanding the Third Military District which included Berlin; General Höppner, in command of an armoured division in Thuringia; Colonel Hans Oster, who made the Abwehr, the O.K.W. Counter Intelligence, a centre of opposition to Hitler; and Ewald von Kleist, a gentleman farmer and descendant of the famous poet who undertook to go to London and see Churchill and Vansittart. Everything depended upon the conspirators' ability to persuade Brauchitsch, Halder, and the other generals that Beck was right and Hitler wrong on the certainty of a general war if Czechoslovakia was attacked. Various soundings were made in London in the hope of securing incontestable proof that Britain and France would support the Czechs, in the event of a German attack. Such evidence as they were able to get, however – including a letter from Mr Churchill – failed to convince Brauchitsch or Halder, and the conspiracy hung fire.[1] On 9 September Hitler held another military conference in Nuremberg. It was a stormy meeting, beginning at ten at night and lasting until half past three in the morning, and was attended by Halder as well as Brauchitsch and Keitel. Hitler was highly critical of the Army's plans, condemning them for failure to provide the concentration of forces which alone would achieve a break-through and secure the quick, decisive success he needed. His aim was to drive at once right into the heart of Czechoslovakia and leave the Czech Army in the rear.[2] X-day was now fixed for 30 September and was to be preceded by a rising in Sudetenland.

Hitler still held to the belief that Britain and France would not go to war over Czechoslovakia. As if to confirm his view, *The*

1. See the full account in J. W. Wheeler-Bennett: *The Nemesis of Power*, pp. 383-424.
2. Notes by Schmundt of the Conference (G.D., D.II, No. 448).

Times, on 7 September, published its famous leader suggesting the possibility of Czechoslovakia ceding the Sudetenland to Germany. When Hitler stood in the spotlights at the huge stadium on the final night of the Rally, all the world was waiting to hear what he would say – and they were not disappointed. His speech was remarkable for a brutal attack on another State and its President such as had rarely, if ever, been heard in peacetime before.

Hitler made no attempt to disguise his anger at the humiliation of 21–2 May, which, he declared, had been deliberately planned by Benes, who spread the lie that Germany had mobilized.

You will understand, my comrades, that a Great Power cannot for a second time suffer such an infamous encroachment upon its rights. . . . I am a National Socialist, and as such I am accustomed on every attack to hit back immediately. I know, too, quite well that through forbearance one will never reconcile so irreconcilable an enemy as are the Czechs; they will only be provoked to further presumption. . . .

Herr Benes plays his tactical game: he makes speeches, he wishes to negotiate, after the manner of Geneva he wishes to clear up the question of procedure and to make little appeasement presents. But in the long run that is not good enough! . . .

I am in no way willing that here in the heart of Germany a second Palestine should be permitted to arise. The poor Arabs are defenceless and deserted. The Germans in Czechoslovakia are neither defenceless nor are they deserted, and people should take notice of that fact.[1]

At every pause the deep baying of the huge crowd gathered under the stars, and the roar of '*Sieg Heil! Sieg Heil! Sieg Heil!*' supplied a sinister background. At last the one-time agitator of the Munich beerhalls had the world for audience. Yet, for all his tone of menace Hitler was careful not to pin himself down; he did not commit himself to precise demands – only 'justice' for the Sudeten Germans – nor to the course of action he would follow if the demands were not made.

The speech was the signal for a rising in the Sudetenland, and there were ugly scenes in Eger and Karlsbad, where several people were shot. But the Czechs did not lose their nerve. The Government proclaimed martial law, put down the rising, and by the 15th had the situation well in hand. Czechoslovakia was not going to disintegrate from within, as Austria had. Henlein fled to Bavaria with several thousand of his followers and organized a Freikorps for raids across the frontier. But, despite German Press accounts under banner headlines of a 'reign of terror', the

1. Speech of 12 September at Nuremberg (Baynes: vol. II, pp. 1,487–99).

withdrawal of Henlein was in fact followed by a pacification of the Sudetenland.

VIII

But Hitler's calculations were not to be proved wrong. The failure of nerve came, not in Prague, but in Paris. Twenty-four hours after Hitler's speech at Nuremberg the French Government reached a point where it was so divided on the question of its obligations to Czechoslovakia that the French Prime Minister, Daladier, appealed to Chamberlain to make the best bargain he could with Hitler. Mr Chamberlain, who had for some time been considering the advantages of an interview with Hitler, at once sent off at eleven o'clock on the same evening (the 13th) a message proposing that he should fly to Germany (if possible the next day), and try to find a basis for a peaceful solution.

Hitler was delighted. *'Ich bin vom Himmel gefallen,'* he exclaimed on reading Chamberlain's message.[1] His vanity was gratified by the prospect of the Prime Minister of Great Britain, a man twenty years older than himself, making his first flight at the age of sixty-nine in order to come and plead with him. Hitler did not even offer to meet him half-way, but awaited him at the Berghof, in the extreme south-east corner of Germany, a journey of seven hours even by plane.

There, at four o'clock on 15 September, Chamberlain was greeted by Hitler at the top of the steps and, after a brief interval for tea, went with him to the study on the first floor where Schuschnigg had been received seven months before. They were accompanied only by Paul Schmidt, the interpreter. Sir Nevile Henderson had taken special pains to exclude Ribbentrop who retorted by refusing to make Schmidt's record of the conference available to Chamberlain afterwards.

Hitler began by a long, rambling account of all that he had done for Germany in foreign policy, how he had restored the equality of rights denied by Versailles, yet at the same time had signed the Pact with Poland, followed by the Naval Treaty with Britain, and had renounced Alsace-Lorraine. The question of the return of the Sudeten Germans, however, was different, he declared, since this affected race, which was the basis of his ideas. These Germans must come into the German Reich. 'He would face any war, even the risk of a world war, for this. Here the limit

1. L. B. Namier: *Diplomatic Prelude*, p. 35.

had been reached where the rest of the world might do what it liked, he would not yield one single step.'

Chamberlain, who had spent most of the interview so far listening and watching Hitler, interrupted to ask if this was all he wanted, or whether he was aiming at the dismemberment of Czechoslovakia. Hitler replied that there were Polish and Hungarian demands to be met as well – what was left would not interest him. The Sudetenland was the one remaining problem, but, he insisted again, he was determined to solve it by one means or another.

He did not wish that any doubts should arise as to his absolute determination not to tolerate any longer that a small, second-rate country should treat the mighty thousand-year-old German Reich as something inferior.

Chamberlain attempted to narrow the problem down to practical considerations: if the Sudetenland was to be ceded to Germany, how was this to be done, what about the areas of mixed nationality, was there to be a transfer of populations as well as a change of frontiers? Hitler became excited.

All this seems to be academic; I want to get down to realities. Three hundred Sudetens have been killed, and things of that kind cannot go on; the thing nas got to be settled at once. I am determined to settle it; I do not care whether there is a world war or not. I am determined to settle it and to settle it soon; I am prepared to risk a world war rather than allow this to drag on.

Outside the autumn day was dying, the wind howled and the rain ran down the window-panes. Up in this house among the mountains two men were discussing the issue of war or peace, an issue that must affect millions of people they had never seen or heard of. It was this thought which preoccupied Chamberlain, and now he too began to grow angry.

'If the Führer is determined to settle this matter by force,' he retorted, 'without waiting even for a discussion between ourselves to take place, what did he let me come here for? I have wasted my time.'

With perfect timing, Hitler hesitated and let his mood change. 'Well, if the British Government were prepared to accept the idea of secession in principle, and to say so, there might be a chance then to have a talk.' Here, Chamberlain felt, was something to bite on at last. According to his own later version, he

declined to commit himself until he had consulted the British
Cabinet; but, according to Schmidt's minute, the Prime Minister
added that 'he could state personally that he recognized the
principle of the detachment of the Sudeten areas'. If Hitler was
prepared to consider a peaceful separation of the Sudeten Germans from Czechoslovakia, then he believed there was a way out,
and would return for a second meeting. Meanwhile he asked
Hitler for an assurance that he would not take precipitate action
until he had received an answer. With all the appearance of
making a great concession, Hitler agreed, knowing perfectly well
that X-day was in any case still a fortnight away.

Here the discussion ended for the time being, and Chamberlain
next day flew back to London without seeing Hitler a second
time.[1]

Hitler, as he later admitted to Chamberlain, never supposed
that the British Prime Minister would be able to secure the
Czechs' agreement to a voluntary surrender of the Sudetenland to
Germany. He saw the interview at Berchtesgaden, not as an
alternative to his intention of destroying Czechoslovakia by force,
but as a further means of ensuring that Britain and France would
not intervene. He had drawn the British Prime Minister into
advocating the cession of the Sudetenland on the grounds of self-
determination; if, as he anticipated, this was rejected by Prague,
in Chamberlain's eyes the responsibility of war would rest on the
unreasonable Czechs, and Britain would be less likely than ever to
go to Czechoslovakia's aid, or to encourage the French to do so.

During the week that followed, therefore, Hitler continued his
preparations to attack Czechoslovakia. On the 17th he authorized
the establishment of the Sudeten German Freikorps, and instructed the Army High Command to look after their needs. On
the 18th the Army reported its plans for the deployment of five
armies against the Czechs, a total of thirty-six divisions, including
three armoured divisions.[2]

Political preparations matched the military. On 20 September
the Slovak People's Party, at Henlein's prompting, put forward a

1. This account is based on Paul Schmidt's official report in G.D.,
D.II, No. 487; Schmidt's account in his book *Statist auf diplomatischer
Bühne*, pp. 394–9; Chamberlain's notes, *Brit. Doc.*, 3rd Series, vol. II, No.
895; Chamberlain's letter to his sister, 19 September, in Keith Feiling: *Life
of Neville Chamberlain* (London, 1946), pp. 366–8; Sir Nevile Henderson,
pp. 149–50.

2. N.D. 388-PS, Item 26.

claim to autonomy for the Slovaks. On the same day Hitler saw the Hungarian Prime Minister and Foreign Minister in Berlin and sharply urged them to present their demands to Czechoslovakia for the return of the districts claimed by Hungary. 'In his opinion,' he added, 'action by the Army would provide the only satisfactory solution. There was, however, a danger of the Czechs submitting to every demand.'[1] On the 21st the Poles delivered a Note in Prague, asking for a plebiscite in the Teschen district, a step followed by the Hungarian Government the next day. By the 22nd the Sudeten Freikorps, armed and equipped in Germany, had seized control of the Czech towns of Eger and Asch.

This same day (22 September) Chamberlain again flew to Germany, and was received by Hitler at Godesberg, on the Rhine. The British delegation were accommodated at the Hotel Petersberg, on one side of the river; Hitler stayed on the other, at the Hotel Dreesen, where he had decided in June 1934 to fly to Munich and begin the Röhm Purge.

Between his first and second meetings with Hitler, Chamberlain had succeeded in getting the agreement of both the British and French Governments to the terms with which he now returned and in forcing the Czechs to accept them (after an initial refusal) by an Anglo-French ultimatum. When he crossed the river to Hitler's hotel in the afternoon, Chamberlain was in an excellent temper. He was prepared to present a plan for the transfer of the Sudeten districts of Czechoslovakia to Germany without a plebiscite, leaving a commission to settle the details including the transfer of populations where no satisfactory line could be drawn. In addition, to remove German fears of Czechoslovakia being used as a base from which to attack Germany, the existing alliances which the Czechs had with Russia and France were to be dissolved, while Britain would join in an international guarantee of Czechoslovakia's independence and neutrality.

When Chamberlain had finished speaking, Hitler inquired whether his proposals had been submitted to the Czech Government, and accepted by them. The Prime Minister replied: 'Yes.' There was a brief pause. Then Hitler said, quite quietly: 'I'm exceedingly sorry, but after the events of the last few days this solution is no longer any use.'

A long and acrimonious debate followed. Chamberlain was

1. Report on the meeting of Hitler with Imredy and Kanya on 20 September (G.D., D.II, No. 554).

both angry and puzzled; he had, he declared, taken his political life in his hands to secure agreement to Hitler's demands – only for Hitler to turn them down. He could see no reason at all why Hitler should regard the situation as so changed in the past week that the solution discussed at Berchtesgaden was no longer applicable. Nor did Hitler give any clear indication of the reasons why he had changed his mind. He talked of the demands of the Poles and Hungarians, the unreliability and treachery of the Czechs; he argued himself into a fury over the wrongs and sufferings of the Sudeten Germans; above all, he insisted on the urgency of the situation and the need for speed. The whole problem, he shouted, must be settled by 1 October. If war was to be avoided, the Czechs must at once withdraw from the main areas to be ceded – these were marked by the Germans on a map – and allow them to be occupied by German forces. Afterwards a plebiscite could be held to settle the detailed line of the frontier, but the essential condition was a German occupation of the Sudetenland, at once.[1]

Messages brought into the conference room reporting the death of more Sudetens that day enabled Hitler to work up his indignation to a new pitch. Yet, as they walked on the terrace at the conclusion of the three hours' discussion, he said to Mr Chamberlain with a complete change of manner: 'Oh, Mr Prime Minister, I am so sorry: I had looked forward to showing you this beautiful view of the Rhine . . . but now it is hidden by the mist.'[2]

A deadlock in the negotiations had now been reached. Chamberlain took note of Hitler's new demands, but he refused to commit himself and withdrew to his hotel across the river.

The question which puzzled the Prime Minister, and which the historian must attempt to answer, was why Hitler acted in this unexpected way. Chamberlain assumed that Hitler's demands for the cession of the Sudetenland had been sincerely meant, but Hitler's real intention, as defined in his directive after the May crisis, was 'to destroy Czechoslovakia by military action'. Hitler had used the Sudeten question simply as a means to create

1. Schmidt's account in G.D., D.II, No. 562, and his book, p. 401; Kirkpatrick's Minute in *Brit. Doc.*, 3rd Series, vol. II, No. 1,033; Henderson: pp. 154–5.

2. André Maurois, *Tragedy in France* (London, 1940), pp. 12–13: Chamberlain himself recounted the incident on his visit to Paris in November 1938.

favourable political conditions for carrying out his objective. But what Chamberlain now offered him was the cession of the Sudetenland as a substitute for the destruction of the Czechoslovak state by force.

There were arguments in favour of accepting Chamberlain's offer, as Hitler saw perfectly well: the risk of a general war, if he persisted; the warnings of the General Staff that Germany was not yet prepared for such a conflict; a solid gain at no expense. But the fact that the Western Powers had been prepared to go as far as this in their anxiety to avoid war confirmed Hitler in his belief that, if he held out and refused to settle for half, he could achieve the whole of his objective without any greater risk. How he would do this remained to be seen: what mattered immediately was to increase the pressure, and this Hitler proceeded to do by adding to his original claim to the Sudetenland the demand for its occupation by the German Army at once.

The next day Chamberlain tried, without success, to persuade Hitler to accept a compromise. An exchange of letters across the river produced no effect. All Chamberlain could do was to ask Hitler to put his new demands in writing together with a map. These he undertook to forward to Prague. For the rest, 'I do not see that I can perform any further service here. I propose therefore to return to England.'

While the memorandum was being prepared, Hitler invited Chamberlain to a final discussion at half past ten on the evening of the 23rd. But there was no modification of his demands; instead a new time limit had now been added, requiring the Czechs to begin evacuation of the territory to be ceded by 26 September, and to complete it by 28 September, in four days' time. The exchanges between the two men had already become tart when Ribbentrop brought the news that the Czechs had ordered mobilization. That, Hitler declared, settled matters. Chamberlain contradicted him: Germany had mobilized first. The argument went to and fro, Hitler excitedly denouncing the Czechs, Chamberlain not concealing his indignation at Hitler's impatience and his anger at the way he had been treated. When Chamberlain described the document he had been given as an ultimatum, Hitler pointed to the fact that it bore the word 'Memorandum' at the top. This was too much for the Prime Minister, who retorted that he was more impressed by the contents than by the title. Hitler, people would say, was already behaving like a conqueror: no, interjected Hitler, 'like an owner with his property'.

Then, once again, with perfect timing, Hitler produced his final 'concession'. 'You are one of the few men for whom I have ever done such a thing,' he declared. 'I am prepared to set one single date for the Czech evacuation – 1 October – if that will facilitate your task.' Seizing a pencil, he altered the dates in the memorandum in his own hand. Chamberlain was impressed. He did not commit himself to do more than submit Hitler's terms to the British and Czech Governments, but he added that 'he had a feeling a relationship of confidence had grown up between himself and the Führer as a result of the conversation of the last few days. . . . He did not cease to hope that the present crisis would be overcome and then he would be glad to discuss other problems with the Führer in the same spirit.

'The Führer thanked Chamberlain for his words and told him that he had similar hopes. As he had already stated several times, the Czech problem was the last territorial demand which he had to make in Europe.'[1] Hitler's last remark, Chamberlain told the House of Commons, was made 'with great earnestness'.

Whatever Chamberlain's personal inclinations may have been, on Sunday 25 September the British Cabinet decided that it could not accept the terms Hitler had offered or urge them on the Czechs. On the 26th the British Government at last gave assurances of support to France if she became involved in war with Germany as a result of fulfilling her treaty obligations, and preparations for war were expedited in both Britain and France.

The British Prime Minister, however, still refused to give up hope and resolved to make one last appeal to Hitler, in the hope of persuading him to moderate the tone of the speech he was due to make in the Berlin Sportpalast on the evening of the 26th. Sir Horace Wilson was at once sent off by plane with a personal letter to the Führer. In this Mr Chamberlain reported the rejection by the Czech Government of the Godesberg Proposals. But, he added, the issue could still be settled by peaceful means if Hitler would agree to direct negotiations between the German and Czech Governments, with the British present as a third party.

1. Kirkpatrick's notes, *Brit. Doc.*, 3rd Series, vol. II, No. 1,033 and 1,073; G.D., D.II, No. 583; Schmidt: pp. 399–407; Henderson: pp. 152–7.

In the interval Hitler had swung back into his most intransigent mood, working his resentment, hatred and impatience of opposition up to the pitch where they would provide him with the necessary stimulus for his speech. This was the mood in which Sir Horace Wilson and the British Ambassador found him when they arrived to present the British Prime Minister's letter at five o'clock on the 26th, three hours before the meeting in the Sportpalast was due to begin. Hitler was so keyed up that he could scarcely bear to remain seated. When Schmidt, the interpreter, who was reading out a translation of the letter, came to the words: 'The Czech Government regard the proposal as wholly unacceptable,' Hitler leapt up, and shouting: 'There's no point at all in going on with negotiations,' made for the door. Only with difficulty could Wilson persuade him to hear them out, and he continued to bark out interruptions. 'The Germans were being treated like niggers; one would not dare treat even the Turks like that. "On 1 October I shall have Czechoslovakia where I want her." If France and England decided to strike, let them. He did not care a farthing.' The utmost the British representatives were able to get out of him was agreement to conduct negotiations with the Czechs, on the basis of their acceptance of the Godesberg Memorandum and a German occupation of the Sudetenland by 1 October. If he was to hold back his troops, Hitler demanded an affirmative reply within less then forty-eight hours, by 2 p.m. on Wednesday 28 September. Time and date, it is clear from the records, were fixed on the spur of the moment. As Sir Horace Wilson left, Hitler urged him to come to the Sportpalast that evening, in order to get an idea of what feeling in Germany was like.[1]

Hitler's speech at the Sportpalast was a masterpiece of invective which even he never surpassed. He began, as his custom was, with a survey of his own efforts to arrive at a settlement with the other Powers in the past five years. He instanced the problems that had already been solved – the familiar catalogue of the Pact with Poland, the Anglo-German Naval Treaty, the renunciation of Alsace-Lorraine, friendship with Italy, the peaceful incorporation of Austria. 'And now before us stands the last problem that must be solved and will be solved. It is the last territorial claim which I have to make in Europe, but it is the claim from which I will not recede and which, God willing, I will make good.' The origin of

1. Kirkpatrick's notes of the interview, *Brit. Doc.*, 3rd Series, vol. ii, No. No. 1,118; Schmidt: pp. 407–8; Henderson: p. 159.

the Czech problem, he declared, was the refusal of the Peace-makers to apply their own principle of self-determination.

This Czech State began with a single lie, and the father of this lie was named Benes. . . . There is no such thing as a Czechoslovak nation, but only Czechs and Slovaks, and the Slovaks do not wish to have anything to do with the Czechs.

From this point Hitler's account became more and more grotesque in its inaccuracy. Having established a rule of terror over the subject peoples, the Slovaks, Germans, Magyars, and Poles, Benes had set out systematically to destroy the German minority; they were to be shot as traitors if they refused to fire on their fellow Germans. The Germans were so persecuted that hundreds of thousands fled into exile; thousands more were butchered by the Czechs. Meanwhile Benes put his country at the service of the Bolsheviks as an advanced air base from which to bomb Germany.

When, Hitler continued, he had insisted that there must be a change, Benes started a still more ruthless persecution of the Sudeten Germans, and brought off the clever trick of 21 May. Protected by Britain, France, and Russia, he believed he could do what he liked. Hitler then gave a wildly exaggerated picture of conditions in the Sudetenland. The daily number of refugees, he claimed, had risen from 10,000 to 90,000 and 137,000,

and today 214,000. Whole stretches of country are depopulated, villages burned down, attempts made to smoke out the Germans with hand-grenades and gas. Herr Benes, however, sits in Prague and is convinced: 'Nothing can happen to me: in the end England and France stand behind me.' And now, my fellow countrymen, I believe that the time has come when one must mince matters no longer. . . . For in the last resort Herr Benes has seven million Czechs, but here there stands a people of over seventy-five millions.

Hitler briefly explained the Godesberg proposals, brushing aside the Czech objection that these constituted a new situation. The Czechs had already agreed to the transfer of the districts demanded; the only difference was the German occupation. In other words: 'Herr Benes's promise must be kept. That is the "new situation" for Herr Benes.'
The Czechs, Hitler declared in his peroration, were working to overthrow the Chamberlain Government in Britain and Daladier

in France; they placed their hopes on Soviet Russia. In this way they still thought to evade fulfilling their promises.

And then I can only say one thing. Now two men stand arrayed one against the other: there is Herr Benes, and here am I. We are two men of a different make-up. In the great struggle of the peoples, while Herr Benes was sneaking about through the world, I as a decent German soldier did my duty. And now today I stand over against this man as a soldier of my people. . . . With regard to the problem of the Sudeten Germans, my patience is now at an end. I have made Herr Benes an offer which is nothing but the execution of what he himself has promised. The decision now lies in his hands: Peace or War. He will either accept this offer and now at last give the Germans their freedom, or we will go and fetch this freedom for ourselves. The world must take note that in four and a half years of war, and through the long years of my political life, there is one thing which no one could ever cast in my teeth: I have never been a coward. Now I go before my people as its first soldier, and behind me – this the world should know – there marches a different people from that of 1918.

We are determined!
Now let Herr Benes make his choice.[1]

Rarely has the issue of war or peace been so nakedly reduced to the personal resentment and vanity of one man.

In the balcony just above Hitler, William Shirer, the American broadcaster, was sitting watching. In his diary he wrote:

For the first time in all the years I've observed him, he seemed tonight to have completely lost control of himself. When he sat down, Goebbels sprang up and shouted: 'One thing is sure: 1918 will never be repeated!' Hitler looked up at him, as if those were the words which he had been searching for all the evening. He leapt to his feet and, with a fanatical fire in his eyes that I shall never forget, brought his right hand, after a grand sweep, pounding down on the table, and yelled with all the power in his lungs: 'Ja!' Then he slumped into his chair exhausted.[2]

The next morning Hitler was still in the same exalted mood; the process of self-intoxication with his own words was still at work. Sir Horace Wilson, calling for a second time just after noon, could do nothing with him. When he asked where the conflict would end, if the Czechs rejected the German demands, Hitler retorted that the first end would be the total destruction of Czechoslovakia. When Wilson then added that the war could scarcely be confined to Czechoslovakia, and that Britain would feel obliged to support

1. Baynes: vol. II, pp. 1,508–27.
2. William L. Shirer: *Berlin Diary* (London, 1941), pp. 118–19.

France if she went to the aid of the Czechs, Hitler twisted his words round:

That means that if France chooses to attack Germany, England feels it her duty to attack Germany also. I can only take note of this communication. . . . If France and England strike, let them do so. It is a matter of complete indifference to me. I am prepared for every eventuality. It is Tuesday today, and by next Monday we shall all be at war.[1]

Two or three times in the course of the interview Hitler shouted: 'I will smash the Czechs,' and when Sir Horace Wilson left he had little doubt that Hitler meant what he said. As soon as Wilson had gone Hitler sent for his adjutant, Schmundt, and at 1 p.m. ordered the movement of the assault units, twenty-one reinforced regiments, totalling seven divisions, up to their action stations. They must be ready to go into action on 30 September. A concealed mobilization was put into operation, including that of five further divisions in Western Germany.[2]

Yet Hitler had not slammed the door. Even at the height of his frenzy in the Sportpalast the night before he had still left open the alternative to war which he had put forward at Godesberg. As the day of the 27th wore on, the pendulum began to swing back from the 'all-or-nothing' mood of the Sportpalast to one of more rational calculation. While Ribbentrop and Himmler were in favour of war, there were others in Hitler's entourage who pressed him to make a settlement, among them Göring. Events began to support their arguments. In particular, the news that Great Britain and France were taking active steps in preparation for war, and Sir Horace Wilson's warning that Britain would support France impressed Hitler more than all Mr Chamberlain's appeals.

At this moment the group of conspirators who planned to carry out a *coup d'état* and seize Hitler by force were making renewed preparations, based on the use of the division commanded by General Brockdorff-Rantzau at Potsdam. This time they were convinced that they would carry Halder, Beck's successor as the Army Chief of Staff, and even perhaps Brauchitsch, the Army Commander-in-Chief, with them. Hitler's decision, of course, cannot have been influenced by a plot of which he

1. Kirkpatrick's notes, *Brit. Doc.*, 3rd Series, vol. II, No. 1,128–9; Schmidt's notes, G.D., D.II, No. 634. Schmidt: pp. 408–9; Henderson: p. 160.
2. N.D. 388-PS, Items 31–3.

remained ignorant, but the conspiracy reveals something of the dismay that was felt in the Army High Command at the risk of a general war – and of this Hitler was perfectly well aware. The main cause of the anxiety felt by the generals was the weakness of the German fortifications and forces in the West. Point was given to this by the report of the German military attaché in Paris on the 27th that by the sixth day of mobilization (which was now in full swing) the French would have deployed sixty-five divisions – against a dozen German divisions at most, some reserve units of doubtful quality.[1] His colleague in Prague reported that the Czech capital was calm and that a million men had been called to the colours.[2]

Meanwhile, during the late afternoon of the 27th, a mechanized division in full field equipment rumbled through the main streets of Berlin, and was greeted with almost complete silence by the crowds, who turned their backs and disappeared into subways rather than look on. For a long time, Hitler stood at the window to watch, and the total lack of enthusiasm – in contrast to the scenes of 1914 – is reported to have made a singularly deep impression on him. Later that evening, at ten o'clock the Commander-in-Chief of the Navy, Raeder, arrived to reinforce the Army's arguments – an appeal that was given added weight by the news, received during the night, that the British fleet was being mobilized.

'The strain upon this one man and upon his astounding will-power,' Mr Churchill wrote, 'must at this moment have been most severe. Evidently he had brought himself to the brink of a general war. Could he take the plunge in the face of an unfavourable public opinion and of the solemn warnings of the Chiefs of his Army, Navy, and Air Force? Could he, on the other hand, afford to retreat after living so long upon prestige?'[3]

Hitler, at any rate, was sufficiently interested in keeping open the line to London to follow his outburst to Sir Horace Wilson with a letter delivered to Mr Chamberlain at 10.30 p.m. on the 27th, in which he sought to defend the attitude he had taken up and to answer the objections of the Czechs to accepting the Godesberg proposals. The letter contained no hint of any modification, but it was skilfully phrased to appeal to Chamberlain, and the closing sentence – 'I leave it to your judgement whether

1. G.D., D.II, No. 647.
2. ibid., No. 646.
3. Winston Churchill: vol. I, p. 246.

... you consider you should continue your effort ... to bring the Government in Prague to reason at the very last hour' – spurred the British Prime Minister to make one final effort.[1]

IX

With the morning of 28 September – 'Black Wednesday' – all hope of avoiding war seemed to have gone. A sense of gloom hung over Berlin, no less than over Prague and Paris and London. Only a few hours remained before the time-limit fixed by Hitler expired; if no satisfactory reply had been received by two o'clock, it was universally believed that a German invasion of Czechoslovakia would follow. Nowhere was the sense of tension greater than at the Reich Chancellery, where in the course of the next hour or two Hitler had to decide on peace or war.

Shortly after eleven o'clock Hitler was asked to receive the French Ambassador. François-Poncet brought an offer which went a good way to meet the Godesberg demands, providing for the immediate occupation of part of the Sudetenland by 1 October and the occupation of the rest in a series of stages up to 10 October. The plan had not yet been accepted by the Czechs, but if it was agreed to by Hitler the French Government was prepared to demand that the Czechs accede to it as well, and would itself guarantee the smooth execution of the occupation.

The decisive move, however, appears to have been an appeal which the British Government addressed to Mussolini. The Duce, who had given general support to Hitler's claims against the Czechs in a recent series of speeches, was now thoroughly alarmed at the prospect of a European war for which Italy was ill-prepared. At the British request he agreed to send Attolico, the Italian Ambassador in Berlin, to Hitler.

Breathless and hatless, Attolico arrived at the Chancellery while Hitler was still engaged with François-Poncet. The Führer agreed to come out to speak to the Ambassador. Mussolini, Attolico began, sent assurances of full support whatever the Führer decided, but he asked him to delay a final decision for twenty-four hours in order to examine the new proposals put forward by Paris and London. Mussolini's appeal made an impression on Hitler; after a slight hesitation he agreed to Attolico's request. When he went back to the French Ambassador he was clearly preoccupied with Mussolini's message and told François-

1. Text of Hitler's letter (G.D., D.II, No. 635).

Poncet briefly that he would let him have a reply early in the afternoon.

The French Ambassador had not long been gone when Sir Nevile Henderson arrived. He met Göring and Neurath, who had both been urging Hitler to accept a settlement, as they came out of the Cabinet room. Henderson brought Chamberlain's reply to Hitler's letter of the night before. In a last appeal the British Prime Minister put forward the suggestion of an international conference to discuss the necessary arrangements to give Hitler what he wanted.[1] Hitler again declined a definite answer; he must consult first with Mussolini. Mussolini, meanwhile, was again on the telephone to Attolico, who was instructed to inform Hitler of the Duce's support for Chamberlain's proposals of a conference and of Italy's willingness to take part in such a meeting. At the same time, Mussolini pointed out, the new proposals brought by François-Poncet, which would form the basis of any discussions, would allow Hitler to march his troops into the Sudetenland by 1 October, the date to which he had publicly committed himself.

Some time between one and two o'clock that afternoon Hitler made his decision. He agreed to Mussolini's suggestion, on condition that Mussolini should be present in person and the conference held at once, either in Munich or Frankfurt. Mussolini accepted and chose Munich. The same afternoon invitations were sent to London and Paris – not, however, to either Prague or Moscow.

Hitler was eager to see Mussolini before the conference began, and early next day, 29 September, he boarded the Duce's train at Kufstein on the old German–Austrian frontier. To Ciano, Prince Philip of Hesse confided: 'The Führer is only half satisfied.' According to Italian accounts, Hitler greeted Mussolini with an elaborate exposition, illustrated with a map, of his plans for a lightning attack on Czechoslovakia, followed by a campaign against France. If these accounts are to be believed, it was Mussolini's influence which persuaded Hitler to give the conference a chance and not to assume that it would fail from the beginning. He quietened Hitler's suspicions with the renewed assurance that, should the conference break down, Italy would support Germany.

The meeting of the two dictators with the British and French Prime Ministers began in the newly built Führerhaus on the

1. Text in *Brit. Doc.*, 3rd Series, vol. II, No. 1,158.

Königsplatz at 12.45 p.m. Hitler, pale, excited and handicapped by his inability to speak any other language but German, leaned a good deal on Mussolini. Indeed, Mussolini seems to have been more at his ease than anyone else and to have played the leading part in the conference, partly because of his ability to speak the others' languages. Hitler, however, left the meeting in little doubt of what was required of it. 'He had already declared in his Sportpalast speech that he would in any case march in on 1 October. He had received the answer that this action would have the character of an act of violence. Hence the task arose to absolve the action from such a character. Action, however, must be taken at once.'[1]

Mussolini provided the Conference with a basis for discussion by producing a memorandum which eventually formed the basis of the Munich Agreement. The history of this Memorandum is of some interest. It had been drafted the day before by Neurath, Göring, and Weizsäcker (the State Secretary in the Foreign Office) in order to forestall Ribbentrop; it had been shown to Hitler by Göring, and then secretly put in the hands of Attolico for dispatch to Rome. Mussolini now brought it out as his own draft, before Ribbentrop could put forward an alternative, and so got the conference over its first hurdle. Attempts by Chamberlain and Daladier to secure representation for the Czechs produced no results: Hitler refused categorically to admit them to the conference. Either the problem was one between Germany and Czechoslovakia, which could be settled by force in a fortnight; or it was a problem for the Great Powers, in which case they must take the responsibility and impose their settlement on the Czechs.

The conference had been so hastily improvised that it lacked any organization. No minutes were taken; the delegations sat in easy chairs scattered round a large circle, and after the adjournment for lunch in the middle of the afternoon ambassadors, officials and adjutants slipped into the room to form an audience lining the walls. The general discussion was constantly breaking down into individual arguments or conversations, and this was facilitated by the difficulties of translation. There were constant interruptions while members of one delegation or another went in and out to prepare alternative drafts. Mr Chamberlain, the ex-Chancellor of the Exchequer, was characteristically obstinate about such questions as compensation for property, a question

1. German F.O. Memorandum on the first meeting between 12.45 and 3 p.m., G.D., D.II, No. 670.

which Hitler, equally characteristically, brushed aside with angry indifference. Finally, in the early hours of the morning of 30 September, agreement was reached, and the two dictators left to the British and French the odious task of communicating to the Czechs the terms for the partition of their country.[1]

X

Even on paper the Munich Agreement contained few substantial variations from the proposals of the Godesberg Memorandum. On 1 October German troops marched into the Sudetenland, as Hitler had demanded, and in carrying out the Agreement the Germans were able to brush aside the few limitations the Western Powers had tried to add. The promised plebiscite was never held and the frontiers when finally drawn followed strategic much more than ethnographical lines, leaving two hundred and fifty thousand Germans in Czechoslovakia, and including eight hundred thousand Czechs in the lands ceded to the Reich. Czechoslovakia lost her system of fortifications – which greatly impressed the German generals when they inspected them – together with eleven thousand square miles of territory. To this must be added crippling industrial losses and the disruption of the Czech railway system. President Benes was forced to go into exile and one of the first acts of the new régime was to denounce the alliance with Russia. On 10 October the Czechs ceded the Teschen district to Poland, and on 2 November Ribbentrop and Ciano dictated the new Czech–Hungarian frontier at a ceremony in the Belvedere Palace at Vienna from which the two other signatories of the Munich Agreement and the guarantors of Czechoslovakia were blatantly excluded.

On the night of the Munich Conference General Jodl wrote in his diary:

The Pact of Munich is signed. Czechoslovakia as a Power is out. . . . The genius of the Führer and his determination not to shun even a world war have again won victory without the use of force. The hope remains that the incredulous, the weak and the doubters have been converted and will remain that way.[2]

1. Sources for the actual conference: Sir H. Wilson's notes, *Brit. Doc.*, 3rd Series, vol. II, No. 1,227; German Memoranda, G.D., D.II, Nos. 670 and 674; Weizsäcker: pp. 153–5; Schmidt: pp. 413–16; François-Poncet: c. 10; Henderson: pp. 166–7.
2. Jodl's diary (N.D. 1,780-PS).

Hitler's prestige rose to new heights in Germany, where relief that war had been avoided was combined with delight in the gains that had been won on the cheap. Whether those who opposed a policy of risking war would ever have carried out their plan to seize Hitler – as General Halder and others subsequently claimed – remains uncertain; but Hitler's success, without war, cut the ground away from under their feet.

Abroad the effect was equally startling, and Mr Churchill described the results of the Munich settlement in a famous speech on 5 October 1938:

At Berchtesgaden . . . £1 was demanded at the pistol's point. When it was given (at Godesberg), £2 was demanded at the pistol's point. Finally the Dictator consented to take £1 17s. 6d. and the rest in promises of goodwill for the future. . . . We are in the presence of a disaster of the first magnitude.

Austria and the Sudetenland within six months represented the triumph of those methods of political warfare which Hitler had so sedulously applied in the past five years. His diagnosis of the weakness of the Western democracies, and of the international divisions which prevented the formation of a united front against him, had been brilliantly vindicated. Five years after coming to power he had raised Germany from one of the lowest points of her history to the position of the leading Power in Europe – and this not only without war, but with the agreement of Great Britain and France. The tactics of legality had paid as big dividends abroad as at home.

The fact that the Prime Minister of Great Britain had twice flown to Germany to intercede with him, and on the third occasion had hurried across Europe with the heads of the French and Italian Governments to meet him at the shortest possible notice, constituted a personal triumph for Hitler. He can scarcely have failed to appreciate the fact that, twenty years after the end of the First World War, he had dictated terms to the victorious Powers of 1918 in the very city in the back streets of which he had begun his career as an unknown agitator.

Yet Hitler was more irritated than elated by his triumph. The morning after the Munich Agreement was signed, when Chamberlain called on the Führer in his Munich flat, Paul Schmidt, who was present to interpret, describes Hitler as moody and preoccupied. The news that Chamberlain had been given an ovation as he drove through the streets of Munich – in contrast to Berlin's sullen reception of the mechanized division – further annoyed him. When Hitler returned to Berlin he exclaimed angrily to his S.S. entourage: 'That fellow Chamberlain has spoiled my entry into Prague.'[1]

After Munich the view gained currency outside Germany that Hitler had been bluffing all the time, that he had always had a 'Munich' in view, and that he laughed up his sleeve when Chamberlain failed to call his bluff and took his threats at face value. This view does not, however, correspond with the impressions of those who saw Hitler at the time. If those impressions are put together it is a different picture of Hitler's state of mind which emerges.

On the view taken here Hitler was genuinely undecided up to noon of 28 September, when he received the message from Mussolini, whether to risk war or not. The hesitation was not, as Chamberlain thought, between getting the Sudetenland by force or by negotiation, but between getting the Sudetenland and overrunning the whole of Czechoslovakia. Hitler had been impressed by the events of 27 September both by the evidence of German lack of enthusiasm for a war and by the urgent warnings from the Army and the Navy of the chance of defeat, but it was not until he received the message from Mussolini that he finally made up his mind to withhold the order for an attack on Czechoslovakia. For the message from Mussolini not only sought to persuade him of the advantages of such a course, but implied, to Hitler's suspicious mind, that if he went on he would go on alone. Göring later told Weizsäcker that 'he knew from Hitler that two reasons had moved him to choose peaceful methods: first, doubts as to the warlike disposition of the German people; and second, the fear that Mussolini might definitely leave him in the lurch'.[2]

Even when he had agreed to the conference Hitler continued to have doubts. The indignation against the Czechs into which he had lashed himself, his pride and sensitivity to prestige, his ingrained dislike of negotiation, his preference for violence, his desire for a sensational success for the new German Army he had created, the recurrent thought of the original plan to secure the whole of Czechoslovakia – all these were factors liable to start up

1. The remark was overheard by Schacht, who referred to it at Nuremberg (N.P., Part XIII, p. 4).
2. Ernst von Weizsäcker: *Memoirs* (English translation, London, 1951), p. 154.

once more the conflict in his mind. In short, Hitler at Munich was still only half convinced that he had taken the right decision, and this is borne out by his behaviour after the Agreement was signed.

The German High Command were only too relieved at avoiding war, and at Nuremberg General Keitel admitted that they 'did not believe themselves to be strong enough at that moment to break through the fortifications of the Czechoslovak frontier'. But Hitler regarded his generals as defeatists. He was more impressed by the arguments of Ribbentrop and Himmler that Germany had failed to exploit the Western Powers' fear of war to the full. The fact that Britain and France had agreed to impose the Munich terms on Czechoslovakia suggested that, if he had held on and ordered his troops to attack, they would never have intervened. By allowing himself to be persuaded into accepting a negotiated settlement, Hitler came to believe that he had been baulked of the triumph he had really wanted, the German armoured divisions storming across Bohemia and a conqueror's entry into the Czech capital. This was still his objective.

It was clear to me from the first moment [Hitler later declared] that I could not be satisfied with the Sudeten territory. That was only a partial solution.[1]

Thus the old conflict, only half suppressed, was revived retrospectively.

The criticism which began to be heard of the Munich Agreement in Great Britain and France, and the fact that the British Government proposed to increase, not reduce, its rearmament programme, soon roused Hitler's anger. At Saarbrücken, on 9 October, he retorted by announcing the strengthening of Germany's western fortifications, adding:

It would be a good thing if people in Great Britain would gradually drop certain airs which they have inherited from the Versailles period. We cannot tolerate any longer the tutelage of governesses. Inquiries of British politicians concerning the fate of Germans within the frontiers of the Reich – or of others belonging to the Reich – are not in place. . . . We would like to give these gentlemen the advice that they should busy themselves with their own affairs and leave us in peace.[2]

For a moment Hitler seems to have considered the possibility of still carrying out his full programme. Some time in the first ten

1. Hitler's speech to his C.-in-C.s, 23 November 1939 (N.D. 789-P S).
2. Baynes: vol. II, pp. 1,532–7.

days of October he sent General Keitel four questions to which he
wanted an immediate reply:

1. What reinforcements are necessary in the present situation to break
all Czech resistance in Bohemia and Moravia?
2. How much time is required for the regrouping or moving up of
new forces?
3. How much time will be required for the same purpose if it is executed after the intended demobilization measures?
4. How much time would be required to achieve the state of readiness
of 1 October?[1]

On reflection Hitler let matters stand for the time being, but his
intention of going a stage further was never in doubt, and a new
directive for the Armed Forces was issued on 21 October which
listed, immediately after measures to defend Germany, preparations to liquidate the remainder of Czechoslovakia.[2]

The well-meaning efforts of the appeasers during the next six
months, far from mollifying, only irritated Hitler further. He
objected to this attempt to put him on his best behaviour, to treat
him as a governess treats a difficult child, appealing to sweet
reason and his better instincts. After Munich he was more
determined than ever not to be drawn into the kind of general
settlement which was the object of Chamberlain's policy. If
England wanted a settlement with Germany it was quite simple,
all she had to do was to give him a free hand in Europe and stop
clucking like a fussy hen about what happened east of the Rhine,
a sphere of influence which Germany now claimed as her own.
Hitler refused to make any concessions in return for the gestures
of appeasement offered to him; he was interested in appeasement
only in so far as it was the equivalent of capitulation and the complete abandonment of British interest in continental affairs.

The speech at Saarbrücken in which he had attacked Churchill,
Eden, and Duff Cooper as warmongers was followed by others in
similar vein, at Weimar on 6 November and at Munich on 8
November. At Munich Hitler declared:

National Socialist Germany will never go to Canossa! If the rest of the
world obstinately bars the way to recognition of our rights by the way of
negotiation, then there should be no surprise that we secure for ourselves our rights by another way.[3]

On the night of 9–10 November a carefully organized pogrom
against the Jewish population throughout Germany was carried

1. N.D. 388-PS, item 48.
2. N.D. C-136.
3. Baynes: vol. II, p. 1,557.

out as revenge for the murder of a Nazi diplomat by a young Jew in Paris. These events produced a reaction of horror and indignation in both Great Britain and the United States. President Roosevelt recalled the American Ambassador in Berlin, and the British Press was unanimous in its condemnation of the Nazi outrages. Hitler flew into a rage. Hatred of the Jews was perhaps the most sincere emotion of which he was capable. To his resentment against Britain was added the fury that the British should dare to express concern for the fate of the German Jews. He now saw London as the centre of that Jewish world conspiracy with which he had long inflamed his imagination, and Great Britain as the major obstacle in his path.

German diplomatic activity during the winter of 1938–9 was directed, not towards London, but towards Paris and Rome.

In the first case his aim seems to have been to detach France from Great Britain. In mid-October, when François-Poncet, the French Ambassador, was about to leave Berlin to take up a new appointment in Rome, Hitler invited him to pay a farewell visit to the Obersalzberg. He received him, not in the Berghof, but in the pavilion he had built six thousand feet up in the mountains. In a famous dispatch François-Poncet has described the scene: the approach up a nine-mile-long road cut through the rock, and the ascent in a lift with double doors of bronze. At the summit he stepped out into an immense circular room surrounded by pillars, with fantastic views of the mountain peaks. 'In the immediate vicinity of the house, which gives the impression of being suspended in space, an almost overhanging wall of bare rock rises up abruptly. The whole, bathed in the twilight of an autumn evening, is grandiose, wild, almost hallucinating.'[1]

Hitler did not disguise his dissatisfaction with the results of Munich and launched into an angry tirade against Great Britain. But he was eminently reasonable on the subject of Franco–German relations, suggesting a joint declaration guaranteeing the existing frontier, and thus confirming Germany's abandonment of any claim to Alsace-Lorraine, together with an agreement to hold consultations on all questions likely to affect mutual relations.

The French Government proved amenable to the suggestion, and the proposed Declaration was signed on 6 December when Ribbentrop visited Paris and had long talks with the French

1. Dispatch of M. François-Poncet, 20 October 1938, *French Yellow Book* No. 18.

Foreign Minister, Georges Bonnet. Ribbentrop later claimed that Bonnet accepted his view that Czechoslovakia was to be considered as lying in the German sphere of interest and no longer an issue for discussion between France and Germany. Whatever the truth of this – and it was indignantly denied by Bonnet – it is obvious that this was the object which the Germans hoped to obtain by their gesture towards France. France's alliances with Poland and the U.S.S.R., Ribbentrop claimed to have told Bonnet, were 'an atavistic remnant of the Versailles mentality'.[1] The price of German friendship, in short, was a disavowal of France's old interest in Europe east of the Rhine.

In the meantime Hitler was at pains to strengthen his relations with Italy. At Munich Ribbentrop had produced a draft for a defensive military alliance between Germany, Italy, and Japan, and at the end of October the German Foreign Minister visited Rome to urge the Duce to put his signature to the treaty.

The Führer is convinced [Ribbentrop told the Italians] that we must inevitably count on a war with the Western Democracies in the course of a few years, perhaps three or four. . . . The Czechoslovak crisis has shown our power! We have the advantage of the initiative and are masters of the situation. We cannot be attacked. The military situation is excellent: as from the month of September (1939) we could face a war with the great democracies.[2]

To please Mussolini, Hitler agreed to a joint German–Italian arbitration of the disputed frontier between Hungary and Slovakia although he had previously resisted the idea. The Italian dictator was wary of committing himself to an outright military alliance, of which he had fought shy throughout the summer and autumn. He resented Ribbentrop's visit to Paris in December and the German–French Declaration at precisely the moment when Italy was raising her own claims to Tunisia, Corsica, and Nice. Yet the very fact that Mussolini was beginning a new quarrel with France forced him back into his old position of dependence on Germany. As Hitler had astutely realized at the time of the Abyssinian War, if Mussolini continued to cherish his bombastic imperial ambitions he would always be forced to come begging to Berlin for support in the end, whether he liked it or not. Sure

1. German Minute of the conversation between Ribbentrop and Bonnet in Paris, 6 December 1938 (G.D., D.IV, No. 370).
2. Ciano's Minute of Ribbentrop's conversation with the Duce and himself, 28 October 1938; *Ciano's Diplomatic Papers*, pp. 242–6. Cf. Schmidt's Minute in G.D., D.IV, pp. 515–20.

enough, at the beginning of the New Year, after two months of hesitation, the Duce suppressed his doubts and instructed Ciano to inform Ribbentrop that he was willing to accept the suggested treaty.

In his speech of 30 January Hitler was lavish in his praise of Fascist Italy and her great leader. It was to be some months yet before the Pact of Steel was actually signed, but Hitler was content: he had Mussolini where he wanted him and the working partnership of the Axis had been reaffirmed.

XI

What would Hitler's next move be? No question more absorbed the attention of every diplomat and foreign correspondent in the winter of 1938–9. Every rumour was caught at and diligently reported.

Immediately after Munich, Dr Funk, Schacht's successor at the Ministry of Economics, went on a tour of the Balkans. His visit underlined the state of economic dependence upon Germany in which all these countries – Hungary, Rumania, Bulgaria, and Yugoslavia – now found themselves. Their political docility was secured by other means besides preferential trade and currency agreements – by the organization of the German minorities; by subsidies to local parties on the Nazi model, like the Iron Guard in Rumania; by playing on internal divisions between different peoples and different classes in the same country; by encouraging the territorial claims of one country, like Hungary, and rousing the fears of another, like Rumania. After the annexation of Austria and the capitulation of Munich these countries had to recognize that they were in the German sphere of influence and must shape their policy accordingly. They could pursue tactics of procrastination and evasion, and still attempt to play off Rome against Berlin, but this was the limit of their independence.

Precisely because of this dependence, however, and the success of Germany's methods of peaceful penetration, it seemed unlikely that Hitler would attempt a *coup* in this direction. It was to the east and north-east, rather than the south-east, that the rumours persistently pointed – the occupation of the rest of Czechoslovakia, the annexation of Danzig, the return of Memel from Lithuania, or – the most interesting possibility of all – the use of the easternmost part of Czechoslovakia, Ruthenia, with its Ukrainian population, as a base from which to stir up discontent among the Ukrainians of the U.S.S.R. and of Poland.

After Munich Hitler did not hesitate to express his disappointment with the Hungarians for failing to press their claims on the Czechs more pertinaciously. He showed considerable impatience with the Hungarian demands on Slovakia, and refused to agree to their annexation of Ruthenia, with a common Hungarian–Polish frontier. Instead an autonomous Ruthenia was set up within the new Czechoslovakia, in the same relationship towards its German patrons as the autonomous Slovakia. The little town of Chust, which was the capital of Ruthenia, soon became the centre of a Ukrainian national movement, eager to bring freedom to the oppressed Ukrainian populations of Poland and of the Soviet Union.

The German game in this backwater of Eastern Europe roused sharp interest in the European capitals, especially in Moscow and Warsaw. Poland and Russia took the threat sufficiently seriously to discover a common interest, despite their inveterate hostility: political and trade talks were initiated, and the Pact of Non-aggression between the two countries reaffirmed.

This Polish–Soviet *rapprochement* may have played a part in persuading the Germans to postpone their plans for a Greater Ukraine. At any rate, Ruthenia, and the uses to which it might be put, began to attract less attention in the New Year. By the end of January it was a different set of anxieties which was beginning to occupy the Foreign Ministries in London and Paris.

On 24 January Lord Halifax, the British Foreign Secretary, wrote an appreciation of the European situation, which was to be laid before President Roosevelt and which was subsequently sent to the French Government as well. Lord Halifax began by saying that he had received a large number of reports about Hitler's mood and intentions.

According to these reports, Hitler is bitterly resentful at the Munich Agreement which baulked him of a localized war against Czechoslovakia and demonstrated the will to peace of the German masses in opposition to the warmongering of the Nazi Party. He feels personally humiliated by this demonstration. He regards Great Britain as primarily responsible for this humiliation, and his rage is therefore directed principally against this country, which he holds to be the chief obstacle now to the fulfilment of his further ambitions.

As early as November there were indications which gradually became more definite that Hitler was planning a further foreign adventure for the spring of 1939. At first it appeared that he was thinking of expansion in the east, and in December the prospect of establishing an independent Ukraine under German vassalage was freely spoken of in Germany. Since then reports indicate that Hitler, encouraged by Ribbentrop, Himmler, and others, is considering an attack on the Western Powers as a preliminary to subsequent action in the east.[1]

The reports of an attack on the west, on Holland, perhaps, or Switzerland, although taken seriously by the British Foreign Office at the time, in fact proved to be without any substance. Hitler was not in a hurry; he preferred to let the situation develop until an opportunity presented itself, and almost certainly it was to the east, not the west, that his attention was directed.

It is in the directives which he issued to the Armed Forces that we have the surest indication of the way in which Hitler's mind was moving. There are three such directives in the six months between Munich and Prague.[2] In the first, issued on 21 October, the Army and the other Forces are ordered to be prepared at all times for three eventualities: the defence of Germany, the liquidation of Czechoslovakia, and the occupation of Memel. On 24 November Hitler added a fourth eventuality, the occupation of Danzig, and on 17 December he instructed the Army to make its preparations to occupy the rest of Czechoslovakia on the assumption that no resistance worth mentioning need be expected.

These are in fact the objectives which Hitler proceeded to realize during the next twelve months. This does not exclude the possibility that the Ukraine may have interested him for a time and been discussed in his entourage, but, so far as we know, it never got to the stage of being reduced to a directive.

In point of time, the preliminary moves for securing Danzig overlap the preparations for the liquidation of Czechoslovakia, but it will be convenient to treat relations with Poland separately and to conclude this chapter, which began with the occupation of Vienna in March 1938, with the occupation of Prague in March 1939.

After the cession to Poland and Hungary of a further 5,000 square miles of territory, with a population of well over a million souls, the Government in Prague was obliged to grant far-reaching autonomy to the two eastern provinces of Slovakia and Ruthenia, each of which had its own Cabinet and Parliament and maintained

1. *Brit. Doc.*, 3rd Series, vol. v, No. 5 and No. 40; Lord Halifax to the British Embassy in Washington, and to the British Embassy in Paris.
2. These are, respectively, N.D., C-136, C-137, C-138.

only the most shadowy relation with the Central Government. Even this did not satisfy the Germans, and the German Foreign Office archives for these months contain a long series of further demands upon the unfortunate Czechs.[1]

When Chvalkovsky, the Czech Foreign Minister, visited Berlin in January 1939, Hitler reproached him with the failure of the Czechs to draw the consequences of what had happened and to break with their past, or to abandon hope of change in the future as a result of international conflict. Unless the Czechs showed a different spirit, he would 'annihilate' them. Then followed a long and humiliating list of further demands.

The German documents in fact leave the clear impression that Hitler was only seeking a favourable opportunity to carry out the destruction of the Czechoslovak State of which he had been baulked at Munich, and that it was for this reason that the Germans steadily refused to give the guarantee for which the Czechs anxiously pleaded.

There were considerable practical advantages to be derived from such a move. The German Army was anxious to replace the long, straggling German–Czech frontier, which still represented a deep enclave in German territory, with a short easily-held line straight across Moravia from Silesia to Austria. The German Air Force was eager to acquire new air bases in Moravia and Bohemia. The seizure of Czech Army stocks[2] and of the Skoda arms works, second only to Krupps, would represent a major reinforcement of German strength. The rearmament of Germany was beginning to impose a severe strain on the German economy and standard of living. The occupation of Bohemia and Moravia would help to alleviate this strain. Czech reserves of gold and foreign currency, Czech investments abroad and the agricultural and manpower resources of the country could be put to good use. At the same time, another cheap success in foreign policy would distract attention from any shortages at home and add to the prestige of the régime.

The role of fifth column, which had been played by the Sudeten Germans in 1938, was now assigned to the Slovaks, assisted by

1. Published in G.D., D.IV, c. 1.
2. Hitler later gave a figure of 1,500 planes (500 front line), 469 tanks, over 500 A.A. guns, 43,000 machine-guns, over a million rifles, a thousand million rounds of rifle and three million rounds of field-gun ammunition, as the total of the loot acquired in March 1939.

the German minority left within the frontiers of the new State. The demand of the Slovak extremists for complete independence had only been intensified by the grant of autonomy after Munich, and was carefully cultivated by the Germans. As early as mid-October 1938 a meeting took place between Göring, two of the Slovak leaders, Durcansky and Mach, and Karmasin, leader of the German minority in Slovakia. After Durcansky had declared that the Slovak aim was complete independence, with very close ties with Germany, Göring assured him that the Slovak efforts would be suitably supported. 'A Czech State minus Slovakia is even more completely at our mercy. Air bases in Slovakia for operations against the east are very important.'[1] On 12 February Hitler received Dr Tuka, the leader of the Slovak National Party, together with Karmasin, in the Reich Chancellery. Encouraged by the Führer, Tuka declared that further association with the Czechs had become an impossibility for the Slovaks. 'I lay the destiny of my people in your hands, my Führer; my people await their complete liberation from you.'[2]

It needed no gift of prophecy to foretell that the state of affairs in Czechoslovakia could not continue indefinitely. The Prague Government had either to act or watch the separatist intrigues in Slovakia and Ruthenia break up the state. On 6 March the President of Czechoslovakia, Hacha, dismissed the Ruthenian Government from office, and, on the night of 9–10 March, the Slovak as well. The next day martial law was proclaimed in Slovakia. Hitler was taken by surprise. He was about to leave for Vienna to take part in the celebrations of the anniversary of the *Anschluss*, while Göring was on holiday at San Remo. It did not take him long, however, to grasp that here was the opportunity for which he had been waiting.

Some of the Slovak leaders seem to have shown a last-minute reluctance to play the part for which they were cast, but they were prodded in the back by Karmasin and the well-organized German minority. Durcansky, one of the dismissed Ministers, was hurried across the border in the German Consul's car. Over the Vienna radio he denounced the new Slovak Government formed by Sidor, and called on the Slovak Hlinka Guard to rise. Arms were brought across the river from Austria and distributed to the Germans, who occupied the Government buildings in Bratislava. The British Consul in the city reported that the en-

1. German Minutes of the conversation, G.D., D.IV, No. 68.
2. ibid., No. 168.

thusiasm of the Slovak population was lukewarm, and continued so even after the declaration of Slovak independence. But Hitler was not interested in what the Slovaks thought; all he wanted was the declaration, and he took drastic measures to get it.

It had already been announced in Berlin on the morning of 11 March that Tiso, the deposed Slovak Premier, had appealed to Hitler. That night (according to the account later put together by the British Minister in Prague[1]) the two chief German representatives in Vienna, Bürckel and Seyss-Inquart, accompanied by five German generals, arrived in Bratislava and pushed their way into a meeting of the Slovak Government. Bürckel is reported to have told the new Premier, Sidor, that they must proclaim the independence of Slovakia at once, or Hitler – who had decided to settle the fate of Czechoslovakia – would disinterest himself in the Slovaks' future.

For the moment Sidor gave an evasive answer, but early the next morning, Sunday the 12th, Tiso, the deposed Premier, requested a further Cabinet meeting. When this met – in the offices of the newspaper *Slovak*, to escape German interference – Tiso told the Cabinet that Bürckel had brought him an invitation from Hitler to go at once to Berlin. This he had been obliged to accept, for the consequences of refusal, Bürckel had added, would be the occupation of Bratislava by German troops and of Eastern Slovakia by the Hungarians. Accordingly he proposed to leave by train for Vienna early on Monday and be back by Tuesday night. No sooner, however, did Tiso reach Vienna than he was bundled into a plane and flown to Berlin.

In the early evening of Monday, 13 March, Hitler received Tiso and Durcansky in the Reich Chancellery. Tiso, a short, stout Catholic priest, who once told Paul Schmidt: 'When I get worked up, I eat half a pound of ham, and that soothes my nerves,' had first to listen to a long, angry speech in which Hitler denounced the Czechs and expressed astonishment at his own forbearance.

The attitude of the Slovaks, Hitler continued, had also been disappointing. After Munich he had prevented Hungary from occupying Slovakia in the belief that the Slovaks wanted independence, and had thereby risked offending his Hungarian friends. The new Slovak Premier, Sidor, however, now declared that he would oppose the separation of Slovakia from Czechoslovakia.

1. *Brit. Doc.*, 3rd Series, vol. IV, No. 473.

He had therefore [Hitler continued] permitted Minister Tiso to come here in order to clear up this question in a very short time: whether Slovakia wished to conduct her own affairs or not. . . . It was not a question of days, but of hours. . . . If Slovakia wished to make herself independent he would support this endeavour, and even guarantee it. If she hesitated . . . he would leave the destiny of Slovakia to the mercy of events, for which he was no longer responsible.[1]

To add point to Hitler's remarks, Ribbentrop conveniently produced a message reporting Hungarian troop movements on the Slovak frontiers.

Tiso was then allowed to go. After further conversations with Ribbentrop, Keppler and other Nazi officials, he rang up Bratislava, to request the summoning of the Slovak Parliament for ten o'clock the next morning, and in the early hours of the morning returned to the Slovak capital. When the Deputies met, Tiso read out a proclamation of independence for Slovakia which he had received from Ribbentrop already drafted in Slovak. Attempts to discuss the proposal were blocked by the leader of the German minority, Karmasin, who warned the Deputies to be careful lest the German occupation should be extended to Bratislava. Whether they liked it or not, the Slovak Deputies had no option but to accept the independence thrust upon them, and by noon on Tuesday, 14 March, the break-up of Czechoslovakia had begun. In the House of Commons the next day Mr Chamberlain gave the internal disruption of the Czechoslovak State by the action of the Slovaks, before the Germans marched in, as the reason why Great Britian could no longer be bound by any obligation to guarantee the frontiers of Czechoslovakia. Once again Hitler had shown his understanding of the value of 'legality'.

XII

Hitler was now ready to deal with the Czechs. According to a report later sent to London by the British Embassy in Berlin,[2] his original plan was for an ultimatum to the Czech Government, with a display of force in support, and it was only on the afternoon of 12 March that he decided to march in and hurriedly withdrew the ultimatum. Whatever truth there was in this report, by 13 March the news from Slovakia had been crowded out of

1. German Minute of the Conversation by Hewel (N.D. 2,802-PS).
2. *Brit. Doc.*, 3rd Series, vol. IV, No. 474.

the front pages of the German Press by violent stories of a Czech 'reign of terror' directed against the German minority in Bohemia and Moravia. 'German Blood Flows again at Brünn', 'Unheard-of Czech Provocation of German Nationality', 'Humiliation of German Honour' – these were the familiar headlines. Not only the wording, the French Ambassador noted, but even the incidents reported were almost identical with those of August 1938: the pregnant woman struck down and trampled on, the German student beaten up, and so on. Despite the efforts of the German minority to provoke the Czechs there was little truth in any of these atrocity stories, apart from a handful of minor incidents. But they served their purpose, not least in helping Hitler to whip up his own indignation.

On Monday the 13th the Czech Government made a last effort to avert German action by a direct appeal to Hitler, and the following day President Hacha and the Foreign Minister, Chvalkovsky, set out for the German capital by train. An hour before they left, the Hungarians presented an ultimatum demanding the withdrawal of all Czech troops from Ruthenia, and the President had not yet crossed the Czech frontier when news reached Prague that German troops had already occupied the important industrial centre of Moravska Ostrava.

In Berlin President Hacha was received with all the honours due to a Head of State, was lodged in the Adlon Hotel and, when he reached the Chancellery, found an S.S. Guard of Honour drawn up in the courtyard. The irony was barely concealed. Not until after 1 a.m. was the President admitted to Hitler's presence, and he was quite unable to discover in advance what would be discussed. He found the Führer in his study, accompanied by Göring, General Keitel, and four other men. Ill at ease, politically inexperienced, old, tired, and without a card in his hand, Hacha tried to soften Hitler's mood by ingratiating himself. He was, he said, an unknown person until recently; had taken no part in politics (he was a judge), had rarely met either Benes or Masaryk and had felt their régime to be alien to him – 'so much so that after the sudden change he had asked himself whether it was really a good thing for Czechoslovakia to be an independent State.' He had no grounds for complaint over what had happened in Slovakia, but he pleaded with the Führer for the right of the Czechs to continue to live their own national life.

When Hacha had finished his abject plea Hitler began to speak.

Once again he reviewed the course of his dealings with the Czechs; once again he repeated the charge that they had failed to break with the old régime of Benes and Masaryk.

Last Sunday, therefore, 12 March, for him the die was cast. . . . He had no longer confidence in the Czech Government. . . . This very morning at 6 a.m. the German Army would invade Czechoslovakia at all points and the German Air Force would occupy all Czech airports. There were two possibilities. The first was that the invasion of the German troops might develop into a battle. This resistance would then be broken by force of arms. The other was that the entry of the German troops should take place in a peaceable manner, and then it would be easy for the Führer to give to the Czechs an individual existence on a generous scale, autonomy and a certain amount of national freedom. . . .

  If it came to a fight, in two days the Czech Army would cease to exist. Some Germans would, of course, also be killed, and this would produce a feeling of hatred which would compel him to refuse any longer to grant autonomy. The world would not care a jot about this. He felt sorry for the Czech people when he read the foreign Press. It gave him the impression expressed by the German proverb: The Moor has done his duty; the Moor may go. . . .

  This was the reason why he had asked Hacha to come here. That invitation was the last good deed he would be able to render to the Czech people. . . . Perhaps Hacha's visit might avert the worst. . . . The hours were passing. At six o'clock (it was then nearly 2 a.m.) the troops would march in. He felt almost ashamed to say that for every Czech battalion a German division would come. The military operation had been planned on the most generous scale. He would advise him to withdraw now with Chvalkovsky, in order to discuss what should be done.

When Hacha asked what could be done in so short a time, Hitler suggested he should telephone to Prague.

Hacha asks whether the purpose of the invasion is to disarm the Czech Army. This might, perhaps, be done in some other way. The Führer says that his decision is irrevocable. Everyone knows what a decision by the Führer means.[1]

At this point Hacha and Chvalkovsky were taken into another room for further talks with Göring and Ribbentrop. During this interlude Göring threatened to destroy Prague by bombing and Hacha fainted. He was revived by an injection from Hitler's doctor, Morell, who had thoughtfully been kept in attendance. Before they returned Hacha was put through to Prague by telephone, and the Czech Government undertook to order no resis-

1. German Minute by Hewel (N.D. 2,798-PS).

tance to the German advance. In the meantime a draft communiqué had been prepared and was ready for Hacha's signature when the Führer received him again in his study shortly before 4 a.m. Its smooth terms were a masterpiece of understatement. The Führer had received President Hacha at the latter's request, and the President 'confidently placed the fate of the Czech people in the hands of the Führer'. Not a word was said of threats or invasion.[1]

Hitler could hardly contain himself. He burst into his secretaries' room and invited them to kiss him. 'Children,' he declared, 'this is the greatest day of my life. I shall go down to history as the greatest German.'[2]

Two hours later German troops crossed the frontier. 'Legality' had been preserved, and when the British and French Ambassadors called at the Wilhelmstrasse to deliver their inevitable protests they were met with the argument that the Führer had acted only at the request of the Czech President, just as the occupation of Austria had been undertaken only in response to the telegram sent by Seyss-Inquart.

By the afternoon of 15 March Hitler was on his way to Prague, where he arrived the same evening, accompanied by Keitel, Ribbentrop, and Himmler. His proclamation to the German people revived the stories of an 'intolerable' reign of terror, which had forced him to intervene to prevent the 'complete destruction of all order in a territory ... which for over a thousand years belonged to the German Reich'.[3] That night he spent in the palace of the Kings of Bohemia with the swastika waving from its battlements. Hitler had paid off another of the historic grudges of the old Hapsburg Monarchy, the resentment of the Germans of the Empire in face of the Czech claim to equality, that impertinent claim he had first rejected in the working-class quarters of Vienna thirty years before.

The next day, sitting in the Hradschin Castle, on the hill overlooking Prague, Hitler reaffirmed the claim of the Germans to the territories of Bohemia and Moravia in which the upstart Czechs had dared to establish their own national state.

For a millennium [he wrote in the Proclamation of 16 March] the territories of Bohemia and Moravia belonged to the *Lebensraum* of the

1. Text of the communiqué, N.D. TC-49.
2. Zoller: op. cit., p. 84.
3. Text in Baynes: vol. ii, pp. 1,585–6.

German people. Violence and stupidity tore them arbitrarily from their ancient historic setting and at last through their inclusion in the artificial construction of Czechoslovakia created a hot-bed of continual unrest. ... The Czechoslovak State has proved its inability to live its own internal life, and in consequence has now fallen into dissolution.[1]

There followed the text of the decree establishing the Protectorate of Bohemia and Moravia.

As a contemptuous sop to the Western Powers, Hitler recalled the 'moderate' Neurath and named him the first Protector. But the real power over the Czechs lay in the hands of the Head of the Civil Administration and the Secretary of State. To these two offices Hitler appointed Henlein and Karl Hermann Frank, the leaders of the Sudeten German Party, as a suitable reward for their services.

On the 16th Tiso sent Hitler a telegram asking him to take Slovakia under his protection, which had been drafted with German help during his visit to Berlin on the 13th. Hitler graciously responded and German troops promptly moved in to guarantee Slovakia's newly won independence. Ruthenia, however, which was no longer of interest to the Germans, was abandoned to the Hungarians. An appeal to Hitler and the proclamation of Ruthenian independence had no effect. Hungarian troops marched in, overrunning all opposition, and soon reached the Polish border, establishing the common frontier between Hungary and Poland which had been the aim of the two countries at the time of Munich.

Hitler did not stay long in Czechoslovakia. After reviewing his troops in Prague and paying a flying visit to Brünn, he was back in Vienna on the 18th. There the Treaty of Protection between Germany and Slovakia was drafted and initialled, before its final signature at Berlin on 23 March. Slovakia granted to Germany the right to maintain garrisons in its territory and promised to conduct its foreign policy in the closest agreement with its Protector. A secret protocol allowed Germany the fullest rights in the economic exploitation of the country.[2]

As the year before in Austria, so now in Czechoslovakia, the speed of the operation staggered the world. By the time the

1. Baynes: vol. ii, pp. 1,586–7.
2. Text of Treaty, N.D. 1,439-PS; Text of Secret Protocol, N.D. 2,793-PS.

British and French Ambassadors arrived to deliver their protests Hitler was already back in Vienna, the Protectorate had been established and the Treaty with Slovakia drawn up. Less than a week after Tiso had been summoned to Berlin, only four days after Hacha's arrival there, the occupation was complete, and German garrisons were established in Prague, Brünn and Slovakia.

Nowhere was the German action more resented than in Rome. Attolico, the Italian Ambassador in Berlin, had only been informed of the German intentions on 14 March, and Ciano wrote in his Diary: 'The Axis functions only in one of its parts which tends to preponderate, and acts entirely on its own initiative with little regard for us.'[1]

The arrival of Philip of Hesse with his usual message of thanks for Italy's unshakeable support scarcely mollified Mussolini. 'The Italians will laugh at me,' he told Ciano; 'every time Hitler occupies a country he sends me a message.' The Duce was gloomy and worried. The prospect of the expansion of German influence down the Danube and in the Balkans, his own chosen sphere of interest, had shaken him badly, but anger was tempered by the calculation that Hitler was now too powerful to oppose and that it was best to be on the winning side. German reassurances that the Mediterranean and Adriatic were Italy's, and that Germany would never meddle there, Mussolini received with appropriate scepticism. The message was very interesting, he remarked to his son-in-law, 'provided we can believe it'. But by the same evening he had swung back in favour of Germany again, expressing violent irritation with the Western Democracies, and declaring: 'We cannot change our policy now. After all, we are not political whores.'

Mussolini was the prisoner of his own policy. Hitler's success roused his envy, yet the more he attempted to imitate the Führer the more dependent he became upon him. A personal letter from Hitler on the twentieth anniversary of the Fascist movement helped to smooth the Duce's ruffled feathers, and by 26 March he was making a speech full of aggressive loyalty to the Axis. If he was to find compensation it must be within the framework of the Axis, not outside it. The Duce's eyes began to wander towards Albania.

1. *Ciano's Diary, 1939–43* (English translation, London, 1947), p. 44.

In London the effects of Hitler's *coup* were more far-reaching. Prague has rightly been taken as the turning point in British foreign policy, the stage at which the British Government set to work, however ineptly, to organize resistance to any further aggressive move by the German dictator. But it is important not to confuse what became clear later, looking back from subsequent events, with what was realized at the time. The British Government had not yet made up their minds to war nor abandoned hope of a general settlement. As Sir Samuel Hoare put it later: 'The lesson of Prague was not that further efforts for peace were futile, but rather that, without greater force behind them, negotiations and agreements with Hitler were of no permanent value.'[1] Attempts at negotiation and a peaceful settlement of Hitler's demands on Poland continued right up to September 1939; the introduction of conscription, the guarantees to Poland and Rumania were not, in themselves, effective measures to check Hitler. But, however inadequate, they marked a shift in British policy and, as a result, a contraction of Hitler's diplomatic freedom of manoeuvre *vis-à-vis* the Western Powers when he attempted to repeat the tactics of Vienna and Prague in the case of Danzig. After Prague, although Hitler was extremely reluctant to recognize it, the chances of further successes on the cheap in foreign policy were steadily diminishing. A chapter was closed. If he persisted in his plans, a new chapter would open in which his triumphs would have to be achieved under new conditions.

Yet it is easy to be misled by this. It was, after all, only a change in the circumstances, not in the character, of Hitler's foreign policy which took place with the occupation of Bohemia and Moravia. Much has been made of the fact that by his seizure of lands inhabited by Czechs, not by Germans, Hitler had now departed from the principle of self-determination to which he had hitherto appealed. It is certainly true that it was this change of front which caught the attention of many people in Western Europe who had hitherto been impressed by Hitler's advocacy of the right of the Germans to self-determination. Thus Sir Nevile Henderson wrote: 'By the occupation of Prague Hitler put himself unquestionably in the wrong, and destroyed the entire arguable validity of the German case as regards the Treaty of Versailles.'[2]

1. Viscount Templewood (Sir Samuel Hoare): *Nine Troubled Years* (London, 1954), p. 377.
2. Henderson: p. 209.

But it is not true, as Henderson goes on to say, that 'after Prague, Nazism ceased to be national and racial, and became purely dynamic and felonious'. Nazism had always been dynamic. Hitler's adoption of the phraseology of national self-determination was no more to be taken seriously than his use of the language of the League when that suited his purpose. A master of opportunism, he used whatever pretext came to hand – equality of rights, the defence of Europe against Bolshevism, the Wilsonian right of self-determination, Germany's need of *Lebensraum*. Prague destroyed a good many illusions outside Germany, but it marked no essential change in Hitler's policy. In November 1937 at the secret conference recorded by Hossbach, Hitler had already named the overthrow of Czechoslovakia and Austria as his two objectives. Hitler had been wrong about the dates and wrong about the circumstances: he had secured both Austria and Czechoslovakia more quickly and more easily than he expected in November 1937. But he had been right about the things that mattered, the objectives to go for and the chances of securing them without intervention by the other Powers. And Austria and Czechoslovakia were only the preliminaries to that programme of eastwards expansion which Hitler had drawn up in the pages of *Mein Kampf*.

Those who had been taken in by the arguments of self-determination made the same mistake as those who had imagined that Hitler would be bound by the Nazi Party Programme or by the policy of 'legality' after he became Chancellor. They failed to recognize that Hitler had only one programme: power, first his own power in Germany, and then the expansion of German power in Europe. The rest was window-dressing. This had been his programme before Prague, as it remained his programme afterwards. The only question was whether the other Powers would let him achieve the German domination of Europe without taking effective action to stop him.

In the spring of 1939, an official of the Propaganda Ministry remarked to a French acquaintance: 'We have before us so many open doors, so many possibilities, that we no longer know which way to turn, or which direction to take.' Hitler, however, knew very well which direction he meant to take: Europe was not to be left wondering for long.

CHAPTER NINE

HITLER'S WAR

1939

I

AFTER the annexation of Austria, Hans Dieckhoff, one of the senior men in the German Foreign Office, remarked to Ribbentrop that Bismarck would have taken years to consolidate his position before making another move. 'Then,' Ribbentrop retorted, 'you have no conception of the dynamics of National Socialism.'

The obvious weakness of Hitler's policy, the fault which destroyed him as surely as it had destroyed Napoleon, was his inability to stop. By the end of 1938 Hitler had transformed Germany's position in international affairs. He had everything to gain by waiting for a year or two before taking another step, sitting back to profit from the divisions and hesitations of the other European Powers, instead of driving them, by the fears he aroused, into reluctant combination. Moreover, a temporary relaxation of the rearmament drive would have had considerable economic benefits for Germany.

A fortnight after the Munich Agreement was signed, however, on 14 October Göring presided over a conference at which he demanded an acceleration of the German rearmament programme. Some weeks later, at a meeting of the Reich Defence Council on 18 November, Göring spoke at length on the need to concentrate all the resources of the nation on raising the level of rearmament from a current index of 100 to one of 300. Everything was to be subordinated to this single task, regardless of the fact, which Göring frankly admitted, that the German economy was already showing the strain of the armament programme.

Alarmed at the financial consequences of Göring's new measures, Schacht, as President of the Reichsbank, presented a memorandum signed by the directors of the Bank, protesting against the Government's reckless expenditure. This was on 7 January 1939. Hitler sent for Schacht and, instead of discussing his memorandum, handed him his dismissal. 'You don't fit into the National Socialist picture,' he told him.[1] As President of the

1. Schacht: *Account Rendered*, pp. 132–7.

Reichsbank Schacht was replaced by the docile Funk, and all but two of the Bank's directors were removed. A secret decree was promulgated abolishing the collegial constitution of the Bank and placing it under the direct orders of the Führer, with the obligation to provide the Government with whatever credits it demanded.

There was no question about the purpose of this rearmament: it was to strengthen Hitler's hand in foreign policy. The liquidation of Czechoslovakia was the first of Hitler's immediate objectives, but this by no means occupied all his attention. The annexation of Austria and the destruction of the Czechoslovak State, as he had made clear in the conference of November 1937, were only the preliminaries to the further development of his foreign policy.

If any country had good reason to fear Germany's intentions it was Poland. At the Peace Settlement of 1919, and afterwards when Germany was weak, the Poles had acquired territory, the loss of which was more resented by the Germans than perhaps any other part of the Versailles Settlement. In order to provide Poland with access to the sea, Danzig was separated from Germany and made into a Free City, where the Poles enjoyed special privileges, while East Prussia was divided from the rest of the Reich by the Polish Corridor. There was justice on both sides. Much of the land regained by Poland has been first seized by Prussia at the time of the Partitions, and was inhabited by Poles. But the Poles, especially in Silesia, had in turn taken more than they could legitimately claim. German governments, long before Hitler, had continually protested against the injustice of Germany's eastern frontiers, and German public opinion was as solid in demanding that they should be redrawn as Polish opinion was in refusing it. The rise of the Nazis to power in Germany had been followed by the steady growth of Nazi influence in Danzig, and it appeared only a question of time before the city was reunited to the Reich.

Yet the first country with which Hitler had signed a Pact of Non-Aggression had been Poland, and for five years he treated Poland in the friendliest fashion, despite the unpopularity of such a policy in Germany. The obvious reason for Hitler's attitude was his need to placate the most suspicious of Germany's neighbours and France's principal ally in Eastern Europe, until he was strong enough to risk her hostility with equanimity. But there is also evidence to show that, as Göring believed, Hitler was anxious to secure Polish support against Russia. With his Austrian outlook on European politics Hitler did not share the traditional North German dislike of the Poles, or the feeling of a common interest with Russia in suppressing an independent Polish State, which had played so large a part in shaping Prussian policy in the past. The essential condition, in Hitler's view, was the willingness of the Poles to accept the restoration of Danzig to Germany and other changes in their western frontiers, in return for which they would eventually find compensation eastwards against Russia.

The question was whether the Polish Government would accept the role of Germany's ally in Hitler's schemes of eastward expansion. This question was the more difficult for the Poles to answer since their own distrust of Russia virtually ruled out the logical alternative to accepting Hitler's offer, that of combining with Russia to present a solid resistance to Germany's ambitions. Polish policy aimed at independence of both her great neighbours, but Poland's strength was inadequate to maintain such a position. The result was to leave Poland isolated, and at the mercy of an agreement between Germany and Russia to partition her territory between them.

Hitler adopted the policy of such an agreement with Russia, however, only after the failure of his first plan, a German–Polish alliance against Russia. Our information of these exchanges between Poland and Germany is derived from *The Polish White Book*,[1] and from the German diplomatic documents.[2] The matter was first broached shortly after Munich, at a time when the Poles were anxious to secure a Hungarian occupation of Ruthenia, and the consequent suppression of the Ukrainian National movement which was causing trouble among their own Ukrainian population. On 24 October 1938, Ribbentrop invited the Polish Ambassador, Josef Lipski, to lunch at the Grand Hotel in Berchtesgaden, and, after listening to his outline of Polish wishes in regard to Ruthenia, suddenly turned the conversation to the question of Polish relations with Germany. The time had come, Ribbentrop declared, for a general settlement of the issues outstanding between the two countries. He put forward proposals for Poland's consideration, of which the two most important were the return of the Free State of Danzig to the Reich, and the construction of a German extra-territorial road and railway

1. *Polish White Book: Official Documents concerning Polish–German and Polish–Soviet Relations, 1933–9* (London, 1940).
2. See especially G.D., D.V.

across the Polish Corridor to link East Prussia with the rest of Germany.

At this stage Ribbentrop was still friendly; he invited Colonel Beck, the Polish Foreign Minister, to come to Germany to discuss the situation, and made a number of additional proposals to Lipski in return for Polish acquiescence in Germany's demands. Besides providing Poland with a free port at Danzig, together with a Polish extra-territorial road and railway, Germany would be prepared to extend the German–Polish Pact and to guarantee her existing frontiers with Poland. The Polish account contains two further suggestions which the Germans took care to omit when they published their White Book.

As a possible sphere for future cooperation between the two countries the German Foreign Minister specified joint action in colonial matters and the emigration of Jews from Poland, *and a joint policy towards Russia on the basis of the Anti-Comintern Pact*. . . . He added that, if the Polish Government agreed to the German conception regarding Danzig and the Motor Road, the question of Ruthenia could be solved in accordance with Poland's attitude to the matter.[1]

There was nothing new in this suggestion of German–Polish cooperation against Russia; it had been made a score of times by Göring in the past five years. So far the invitation had been evaded by Beck, and Hitler had not been pressing. But the introduction of Danzig put the whole matter in a different light. As Beck later told Lipski, at the time the negotiations were being conducted for the original German–Polish Agreement of January 1934, Marshal Pilsudski had laid down the axiom that Danzig was the surest criterion for Germany's intentions towards Poland. For the first time the question of Danzig had been raised between the two Governments, and Beck could have little doubt that Ribbentrop's proposals were being made with a sense of immediacy which had been lacking from Göring's expansive gestures.

The success of Beck's policy of independence had so far rested on the fact that neither Germany nor the Soviet Union had wished to bring pressure to bear on the Poles; it was now to be subjected to its first real test. Hitler limited his demands in the first place to Danzig and a road and railway across the Corridor, but not a single Pole believed that, once these had been conceded, Hitler would not demand the cession of the provinces of Posen and Polish Silesia. Nor did Beck consider Ribbentrop's vague offer of alliance against Russia at all seriously, since he saw quite

1. *Polish White Book*, pp. 47–8. (Author's italics.)

correctly that it would reduce Poland to the subordinate status of a German satellite. On the other hand, although he did his best to renew such links as he had with Moscow – a joint statement of Russo-Polish friendship was issued on 26 November and trade talks begun – he was equally opposed to becoming too dependent upon Russia either. The most he could do was to try to persuade the Germans not to press their demands, at the same time making it clear to them that any attempt to annex Danzig by force would lead to war.

A further conversation between Ribbentrop and Lipski took place on 19 November, and was followed by the visit of Beck to Berchtesgaden for talks with Hitler and his Foreign Minister at the beginning of January. At the end of January Ribbentrop went to Warsaw. In the course of these conversations, which were still conducted in a friendly atmosphere, the position of both sides was more clearly defined. Hitler declared that a strong Poland was an absolute necessity for Germany. 'Every Polish division engaged against Russia was a corresponding saving of a German division.'[1] But 'Danzig is German, will always remain German, and will sooner or later become part of Germany'.[2] In return for Danzig and the grant of extra-territorial communications with East Prussia, Hitler was prepared to offer the fullest safeguards for Poland's economic interests in the city, and a German guarantee of Poland's frontiers.

However carefully wrapped up, Beck's reply was a blank refusal. He was willing to discuss a German–Polish agreement about Danzig to replace the existing League of Nations régime, but not to consider the return of Danzig to the Reich. He was prepared to improve German communications with East Prussia, but not to agree to an extra-territorial road across the Corridor. Ribbentrop's persistence entirely failed to alter Beck's attitude. The Polish Foreign Minister protested, with some reason, that on both issues Polish opinion was too strong to allow him to give any other reply, even if he had wished to.

It was unlikely that Hitler would allow this situation to continue indefinitely. On 24 November, after Ribbentrop's second conversation with Lipski, he revised his secret Directive to the Armed Forces to provide for a further contingency: a lightning occupation of Danzig by German forces, for which plans were

1. Beck's Minute of his conversation with Hitler at Berchtesgaden, 5 January 1939. *Polish White Book*, No. 48.
2. G.D., D.V, No. 119.

to be submitted by 10 January.[1] Although he knew nothing of this, after his conversations at Berchtesgaden Beck told Ribbentrop that he was in a pessimistic mood. 'Particularly in regard to the Danzig question, as it had been raised by the Chancellor, he saw no possibility whatever of agreement.'[2] But, for the moment, it suited Hitler not to press his demands on Poland. He had first to complete the liquidation of Czechoslovakia. At Berchtesgaden he assured Beck that there would be no *fait accompli* in Danzig, and in his speech of 30 January he made his customary friendly reference to Poland and the five-year-old German–Polish Agreement. After that there was silence for the next seven weeks.

Then came the occupation of Bohemia-Moravia, and the German assumption of a protectorate over Slovakia. At once the situation was transformed. Although the Hungarian occupation of Ruthenia removed Polish anxieties about the Ukrainian National movement, German garrisons in Slovakia on the southern flank of Poland (there were already German troops on Poland's northern and western frontiers) were taken in Warsaw as a step explicitly directed against Polish security. The deliberate neglect of the Germans to inform them in advance increased the Polish Government's alarm.

Nor was this the end of the surprises Germany had in store for Poland. Immediately after the occupation of Prague, Ribbentrop presented an ultimatum to the Lithuanian Government demanding the return of the Memelland, a strip of territory on the northern frontier of East Prussia which Germany had lost by the Treaty of Versailles. No country was more interested than Poland in any change in the *status quo* along the Baltic coast, yet Ribbentrop again refused to give any information beforehand to the Polish Ambassador.

There was no question of Lithuanian resistance to Germany, and a week after reviewing his troops in Prague Hitler arrived in Memel by sea to acclaim the return of the city to the Reich. 'You have returned,' he told the Memellanders, 'to a mighty new Germany . . . a Germany determined to be the mistress of her own destiny and herself to fashion that destiny, even if that should not please the world without. For this new Germany today over eighty million Germans take their stand.'[3]

For the moment the focus of Western anxieties was Rumania,

1. N.D. C-137.
2. *Polish White Book*, No. 49.
3. Speech at Memel, 23 March 1939 (Baynes; vol. II, pp. 1,588–9).

where Herr Wohltat was engaged in negotiating a far-reaching economic agreement on behalf of the Reich. On 17 March the Rumanian Minister in London, M. Tilea, saw Lord Halifax and spoke in alarming terms of a German ultimatum and the possibility of a German invasion of his country. Whether Tilea's information was accurate or not, his action was swiftly repudiated by the Rumanian Government, which, on 23 March, proceeded to sign the Agreement with Germany without further demur. Since the Treaty established a dominant position for Germany in the development of Rumania's very considerable agricultural and mineral resources, it appeared unlikely that Hitler would make a further move in that direction. The Hungarians, whose eagerness to recover Transylvania had been encouraged by the Germans as an additional way of squeezing the Rumanians, were abruptly reined back, and an uneasy peace descended on the Balkans.

For it was on Poland that Hitler's attention was now fixed, and even before the annexation of Memel and the signing of the Treaty with Rumania the Germans had renewed their proposals in a peremptory tone. On 21 March, Ribbentrop again asked the Polish Ambassador to call on him. The interview seems to have been conducted with some acerbity on both sides. Lipski complained of the German action in Slovakia, which had been undertaken without a word to the Poles. Ribbentrop replied that, if the matter of Danzig and the extra-territorial road and railway to East Prussia could be settled to Germany's satisfaction, the Slovak question could doubtless be dealt with in such a way as to remove Polish anxieties. But a settlement of the issues between Germany and Poland could no longer be delayed. The Führer had been disagreeably surprised at the failure of the Poles to make any constructive reply to his proposals, and it was important that he should not come to the conclusion that Poland was rejecting his offer. For that reason it would be advisable for Colonel Beck to come to Berlin as soon as possible, and for the Ambassador to report to Warsaw at once.

The terms of the German offer remained the same, and Lipski records that Ribbentrop 'emphasized that obviously an understanding between us would have to include explicit anti-Soviet tendencies. . . .'[1] Hitler was now determined to press the Poles hard, but he was still thinking in terms of a peaceful settlement which would bind the Poles more closely to Germany. This is

1. *Polish White Book*, No. 61. The German account of the meeting, which omits any mention of Russia, is given in G.D., D.VI, No. 61.

confirmed by the record of a talk which Hitler had with the Commander-in-Chief of the Army, General von Brauchitsch, on 25 March.

The Führer [Brauchitsch noted] does not wish to solve the Danzig question by the use of force. He would not like to drive Poland into the arms of Great Britain by doing so. . . .

For the time being the Führer does not intend to solve the Polish question. It should now be worked on, but a solution in the near future would have to be based on exceptionally favourable political conditions. In that case Poland will be knocked out so completely that it need not be taken into account as a political factor for the next few decades. The Führer has in mind as such a solution a border-line advanced from the eastern tip of East Prussia to the eastern tip of Upper Silesia. Evacuation and re-settlement are questions that remain open. The Führer does not want to go into the Ukraine. Possibly one could establish a Ukrainian State. But these questions also remain open.[1]

Brauchitsch's notes afford some insight into Hitler's mind at this time, immediately after Prague and Memel. Danzig was the next problem to be dealt with, but at this stage Hitler did not intend – as he had always intended with the Sudetenland in the case of Czechoslovakia – to use Danzig as a pretext for the destruction of the Polish State. He would have been glad enough to recover Danzig without making enemies of the Poles. On the other hand, he was not prepared to wait indefinitely for the Poles, and, if he had to use force, then characteristically he would impose a really drastic settlement upon the Poles, the outline of which he had ready at the back of his mind. Everything depended upon the answer the Poles gave him in the next few days.

II

On Sunday 26 March Lipski, newly returned from Warsaw, handed Ribbentrop the Polish reply to the proposals renewed on 21 March. The Polish Government was prepared to discuss Danzig as well as German communications with East Prussia, and was anxious to reach a settlement with Germany on both; but the German demands, the return of Danzig and the extra-territorial road and railway, were unacceptable and were once again rejected. Ribbentrop received Lipski coldly and began to threaten. The Poles had been taking mobilization measures. 'It reminded him of certain risky steps taken by another State

1. N.D., R-100.

(obviously he was thinking of Czechoslovakia). He added that all aggression on our part (against Danzig) would be an aggression against the Reich.'[1]

The next day Ribbentrop summoned Lipski for a further interview, told him the Polish counter-proposals were wholly unsatisfactory, began blustering about Polish outrages against the German minority in Poland and warned him that the German Press could hardly be restrained much longer from answering Polish attacks. On 28 March Beck sent for the German Ambassador in Warsaw and replied to Ribbentrop's statement on Polish aggression against Danzig with the announcement that the Polish Government would equally regard any attempt by the Germans, or by the Danzig Senate, to change the *status quo* in the Free City as an act of aggression against Poland.

THE GERMAN AMBASSADOR: You want to negotiate at the point of the bayonet!
COLONEL BECK: That is your own method.[2]

So far the exchanges between Germany and Poland had followed a course which, if not that desired by Hitler, had certainly been foreseen by him. The next stage, foreshadowed by Ribbentrop's threatening tone on 26 and 27 March, was to be the application of pressure to the recalcitrant Poles. At this stage, however, the situation was complicated by the unexpected intervention of the British Government, which, to Hitler's anger, refused to mind its own business and disinterest itself in what was happening in Eastern Europe. Alarming reports were reaching London of German preparations for immediate action against Danzig and Poland. This time British intervention did not take the form it had taken in September 1938 of offering to secure satisfaction for Germany's demands with the object of avoiding war. On 31 March the British Prime Minister announced in the House of Commons: 'In the event of any action which clearly threatens Polish independence, and which the Polish Government accordingly consider it vital to resist with their national forces, H.M. Government would feel themselves bound at once to lend the Polish Government all support in their power.' The French Government associated themselves with the British in these assurances.

1. Lipski's Report to Beck, *Polish White Book*, No. 63.
2. *Polish White Book*. No. 64.

Mr Chamberlain's sudden decision to offer an unconditional guarantee to Poland, followed within a fortnight by similar guarantees to Rumania and Greece, was criticized in Great Britain at the time, and has continued to be criticized since, as a maladroit method of meeting the threat of further German aggression. But this criticism, however just, does not alter the fact that, from Hitler's point of view, he was now confronted with a new situation, principally as a result of his decision to overrun the remainder of Czechoslovakia only six months after the Munich Agreement.

Hitler was both surprised and angered by the British Government's declaration. Admiral Canaris, who was with him soon after the news came from London, reported that he flew into a passion, hammered on the table-top, and stormed up and down the room. 'I'll cook them a stew that they'll choke on,' he shouted.[1] When he spoke at Wilhelmshaven on 1 April, the day after Chamberlain's announcement in the House, he insisted excitedly that he was not to be turned from the path he had chosen. Germany could not submit to intimidation or encirclement.

When folk in other countries say that now they are arming and that they will continuously increase their armaments, then to these statesmen I have only one thing to say: 'Me you will never tire.' I am determined to continue to march on this path, I am convinced that we shall advance faster than the others. . . . If anyone should really wish to pit his strength against ours with violence, then the German people is in the position to accept the challenge at any time: it is ready, too, and resolved. . . .[2]

In the same mood Hitler issued a new directive to his commanders on 3 April which listed as the three contingencies for which they were to prepare, the defence of the frontiers, Operation White (war with Poland), and the seizure of Danzig. Plans for Operation White, the aim of which was set as the smashing of the Polish armed forces, were to be ready by 1 September 1939, the actual date of the German invasion of Poland. German policy, the directive stated, continued to be based on the avoidance of trouble with Poland. But 'should Poland reverse her policy towards Germany and adopt a threatening attitude towards the Reich, we may be driven to a final settlement, notwithstanding the existing Pact with Poland'.[3] For the moment, however, Hitler

1. Canaris's account is repeated by H. B. Gisevius: *To the Bitter End* (London, 1948), p. 362.
2. Baynes: vol. ii, pp. 1,590–602.
3. N.D. C-120.

seems to have been at a loss how to proceed. This time the British Prime Minister showed no disposition to fly to Germany, and the Polish Foreign Minister, instead of coming to Berlin as Ribbentrop had demanded, visited London, where agreement was announced on the preparation of a pact of mutual assistance between Great Britain and Poland. Remarking on the signs of hesitation in Berlin, the French Chargé d'Affaires reported to Paris on 11 April:

For the first time the Third Reich has come up against a categorical no; for the first time a country has clearly expressed its determination to oppose force by force, and to reply to any unilateral movement with rifles and guns. This is the kind of language that is understood in Germany. But they have not been used to hearing it for a long time. It has also been difficult for them to believe their ears, and they still do not despair of wearing down Polish resistance in the long run.[1]

Grégoire Gafencu, the Rumanian Foreign Minister, who paid a visit to the Chancellery about this time (on 19 April, the eve of Hitler's fiftieth birthday), found him determined but calm on the subject of Poland. It was the mention of England which brought him out of his chair, pacing up and down the room and shouting out his resentment. Why, he demanded, were the British so obstinate that they could not see he wanted to arrive at an agreement with them? 'Well, if England wants war, she can have it. It will not be an easy war, as they like to think, nor a war fought in the way the last one was. England will not have the whole world on her side; this time, half at least will be on our side. And it will be a war of such destructiveness as no one has imagined. How can the English imagine what a modern war will be like when they are incapable of putting two fully equipped divisions in the field?'[2]

Some of the anger which Hitler felt at this check came out in his speech to the Reichstag at the end of the month. On 14 April, following the Italian invasion of Albania on the 7th, President Roosevelt had addressed a message to Mussolini and Hitler, asking if they were willing to give assurances against aggression to a long list of thirty countries. It was announced in Berlin that Hitler would reply to the President on 28 April.

Hitler began his speech with a lengthy and elaborate defence of his foreign policy, up to the present. This is so frequent a feature

1. M. de Vaux St Cyr to M. Bonnet, 11 April 1939; *French Yellow Book*, No. 97.
2. Grégoire Gafencu: *Derniers Jours de l'Europe* (Paris, 1946), p. 89.

of his speeches on foreign policy as to suggest that this act of self-justification, always beginning with the iniquities of the Treaty of Versailles, was psychologically necessary, in order to kindle the indignation and conviction with which he could defend the most blatant acts of aggression.

After describing his action in Czechoslovakia as a service to peace, Hitler passed to a consideration of German relations with Great Britain and with Poland. For Great Britain he had nothing but feelings of friendship and admiration, but friendship could only survive if it was placed upon the basis of mutual regard for each other's interests and achievements. This the British refused to recognize. The British now accepted war with Germany as inevitable, and had begun their old game of encircling Germany. With this the basis for the Anglo-German Naval Treaty of 1935 had been destroyed, and he had therefore decided to make a formal denunciation of it.

With Poland, too, Hitler declared, he had been only too anxious to reach a settlement. Poles and Germans had to live side by side, whether they liked it or not, and he had never ceased to uphold the necessity for Poland to have access to the sea. But Germany also had legitimate demands, for access to East Prussia and for the return of the German city of Danzig to the Reich. To solve the problem Hitler had made an unprecedented offer to Poland, the terms of which he now repeated, with the careful omission of the German invitation to join in a bloc directed against Russia. The Poles, however, had not only rejected his offer, but had begun to lend themselves – like the Czechs the year before – to the international campaign of lies against Germany. In these circumstances the German–Polish Agreement of 1934 had no longer any validity, and Hitler had therefore decided to denounce this too. He was careful to add, however, that the door to a fresh agreement between Germany and Poland was still open, and that he would welcome such an agreement, provided it was upon equal terms.

Throughout this speech Hitler spoke in violent terms of the 'international warmongers' in the Democracies, whose one aim was to misrepresent German aims and to stir up trouble. He boasted of the part German and Italian forces had played in Franco's victory, and exalted the strength of the Axis, congratulating Mussolini on the occupation of Albania and the establishment of order in a territory which naturally belonged to Italy's *Lebensraum.*

Hitler had by now worked himself into the state of mind in which he was prepared to give President Roosevelt his answer. The second half of his speech was marked by a display of sarcasm which produced roars of applause from the Reichstag, and from the delighted Göring, who presided. It is not difficult to pull holes in Hitler's argument when it is set down in cold print, or to point to the cheapness of his retorts, but to see and hear it brought to life on the film is to be struck once again by Hitler's mastery of irony and every other trick of the orator. As he delivered it, and as Germany heard it over the radio, it was a masterpiece of political propaganda, directed with equal skill at his German audience and at public opinion in the U.S.A.

The American President had read him a lesson on the wickedness and futility of war: who should know better, Hitler retorted, than the German people, who had suffered from the oppression of an unjust peace treaty for twenty years? Mr Roosevelt believed that all problems could be solved round the conference table: yet the first nation to express distrust of the League of Nations was the U.S.A., which refused to join it from the beginning. 'The freedom of North America was not achieved at the conference table, any more than the conflict between the North and South.' Mr Roosevelt's view, though it did him credit, found no support in the history of his own country, or of the rest of the world.

President Roosevelt pleaded for disarmament: the German people, trusting in the promises of another American President, had laid down their arms once before, only to be shamelessly treated by their enemies in the Peace Conference that followed. Germany was the one nation that had disarmed, only to see the other States repudiate their promises: the German people had had enough of unilateral disarmament.

Mr Roosevelt was much concerned about German intentions in Europe. If Germany inquired about American policy in Central and South America she would be referred to the Monroe Doctrine and told to mind her own business. None the less, Hitler had approached each of the States mentioned by the President and had asked them if they felt threatened by Germany, and if they had asked the American President to request guarantees on their behalf. The reply in all cases had been negative. Not all the States mentioned by the President, however, had been able to reply. In Syria and Palestine the views of the inhabitants could not be ascertained owing to the occupation by French and British – not German – troops. The German Government was still willing to

give assurances against aggression to any of the States referred to
by the President, provided only that they came forward and
asked for such assurances themselves.

Mr Roosevelt! I fully understand that the vastness of your nation and
the immense wealth of your country allow you to feel responsible for the
history of the whole world and for the history of all nations. I, sir, am
placed in a much smaller and more modest sphere.

I once took over a State, which was faced by complete ruin, thanks to
its trust in the promises of the rest of the world and to the bad régime of
democratic governments. . . .

Since then, Mr Roosevelt, I have only been able to fulfil one simple
task, I cannot feel myself responsible for the fate of the world, as this
world took no interest in the pitiful fate of my own people. I have regarded myself as called upon by Providence to serve my own people alone.
. . . I have lived day and night for the single task of awakening the
powers of my people, in view of our desertion by the rest of the world. . . .

I have conquered chaos in Germany, re-established order, enormously
increased production. . . . I have succeeded in finding useful work once
more for the whole of seven million unemployed. . . . Not only have I
united the German people politically, but I have also rearmed them. I
have also endeavoured to destroy sheet by sheet the treaty which in its
448 articles contains the vilest oppression which peoples and human
beings have ever been expected to put up with.

I have brought back to the Reich provinces stolen from us in 1919, I
have led back to their native country millions of Germans who were
torn away from us and were in misery, I have re-established the historic
unity of German living-space – and, Mr Roosevelt, I have endeavoured
to attain all this without spilling blood and without bringing to my
people, and consequently to others, the misery of war.

I, who twenty-one years ago was an unknown worker and soldier of
my people, have attained this, Mr Roosevelt, by my own energy. . . .
You, Mr Roosevelt, have a much easier task in comparison. You became
President of the United States in 1933 when I became Chancellor of the
Reich. From the very outset you stepped to the head of one of the largest
and wealthiest States in the world. . . . You have at your disposal the
most unlimited mineral resources in the world. . . . In spite of the fact
that the population of your country is scarcely one-third greater than
the number of inhabitants in Greater Germany, you possess more than
fifteen times as much living-space. Conditions prevailing in your country
are on such a large scale that you can find time and leisure to give your
attention to universal problems.

Your concerns and suggestions, therefore, cover a much larger area
than mine, because my world, Mr Roosevelt, in which Providence has
placed me and for which I am therefore obliged to work, is unfortunately
much smaller – although for me it is more precious than anything else,
for it is limited to my people.

I believe, however, that this is the way in which I can be of the most service to that for which we are all concerned, the justice, well-being, progress and peace of the whole human community.[1]

This speech of 28 April 1939 is one of the most effective defences Hitler ever made of his use of the power he had secured in 1933. Nor does it require much imagination to see how powerfully the argument of Hitler's closing passage must have appealed to the German people. Yet Hitler's real skill lay in his evasion of the simple question which President Roosevelt had posed: was Nazi Germany entertaining further schemes of aggression?

To this question Hitler, for obvious reasons, preferred to give no clear answer. Instead, he confused the issue by repeating his own highly selected and exaggerated account of the history of Germany since 1918, by pointing to the inconsistencies and short-comings of his critics, and by playing upon that historical pariah-complex of self-pity and self-justification which the German people had developed after the defeat of 1918. Even to question his intentions was made to appear as part of that denial of equal rights to the German people upon which he had fed his own and his audiences' indignation for so long.

From the point of view of the immediate situation the speech marked the close, rather than the opening, of a period of activity on Hitler's part. Having answered Polish obduracy and the British guarantees by the denunciation of the Naval Treaty and the German–Polish Pact, Hitler was content to sit back and wait. Even with the Poles the door had been left open to further negotiations, if the Poles should change their minds.

This attitude was not altered after Beck's reply to Hitler in his speech to the Polish Diet on 5 May. Rejecting Hitler's account of the negotiations between Poland and Germany and reaffirming Poland's determination not to agree to the German demands, Beck spoke of 'various other hints made by representatives of the Reich Government which extended much further than the subjects of discussion. I reserve the right to return to this matter if necessary.'[2] This covert reference to suggestions of a joint German–Polish front against Russia, and Beck's declaration that peace could be bought too dearly, if it was at the price of national honour, did not, however, stir Hitler to reply. The German Press,

1. Full text in *Documents on International Affairs, 1939–46* (London, 1951), vol. I, March–September 1939, pp. 214–56.
2. *Polish White Book*, No. 77, Report of Beck's Speech.

too, was kept under restraint. Reporting to Paris early in May, the French Ambassador in Berlin wrote:

As far as the actual substance of the dispute is concerned, the two parties remain in their respective positions. Each maintains that it is up to the other to make a gesture. Actually, on the German side, they anticipate that Poland will soon grow tired of her 'heroic' attitude, will exhaust herself financially and morally, and that she will be given to understand from London and Paris that nobody is anxious to fight for the sake of Danzig. 'Danzig is not worth a European war' – this seems to be the catch-phrase of German propaganda.[1]

III

There were no further negotiations with the Poles before the outbreak of war and none with the British until the middle of August. Throughout the summer of 1939, from the end of April to August, Hitler was little to be seen in public, made no important pronouncements and only came infrequently to Berlin. Most of the time he spent at Berchtesgaden. He could have devised no better tactics for the occasion. The measures hastily improvised by the Chamberlain Government had been due to the sense of urgency created by his action in Czechoslovakia and the Memelland. Once the tension relaxed, the feeling of compulsion disappeared, and there was a good chance that London and Paris might be tempted to reduce rather than extend the obligations they had assumed. The British Government was still eager to avoid war and find a settlement, while in Paris the currents of appeasement and defeatism still ran strongly beneath the surface. Nor was the guarantee which had been given to Poland of practical value, unless the Russians could be brought in as well. No effective opposition to Germany could be organized in Eastern Europe without the Soviet Union.

The Chamberlain Government was reluctant to accept such a conclusion, and still more reluctant to act upon it. Although, under strong pressure from their critics, they opened negotiations in Moscow, they pursued them without conviction. The Russians, on their side, looked upon Western policy with distrust and were determined not to accept any obligations towards Poland except as part of a mutual assistance pact binding Britain and France as well as themselves to the defence of Eastern Europe including

1. M. Coulondre to M. Bonnet, 9 May 1939; *French Yellow Book*, No. 125.

the Soviet Union. Even if the British were prepared to undertake such a commitment – and they were not – they were confronted with the refusal of the Poles and the other peoples living between Germany and Russia to accept help from a country they regarded with as much suspicion as the Germans.

Here was a situation from which Hitler not find it hard to extract profit. 'During the next four months,' wrote Sir Nevile Henderson, 'the chief impression which I had of Hitler was that of a master chess-player studying the board and waiting for his opponent to make some false move which could be turned to his advantage.'[1]

Throughout the summer the remilitarization of Danzig, the training of the local S.S. and S.A. with arms smuggled across the frontier, and a series of incidents designed to provoke the Poles, continued with little remission. In the middle of June, Goebbels appeared in the city and made two violent speeches, reaffirming the German claim to its return.

While pressure was kept up on Poland, German propaganda through the radio and the Press hammered home the argument that Danzig was not worth a war, and that war was only likely because of the obstinacy of the Poles. In their turn the Poles were warned not to trust their new friends, the British, who would soon tire of their energetic attitude, and sell them down the river, as they had sold the Czechs at Munich.

The centre of diplomatic activity during the summer was not Berlin, but Moscow. From time to time, however, Weizsäcker, the State Secretary at the Wilhelmstrasse, saw the British and French Ambassadors in Berlin in order to sound them out. His arguments always followed the same course: the rashness of Britain and France in handing over the decision of peace or war to an irresponsible people like the Poles. Britain, he told Henderson on 13 June, had abandoned her traditional policy of no continental entanglements. 'Instead of this, Britain was now committing herself more and more on the Continent, and permitting the Poles to gamble with the destiny of Great Britain.'[2]

Meanwhile, relations with the other States in the German sphere of influence were strengthened, in order to keep Poland isolated. The visit of the Hungarian Prime Minister and Foreign Minister to Berlin, at the end of April, was followed by the State visit of

1. Henderson: *Failure of a Mission*, p. 228.
2. G.D., D.VI, No. 521.

Prince Paul, the Regent of Yugoslavia, at the beginning of June. Hitler laid himself out to please, and, in addition to a gala performance at the Opera and a State banquet, there was an impressive military review. A month later the Bulgarian Prime Minister was fêted in the German capital. The Germans showed an equal interest in the Baltic. The Pact of Non-Aggression signed with Lithuania after the cession of Memelland was matched by similar pacts with Latvia and Estonia, the governments of which had already communicated to London their wish to be left out of any attempt to organize collective security in Eastern Europe.

Hitler's greatest success, however, was his alliance with Italy. The invasion of Albania in April, which Mussolini and Ciano regarded as the assertion of Italian independence, only bound them more closely to the Axis. Hitler was delighted: the Italian action underlined the common interest of the two dictatorships in face of the defenders of the *status quo*, Great Britain and France. The Germans now began to press for the signature of the military alliance which Mussolini had so far evaded. Ciano was uneasy about the state of German–Polish relations. After conversations with Göring in April, he noted in his diary that Göring's remarks about Poland were reminiscent of the tone used at other times about Austria and Czechoslovakia. These anxieties were increased by the reports of Attolico, the Italian Ambassador in Berlin. Ciano, therefore, invited Ribbentrop to come to Italy, in the hope of learning what was in Hitler's mind, and set off for their meeting at Milan (on 6 May) with a memorandum in which the Duce laid great stress on Italy's need of peace for a period of not less than three years.

Ciano found Ribbentrop reassuring. He did not disguise Hitler's determination to recover Danzig and secure his motor road to East Prussia, but he was sympathetic to Mussolini's insistence on the need to defer war. 'Germany, too,' he remarked, 'is convinced of the necessity for a period of peace, which should not be less than four or five years.'[1]

After dinner Ciano telephoned to Mussolini and reported that the conversations were going well. Thereupon the Duce, on the spur of the moment, apparently swayed by a gust of anti-British irritation after a year's hesitations and doubts, ordered Ciano to publish the news that an Italo-German alliance had been agreed upon. Ribbentrop would have preferred to wait until he could bring in Japan as well, but when he telephoned to Hitler he found

1. Ciano's Minutes, *Ciano's Diplomatic Papers*, pp. 282–7.

the Führer eager to seize the chance offered by Mussolini's sudden change of mind, and dutifully agreed in turn. The announcement of the alliance, Hitler was convinced, would further weaken the British and French resolution to stand by Poland, and he took care to draft the agreement in the most far-reaching terms. The Italians accepted the German draft with very few changes, and on 21 May Ciano arrived in Berlin for the formal signature of the Pact of Steel.

Hitler looked upon the Pact as a triumph for his diplomacy, and great publicity was given to the ceremony at which it was signed. The Chancellery was crowded with brilliant uniforms, resplendent with decorations. Ciano had invested Ribbentrop with the Collar of the Annunziata the evening before, thereby making him the cousin of the King of Italy, and seriously offending Göring, who noisily declared that he should have received the decoration as the real architect of the Alliance. Hitler, in the best of tempers, presided while the two Foreign Ministers affixed their signatures. He had every reason to be pleased with himself.

The preamble of the Treaty announced that 'the German and Italian nations are determined to act side by side and with united forces for the securing of their living-space and the maintenance of peace'.

Article II: Should the common interest of the contracting parties be endangered by international events of any kind whatever, they will immediately enter into discussions over the measures to be taken for the protection of these interests.

If the security or vital interests of one of the contracting parties be threatened from outside, the other will give the threatened party full political and diplomatic support in order to set aside this threat.

Article III: If, contrary to the wishes and hopes of the contracting parties, it should happen that one of them is involved in hostilities with another Power or Powers, the other contracting party will come immediately to its side as ally and support it with all its military forces on land, sea, and in the air. . . .

Article V: The contracting parties undertake now that in the event of a war conducted in common they will conclude an armistice and peace only in full agreement with each other.[1]

The Alliance was followed by an agreement on the vexed question of the South Tyrol, which was intended as a gesture on Hitler's part towards his Italian friends. Hitler agreed to the

1. Text of the Treaty in *Documents on International Affairs, 1939–46*, vol. I, pp. 168–70.

transfer of all persons of German nationality from the South Tyrol to the Reich, thereby showing complete disregard for the principle of nationality to which he had so often appealed, but complete consistency with the views he had expressed in *Mein Kampf.*

Mussolini's chief anxiety, however, continued to be the possibility of war. On 30 May, the day before General Cavallero left Rome to serve on the military commission set up under the new Pact, the Duce gave him a secret memorandum for Hitler which repeated many of the points Mussolini had laid down in his memorandum for Ciano before the Milan meeting. He re-emphasized Italy's need of a preparatory period of peace extending as far as the end of 1942, and spoke of the advantages to be gained by further undermining of the Western Powers' will to resist. Hitler's reply was a vague suggestion that he should meet the Duce for a discussion some time in the near future. Beyond that he made no comment, and his silence seems to have been accepted by the Italians as assent.

Had Mussolini been present when Hitler met his senior Army, Navy, and Air Force officers on 23 May, the day after the Pact of Steel had been signed, his anxiety would have been vastly increased. The meeting, like that of November 1937, was held in the Führer's study in the Reich Chancellery. The audience this time numbered fourteen, all from the Services. Among those present were Göring, Generals von Brauchitsch, Keitel, and Halder, and Admiral Raeder; the record of Hitler's remarks was taken by his adjutant, Lieutenant-Colonel Schmundt.

Hitler began from the same premises as in November 1937: the problem of *Lebensraum,* and the need to solve it by expansion eastwards. Once again he ruled out a colonial solution as an alternative. This time, however, he passed rapidly over the assumptions on which his views were based, and came almost at once to the military problem.

War, Hitler told his officers, was inevitable.

Further successes can no longer be attained without the shedding of blood. . . .

Danzig is not the object of our activities. It is a question of expanding our living-space in the east, of securing our food-supplies, and of settling the Baltic problem. . . . There is no question of sparing Poland and we are left with the decision: To attack Poland at the first suitable opportunity.

We cannot expect a repetition of the Czech affair. There will be war. Our task is to isolate Poland. The success of this isolation will be decisive. ... There must be no simultaneous conflict with the Western Powers.

If it is not certain that German–Polish conflict will not lead to war in the west, the fight must be primarily against England and France.

Basic principle: Conflict with Poland – beginning with an attack on Poland -- will only be successful if the Western Powers keep out. If this is impossible, then it will be better to attack in the west and incidentally to settle Poland at the same time.[1]

Hitler then went on to discuss the character of a war with the British, whom he described as the driving force against Germany, and of whose strength he spoke with appreciation. It would, he declared, be a life-and-death struggle and probably of long duration. 'The idea that we can get off cheaply is dangerous; there is no such possibility. We must burn our boats. It is no longer a question of right or wrong, but of life or death for eighty million human beings.'

Much that Hitler said about the conduct of a war with Britain is of interest in the light of events a year later. He saw the Ruhr as Germany's vital point, and so made the occupation of Holland and Belgium, to protect the Ruhr, a first objective. Britain's weakness was her need of sea-borne supplies. The Army's task, therefore, must be to overrun the Low Countries and France in order to provide bases from which the Navy and Air Force could blockade Britain and cut off her supplies. Analysing the lessons of the First World War, Hitler argued that a wheeling movement by the German Army towards the Channel ports at the outbreak of war – instead of towards Paris – might well have been decisive. This was in fact to be his own strategy in 1940.

Hitler's object was still, as it had always been, continental expansion eastwards. The chief obstacle to his plans he now saw as England, not France as in *Mein Kampf*: indeed, there is barely a mention of France throughout Schmundt's minutes. War between Germany and Great Britain, Hitler was convinced, could not be avoided. On the other hand, he was not anxious to begin it yet. His immediate object, as it had been the year before in the case of Czechoslovakia, was a localized war to settle with Poland. This time there could be no question of a repetition of Munich: war was certain. The great question was whether Poland could be isolated and the war limited. This was his aim, but conceivably

1. N.D. L-79, *Documents on International Affairs, 1939–46*, vol. I, pp. 271–7.

he might fail. In that case Poland would be reduced to a side-issue, and the real struggle would be with the Western Powers. There was one other case in which it would be necessary to attack Britain and France at once: if they succeeded in establishing an alliance with Russia. But Hitler did not take this possibility very seriously and he expressed the belief that Russia might well disinterest herself in the fate of Poland altogether.

For all his air of finality on this occasion, Hitler took care to keep and exploit his freedom of diplomatic manoeuvre during the summer. War was not inevitable until the moment when the German armies crossed the Polish frontier on the morning of 1 September. But, granted Hitler's purpose of pursuing an expansionist policy, it was a sober and shrewd calculation of the risks. Its weakness was Hitler's failure to push his predictions far enough into the future, and to reckon with the importance of the U.S.A., or the strength of the Soviet Union. But, in the short run, Hitler was quite right in thinking that he could ignore both America and Russia, while his estimate of France's weakness and his grasp of how to attack Britain were to prove well-founded.

As it happens, we have a precise account of what German rearmament had achieved so far, given in a lecture by General Thomas, Head of the War Economy and Armaments Office, at the Foreign Office the day after Hitler's conference.[1] From the Peace Treaty army of seven infantry and three cavalry divisions, which Hitler had found on taking office, the German Army had been expanded to a peacetime strength of thirty infantry divisions (including four fully motorized and three mountain divisions), five newly equipped Panzer divisions, four light divisions, and twenty-two machine-gun battalions. In four years its peacetime strength had been increased from seven to fifty-one divisions, compared with an expansion from forty-three to fifty divisions in the period from 1898 to 1914.

Behind these forces there stood a steadily increasing number of reserves and the most powerful armaments industry in the world, which in time of peace had already equalled, and in part excelled, the production performances of the First World War. Nor had the Army been built up at the expense of the other branches of the armed forces. Since 1933 the German Navy had put into service two battleships of 26,000 tons; two armoured cruisers of 10,000 tons; seventeen destroyers, and forty-seven

1. N.D. EC-28, 24 May 1939.

U-boats. It had launched, and was engaged on completing, two more battleships of 35,000 tons (actually much larger, for one of them was the *Bismarck*); four heavy cruisers of 10,000 tons; an aircraft carrier; five destroyers, and seven U-boats. The German Air Force, which had been entirely built up since 1933, now had a strength of 260,000 men, with twenty-one squadrons consisting of 240 echelons. Its anti-aircraft forces, equipped with four standard types of A.A. guns, numbered close on three hundred batteries.

Such was the backing of force which Hitler had provided for his diplomacy. If, numerically, the number of divisions Germany could put in the field was still smaller than that of the French or Russian Armies, in quality, leadership, and equipment it was almost certainly an instrument without equal – and this time Hitler was determined to put it to use. By 15 June, he had the Army's plan for operations in Poland.[1] Brauchitsch defined the object of the operation as 'to destroy the Polish armed forces. The political leadership demands that the war should be begun by heavy surprise blows and lead to quick successes.' All preparations were to be complete by 20 August. On 22 June the O.K.W. presented a detailed timetable for the attack, for which reserves were to be called up on the pretext of autumn manoeuvres.[2] On the 24th, the Army was ordered to prepare plans for capturing the bridges over the Lower Vistula intact.[3] On the 23rd, Göring presided over a meeting of the Reich Defence Council attended by thirty-five ministers, generals and officials. The main items on the agenda were all connected with Hitler's decision to draft seven million men in the mobilization for war. Concentration camp prisoners and workers from Bohemia-Moravia would be used to augment Germany's manpower resources. Two further meetings of the Council were held in July.[4] A month later, on 27 July, the order was drafted for the occupation of Danzig, only the date being left blank for the Führer to write in.[5]

IV

Yet Hitler was in no hurry to move. Three months had passed since his speech of 28 April (from which, it was later noticed, he had omitted his customary attack on the Soviet Union). For three months the resolution of the Poles, and the determination

1. N.D. C-142.   2. N.D. C-126.   3. N.D. C-120.
4. N.D. 3787-PS.   5. N.D. C-30.

of the British and French to stand by their guarantees, had been subjected to strains, but had not been weakened. Only in one direction could Hitler see an opening, in Moscow. The British Government first broached the idea of negotiations to the Russians in the middle of April. On the 16th of that month, Litvinov made a formal proposal for a triple pact of mutual assistance to be signed by Britain and France and the U.S.S.R. and supported by a military convention. After three weeks' delay (during which Litvinov was turned out of office) the British virtually rejected the Russian proposal and it was not until 27 May, under strong pressure from many sides in London, that Chamberlain instructed the ambassador to put forward counter-proposals from the British and French governments.

Despite a specific Russian invitation, neither the British Foreign Secretary (Halifax) nor any other minister went to Moscow to conduct the negotiations. These made little progress during June, and on the 29th of that month Russian impatience was expressed in a special article written by Zhdanov and published by *Pravda* with the headline: 'British and French Governments Do Not Want a Treaty on the Basis of Equality for the U.S.S.R.'

None of this was missed in Germany. Hitler was very well-informed about the difficulties and suspicions on both sides. Without the support of Russia, the one Great Power near enough to give active help to Poland, the Anglo-French guarantees must lose much of their value. True, France and Britain could still attack Germany from the west; but this would not prevent the German Army overrunning Poland, and presenting the Western Powers with a *fait accompli* which would make their continuation of the war futile. Could Germany do anything to hinder the progress of the Moscow talks? Better still, was there a possibility of substituting for an agreement between Russia, Britain and France a Russo-German agreement, which would guarantee Russia's neutrality in the event of a war between Germany and Poland? In that case, it could be argued, Britain and France would be forced to recognize the impossibility of coming to the aid of Poland, and would either put pressure on the Poles to accept the German demands or disinterest themselves in what happened to Poland.

These possibilities were already being canvassed in the group around Hitler as early as March and April. During the winter attempts had been made to start negotiations for the renewal of the Russo-German economic agreement (which expired at the end of 1938). At first these made little progress but were later to provide a convenient means for each side to sound out the other's intentions. Stalin's speech of 10 March, with its warning that the U.S.S.R. would not let itself be manoeuvred by the Western Powers into a war with Germany, was carefully noted in Berlin, and in April, Göring and Mussolini agreed that it would be a good thing to put out feelers towards Moscow.[1] The very next day (17 April), the Soviet Ambassador made the first call at the German Foreign Office since his appointment nearly a year before and asked Weizsäcker point-blank what he thought about German–Russian relations: in the Russian view, ideological differences need not affect them and the Soviet Union had refrained from exploiting the present friction between Germany and the Western Powers. On 3 May Molotov replaced Litvinov (the man most closely identified with the policy of collective security and cooperation with the Western Powers) as Commissar for Foreign Affairs. Two days later, the Soviet Chargé d'Affaires, Astakhov, asked Schnurre, the German expert conducting the economic negotiations, 'whether this event would cause a change in our attitude towards the Soviet Union'.[2] These Russian soundings were repeated several times in the course of May.

The basis for a deal was obvious. In the long run war between Germany and Russia was inevitable, so long as Hitler persisted in looking for Germany's living-space in the east. But in the short run, the last thing Hitler wanted was to become involved with Russia while he was still occupied with Poland. Stalin, on his side, was eager to avoid or at least postpone any clash with Germany as long as possible. In default of an alternative, Stalin had put forward various schemes for collective security, but he had an inveterate distrust of the Western Powers, doubted their determination to resist Hitler if put to the test and suspected them of trying to embroil the Soviet Union with Germany as a way of weakening both régimes.

In such a frame of mind, Stalin was likely to look on a separate deal with Germany as very much to Russia's advantage. It would enable him to buy time at the expense of Poland, and possibly secure important territorial and strategic advantages in Eastern Europe as part of his price. These could be used to strengthen the Soviet Union against the day when Hitler might feel free to put his designs against Russia into operation. Even after the

1. G.D., D.VI, No. 211.
2. ibid., No. 332.

German attack on the U.S.S.R. in 1941, Stalin was still prepared to justify the Pact of 1939 along these lines.[1]

The obstacles in the way were twofold: the extreme distrust each side entertained towards the other, and the public commitments each had undertaken against the other. Hitler had made anti-Bolshevism a principal item of his propaganda stock-in-trade for twenty years, both in Germany and abroad; he had built up his foreign relations around the Anti-Comintern Pact, and, quite apart from propaganda, he had always looked towards Russia as the direction of Germany's future expansion. Next to anti-Semitism, with which it was partly identified, anti-Bolshevism had been the most consistent theme in his career. However opportunist his attitude, and however cynical his intentions towards Russia once the Pact had served its purpose, Hitler was bound to hesitate in face of such a repudiation of his own past.

But how seriously were such arguments to be taken? Once they had recovered their breath most people would be far more impressed by his astuteness in getting the Russians to sign than troubled about his inconsistency. A *rapprochement* with Russia would even be welcomed in certain quarters. In the German Army, always preoccupied with the danger of a war on two fronts, there had always been a school of thought which followed General von Seeckt's view and favoured active collaboration with Russia. In the German Foreign Office, too, a policy of friendship with Russia had not lacked advocates after 1918, and had found expression in the Treaty of Rapallo in 1922, when the two countries had formed a common front against the victor powers. (Von der Schulenberg, the German Ambassador in Moscow in 1939, was one of the last disciples of von Maltzan and Brockdorff-Rantzau, the architects of the Rapallo policy.) To those who were struggling with the economic problems of the Four-Year Plan, the ability to draw upon Russian resources in raw materials would be a godsend. Finally, there was the argument which weighed most of all with Hitler – this was the surest way to isolate Poland, to deter the Western Powers from interfering, and to keep any conflict localized.

The evidence suggests that Ribbentrop was an early advocate of a deal with Russia, while Hitler was slower to make up his mind and more wary. On or about 25 May Ribbentrop held a meeting in his country house at Sonnenburg attended by the

1. cf. Stalin's broadcast of 3 July 1941 in J. V. Stalin: *On the Great Patriotic War of the Soviet Union* (London, 1948).

State Secretary Weizsäcker and Gauss, the legal expert of the German Foreign Office. Draft instructions were drawn up for the German Ambassador in Moscow who was to approach Molotov and tell him: 'The time has come to consider a pacification and normalization of German–Soviet foreign relations.'[1] Hitler, however, first held up, then cancelled, these instructions. On the 26th, Weizsäcker telegraphed to the Ambassador to maintain 'an attitude of complete reserve'.[2] It was the opinion in Berlin, he wrote the next day, that an Anglo-Russian agreement would not be easy to prevent and that German intervention might 'perhaps call forth a peal of Tartar laughter'.[3] Then on the 30th Hitler changed his mind and Weizsäcker cabled: 'Contrary to the tactics hitherto planned we have now, after all, decided to make a certain degree of contact with the Soviet Union.'[4]

The Germans found the Russians tough and suspicious negotiators. Talks were conducted with Molotov and Mikoyan throughout June, but on the 29th Hitler ordered the German Ambassador to hold his hand. A pause of three weeks followed.

Then on 18 July the Russians took the initiative in proposing a renewal of the economic talks, and on the 22nd Weizsäcker instructed the German Ambassador to pick up the threads of the political negotiations 'without in any way pressing the matter'.[5]

Four days later, on the evening of 26 July, Schnurre, who was in charge of the trade talks on the German side, took Astakhov, the Soviet Chargé, and Babarin, the head of the Russian Trade Mission, out to dinner.

Schnurre's instructions were to raise once more the possibility of political, as well as economic, negotiations. 'What could England offer Russia?' he asked his two guests. 'At best, participation in a European war and the hostility of Germany, but not a single desirable end for Russia. What could we offer, on the other hand? Neutrality and staying out of a possible European conflict, and, if Moscow wished, a German–Russian understanding on mutual interests which would work out to the advantage of both countries.'[6]

Weizsäcker followed up Schnurre's conversation by instructing the German Ambassador to see Molotov and discover the Russian reaction to Schnurre's remarks. If it was favourable, Schulenberg was authorized to go a step further.

1. G.D., D.VI, No. 441.   2. ibid., No. 442.
3. ibid., No. 446.   4. ibid., No. 452.   5. ibid., No. 700.
6. Schnurre's Report, ibid., No. 729.

We would be prepared, however the Polish question may develop, whether peacefully as we desire, or in some other way that is forced upon us, to safeguard all Soviet interests and to come to an understanding with the Government in Moscow.[1]

Two days later, 31 July, for the first time, there was a note of urgency in the German Foreign Office instructions. Schulenberg was to report the date and time of his next interview with Molotov: 'We are anxious for an early interview.'[2]

One reason for urgency may well have been the news which the German Ambassador in Paris reported on the 28th, that France and Britain had agreed to military staff talks in Moscow. But the undistinguished composition of the Western missions, when they were announced, and the fact that they were to proceed not by plane but by slow boat, suggested – quite correctly – that both the British and the French Governments approached the military talks with as little conviction as the political. By contrast the Germans appeared at last to have made up their minds. On 2 August Ribbentrop himself saw Astakhov in Berlin and the next day telegraphed to Schulenburg:

I expressed the German wish for remoulding German–Russian relations and stated that from the Baltic to the Black Sea there was no problem which could not be solved to our mutual satisfaction. ... I declared myself ready for such conversations if the Soviet Government would inform me that they also desired to place German–Russian relations on a new and definitive basis.[3]

In his dispatch of 27 July, the French Chargé d'Affaires in Berlin had reported that Hitler had apparently not yet reached a decision, and was still balancing between Ribbentrop's view that Germany could secure her demands without risk of a general war and Göring's that any further move by Germany was bound to lead to a conflict with the Western Powers. Now, on 3 August, M. de St Hardouin wrote: 'In the course of the last week a very definite change in the political atmosphere has been observed in Berlin. ... The period of embarrassment, hesitation, inclination to temporization or even to appeasement, which had been observable, has been succeeded by a new phase.'[4]

The most obvious sign of this change was the renewal of the German press campaign against Poland, which had been damped

1. Schnurre's Report, ibid., No. 736, 29 July 1939.
2. ibid., No. 744, 31 July.   3. ibid., No. 758.
4. M. de St Hardouin to M. Bonnet, 3 August 1939; *French Yellow Book,* No. 180.

down since June. The scope of the campaign was now enlarged to include German claims not merely to Danzig, but to the whole of the Corridor, and even Posen and Upper Silesia, claims which were supported by a steady stream of reports describing Polish oppression of the German minority in these provinces.

At the same time the interference of the Germans in Danzig with the Polish customs and frontier guards in the Free Territory, and Polish economic reprisals, led to the most serious crisis so far in the dispute over the city. When the Danzig authorities notified a number of the Polish customs officers that they would be prevented from carrying out their duties, the Polish Government, alarmed at the undermining of their rights, sent an ultimatum demanding the withdrawal of the order under a time limit. The reply was a denial that any such order had been issued. The affair did not rest there. On 7 August, Forster, the Gauleiter of Danzig, was summoned to the Obersalzberg, and on his return told Carl Burckhardt, the League High Commissioner, that Hitler had reached the extreme limits of his patience. This was followed by a sharp exchange of notes between the Polish and German Governments, each warning the other of the consequences of further intervention.

On the 11th, when Burckhardt himself visited Hitler, the Fuehrer threatened that 'if the slightest thing was attempted by the Poles he would fall upon them like lightning with all the powerful arms at his disposal, of which the Poles had not the slightest idea. M. Burckhardt said that that would lead to a general conflict. Herr Hitler replied that if he had to make war he would rather do it today than tomorrow, that he would not conduct it like the Germany of Wilhelm II, who had always had scruples about the full use of every weapon, and that he would fight without mercy up to the extreme limit.'[1]

Threats on the one hand, and on the other a disarming reasonableness. 'If the Poles leave Danzig absolutely calm,' he told Burckhardt, 'then I can wait.' He would still be content with the terms he had set out on 26 March: it was the Poles who refused to negotiate. 'I want nothing from the west . . . But I must have a free hand in the east . . . I want to live in peace with England and to conclude a definite pact; to guarantee all the English possessions in the world and to collaborate.' This was a characteristic

1. Report of M. Carl Burckhardt, High Commissioner of the League at Danzig (Geneva, 19 March 1940), printed in *Documents on International Affairs, 1939–46*, vol. I, pp. 346–7.

display of Hitler's diplomacy, with its ingenious alternation of threats and conciliation; and as he calculated, every word he said to Burckhardt was reported to London.[1]

In Rome, meanwhile, the danger of war aroused increasing anxiety. The reports of Attolico, the Italian Ambassador in Berlin, were alarming. For some time Mussolini had been pressing his brother dictator to meet him. In July Hitler agreed to 4 August at the Brenner, but his reaction to an Italian suggestion for an international conference (in which Mussolini saw himself repeating his Munich success) was unfavourable, and the meeting was postponed. Alarmed at the Germans' silence about their plans (the usual sign that they meant to spring a surprise on their allies) Ciano urgently requested Ribbentrop to meet him at Salzburg on 11 August. 'Before letting me go,' Ciano recorded in his Diary, 'Mussolini recommends that I should frankly inform the Germans that we must avoid a conflict with Poland, since it will be impossible to localize it, and a general war would be disastrous for everybody. Never has the Duce spoken of the need for peace so unreservedly and with so much warmth.'[2]

When they met at Fuschl, Ribbentrop's estate outside Salzburg, the two Foreign Ministers spent altogether ten hours in each other's company. Ciano pleaded with all the eloquence at his command for a peaceful settlement of the dispute with Poland; he found himself up against a brick wall. Ribbentrop proclaimed a German–Polish conflict inevitable.

I must add [Ciano reported] that he gives the impression of an unreasonable, obstinate determination to bring about this conflict. . . . He starts from two assumptions which it is useless to discuss with him, since he answers by repeating the same axioms, and avoiding any discussion. These axioms are: (1) That the conflict will not become general. . . . (2) That, even should France and Britain wish to intervene, they are faced with the physical impossibility of injuring Germany or the Axis, and that the conflict would be certain to finish with the victory of the totalitarian Powers.[3]

Ciano's suggestion of a settlement by conference was brushed aside. Ribbentrop refused, however, to tell Ciano what Germany proposed to do – 'all decisions were still locked in the Führer's impenetrable bosom.' So convinced was he that the Western

1. *Brit. Doc.*, 3rd Series, vol. VI, No. 659.
2. *Ciano's Diary, 1939–43*, p. 123.
3. Ciano's Minutes, *Ciano's Diplomatic Papers*, pp. 297–9.

Powers would not intervene that, in the course of one of their meals, he wagered Ciano a collection of old armour against an Italian painting that he would be proven right. Four years later, sitting in gaol at Verona, waiting to be shot by the Germans, Ciano reflected with some bitterness that Ribbentrop had neglected to pay his debt.

Ciano described the atmosphere of his talks with Ribbentrop as icy. Hitler, whom he was taken to see the following day at the Berghof, was more cordial, but appeared equally implacable in his decision. He was already lost in military calculations, and received Ciano with his staff-maps spread out on the table before him. The first part of the interview was entirely taken up with Hitler's demonstration of the strength of Germany's military position. 'After the conquest of Poland (which could be expected in a short time) Germany would be in a position to assemble for a general conflict a hundred divisions on the West Wall.' As for Poland, she was too weak to withstand the German attack, and Hitler repeated Ribbentrop's suggestion that Italy should take advantage of the occasion to dismember Yugoslavia.

In reply Ciano set out with a wealth of detail Italy's weakness and lack of preparations for war, complaining that, despite the alliance so recently signed, the Germans had never informed their allies of the gravity of the situation or of their own intentions. But Hitler, he noted, listened with a far-away look.

Actually [Ciano wrote in his Diary] I feel that, as far as the Germans are concerned, an alliance with us means only that the enemy will be obliged to keep a certain number of divisions facing us, thus easing the situation on the German war fronts. . . . The fate that might befall us does not interest them in the least. They know that the decision will be forced by them rather than by us.[1]

Hitler offered a variety of reasons for his decision to attack the Poles, none of which Ciano took very seriously. But Hitler was quite precise about dates. The whole campaign must be concluded by 15 October, when the rains and mud could be expected. The question whether to attack or not would have to be settled by the end of August at the latest. 'The Führer was determined to use the opportunity of the next political provocation . . . to attack Poland within forty-eight hours and to solve the problem in that way.'[2]

1. *Ciano's Diary*, pp. 124–5.
2. Schmidt's Minutes, N.D. 1871-PS. Another German version in N.D. TC-77. Ciano's account in *Ciano's Diplomatic Papers*, pp. 299–303.

Ciano did his best to argue with Hitler but without effect. Convinced that the Western Powers would not intervene, Hitler was prepared to dispense with Italian aid, and said so. He agreed to consider Ciano's suggestion of the offer of an international conference, but obviously only as a matter of form. While they were still talking a telegram arrived from Moscow announcing Russian agreement to the dispatch of a German delegation to negotiate. This telegram has never been discovered and the whole incident bears all the marks of having been staged for Ciano's special benefit: it confirmed the impression that everything had been decided already, and that Hitler only continued to listen to the views of his Italian allies out of politeness.

The next day, 13 August, when the conversation was renewed, Ciano made no further effort to alter Hitler's mind. Hitler finally disposed of the suggestion of a conference and spent the rest of the time repeating what he had said the day before, with renewed emphasis on his belief that Britain and France would bluster but do nothing more. He added that, if they should intervene, this would show that they had already decided to move against the Axis, and were not in any case prepared to allow the Axis Powers the further period of preparation which Mussolini desired. 'The Western Democracies were dominated by the desire to rule the world, and would not regard Germany and Italy as their class. This psychological element of contempt was perhaps the worst thing about the whole business. It could only be settled by a life-and-death struggle.'[1]

Ciano confined himself to confirming the date. The campaign, Hitler replied, would be over in a fortnight, and a further month would be required for the final liquidation of Poland; the whole affair could be settled between the end of August and the middle of October. Hitler added the usual assurances that the Mediterranean was Italy's sphere in which he would never seek to interfere, and declared himself fortunate to have been born 'at a time in which, apart from himself, there was one other statesman who would stand out as great and unique in history; that he could be this man's friend was for him a matter of great personal satisfaction'.

Ciano was not taken in. 'I return to Rome,' he wrote in his Diary, 'completely disgusted with the Germans, with their leader, and with their way of doing things. They have betrayed us and

1. German Minute, N.D. TC-77. Ciano's account in *Ciano's Diplomatic Papers*, pp. 303-4.

lied to us. Now they are dragging us into an adventure which we do not want and which may compromise the régime and the country as a whole.'[1]

There is no need to look far for an explanation of the indifference Hitler and Ribbentrop showed towards the ally they had welcomed with such effusiveness three months before. It was the prospect of an agreement with Russia which now dazzled the Führer and his Foreign Minister. There was always a strong element of personal feeling in all Hitler's policies; he was eager to score off his opponents, to repay in the most dramatic form possible the check he had experienced in the spring. To sign a treaty with a government he had hitherto treated with unremitting hostility, at the very moment when the British and French Missions were still negotiating in the Russian capital – this was the sort of *coup* which appealed to his vanity.

Yet the agreement had still to be negotiated, and was far from being so certain as Ribbentrop had suggested to Ciano. The Russians were in no hurry, and in the latest communication which the Germans had received spoke of discussions 'to be undertaken only by degrees'.[2] Hitler, with his eyes on the deadline he had fixed for the attack on Poland, began to press for the negotiations to start at once. On 14 August Ribbentrop telegraphed to the German Ambassador in Moscow, instructing him to see Molotov – if possible, Stalin – and to suggest that he should himself come to Moscow for direct discussions with the Russian Government. He was to add, as a further inducement, that in the opinion of the Reich Government 'there is no question between the Baltic and the Black Seas which cannot be settled to the complete satisfaction of both countries. Among these are such questions as: the Baltic Sea, the Baltic area, Poland, South-Eastern questions, etc.'[3]

At last the Germans had come out into the open, but Molotov was not to be hurried. When Schulenburg conveyed Ribbentrop's offer to come to Moscow, he remarked that such a visit 'required adequate preparation in order that the exchange of opinions might lead to results'. Were the Germans, for instance, prepared to exercise pressure on the Japanese and persuade them to adopt a different attitude towards Russia? Did the Germans wish to conclude a pact of non-aggression? Would they agree to a joint guarantee of the Baltic States? All such matters, he concluded,

1. *Ciano's Diary*, p. 125.
2. G.D., D.VII, No. 50.   3. ibid., No. 56.

'must be discussed in concrete terms so that, should the German Foreign Minister come here, it will not be a matter of an exchange of opinions, but of making concrete decisions'.[1]

Nothing suited Hitler better. Ribbentrop at once replied, accepting Molotov's suggestions unconditionally and adding that he was ready to come at any time after Friday 18 August with full powers to conclude a treaty.

The Russians, too, were nearer a decision. The military talks with the British and French had reached a deadlock and were adjourned on 17 August; they were never seriously resumed. The Russians, however, meant to take full advantage of the Germans' eagerness. When Molotov received the German Ambassador the same day, the 17th, he told him that they must proceed 'by serious and practical steps'. First, they must conclude the trade agreement which had been hanging fire for several months; then they could turn to a non-aggression pact. But this in turn must be accompanied 'by a special protocol defining the interests of the contracting parties in this or that question of foreign policy'. Finally, Molotov made no reference to Ribbentrop's specific proposal of a date for his visit.[2]

Molotov's tactics only added to Hitler's impatience. The trade treaty would be signed at once, Ribbentrop telegraphed back; what mattered was his immediate departure for Moscow.

Please emphasize [he told the Ambassador] that German foreign policy has today reached a historic turning point. Please press for a rapid realization of my journey and oppose any fresh Russian objections. You must keep in mind the decisive fact that an early outbreak of open German-Polish conflict is possible and that we, therefore, have the greatest interest in having my visit to Moscow take place immediately.[3]

The next day, the 19th, Hitler gave orders for twenty-one U-boats to take up positions in the North sea and for the two German battleships, *Graf Spee* and *Deutschland*, to sail for Atlantic waters. That evening a telegram from Schulenberg at last brought the Russian Government's agreement to Ribbentrop's meeting – but only a week after the signature of the trade treaty, on 26 or 27 August.

Hitherto, although the diplomatic exchanges had been conducted from the Obersalzburg under his eye, Hitler had left the actual negotiations to Ribbentrop. Now, faced with a delay which might disrupt the timetable he had laid down, Hitler swallowed his pride and brought himself to ask a personal favour

1. G.D., D.VII, No. 70   2. ibid., No. 105.   3. ibid., No. 113.

of Stalin, the head of the Bolshevik state which he had proclaimed the irreconcilable enemy.

Accepting Molotov's draft of a non-aggression pact and promising that Ribbentrop would be authorized to sign this as well as the protocol for which the Russians were asking, he urged Stalin to receive

my Foreign Minister on Tuesday 22 August but at the latest on Wednesday 23 August. The tension between Germany and Poland has become intolerable. . . . A crisis may arise any day. . . . In my opinion, it is desirable in view of the intentions of the two states to enter into a new relationship, not to lose any time. . . . A longer stay by the Foreign Minister in Moscow than one to two days at most is impossible in view of the international situation. I should be glad to receive your early answer.   Adolf Hitler[1]

Hitler's telegram was sent off on the afternoon of Sunday the 20th. Throughout the rest of Sunday and all day Monday Hitler waited on tenterhooks for Stalin's reply. Would the Russians still go through with the deal? Would they agree to his need for a quick decision? Worst of all, would they, at the last moment, reach agreement with the British and French? Unable to sleep, Hitler rang up Göring in the middle of the night to express his anxiety at the long time Stalin was taking to decide.

At last, on the Monday morning, Schulenburg telegraphed Stalin's reply:

To the Chancellor of the German Reich, A. Hitler:
I thank you for your letter. I hope that the German–Soviet Non-Aggression Pact will mark a decided turn for the better in the political relations between our two countries. . . .

The Soviet Government has authorized me to inform you that it agrees to Herr von Ribbentrop's arriving in Moscow on 23 August.
                                                                         J. Stalin[2]

The pact itself presented no difficulties: Hitler had already accepted Molotov's draft. But the Russians had added a postscript to the text: 'The present pact shall be valid only if a special protocol is signed simultaneously covering the points in which the High Contracting Parties are interested in the field of foreign policy.'[3]

To put it in crude terms, the Soviet Government did not propose to sign until it learned what its share of the spoils was going to be, and how Eastern Europe was to be parcelled up. It was to

1. G.D., D. VII, No. 142.   2. ibid., No. 159.   3. ibid., No. 133.

complete this process of horse-trading that Ribbentrop was now to fly to Moscow. But to Hitler the one thing that mattered was the Pact. For the Pact, whatever its precise wording, would mean the neutrality of Russia, an end to any threat of a British–French–Russian agreement to block German designs in Eastern Europe, and the isolation of Poland. If concessions had to be made to Russia at this stage, they could always be retracted later: Hitler had never found it difficult to repudiate agreements which had outlived their usefulness. To get Stalin's signature he was prepared to promise anything, and without a moment's hesitation he signed the scrap of paper conferring plenipotentiary powers on Ribbentrop, adding only the proviso that whatever agreements he entered into should come into force as soon as they were signed.[1] Armed with this authority, within a few hours Ribbentrop was on his way by plane to Moscow.

V

Ribbentrop left early on the morning of the 22nd. Later that day one after another of the senior commanders of the Armed Services drove up the mountain road to the Berghof for a conference specially summoned by the Führer. They found him in his most exultant mood, the Man of Destiny who held the issue of peace or war in his hands. Outside it was a hot, peaceful summer day in the mountains; inside the house Hitler stood behind a large desk, while the officers sat in a half-circle before him. No discussion was permitted; they were there to listen. According to one version, Hitler broke off his address to entertain the generals to a meal, and went on with his talk afterwards. No official record was kept, but surreptitious notes were taken by more than one officer, and these, while not a verbatim account of Hitler's words, supply a substantial version of what he said.[2]

It was clear to me that a conflict with Poland had to come sooner or later. . . . I wanted first of all to establish a tolerable relationship with Poland in order to fight against the West. But this plan, which appealed to me, could not be executed. . . . It became clear to me that, in the event of a conflict with the West, Poland would attack us. . . and in certain circumstances a conflict with Poland might come at an inopportune moment.

I give as reasons for this conclusion:

1. G.D., D. VII, No. 191.
2. The version of Hitler's remarks used here is that printed in G.D., D.VII, Nos. 192 and 193.

First of all, two personal factors: My own personality and that of Mussolini. All depends on me, on my existence, because of my political talents. Probably no one will ever again have the confidence of the whole German people as I have. There will probably never again be a man with more authority than I have. My existence is, therefore, a factor of great value. But I can be eliminated at any time by a criminal or a lunatic.

The second personal factor is the Duce. His existence is also a decisive factor. If anything happens to him, Italy's loyalty to the alliance will no longer be certain. . . .

On the other side, a negative picture. . . . There is no outstanding personality in England or France.

For us it is easy to make decisions. We have nothing to lose; we have everything to gain. Our economic situation is such that we cannot hold out for more than a few years. Göring can confirm this. We have no other choice; we must act. Our opponents will be risking a great deal and can gain only a little. Britain's stake in a war is inconceivably great.

Hitler then turned to the political factors which favoured Germany. There was tension in the Mediterranean, in the Far East, and this was bound to preoccupy Britain. The British Empire had emerged in a weakened state from the last war; France's position had also deteriorated. As for the other States, none of them would move. 'All these fortunate circumstances will no longer prevail in two or three years. No one knows how much longer I shall live. Therefore, better a conflict now.'

Hitler repeated his view that the chances of British and French intervention were slight, and that it was necessary to accept the risk. In any case, neither Britain nor France was in a position to fulfil her obligations to Poland.

The West has only two possibilities in a fight against us:
1. Blockade: it will not be effective because of our autarky and because we have sources of supply in Eastern Europe. 2. Attack in the west from the Maginot Line: I consider this impossible. . . .

The enemy had another hope, that Russia would become our enemy after the conquest of Poland. The enemy did not reckon with my great strength of purpose. Our enemies are small fry. I saw them in Munich. I was convinced that Stalin would never accept the English offer. . . . Litvinov's dismissal was decisive. . . . The day after tomorrow Ribbentrop will conclude the treaty. Now Poland is in the position in which I wanted her.

We need not be afraid of a blockade. The East will supply us with grain, cattle, coal, lead, and zinc. It is a mighty aim which demands great efforts. I am only afraid that at the last minute some swine or other will produce a plan of mediation. The political objective goes farther. A beginning has been made with the destruction of England's hegemony.

The way will be open for the soldiers after I have made the political preparations.

In the second part of his talk Hitler returned to the need for iron resolution.

Things can also work out differently regarding England and France. It is impossible to prophesy with any certainty. I am expecting an embargo on trade, not a blockade. Furthermore, other relations will be broken off. The most iron determination on our part. No shrinking back from anything.

A long period of peace would not do us any good. . . . It is not machines that fight each other, but men. . . . Spiritual factors are decisive. . . . In 1918 the nation collapsed because the spiritual prerequisites were insufficient.

The destruction of Poland has priority. The aim is to eliminate active forces, not to reach a definite line. Even if war breaks out in the West, the destruction of Poland remains the priority. A quick decision in view of the season.

I shall give a propagandist reason for starting the war, no matter whether it is plausible or not. The victor will not be asked afterwards whether he told the truth or not. When starting and waging war it is not right that matters, but victory.

Close your hearts to pity. Act brutally. Eighty million people must obtain what is their right. Their existence must be made secure. The strongest man is right. The greatest harshness.

With this exhortation Hitler dismissed his generals. The order for the start of hostilities, he added, would be given later: the probable time would be dawn on Saturday, 26 August.

Hitler stayed on at the Berghof, waiting for news from Moscow, for the rest of the 22nd and for the whole of Wednesday the 23rd. It was here that Henderson, the British Ambassador, found him on Wednesday afternoon after flying from Berlin. On the previous day the British Cabinet had met to discuss the announcement that Germany and Russia were about to conclude a Pact of Non-Aggression. The news had less effect than Hitler had expected. Alliance with Russia had been the policy of Chamberlain's critics – Churchill, Lloyd George, and the Labour Party. Chamberlain himself had been reluctant to start negotiations; dislike of the Soviet Union was strong in the Conservative Party and there was considerable satisfaction that the Russians had now 'shown themselves in their true colours'. An official communiqué announced: 'The Cabinet had no hesitation in deciding such an event would in no way affect their obligation to Poland, which they have repeatedly stated and which they are determined to fulfil.' To leave no doubt that they meant what they said, the British Government began to call up reservists and ordered their Ambassador in Berlin to deliver to Hitler personally a letter from the Prime Minister.

It has been alleged [Mr Chamberlain wrote] that if H.M. Government had made their position more clear in 1914 the great catastrophe would have been avoided. Whether or not there is any force in this allegation, H.M. Government are resolved that on this occasion there shall be no such tragic misunderstanding.

If the case should arise, they are resolved, and prepared, to employ without delay all the forces at their command, and it is impossible to foresee the end of hostilities once engaged.[1]

Having stated this, however, Mr Chamberlain went on to express the view that there was no issue between Germany and Poland which could not be settled by negotiation, and to offer suggestions of ways in which such negotiations might be begun.

The gist of Chamberlain's letter had been communicated to Hitler in advance: if the warning it contained took him by surprise, its effect on him was at once relieved by the repetition of Chamberlain's familiar offer to continue his search for a peaceful settlement. Far from being impressed, he had no sooner received the Ambassador than he launched into a violent tirade against the British upon whom he laid the main blame for the crisis: it was the British guarantee to Poland, he declared, which had prevented the whole affair being settled long ago. He gave the wildest account of Polish excesses against the German minority in Poland, refused even to consider the suggestion of negotiations, and bitterly reproached the British for the way in which they had rejected his offers of friendship.

To all appearance Hitler was a man whom anger had driven beyond the reach of rational argument, yet Weizsäcker, who was present, records: 'Hardly had the door shut behind the Ambassador than Hitler slapped himself on the thigh, laughed and said: "Chamberlain won't survive that conversation; his Cabinet will fall this evening." '[2]

At a second interview, later in the afternoon, Henderson found

1. The British Blue Book (Cmd 6106): *Documents concerning German-Polish Relations and the Outbreak of Hostilities between Great Britain and Germany* (London, 1939), No. 56.
2. Weizsäcker: p. 203.

the Chancellor in a calmer frame of mind, but as unprepared as before to make a single concession. 'I spoke of the tragedy of war,' Henderson reported, 'and of his immense responsibility, but his answer was that it would be all England's fault.' It would have needed a different man from Henderson to convince Hitler that the British Government had made up its mind to resist him. According to the German minute of their conversation, 'the Ambassador declared that Chamberlain had always been a friend of Germany. . . . The proof of his friendship was to be found in the fact that he had refused to have Churchill in the Cabinet. The hostile attitude to Germany did not represent the will of the British people.

'The Führer assured the Ambassador that he did not include him personally among the enemies of Germany. . . . However, as far as he was concerned, the position was very simple. He was now fifty; therefore, if war had to come, it was better that it should come now than when he was fifty-five or even sixty years old. There could only be understanding or war between England and Germany. England would do well to realize that as a front-line soldier he knew what was war and would utilize every means available. . . . "At the next instance of Polish provocation," the Führer continued, "I shall act. The questions of Danzig and the Corridor will be settled one way or the other".'[1]

In his reply to Chamberlain, Hitler took note of the British intention to fulfil their guarantee to Poland, but this, he added, could make no difference to his determination: 'Germany, if attacked by England, will be found prepared and determined.'

It is unlikely that Hitler believed the British would put his determination to the test. Confident that the actual conclusion of the Pact between Germany and Russia would shake the resolution of the Western Powers, on the evening of his interview with Henderson (the 23rd) Hitler fixed the date for the attack on Poland at 4.30 a.m. on Saturday the 26th.

The news from Moscow was good. After leaving Berlin on the 22nd and spending the night at Königsberg, Ribbentrop reached the Russian capital at noon on the 23rd. He drove almost immediately to the Kremlin for his first talk with Stalin and Molotov, and when he got back to the German Embassy for a

1. Henderson's account is given in the British Blue Book, No. 58, and the German in G.D., D.VII, No. 200. Hitler's reply in *Brit. Doc.*, 3rd Series, vol. VII, pp. 216–19.

hurried dinner he was in the best of humours: everything was going well, agreement would be reached before the evening was out.

In his second conversation Ribbentrop engaged on a *tour d'horizon* with Stalin and Molotov. Their conversation ranged over Japan, Italy, Turkey, England, France, and the Anti-Comintern Pact. A little embarrassed, perhaps, at the reference to the Pact which was his own diplomatic masterpiece, Ribbentrop 'observed that the Anti-Comintern Pact was basically directed not against the Soviet Union, but against the Western Democracies. He knew that the Soviet Government fully recognized this fact. Herr Stalin interposed that the Anti-Comintern Pact had in fact frightened principally the City of London and the small British merchants.'

The evening appears to have been passed in the most cordial atmosphere. When toasts were drunk, 'Herr Stalin spontaneously proposed a toast to the Führer: "I know how much the German nation loves its Führer; I should therefore like to drink his health."'[1] By then the serious business had been transacted, and copies of the Agreement were being prepared for signature.

The first document was a straightforward Pact of Non-Aggression. In the event of either party becoming involved in war, each agreed to give no help to the other's enemies; nor was either to participate in any grouping of Powers aimed directly or indirectly at the other. Constant consultation and the settlement of differences by arbitration were provided for, the treaty being concluded in the first place for ten years, with a possibility of extension.

To the public treaty was appended a protocol of the utmost secrecy, which only became known after the war. By this Germany and Russia agreed to divide the whole of Eastern Europe into spheres of influence, the limits of which were outlined in three clauses. In the first, Finland, Estonia, and Latvia were recognized to lie in the Soviet sphere, Lithuania and Vilna in the German. In the second, a partition of Poland was foreshadowed along the line of the Rivers Narew, Vistula, and San. 'The question of whether the interests of both parties make desirable the maintenance of an independent Polish State, and how such a State should be bounded, can only be definitely determined in the course of further political developments.' In the third article Russia stated her interest in the Rumanian province of Bessarabia. Ribbentrop, with an eye to German economic interests in that part of the

1. German Minute of the discussions; G.D., D.VII, No. 213.

world, was content to declare Germany's 'complete political disinterestedness in these areas'.[1]

In the early hours of the 24th both documents were signed, and by one o'clock in the afternoon Ribbentrop was on his way back to Berlin. He had been in Moscow just twenty-four hours. Delighted with the reception he had been given and triumphant at the result of his visit, he returned to Berlin filled with enthusiasm for Germany's new friends. Stalin was less easily carried away. As the German delegation left the Kremlin he took Ribbentrop by the arm and repeated: 'The Soviet Government takes the new Pact very seriously. I can guarantee on my word of honour that the Soviet Union will not betray its partner.' The doubts were barely concealed.

Ribbentrop returned to Berlin in the firm belief that he brought with him an agreement which gave Hitler a free hand to deal the Poles a blow from which they would not recover for fifty years. To get this Ribbentrop had been prepared to risk straining Germany's relations with the Italians and the Japanese,[2] to make nonsense of the Anti-Comintern Pact of which he had himself been the architect, and to grant sweeping concessions to the Russians in Easten Europe. Immediately, these appeared a small price to pay for one of the most dramatic diplomatic *coups* in history, which at a blow wrote off the Franco-Soviet Alliance of 1935, the long-drawn-out negotiations of the British and French in Moscow, and – as Ribbentrop was quite convinced – the British and French guarantees of support to Poland.

Hitler had already returned to Berlin on the 24th, and was there waiting to greet his Foreign Minister as 'a second Bismarck' – a remark that indicates clearly enough the unique place in German history which he now claimed for himself.

That evening he spent with Göring and Weizsäcker, listening to Ribbentrop's account of his reception in Moscow. The 'second Bismarck' was still under the impression of his visit to the Kremlin, where, he told Hitler, he 'felt more or less as if he were among old Party comrades'.

The news from London, however, was disappointing. Parliament had met on the 24th and had unanimously applauded firm

1. Text of Treaty and of the additional Protocol, G.D., D.VII, Nos. 228–9.
2. The news of the Pact led to the fall of the Japanese Government and to strong Japanese protests in Berlin.

statements by the Prime Minister and Foreign Secretary. Chamberlain's government had not fallen and the news of the Nazi–Soviet Pact had so far failed to produce the expected results.

The attack on Poland was now due to start in thirty-six hours. After talking to Göring, Ribbentrop, and one or two of the generals, Hitler let the orders stand but determined to make one further effort to detach the Western Powers from the Poles.

This last approach to London was made by two separate means. The first was the dispatch of an unofficial envoy to sound out the British by the back door. On the morning of the 25th Herr Birger Dahlerus, a Swedish friend of Göring's, who had brought about a meeting between Göring and a group of English business men earlier in the month, left by plane for London and saw Lord Halifax later that afternoon. Herr Dahlerus believed his mission to be that of finding some means to avert war and acted in all good faith. What he took to London, however, was no new offer for a solution of the crisis over Poland, but simply an assurance of Hitler's willingness to come to an agreement with England. At the same time Hitler proposed to make a more direct approach through the British and French Ambassadors.

Hitler's first task, however, on the morning of the 25th, was to dispatch a long and somewhat embarrassed letter to Mussolini, with a tardy explanation of the negotiations in Moscow and assurances that the Pact with Russia could only strengthen the Axis. The end of the letter suggested that war was imminent: 'No one can say what the next hour may bring. . . . I can assure you, Duce, that in a similar situation I would have complete understanding for Italy, and that in any such case you can be sure of my attitude.'[1] Having made this bid for Mussolini's support, Hitler summoned the British Ambassador to the Reich Chancellery for half past one.

In a wholly different mood from that in which he had greeted the Ambassador at Berchtesgaden forty-eight hours before, Hitler began by recalling Henderson's hope, expressed at the end of their last conversation, that an understanding between Britain and Germany might still be possible. He had also (he said) been impressed by the speeches of the British Prime Minister and Foreign Minister in Parliament the day before. 'After turning things over in his mind once more he desired to make a move as regards England which should be as decisive as the step taken in regard to Russia, the result of which had been the recent Pact.' Chamber-

1. G.D., D.VII No. 266.

lain's speech could not affect German policy towards Poland one iota. But Hitler spoke with regret of the general war to which it seemed the British attitude must now lead.

After naming certain conditions – the eventual fulfilment of Germany's colonial demands, the preservation of his special obligations to Italy, and his refusal ever to enter into a conflict with Russia – Hitler then made his offer: a German guarantee of the existence of the British Empire, with the assurance of German assistance, irrespective of where such assistance might be required. With this he coupled his willingness to accept a reasonable limitation of armaments, and to regard Germany's western frontiers as final.[1]

Hitler added a few more characteristic touches – 'that he was by nature an artist not a politician, and that once the Polish question was settled he would end his life as an artist and not as a warmonger; that he did not want to turn Germany into nothing but a military barracks; that once the Polish question was settled he himself would settle down',[2] and so on. But these did not alter the essentials of his offer, which, reduced to simple terms, was a bribe in return for looking the other way while he strangled Poland. In Hitler's own mind it was, no doubt, an exact parallel to the bribe which he had persuaded Stalin to accept two days before. The one condition was a free hand over Poland. When Henderson tried to bring Poland back into the picture, insisting that 'the British Government could not consider his offer unless it meant at the same time a peaceful settlement with Poland, Herr Hitler said: "If you think it useless, then do not send my offer at all."' Finally, Henderson agreed to transmit the offer to London, Hitler urging him to spare no time and offering to put a German plane at his disposal, so that he could fly to London and add personal representations to Hitler's message.

Hitler had still two more visitors to receive that afternoon. The first was Attolico, the Italian Ambassador, from whom he was expecting a reply to the letter he had sent Mussolini earlier in the day. When he learned that no reply had yet reached Berlin he showed keen disappointment, and sent Ribbentrop to telephone Ciano.

At half past five the French Ambassador, Coulondre, arrived. In the case of France, Hitler had no such offer to make as he had just communicated to Henderson, but once again he insisted upon

1. G.D., D.VII, No. 265. Cf. British Blue Book, No. 68.
2. Sir N. Henderson to Viscount Halifax, British Blue Book, No. 69.

his belief that there was no issue between France and Germany which could justify shedding the blood of 'two equally courageous peoples'. 'I say again, it is painful to me to think we might come to that. . . . But the decision does not rest with me. Please tell this to M. Daladier.'[1]

At this point the exact sequence of events is not clear. Either just before, or just after, the interview with Coulondre a message was brought in to Hitler announcing the signature in London of the Pact of Mutual Assistance between Britain and Poland. Schmidt says it was before Coulondre arrived, and this would explain Hitler's anxiety, which Coulondre as well as Schmidt noticed, to cut the interview short. Whenever it arrived it was a piece of news which was bound to make a sharp impression on Hitler. The final signature of the Agreement had been held up for months by one delay or another: the fact that it should be signed on this very day, after Hitler had made his final offer to Great Britain, meant that his latest attempt to drive a wedge between the British and the Poles had failed. After he had read the report Hitler sat for some time at his desk brooding over it.[2]

The news from London was followed by a second piece of unwelcome news, this time from Rome. Hitler's message of the morning of the 25th, with its hint of imminent action against Poland, had found Mussolini still in a state of painful hesitation. On his return from Berchtesgaden, twelve days before, Ciano had urged on the Duce the need to recover his independence of Germany, while there was still time. 'The Duce's reactions,' he noted in his Diary, 'are varied. At first he agrees with me. Then he says that honour compels him to march with Germany. Finally, he states that he wants his share of the booty in Croatia and Dalmatia.'[3]

On the 18th Ciano records:

A conversation with the Duce: his usual shifting feelings. He still thinks it possible that the democracies will not march, and that Germany might do good business cheaply, from which business he does not want to be excluded. Then, too, he fears Hitler's rage. He believes that a denunciation of the Pact of Steel might induce Hitler to abandon the Polish question in order to square accounts with Italy. This makes him nervous and disturbed.[4]

1. M. Coulondre to M. Bonnet, 25 August 1939; *French Yellow Book*, No. 242.
2. Schmidt, p. 451.
3. *Ciano's Diary*, p. 125.
4. ibid., p. 128.

The Pact with Russia greatly impressed both Mussolini and Ciano, and the Duce swung back to his most belligerent mood. Yet even Mussolini could not ignore the poor state of the Italian Army and the lack of preparations for a major war. Finally, he was persuaded, if not to break with Hitler, at least to decline to go to war at this stage. This was the message which Attolico now brought to the Reich Chancellery shortly after Coulondre had left.

After expressing his satisfaction at the agreement with Russia, Mussolini wrote:

As for the *practical* position of Italy, in case of a military collision, my point of view is as follows: If Germany attacks Poland, and the conflict remains localized, Italy will afford Germany every form of political and economic assistance which is requested. If Germany attacks, and Poland's allies open a counter-attack against Germany, I wish to warn you now that it would be better if I did not take the *initiative* in military operations in view of the *present* situation of Italian war preparations. ... Our intervention can, however, take place at once if Germany delivers to us immediately the military supplies and the raw materials to resist the attack which the French and English would direct against us.

By way of defending his decision, Mussolini added: 'At our meetings the war was envisaged for after 1942 and at such time I would have been ready on land, on sea, and in the air according to our agreed plans.'[1] But for the moment, Italy would not march.

After the way he had treated the Italians and his refusal to take them into his confidence Hitler had little reason to be surprised at the Italians' decision but he did not disguise his disappointment. Abruptly dismissing Attolico, he declared, 'The Italians are behaving just as they did in 1914.' Added to the news from London the effect of Mussolini's reply was to convince Hitler that he must give himself more time. As Schmidt showed Attolico out of the Chancellery he passed Keitel hurrying in to see Hitler, and when he met him on his way back he heard the general excitedly instructing his adjutant with the words: 'The order to advance must be delayed again.'[2] Less than twelve hours before zero-hour the invasion was halted. It was only by the narrowest margin.

1. *Hitler e Mussolini, Lettere e Documenti* (Milan, 1946), No. 2: translation in *Documents on International Affairs, 1939–46*, vol. I, pp. 188–9.
2. Schmidt: p. 453.

Many units were already on the move. General Petzel's I Corps in East Prussia did not get the countermanding order until half past nine and its forward troops were stopped with difficulty. Detachments of Kleist's Corps further south had reached the Polish frontier and were only halted by a staff officer who used a scouting plane to make an emergency landing on the border.

VI

The strain on Hitler at this point was intense. But, haggard and preoccupied though he appeared, he had lost neither his nerve nor his skill in political calculation.

His calculations ranged over three possibilities. The first was, in some form or other, a repetition of what had happened the previous year with the Czechs: political pressure by the British and the French Governments on the Poles leading to Polish acceptance of the German demands – demands which, Hitler must have reflected, could be increased or modified as the occasion suggested.

The second, which might well develop if the Poles were obstinate in resisting the pressure of their Allies to reopen negotiations with the Germans, was a breach between Warsaw and the Western Powers, leaving the German Army free to conduct a swift and localized campaign in the East.

The third possibility was an attack on Poland without first securing the non-intervention of Britain and France. This involved the risk of a general European war but this was a limited risk, for, if the Germany army could overrun Poland with sufficient speed, Hitler was convinced that he could confront the Western Powers with a *fait accompli* before hostilities began in earnest.

These were the three possibilities, in various combinations, which Hitler turned over in his mind and sought to manipulate in the nine days which remained between the postponement of the attack on the evening of the 25 August and the British declaration of war on 3 September. To understand Hitler's mind and the twists of this final phase of his diplomacy it is important to remember that he kept all three possibilities open and did not commit himself to a choice between them – not even after the attack on Poland had begun – until the British Government finally made up its mind to declare war.

All the time Hitler went on probing the strength of the opposition he had encountered, searching for a weak point, trying to gauge how far he could go, exploring every possibility that turned up. As at every crisis in his career – in 1932, in June 1934, in September 1938 – he listened to the arguments which went on around him, appearing to side first with one, then with another, but all the time reserving decisions to himself; pouring out a stream of words in which recrimination, self-justification, misrepresentation, and grotesque exaggeration were all jumbled together, but revealing his inner mind to no one, waiting for the opportunity and the intuitive impulse to carry him forward.

Less than twenty-four hours after he had postponed the attack on Poland, Hitler fixed a new zero hour and thereafter did not depart from it. On the afternoon of the 26th, General Halder noted in his diary:

15.22   Get everything ready for morning of 7th Mobilization Day (by telephone from Reich Chancellery)
  1. Attack starts September 1
  2. Führer will let us know at once if we are not to strike
  3. Führer will let us know if further postponement is necessary
  4. It is intended to force Poland into an unfavourable position for negotiations and so achieve maximum objective [Henderson]
  Führer very calm and clear.
  Rumour has it that England is disposed to consider comprehensive proposal. Details when Henderson returns. . . .
  Plan: we demand Danzig, corridor through Corridor, and plebiscite on the same basis as Saar. England will perhaps accept, Poland probably not. *Wedge between them!*[1]

Halder's phrase 'Wedge between them' is the best guide to the confused negotiations that follow. They fall into three groups: those with Rome, those with Paris, and those with London. Of these, the last, which involved a double approach, officially through the British Embassy and unofficially through Herr Dahlerus, are by far the most important.

First the exchanges with Rome and Paris, which can be summarized briefly.

Hitler's immediate reply to Mussolini had been to ask him what he needed to complete his preparations, in order to see whether Germany could supply the deficiencies. The Italian answer was such as to rule out any hope of this. After helping to draw up the list of Italy's needs, Ciano wrote: 'It's enough to kill

1. G.D., D.VII, pp. 565–6.

a bull – if a bull could read it.'[1] Hitler's reply was again prompt. Some of the Italian demands could be met, but not before the outbreak of hostilities. Italy's decision, however, could not alter his own:

As neither France nor Britain can achieve any decisive successes in the West, and as Germany, thanks to the agreement with Russia, will have all her forces free in the East after the defeat of Poland. . . I do not shrink from solving the Eastern question even at the risk of complications in the West.[2]

The Duce, Ciano reports, was beside himself at the poor figure he was obliged to cut.

I leave to you to imagine [he telegraphed to Hitler] my state of mind in finding myself compelled by forces beyond my control not to afford you real solidarity at the moment of action.

The tone of Hitler's answer was resigned:

Duce,
I have received your communication on your final attitude. I respect the reason and motive which led you to take this decision. In certain circumstances it can nevertheless work out well.
In my opinion, however, the prerequisite is that at least until the outbreak of the struggle, the world should have no idea of the attitude Italy intends to adopt.

Hitler contented himself with three further requests to his Italian ally: support for Germany in the Italian press and broadcasts; the immobilization of as large British and French forces as possible; and, as a great favour, Italian manpower for industrial and agricultural work.

But, Duce, the most important thing is this: If, as I have said, it should come to a major war, the issue in the East will be decided before the two Western Powers can score a success. Then, this winter, at the latest in the spring, I shall attack in the West with forces which will be at least equal to those of France and Britain. . . .[3]

In the hope of saving face, Mussolini revived his suggestion of a conference and at the last moment, on the evening of 31 August, offered to act as mediator. Hitler thanked Mussolini for his

1. The Italian demands included six million tons of coal, two million tons of steel, seven million tons of oil, one million tons of timber, and 150 A.A. batteries.
2. Hitler to Mussolini, 26 August, 3.08 p.m. (G.D., D.VII, pp. 313–14).
3. Hitler to Mussolini, 27 August, 12.10 a.m. (ibid., pp. 346–7).

trouble but declined to be drawn. To Attolico he said that he was 'not in the mood to be slapped in the face time and again by Poland, and does not want to bring the Duce into an uncomfortable position through acceptance of his mediation. . . . To the question of Attolico whether herewith everything is at an end, the Führer answered yes.'[1] There was no open breach between the Axis partners, but Hitler refused to alter his plans in order to save Mussolini's reputation. The Pact of Steel had failed to provide the support he had expected, he was not going to let it act as a brake.

Apart from a letter to Daladier, in which he repeated with considerable skill the argument that Danzig and Poland did not represent a sufficient issue to justify war between France and Germany, Hitler paid little attention to France in the final stages of the crisis. Coulondre, indeed, did not see the Chancellor again after the 26th, until he presented the French ultimatum on the evening of 1 September. Hitler judged, correctly, that it was on London that everything, including the French decision, would depend.

On the evening of the 26th Dahlerus returned from London, bringing with him a letter which he had persuaded Lord Halifax to write to Göring expressing Britain's desire for peace and wish to come to an understanding with Germany. Halifax's letter was couched in the most general and non-committal terms. None the less, when Dahlerus read it to Göring, whom he found on his private train *en route* for his headquarters outside Berlin, the Field-Marshal declared it to be of enormous importance and drove back to Berlin with Dahlerus to see Hitler. When they reached the Chancellery at midnight the building was in darkness and Hitler in bed, but Göring insisted on waking him up. Dahlerus, kept waiting in an ante-room, had time to notice the exquisite carpets – always a weakness of Hitler's – and the masses of orchids. Then he was shown in.

Entirely ignoring the letter Dahlerus had brought from London, Hitler began with a twenty-minute lecture justifying German policy and criticizing the British. After that he spent half an hour eagerly questioning Dahlerus about the years he had passed in England. Only then did he return to the current crisis, becoming more and more excited, pacing up and down and boasting of the

1. German Minute of Hitler's talk with Attolico at 7 p.m., 31 August 1939 (N.D. 1889-PS).

armed power he had created, a power unequalled in German history.

When Hitler had finished Dahlerus got his chance to say something.

Hitler listened without interrupting me . . . but then suddenly got up, and, becoming very excited and nervous, walked up and down saying, as though to himself, that Germany was irresistible. . . . Suddenly he stopped in the middle of the room and stood there staring. His voice was blurred, and his behaviour that of a completely abnormal person. He spoke in staccato phrases: 'If there should be war, then I shall build U-boats, build U-boats, U-boats, U-boats, U-boats.' His voice became more indistinct and finally one could not follow him at all. Then he pulled himself together, raised his voice as though addressing a large audience and shrieked: 'I shall build aeroplanes, build aeroplanes, aeroplanes, aeroplanes, and I shall annihilate my enemies.' He seemed more like a phantom from a story-book than a real person. I stared at him in amazement and turned to see how Göring was reacting, but he did not turn a hair.

A little later Hitler walked up to Dahlerus and said: 'Herr Dahlerus, you who know England so well, can you give me any reason for my perpetual failure to come to an agreement with her?' When Dahlerus replied, with some diffidence, that it was the English people's lack of confidence in Hitler personally and in his régime, 'Hitler flung out his right arm, striking his breast with his left hand, and exclaimed: "Idiots, have I ever told a lie in my life?"'

The upshot of the meeting was that Dahlerus agreed to return to London with a new offer from Hitler to the British Government. It comprised six points:

1. Germany wanted a pact or alliance with Britain.
2. England was to help Germany to obtain Danzig and the Corridor, but Poland was to have a free harbour in Danzig, to retain Gdynia and a corridor to it.
3. Germany would guarantee the Polish frontiers.
4. Germany was to have her colonies, or their equivalent, returned to her.
5. Guarantees were to be given for the German minority in Poland.
6. Germany was to pledge herself to defend the British Empire.

Dahlerus was not allowed to write these points down, but both Hitler and Göring appeared to attach a great deal of importance to the message he was to take.[1]

1. This account is based upon Birger Dahlerus: *The Last Attempt* (London, 1948), c. 6. Cf. also *Brit. Doc.*, 3rd Series, vol. VII.

Dahlerus reached London again just after midday on Sunday the 27th, and was at once taken, by a roundabout route, to No. 10 Downing Street. The British Government had now two different sets of proposals before them, the first the offer Hitler had made to Henderson on the 25th, to which no reply had yet been sent, and the second, that now brought by Dahlerus. There were considerable differences between the two. In the first Hitler had offered to guarantee the British Empire, but only after he had settled with Poland. Now the six points brought by Dahlerus suggested that Hitler was now prepared to negotiate through the British for the return of Danzig and the Corridor, guarantee Poland's new frontiers, and then pledge herself to defend the British Empire. This advance between the 25th and the 26th no doubt represented a new bid by Hitler to divide the opposition. The circumstances in which the proposals had been thrown together, however, made the British Government sceptical as to their value. It was finally agreed that Dahlerus should return to Berlin with a reply to the second offer, and report on its reception by Hitler, before the official reply to the first offer was drafted and sent over by Henderson on the 28th.

So, once again, Dahlerus flew back to Berlin, and soon after eleven o'clock on the Sunday night delivered the British Government's message to Göring. In principle the British were willing to come to an agreement with Germany, but they stood by their guarantee to Poland; they recommended direct negotiations between Germany and Poland to settle questions of frontiers and minorities, stipulating that the results would have to be guaranteed by all the European Powers, not simply by Germany; they rejected the return of colonies at this time, under threat of war, though not indefinitely; and they emphatically declined the offer to defend the British Empire. Göring at once went off to Hitler, this time alone. To Dahlerus's surprise, Hitler accepted the British terms. Provided the official British reply corresponded with his report, there was no reason, Göring told Dahlerus, to suppose that an agreement could not be reached. Dahlerus got the British Chargé d'Affaires out of bed at 2 a.m. and sent an account of his reception off to London.

Dahlerus made it clear that Hitler suspected the Poles would try to avoid negotiations. 'Reply should therefore contain clear statement that the Poles have been strongly advised to immediately establish contact with Germany and negotiate.'[1] Lord

1. *Brit. Doc.*, 3rd Series, vol. VII, No. 406.

Halifax acted on this and through the British Ambassador in Warsaw secured Beck's agreement to start negotiations with Germany at once, in time to incorporate this in the official reply Henderson was waiting to take back to Germany.

Sir Nevile Henderson flew back to Berlin on the evening of Monday the 28th, and was received in state, with a guard of honour and a roll of drums, when he presented himself at the Chancellery at half past ten o'clock. Despite further outbursts on Hitler's part against the Poles, the interview was conducted in a reasonable manner. The official reply which Henderson brought with him confirmed the report which Dahlerus had given, but it made perfectly clear that 'everything turns upon the nature of the settlement with Poland and the method by which it is reached'. The British politely declined Hitler's bribe: 'They could not, for any advantage offered to Great Britain, acquiesce in a settlement which put in jeopardy the independence of a State to whom they have given their guarantee.' Britain would maintain her obligations to Poland, and must, in any case, insist that any settlement arrived at should be guaranteed by the other European Powers as well as by Germany. 'In the view of H.M. Government, it follows that the next step should be the initiation of direct discussions between the German and Polish Governments.'[1] The British Government had secured the agreement of the Polish Government to such discussions: they now asked the German Government if they too were prepared to negotiate.

For the moment Hitler gave no reply, but promised one on the following day, Tuesday 29 August, after he had talked matters over with Ribbentrop and Göring.

Having got the British and the Poles' offer to start negotiations, Hitler characteristically put up his demands, exactly as he had at Godesberg a year before. The German reply, handed to Henderson at 7.15 p.m. on 29 August began with a lengthy indictment of the Poles, their refusal of the German demands, the provocation and threats they had since offered to Germany, and their persecution of the German minority – a state of affairs intolerable to a Great Power. All this was skilfully used to heighten the effect of the concession Hitler was ready to make in order to win Britain over.

Though sceptical as to the prospects of a successful outcome [of direct

1. Text of the reply in British Blue Book, No. 74.

talks with the Poles], the German Government are nevertheless prepared to accept the English proposal and to enter into direct discussions . . . solely as a result of the impression made upon them by the written statement received from the British Government that they too desire a pact of friendship. . . .

The German Government, accordingly, in these circumstances agrees to accept the British Government's offer of their good offices in securing the dispatch to Berlin of a Polish emissary with full powers. They count on the arrival of this Emissary on Wednesday 30 August.[1]

The catch was in the last two lines: the Polish emissary was to leave at once and reach Berlin the following day – and he was to come provided with full powers. If the Poles accepted, it meant capitulation. To send a plenipotentiary to Berlin, with full powers to commit the Polish Government, was to invite a repetition of what had happened to the Austrian Chancellor, Schuschnigg, and to President Hacha. But if the Poles refused, Hitler hoped, the British and French might come to regard them in the same light as Benes and the Czechs the year before, as the sole obstacles to a peaceful settlement, which Germany was only too eager to sign. After all, was Danzig worth a war?

When Henderson remarked that this sounded remarkably like an ultimatum, Hitler denied it heatedly – as he had at Godesberg. As the Ambassador prepared to leave, however, Hitler renewed the pressure. '"My soldiers," he added, "are asking me Yes or No?" . . . They were telling him that one week had already been lost and that they could not afford to lose another, lest the rainy season in Poland be added to their enemies.'[2]

The entry in General Halder's diary for the 29th affords another insight into Hitler's tactics:

Poles directed by English to go to Berlin as required by Germans. Führer wants them to come tomorrow.
Basic principles: Raise a barrage of demographic and democratic demands . . .
30·8 Poles in Berlin
31·8 Blow up
 1·9 Use of force.[3]

This time the British Government did not fall into the trap. Although they continued to work for negotiations between Germany and Poland and to urge this course in Warsaw, they

1. G.D., D.VII, No. 421.
2. Henderson: *Failure of a Mission*, p. 267.
3. G.D., D.VII, Appendix I, p. 567.

declined to put pressure on the Poles to comply with Hitler's demand for a plenipotentiary within twenty-four hours, a condition which Halifax described as wholly unreasonable. A last attempt by Göring to influence the British by sending Dahlerus to London on the 30th failed to alter the situation. When Dahlerus asked about the size of the plebiscite area, Göring seized an old atlas, tore out a page and marked it in with a coloured pencil. Dahlerus noticed that Göring's way of conducting affairs of state was so reckless that he included the city of Lodz in the 'German area' which he marked, although it lay sixty miles east of the old pre-1914 Prussian frontier.

Dahlerus repeated in London Hitler's desire for peace and for a settlement with Britain. But Chamberlain and Halifax, though deeply troubled, held to the view they had expressed in their Note of 28 August, that the prerequisite of an agreement between Germany and Great Britain was a settlement between Germany and Poland and that 'everything turns upon the nature of the settlement and the method by which it is reached.'

During the course of Wednesday the 30th a precise statement of the German claims against Poland was for the first time drawn up under sixteen heads. It included the return of Danzig; a plebiscite, under international control, on the Corridor; extra-territorial communications between Germany and East Prussia, and between Poland and Gdynia; an exchange of populations; and the guarantee of minority rights. Hitler himself later said in Schmidt's presence: 'I needed an alibi, especially with the German people, to show them that I had done everything to maintain peace. That explains my generous offer about the settlement of Danzig and the corridor.'[1]

The sixteen points had another use as well. They might tempt the British to put pressure on the Poles and sow distrust between London and Warsaw.

When Henderson arrived to present the British reply to Ribbentrop at midnight on 30–31 August, he was greeted with a violent display of temper. Emulating his master, Ribbentrop shouted at the Ambassador, and although he referred to the sixteen points, refused to let him see the text on the grounds that the time-limit for negotiations with the Poles had elapsed. All Ribbentrop would agree to do was to read them out to Henderson,

1. Schmidt: p. 460.

but Göring took care to see that a copy was provided by Dahlerus next morning.

Henderson had already been sufficiently impressed by the 'generosity' of the German terms to get Lipski, the Polish Ambassador, out of bed at 2 a.m. and urge him to take steps to start negotiations. Later on the 31st the Polish Government, pressed by the British and French, did in fact instruct Lipski to seek an interview with Ribbentrop. But the Poles were not prepared to accept German dictation, and Lipski's instructions were simply to inform the Germans that the British suggestion of direct negotiations was being favourably considered by the Polish Government, and that they would send a reply in a few hours.

Immediately on receiving this message from Warsaw, Lipski requested an interview with Ribbentrop. This was at 1 p.m. But the Germans had already broken the Polish diplomatic cipher and knew that Lipski was not empowered to act as a plenipotentiary and agree to Hitler's demands on the spot. Hitler was not interested in negotiations, only in a Polish capitulation. Lipski was kept waiting without an answer until after 6 o'clock, and it is possible that he was only received then because of 'the urgent desire of the Duce' expressed in a special message from Rome. The interview, when it finally took place, did not last long. Since Lipski had not come with plenipotentiary powers to accept the German proposals, the Foreign Minister brusquely informed him there was no further point in talking and ended the interview.

There is an unreal atmosphere about all these eleventh-hour negotiations, an air of urgent futility in the telegrams passing between London and Warsaw, Berlin and London, London and Paris, Paris and Rome. Even at the time those who were engaged in these diplomatic activities found it difficult to believe that they had any point. As in a badly managed play, anticlimax had preceded the denouement, and there was only relief when the curtain finally came down.

There was not much longer to wait. The High Command of the Army was pressing Hitler for a decision one way or the other. They had little doubt what the decision would be. Halder's forecast on the 29th was not far wrong. The Poles did not come to Berlin after all, but the date was right. Half an hour after noon, on Thursday 31 August, Hitler signed 'Directive No. 1 for the Conduct of the War'.

Every preparation was complete, even down to the necessary 'incidents'. Since 10 August one of Heydrich's S.S. men, Naujocks, had been waiting at Gleiwitz, near the Polish frontier, in order to stage a faked Polish attack on the German radio station there. At Oppeln he got in touch with Müller, the head of the Gestapo. 'Müller,' Naujocks explained in an affidavit taken after the war, 'had twelve or thirteen condemned criminals who were to be dressed in Polish uniforms and left dead on the ground. For this purpose they were to be given fatal injections by a doctor employed by Heydrich. Then they were also to be given gunshot wounds. After the incident, members of the Press and other persons were to be taken to the scene of the incident.'[1] At 8 p.m. on 31 August Naujocks picked up one of these men, already unconscious, near the Gleiwitz radio station, seized the station as he had been ordered, broadcast a short proclamation and fired a few pistol shots, leaving the body behind. Naujocks's story is confirmed by General Lahousen, of the German Counter-Intelligence, whose job it was to provide the Polish uniforms. The 'attack' on Gleiwitz was one of the Polish infringements of German territory cited by the Germans as the justification for their attack the next day.

While these 'incidents' were being staged on the frontier, at nine o'clock on the Thursday night, the Berlin radio broadcast the sixteen points of the German demands as proof of the moderation and patience of the Führer in face of intolerable provocation. The Poles were represented as stubbornly refusing to undertake negotiations, and the sixteen points as the German offer which had been 'to all intents and purposes rejected'. The use of the Points as an alibi now became clear: even a seasoned foreign correspondent like William Shirer admits that he was at first taken aback by their reasonableness.

Away to the east of Berlin, tanks, guns, lorries, and division after division of troops were moving up the roads towards the Polish frontier all through the night. It was a beautiful, clear night. At dawn on 1 September, the precise date fixed in the Führer's directive at the beginning of April, the guns opened fire. Hitler's war had begun. Not for five and a half years, until he was dead, were they to be silenced.

1. Naujocks's Affidavit, N.D. 2,751-PS.

VII

On 1 September 1939 there were no scenes of enthusiasm, no cheering crowds in Berlin like those in Munich in which Hitler had heard the news of the declaration of war twenty-five years before. When he drove to address the Reichstag at the Kroll Opera House at 10 a.m. the streets were emptier than usual. Most of those who turned to watch the line of cars accompanying the Führer stared in silence.

Hitler's speech to the Reichstag was on a characteristic note of truculent self-defence. Not only was the whole blame for failure to reach a peaceful settlement thrown on the Poles, but they were actually accused of launching an offensive against Germany, which compelled the Germans to counter-attack.

For two whole days I sat with my Government and waited to see whether it was convenient for the Polish Government to send a plenipotentiary or not. . . . But I am wrongly judged if my love of peace and my patience are mistaken for weakness or even cowardice. . . . I have, therefore, resolved to speak to Poland in the same language that Poland for months past has used towards us. . . . This night for the first time Polish regulars fired on our own territory. Since 5.45 a.m. we have been returning the fire, and from now on bombs will be met with bombs.[1]

It was not one of Hitler's best speeches. He made a great deal of the Pact with Russia, but was uncertain in his attitude towards the Western Powers, disclaiming any quarrel with France or Britain and insisting on his desire for a final settlement with both. He was also clearly embarrassed by the need to refer to Italy. Towards the end he declared:

I am asking of no German man more than I myself was ready to do throughout four years. There will be no hardships for Germans to which I myself will not submit. My whole life belongs henceforth more than ever to my people. I am from now on just the first soldier of the German Reich. I have once more put on that coat that was the most sacred and dear to me. I will not take it off again until victory is secured, or I will not survive the outcome.

He then announced that, if anything should happen to himself, Göring would be his successor, and after him, Hess.

The nomination of Göring was as much a purely personal

1. Text in Adolf Hitler: *My New Order*, edited by Raoul de Roussy de Sales (N.Y., 1941), pp. 683–90.

decision on Hitler's part as the decision to attack Poland. No Cabinet had now met for two years past, and anything that could be called a German Government had ceased to exist. By assuming the right to name his own successor Hitler demonstrated the arbitrary character of the rule which he exercised over Germany: this was to be intensified during the course of the war which had now begun.

Shortly after Hitler's return from the session of the Reichstag, Göring took Dahlerus to see him in the Chancellery. They found Hitler alone in a small room. 'His calm,' Dahlerus writes, 'was skin-deep, but I could see that he was nervous and upset inside. He was obviously determined to snatch at every argument, however far-fetched, that would serve to absolve him personally for the decisions he had made.'

This time Hitler's self-justification took the form of recriminations against the British for their refusal to come to terms with him.

He grew more and more excited, and began to wave his arms as he shouted in my face: 'If England wants to fight for a year, I shall fight for a year; if England wants to fight two years, I shall fight two years. ...' He paused and then yelled, his voice rising to a shrill scream and his arms milling wildly: 'If England wants to fight for three years, I shall fight for three years....' The movements of his body now began to follow those of his arms, and when he finally bellowed: '*Und wenn es erforderlich ist, will ich zehn Jahre kämpfen,*'[1] he brandished his fist and bent down so that it nearly touched the floor. The situation was highly embarrassing, so embarrassing in fact that Göring reacted perceptibly to the spectacle Hitler was making of himself by turning on his heel so that he had his back to both of us.[2]

Hitler was still not convinced that Britain and France would intervene and the delay in their declaration of war strengthened his belief. Although Warsaw, and other Polish cities had been under heavy bombardment since dawn on 1 September, the British and French Governments were slow to put their alliance with the Poles into effect. Dahlerus was once more employed to keep open a line of communication with London and suggest that a Polish capitulation, even now, might spare Europe a general war.

Dahlerus's telephone calls to the Foreign Office made little

1. 'And, if necessary, I will fight for ten years.'
2. Birger Dahlerus: pp. 119-20.

impression; a more serious attempt at mediation, however, came from Mussolini. The Duce made one last effort to bring the British and French and Germans together for another Munich conference, from which, no doubt, the Poles would have been excluded as the Czechs had been. The British and French ambassadors delivered a warning to Ribbentrop on the evening of 1 September that they would fulfil their obligations to Poland unless the Germans at once suspended hostilities. But no further action followed during the 2nd and Mussolini tried throughout the day to get agreement on an armistice, leaving the armies in their existing positions and to be followed immediately by a conference in which (he assured Hitler) 'settlement of the Polish–German dispute . . . would certainly be favourable to Germany'.[1] The British, however, were not prepared to accept Mussolini's offer of mediation, unless Hitler first withdrew his troops to the German frontier. At that, even Mussolini gave up. Hitler might still hope that the British and French Governments would not nerve themselves to declare war but he was not prepared to make the slightest concession to win them over. Long before their intervention could be effective, he calculated (and not without reason), the Poles would be crushed, a belief he had already expressed to Weizsäcker on 29 August – 'In two months Poland will be finished, and then we shall have a great peace conference with the Western Powers.'[2]

The halting resolution of the British Government was stiffened by an angry debate in the House of Commons on the evening of 2 September. Telephoning to the still irresolute French immediately afterwards, Chamberlain told Daladier:

The situation here is very grave. . . . There has been an angry scene in the House. . . . If France were to insist on forty-eight hours to run from midday tomorrow, it would be impossible for the Government to hold the situation here.[3]

If the French could not make up their minds, Halifax told Bonnet, Britain would have to act on her own. The House of Commons was to meet at noon on Sunday the 3rd, and as the French Ambassador in London confirmed, Chamberlain risked being

1. G.D., D.VII, No. 535.
2. Weizsäcker: pp. 208 and 214.
3. Cadogan's Minute of the telephone conversation, *Brit. Doc.*, 3rd Series, vol. VII, No. 740.

turned out of office if he could not give a definite answer to his critics.

The British Government could wait no longer. At nine o'clock on Sunday morning, the 3rd, Sir Nevile Henderson presented himself at the Wilhelmstrasse to deliver their ultimatum: unless satisfactory assurances of German action to call off the attack on Poland were received by 11 a.m. a state of war would exist between Britain and Germany from that hour.

Ribbentrop was 'not available' to receive the British Ambassador. He sent Paul Schmidt, the interpreter, to act in his place, and it was Schmidt who brought the message across to the Chancellery immediately afterwards. Pushing through the crowd of Nazi leaders who filled the ante-room, he entered the Führer's study.

Hitler was sitting at his desk and Ribbentrop stood by the window. Both looked up expectantly as I came in. I stopped at some distance from Hitler's desk, and then slowly translated the British Government's ultimatum. When I finished, there was complete silence.

Hitler sat immobile, gazing before him. He was not at a loss, as was afterwards stated, nor did he rage as others allege. He sat completely silent and unmoving.

After an interval, which seemed an age, he turned to Ribbentrop, who had remained standing by the window. 'What now?' asked Hitler with a savage look, as though implying that his Foreign Minister had misled him about England's probable reaction.[1]

Ribbentrop's only answer was to explain that they could now expect a French ultimatum.

Outside, in the ante-room, Schmidt's news was also received in silence. Göring contented himself with the remark: 'If we lose this war, then God help us!' Goebbels stood apart, lost in his own thoughts and saying nothing.

Hitler's embarrassment was soon relieved by the remarkable progress of the German armies in Poland. This seems to have been almost the only campaign of the Second World War in which the German generals did not have to submit to Hitler's direct interference. Hitler's interest in what was happening, however, was so great that he at once left Berlin for the Eastern Front. Before setting out he issued a Proclamation to the German People in which he pointed to the British policy of the Balance of Power and the encirclement of Germany as the ultimate causes of the

1. Schmidt: p. 464.

war, but assured the German people that this time there would be no repetition of 1918.

Hitler established his headquarters in his special train near Gogolin. Every morning he set out by car to drive up to the front line. On 18 September, he moved to the luxurious Casino Hotel at Zoppot, on the Baltic, and from there made his triumphal entry into Danzig the following day.

Despite the utmost bravery the Polish forces were overwhelmed by the speed and impetus of the German armoured and motorized divisions, supported by an air force which had swept all opposition out of the skies in the first two or three days. This was the first time the world had heard of the *Blitzkrieg*: Hitler had not been bluffing when he promised to restore Germany's military power. By the end of the second week the Polish Army had virtually ceased to exist as an organized force. Warsaw and Modlin alone held out, much to Hitler's anger. William Shirer, the C.B.S. Correspondent, who heard him speak at Danzig, reported that Hitler had waited in the hope of making his speech in Warsaw, and was furious with the Poles for spoiling the effect.

Hitler was certainly in no mood to hold out any olive-branches. After the inevitable justification of his actions, Hitler turned angrily upon the British warmongers, who, he declared, had manoeuvred the Poles into provoking and attacking Germany. Poland would never rise again in the form of the Versailles Treaty: that was guaranteed, not only by Germany, but by Russia as well. Poland, however, was only the pretext; the real British motive was hatred of Germany. Hitler thereupon burst into a series of threats. However long the war went on, Germany would never capitulate. 'Today you have the Germany of Frederick the Great before you. . . . This Germany does not capitulate. We know too well what would be in store for us: a second Versailles, only worse.'[1]

The authentic Hitler touch appears in his references to the Poles. Poland, like Czechoslovakia, was dismissed as an artificial creation. Like Ludendorff, coming to Vilna in 1915,[2] Hitler was full of the Germans' historical mission in Eastern Europe:

Thirty years would have been sufficient to reduce again to barbarism those territories which the Germans, painstakingly and with industry and thrift, had saved from barbarism. . . . The fate of Germans in this State was horrible. There is a difference whether a people of lower

1. Text in *My New Order*, pp. 693–706.
2. See above, pp. 317–18.

cultural value has the misfortune to be governed by a culturally significant people, or whether a people of high cultural value has forced upon
it the tragic fate of being oppressed by an inferior. . . . What was for us
and also for me most depressing was the fact that we had to suffer all
this from a State which was far inferior to us. . . .

It was in this same spirit of contempt for the Poles as a people
of inferior culture and inferior rights that Hitler was already
beginning to discuss the future of the territories he had overrun.
The record of a discussion on board the Führer's train at Ilnau
on 12 September shows Hitler to have been still undecided
between the complete partition of Poland with Russia, and the
establishment of a small, nominally independent Polish State, not
unlike Napoleon's Grand Duchy of Warsaw. Hitler was inclined
to favour the second alternative, possibly combining it with the
formation of a separate Ukrainian State out of the south-eastern
provinces of Poland. But at this point Russia's views had also to
be taken into account.

The speed of the German advance in Poland took the Soviet
Government by surprise. They had hastily to change their own
plans, and to prepare for an immediate occupation of the territory
allotted to them by the August Agreement. This was begun on 17
September and completed within a few days. The German and
Russian armies met at Brest-Litovsk, the town in which Germany
had dictated peace to the young and harassed Soviet Republic in
1918. The Russian advance brought Soviet troops to the frontiers
of Hungary, news which raised the utmost alarm throughout the
Balkans and in Rome. What was to become of the Poles? This
question now demanded an urgent answer and after unsuccessfully trying to persuade Stalin or Molotov to come to Berlin,
Ribbentrop left for a second visit to Moscow on 27 September.
It was Stalin who now took the initiative and, in the three meetings held in the Kremlin on 27 and 28 September, largely succeeded in altering the August Agreement to his own satisfaction.
Stalin's first demand was the abandonment of any idea of an
independent Polish State which might create friction between
Germany and the U.S.S.R. – a polite way of saying that it might
be used by Germany against Russia. Instead, Poland was to be
entirely divided between the two Powers. Stalin's second demand
was the inclusion of Lithuania in the Russian, instead of the
German, sphere of influence. In return, he was prepared to make
concessions in Central Poland, ceding the Province of Lublin and

part of the Province of Warsaw to the Germans, although these lay to the east of the original line of partition. He was also prepared, when Russia moved into Lithuania, to adjust the frontier of East Prussia, to Germany's advantage, in the Suwalki triangle. Stalin had already made it clear in a conversation with the German Ambassador on 25 September that he proposed to 'take up immediately the solution of the problem of the Baltic countries', and that he expected the unstinted support of the German Government in reaching settlements with Estonia, Latvia, and Lithuania which would give Russia what she wanted in the way of naval and air bases on the Baltic. Still suspicious of German intentions, Stalin had clearly decided to secure the maximum advantage from Hitler's new policy at once, before Hitler changed his mind again. So skilfully did he play his hand that the final result of the German campaign in Poland was to strengthen the Russian, even more than the German, position in Eastern Europe, and to hand over to the Soviet Union half Poland and the three Baltic States. The Germans had even to withdraw their troops from the oil region of Borislav-Drohobycz, which they were eager to acquire, but which Stalin insisted on retaining in the Soviet half of Poland. The only concession offered in return was a Russian promise to export to Germany a quantity of oil equal to the annual production of the area.

Hitler can scarcely have enjoyed the price he had to pay for agreement with Russia, especially in the Baltic States, traditional outposts of German civilization in the East which had now to be abandoned to the Slavs. Yet there was no hesitation on the German side, and Ribbentrop, after referring the final decision to the Führer, was authorized to sign before he left Moscow on the 29th and to accept Stalin's demands *en bloc*.

Why did Hitler attach so much importance to maintaining good relations with Russia? Partly, no doubt, as his speech of 19 September shows, because he realized that London and Paris were still counting on a quarrel between Germany and Russia. Partly because he hoped to secure economic aid from Russia which would help to defeat the British blockade. The main reason, however, was the advantage which Hitler saw in shelving the problems of Eastern Europe, at least for a time, and leaving himself free to concentrate all his attention and forces on dealing with the West.

VIII

Ostensibly, Hitler still held the view that, after the defeat and partition of Poland, no further cause for war existed between Germany and the two Western Powers. In a joint communiqué published in Moscow on 28 September Ribbentrop and Molotov expressed the view that, 'after the definite settlement of the problems arising from the collapse of the Polish State . . . it would serve the true interest of all peoples to put an end to the state of war existing between Germany on the one side, and England and France on the other'.[1] The same argument was given great prominence in the German Press and radio, and there is every indication that the German people would have warmly welcomed peace after the successes in the east. The Army leaders, too, were strongly in favour of avoiding a war with the Western Powers, and of arriving at a compromise settlement. The plans which the Army High Command submitted to Hitler at the end of September visualized the deployment of German troops in the west on strictly defensive lines.

The talk of a peace offensive, which was widespread in Berlin after Hitler's return from Poland in the last week of September, found a fervent echo in Rome. The elimination of Catholic Poland, a country for which Italians felt a traditional friendship; the advance of Russia to the threshold of the Balkans; Hitler's neglect of Italy for his new-found Russian friends; the feeling of being left out and no longer informed of what was afoot, greatly increased the mixed emotions of chagrin, envy, and resentment with which the Duce had watched Hitler's success in the past month. Mussolini was eager for peace, if only to save his own face. He was also anxious to discover Hitler's intentions, and an invitation to Ciano to visit Berlin immediately after Ribbentrop's return from Moscow was at once accepted.

Ciano found Hitler in a very different mood from that in which he had last seen him at the Berghof seven weeks before. 'At Salzburg,' he wrote in his Diary, 'the inner struggle of this man, decided upon action but not yet sure of his means and of his calculations, was apparent. Now, he seems absolutely sure of himself. The ordeal he has met has given him confidence for future ordeals.'[2]

1. *Nazi–Soviet Relations*, p. 108.
2. *Ciano's Diary, 1939–43*, p. 162.

Ciano's record of his conversation on 1 October leaves no doubt that, while still nominally committed to a peace offer, Hitler was already thinking in terms of its failure and the deliberate extension of the war to the west. The effect of the victories he had won over Poland had been to sharpen his taste for more. The inactivity of the Western Powers during the Polish campaign presented itself not as an opportunity for a negotiated peace, but as further evidence of their feebleness, an invitation to rid himself of their interference for good. The hesitations which had beset him during the month before the attack on Poland were now, as Ciano recognized, replaced by a serene self-confidence. The Pact with Russia, which had given him a free hand in Poland, now guaranteed his freedom of action in the west, without the need to worry about his rear. The fact that Hitler no more trusted the Russians than they trusted him was an additional argument for settling with France and Britain as soon as possible, before he had again to look to Germany's eastern frontiers.

Ciano summed up his impressions of his visit in these words: 'If I were to state that the Führer unreservedly prefers a solution by war to a possible political agreement, it would be arbitrary and perhaps imprudent of me. . . . Today, to offer his people a solid peace after a great victory, is perhaps an aim which still tempts Hitler. But if in order to reach it he had to sacrifice, even to the smallest degree, what seem to him the legitimate fruits of his victory, he would then a thousand times prefer battle. Certainty of his superiority over the adversary is a factor which encourages his intransigence, just as the influence of Ribbentrop who does not conceal his extreme views, has the effect of making the Führer's attitude more rigid towards the Western Powers.'[1]

Thus the much-advertised peace offer of 6 October, to which so much importance had been attached in advance, was largely discounted by Hitler before it was made. Hitler's main purpose in making the speech seems to have been to carry German opinion with him, and convince the German people that, if the war continued, it was through no fault of his. The unpopularity of the war and the longing for peace impressed everyone who was in Berlin in the autumn of 1939. It was, almost certainly, with this undercurrent of disaffection in view that the German Press had been ordered to build up Hitler's peace offer in advance, and that Hitler now presented himself in his most plausible mood.

1. Ciano's Minute, *Ciano's Diplomatic Papers*, pp. 309–16.

Hitler had flown to Warsaw the day before to review the victorious German troops. Full of pride at what he had seen, he opened his speech to the Reichstag with an exultant description of the triumph of German arms – 'in all history there has scarcely been a comparable military achievement'. There followed a long passage in which Hitler made a venomous attack upon the Polish nation and its leaders – 'this ridiculous State' – ending with a grossly distorted account of German–Polish relations, in which a deliberate campaign of atrocities was represented as rising to new heights of infamy after the British guarantee. Only when he had vented these twin emotions of arrogance and hatred did Hitler turn to review the present situation.

He began by underlining the importance of Germany's new relationship with Russia – the turning-point in German foreign policy. He repudiated any suggestion of 'fantastic' war-aims directed to the establishment of German domination in the Ukraine, Rumania, or even the Urals: on the contrary, Germany and Russia had clearly defined their respective spheres of interest, in order to prevent any friction arising between them. Where the League of Nations had totally failed to provide the much-promised revision of the Peace Treaties, Germany and Russia had carried out a resettlement which had removed part at least of the material for a European conflict.

Hitler pointed to the new settlement with Poland as the culminating achievement in his policy of ridding Germany of the fetters fastened on her by the Treaty of Versailles. This last revision of the Treaty, too, could have been brought about in the same peaceful way as in the other cases, but for the malignant opposition of the warmongers abroad. Hitler then proceeded to recite all the efforts he had made to improve relations and live in peace with Germany's neighbours.

My chief endeavour has been to rid our relations with France of all trace of ill-will and render them tolerable for both nations. . . . Germany has no further claims against France, and no such claim shall ever be put forward. I have refused even to mention the problem of Alsace-Lorraine. . . . 1 have always expressed my desire to bury forever our ancient enmity and bring together these two nations, both of which have such glorious pasts.. . . I have devoted no less effort to the achievement of an Anglo-German understanding, nay, more than that, of an Anglo-German friendship. . . . I believe even today that there can only be real peace in Europe and throughout the world if Germany and England come to an understanding. . . .

Why should this war in the west be fought? For the restoration of

Poland? The Poland of the Versailles Treaty will never rise again. This is guaranteed by two of the largest States in the world.

Hitler made it quite clear that the reorganization of Central Europe was a subject on which he would not permit 'any attempt to criticize, judge or reject my actions from the rostrum of international presumption'. But the future security and peace of Europe was a matter which must be settled by international conference and agreement. One day such a conference would have to meet and these problems would have to be tackled.

If, however, these problems must be solved sooner or later, then it would be more sensible to tackle the solution before millions of men are first uselessly sent to their death. . . . Continuation of the present state of affairs in the west is unthinkable. Each day will soon demand increasing sacrifices. . . . One day there will again be a frontier between Germany and France, but instead of flourishing towns there will be ruins and endless graveyards. . . .

If, however, the opinions of Messrs Churchill and his followers should prevail, this statement will have been my last. Then we shall fight, and there will never be another November 1918 in German history.[1]

Every paper in Germany at once broke into headlines: 'Hitler's Peace Offer. No war aims against France and Britain. Reduction of armaments. Proposal of a conference.'[2] As propaganda it was a well-turned trick; as a serious offer of peace it was worthless, since it contained not a single concrete proposal other than – by implication – general recognition of Germany's conquests as the basis of any discussion. When Daladier replied on 10 October and Chamberlain on the 12th, they left no doubt that they were not prepared to consider peace on terms which, as Chamberlain put it, began with the absolution of the aggressor. On the 13th an official German statement announced that Chamberlain had rejected the hand of peace and deliberately chosen war. Once again Hitler had established his alibi.

It was scarcely more than that. On 9 October, three days before Chamberlain spoke, Hitler drew up a lengthy memorandum for his Commanders-in-Chief in which he wrote: 'The German war aim is a final military settlement with the West, that is, the destruction of the power and ability of the Western Powers ever again to oppose the State Consolidation and further development of the German people in Europe. As far as the outside world is concerned, this aim will have to undergo various propaganda

1. Text in *My New Order*, pp. 721–56.
2. Taken from the *Völkischer Beobachter*.

adjustments, necessary from a psychological point of view. This does not alter the war aim. That is and remains the destruction of our western enemies.'[1]

On 27 September Hitler had already informed his three Commanders-in-Chief and General Keitel that he intended to attack in the west. His memorandum of 9 October appears to have been written in defence of this intention. The same day he signed Directive No. 6, the first paragraph of which presented his decision in more guarded language: 'If it should become apparent in the near future that England, and, under England's leadership, France, are not willing to make an end of the war, I am determined to act actively and aggressively without much delay.'[2]

Thus, a month after launching the attack on Poland, Hitler had rejected his earlier idea of a peace settlement, once Poland had been overrun, in favour of the deliberate extension of the war to the west. So far as Hitler is concerned, it is at this point – the end of September or the beginning of October – rather than a month earlier, when the actual fighting began, that he made up his mind to turn a single campaign into a European war. This had been present in Hitler's mind as a possibility in August, and in his more excited moments he had been inclined, even then, to declare that if the British and French wanted war they could have it, and the sooner the better. The scales had finally been tipped by three developments during September. The first was the speed and ease with which the German Army had eliminated Poland. The second was the passivity of the French and British during the Polish campaign, despite the heavy superiority of the French Army in numbers when compared with the small German forces retained in the west: this confirmed his conviction that they lacked the will to fight. The third was the German–Russian Agreement signed by Ribbentrop: this afforded him the opportunity to turn west without worrying about his eastern frontiers and to knock out France and Britain before he gathered all his forces for the decisive gamble, the opening of the gateway to the east as the direction of Germany's future expansion.

Neither agreement with Russia nor the decision to attack in the west represented any change in Hitler's ultimate intention to carve out Germany's *Lebensraum* in the east. The elimination of French and British opposition was a prerequisite, not a substitute, for his

1. N.D. L-52. Cf. further below, pp. 563–4.
2. N.D. C-62.

eastern ambitions. While Ribbentrop talked enthusiastically of the future of German–Russian cooperation Hitler kept his own counsel, and there is no reason to suppose that he ever abandoned the ideas he had expressed fifteen years before in *Mein Kampf*. But he was in no hurry to attack Russia, that remained in the future and he was prepared to draw every advantage he could from the new relationship with Moscow, in particular the inestimable advantage of settling with the West first without the danger of war on two fronts. Hitler was the last man to pin himself down in advance, he was prepared to change course and adapt himself to any new circumstance that appeared, but the drift of his ideas is clear enough: deal with Poland before turning west; deal with France and Britain, before turning back to the east.

To a man of Hitler's hesitations the decision to resort to war at the beginning of September represented a severe psychological test. He had supported himself with the assurance that it was only a localized war on which he was embarking. But now that the ordeal was past, now that military success had proved both so easy and so gratifying, his confidence bounded up and he let his ideas expand. Instead of waiting to see what the Western Powers were going to do, he would take the initiative himself. It was a pattern which had repeated itself again and again throughout the years since 1933. Success and the absence of resistance tempted Hitler to reach out further, to take bigger risks and to shorten the intervals between his *coups*. The curve had mounted steadily from the withdrawal from the League in October 1933 through the announcement of conscription and the remilitarization of the Rhineland, to Austria, Munich, and Prague. With the change from political to open warfare Hitler had begun to trace a new line, but already it was beginning to follow the same characteristic contour: the three weeks' local war in Poland was now to be followed by a war in the west in which at least four countries were bound to be involved besides Germany. Released, as Ciano noted, from the hesitation and anxieties of the time before he had risked war, he was already on the way to that assumption of his own infallibility which marked the deterioration of his judgement.

BOOK III

WAR-LORD
1939–45

CHAPTER TEN

THE INCONCLUSIVE VICTORY
1939–40

I

WITH the beginning of the war Hitler became more and more immersed in the political and strategical calculations by which he hoped to win it. His appearances in public became infrequent; his time was taken up with diplomatic and military conferences, and such private life as he had ever enjoyed was sacrificed to the claims of a position in which he bore the sole responsibility for every decision that had to be taken. If it is difficult at times in the intricate history which follows to detect the figure of the man, this is not due solely to the character of the records which have survived – minutes of conferences, diplomatic exchanges, and military directives: it corresponds to the actual conditions of his life during these years. The human being disappears, absorbed into the historic figure of the Führer. Only in the last two years of his life, as the magic begins to fail, is it possible to discover again the mortal and fallible creature beneath.

While therefore the present study makes no pretence to be a history of the war, it must necessarily, for the greater part of this section, be principally concerned with Hitler as the war-lord of Nazi Germany, with the situations that confronted him and with the decisions that he took.

In the autumn of 1939 Hitler was well aware that the professional soldiers were opposed to extending the war by an attack in the west, particularly at the time he proposed, in the closing months of the year. Before he could develop his plans he had to master this opposition, and to this end he drafted a memorandum setting out his views and read it to the three Commanders-in-Chief, Halder, and Keitel at a conference held on 10 October.

The memorandum was a well-constructed piece of work. It began with the defensive argument that Germany must strike in the west in order to prevent the occupation of Belgium and Holland by the French, and sought to prove that time was on the side of the enemy, not least because of the uncertainty of Russia's intentions.

'By no treaty or pact,' Hitler wrote, 'can a lasting neutrality of Soviet Russia be insured with safety. At present all reasons speak against Russia's departure from this state of neutrality. In eight months, one year, or several years this may be altered.'[1]

As he got into his stride Hitler dropped the argument of a preventive occupation of the Low Countries and described the primary aim of the operations he proposed as the total destruction of the enemy's forces. The detailed passages, with their emphasis on mobility, speed and the concentration of armour, show Hitler already thinking in the terms which were to bring such success when translated into action in May and June 1940.

In his eagerness to launch the attack during the autumn Hitler insisted that the process of refitting and reinforcing formations used in Poland must be carried out with a speed which might leave much to be desired. If necessary, the attacking forces must be prepared to go on fighting right into the depths of the winter – and they could do this, he argued, so long as they kept the fighting open and did not let it become a war of positions. The key was the armoured divisions. 'They are not to be lost among the endless rows of houses in Belgian towns. It is not necessary for them to attack towns at all but . . . to maintain the flow of the army's advance, to prevent fronts from becoming stable by massed drives through weakly held positions.' With this always in mind, the German Army was to sweep across Holland, Belgium, and Luxembourg, and destroy the opposing forces before they could form a coherent defensive front. Hitler concluded by stressing the need for improvisation 'to the utmost'. As for the time of the attack, 'the start cannot take place too early'.

Hitler's arguments did not convert the opposition in the Army. To extend the war gratuitously, when all that was necessary was to stand on the defensive; to force Britain and France to fight, when inaction might well produce a compromise settlement, seemed to the generals an irresponsible gamble. They did not share Hitler's confidence in the superiority of the German Army over the French; and they were sceptical of the claims which Hitler made for their advantage in armour and in the air. If the gamble failed to come off, and no quick victory was obtained, Germany would find herself involved in a second world war, for which, they felt, her resources were inadequate.

Recognizing that Hitler was unlikely to tolerate independent views on the undesirability of extending the war, Brauchitsch (the

1. N.D. L-52.

C.-in-C. of the Army) and Halder (the Chief of Staff) made the most of technical arguments – the problem of re-equipping the Army and transferring it from Poland to the west; the risks of a winter campaign, and the strength of the forces opposing them. Just as Hitler camouflaged his belief that he could get away with another act of aggression by talking of the danger of waiting for the Allies to move first, so the generals disguised their distrust of Hitler's leadership by playing up the practical difficulties. In the background the same group of men who had urged Brauchitsch and Halder to remove Hitler by force in 1938 was again active – among them General Beck, the former Chief of Staff; Goerdeler; Hassell, the former Ambassador in Rome; General Oster, of the Counter-Intelligence (the Abwehr); and General Thomas, Head of the War Economy and Armaments Office.

A lull followed, during which the generals began to hope that they had dissuaded Hitler from going on with his plans. But at the end of October Hitler announced that the attack would begin on 12 November, and Brauchitsch, as Commander-in-Chief of the Army, was faced with the choice between giving orders for an offensive which he believed was bound to end disastrously for Germany, and organizing a putsch against the man who was the Commander-in-Chief of the German Armed Forces and the Head of the State.

The one institution in Germany which possessed the authority and disposed of the forces to carry out a *coup d'état* was the Army. As a result the history of the active German Opposition is a history of successive attempts to persuade one or other of the military leaders to use armed force against the Nazi régime. It may well be argued that to expect the commander-in-chief of any army to stage a mutiny in time of war is to ask more than is reasonable. Whatever view is taken of the difficult problem of moral responsibility, however, the fact is clear enough that, as in September 1938, the Army leaders refused to take the action demanded of them by the Opposition group.

For a few days at the beginning of November the conspirators were hopeful. Their argument that, if Hitler were removed, it would be possible to reach a settlement with the Western Powers and save Germany from the disaster of another 1918, appeared to be making an impression on the Army High Command, who were badly shaken by Hitler's announcement of a definite date for the offensive in the west. Discussions were held with the Army

Chief of Staff, General Halder, and his deputy, General Stülpnagel, on 2 and 3 November, and General Oster was assured that preparations for a military putsch had been made, if Hitler should insist on giving the final order for the attack. A meeting between General Brauchitsch and Hitler was fixed for Sunday, 5 November, after which the Army leaders promised a final decision.

The interview between Hitler and Brauchitsch took place in the Reich Chancellery; it did not last long. Hitler listened quietly enough as Brauchitsch set out his anxieties over the proposed attack, but when the Commander-in-Chief remarked that the spirit of the German infantry in Poland had fallen far short of that of the First World War, Hitler flew into a rage, shouting abuse at Brauchitsch and forbidding him to continue with his report. Under this direct attack the Commander-in-Chief, who seems to have been not far from a nervous breakdown, crumpled up. Furious at the defeatism of the High Command, Hitler peremptorily ordered the preparations to continue and the attack to begin at dawn on the day fixed, 12 November.

Neither Hitler himself nor Himmler seems to have guessed the length to which talk of a putsch had gone at the Army Headquarters in Zossen. But they scarcely needed to worry. After the dressing-down he received from Hitler, Brauchitsch (and Halder) hastily disavowed all interest in the conspiracy. Chance offered them a way out. On 7 November the attack had to be postponed, owing to an unfavourable weather forecast, and the High Command was able to make use of the same excuse to secure further postponements throughout the winter, without raising the main issue.

While the conspirators of the Opposition group around Beck and Oster had been trying, with diminishing hopes, to stir the Army High Command to action, they were startled by the news that a bomb explosion had wrecked the Bürgerbräukeller in Munich a short time after Hitler had finished speaking there on the anniversary of the 1923 putsch. Two British Secret Service agents, Captain Payne Best and Major R. H. Stevens, who, it was suggested, knew of the plot, were simultaneously kidnapped on the Dutch border, and a German carpenter, by the name of George Elser, was arrested on the Swiss frontier, with a marked photograph of the interior of the hall in his possession.

It is not surprising that the Opposition were startled by this news, for in fact the attempt on Hitler's life was organized by the Gestapo as a means of raising the Führer's popularity in the country. Elser, a skilled cabinet-maker, who had drifted into the company of a group of Communists, had been picked up by the Gestapo in the concentration camp at Dachau, where he had been sent for 're-education'. He was offered his freedom if he would do what he was told, and was taken twice by night to the Bürgerbräukeller in Munich. There he was ordered to build an explosive charge into one of the pillars close to the spot where Hitler would be standing during his speech. An alarm-clock was placed with the explosive, but had no connexion with the fuse, which could only be started by electric current from outside.

One of the fixed dates in the Nazi calendar was 8 November, the day on which Hitler never failed to appear in Munich for his annual reunion with the Old Fighters. This time he attended the celebrations in the Bürgerbräu as usual, but cut short his speech and left early. He had not been gone very long when a tremendous explosion wrecked the hall, killing several Party members and injuring many more.

Hitler's secretary, who was on the train taking the Führer back to Berlin, has described how the news reached them at Nuremberg. It is possible that he had not been told of what was planned. At any rate, he immediately seized on his escape as proof of providential intervention. His eyes blazing with excitement, he leaned back in his seat and announced: 'Now I am content! The fact that I left the Bürgerbräu earlier than usual is a corroboration of Providence's intention to allow me to reach my goal.'[1]

Goebbels made the utmost use of the incident to stir up resentment against those who were lukewarm towards the war, and to portray Hitler as an inspired leader whose intuition alone had preserved him from death. Elser, who had been given the photograph of the Bürgerbräukeller and released a quarter of a mile from the Swiss border, was arrested as soon as he tried to cross it. The German Press seized on his Communist connexions, and a lurid picture was drawn of a conspiracy in which Otto Strasser as well as the British Secret Service figured prominently. At one time a big trial was to have been staged, with the two kidnapped British agents in the dock, and Elser as the chief witness carefully coached to prove that the assassination had been organized by the British. The fact that the trial was never held suggests that, in some way, the Gestapo gambit had failed. The timing had been

1. A. Zoller: *Hitler Privat*, p. 181.

a little too perfect, and the German people remained stolidly sceptical of their Führer's providential escape.[1]

Hitler had postponed the attack in the West, but he had not abandoned his plans. On 20 November Directive No. 8 ordered the state of alert to be maintained, so that immediate advantage could be taken of any improvement in the weather, and on 23 November Hitler summoned the principal commanding officers of the three services to the Chancellery for another conference similar to those of 23 May and 22 August. Once again we are fortunate to have an account of what Hitler said, which was made at the time and captured after the war.[2]

The arguments which Hitler used were the same as those he had put forward on 10 October, but he spoke more freely, and the arguments were driven home with greater force. He began by reproaching the generals for their lack of faith in his earlier decisions, the occupation of the Rhineland and the *Anschluss*. 'The number of people who put trust in me was very small.'

The next step was Bohemia, Moravia, and Poland. It was clear to me from the first moment that I could not be satisfied with the Sudeten territory. That was only a partial solution. The decision to march into Bohemia was made. Then followed the establishment of the Protectorate and with that the basis for the conquest of Poland was laid. I was not quite clear at that time whether I should start first against the East and then against the West or vice versa. By the pressure of events it came first to the fight against Poland. One might accuse me of wanting to fight and fight again. In struggle I see the fate of all beings. Nobody can avoid fighting if he does not want to go under.

Hitler laid great stress on the fact that for the first time since the foundation of the German Empire by Bismarck, Germany had no need to fear a war on two fronts. The Pact with Russia brought no security for the future but for the present the situation was favourable to Germany. The same was true of Italy, where everything depended upon Mussolini's survival. After a rapid survey of other political factors, Hitler drew this conclusion:

Everything is determined by the fact that the moment is favourable now: in six months it may not be so any more. As the last factor I must in all

1. This account is based on that given by Captain Payne Best, one of the British officers kidnapped on the Dutch frontier. Captain Best got Elser's story from him during their time in prison. Cf. S. Payne Best: *The Venlo Incident* (London, 1950), pp. 128–36.
   2. N.D. 789-PS.

modesty name my own person: irreplaceable. Neither a military nor a civil person could replace me. Assassination attempts may be repeated. I am convinced of my powers of intellect and decision. ... Time is working for our adversaries. Now there is a relationship of forces which can never be more propitious, but can only deteriorate for us. ...

My decision is unchangeable. I shall attack France and England at the most favourable and quickest moment. Breach of the neutrality of Belgium and Holland is meaningless. No one will question that when we have won.

The closing passages show Hitler in an exalted mood. Carried away by his theme, he was disarmingly candid:

Every hope of compromise is childish: Victory or defeat! The question is not the fate of National Socialist Germany, but who is to dominate Europe in the future. ... No one has ever achieved what I have achieved. My life is of no importance in all this. I have led the German people to a great height, even if the world does hate us now. I am setting this work on a gamble. I have to choose between victory and destruction. I choose victory.

The spirit of the great men of our history must hearten us all. ... As long as I live I shall think only of the victory of my people. I shall shrink from nothing and shall destroy everyone who is opposed to me. I have decided to live my life so that I can stand unashamed; if I have to die I want to destroy the enemy. ... In the last years I have experienced many examples of intuition. Even in the present development I see the prophecy. If we come through this struggle victoriously – and we shall – our time will enter into the history of our people. I shall stand or fall in this struggle. I shall never survive the defeat of my people. No capitulation to the forces outside; no revolution from within.

Although Hitler had designed the whole occasion in order to stamp the impression of an inspired leadership upon his commanders, it is difficult to believe that he was still only acting a part; the megalomania of the later years is already evident. He failed to convince the senior generals – Brauchitsch unsuccessfully offered his resignation after the meeting – but it was certain that the vacillating doubts of the High Command would prove insufficient to halt Hitler in a mood which had been hardened into reckless determination by his victory in Poland. All that the generals could do was to make use of the continued bad weather to delay the start of the offensive until well into 1940.

Meanwhile the impression which Hitler had formed of the lack of enthusiasm for war among his senior commanders, and the suspicion that they were prepared to use any pretext to avoid a clear-cut military decision, strengthened the feelings of distrust with which he was coming to regard the professional soldiers. The clash between Hitler and his generals in the winter of 1939–40, as most of them subsequently realized, bore fruit in his refusal ever again to let himself be influenced by their advice, even in military matters. When the attack in the west was followed, not by the disaster they had foretold, but by the most startling victories of the war, Hitler was encouraged to believe that his judgement was as superior to theirs in strategy, and even tactics, as he had always known it to be in politics – with disastrous results for both Hitler and the Army.

II

Throughout the autumn and winter of 1939–40 Hitler's mind was filled with the prospects of the offensive which he meant to launch in the west. Despite the successive postponements, he still thought of the attack as no more than a few days distant, and not until the New Year did he reluctantly agree to defer it to the spring or early summer. His mood was bellicose: in December Weizsäcker heard him say that a campaign in the west 'would cost me a million men, but it would cost the enemy that too – and the enemy cannot stand it'.[1] In the meantime, however, politics forced themselves on his attention, in particular the awkward problems raised by German relations with Italy and with Russia.

The brief honeymoon period of the Pact of Steel was long since over. The alliance was popular in neither country, and Hitler admitted at the meeting with his commanders on 23 November that Italy's reliability depended solely upon Mussolini's continuation in power. The Duce's own attitude was far from stable. On 20 November Ciano noted in his diary: 'For Mussolini, the idea of Hitler's waging war and, worse still, winning it, is altogether unbearable.'[2] A month later, on 26 December, Mussolini was hoping for a German defeat, and told Ciano to let the Dutch and Belgian Governments know surreptitiously that their countries were threatened with an imminent German invasion.

At other times Mussolini swung round and talked of intervening on Germany's side. But the ill-concealed contempt which many Germans felt for their 'non-belligerent' ally kept Mussolini's resentment alive, while German policy on a number of important issues was strongly criticized in Rome. Hitler's agreement with Russia; the elimination of even a reduced Polish State,

1. Weizsäcker: p. 219.   2. *Ciano's Diary*, p. 176.

in deference to Russian wishes; German silence when Russia attacked Finland; German behaviour in carrying out the settlement over the South Tyrol – all these were the subject of Italian grievances. When the Russians invaded Finland at the beginning of December, Ciano noted that there were demonstrations against the Soviet Union in a number of Italian towns – 'the people say "Death to Russia" and really mean "Death to Germany".'[1]

A visit to Rome by Ley at the beginning of December did nothing to remove Italian suspicions. Far from it, for on 16 December Ciano made a two-hour speech before the Fascist Chamber of Corporations which went further than ever before in its implied criticism of Italy's ally. Three weeks later Mussolini sent Hitler a letter which represents the high-water mark of Mussolini's independence towards his brother-dictator.

He began by expressing his 'profound conviction' that, even if she had the aid of Italy, Germany could not bring Britain and France 'to their knees or even divide them. To believe that is to delude oneself. The United States would not permit a total defeat of the democracies'. For this reason, he urged Hitler, it was better to seek a compromise than 'to risk all, including the régime' in trying to defeat them. 'Unless you are irrevocably resolved to prosecute the war to a finish, I believe that the creation of a Polish state . . . would be an element that would resolve the war and constitute a condition sufficient for the peace.'

The main burden of Mussolini's letter was the unfortunate consequences of Hitler's Pact with Russia – discontent in Spain and Italy; the sacrifice of Finland in a war for which Italian volunteers had come forward in thousands, as well as the failure to preserve an independent Polish State. Opposed to an extension of the war in the west, Mussolini urged Hitler to turn back and seek Germany's *Lebensraum* in the east, in Russia.

No one knows better than I [he wrote], that politics has to admit the demands of expediency. This is true even of revolutionary politics. . . . Nonetheless, the fact is that in Poland and the Baltic it is Russia which has been the great beneficiary of the war – without firing a shot. I, who was born a revolutionary and have never changed, I say to you that you cannot sacrifice the permanent principles of your revolution to the tactical needs of a passing phase of policy. I am sure that you cannot abandon the anti-Bolshevik and anti-Semitic banner you have brandished for twenty years . . . and I have a duty to perform in adding that

1. *Ciano's Diary*, p. 180.

one step further in your relations with Moscow would have catastrophic results in Italy.[1]

Mussolini's letter was not only evidence of the troubled state of the relations between the two allies; its arguments touched on a side of his own policy – the Nazi–Soviet Pact – about which Hitler was never altogether at ease.

The major problem in Germany's relations with Russia was no longer represented by Poland. After the partition, while part of the western half of Poland was annexed to the Reich, the rest was formed into the Government-General, under Hans Frank, once the Party's defence-lawyer in the lean years before they came to power. On 7 October, the day after his so-called 'peace speech', Hitler appointed Himmler as Head of a new organization, the R.K.F.D.V., the Reich Commissariat for the Strengthening of German Folkdom.[2] Its first task was to carry out the deportation of Poles and Jews from the provinces annexed to Germany. 1,200,000 Poles and 300,000 Jews were moved in the first year under such conditions that many died on the way.

In the Government-General to which they were deported, Frank, besides recruiting forced labour and stripping the country of food and supplies, undertook the responsibility for the 'Extraordinary Pacification Action',[3] the liquidation of the Polish educated class as a deliberate act of policy. The treatment of the Jews was handed over to Himmler and the S.S. 'The final solution of the Jewish problem', that sinister and terrible phrase, was the cover name used to disguise S.S. plans for the extermination of all men, women, and children of Jewish blood in Europe: its first phase was put into operation in the Polish Government-General where, at Auschwitz, close on a million human beings perished before the end of the war.[4] Poland, in fact, became the working model of the Nazi New Order based upon the elimination of the Jews and the complete subjugation of inferior races, like the Slavs, to the Aryan master-race represented by the S.S.

Whatever fears, therefore, the Russians may have had that

1. Mussolini to Hitler, 4 January 1940. *Hitler e Mussolini*, pp. 33–9.
2. For an account of its activities, see Rober L. Koehl: *R.K.F.D.V.: German Resettlement and Population Policy, 1939–45* (Cambridge, Mass., 1957).
3. *Ausserordentliche Befriedigungsaktion.*
4. This figure is taken from Gerald Reitlinger: *The Final Solution* (London, 1953), p. 460.

Hitler would use the Poles living under German rule to stir up trouble among those living under Soviet rule were soon removed by the brutal way in which the Germans treated all Poles. The test of German–Russian relations in the winter of 1939–40 was not Poland, but Finland. Hitler had accepted the absorption of the three Baltic States into the Russian sphere of influence and the painful sequel of the evacuation of the long-established German population from those countries. Now he had to sit by silently while the Russians used force to coerce the Finns, a people who had close ties with Germany and whose brave resistance to the Russians inevitably roused admiration. The role of a neutral was humiliating for the man who had continually summoned all Europe to join him in throwing back the Bolshevik horde. Germany, however, expressed complete disinterest in the fate of Finland, and the Foreign Office instructed all German missions abroad to avoid any gesture of sympathy with the Finns or criticism of the Russians.

Hitler can scarcely have been blind to the fact that the measures taken by Russia to strengthen her position in the Baltic were obviously aimed at defending herself against an attack by Germany. Yet, without indulging in Ribbentrop's infatuated dreams about the future of German–Russian friendship, he still judged the price of cooperation with the Soviet Union to be worth paying. The advantages on which he counted were threefold: economic, political, and strategic.

Further economic agreements between the two countries were signed on 24 October 1939 and 11 February 1940. So important were the Russian supplies of raw materials for Germany that, on 30 March, Hitler ordered the delivery of German equipment to the U.S.S.R. to be given priority over deliveries to Germany's own Armed Forces. In return the Soviet Union supplied Germany in the first year with a million tons of cereals, half a million tons of wheat, 900,000 tons of oil, 500,000 tons of phosphates, 100,000 tons of cotton, as well as smaller amounts of other raw materials, and transported a million tons of soya beans from Manchuria.[1]

Collaboration was extended from the economic to the political field. In the autumn of 1939 Russian propaganda and the Communist parties abroad gave support to the German thesis that the responsibility for continuing the war rested upon the Western Powers – the so-called Peace Offensive. The two Governments

1. N.D. 2,353-PS. Material collected for an Official History of the German War Economy.

cooperated in bringing pressure to bear on Turkey to prevent the Turks from abandoning their neutrality, while the division of North-eastern Europe into spheres of influence was put into effect without a hitch.

But the supreme advantage, which Hitler rated above everything else, was strategic: the possibility of making his attack in the west without worrying about the defence of Germany's eastern frontiers. Not only was he able to avoid a war on two fronts, but he was able to concentrate practically the whole of his available forces in the west. During the 1940 campaign only seven German divisions were retained in the east to guard the long line between the Baltic and the Carpathians, and two of these were transferred to the west in the course of the campaign. After the war Göring estimated the Pact with Russia to have been worth fifty divisions to Hitler, the number of troops he would otherwise have had to keep in the east. The Pact with Russia was in fact as much an indispensable condition of Hitler's attack in the west as of the attack on Poland.

Like Stalin, Hitler was taking advantage of a situation which neither side expected to last long. For the moment the balance of advantage appeared to be in Stalin's favour, but Hitler was undismayed. If he could use Russian neutrality to inflict a defeat upon the Western Powers, he would more than redress the balance. Russia's gains in Eastern Europe and the Baltic would be forgotten if he could overrun the Low Countries and France, drive the British Army into the sea and dictate terms in the west. In any case, Russia's gains need not be regarded as permanent. On 17 October 1939, when talking to Keitel about the future of Poland, Hitler had made one exception to the general policy of neglect to be followed in the Government-General:

The territory is important to us [he told Keitel] from a military point of view as an advanced jumping-off point and can be used for the strategic concentration of troops. To that end the railroads, roads and lines of communication are to be kept in order.[1]

Hitler had shelved his eastern ambitions for the present but he had not forgotten them.

III

On 10 January 1940 Hitler ordered the attack in the west to begin on the 17th, that day week, at fifteen minutes before sunrise.

1. N.D. 864-PS.

Three days later he once again postponed it, and the last order in the captured file of postponements speaks of 20 January as the probable D-day: after that there is silence until May.

The very day of Hitler's decision – 10 January – a German Air Force staff officer made a forced landing in Belgium while flying from Münster to Cologne. He had with him the complete operational plan for the opening of Hitler's offensive, and although he burnt part of it, enough fell into Belgian hands to alarm the Germans. This settled the matter, to the barely disguised relief of the High Command. Until the winter was over, and new plans could be prepared, Hitler at last agreed that there was no further point in postponing the start of the operation from day to day.

Hitler was partly reconciled to this decision by the interest he began to feel in a new project, the initiative for which came from the Naval High Command. The Commander-in-Chief of the German Navy, Admiral Raeder, had been disappointed by the outbreak of war in 1939. By 1944, he believed, there would have been a 'good chance of settling the British question conclusively'; but in 1939 the German Navy had neither sufficient surface ships nor U-boats to make a serious challenge to British naval supremacy.

Searching for a means of increasing the Navy's power of attack against Britain's sea-routes, Raeder hit on the idea of securing bases in Norway. On 3 October he asked his Naval Staff to prepare answers to a number of questions on Norway, and on 10 October he made the suggestion to Hitler at one of the Führer's conferences on naval affairs.[1] Hitler was not much interested. At that time he was absorbed in the plans for invading the Low Countries and France, which he expected to put into operation in November, and the Norwegian project was not mentioned again until the middle of December.

By December the situation had been transformed by the Russian attack on Finland. Allied aid for the Finns was under discussion in London and Paris, and the possibility of British and French troops being sent to Finland through Norway, even of an allied occupation of Norway, was taken seriously by the Germans. The most vulnerable link in Germany's war economy was her dependence on supplies of iron-ore from Sweden. In 1940 these

1. The German Naval Archives – including the records of Hitler's wartime conferences with his C.-in-C.s at which the C.-in-C. of the Navy was present – were captured in their entirety at the end of the war.

supplies were expected to account for eleven and a half million out of Germany's total consumption of fifteen million tons. During the winter months, the Gulf of Bothnia was frozen and the only route open was through Narvik and down the long Atlantic seaboard of Norway. By occupying Norway the Western Powers could not only interfere with this vital traffic, but could block the movement of German ships from the Baltic into the North Sea and the Atlantic.

Raeder was able to use these facts to support his argument for Germany forestalling the British by securing control of Norway first. At the same time he suggested a means of doing this which at once attracted Hitler. Through Rosenberg, who held the obscure post of head of the Party's Foreign Policy Bureau, and who had always been interested in the Nordic peoples of Scandinavia, the Admiral had been put in touch with Quisling and Hagelin, the leaders of the small Norwegian Nazi Party known as the Party of National Unity. Quisling, a former General Staff officer and Norwegian Minister of War from 1931 to 1933, encouraged the belief that, with German support, he would be able to carry out a *coup d'état*. In this way the German forces needed could be reduced to proportions which would not disturb the main concentration on the western frontier or endanger the plans already made to attack France.

Hitler was sufficiently impressed by Raeder's argument to see Quisling three times between 14 and 18 December, and to give orders for German support to be made available to him. Hitler preferred the method of the *coup d'état* because of its obvious economy, but, in case of its failure, he agreed to plans being prepared for an occupation of Norway by force. He had still not committed himself, but the final postponement of the offensive in the west, in the middle of January, freed his hands, and was followed on 27 January by the establishment of an inter-services staff to work out the details. The occupation of Denmark was to be carried out at the same time as the operation against Norway.

While these preparations were being made in Berlin, in London Churchill, as First Lord of the Admiralty, was urging a reluctant Cabinet to give the British Navy permission to lay mines in Norwegian territorial waters and so interfere with their use by the Germans for the transport of iron-ore from the port of Narvik. The Cabinet refused to agree, but on 17 February the British destroyer *Cossack* intercepted the German prison-ship

Altmark in Norwegian waters and rescued a number of British prisoners. This incident roused Hitler's anger and put an end to any hesitation. He demanded the immediate appointment of a commander for the expedition and agreed at once to see the man proposed by Keitel, General Nikolaus von Falkenhorst, who had served in Finland in 1918 and who was at that time in command of an army corps at Coblenz.

Falkenhorst came to Berlin on 20 February. Hitler saw him for a few minutes before his daily military conference and gave him instructions to take over the preparations for the occupation of Norway. He gave three reasons for his decision: to keep the British out of the Baltic, to give greater freedom of operation to the German Navy, and to protect the ore-route down the Norwegian coast. Falkenhorst, a little bewildered by his new commission, was then dismissed and told to return at five o'clock the same afternoon with his plans ready to lay before the Führer. He bought a Baedeker and retired to his hotel bedroom. By five o'clock he had a rough plan sketched out, sufficient to satisfy Hitler, and before he returned to Coblenz his new command had been confirmed.

In the week that followed the interview with Falkenhorst, Jodl's Diary shows the greatly increased interest Hitler was now taking in the Norwegian expedition. The force to be employed was to be kept as small as possible, and Falkenhorst was given no more than five divisions. But the part to be played by Quisling had dwindled into insignificance, and the Germans were preparing to carry out a military occupation, relying on surprise to supplement the small forces Hitler was willing to spare.

The risks involved in such an operation were great. As Raeder pointed out to Hitler in a conference on 9 March, it was contrary to all the principles of naval warfare to attempt such an undertaking without command of the sea. Everything, therefore, depended upon the element of surprise. Reports of British and French preparations for the occupation of Norwegian ports as part of the plan to come to Finland's aid kept the German High Command in a state of constant alarm lest they should be forestalled by the Allies.

Their anxiety was relieved when the Finns were driven to ask the Russians for an armistice. This was signed on 12 March, and the danger of an Anglo-French landing receded. But, having gone so far, Hitler refused to turn back. Raeder admitted at a conference on 26 March that the danger of a British landing in Norway was no longer acute, but added that, in his opinion, Germany would sooner or later have to carry out an occupation of Norway and that the moment was favourable. Hitler entirely agreed. 'Exercise Weser' (Norway) was to come before 'Case Yellow' (the code name for the attack in the west), and the preparations were to go forward whether the Allies proceeded with their plans or not. A week later, on the afternoon of 2 April, Raeder, Göring, and Falkenhorst reported that the preparations were complete, and Hitler confirmed the order for operations to begin on 9 April.

Evidence of the German concentration of troops and naval forces along the Baltic coast in March and early April was not taken seriously by the Norwegian and Danish governments, and as late as 5 April, when the German supply ships had already put to sea, Chamberlain made the unhappy remark that Hitler had 'missed the bus'. The Germans, therefore, enjoyed the advantage of complete surprise and Hitler gave nothing away. He made a number of speeches in the first three months of 1940, but they revealed nothing of his intentions.

The first of these speeches was made on 30 January, when Hitler celebrated the first seven years of his rule by appearing at the Sportpalast in Berlin. He poured elaborate scorn on the Allied war-aims. 'No nation,' he declared, 'will burn its fingers twice. The trick of the Pied Piper of Hamelin works only once. The apostles of international understanding cannot once again betray the German nation.'

On 24 February he appeared in Munich, on the twentieth anniversary of his first appearance at a big public meeting. Considering the opportunity this offered, his speech was disappointing. He was obviously aware that the war was none too popular in Germany, but the argument was laboured and he constantly returned to the same points without making them more convincing. Only at the end of his speech was there a touch of the old Hitler.

'It is the leadership of the German nation that counts,' he told his audience of the Nazi Old Guard. 'If in those days a certain Adolf Hitler had been Chancellor of the German Reich, instead of a musketeer in the German Army, do you believe that the capitalist idols of international democracy would have won?' In the same passage Hitler described himself as 'the flint that strikes the spark out of the German nation'.[1] In the first winter of the

1. *My New Order*, pp. 783–8.

war, however, there were few sparks to be struck out of the German people.

From Munich Hitler returned to Berlin, where he signed the preliminary directive for 'Exercise Weser' on 1 March, and received Sumner Welles, the U.S. Under-Secretary of State, on the 2nd. The purpose of Welles's visit was to sound out the possibilities for the re-establishment of peace before the conflict began in earnest, and in particular to strengthen the reluctance of the Italians to be drawn into the war. Neither purpose commended itself to Hitler, and Sumner Welles's reception in Berlin was cool.

The American envoy's visit to Berlin, as he soon recognized, was a waste of time. Hitler was not to be diverted from the decisions he had already made. But there was some slight hope of keeping Mussolini out of the war, and Welles returned to Rome after visits to Paris and London. The possibility that in Rome he would find a more sympathetic audience than in Berlin caused Hitler some anxiety. The Duce's letter of January had been left unanswered for two months: now, quite unexpectedly, the German Ambassador informed Ciano on 8 March that Ribbentrop would arrive in Rome in two days' time, before Welles returned, bringing with him Hitler's long-delayed reply.

The letter was couched in the most cordial terms, and Hitler played skilfully on the conflict in Mussolini's mind between fear and the desire to play a historic role.

I believe, Duce, that there can be no doubt that the outcome of this war will also decide the future of Italy . . . that sooner or later, fate will force us after all to fight side by side, that you will likewise not escape this clash of arms . . . and that your place will then more than ever be at our side, just as mine will be at yours.[1]

Although inclined to object on some points – notably on relations with Russia – Mussolini accepted the German argument without dispute.

The Führer is right [he told Ribbentrop] when he states that the fates of the German and Italian nations are bound up together. . . . It is in practice impossible for Italy to keep out of the conflict. At the given moment she will enter the war and will conduct it along with Germany and in line with her.[2]

1. G.D., D.VIII, No. 663.
2. Ribbentrop's conversations with Mussolini, in *Ciano's Diplomatic Papers*, pp. 339–59.

Ribbentrop failed to pin Mussolini down to a specific date, but he made good use of Italian resentment at the effect of the British blockade. In particular the sudden ability of the Germans to find up to twelve million tons of coal a year, and the trucks to move it, left a considerable impression on the Italians. To clinch matters, Ribbentrop invited Mussolini to meet Hitler on the Brenner at any time after 19 March.

Even Ciano admitted that Ribbentrop had succeeded in re-inforcing the Axis by his visit. He still hoped that Mussolini would keep Italy out of the war, but Sumner Welles, who saw Mussolini again on 16 March, was impressed by the change in the Duce. 'He did not seem to be labouring under the physical or mental oppression which had been so obvious during my first conversation with him. . . . He seemed to have thrown off some great weight. Since that time I have often wondered whether, during the two weeks which had elapsed since my first visit to Rome, he had not determined to cross the Rubicon, and during Ribbentrop's visit had not decided to force Italy into the war.'[1]

As soon as he returned to Berlin, Ribbentrop telephoned to Rome to ask for the Brenner meeting to be brought forward to the 18th. Mussolini cursed – 'These Germans are unbearable; they don't give one time to breathe or to think matters over' – but he agreed. Ciano wrote that the Duce still hoped to persuade Hitler to desist from his attack in the west, but he added gloomily: 'It cannot be denied that the Duce is fascinated by Hitler, a fascination which involves something deeply rooted in his make-up. The Führer will get more out of the Duce than Ribbentrop was able to.'[2]

However much he might try to bolster up his resolution, Mussolini could not overcome the sense of inferiority he felt in face of Hitler. As Ciano saw, the sole successes which Mussolini valued were military successes. Hitler had dared to risk war, and he had not. Hitler had only to play on this feeling of humiliation to stimulate the Duce's longing to assert himself and revive his flagging belligerency. When they met on the Brenner, high up in the snow-covered mountains – their first meeting since Munich – Hitler overwhelmed Mussolini with a flood of talk, describing at length the course of the Polish campaign and the German preparations for the attack in the west. Mussolini had little chance

1. Sumner Welles: *The Time for Decision* (N.Y., 1944), p. 138.
2. *Ciano's Diary*, pp. 220–1.

of saying anything, yet he used the few minutes that were left him to re-affirm his intention of coming into the war.

The Duce repeated that, as soon as Germany has by her military operations created a favourable situation, he would lose no time in intervening. Should the German advance develop with a slower tempo, the Duce would wait until the moment when his intervention at the decisive hour could be of real use to Germany.[1]

Back in Rome the Duce might grumble at the way in which Hitler talked all the time, but face to face with him he was unable to conceal an anxious deference. Hitler handled him with skill. The impression of German strength which he created and the confidence with which he spoke stirred Mussolini's old fear of being left out at the division of the spoils. As the two dictators parted on the station platform, Hitler could congratulate himself on the ease with which he had re-asserted his ascendancy: three months later Italy entered the war.

I V

Hitler said not a word to Mussolini of his intention of attacking Norway – further proof, if it were needed, of the disdain with which he treated his Italian allies. From the beginning of April, however, all his attention was directed to the Baltic and the north.

Meanwhile, exactly one day after Hitler confirmed 9 April as the date for 'Exercise Weser', the British Cabinet at last authorized the Royal Navy to mine Norwegian waters, an operation fixed for 8 April. In case of German counter-action, British and French forces were embarked to occupy the very same Norwegian ports selected by the German Navy as its own objectives. Thus, between 7 and 9 April, two naval forces were converging on Norway, and the scraps of news which reached Berlin of British preparations heightened the atmosphere of tension in Hitler's headquarters. Raeder was staking virtually the whole German fleet on the Norwegian gamble, and if it had the ill-luck to encounter the British fleet in any force, disaster could follow within a few hours.

In fact, a German transport was sunk, and the German cruiser *Hipper* brought to action by a British destroyer on the 8th. But the operation went on, and the tactics of surprise proved brilliantly successful. Oslo, Bergen, Trondheim, Stavanger, and Narvik

1. *Ciano's Diplomatic Papers*, p. 365.

were captured at a blow. Quisling's *coup* was a miserable failure; the Norwegian King and Government escaped, and six weeks' hard fighting lay ahead before the Allied troops, now hurriedly landed, were driven out. None the less, the British had been taken by surprise and 'completely outwitted' (the phrase is Churchill's) on their own native element of the sea. The British Navy inflicted considerable losses on the German forces, but these were not much greater than Raeder had anticipated, and they were a small price to pay for safeguarding the iron-ore supplies, securing the Baltic, and breaking out into the Atlantic, with bases along the whole of the Norwegian coast at the disposal of the German Navy and the German Air Force.

From the beginning Hitler had taken a close personal interest in the Norwegian expedition. Falkenhorst was directly responsible to him, and Hitler's own command organization (the O.K.W., the Supreme Command of the Armed Forces) replaced the Army High Command (O.K.H.) for the planning and direction of operations. This led to considerable friction and departmental jealousy. More important still was the way in which it foreshadowed future developments. For Norway marks the beginning of that continuous personal intervention in the daily conduct of operations which was more and more to absorb Hitler's attention and drive his generals to distraction.

Hitler's temperament was singularly ill-fitted for the position of a commander-in-chief. He easily became excited, talked far too much and was apt to blame others for his own mistakes, or for adverse circumstances out of their control. These faults were particularly noticeable in April 1940, as Jodl's Diary shows, for at the back of Hitler's mind was the fear that unexpected difficulties in Norway might force him to postpone the attack in the west once again. This still remained the main objective, compared with which Norway was only a side-show.

Fortunately for Hitler, his gamble on time came off, and at the end of April he felt sufficient confidence in the outcome of the Norwegian operations to fix a provisional date for the opening of the western campaign in the first week of May. A slight delay due to bad weather caused a change from 8 May to 10 May, a decision which threw Hitler into a state of agitation. But this proved to be the final postponement, and at dawn on 10 May 1940 the battle in the west was joined at last.

Little though Hitler may have realized it then, he owed his success in the Battle of France more than anything else to the long delay in opening the attack which had so much irked him at the time.

The original plan for the attack had assigned the chief role to the most northerly of the three German Army Groups in the west, Army Group B under von Bock. This was to carry out a wide sweeping movement through the Low Countries, supported by Army Group A (Rundstedt), which held the centre of the German line opposite the Ardennes, and by Army Group C (Leeb), which held the left wing facing the Maginot Line. For this purpose virtually the whole of the German panzer forces were assigned to Bock on the right wing.

There were solid arguments against such a plan. It was a repetition of the German advance in 1914 and so unlikely to take the Western Allies by surprise, and it meant sending the tank forces into country broken by innumerable canals and small rivers. Here they would come into head-on collision with the pick of the British and French armies advancing into Belgium, and even if the Germans succeeded in forcing them back they would only be driving the Allies nearer to their fortified positions and their supply bases.

The French High Command had framed their own plans to meet precisely such an opening move and, had Hitler adhered to the original scheme, events might conceivably have followed the dictation of the French rather than of the Germans. But an alternative plan had already been worked out by the Chief of Staff of Rundstedt's Army Group A, General von Manstein. Manstein argued that the decisive thrust should be made not on the German right wing, where the Western Allies would almost certainly expect it, but in the centre, through the Ardennes, aiming at Sedan and the Channel coast. Such a move would take the French completely by surprise, for they (like many of the German generals) had written off the Ardennes as unsuitable for tank operations, and this part of the French Front was more weakly defended than almost any other. If the tanks could once get through the wooded hills of the Ardennes they would be out into the rolling country of northern France, which was well-suited to a rapid advance. Finally, if the German plan proved successful, it would destroy the hinge upon which the British and French advance into Belgium depended, severing their lines of communication, cutting them off from France and forcing them into a trap with their backs to the Belgian coast.

Manstein's suggestion was frowned on by the Army High Command, but, thanks to the delays to which the start of the operation was subject, Manstein succeeded in getting his scheme brought to Hitler's attention.

Manstein's proposals had precisely those qualities of surprise and risk to which Hitler attached so much importance, and in the course of February he ordered the whole plan of attack to be recast along Manstein's lines, transferring the all-important panzer forces from the right wing to the centre under von Rundstedt.

This change proved decisive. The opposition of the Army High Command, supported by the aggrieved Bock, was not easily overcome, and professional jealousy succeeded in getting Manstein transferred to the command of an infantry corps, where he played a minor part in the offensive. But by March Manstein's plan had become Hitler's own – he seems to have believed that he had thought of it himself – and by May the new orders were ready to to be put into operation.

The German Army which invaded the Low Countries and France on the morning of 10 May consisted of eighty-nine divisions, with a further forty-seven held in reserve. It included the formidable weapon of ten panzer divisions, with three thousand armoured vehicles, a thousand of which at least were heavy tanks. The first sensational success was the overrunning of the Dutch and Belgian defence systems. The key to this was the use of small forces of highly trained parachute and glider troops which captured the vital bridges before they could be destroyed, together with the famous fortress of Eben Emael on the Albert Canal. Hitler had personally conceived the most important points in the plans for the use of the airborne troops. It had been his idea to capture Eben Emael by landing on the roof a detachment of less than a hundred parachute engineers equipped with a powerful new explosive, a success built up by German propaganda as a demonstration of the power of Germany's secret weapons.

But the crux of the operation, still unsuspected by the Western Powers, was the thrust through the Ardennes. Rundstedt's Army Group, ranged along the frontier from Aachen to the Moselle, disposed of forty-four divisions, including three panzer corps under the command of General von Kleist. The armoured column was over a hundred miles long, stretching back fifty miles the other side of the Rhine.

The plan worked with extraordinary success. The German armour quickly traversed the Ardennes, passed the French frontier on 12 May and were over the Meuse on the 13th. The High Command indeed became alarmed at the ease with which Kleist was advancing.

Hitler shared this anxiety. He was preoccupied with the possibility of a French counter-attack from the south, and personally intervened to halt the advance of General Guderian's leading panzer divisions, which had reached the Oise on the night of the 16th. A note in Halder's diary on 17 May reads:

Führer is terribly nervous. Frightened by his own success, he is afraid to take any chance and so would rather pull the reins on us.

The next day Halder wrote:

Every hour is precious, Führer's H.Q. sees it quite differently. Führer keeps worrying about south flank. He rages and screams that we are on the way to ruin the whole campaign. He won't have any part in continuing the operation in a westward direction.[1]

The halt, however, was only temporary. The motorized infantry was quick in following up, and on the evening of the 18th Hitler was persuaded to allow the tanks to resume their advance. Backed by an irresistible superiority in the air, the German armoured thrust broke right through the French front and threw the Allied plans into confusion. While the British Army and the best of the French divisions were fighting fiercely in Belgium, they were cut off to the south by the German dash for the coast, and on the night of 20 May received the news that the Germans had reached the mouth of the Somme at Abbeville. A week later the Belgian King ordered his Army to cease fighting. The British Expeditionary Force and the First French Army were caught in a trap between the converging forces of Bock's Army Group on the north and Rundstedt's on the south.

The German plan of encirclement was only defeated by the brilliant improvisation of the Dunkirk evacuation. Between 27 May and 4 June a total of 338,000 British and French troops were got away by sea from the beaches and harbour of Dunkirk. Yet the possibility of such an evacuation might well have been denied to the British if Guderian's tanks had not been ordered to halt a few miles south of Dunkirk on 24 May, at a time when the British

1. Quoted in B. H. Liddell Hart: *The Other Side of the Hill* (3rd edition, London, 1951), pp. 190–1.

Army had not yet fought its way back to the coast and there was nothing to prevent the Germans capturing the last escape-port open to the B.E.F.

There seems little doubt that the Commander-in-Chief of the German Army and the Chief of Staff, Brauchitsch and Halder, were opposed to any halt, but there is evidence, despite his later denials, that Rundstedt, commanding Army Group A, was in favour. Göring, whose vanity made him eager to press the claims of his Air Force, urged Hitler to leave the elimination of the trapped British and French armies to the Luftwaffe: it would be better for the Führer's prestige if the whole credit for the victory now within their grasp did not rest with the Army generals. Hitler himself was set upon avoiding the stalemate which had followed the Battle of the Marne in 1914: his objective was the defeat of the French army and he wanted at all costs to preserve his armoured force for the next phase of the offensive which would decide the battle for Paris and France. If the French were knocked out of the war, he was confident that the British would come to terms.

Whatever the mixture of motives, after an angry interview with Brauchitsch and Halder on the afternoon of 24 May, Hitler insisted on holding back the German tanks. Forty-eight hours later he reversed his decision, and on 27 May the panzer troops were allowed to resume their advance. But by then it was too late. The British had used the unexpected respite to strengthen their defences and were able to hold off the Germans long enough to complete their evacuation. The first of Hitler's military mistakes was to have momentous consequences for the future of the war.

At the time, however, the failure at Dunkirk appeared slight beside the continuing news of German successes. So Mussolini, as well as Hitler, judged. Fear of the consequences of going to war gave place in the Duce's mind to fear of arriving too late. Gauging the mood of his brother dictator with skill, Hitler found time in the midst of his preoccupations to write a series of letters to Mussolini in which he poured scorn on the feebleness of the British and French. Mussolini's replies were each more enthusiastic than the last, culminating in the announcement, delivered by the Italian Ambassador on 31 May, that Italy would declare war in the next few days. The date finally agreed on was 10 June, and hostilities began on the 11th.

Hitler was delighted at Mussolini's decision. He undoubtedly

overrated Italy's value as an ally, and great efforts were made by
Goebbels to convince the German people of the importance of
Italian intervention. The German people, however, showed no
more enthusiasm for the alliance than the Italians. Mussolini's
timing, indeed, was so bad that his declaration of war in June
1940 made their new allies appear even more contemptible in
German eyes than the Italian failure to fight in September 1939.

Meanwhile, on 5 June, the German Army renewed the attack
by driving south across the Somme. The French had lost something like thirty divisions, nearly a third of their Army, in the
fighting in Belgium, and only two out of the fourteen British
divisions now remained in France. With his depleted forces,
General Weygand had to face a numerically superior German
Army, elated by its victories, provided with overwhelming air
support and led by armoured formations against which the
French had no defence. In eleven days the battle was over. On
14 June Paris was occupied by the Germans and the panzer
divisions were racing for the Rhône Valley, the Mediterranean,
and the Spanish frontier. On the evening of 16 June M. Reynaud
resigned, and the same night Marshal Pétain formed a new French
Government, whose sole aim was to negotiate an armistice. Less
than six weeks after the opening of the campaign Hitler was on
his way to Munich to discuss with Mussolini the terms to be
imposed on France.

V

Since the beginning of the Norwegian campaign on 9 April
Hitler's troops had overrun Norway, Denmark, Holland,
Belgium, Luxembourg, and France, had successfully defied the
power of the British Navy, driven the British Expeditionary
Force into the sea, and inflicted a shattering defeat on the army
of Napoleon and Foch. For more than four years between 1914
and 1918 the old German Army had fought at terrible cost and
without success to effect the break-through on the Western Front
which Hitler had achieved in little more than a month with very
small losses.

Before the war Hitler had scored a series of political triumphs,
culminating in the Nazi–Soviet Pact, which could challenge comparison with the diplomacy of Bismarck. Now he had led the
German Army to a series of military triumphs which eclipsed the
fame of Moltke and Ludendorff and challenged comparison with

the victories of Frederick the Great and even Napoleon. Hitler, the outsider who had never been to a university or a staff college, had beaten the Foreign Office and the General Staff at their own game.

It is customary to decry this achievement, to point, for instance, to the luck Hitler had in encountering such weakness and incompetence on the other side, to his good fortune in finding a Manstein to construct his plan of campaign for him and men like Guderian to put it into operation. But this is only a part of the truth. If there was weakness and incompetence on the other side, it was Hitler who divined it. He was the one man who consistently refused to be impressed by the military reputation of France, the one man who insisted that a quick victory in the west was possible, and who forced the Army against his generals' advice to undertake a campaign which was to prove the most remarkable in its history. If Manstein designed the plan of campaign it was Hitler who took it up. If Guderian was the man who showed what the German panzer divisions could do when used with imagination it was Hitler who grasped the importance of armour, and provided the new German Army with ten such divisions at a time when there was still strong opposition inside the Army itself to such ideas. If Hitler, therefore, is justly to be made responsible for the later disasters of the German Army, he is entitled to the major share of the credit for the victories of 1940: the German generals cannot have it both ways.

But what use did Hitler intend to make of his victory? Hitler had never looked to the west for the future expansion of Germany, but always to the east. The conflict with Britain and France arose not from any demands he had to make on the Western Powers themselves, but from their refusal to agree to a free hand for Germany in Central and Eastern Europe. This had been the issue between Britain and Germany throughout 1938 and 1939, over Czechoslovakia no less than over Poland, and it remained the issue now, in 1940.

So far the problem had baffled Hitler. Bribes, in the form of the Naval Agreement of 1935 and the guarantee of the British Empire which he offered in 1939, had failed to overcome British opposition, and in September 1939 this opposition had been carried to the point of declaring war on Germany. Hitler, however, far from abandoning his hopes of a settlement with Great Britain as a result of the war, looked upon the victories he had won in Poland and the west as clearing the ground for such an agreement. The

British had now, he felt, lost any reason for continuing to adhere to their former policy. Their last ally on the Continent had gone, their Army had been driven into the sea, they must now surely accept the impossibility of preventing a German hegemony in Europe and, like sensible people, come to terms – the more so as Hitler had no desire, at this stage, to interfere with their independence or their Empire. For his part, he was perfectly ready to conclude an alliance with Great Britain and to recognize the continued existence of the British Empire, which [he told Rundstedt] must be looked on, together with the Catholic Church, as one of the corner-stones of Western civilization. England would have to return the German colonies and recognize Germany's dominant position in Europe, but that was all.

In this frame of mind, preoccupied with the chances of a compromise peace with Great Britain and daily expecting to receive an approach from London, Hitler turned to the question of the armistice with France. A final settlement with France could be allowed to wait until the end of the war, but the character of the armistice terms offered to France now might have considerable influence on the British. In particular, a French decision to continue the fight from North Africa or the departure of the French Fleet to join the Royal Navy would strengthen the British determination to go on fighting themselves. On the other hand, French acceptance of the German armistice terms might well make the British think twice.

Mussolini was in a very different mood. He was eager to become the heir of the French Empire in North Africa and to secure the mastery of the Mediterranean. His claims extended to Nice, Corsica, French Somaliland, and Tunisia; an Atlantic outlet in Morocco; the acquisition of Malta and the replacement of Britain by Italy in Egypt and the Sudan. As guarantees, the Duce wanted to occupy the whole of French territory and to enforce the surrender of the French fleet. But, as he confessed with some bitterness to Ciano on the train to Munich, Hitler had won the war and Hitler would have the last word.

The German reception of the Italians was cordial, but Ribbentrop made it quite plain that Hitler would not agree to make demands of the French which might drive them to continue the war from North Africa or England. Above all, the powerful and undamaged French fleet must be prevented from joining the British. For this reason, no less than for the effect on British opinion, Mussolini's annexationist ambitions would have to be deferred. Hitler proposed to occupy only three-fifths of France, to allow a French Government in Unoccupied France, to promise not to make use of the French fleet during the war and to leave the French colonies untouched.

These were heavy blows for Mussolini, but after only a week's campaign, during which the Italian troops had not distinguished themselves, he was in no position to argue. When Ciano, taken aback by Ribbentrop's sudden enthusiasm for peace, asked him: 'Does Germany at the present moment prefer peace or the prosecution of the war?' Ribbentrop replied without hesitation: 'Peace.'[1] Faithfully echoing Hitler's opinions on the value of the British Empire, Ribbentrop told his Italian colleague in confidence that Britain had already been informed of the Führer's conditions through Sweden. Hitler agreed not to conclude an armistice with France until she had come to terms with Italy as well, but he declined Mussolini's suggestion of joint German–Italian negotiations with the French. He had no intention of sharing his triumph.

From Munich, where the talks with Mussolini and Ciano had taken place on 18–19 June, Hitler flew back to his Field Headquarters at Bruly-le-Pêche, and the final terms of the armistice were drafted on the 20th. Paul Schmidt and the translators worked all night by candle-light in a little village church to complete the French version, with Keitel, and sometimes Hitler, coming in to see what progress they were making.

For the signing of the armistice Hitler had appointed the exact place in the Forest of Compiègne, north-east of Paris, where Foch had dictated the terms of capitulation to the German delegation on 11 November 1918. The old restaurant car in which the negotiations had taken place was brought out from its Paris museum and set up on the identical spot it had occupied in 1918.

It was a hot June afternoon, with the sun casting shadows through the elms and the pines, when Hitler – in uniform, with the Iron Cross on his chest – stepped out of his Mercedes and strode into the clearing. He was accompanied by an impressive retinue, Göring, with his Field-Marshal's baton, Keitel, Brauchitsch, Raeder, Ribbentrop, and Hess. Silently he led the little procession up to the block of granite on which the French inscription read: 'Here on 11 November 1918 succumbed the criminal pride of the

1. *Ciano's Diplomatic Papers*, pp. 372–5.

German Reich . . . vanquished by the free peoples which it tried to enslave.' Fifty yards away, in the shelter of the trees, William Shirer, the C.B.S. Correspondent, was watching intently through field-glasses. As Hitler turned Shirer caught his expression, a mixture of scorn, anger, hate, and triumph:

He steps off the monument and contrives to make even this gesture a masterpiece of contempt. . . . He glances slowly round the clearing. . . . Suddenly, as though his face were not giving quite complete expression to his feelings, he throws his whole body into harmony with his mood. He swiftly snaps his hands on his hips, arches his shoulders, plants his feet wide apart. It is a magnificent gesture of defiance, of burning contempt for this place and all that it has stood for in the twenty-two years since it witnessed the humbling of the German Empire.[1]

Shortly afterwards the French delegates arrived. Hitler received them in silence. He stayed to listen to the reading of the preamble, then rose, gave a stiff salute with his outstretched arm, and, accompanied by his retinue, left the railway car. As he strode back down the avenue of trees to the waiting cars the German band played the German national anthem, *Deutschland über Alles*, and the Nazi Horst Wessel Song. The one-time agitator, who told the Munich crowds in 1920 that he would never rest until he had torn up the Treaty of Versailles, had reached the peak of his career. He had kept his promise: the humiliation of 1918 was avenged.

No other tourist has ever paid his first visit to Paris as a conqueror. Hitler combined both roles. He came at the end of the month, made a tour of the sights, went up the Eiffel Tower and stood in rapt contemplation before the tomb of Napoleon in the Hôtel des Invalides. Paris, however, did not impress him as much as the Italian cities, not even as much as Vienna, and he was critical of its architecture. 'I paid my visit [to the Opera] very early in the morning, between six and nine . . . The first newspaper seller who recognized me stood there and gaped. I still have before me the mental picture of that woman in Lille who saw me from her window and exclaimed: "The Devil."

'Finally, we went up to the Sacré Coeur. Appalling! But Paris remains one of the jewels of Europe.'[2]

Early in July, Hitler returned to his headquarters near Freudenstadt, in the depths of the Black Forest, and was back in Berlin to receive Ciano on the 7th.

1. William Shirer: *Berlin Diary*, p. 331.
2. *Hitler's Table Talk* (29 October 1944), pp. 98–9.

With France Hitler had every reason to be satisfied. The French Government had been relieved by the comparative moderation of the German demands, and the armistice was signed without further difficulty. But the news which Hitler had been waiting for since the middle of June, a sign from London that the British were willing to consider peace negotiations, still failed to come. Tentative soundings through the neutral capitals produced no result. On 18 June Churchill, speaking in the House of Commons, declared the Government's determination to fight on, whatever the odds, 'so that, if the British Empire and its Commonwealth last for a thousand years, men will still say: "This was their finest hour".' On 3 July the British Government underlined its resolve by ordering the British Navy to open fire on the French warships at Oran. Hitler continued to postpone the speech he was to make to the Reichstag in order to give England sufficient time to make the decision he hoped for, but he was much less confident than he had been at Munich in June. Ciano found him in a divided mind, unwilling to commit himself to any course, but prepared to admit the possibility that the war would have to continue.

Hitler waited another twelve days and then at last summoned the Reichstag for 19 July, more than a month after the collapse of France. The month's silence left little doubt that the British, to Hitler's genuine astonishment and even regret, were resolved to continue the war. After waiting in vain for a move on the part of the British Government Hitler decided to make a direct appeal himself, as a last gesture.

It almost causes me pain [he told the Reichstag] to think that I should have been selected by Fate to deal the final blow to the structure which these men have already set tottering. . . . Mr Churchill ought perhaps, for once, to believe me when I prophesy that a great Empire will be destroyed – an Empire which it was never my intention to destroy or even to harm. . . .

In this hour, I feel it to be my duty before my own conscience to appeal once more to reason and common sense in Great Britain as much as elsewhere. I consider myself in a position to make this appeal since I am not the vanquished begging favours, but the victor speaking in the name of reason. I can see no reason why this war must go on.[1]

The occasion was a splendid one, marked by the promotion of Göring to the special rank of Reichsmarshal and of twelve generals to be field-marshals. Hitler himself was at the top of his

1. *My New Order*, pp. 809–38.

form as an orator, speaking with more control than usual and conveying an unusual sincerity in what he said. Outwardly, it was a scene of triumph, yet the impression left at the end was one of uncertainty, and Ciano reported that there was ill-concealed disappointment among the Germans he met at the unfavourable British reaction to Hitler's offer.

It is doubtful whether Hitler himself, by this time, expected anything else. He had already issued the directive for the invasion of Britain three days before his speech. This was the obvious answer: if Britain would not come to terms she must be forced to submit. So, throughout the rest of the summer of 1940 and well into the autumn, the preparations for a direct assault on the British Isles continued, and all the world waited for the news that Hitler had launched his invasion armada across the Channel.

VI

How then did it come about that, five months after his speech to the Reichstag, Hitler signed the order for the invasion, not of Britain, but of the Soviet Union? Why did he change his mind, why did he make the mistake of attacking Russia before he had finished with Britain, thereby deliberately incurring the dangers of a war on two fronts?

One answer which has been given to these questions is that Hitler never seriously intended to carry out an invasion of Britain, that 'Operation Sea-Lion'[1] was an elaborate bluff designed to bring pressure to bear on the British to come to terms and dropped when they refused to be frightened into capitulation. This is the view which Rundstedt, who was appointed to command the invasion force, took after the war. 'Among ourselves,' his chief of operations, Blumentritt, told Liddell Hart, 'we talked of it as a bluff.'[2] The German military and naval records of the time, however, do not bear this out: the answer to be pieced together from these is a different one.[3]

Until the summer of 1940 Hitler had never seriously considered how a war against Britain could be fought and won. This is not as paradoxical as it may seem at first sight. His quarrel with the

1. The code name for the invasion of Britain.
2. Liddell Hart, op. cit., p. 222.
3. See the excellent account given by Ronald Wheatley: *Operation Sea-Lion* (London, 1958); and, Walter Ancel, *Hitler confronts England* (Durham N.C., 1960).

British arose solely from their refusal to allow him a free hand in Europe. Once that was settled, he had no further claims against them, apart from the return of the former German colonies. Any territorial or economic gains which Germany might acquire in the west were secondary to the prime object of the campaign against the Western Powers, to free German energies for the policy from which Hitler had never wavered since he wrote *Mein Kampf* – the historic policy of expansion in the East.

Once the French had been defeated and the British thrust out of continental Europe, Hitler had no further interest in continuing the war in the West and no plans had been made for a subsequent attack on Britain. It is true that, as early as November 1939, Admiral Raeder had set his naval staff to work on the problems involved in crossing the English Channel, but his attempts to arouse Hitler's interest at conferences on 21 May and 20 June proved unsuccessful. Until the end of June Hitler's view of the future was based on the assumption that the British would be willing to come to terms.

It was not until 2 July that Keitel issued instructions to the three services to prepare plans and not until 16 July that Hitler signed his own directive fixing the middle of August as the date by which preparations must be completed. Even then the opening sentences revealed Hitler's reluctance: 'As England, in spite of the hopelessness of her military position, has so far shown herself unwilling to come to any compromise, I have decided to begin to prepare for, and if necessary to carry out, an invasion of England.'[1]

Once planning began, it was clear that the problems to be overcome were formidable. Five days after signing the directive of 16 July, Hitler spoke to Raeder in realistic terms of what would be involved.

The invasion of Britain is an exceptionally daring undertaking, because even if the way is short this is not just a river crossing, but the crossing of a sea which is dominated by the enemy. This is not a case of a single-crossing operation as in Norway; operational surprise cannot be expected; a defensively prepared and utterly determined enemy faces us and dominates the sea area which we must use. For the Army forty divisions will be required; the most difficult part will be the continued reinforcement of military stores. We cannot count on supplies of any kind being available to us in England. The prerequisites are complete mastery of the air, the operational use of powerful artillery in the Straits

1. N.D. 442-PS.

of Dover and protection by minefields. The time of the year is an important factor too. The main operation will therefore have to be completed by 15 September. . . . If it is not certain that preparations can be completed by the beginning of September, other plans must be considered.[1]

Raeder needed no convincing of the difficulties in the way of a successful invasion. Not only was he powerfully impressed by Germany's naval inferiority, but he saw no possibility at all of providing sufficient transports for the forty divisions which the Army planned to land. An acrimonious debate followed between the Army and the Navy on the number of divisions to be put across the Channel and the width of the front on which landings were to be made.

When the Navy insisted that the invading force be cut from forty to thirteen divisions, landing on a much shorter front – conditions which Halder described as suicidal: 'I might just as well put the troops that have landed straight through a sausage machine' – an attempt was made to substitute air power for the sea power which Germany lacked. As early as 1 August, after a conference at the Berghof the previous day, a revised directive, while still requiring preparations to be continued for landing on a broad front, made it plain that the Führer's final decision on landing the invasion would only be taken eight to fourteen days after the air attack had begun: 'his decision will depend largely on the outcome of the air offensive.'[2]

In mid-August Hitler finally accepted the Navy's arguments against attempting a landing on the scale originally planned. In effect, this meant reducing invasion to a subordinate role dependent upon the ability of the Luftwaffe to strike a decisive blow first at the British power and will to defend themselves. Goering had no doubts that it could and, on 13 August, 1,500 German aircraft took part in the opening attack of 'Operation Eagle' planned to eliminate the R.A.F.

On 1 September the movement of shipping to the German embarkation posts began, and operation schedules were issued on the 3rd. But when Raeder saw Hitler on the 6th, he found him inclined to regard 'Operation Sea-Lion' as unnecessary: 'he is finally convinced that Britain's defeat will be achieved, even without the landing'.

The day after Raeder saw Hitler, on 7 September, the German

1. *Führer Conferences on Naval Affairs*, 1939: Conference of 21 July 1940.
2. *Führer Conferences on Naval Affairs*, 1 August 1940.

Air Force made the first of its mass raids on London, with 625 bombers escorted by 648 fighters, the heaviest attack ever delivered on a city. Further night raids followed and on Sunday, the 15th, the Luftwaffe set out to deliver a final assault on the battered capital. This was the climax of the Battle of Britain. The switch from attacks on the R.A.F. to the bombing of London had been made partly as a reply to British raids on Berlin, partly as a deliberate policy of striking at the morale of the civilian population. It proved to be a major mistake in tactics. The week's comparative respite gave the R.A.F. Fighter Command the chance to recover when it had been on the verge of exhaustion: on the 15th it broke up the waves of German bombers and drove them off with heavy losses to the attackers.

The bombing of London and other British cities continued far into the winter, but by daylight at least the R.A.F. had shown that it was still master of the skies over Britain. Thus the conditions for a successful landing were still lacking. Two days later 'Operation Sea-Lion' was postponed indefinitely, and on 12 October a brief directive announced:

The Führer has decided that from now until the spring, preparations for Sea-Lion shall be continued solely for the purpose of maintaining political and military pressure on England.

Should the invasion be reconsidered in the spring or early summer of 1941, orders for a renewal of operational readiness will be issued later....

Keitel[1]

In practice this was the end of the project and, after being shelved for a year, 'Operation Sea-Lion' was quietly cancelled in January 1942.

The course of events summarized in the last two pages suggest three conclusions.

First, it is clear that Hitler was slow and reluctant to admit that a further campaign would be necessary to force the British to come to terms.

Second, once he had reached this conclusion and serious planning began, German naval inferiority forced Hitler to substitute for the original full-scale invasion with forty divisions a plan for defeating Britain by air attack in which the landing of sea-borne troops would occur only after the British resistance had been broken and their defences crippled by the Luftwaffe.

Third, Hitler decided to postpone and then to abandon

1. Martienssen: *Hitler and his Admirals*, pp. 90–1.

'Operation Sea-Lion' not because his bluff had been called, but because it had become clear that the Luftwaffe was no more able than the Navy to create the conditions in which German troops could be put across the Channel and carry out the occupation of the island.

But already, before the issue was decided by the failure of the Luftwaffe, Hitler was beginning to ask himself whether the final defeat of the British, if it was not to be quickly obtained, need hold up the further plans which he was revolving in his mind. According to General Jodl, at the height of the fighting in the West Hitler expressed his determination to deal with Russia as soon as the military situation made it at all possible. Hitherto he had always made it a condition of any attack on Russia that Germany must first be secure against intervention from the west. In his speech to the generals on 23 November 1939 he had repeated this condition, first laid down in *Mein Kampf*: 'We can oppose Russia only when we are free in the west.'

But, with Britain expelled from the Continent and left without an ally, was this not already as good as settled?

Hitler was prepared to wait until the autumn to see if the British could be brought to admit defeat openly, but not longer. In the meantime, before July was out, even before the Luftwaffe had begun its all-out offensive against the British, he gave orders to start preliminary planning for an attack on Russia.[1]

Hitler was strengthened in his resolve not to delay a settlement with Russia too long by the advantage which the Russians were taking of his preoccupation with the west. In June 1940 while the Battle of France was still in progress, the Soviet Government annexed the Baltic States without informing the Germans in advance, and followed this by heavy pressure on Rumania to make a further cession of territory. Always sensitive to any change in the east, Hitler's suspicions of the Russians mounted in proportion to the treachery of his own intentions.

For a moment in July, under the impression of the victories he had won in the west, Hitler was tempted to leave the British to sit behind their island defences and turn eastwards at once, launching an attack on Russia in the autumn of 1940. Keitel, however, was

1. There is an obvious parallel with Napoleon in 1805 the French Emperor started planning the march eastwards which was to lead to Austerlitz while still maintaining his preparations for the invasion of Britain from the camp at Boulogne. For the stages in the preliminary planning of 'Operation Barbarossa', the invasion of Russia, see pp. 598–9 below.

able to persuade his master that practical considerations alone – the impossibility of building up the forces required in so short a time – ruled this out. The proposal for the invasion of Russia was nevertheless only postponed, not abandoned.

At a discussion on the last day of July Halder records Hitler as saying:

> In the event that invasion does not take place, our efforts must be directed to the elimination of all factors that let England hope for a change in the situation. . . . Britain's hope lies in Russia and the U.S.A. If Russia drops out of the picture, America, too, is lost for Britain, because the elimination of Russia would greatly increase Japan's power in the Far East. . . . Decision: Russia's destruction must therefore be made a part of this struggle. . . . The sooner Russia is crushed the better. The attack will achieve its purpose only if the Russian State can be shattered to its roots with one blow. . . . If we start in May 1941, we will have five months in which to finish the job.[1]

Hitler still put the invasion of Britain in the front of his argument but he was already looking ahead to an attack on Russia in 1941, whether the British capitulated first or not.

Until this was settled, one way or the other, Hitler did not advertise his intentions. The Commander-in-Chief of the Navy, Admiral Raeder, in a memorandum written in January 1944, admitted that he had no idea in September 1940 of what was in Hitler's mind, although he later came to believe that at that time 'the Führer was already firmly resolved on a surprise attack against Russia, regardless of what was the Russian attitude to Germany.' The Commander-in-Chief of the Air Force, Göring himself, was also kept in the dark until November. The Luftwaffe maintained its attacks on London and other big cities well into the winter of 1940–1 and Hitler was perfectly willing to see whether the heavy German air-raids might not shake the British resolution to continue the war.

In the meantime, however, the planning of Operation Barbarossa went steadily forward independently of a decision on the operation against Britain. On 29 July General Jodl visited the O.K.W.'s operations staff at Bad Reichenhall, and told its head, General Warlimont, that Hitler had made up his mind to prepare for war against Russia.

At a later date [Warlimont testified after the war] I talked with Hitler myself. He had intended to begin the war against the U.S.S.R. as early as the autumn of 1940, but he gave up this idea. The reason was that the

1. Halder's Diary, 31 July.

strategic position of the troops at that time was not favourable for the purpose. The supplies to Poland were not good enough; railways and bridges were not prepared; the communication lines and aerodromes were not organized. Therefore, the order was given to secure the transport and to prepare for such an attack as would eventually be made.[1]

Warlimont's Staff at once set to work, and on 9 August got out the first directive (*Aufbau Ost*) to start work in the deployment areas in the east for the reception of the large masses of troops which would be needed.[2]

At roughly the same time Hitler also gave orders to the Army General Staff under Halder, quite independently of Warlimont's team, to prepare a plan of campaign for operations against the Soviet Union. Early in August Halder saw the German military attaché in Moscow, Koestring, told him in confidence of what was afoot and warned him to be ready to answer a lot of questions.[3] On 3 September 1940, when General Paulus took over the office of Quartermaster-General of the Army, he found a skeleton operational plan for the offensive already in existence and this was completed by the beginning of November.[4] The plan was presented to Hitler by General Halder on 5 December, and Hitler then gave it his approval, stressing that the primary aim was to prevent Russian armies withdrawing into the depths of the country and to destroy them in the first encounter. The number of divisions to be committed was fixed at 130 to 140 for the entire operation.[5]

The movement of troops to the east began in the summer of 1940. In November the Economic Section of the O.K.W. (the Wirtschaftsrüstungsamt) set to work on the economic preparations for the attack. A special department for Russia was established and among its tasks was a survey of the whole of Russian industry (especially the arms industry) and of the sources of raw material supplies (especially of petroleum).[6]

Thus, when Hitler came finally to express his intention of invading Russia in the directive of 18 December, it was no hastily improvised decision, but one which already had behind it

1. Warlimont's affidavit, N.P., Part vi, p. 237.
2. Warlimont's testimony, N.D. 3,031-PS, 3,032-PS, and a further affidavit in N.C.A., Supp. B, pp. 1,634–7.
3. Koestring's Affidavit, N.D. 3,014-PS.
4. Paulus's evidence at Nuremberg, N.P., Part vi, p. 240.
5. War Diary of the O.K.W. Operations Staff, N.D. 1,799-PS.
6. N.D. 2,353-PS.

several months of hard work by the planning departments of the
O.K.W. and the O.K.H.

VII

There was a third possibility, an alternative to the invasion of
either Britain or Russia, which Admiral Raeder persistently urged
Hitler to consider – the Mediterranean, and the adjacent territories of North Africa and the Middle East. Here, Raeder argued,
was the most vulnerable point in Britain's imperial position, the
weak link against which Germany ought to concentrate all her
strength.

As he developed his case in two discussions with Hitler, on 6
and 26 September, Raeder brought forward additional arguments,
the economic importance of this area for supplying the raw
materials Germany so badly needed, and the dangers of a British,
or even American, landing in French West Africa by way of
the Spanish and Portuguese islands in the Atlantic. At the second
of these conferences Raeder made certain concrete proposals.
Gibraltar and the Canary Islands should be secured, and the protection of North-west Africa strengthened in cooperation with
Vichy France. At the same time, the Germans, in cooperation
with Italy, should launch a major offensive against Suez, and
from there advance northwards through Palestine and Syria to
Turkey.

This was nothing less than an alternative pattern for the future
of the war to that which was already forming in Hitler's mind, and
Raeder acknowledged as much when he added that, if his plans
were successfully carried out, 'it is doubtful whether an advance
against Russia in the north will be necessary'. There was much to
be said for his proposals. They kept Britain in the centre of the
picture as the chief enemy, a natural conclusion for the German
Naval Staff; they made full use of Germany's alliances with Italy
and Spain, and the projected operations were much more within
the compass of German strength than the conquest of Russia
proved to be. Göring, who was normally on the worst of terms
with Raeder, strongly supported his view, and if Hitler had
appreciated the importance of sea-power he would have recognized the force of the Admiral's arguments.

At the time Raeder believed he had more than half convinced
Hitler. The Führer showed interest in his suggestions, expressed
general agreement and undertook to discuss them with Mussolini

and possibly with Franco. Nor were these promises left unfulfilled. In the last four months of 1940 Hitler devoted considerable time and energy to plans for operations in the Western Mediterranean. None the less, Raeder later came to the conclusion, as we have seen, that Hitler's mind was already firmly made up on the invasion of Russia at the time of these September discussions, and Hitler's interest in the Mediterranean, it subsequently became clear, was governed by very different assumptions from those of the German Naval Staff.

Hitler's aims in the Mediterranean and African theatres were two-fold. The first was to add to Britain's difficulties by closing the Mediterranean to her shipping and so bring additional pressure on her to come to terms. In other words, operations in this area were to serve the same purpose as the continued threat of invasion and the heavy bombing of British towns. The objectives, however, were limited: the last thing Hitler wanted to do was to launch out on a major offensive in the south when the concentration of troops in the east was already beginning.

Hitler's second purpose was defensive, to safeguard North-west Africa and the Atlantic islands – the Cape Verde group, the Azores, the Canaries, and Madeira – against possible Allied landings. He was alive to the threat that the British, and possibly the Americans, might turn the defensive front he had established along the western coastline of Europe by using the Atlantic islands as a stepping-stone to West Africa, and Africa as the back door to Europe. The greater part of West Africa belonged to the French colonial empire, the allegiance of which remained uncertain. In August French Equatorial Africa had declared for General de Gaulle, and in September the Free French, with British support, attempted to capture Dakar. Two years later the American and British landings in Morocco were to show that Hitler had not been wrong in foreseeing the direction in which they would make their attack on the 'Fortress Europe'. The British were not yet prepared to undertake such operations, but it was a common-sense precaution on Hitler's part to forestall them. If, at the same time, Vichy could be persuaded to strengthen the defences of the French Empire, so much the better.

From beginning to end, however, Hitler looked to Franco's Spain to undertake the main responsibility in the western Mediterranean, and, less hopefully, to Vichy France for the defence of North-west Africa, just as he insisted that the burden of operations in the eastern Mediterranean must fall on Italy. At no time did he contemplate the use of German forces in anything more than a supporting role – specialist troops and a few squadrons of dive-bombers to assist in the capture of Gibraltar, at the most a division or two to stiffen the Spanish and Italian Armies. There is no evidence at all that he ever thought of the Mediterranean as a main theatre of operations for Germany, or that he seriously considered Raeder's proposals as an alternative to his own plan for attacking Russia. What he did was to single out, against Raeder's advice, those parts – notably the attack on Gibraltar and its corollary, the occupation of the Atlantic islands – which fitted in with, and would not disturb, his own very different view of the future of the war. At the same time, he did all he could to secure the entry of Spain, and if possible France as well, into the war in order to safeguard the west and keep Britain fully occupied while he turned to the east.

Even these limited objectives proved to be beyond Hitler's power to achieve, largely because of the superior skill of the Spanish dictator in avoiding the trap, into which Mussolini had fallen, of identifying his régime too closely with a German alliance.

General Franco had first expressed his willingness to enter the war in June 1940 at a time when it seemed likely that the war was about to end and the division of the spoils about to begin. As the summer wore on, however, and the capitulation or invasion of Britain failed to take place, Franco's enthusiasm cooled and he began to lay stress on the conditions which were a prerequisite of Spanish intervention. These included territorial claims – French Morocco, part of Algeria (Oran), and the enlargement of the Rio de Oro and Spanish Guinea – as well as demands for large-scale economic assistance in grain and petroleum, and the provision of military equipment. In September 1940 Franco sent his future Foreign Minister, Serrano Suñer, to Berlin, partly in order to allay the growing German irritation with Spain and partly in order to spy out the land.

Suñer's discussions with Ribbentrop set the pattern of German–Spanish exchanges for the next six months. On the one hand, Ribbentrop pressed him hard for a definite date by which Spain would enter the war; on the other, he described the Spanish demands for aid as excessive, and was evasive on the question of Morocco and Spain's other territorial claims. In his turn, Suñer avoided any definite commitments and continued to insist that Spain's demands must be met before she could risk intervention.

Like most people who had to deal with the German Foreign Minister, Suñer took a violent dislike to Ribbentrop, to his preposterous vanity and to his overbearing methods in trying to get his own way. Hitler made a different impression on him. The first interview, on 17 September, was carefully staged. After he had passed through the portico of the massive new Reich Chancellery, with its row of Doric columns, and crossed the vast marble gallery which stretched into the distance, he was ushered into the Führer's presence. Hitler had assumed the role of the 'world-historical' genius for the occasion, exhibiting the calm confidence of the master of Europe and leaning over the maps to demonstrate with assured gestures the ease with which he could take Gibraltar. He greeted Suñer with the famous magnetic stare, and walked across the room with carefully controlled, cat-like steps. His glance took in whole continents, and he spoke of organizing Europe and Africa as a single bloc for which he would proclaim a new Monroe Doctrine of non-intervention. Unlike Ribbentrop, he took care neither to utter any complaints nor to exert pressure on his visitor.

For the rest of Suñer's visit everything possible was done to impress him with the power and efficiency of the Third Reich. At the end, exhausted and oppressed, the Spanish Minister escaped with relief to the more congenial atmosphere of Italy. But before he left, Suñer had a second interview with Hitler, in which the Führer, dropping the impressive part he had played at their first meeting, displayed a childlike pleasure in the gift Franco had sent him and astonished the Spaniard by his lack of dignity and by the unaffected behaviour of a German *petit bourgeois*. This contrast between the grandiose pretensions of the régime and the underlying vulgarity and childishness of its rulers was the most permanent impression which Suñer carried away from his visit to Berlin.[1]

From the point of view of the war nothing had been decided. When Ribbentrop visited Rome he spoke in confident terms of Spain's intervention, possibly within four weeks' time. But when Ciano saw Hitler in Berlin on 28 September he found him in a pessimistic mood. Hitler complained of the long list of Spanish demands: 'he was not convinced that Spain had the same intensity of will for giving as for taking'. To promise French Morocco to Spain was to incur the risk of the French authorities in North Africa concluding an agreement with Britain. It would be better,

1. cf. Serrano Suñer: *Entre les Pyrénées et Gibraltar* (Paris, 1948), c. 12.

Hitler believed, to leave the French in Morocco and persuade them to defend it against the British. In any case, the Spaniards refused to commit themselves to a precise date, even if they were to receive all they asked for.

A week later, on 4 October, Hitler and Mussolini met on the Brenner to review the situation. This time Hitler gave a double reason for refusing to cede French Morocco to Spain. The first, which Ribbentrop had already made clear to Suñer, was his plan for a large German empire in Central Africa, for which part of the Moroccan coast would be needed as an intermediate base. The second was his fear that such a step would lead the French colonies in North and West Africa to join de Gaulle. Hitler developed the corollary of his second theme, collaboration with France, at some length, much to the irritation of Mussolini, who feared that Vichy might be ingratiating itself with Hitler, and so depriving him of his anticipated reward, the major share of the French colonial empire. In the middle of October Mussolini wrote to Hitler in reproachful tones of France, 'who thought, because she had not fought, that she had not been beaten'. The idea of drawing France more fully into the Axis camp, however, continued to intrigue Hitler, despite the Duce's protests, and towards the end of October he resolved to clear up his difficulties with Spain and France by a personal visit to Franco on the Spanish frontier and a meeting with the leaders of Vichy France on the way.

VIII

Much to Hitler's surprise, the meeting with Franco proved to be one of the few occasions since he had become the Dictator of Germany on which Hitler found himself worsted in a personal encounter. The memory of his failure never ceased to vex him. For Hitler went out of his way to flatter the Spanish leader. He put himself to the trouble of a long journey across France and he offered Spain immediate aid in the capture of Gibraltar. Admittedly, Hitler was unwilling to agree to the cession of French Morocco, if only because he wanted to keep Vichy in play. Nevertheless, he was confident that with vague promises for the future and with the impression which his dynamic personality was bound to leave on Franco he would succeed in persuading the Spaniards to agree to enter the war in the near future and play the part for which he had cast them.

The two dictators met at the Spanish frontier town of Hendaye on 23 October. Hitler began with an impressive account of the strength of Germany's position and the hopelessness of England's. He then proposed the immediate conclusion of a treaty, by which Spain would come into the war in January 1941. Gibraltar would be taken on 10 January by the same special troops which had captured the Belgian fortress of Eben Emael, and would at once become Spanish.

To Hitler's mounting irritation, however, Franco appeared to be unimpressed by all that he had just heard. Hitler completely failed to establish that ascendancy over the Caudillo which he never failed to exercise over the Duce. Instead Franco began to insist on Spain's need of economic and military assistance, and to ask awkward questions about Germany's ability to give either in the quantities required. He even ventured to suggest that, if England were conquered, the British Government and Fleet would continue the war from Canada with American support. Barely able to control himself, Hitler at one point stood up and said there was no point in continuing the talks, only to sit down and renew his efforts to win Franco over.

The departure of the trains was delayed for two hours, and Ribbentrop stayed on until the morning to work out a draft treaty which would satisfy the Spaniards. But neither Hitler nor Ribbentrop could get Franco to commit himself to anything beyond vague generalities. The Führer for once had to admit defeat, after a conversation lasting nine hours; 'rather than go through which again', he told Mussolini, 'he would prefer to have three or four teeth taken out'. Ribbentrop, who had missed a night's sleep to no purpose, was even more incensed. Racing across France to join Hitler, he spent his time in cursing 'that ungrateful coward Franco who owes us everything and now refuses to join us'.[1]

By contrast, Hitler's interview with Pétain at Montoire on the following day appeared to go well. The aged Marshal of France was one of the few men who ever impressed Hitler, perhaps because, like Lloyd George, he had played a prominent part in the defeat of Germany in 1918. To Mussolini Hitler described Laval as 'a dirty democratic politician, a man who doesn't believe in what he says', but for Pétain he had only praise.

Although he expressed regret about the painful circumstances in which they met, Hitler made no attempt to disguise the

1. Schmidt: op. cit., p. 503.

difficulty of France's position. 'Once this struggle is ended,' he told the Marshal, 'it is evident that either France or England will have to bear the territorial and material costs of the conflict.' When, however, Pétain expressed himself ready to accept the principle of collaboration, it was agreed that the Axis Powers and France had an identical interest in seeing Britain defeated as soon as possible and that France should support the measures they might take to this end. In return, Hitler agreed that France should receive compensation for territorial losses in Africa from Britain and be left with an empire equivalent to the one she still possessed.[1]

On the surface this promised well, but all the details remained to be worked out, and Pétain's comment to a friend has often been quoted: 'It will take six months to discuss this programme and another six months to forget it.'[2]

Hitler seems to have been satisfied for the moment. He told Mussolini that he was convinced that the fight between Vichy and de Gaulle was genuine, and that 'the support of France will be of great interest and great help to the Axis, not so much from a military point of view as from the psychological effect which it will have on the British when they see a compact continental bloc against England being formed'.[3]

The meeting with Mussolini at which this was said took place almost immediately after Hitler had seen Franco and Pétain. Its occasion was an item of news which took Hitler by surprise and was to prove the turning-point in his plans for the Mediterranean and Africa.

On 28 October the Italians attacked Greece, not merely without Hitler's agreement, but in flat contradiction of his wishes. This was an event which affected the whole future of the war. Its full consequences will have to be discussed later. Here we are concerned only with its effects on Hitler's interest in the southern theatre of operations.

These did not at first appear to be great. True the Italian setbacks in Greece faced Hitler with the prospect of having to come to Mussolini's aid in the Balkans. This, and the improvement in Britain's position as a result of her occupation of Crete and a number of the Aegean Islands certainly put an end to any idea of German offensive operations in the eastern Mediterranean. Even

1. Text of the Montoire Agreement in W. L. Langer: *Our Vichy Gamble* (N.Y., 1947), pp. 94–6.
2. *Procès du Maréchal Pétain* (Paris, 1945), p. 313: Estèbe's evidence.
3. *Ciano's Diplomatic Papers*, p. 400.

German aid for the Italian drive on Suez, which was the most to which Hitler had ever agreed, was now held back; it was only to be given, if at all, after the Italians had reached Mersa Matruh. But the military conference of 4 November and the directive of 12 November in which these decisions were embodied, confirmed the plans for action in the western Mediterranean.

Orders were given for 'Operation Felix'[1] to be carried out with German troops supporting the Spaniards in the assault on Gibraltar. To fend off any British counter-attack, other German troops were to occupy the Portuguese Cape Verde Islands by air; small forces were to be landed to strengthen the Spanish defence of the Canaries; and three German divisions were to be sent to the Spanish–Portuguese frontier. The possibility of occupying the Azores and Madeira was also to be investigated.

In view of the uncertainties of the situation these were bold decisions. Yet only small forces were involved. Hitler, it soon appeared, was still relying on Spain's intervention, and a memorandum prepared by the Naval Staff on 14 November showed how little Hitler's plans, even at their boldest, corresponded with the Navy's view of what ought to be undertaken in the Mediterranean. Criticizing 'Operation Felix' as insufficient, the Naval Staff argued that Germany must fight for the African area as 'the foremost strategic objective' and, at the same time as she closed the western Mediterranean, herself launch an offensive against Suez, occupy Greece and march through Turkey.

There was never any prospect that Hitler would adopt such a plan. Although, later, German troops occupied Greece and Crete, and led the Italians in the drive for Suez, Hitler regarded all these operations as either defensive in character or as entirely secondary to the main theatre of war in the east. At the end of the directive of 12 November he added that, irrespective of the results of the forthcoming discussions with Molotov, 'all preparations for the east which have been verbally ordered will be continued'. 'Operation Felix' was compatible with these preparations: Raeder's proposals were not.

Soon afterwards 'Operation Felix', too, had to be first postponed, then virtually abandoned. During November Hitler pressed Franco hard, but the Spaniards warily refused to give any definite commitment and proved fertile in finding excuses. On 7 December Admiral Canaris presented the Spanish dictator with

---

1. 'Operation Felix': the projected occupation of Gibraltar and the Atlantic islands.

a proposal from Hitler to send German troops across the frontier on 10 January and begin operations against the British on that date. This time Franco gave Hitler a blunt refusal. He had little confidence in the plans suggested, he replied, which would only lead to a British or American occupation of the Atlantic islands. Nor was Spain in an economic condition to enter the war yet. The sudden opening of the first British Desert Offensive and the victory of Sidi Barrani in the second week of December confirmed all Franco's doubts. The war, it appeared, was far from over, and the Italian Army was soon in full retreat across the desert. Forced to recognize his failure with Franco, on 11 December Hitler issued the brief notice: '"Operation Felix" will not be carried out as the political conditions no longer obtain.'

For a moment Hitler even feared that the British successes might lead to the break-away of the French colonial empire under General Weygand, and on 10 December he ordered preparations to be made for an emergency operation, 'Attila', which would secure, if necessary, the occupation of the whole of France and the capture of the French Fleet and Air Force. Weygand made no move, but on 13 December Laval, the advocate of collaboration, was dismissed from his office in the Vichy Government and placed under arrest. The Germans soon secured his release, but not his return to office, and Marshal Pétain stubbornly refused to go to Paris to receive the ashes of the Duke of Reichstadt, Napoleon's son, which Hitler had ordered to be sent from Vienna as a symbolic gesture to the French. The Montoire promises of collaboration were evidently worthless, and on Christmas Eve Hitler gave Admiral Darlan, the Vichy Minister of Marine, a taste of his temper in an angry interview at Beauvais. 'Operation Attila' was not carried out, although the troops were held in readiness to the spring of 1941. None the less Hitler had to abandon the hopes he entertained in the autumn of 1940 of winning the French over to active cooperation against the British, and in the event Montoire proved to have been as much a failure as Hendaye.

In the New Year Hitler made one final effort to persuade Franco to come into the war, writing personally to the Caudillo on 6 February and invoking Mussolini's intervention as well. Neither approach had any effect. Mussolini met Franco at Bordighera on 12 February 1941, but, far from changing the

Spanish point of view, only echoed Franco's complaints of Hitler's illusions about France. Hitler's own letter to Franco was strongly worded.

About one thing, Caudillo [he wrote], there must be clarity: we are fighting a battle of life and death and cannot at this time make any gifts. . . .

The entrance of Spain into this struggle has certainly not been conceived of as exclusively to the benefit of German and Italian interests. . . . Spain will never get other friends than those given her in the Germany and Italy of today, unless it becomes a different Spain. This different Spain, however, could only be the Spain of decline and final collapse. For this reason alone, Caudillo, I believe that we three men, the Duce, you, and I, are bound together by the most rigorous compulsion of history, and that thus we in this historical analysis ought to obey as the supreme commandment the realization that, in such difficult times, not so much an apparently wise caution as a bold heart can save nations.[1]

Three weeks later Hitler received Franco's reply. The Caudillo was profuse in his protestations of loyalty.

'We stand today,' he wrote, 'where we have always stood. . . . You must have no doubt about my absolute loyalty to the realization of the union of our national destinies with those of Germany and Italy.'[2]

But he maintained that attitude of polite evasion which, throughout the negotiations, had baffled Hitler's clumsy efforts to pin him down, and he still refused to commit himself.

With that Hitler had to be content. 'I fear,' he wrote to Mussolini, 'that Franco is making the greatest mistake of his life.' The Spanish dictator, indeed, was to appear high on the list of those who disappointed the Führer by their failure to fulfil the historic role for which he had cast them. It was a stigma which that wily politician knew how to bear with fortitude and eventually to turn to profit.

1. *The Spanish Government and the Axis,* pp. 28–33.
2. ibid.

CHAPTER ELEVEN

'THE WORLD WILL HOLD ITS BREATH'
1940–1

I

LOOKING back over the six months since the defeat of France, Hitler could hardly avoid a feeling of angry frustration. The triumphs of the summer had been frittered away in a succession of failures. The British had refused to come to terms; the Spaniards and the French had proved elusive and unreliable; Gibraltar remained untaken, and the French colonial empire unsecured. Since the armistice at Compiègne nothing had gone right in the west.

At first sight the situation in the east was scarcely more promising. It was in the east, however, that Hitler was to recover the initiative in the spring of 1941, sweeping the British once more into the sea, over-running the Balkans and astonishing the world by the force of the attack which he let loose against Russia. This is the history we have now to trace, from June 1940 to June 1941.

In the summer of 1940 the Russians, alarmed by the extent of the German victories in the west, had hurriedly taken advantage of Hitler's preoccupation to occupy the whole of their sphere of influence under the 1939 Agreement. In June Russian troops marched into the Baltic States of Estonia, Latvia, and Lithuania, and in August all three were incorporated in the Soviet Union. The Russians followed their action in the north by an ultimatum to Rumania at the end of June, demanding the cession of the two provinces of Bessarabia and the Northern Bukovina. Hitler could only advise the Rumanians to comply, but henceforward he was determined to prevent any further Russian move towards the west.

His immediate object was to avoid the development of a situation in the Balkans which would provide the Soviet Government with an excuse for intervention. The danger came from Rumania's neighbours, whose territorial ambitions had been aroused by the Russian acquisition of Bessarabia. The Bulgarian claim to the South Dobrudja was soon settled, but the Hungarian demand for Transylvania was more than Rumanian national pride would accept, and relations between the two States rapidly deteriorated to a point where war was a possibility.

Rumanian oil was essential to Germany, and Hitler could not afford to see Russian troops occupying the oilfields in the event of the Rumanian State disintegrating. Behind the scenes, therefore, he used his influence to bring the Hungarians and the Rumanians into a more reasonable frame of mind, and, when advice proved ineffectual, Ribbentrop summoned both parties to Vienna at the end of August to accept a settlement dictated by the two Axis Powers.

Neither Hungary nor Rumania regarded the settlement as satisfactory. Ribbentrop only obtained the Hungarians' consent by shouting at them in a threatening manner, while the Rumanian Foreign Minister, Manoilescu, fell across the table in a faint when he saw the line of partition which Ribbentrop had drawn. But Hitler was indifferent to Hungarian or Rumanian feelings. What mattered was to secure the oilfields: to make doubly sure, he offered Rumania a guarantee of her new frontiers and secretly ordered a force of twelve divisions to be prepared for open intervention, if required.

The crisis, in fact, ended very much to Hitler's advantage. A few days after the Vienna Award, King Carol abdicated in favour of his son, and General Antonescu, an admirer of the Führer, became Rumanian Prime Minister. Before the end of September Antonescu, who was soon to become one of Hitler's favourites, set up a dictatorship, adhered to the Axis Pact (23 September) and 'requested' the dispatch of German troops to help guarantee the defence of Rumania against Russia. A secret order from the Führer's H.Q. on 20 September directed:

The Army and Air Force will send Military Missions to Rumania. To the world their tasks will be to guide friendly Rumania in organizing and instructing her forces.

The real tasks – which must not become apparent either to the Rumanians or to our own troops – will be:

(*a*) To protect the oil district against seizure by third Powers or destruction.

(*b*) To enable the Rumanian forces to fulfil certain tasks according to a systematic plan worked out with special regard to German interests.

(*c*) To prepare for deployment, from Rumanian bases, of German and Rumanian forces in case a war with Soviet Russia is forced on us.[1]

The reorganization of the Rumanian Army on German lines

1. N.D. C-53.

began in the autumn of 1940, and the German Military Mission was followed by German troops, including A.A. regiments to protect the oilfields, and the 13th Panzer Division which was transferred for training. Hitler had soon established a hold over Rumania as a satellite State which was not to be shaken until the end of the war.

These German moves were far from welcome in Moscow. On 1 September Molotov summoned the German Ambassador and described the Vienna Award as a breach of the Nazi–Soviet Pact, which provided for previous consultation. Molotov took equal exception to the German guarantee to Rumania, which, he pointed out, was universally taken to be directed against the U.S.S.R.

These protests, however, Hitler could afford to discount, although he offered a sop in the form of Russian membership of the new Danubian Commission, from which the Soviet Union had originally been excluded. Much more serious was the resentment with which the establishment of a German protectorate over Rumania was received in Rome.

Mussolini had for long entertained ambitions to extend Italian influence in the Balkans and along the Danube, ambitions to which he had always recognized that the growth of German power must be a threat. It was fear of German expansion towards the south-east which had led him originally to oppose the *Anschluss*, and all Hitler's fair words had failed to eradicate the suspicion with which he watched any German move in the direction of the Danube or the Adriatic. Hitler was well aware of Mussolini's ambitions in the Balkans and of his sensitivity to German rivalry in this area. He was also alive to the possibility of Mussolini taking action there to forestall him. At the interview he had with Ciano on 7 July 1940 Hitler was at pains to impress on the Italian Minister the need to delay any such action in the case of Yugoslavia, a country long marked down by the Duce as an object of his imperial designs. This warning was renewed in the succeeding weeks and extended to Greece, the other possible objective of an Italian move. In both cases the same reason was given, the danger of Balkan complications at this time – although Hitler added that he accepted as a matter of course Mussolini's right to settle his claims on Yugoslavia and Greece as soon as the situation became more settled.

These German hints were not much to the Duce's liking – 'It is a complete order to halt all along the line,' Ciano complained. But ostensibly the Italians agreed, and in a letter of 27 August Mussolini assured Hitler that the measures he had taken on the Greek and Yugoslav frontiers were purely defensive: all the Italian resources would be devoted to the attack on Egypt. Hitler took care to associate the Italians with him in the settlement imposed on Hungary and Rumania, and when Ribbentrop visited Rome in the middle of September he repeated that 'as far as Greece and Yugoslavia are concerned, it is a question of exclusively Italian interests. . . . Yugoslavia and Greece are two zones of Italian interest in which Italy can adopt whatever policy she sees fit with Germany's full support.'[1] Mussolini did not conceal his intention of attacking Greece; the Greeks, he told Ribbentrop, were to Italy what the Norwegians had been to Germany before the April expedition. But he spoke of it as an operation to be undertaken after Britain had been driven out of the eastern Mediterranean.

German–Italian cooperation at this time appeared to be closer than usual, and Mussolini readily fell in with Ribbentrop's proposal of a new Tripartite Pact to be signed by Germany, Italy, and Japan. Ribbentrop had first put forward this suggestion as long ago as October 1938, and he repeated in September 1940 the same arguments he had used then, the effect such an alliance would have in strengthening isolationist opinion in America in its opposition to Roosevelt's policy. Ribbentrop admitted that the Pact might also have an effect on Russia, but added that it had now become clear that the policy of friendship with Russia could only be pursued within well-defined limits.

At the end of September Ciano travelled to Berlin for the signature of the Pact. Every effort was made to impress its importance on the minds of a people who were becoming more sceptical as the war entered its second year, and the ceremony was given the utmost publicity by the German propaganda machine. A week later another meeting between the Führer and the Duce on the Brenner Pass appeared to confirm the solidarity of the Axis partnership.

'Rarely,' Ciano wrote in his journal, 'have I seen the Duce in such good humour as at the Brenner today. The conversation was cordial and the conversations were certainly the most interesting of all so far. Hitler put at least some of his cards on the table and

1. Ciano's Minute, 19 September 1940; *Ciano's Diplomatic Papers*, pp. 389–93.

talked to us about his plans for the future. . . . Hitler was energetic and again extremely anti-Bolshevist. "Bolshevism," he said, "is the doctrine of people who are lowest in the scale of civilization."[1] What Hitler did not mention, however, was the steps he was already taking to secure German control over Rumania.

When the movement of German troops became known during the next week, Mussolini's anger at Hitler's duplicity showed how fragile were the bonds of confidence between the two régimes. Once again the Italian dictator felt that Hitler had stolen a march on him. Belated attempts to send an Italian contingent as well were unsuccessful, and the indignant Duce burst out to Ciano:

Hitler always faces me with a *fait accompli*. This time I am going to pay him back in his own coin. He will find out from the newspapers that I have occupied Greece. In this way the equilibrium will be re-established. I shall send in my resignation as an Italian if anyone objects to our fighting the Greeks.[2]

On 15 October, little more than a fortnight after the Axis partnership had been ostentatiously strengthened by the Tripartite Pact, Mussolini issued orders to prepare for an attack on Greece in deliberate disloyalty to his own assurances to the Germans and in the same childish mood of pique which had led to the occupation of Albania as a tit-for-tat after Hitler's march into Prague.

This time the consequences were more serious. The role which Hitler had assigned the Italian forces in his strategic plan was the invasion of Egypt, and on 13 September the Italian Army under Graziani had crossed the Egyptian frontier and begun a slow advance eastwards. Even against the scanty British forces opposing them this soon proved to be a task demanding all the resources Mussolini could command, and Marshal Badoglio, the Chief of the Italian General Staff, was firmly set against any extension of Italy's commitments. Mussolini refused to listen; his sorely bruised vanity demanded a bold *coup* to restore Fascist prestige, and early on 28 October Italian troops began the invasion of Greece from Albania.

Not until the last minute was Mussolini willing to inform Hitler of his intention. A long letter written on 19 October did not reach Berlin until the 24th and was only communicated to Hitler personally late that night after his interview with Pétain at Montoire. He did not need to look at a map to realize the implications of Mussolini's move. At precisely the moment when he

1. *Ciano's Diary*, pp. 259–6.   2. *Ciano's Diary*, p. 297.

had succeeded in pacifying the Balkans by the virtual occupation of Rumania, the Italians were about to set the whole peninsula in turmoil again by their ill-timed attack. Bulgaria and Yugoslavia, both with claims on Greece, were bound to be aroused; Russia would be provided with a further pretext for intervention, while the British would almost certainly land in Greece and acquire bases on the European shores of the Mediterranean. On top of his unsatisfactory interview with Franco on the 23rd the news from Rome strained Hitler's temper to the limit. Yet the manner in which Mussolini had acted was a clear enough indication of the resentment he felt at high-handed behaviour by the Germans, and Hitler, quick to see the danger of alienating his one reliable ally after his failure to bring Spain into the war, for once hesitated to intervene too forcefully. He resolved to go to Italy in the hope that a personal appeal to the Duce before the attack began might persuade him to change his mind.

A meeting was hurriedly arranged at Florence, and the Führer's special train, in which he had journeyed to the Spanish frontier, was re-routed to the south, passing through a snowy landscape which, Paul Schmidt remarks, corresponded well with the chilly mood of those inside. Two hours before he reached Florence Hitler was informed that Italian troops had begun the assault that morning, and Mussolini, smirking with self-satisfaction, could not wait to leave the station platform before announcing his first successes.

It is an interesting sidelight on Hitler's character that, in such provocative circumstances, he controlled himself without difficulty and throughout the talks which followed in the Pitti Palace showed no trace of his real feelings. On the contrary, he began by offering the Duce Germany's full support in the new campaign and placed German parachute troops at his disposal if they should be required for the occupation of Crete. He followed this with a long report to his Italian partner on his negotiations with Spain and Vichy France – clever tactics in view of Mussolini's suspicion of France – and ended with a belated but reassuring account of his relations with Rumania. At the conclusion of his report Ciano wrote, evidently with some relief: 'The meeting ends with the expression of the perfect agreement between Italy and Germany on all points.'[1]

Appearances had been preserved. But 'Hitler went north that afternoon', his interpreter Paul Schmidt wrote in his memoirs,

1. Ciano's Minute; *Ciano's Diplomatic Papers*, pp. 399–404.

'with bitterness in his heart. He had been frustrated three times – at Hendaye, Montoire, and now in Italy. In the lengthy winter evenings of the next few years, these long exacting journeys were a constantly recurring theme of bitter reproaches against un-grateful and unreliable friends, Axis partners, and "deceiving" Frenchmen.'[1] His actions on returning to Germany show that he had no illusions about the problems with which the Italians' blunder confronted him. New orders, discussed during the first ten days of November, were issued in the directive of 12 November.[2]

Although the dispatch of German forces to the support of the Italian drive on Suez was to be considered only after the Italians had reached Mersa Matruh, provision was made for the rapid transfer of a German armoured division to North Africa if necessary. Meanwhile the German forces in Rumania were to be reinforced, and an Army Group of ten divisions assembled to march into Greek Thrace if the need should arise. Hitler still hoped to be able to carry 'Operation Felix' out against Gib-raltar, but it is evident that he anticipated trouble in the Balkans, either from British air attacks on Rumania or from an Italian failure in Greece, and was already making preparations to meet it in advance.

Hitler, moreover, had to look still further ahead. Perhaps the most significant paragraph in the directive of 12 November is the instruction already quoted, 'to continue all preparations for the east already verbally ordered.' The plans for an attack on Russia, on which the Army General Staff had been engaged since August, were now taking shape. While his immediate anxiety, therefore, was the possibility of a British landing in Greece and an Italian collapse, Hitler was bound to view any action he might be obliged to take in the context of his larger design.

II

Russian suspicions had already been aroused, not only by the guarantee given to Rumania, but also by renewed German interest in Finland, at the other end of the potential Eastern Front. Towards the end of September, an agreement was reached between the German and Finnish Governments for the movement of German troops through Finland to the outlying garrisons in Northern Norway. When the German Chargé d'Affaires in

1. Schmidt, op. cit., p. 506.   2. N.D. 444-PS.

Moscow called on Molotov on 26 September to offer assurances about the Tripartite Pact to be signed the next day, he was pressed by the Soviet Foreign Minister to provide a copy of the agreement recently concluded between Germany and Finland, 'including its secret portions'. The German Foreign Office at once complied with the Russian request, but Molotov was not satisfied, asking for more information about the agreement and about the dispatch of a German Military Mission to Rumania. Anxious to allay Russian fears, Ribbentrop thereupon took the step of proposing a further meeting between Molotov and himself, and in a letter to Stalin, dated 13 October, suggested that Molotov should visit Berlin. After a week's consideration Stalin accepted the invitation, and it was agreed that Molotov should come to Berlin in the first half of November. The extension of the war to the Balkans in the meantime, and the possibility of German intervention in Greece – which would necessitate the passage of German troops through Bulgaria – added to the importance of the Soviet Foreign Minister's visit.

Molotov arrived in the German capital on 12 November, and after a preliminary talk with Ribbentrop was received by Hitler the same day. The Führer at once placed the discussion on the most lofty plane:

In the life of peoples it was indeed difficult to lay down a course for development over a long period in the future, and the outbreak of conflicts was often strongly influenced by personal factors; he believed nevertheless that an attempt had to be made to fix the development of nations, even for a long period of time, in so far as that was possible, so that friction could be avoided and the elements of conflict precluded so far as was humanly possible. This was particularly in order when two nations such as the German and Russian nations had at their helm men who possessed sufficient authority to commit their countries to a development in a definite direction. . . .[1]

Hitler went on for a long time in the same characteristic high-flown vein. Molotov, a cold and stubborn negotiator, precise to the point of pedantry, waited for him to finish; then, in equally characteristic fashion, ignoring Hitler's attempts to bewitch him with his 'world-historical perspectives' of the future, he asked a series of pointed questions about German–Russian cooperation

1. The German Minutes of Molotov's conversations in Berlin are printed in G.D., vol. XI, pp. 533–70, from which all the following quotations are taken.

in the present. 'The questions hailed down upon Hitler,' Paul Schmidt, who kept the minutes of the meeting, afterwards recalled. 'No foreign visitor had ever spoken to him in this way in my presence.'

What were the Germans doing in Finland, which had been assigned to the Russian sphere of influence in their earlier agreement? What was the meaning of the New Order in Europe and in Asia and what part was the Soviet Union to play in it? What was the significance of the Tripartite Pact? 'There were also issues to be clarified regarding Russia's Balkan and Black Sea interests with respect to Bulgaria, Rumania and Turkey.' On all these points, Molotov said, he would like to have explanations.

Hitler was so taken aback that he made the excuse of a possible air raid and broke off the discussion until the following day.

When they met again next morning, Hitler made an effort to forestall Molotov's remarks by admitting that the necessities of war had obliged Germany to intervene in areas where she had no permanent interests. 'Thus, for instance,' he told Molotov, 'Germany has no political interests whatsoever in the Balkans and is active there at present exclusively under the compulsion of securing for herself certain raw materials.'

Hitler accepted the fact that Finland was a part of the Russian sphere of influence as defined at Moscow, but he insisted that for the duration of the war Germany had economic interests in Finland's nickel and lumber which she expected to be considered. At the same time he pointed out that Germany had lived up to her side of the Agreement, while Russia had occupied the Northern Bukovina and part of Lithuania, neither of which had been mentioned in the Agreement at all. Germany accepted these revisions because they were in Russia's interests; she expected Russia to show the same consideration for her temporary interests in Finland and Rumania.

This was an argument which Molotov was not prepared to admit and a sharp exchange followed. When Molotov pressed for the withdrawal of German troops from Finland, Hitler pointedly asked if Russia intended to go to war against Finland. 'There must be no war in the Baltic,' he insisted. 'It would put a heavy strain on German–Russian relations.' What more did Russia want in Finland, he asked. 'A settlement on the same scale as in Bessarabia,' was Molotov's reply – in effect, annexation. Hitler made no direct comment, but repeated: 'There must be no war with Finland because such a conflict might have far-reaching repercussions.' Unmoved, Molotov retorted: 'A new factor has been introduced into the discussion by this position.'

Hitler was obviously rattled by Molotov's persistence, but he made a determined effort to keep his temper and bring the discussion round to 'more important problems'.

After the conquest of England, the British Empire would be apportioned as a gigantic world-wide estate in bankruptcy of forty million square kilometres. In this bankrupt estate there would be for Russia access to the ice-free and really open ocean. Thus far, a minority of forty-five million Englishmen had ruled the six hundred million inhabitants of the British Empire. He was about to crush this minority. . . . Under these circumstances there arose world-wide perspectives. . . . All the countries which could possibly be interested in the bankrupt estate would have to stop all controversies among themselves and concern themselves exclusively with the partition of the British Empire.

Once again Molotov sat impassively while the Führer used all his skill to distract his attention. But as soon as Hitler finished, Molotov resumed where he had left off: the next question was the Balkans and the German guarantee to Rumania, 'aimed against the interests of Soviet Russia, if one might express oneself so bluntly'. With mounting impatience, Hitler went over the familiar ground again: Germany had no permanent interests in the Balkans, wartime needs alone had taken her there, the guarantee was not directed against Russia, and so on.

If Germany would not revoke her guarantee to Rumania, Molotov then asked, what would she say to a Russian guarantee to Bulgaria? Hitler was at once on his guard. 'The question would first arise whether Bulgaria had asked for a guarantee. He did not know of any such request by Bulgaria.' When Molotov pressed him, Hitler refused to commit himself, although he conceded that Germany, as a Danubian Power, was only indirectly interested in the passage into the Black Sea, adding ominously that 'if she were looking for sources of friction with Russia, she would not need the Straits'.

With this, Hitler's part in the talks ended, leaving him in a state of violent irritation. Franco had only angered him by evasion, Molotov had answered back and argued with him, a liberty which Hitler never forgave and which had already cost others their lives. That night he was unexpectedly absent from the banquet which Molotov gave to his hosts in the Russian Embassy.

Half-way through the banquet a British air-raid drove the two foreign ministers to take shelter below ground. Ribbentrop with characteristic maladroitness seized the occasion to confront Molotov with the draft of a new agreement which would have brought the Soviet Union into the Tripartite Pact.

The core of the treaty was Article I I, an undertaking to respect each other's natural spheres of influence. The significance of this was made clear by two accompanying protocols both of which were to remain secret. The first defined the Four Powers' spheres of influence.

Germany declares that, apart from territorial revisions in Europe to be carried out at the conclusion of peace, her territorial aspirations centre in the territories of Central Africa.

Italy declares that, apart from territorial revisions in Europe, her territorial aspirations centre in the territories of northern and north-eastern Africa.

Japan declares that her territorial aspirations centre in the area of eastern Asia to the south of the Island Empire of Japan.

The Soviet Union declares that its territorial aspirations centre south of the national territory of the U.S.S.R. in the direction of the Indian Ocean.

The Four Powers declare that, reserving the settlement of specific questions, they will mutually respect these territorial aspirations and will not oppose their achievement.

If he could persuade Molotov and Stalin to accept such a settlement, Hitler believed that he would be able to divert Russia from her historic expansion towards Europe, the Balkans and the Mediterranean – areas in which she was bound to clash with Germany and Italy – southwards to areas such as the Persian Gulf and the Indian Ocean, where Germany had no interest and where Russia would at once become embroiled with the British. It was a bold but transparent proposal which cut right across both the traditions and the interests of Russia. Hitler and Ribbentrop hoped, however, to make it more attractive by the second protocol, which promised German and Italian cooperation in detaching Turkey from her commitments to the West and winning her over to collaboration with the new bloc of Powers. As a part of this process, Ribbentrop proposed a new régime for the Straits to replace the Montreux Convention. In addition, the German Foreign Minister spoke in vague but tempting terms of German help in securing for Russia a Non-Aggression Pact with Japan, as a result of which Japan might be persuaded to recognize the Soviet spheres of influence in Outer Mongolia and Sinkiang and to do a deal over the island of Sakhalin, with its valuable coal and oil resources.

Molotov, who had had no chance to examine the draft in advance, was the last man to let himself be carried away by Ribbentrop's barnstorming diplomacy. His reply made it unmistakably clear that Russia was not prepared to disinterest herself in Europe. Not only Turkey and Bulgaria,

but the fate of Rumania and Hungary was also of interest to the Soviet Union and could not be immaterial to her under any circumstances. It would further interest the Soviet Government to learn what the Axis contemplated with regard to Yugoslavia and Greece, and likewise what Germany intended with regard to Poland. . . . The Soviet Government was also interested in the question of Swedish neutrality . . . and the question of the passages out of the Baltic Sea. The Soviet Government believed that discussions must be held concerning this question similar to those now being conducted concerning the Danubian Commission.

Ribbentrop, complaining that he had been 'queried too closely' by his Russian colleague, made one last effort to pull the conversation back to the agenda which he had proposed. 'He could only repeat again and again that the decisive question was whether the Soviet Union was prepared and in a position to co-operate with us in the great liquidation of the British Empire.'

But Ribbentrop's last exasperated plea met with no more response than Hitler's. To Ribbentrop's repeated assurances that Britain was finished, Molotov replied: 'If that is so, why are we in this shelter and whose are these bombs which fall?'[1] 'M. Molotov had to state,' the German Minute ends, 'that all these great issues of tomorrow could not be separated from the issues of today and the fulfilment of existing agreements. The things that were started must first be completed before they proceeded to new tasks.'

On 25 November, less than a fortnight after Molotov's visit to Berlin, the Soviet Government sent an official reply accepting Ribbentrop's suggested Four-Power Pact, on condition that the Germans agreed to a number of additional demands. These included the immediate withdrawal of German troops from Finland; a mutual assistance pact between Russia and Bulgaria, including the grant of a base for Russian land and naval forces within range of the Straits; a further Russian base to be granted

1. Stalin's account to Churchill in Moscow, Churchill, op. cit., vol. ii, p. 518.

by Turkey on the Bosphorus and Dardanelles; and Japan's renunciation of her rights to coal and oil concessions in northern
Sakhalin. Provided these claims were accepted, Russia was prepared to sign the Pact, rewriting the definition of her own sphere
of expansion to make its centre the area south of Baku and Batum
in the general direction of the Persian Gulf.[1]

No reply was ever sent to the Soviet counter-proposals, despite
repeated inquiries from Moscow and German assurances that the
Russian Note was being studied. Hitler's offer had been designed
to divert Russia away from Europe. Once it became clear from
Stalin's reply that Russia insisted on regarding Eastern Europe as
within her sphere of influence, Hitler lost interest in any further
negotiations. If he had still entertained any doubts about giving
the order to prepare for 'Operation Barbarossa' before Molotov's
visit he had none left after it. Immediately after his final talk with
Molotov Hitler saw Göring and told him of his intention to
attack Russia in the spring. Göring, who supported Raeder's
view that Germany's first object should be to clear the British out
of the Mediterranean, attempted to dissuade Hitler, but his arguments made no impression.

Hitler now reinforced his determination to invade Russia and
thus secure Germany's future *Lebensraum* in the east by the
argument, of which he soon convinced himself, that Russia was
preparing to attack Germany. Russian objections to German
intervention in Finland and the Balkans were twisted into evidence of a Russian intention to cut off German iron-ore supplies
from Sweden and oil supplies from Rumania. From this it was
only a step to postulating the existence of an agreement between
Russia and Great Britain. Thus Germany was once more threatened with encirclement, and Hitler was able to adopt the indignant attitude of the innocent man driven to defend himself. This
was the pretext he used to justify his action to the German people
in the proclamation published on the morning of the attack in
June 1941; this was the defence repeated again and again by
Hitler's lieutenants at the Nuremberg Trials. The captured German papers reveal this for the lie it was, and document, step by
step, the systematic preparation of an act of aggression against a
people whose government to the last day was anxious to avoid
giving any pretext for war to the German dictator.

1. Russian Note in *Nazi–Soviet Relations*, pp. 258–9.

III

The history of the preliminary measures for 'Operation Barbarossa' is complicated by Hitler's simultaneous preparation of operations in the Balkans, forced on him by Mussolini's blunder in invading Greece.

In a letter which he wrote to Mussolini on 20 November 1940, Hitler told the Duce frankly that he had come to Florence in the hope of dissuading him from an attack on Greece at that time, and that the consequences of the Italian action were grave. The reluctance of Bulgaria, Yugoslavia, Turkey, and Vichy France to commit themselves had been fortified; Russian alarm about the Balkans and the Straits had been increased, while Britain had been given the opportunity to secure bases in Greece from which to bomb Rumania and southern Italy.

The measures with which Hitler proposed to meet these difficulties were comprehensive. Spain must come into the war at once and, with limited German help, seize Gibraltar and guarantee North-west Africa. Russia must be turned away from the Balkans, Turkey persuaded to stop any threats against Bulgaria, Yugoslavia induced to collaborate with the Axis against Greece, and Rumania pressed to accept German reinforcements. To these political tasks, Hitler added increased air attacks on the British Navy and its bases in the eastern Mediterranean, in which the German Air Force would assist the Italians. The German squadrons must, however, be sent back by 1 May at the latest, and land operations against Egypt would have to be abandoned for the time being. The principal military effort would go into a German attack to clear the British out of Thrace, which could be mounted by March 1941, but not before.

Mussolini's comment on reading Hitler's letter was brief: 'He has really smacked my fingers.' In his reply, however, he accepted Hitler's proposals.

Ciano, who had seen Hitler at the Berghof a few days before, reported that Hitler was genuinely worried about the situation created by Mussolini's blunder, but became more cheerful when Ciano agreed to negotiations to win over Yugoslavia, the other object of Mussolini's ambitions.

Hitler obviously regarded an arrangement with Yugoslavia as the key to the Balkan situation; nor was he far wrong in this, since it was the unexpected and heroic action of the Yugoslavs at the end of March 1941 which did more than anything else to throw his plans awry.

When Ciano saw him at Vienna on 20 November Hitler was still full of Yugoslavia, and, satisfied that the Duce would now agree, he declared: 'From this city of Vienna, on the day of the *Anschluss*, I sent Mussolini a telegram to assure him that I could never forget his help. I confirm it today, and I am at his side with all my strength.'[1] There were tears in his eyes as he spoke; this time even Ciano was embarrassed by the Führer's mock-heroics.

Meanwhile Hitler was engaged in securing the political prerequisites for his intervention in Greece. A succession of Balkan rulers was imperiously summoned to Germany: King Boris of Bulgaria on 17 November; then the Rumanian dictator, General Antonescu; and at the end of the month, Cinkar-Marcovitch, the Yugoslav Foreign Minister. On 5 December Hitler wrote again to Mussolini. Yugoslavia and Bulgaria were proving difficult – the latter under Russian pressure – but he had hopes of bringing them over, and Mussolini was much relieved at the more confident tone of the letter.

Unfortunately for Mussolini, the degree of Fascist incompetence had not yet been fully revealed. On 7 December the Italian Ambassador, newly returned from Rome, saw Ribbentrop and begged for immediate help to relieve the situation in Albania where the Italians were in danger of a complete rout. When Hitler received the Ambassador the next day and asked for an early meeting with the Duce, Mussolini refused to face him. To add to the Duce's troubles, the Battle of Sidi Barrani, which began on 9 December, led to the collapse of the Italian threat to Egypt and the headlong retreat of Graziani's forces back across Libya.

In this crisis Hitler kept his head. He refused to be diverted from his main objectives. Between 10 December and 19 December he issued a series of orders which were designed not only to prop up his failing Italian ally, but to carry out his long-range plans. Undeterred by the set-backs in Albania and North Africa, he chose this moment to draw up the first major directive for the invasion of Russia in six months' time.

On 10 December Hitler ordered formations of the German Air Force to be moved to the south of Italy, from where they were to attack Alexandria, the Suez Canal, and the Straits between Sicily

1. *Ciano's Diary*, p. 309.

and Africa. Preparations were also to be pushed forward for the dispatch of an armoured division to Libya.

On 13 December Directive No. 20 for the invasion of Greece ('Operation Marita') was issued. A German task force was to be formed in Rumania ready to thrust across Bulgaria as soon as favourable weather came, and to occupy the Thracian coast of Greece. A maximum of twenty-four divisions was to be committed, and these were to be ready for use in a new undertaking as soon as the operation was completed. The first objective was to deny the British air bases in Thrace, from which they could bomb Rumania and Italy, but if necessary the operation was to be extended to the occupation of the whole of the Greek mainland.

On 18 December Hitler signed Directive No. 21 for 'Barbarossa':

The German Armed Forces must be prepared to crush Soviet Russia in a quick campaign even before the end of the war against England. For this purpose the Army will have to employ all available units with the reservation that the occupied territories must be safeguarded against surprise attack. . . .
Preparations requiring more time to start are to be begun now – if this has not yet been done – and are to be completed by 15 May 1941 . . . The ultimate objective of the operation is to establish a defence line against Asiatic Russia from a line running approximately from the Volga River to Archangel.[1]

The new directive which laid down the lines of the German advance also made it clear that the active cooperation of Finland, Hungary, and Rumania was counted on from the beginning. That same month of December both the Chief of the Finnish General Staff and the Hungarian Minister of War visited Germany. General Antonescu, who had already seen Hitler in November, came to Berchtesgaden a second time in January 1941.

Finally, on 19 December, Hitler saw the Italian Ambassador and promised increased economic aid for Italy, on condition that German experts should go to Italy and advise on its use. In return more Italian workmen were to be sent to Germany. This was one more step in the reduction of Italy to the status of a German satellite.

With these measures put in train, Hitler was confident that he could master the crisis and still be ready for the attack on Russia by 15 May, the date fixed for the completion of preparations. He said nothing of such a possibility to Mussolini, but the letter

1. N.D. 446-PS.

which he wrote to the Duce on the last day of 1940 was cordial in tone and made no reference to the recriminations he had darted at the unfortunate Italian Ambassador earlier in the month.

Duce,
At the moment when this year comes to an end I feel the need to express to you, from the bottom of my heart, my good wishes for the year about to dawn. I feel the more compelled to give this proof of friendship since I imagine that recent events have perhaps lost you the support of many people, unimportant in themselves, but whose attitude has made you more sensitive to the genuine comradeship of a man who feels himself bound to you alike in good or bad times, in adversity as much as in prosperity.[1]

After this not altogether felicitous opening Hitler did his best to encourage Mussolini and to assure him of his own unshaken confidence in the future. He ended by offering to meet him whenever the Duce felt it to be necessary.

Early in the New Year the chiefs of the three Services were summoned to the Berghof, where a war council lasting two days was held, on 8–9 January 1941. Hitler reviewed what could be done for Italy, and this time ordered a force of two and half divisions to be made ready for service with the Italians in Albania. The need for its use there never arose, but within the limits of what could be spared Hitler was obviously anxious to do what he could to aid Mussolini.

Hitler's general mood was still one of confidence.

The Führer [the Minutes record] is firmly convinced that the situation in Europe can no longer develop unfavourably for Germany even if we should lose the whole of North Africa. . . . The British can hope to win the war only by beating us on the Continent. The Führer is convinced that this is impossible.[2]

Britain, Hitler concluded, only went on fighting because of the hopes she entertained of American and Russian intervention, and he described Stalin as 'a cold-blooded blackmailer who would, if expedient, repudiate any written treaty at any time. . . . A German victory has become unbearable for Russia. Therefore she must be brought to her knees as soon as possible.'[3]

Ten days later Mussolini visited the Berghof. He was most reluctant to make the journey and went on board the train in a

1. *Hitler e Mussolini*, p. 83.
2. *Führer Conferences on Naval Affairs*, 1941, pp. 12–13.
3. Halder's Diary, 16 January 1941.

bad temper. Smarting under the humiliations of Libya and Greece, he looked forward without relish to the Germans' patronizing condolences. To the Duce's and Ciano's surprise Hitler behaved with tact and impressed both of them with the cordiality of his greeting. When the train pulled up in the village station of Puch, Hitler was there in person on the snow-covered platform. The Italians were at once driven up into the mountains and spent two days as Hitler's guests at the Berghof.

Mussolini found Hitler in a very anti-Russian mood, and Ribbentrop called a sharp halt to ill-timed Italian attempts to improve their relations with Moscow. On the second day of the visit, Monday 20 January, Hitler made a speech of two hours on his coming intervention in Greece which much impressed the Italian military men by the grasp of technical matters it displayed. The Führer's exposition ranged over the whole of Europe, Africa, and the Middle East. Demonstrating his points with expressive gestures on the map, he impressed upon his audience the picture of a master of strategy who had foreseen every possibility and who was in complete command of the situation. He did not reveal his intention of attacking Russia, but he did not conceal his intense distrust of his nominal ally.

Though we have very favourable political and economic agreements with Russia, I prefer to rely on the powerful means at my disposal. . . . As long as Stalin lives, there is probably no danger; he is intelligent and careful. But should he cease to be there, the Jews, who at present occupy only second- and third-rank positions, might move up again into the first rank. The Russians are continually trying to work out new demands which they read into the agreements. . . . It is therefore necessary to keep a constant eye on the Russian factor and to keep on guard by means of strength and clever diplomacy.[1]

Mussolini returned, not only relieved by his reception, but – so Ciano reported – in the mood of elation which a meeting with Hitler frequently produced in him. Alfieri, the Italian Ambassador in Berlin, who had accompanied the party, was less sure. Mussolini, he believed, was profoundly resentful at the position of dependence in which he now found himself placed.

Hitler's concealment of his plans for 'Barbarossa' during his talks with Mussolini has already been remarked. It could, of course, be argued that Italy was in no position in 1941 to give any help at all in the operations about to begin in Eastern Europe. But this argument could certainly not be applied to the second of

1. N.D. C-134.

Hitler's partners in the Tripartite Pact, Japan, whose relations with the U.S.S.R. had balanced precariously on the edge of war since the Japanese invasion of Manchuria in 1931. For ten years Japan and Russia had eyed each other with mutual suspicion and hostility. Yet Hitler made no effort to bring Japan into the war he was proposing to wage against Russia; on the contrary, he did everything he could to divert her away from Russia's Far Eastern territories towards the south.

From beginning to end the Japanese showed great reserve in their dealings with the Third Reich. It had taken Ribbentrop a long time to secure the Japanese alliance, which he regarded as one of his diplomatic masterpieces, and it was only under the impression of the German victories of 1940 that the Japanese were brought to sign the Tripartite Pact. In February 1941 Ribbentrop invited the Japanese Ambassador, Oshima, to his country estate at Fuschl and had a long talk with him on the future of German–Japanese cooperation. Following this, on 5 March, Hitler issued his Basic Order No. 24, 'Regarding Collaboration with Japan'. Finally, at the end of the month, the Japanese Foreign Minister, Matsuoka, visited Berlin and had a number of conversations with Hitler and Ribbentrop. From these records it is possible to reconstruct the policy which Hitler was urging on his Japanese allies in the spring of 1941.

Hitler wanted Japan to enter the war at the earliest possible moment, but it was against England, not against Russia, that he sought her cooperation. The war in Europe, Hitler and Ribbentrop assured Matsuoka, was virtually over; it was only a question of time before Britain was forced to admit that she had been defeated. An attack by Japan upon Singapore would not only have a decisive effect in convincing Britain that there was no further point in continuing the war, it would also provide the key to the realization of Japanese ambitions in Eastern Asia at a time when circumstances formed a unique combination in her favour. 'There could never in human imagination,' Hitler told Matsuoka, 'be a better condition for a joint effort of the Tripartite Pact countries than the one which had now been produced. . . . Such a moment would never return. It was unique in history. . . .'[1]

Hitler admitted that there were risks, but he dismissed them as slight. England had her hands full and was in no position to defend her possessions in Asia. America was not yet ready, and an

1. Hitler–Matsuoka meeting of 27 March 1941, *Nazi–Soviet Relations*, pp. 289–98.

attack on Singapore would strengthen the tendency towards non-intervention in the United States. If, none the less, America should attack Japan it would show that such a course had already been decided on. In that case, Japan could rely on German support. As for Russia, Hitler forbade any mention of his intention to invade the U.S.S.R., but he allowed Ribbentrop to hint at the preparations Germany was making in the east, and to give an explicit assurance that Germany would at once attack Russia if she moved against Japan. 'The Führer was convinced,' Ribbentrop added, 'that in case of action against the Soviet Union there would in a few months be no more Great Power of Russia.'[1]

In all their conversations Hitler and Ribbentrop persistently urged on Matsuoka the importance of an attack on Singapore at the earliest possible date. 'Japan would best help the common cause,' Ribbentrop declared, 'if she did not allow herself to be diverted by anything from the attack on Singapore,' and he asked the Japanese Foreign Minister for maps of the British base, 'so that the Führer, who must certainly be considered the greatest expert of modern times on military matters, could advise Japan as to the best method for the attack on Singapore.'[2] Japan, in short, was to play in the Far East the role for which Hitler had cast Franco's Spain and Mussolini's Italy: the capture of Singapore was the Far Eastern version of the capture of Gibraltar and the drive on Suez.

Had Hitler succeeded in persuading his allies to fall in with his plans, Britain's strength would have been stretched to the limit. This time it was not his strategy but his diplomacy that was at fault. Between the defeat of France and the attack on Russia, Hitler conducted a considerable number of diplomatic negotiations: it is a striking fact that, in every case where he was unable to use the threat of force if his wishes were not met, these negotiations failed. Spain, Italy, Vichy France, and now Japan, all in one way or another preferred to go their several ways, and chose different paths from those the Führer had mapped out for them. It is not difficult to see why. Hitler's overbearing manner and his total inability to cooperate with anyone on equal terms; Ribbentrop's belief that the most effective method of diplomacy was to nag and, if possible, to threaten, produced in most of their visitors only a feeling of relief when the interview came to an end.

1. Ribbentrop–Matsuoka, 27 March 1941; ibid., pp. 281–8.
2. Ribbentrop–Matsuoka, 29 March 1941; ibid., pp. 303–11.

No one who has read through even the German records of these conversations would ever be surprised that they failed. It was too patent on every occasion why the Germans wanted what they were asking for, too obvious who was to benefit from it. Ciano was no doubt a prejudiced witness, but he was right when he wrote in his diary: 'I wish to add that, in my opinion, if Spain falls away the fault rests in great part with the Germans and their uncouth manners.'[1]

To clumsiness the Germans added falseness. Hitler and Ribbentrop deceived their allies, even when there was no need. Nothing so much angered Mussolini as the fact that his allies told him lies and then sprang surprises on him. If Mussolini's invasion of Greece was a blunder for which the Nazis had eventually to pay a high price, Hitler had only himself to blame for the way in which he had misled his partner and then stolen an advantage over him in Rumania. Hitler showed surprising loyalty to Mussolini, but it never extended to trusting him. His golden rule in politics remained: Trust nobody.

It is not surprising, therefore, that Hitler should have concealed his purpose to attack Russia from the Japanese Foreign Minister. What is striking is that he should have made no effort to secure Japanese support in case of such a conflict. Instead, the possibility of a clash between Germany and Russia was represented as an additional reason for Japan to launch out to the south, away from her uneasy frontier with the Soviet Union. It is one more piece of evidence pointing to the confidence which Hitler felt in his ability to conquer Russia, as he had conquered France, in a single campaign and without the need of help from outside which, when victory had been won, might prove an embarrassment. Meanwhile, Matsuoka was sufficiently deceived to ignore the hints Ribbentrop dropped, with the result that when Germany attacked Russia three months later his failure to warn the Japanese Government led to his fall. Thereby Hitler lost his best ally in the Tokyo Cabinet, and the Japanese quickly made up their minds to follow their own plans and keep the Germans in ignorance. As in the case of the Italian attack on Greece, the Germans had little justification either for surprise or complaint.

IV

His absorption in the war left Hitler with less and less time for public appearances on other than military occasions. In the whole

1. *Ciano's Diary*, 18 January 1941, p. 330.

of 1940 he made only seven speeches of any importance, even less in succeeding years, a fact of some importance when it is recalled how great a part Hitler's oratory played in the history of the years before the war.

In the winter of 1940–1 Hitler still observed the routine occasions: 4 September, the opening of the Winter Help Relief Campaign; 8 November, the anniversary of the Munich putsch, 30 January, the anniversary of his Chancellorship; 24 February, the anniversary of his first big speech in Munich; 16 March, Memorial Day for those killed in the war. Apart from these fixed dates he made only one big speech, on 10 December, in the Berlin armaments works of Rheinmetall-Borsig.

Both the place and the time of the year suggest that Hitler's object on this last occasion was to check the mood of pessimism which Ciano and other observers had noticed in Berlin in the early autumn, and which was spreading as the second winter of the war advanced, without sight of the end so widely expected in the summer. The speech certainly shows all Hitler's old skill as an agitator, and is a companion piece to the famous speech he made to the Industry Club at Düsseldorf in January 1932.[1] Just as then he had set himself to convince an audience of industrialists and business men, so now every sentence was carefully directed to a working-class audience in the city which had once been a stronghold of the German Marxist parties.

Hitler drew the picture of Germany's enemies in terms of an international class-war. Britain and America were rich nations, countries ruled by capitalists in which, despite their wealth, unemployment was to be reckoned in millions; countries in which the working class was blatantly exploited and profits valued more highly than labour. These were the two worlds now face to face. For, on the other side, was a National Socialist Germany in which unemployment had been ended, and in which work, not money, was the supreme value. 'Today the only question for us is where to find workers' – so completely had the problem of unemployment been solved. In Germany the economic system had been subordinated to the needs of the people; dividends and directors' fees had been limited; in political life and in the new German Army all social prejudices had been abolished.

If in this war everything points to the fact that gold is fighting against work, Capitalism against peoples, and Reaction against the progress of

1. See above, pp. 196–9.

humanity, then work, the peoples and progress will be victorious. Even the support of the Jewish race will not avail the others.

Yet, Hitler declared, he had wanted neither to rearm nor to go to war.

Who was I before the Great War? An unknown nameless individual. What was I during the war? A quite inconspicuous, ordinary soldier. I was in no way responsible for the Great War. However, who are the rulers of Britain today? They are the same old gang who were warmongering before the Great War, the same Churchill who was the vilest agitator amongst them during the Great War. . . .
    When we have won this war it will not have been won by a few industrialists or millionaires, or by a few capitalists or aristocrats, or by a few bourgeois, or by anyone else. Workers, you must look upon me as your guarantor. I was born a son of the people; I have spent all my life struggling for the German people. . . .
    When this war is ended Germany will set to work in earnest. A great 'Awake' will sound throughout the country. Then the German nation will stop manufacturing cannon and will embark on the new work of reconstruction for the millions. Then we shall show the world for the first time who is the real master – Capitalism or work. Out of this work will grow the great German Reich of which great poets have dreamed. . . . Should anyone say to me: 'These are mere fantastic dreams, mere visions,' I can only reply that when I set out on my course in 1919 as an unknown, nameless soldier, I built my hopes for the future upon a most vivid imagination. Yet all has come true.[1]

This theme of National Socialist Germany against the capitalist plutocracies was one which Hitler had already sketched in his Winter Help Speech of September. This was the speech in which Hitler promised the German people reprisals for the air-raids which, he declared, the British had begun. With his voice rising to a scream he shouted:

If the British Air Force drops two or three or four thousand kilograms of bombs, we will drop a hundred and fifty, a hundred and eighty, two hundred thousand, three hundred thousand, four hundred thousand kilograms, and more in a single night. If they say that they will carry out large-scale attacks on our cities, we will blot out theirs. The hour will come when one of us will crack – and it will not be National Socialist Germany.[2]

At this point, Shirer noted, Hitler had to stop because of the hysterical applause from his audience, which consisted mainly of German nurses and social workers.

1. *My New Order*, pp. 873–99.   2. ibid., p. 848.

No matter what happens, England will be broken. That is the only time-table I have. And if today, in England, people are inquisitive and ask: 'But why doesn't he come?' – they may rest assured: he'll come all right.'[1]

Hitler's last big speech of the winter was delivered in the Berlin Sportpalast, the scene of so many Nazi triumphs in 1931 and 1932, on the eighth anniversary of his Chancellorship. It was a speech which bore throughout the mark of that curious ambivalent mixture of attraction and hatred which is so often to be noted in Hitler's attitude towards Britain.

Behind the mask of liberty and democracy, he declared, the British had created in their Empire an unparalleled system of oppression and exploitation. Under the slogan of the 'Balance of Power' they had kept Europe divided, playing off one state against another. The rise of a united Germany had put an end to the British game, and after the set-back of 1918 a new and stronger Germany had arisen to confront the British.

Does England think I have an inferiority complex with regard to her? They swindled and duped us in those days (1918), but we were never defeated by British soldiers. . . . In those days it was Imperial Germany to which they objected; today it is National Socialist Germany. In reality it is whatever Germany happens to exist.

Yet in the next minute Hitler continued:

I have offered Britain my hand again and again. It was the very essence of my programme to come to an understanding with her. We have never demanded anything from them and we have never insisted on anything. I repeatedly offered them my hand, but always in vain. . . .

Even after the war had begun there were possibilities for an agreement. Immediately after the Polish campaign I again offered my hand. I demanded nothing from France or Britain. Still all was in vain. Immediately after the collapse of the west I again offered my hand to Britain. They literally spat on me. . . .

We have been drawn into war against our will. No man can offer his hand more often than I have. But if they want to exterminate the German nation, then they will get the surprise of their lives.

Hitler's peroration repeated the picture of the two worlds and added the oldest theme of all his speeches, the Jews.

I am convinced [he ended] that 1941 will be the crucial year of a great New Order in Europe. The world shall open up for everyone. Privileges for individuals, the tyranny of certain nations and their financial rulers

1. *My New Order*, p. 855.

shall fall. And, last of all, this year will help to provide the foundations of a real understanding among peoples, and with it the certainty of conciliation among nations.

When the other world has been delivered from the Jews, Judaism will have ceased to play a part in Europe. . . . Those nations who are still opposed to us will some day recognize the greater enemy within. Then they will join us in a combined front, a front against international Jewish exploitation and racial degeneration.[1]

It was an authentic touch of the old Hitler, the raw anti-Semitic, anti-capitalist agitator of Munich in the 1920s.

Yet it was on his military rather than his political gifts that Hitler now relied, and with the spring of 1941 he looked forward eagerly to the moment when he could once more give the order to advance on Russia, the greatest of all his schemes, as a necessary preliminary to which he had now come to accept sweeping the British out of Greece and the Balkans.

Between Germany and Greece lay four countries – Hungary, Rumania, Yugoslavia, and Bulgaria – whose compliance had to be secured before Hitler could reach the Greek frontier. Hungary and Rumania had already accepted the status of German satellites, and throughout the winter months German troop trains steadily moved across Hungary to Rumania, where a task force of nearly seven hundred thousand men was built up. In Bulgaria a sharp tussle for influence took place between the Germans and the Russians. The Germans won, and on the night of 28 February German forces from Rumania crossed the Danube and began to occupy key positions throughout the country. The following day Bulgaria joined the Tripartite Pact.

Yugoslavia proved more difficult. Recognizing this, Hitler did not ask for the passage of German troops, but he put strong pressure on the Yugoslav Government to follow the example of Hungary, Rumania, and Bulgaria in acceding to the Tripartite Pact. In the middle of February the Yugoslav Prime Minister and Foreign Minister went to Berchtesgaden, and on 4–5 March the Prince Regent Paul also paid a secret visit to the Führer. Hitler's bribe was the offer of Salonika, and it was taken. On 25 March, Tsetkovitch, the Yugoslav Foreign Minister, signed the Pact in Vienna.[2] Ciano, who had come to Vienna for the occasion, found

1. Speech of 30 January 1941; *My New Order*, pp. 901–24.
2. See the account by R. L. Knéjévitch: 'Prince Paul, Hitler and Salonika,' in *International Affairs*, January 1951, pp. 38–44.

Hitler in good form. Yugoslavia's accession to the Axis greatly simplified the military problem. Given favourable weather, he told Ciano, the decision in Greece could be brought about in a few days. The sharp eyes of Winston Churchill did not miss the fact, reported by British agents, that, immediately on Yugoslavia's agreement, three of the five German armoured divisions which had moved southwards through Rumania were switched north to Cracow in Poland.

Hitler's satisfaction, however, was premature. On the night of 26-7 March a group of Yugoslav officers, rebelling against their Government's adherence to the Axis cause, carried out a *coup d'état* in Belgrade in the name of the young King Peter II.

The Belgrade *coup* upset the Germans' calculations, but what really roused Hitler's fury was the insolence of a nation which ventured to cross him. To his imperious temper this was intolerable, and must be paid for by the most terrible punishment he could inflict. A hurried council of war summoned to the Chancellery learned of the Führer's decision while the Japanese Foreign Minister, Matsuoka, was kept waiting in another room. Hitler did not stop to consider coolly how far the situation was altered by what had happened in Belgrade. Determined to destroy those who had dared to cross him, he took the decision, then and there, to postpone the attack on Russia up to four weeks, so completely was he prepared to sacrifice everything to the satisfaction of his desire for revenge.

'The Führer is determined,' the official record of the meeting runs, 'to make all preparations to destroy Yugoslavia militarily and as a national unit, without waiting for any possible declarations of loyalty from the new government.'[1]

The decision to postpone the attack on Russia for the sake of punishing the Yugoslavs was a grave one, but Hitler made it without hesitation, so fierce was his resentment. Never was the man's essential character more clearly illuminated. The brutal tone of the orders reflects this mood. Not content with taking steps to ward off any threat to his plans from Yugoslavia, he was bent upon the entire destruction of the state and its partition. The blow, he insisted, must be carried out with 'merciless harshness'.

The military preparations for this new and unexpected campaign had to be improvised, but Hitler issued his directive that very day, and again included the sentence: 'Yugoslavia, despite

1. N.D. 1746-PS.

her protestations of loyalty, must be considered as an enemy and crushed as swiftly as possible.'[1] General Jodl spent the rest of the day and most of the night in the Chancellery working out plans, and at four o'clock on the morning of 28 March was able to give the liaison officer with the Italian General Staff a memorandum on the joint measures to be taken. Hitler had already written to Mussolini on the evening of the 27th, requesting him to halt operations in Albania for the next few days and to cover the Yugoslav–Albanian frontier. Mussolini's agreement was received in the early hours of the 28th. At the same time imperious messages had been sent to Hungary and Bulgaria, and General von Paulus hastily dispatched to Budapest to coordinate the military measures to be taken by the satellite forces against the isolated Yugoslavs. Hitler's political preparations contained provision not only for stirring up the hatred and greed of Yugoslavia's neighbours, but also for disrupting the Yugoslav State internally by appealing to the Croats, whose grievances against the Belgrade Government had long been fostered by Nazi agents.

By 5 April, ten days after he had received the news of the *coup d'état*, Hitler had completed his preparations, and at dawn on the 6th, while German forces pushed across the frontiers, squadrons of German bombers took off for Belgrade to carry out a methodical operation lasting three whole days and designed to destroy the Yugoslav capital. Flying at rooftop height, the German pilots systematically bombed the city without fear of intervention. More than seventeen thousand people were killed in an attack to which the name 'Operation Punishment' had been given.

Simultaneously, other German divisions operating from Bulgaria began the invasion of Greece. Both operations, mounted with overwhelming force, were rapidly carried to success. On 17 April the Yugoslav Army was driven to capitulate; six days later the Greeks, after their six months' heroic resistance to the Italians, were forced to follow suit. On 22 April the British troops, who had landed in Greece less than two months before, began their evacuation. On the 27th the German tanks rolled into Athens, and on 4 May Hitler presented his report to a cheering Reichstag. The Balkan war, which Mussolini had begun in an attempt to assert his independence, had ended in a German triumph which completely eclipsed the Italian partner of the Axis, and which was by implication a public humiliation of the Duce, who had been driven by his failures to turn to Germany for help.

1. N.D. C-127.

In his speech to the Reichstag Hitler did his best to disguise this unpalatable fact:

I must state categorically that this action was not directed against Greece. The Duce did not even request me to place one single German division at his disposal for this purpose. . . . The concentration of German forces was therefore not made for the purpose of assisting the Italians against Greece. It was a precautionary measure against the British attempt to entrench themselves in the Balkans.[1]

Hitler declared, with some truth, that he had never wanted war in the Balkans and put the blame upon the British, who had tried to make use of Yugoslavia and Greece as they had of Poland and Norway. Only one phrase betrayed his real feelings:

You will surely understand, gentlemen, that when I heard the news of the *coup d'état* in Belgrade, I at once gave orders to attack Yugoslavia. To treat the German Reich in this way is impossible.

The real relationship between Berlin and Rome, however, was revealed by the partition of Yugoslavia. The new frontiers were drawn by the Führer in a directive issued on 12 April. Not until 21 April, when he was summoned to Vienna, did Ciano learn what would be Italy's share. Yugoslavia as a state had been wiped off the map, and her territories divided up among her conquerors. But Italy's claims were treated on a level with those of the other satellites, and the Duce had perforce to accept Hitler's unilateral decisions.

Italian dependence upon Germany was further emphasized by the course of events in North Africa. There the continuing Italian failure to check the British advance led to the loss of Bardia on 5 January and of Benghazi on 6 February. The British conquest of Cyrenaica was complete. At a conference with his generals on 3 February Hitler discounted the military danger in losing North Africa, but he was worried about the effect on Italy.

Britain [he remarked] can hold a pistol to Italy's head and force her either to make peace and retain everything, or after the loss of North Africa to be bombarded. . . . We must make every effort to prevent this. Italy must be given support. We are already doing this in *Marita*. We must, however, attempt to render effective assistance in North Africa.[2]

The steps which Hitler ordered to make good this decision

1. *My New Order*, pp. 948–63.   2. N.D. 872-PS.

proved as successful in Africa as they had in Greece – from Hitler's point of view almost embarrassingly successful. Recognizing that support from the air was no longer enough, he reluctantly agreed to the transfer of an armoured division from the Balkans and secured Mussolini's consent to the creation of a unified command of all mechanized and motorized forces in the desert under a German general. For this post Hitler chose Rommel, and Rommel took not only the British, but the German High Command, by surprise. Ordered to submit plans for consideration by 20 April, he actually began his attack on 31 March, and by 12 April had driven right across Cyrenaica and recaptured Bardia within a few miles of the Egyptian frontier.

Indeed, by the early summer of 1941, the situation in the eastern Mediterranean had been changed out of recognition. The British had been thrown out of Greece and pushed back to the Egyptian frontier. In Iraq the pro-German Prime Minister, Rashid Ali, led a revolt against the British garrison, and at the beginning of May appealed to Hitler for help for which Syria, under the authority of Vichy, provided a convenient base. Finally, between 20 May and 27 May, German parachute troops captured the island of Crete.

With the small British forces available stretched to the limit to hold Egypt, Palestine, and Iraq, it appeared to the German Naval Staff and to Rommel that it needed only a sharp push to destroy the whole edifice of Britain's Middle Eastern defence system. Accordingly, on 30 May, Raeder revived his demand for a 'decisive Egypt–Suez offensive for the autumn of 1941 which [he argued] would be more deadly to the British Empire than the capture of London'. A week later the Naval Staff submitted a memorandum to Hitler in which, while accepting the decision to attack Russia as an unalterable fact, they urged that this 'must under no circumstances lead to the abandonment or reduction of plans, or to delay, in the conduct of the war in the eastern Mediterranean'. The anxiety revealed in Mr Churchill's and General Wavell's dispatches at this time lends retrospective support to the German Naval Command's arguments. Even a quarter of the forces then being concentrated for the attack on Russia could, if diverted to the Mediterranean theatre of war in time, have dealt a fatal blow to British control of the Middle East.

But Hitler refused to see his opportunity; his intuition failed him. With his mind wholly set upon the invasion of Russia, he declined to look at the Mediterranean as anything more than a sideshow which could be left to the Italians with a stiffening of German troops. In vain both Raeder and Rommel tried to arouse his interest in the possibilities open to him in the south. He was not to be moved, he preferred to dictate rather than take advantage of events. It was to prove one of the supreme blunders of his strategy.

Hitler's mind had been made up at the beginning of the year. On 15 February he announced that any large-scale operations in the Mediterranean must wait until the autumn of 1941, when the defeat of Russia would have been accomplished. Then Malta could be taken and the British expelled from the Mediterranean – but not before. This decision was inflexible. Hitler repeated it to Ciano at Münchenkirchen in April, and Göring admitted that at the time of the capture of Crete 'everything was being prepared for the invasion of Russia and nobody thought of going into Africa'.[1] Crete was the end of the operations in the Balkans, not a stepping-stone to Suez and the Middle East. On 25 May Hitler gave orders to support Rashid Ali's revolt in Iraq, but help was to be limited to a military mission, some assistance from the German Air Force and the supply of arms. The directive made perfectly clear the strict limitations to be observed:

The Arab Freedom Movement is our natural ally in the Middle East against England. . . . I have decided, therefore, to encourage developments in the Middle East by supporting Iraq. Whether – and if so by what means – it may be possible afterwards to launch an offensive against the Suez Canal and eventually oust the British finally from their position between the Mediterranean and the Persian Gulf cannot be decided until 'Operation Barbarossa' is complete.[2]

The utmost Raeder could do was to extract from Hitler promises of a major effort in the Mediterranean and Middle Eastern theatre of war after Russia had been defeated. Hitler was lavish in such promises, including an attack on Egypt from Libya, an advance into Asia Minor from Bulgaria, and the invasion of Persia from positions to be won in Transcaucasia. But the condition was the same in each case – not until Russia had been defeated.

1. Göring's Interrogation, 29 August 1945; N.C.A., Supp. B, p. 1,108.
2. Führer Directive, No. 30, 25 May 1941; *Führer Conferences on Naval Affairs*, 1941, pp. 50–2.

V

All this time the building up of the German forces in the east had steadily continued. On 3 February General Halder presented the Army's detailed estimate of the situation to the Führer. The huge forces to be engaged and the vast distances to be covered excited his imagination. According to Halder's later account, he and Brauchitsch attempted to express doubts but were shouted down. That may be so, but there is no record of this either in the minutes of the conference or in Halder's diary. Hitler was in no mood to listen to doubts. He insisted that the Russians must be prevented from falling back into the depths of their country. Everything depended upon the encirclement of the main Russian forces as near to the frontier as possible. 'It is essential to wipe out large sections of the enemy and not to put them to flight.'[1] The participation of Finland, Rumania, and Hungary in the attack was assured, but Hitler added that – with the exception of Rumania – agreements could be made only at the eleventh hour, in order to keep the secret well guarded. After examining the operational plans for each Army Group, Hitler expressed himself as satisfied. 'It must be remembered,' he declared, 'that the main aim is to gain possession of the Baltic States and Leningrad. . . . When "Barbarossa" begins, the world will hold its breath and make no comment.' By a double bluff, meanwhile, the concentration of German troops in the east was to be represented as a feint to disguise renewed German preparations for the invasion of England and the attack on Greece.

A month later, early in March, Hitler held another military conference, to which he summoned all the senior commanders who were to take part in the attack. Hitler presented the invasion as a step forced on him by Russia's imperialistic designs in the Baltic and the Balkans. A Russian attack on Germany was a certainty, he assured them, and must be forestalled. A secret agreement had even been arrived at between Russia and England, and this was the reason for the British refusal to accept German peace offers.

The war against Russia [Hitler continued] will be such that it cannot be conducted in a chivalrous fashion. This struggle is one of ideologies and racial differences and will have to be conducted with unprecedented,

1. Minutes of the Führer's conference on 3 February 1941; N.D. 872-PS. Cf. General Halder: *Hitler as War Lord* (London, 1950), pp. 19–21.

merciless and unrelenting harshness. All officers will have to rid themselves of obsolete ideologies. I know that the necessity for such means of
waging war is beyond the comprehension of you generals but ... I
insist absolutely that my orders be executed without contradiction. ...
The [Russian] commissars are the bearers of an ideology directly opposed
to National Socialism. Therefore the commissars will be liquidated.[1]

If Halder is to be believed, Hitler added that breaches of international law by German soldiers were to be excused since Russia
had not participated in the Hague Convention and had no rights
under it. Halder's account is certainly in keeping with Hitler's
later orders, and according to Brauchitsch a number of the
generals protested to him after the conference that such a way of
waging war was intolerable. The most Brauchitsch felt able to do
was surreptitiously to issue an order instructing officers to preserve
strict discipline and to punish excesses.

The generals were even more disturbed at the proposals for the
administration of the territories occupied in the east. These, as
they were set out in a special directive issued on 13 March, provided that 'in the area of operations, the Reichsführer S.S.
(Himmler) is entrusted, on behalf of the Führer, with special
tasks for the preparation of the political administration, tasks
which result from the struggle which has to be carried out
between two opposing political systems. Within the limits of these
tasks, the Reichsführer S.S. shall act independently and under
his own responsibility'.[2] While Himmler carried out these tasks,
the areas under occupation were to be sealed off: not even 'the
highest personalities of Government or Party' were to be
admitted.

Although the authority of the Army Commander-in-Chief was
formally safeguarded, this could only mean that Himmler and
the S.S. were to be given a free hand to stamp out all traces of
the Soviet system. The directive also provided for handing over the
areas occupied to the political administration of special commissioners appointed by Hitler himself, and for the immediate
economic exploitation of the territory seized under the direction
of Göring. Even the most unpolitical of German generals can
have had little doubt what all this amounted to. Hitler was taking
steps in advance to make sure that no scruples or conservatism on
the part of the Army Commanders should stand in the way of the

1. Affidavit of General Halder, N.C.A., vol. VIII, pp. 645–6.
2. N.D. 447-PS.

treatment of the occupied territories on thorough-going National Socialist lines.

On 20 April Hitler appointed Alfred Rosenberg, the half-forgotten figure who had played a great part in forming his views on German expansion in the east, as Commissioner for the East European Region. It was an unhappy choice. Himmler, in his capacity as Reichsführer of the S.S. corps d'élite, already claimed the responsibility for laying the racial foundations of the New Order in the east, and this claim had been recognized in the directive of 13 March which has already been quoted. Göring was equally outraged by Rosenberg's appointment: in his capacity as Plenipotentiary for the Four-Year Plan he claimed the right to organize the economic exploitation of the territories in the east so as to guarantee Germany's present and future needs in food and raw materials. This claim, too, was confirmed by Hitler in a secret decree of 20 May, despite Rosenberg's protests. Against two such powerful empire builders as Himmler and Göring, Rosenberg was quite unable to defend his own position, and there was thus from the beginning a conflict of authority in the east between the Army, Himmler, Göring, and the nominal Commissioner, Rosenberg, which only became worse as time went on.

The ruthlessness of the German treatment of the occupied territories in the east was not fortuitous; it was part of a methodical system of exploitation and resettlement planned in advance and entered upon with a full appreciation of its consequences. This can be well illustrated from a directive of Göring's Economic Staff East, dated 23 May 1941, and dealing with the future of Russian agriculture. The overriding need was defined as the use of the food-producing areas of the east to supplement Germany's and Europe's supplies both during and after the war. This was to provide one of the economic foundations of the European New Order, and the methods by which it was to be secured are set out at length. The directive goes on to discuss the consequences for Russia's industrial population:

The German Administration in these territories may well attempt to mitigate the consequences of the famine which will undoubtedly take place, and to accelerate the return to primitive agricultural conditions. ... However, these measures will not avert famine. Many tens of millions of people in the industrial areas will become redundant and will either die or have to emigrate to Siberia. Any attempt to save the population there from death by starvation by importing surpluses from the Black Soil Zone would be at the expense of supplies to Europe. It would reduce Germany's staying-power in the war, and would undermine Germany's and Europe's power to resist the blockade. This must be clearly and absolutely understood.[1]

A memorandum summarizing the discussion at a meeting of state secretaries called to consider plans for 'Barbarossa' on 2 May begins in similar fashion: 'The war can only be continued if all the armed forces are fed by Russia in the third year of the war. There is no doubt that as a result many millions of people will be starved to death if we take out of the country the things we need.'[2]

This, it should be pointed out, is not Hitler talking late at night up on the Obersalzberg; this is the translation of those grim fantasies into the sober directives and office memoranda of a highly organized administration, methodically planning economic operations which must result in the starvation of millions. Not far away, in the offices of Himmler's S.S., equally methodical calculations were being made of how this process could be accelerated by the use of gas chambers (including mobile vans) for the elimination of the racially impure.

On 30 April with the Balkan operations completed, apart from the pendant of Crete, Hitler fixed 22 June as the new date for the opening of the attack in the east. By May the armoured divisions which had overrun Greece were on their way north to join the concentration of German troops in Poland, and an ominous lull settled over the battle fronts. After his report to the Reichstag on 4 May Hitler returned to the Berghof, and it was there that he received the news of one of the strangest incidents of the whole war.

At 5.45 p.m. on Saturday 10 May Rudolf Hess took off in a Messerschmidt fighter from an aerodrome near Augsburg and flew alone over the North Sea in the direction of Scotland. His intention was to seek out the Duke of Hamilton, a serving officer in the Royal Air Force, whom he had met very briefly during the Berlin Olympic Games of 1936. Through the Duke he hoped to be put in touch with political circles in London and to negotiate a peace between Great Britain and Germany. Hess was one of the highest figures in the Nazi Party hierarchy, a close friend of Hitler's since the early 1920s, and the man who had helped him to write Part I of *Mein Kampf* while they were imprisoned in Landsberg Gaol after the 1923 putsch. In time Hess had become

1. N.D. EC-126.   2. N.D. 2718-PS.

a Reich Minister and in 1933 had been made Deputy of the Führer for all Party affairs. A man of no great ability, his chief claim to an important position in the Party was his dog-like devotion to Hitler, to whose inner circle of intimates he had belonged for many years. He was not only constantly seen with him on all Party occasions, but he echoed all that Hitler said, believed unshakeably in the Führer's genius, and accepted the Nazi creed in entire seriousness.

In the last few years, however, especially after the beginning of the war, Hess had fallen into the background. He held no important office in the State or Armed Forces, and the routine transaction of Party business had no longer any interest for Hitler. Not only was Hitler now almost entirely occupied with the conduct of the war, but Hess saw his own position being undermined by the growing influence of Hitler's personal secretary, Martin Bormann. As a result he became resentful and frustrated. He cast around for some means, some sensational act of devotion, whereby he could restore his position and recapture the favour of the leader whom he worshipped. Convinced that he understood Hitler's mind as none of the later upstarts could, he determined as early as the summer of 1940 to fly to Britain and by a dramatic *coup* to bring off the negotiated peace which had so far eluded the Führer.

The flight on 10 May was actually the fourth of Hess's attempts to carry out his idea. After parachuting from his plane near Eaglesham in Scotland and being arrested, Hess succeeded in getting in touch with the Duke of Hamilton, who at once reported the strange news to Churchill. Hess's views proved to be perfectly straightforward. He was convinced that Hitler would defeat England, but he also believed that Hitler, reluctant to destroy the British Empire, still preferred to make a settlement with her. He therefore proposed that he should undertake negotiations in order to conclude a peace on the following lines: Britain was to give Germany a free hand in Europe, and in return Germany would agree to respect the integrity of the British Empire – after the return of the former German Colonies. Hess made it clear that he did not include Russia in Europe, and added that Hitler had certain demands which Russia would have to meet: there was no truth, however, in the rumours of an imminent German attack on Russia. To these conditions Hess added the stipulation that Hitler could never negotiate with the existing British Government, or with any government which contained

Churchill; later he included the simultaneous conclusion of a peace with Italy.

This was the end of the affair so far as Hess and the British were concerned. Once his purpose and proposals had been elicited he was treated as a prisoner of war. No negotiations were ever begun or even contemplated on the British side, and he remained in confinement until the Nuremberg Trials, at which he was sentenced to imprisonment for life.

To Hitler, who had known nothing of Hess's preparations, the news came as a shock. According to Schmidt, it was 'as if a bomb had struck the Berghof'.[1] Hitler was both angry and mystified. Hess had left a long and rambling letter behind, and Keitel later described how he found him walking up and down in his study at the Berghof, tapping his forehead and declaring that Hess must have been crazy. Hitler certainly never took the mission at all seriously; his one concern was how to handle the news of the flight in such a way as to cause least embarrassment to his régime. The fact that his own deputy and devoted follower had flown to Britain could be highly damaging to his prestige, and although Hitler was inclined to believe that Hess had acted quite sincerely while suffering from some mental derangement, he stripped him of his offices, appointed Martin Bormann as deputy leader of the Party in his place, and gave orders that, if Hess returned to Germany, he was to be shot at once. Intensive inquiries, however, failed to uncover any conspiracy. It became clear that Hess had acted entirely on his own initiative and had not even told his wife.

Hess said nothing to his interrogators of Hitler's intention of invading Russia, probably because he did not know of it himself. His flight had no connexion with the events which were so soon to follow. He had first thought of his plan in 1940, and in his mind it was to be the conclusion to the war in the west, in no sense a preliminary to the campaign in the east. In Moscow suspicion persisted long afterwards that Hess had come on a mission to conclude peace with Britain before Hitler turned east and launched his invasion of Russia with British support, or at least with British compliance. There is no evidence at all in favour of such a view. Far from waiting to see whether Hess was successful in his mission or not, Hitler dismissed it as a mad idea, and on 12 May, two days after Hess's flight, fixed the date for the opening of 'Barbarossa'.

1. Schmidt, op. cit., p. 537.

To Hitler's relief and surprise the British made no effort to extort revelations from Hess or to invent them, and within a few days the news had lost its interest. By the time he met Mussolini at the beginning of June, Hitler was ready to weep for his lost comrade. Despite its sensational character, the Hess episode was, as Churchill justly remarks, an incident of little importance.

VI

The few remaining weeks were an anxious time for Hitler. Rumours of an impending attack on the Soviet Union were rife, and, conscious of his own duplicity, Hitler watched carefully for any sign of a Russian move to forestall it.

In order to camouflage his intentions Hitler ordered Russian orders for goods placed in Germany to be fulfilled and deliveries maintained till the last moment. A new trade treaty had been concluded in January 1941, and the Russians continued to make a prompt dispatch of raw materials and food to Germany up to the day of the attack. Schnurre, the chief German economic negotiator, reported in April 1941, that, after difficulties during January and February, 'deliveries in March rose by leaps and bounds'.[1] A month later he wrote: 'I am under the impression that we could make economic demands in Moscow which would go even beyond the scope of the treaty of 10 January 1941.'[2]

Indeed, in the last three months before the attack, the Soviet Government, while building up its defences in the west, did everything it could to conciliate and appease the Germans. When Matsuoka, on his return to Tokyo, passed through Moscow in April, Stalin made an unexpected appearance at the station to see him off and publicly asked for the German Ambassador. When Schulenburg presented himself, Stalin put his arm round his shoulders and declared: 'We must remain friends and you must now do everything to that end.' Later Stalin turned to the German military attaché and remarked: 'We will remain friends with you – in any event.'[3] The German Ambassador had no doubt that this unusual display on Stalin's part had been specially contrived to impress those present with Russo-German friendship. At almost the same time the Russian Government suddenly accepted the

1. Schnurre's Memorandum of 5 April 1941: *Nazi–Soviet Relations* pp. 318–19.
2. Schnurre's Memorandum of 15 May 1941; ibid., pp. 339–41.
3. Schulenburg's Report to the German Foreign Office, 13 April 1941; ibid., pp. 323–4.

German proposals for settling frontier questions arising out of the Soviet annexation of Lithuania.

Early in May Stalin took over the Chairmanship of the Council of People's Commissars, a step universally regarded as indicating the prospect of a crisis with which only Stalin himself could deal. Immediately afterwards, however, on 8 May, Tass denied reports of troop concentrations in the west; on 9 May the U.S.S.R. withdrew its recognition from the legations of the exiled Governments of Belgium, Norway, and Yugoslavia, and on 12 May established relations with the pro-Nazi Government of Rashid Ali in Iraq. All through this period the Soviet Press was kept under the strictest restraint in order to avoid provocation, and as late as 14 June Tass put out a statement categorically denying difficulties between Germany and Russia.

On 28 April Count von der Schulenburg, the German Ambassador, in Moscow, saw Hitler and tried to convince him that there was no danger of an attack on Germany by Russia. Weizsäcker, the State Secretary, supported Schulenburg's views.

If every Russian city reduced to ashes [he wrote to Ribbentrop] were as valuable to us as a sunken British warship, I should advocate the German–Russian war for this summer. But I believe that we would be the victors over Russia only in a military sense, and would on the other hand lose in an economic sense. . . . The sole decisive factor is whether this project will hasten the fall of England.[1]

On 6 and 7 June the Naval War Diary records further dispatches from Schulenburg:

Russia will only fight if attacked by Germany . . . Russian policy still strives as before to produce the best possible relationship to Germany. . . . All observations show that Stalin and Molotov are doing everything to avoid a conflict with Germany. The entire behaviour of the Soviet Government, as well as the attitude of the Press, which reports all events concerning Germany in a factual manner, support this view. The loyal fulfilment of the economic treaty with Germany proves the same thing.[2]

There is, in fact, not a scrap of evidence to show that, in the summer of 1941, the Soviet Government had any intention of attacking Germany. Warnings from the British (who knew the date fixed for the invasion before the end of April) were dismissed by the Russians as trouble making. The Russians' one anxiety, as Schulenburg correctly reported, was to avoid trouble with the

1. Weizsäcker's Memorandum of 28 April 1941; ibid., pp. 333–4.
2. N.D. C-170.

Germans. But Hitler refused to listen to his Ambassador; he was interested only in reports that could be used to support the pretext for his decision, a decision reached long before without regard to Russia's attitude or the threat which he now alleged of Russian preparations to strike westwards.

In May Antonescu paid his third visit to Hitler, this time at Munich, and agreed that Rumania should take part in the attack. At the end of the month the Finnish Chief of Staff spent a week in Germany to discuss detailed arrangements for cooperation between the two armies. Still Hitler said nothing to Mussolini. When they met at the Brenner on 2 June the most that Ribbentrop admitted was that Russo-German relations were not so good as they had been. Stalin, he told Ciano, was unlikely to commit the folly of attacking Germany, but if he did the Russian forces would be smashed to pieces. In a general survey of the situation, Russia was only mentioned by the way. Hitler and Ribbentrop were more concerned to reassure Mussolini about Admiral Darlan's visit to Berchtesgaden in May and his attempt to interest Hitler again in the possibilities of Franco-German collaboration in North Africa and the Middle East.

A fortnight later Ribbentrop was more forthcoming, or more indiscreet. He met Ciano at Venice on 15 June to arrange the adherence of the puppet state of Croatia to the Tripartite Pact. As they went to dinner in their gondola Ciano asked his colleague about the rumours of an impending German attack on Russia.

'Dear Ciano,' was Ribbentrop's expansive reply, 'I cannot tell you anything as yet because every decision is locked in the impenetrable bosom of the Führer. However, one thing is certain: if we attack, the Russia of Stalin will be erased from the map within eight weeks.'[1]

From Venice Ribbentrop sent a telegram to Budapest warning the Hungarians to be ready. On 18 June a Non-Aggression Pact between Germany and Turkey was announced and Hitler wrote a last letter to Antonescu outlining the duties of the German forces in Rumania. On the 14th Hitler had summoned a conference of his commanders-in-chief in the Reich Chancellery. The meeting lasted from eleven in the morning to half past six in the evening, with lunch in the middle. The generals showed none of the doubts they later claimed to have felt about the Russian 'adventure'. The professional soldiers' underestimate of the strength of the

1. *Ciano's Diary*, p. 559.

Soviet forces and the difficulties of the campaign was as great as Hitler's. Now, one after another they explained their operational plans to the Führer, while Hitler nodded his approval, occasionally suggesting some alterations, but only of a minor character. Satisfied with the preparations that had been made, in the following week Hitler left for his new headquarters, Wolfsschanze ('Wolf's Lair'), near Rastenburg in East Prussia.

There, on 21 June, the eve of the attack, he dictated a letter to Mussolini. It was the first official news Mussolini had been given of his intentions.

Duce!
I am writing this letter to you at a moment when months of anxious deliberation and continuous, nerve-racking waiting are ending in the hardest decision of my life. I believe – after seeing the latest Russian situation map and after appraisal of numerous other reports – that I cannot take the responsibility for waiting longer, and above all, I believe that there is no other way of obviating the danger – unless it be further waiting, which, however, would necessarily lead to disaster in this or the next year at the latest.

As so often before, Hitler proceeded to justify himself at length. Britain had lost the war, but held out in the hope of aid from Russia. On their side, the Russians, reverting to their old expansionist policy, prevented Germany from launching a large-scale attack in the west by a massive concentration of forces in the east. Until he had safeguarded his rear, Hitler declared, he dared not take the risk of attacking England.

Whatever may now come, Duce, our situation cannot become worse as a result of this step; it can only improve. Even if I should be obliged at the end of the year to leave sixty or seventy divisions in Russia, that is only a fraction of the forces I am now continually using on the Eastern Front.[1]

Once again Mussolini was roused in the middle of the night with the usual urgent message from the Führer. 'I do not disturb even my servants at night,' he grumbled to Ciano; 'but the Germans make me jump out of bed at any hour without the least consideration.'[2] While the Duce was still reading Hitler's letter the attack was already beginning. From the Arctic Circle to the Black Sea more than a hundred and fifty German, Finnish, and

1. *Hitler e Mussolini*, pp. 99–104.
2. *Ciano's Diary*, p. 365. Ten days later, the Duce added: 'I hope for only one thing, that in this war in the east the Germans lose a lot of feathers.'

Rumanian divisions were pressing forward across the Russian frontiers. The German forces, divided into three Army Groups commanded by Leeb, Bock, and Rundstedt, included nineteen armoured divisions and twelve motorized, supported by over 2,700 aircraft.

In the 1920s Hitler, then an unsuccessful Bavarian politician, whose political following numbered no more than a few thousands, had written at the end of *Mein Kampf*:

And so we National Socialists consciously draw a line beneath the foreign policy tendency of our pre-war period. We take up where we broke off six hundred years ago. We stop the endless German movement towards the south and west of Europe, and turn our gaze towards the lands of the east. At long last we put a stop to the colonial and commercial policy of pre-war days and pass over to the territorial policy of the future. But when we speak of new territory in Europe today we must think principally of Russia and her border vassal states. Destiny itself seems to wish to point out the way to us here. . . . This colossal Empire in the east is ripe for dissolution, and the end of the Jewish domination in Russia will also be the end of Russia as a state.[1]

At dawn on 22 June 1941, one year to the day since the French had signed the armistice at Compiègne, Hitler believed that he was about to fulfil his own prophecy. He concluded his letter to Mussolini with these words:

Since I struggled through to this decision, I again feel spiritually free. The partnership with the Soviet Union, in spite of the complete sincerity of my efforts to bring about a final conciliation, was nevertheless often very irksome to me, for in some way or other it seemed to me to be a break with my whole origin, my concepts and my former obligations. I am happy now to be delivered from this torment.[2]

It was to prove an irrevocable decision.

1. *Mein Kampf*, part II, c. 14.
2. Text of the letter in *Nazi–Soviet Relations*, pp. 349–53.

CHAPTER TWELVE

THE UNACHIEVED EMPIRE

1941–3

I

AT the time Hitler gave two reasons for his decision to attack Russia: the first, that Russia was preparing to attack Germany in the summer of 1941; the second, that Britain's refusal to acknowledge defeat was due to her hopes of Russian and American intervention, and that Britain had actually entered into an alliance with Russia against Germany. The way to strike at Britain was thus to destroy her hopes of Russian aid.

At most these arguments reinforced a decision already reached on other grounds. Hitler invaded Russia for the simple but sufficient reason that he had always meant to establish the foundations of his thousand-year Reich by the annexation of the territory lying between the Vistula and the Urals.

The novelty lay not so much in the decision to turn east as in the decision to drop the provision he had hitherto regarded as indispensable, a settlement with Britain first. Forced to recognize that the British were not going to be bluffed or bombed into capitulation, Hitler convinced himself that Britain was already virtually defeated. She was certainly not in a position, in the near future, to threaten his hold over the Continent. Why then waste time forcing the British to admit that Germany should have a free hand on the Continent, when this was already an established fact to which the British could make no practical objection? This argument was confirmed by the conviction, based on the experience of the campaigns of 1939 and 1940, that the German Armed Forces under his direction were invincible.

Most important of all was the belief, a result partly of this conviction, partly of an underestimate of Russian strength, that the Soviet armies could be defeated in a single campaign. Hitler knew that he was taking a risk in invading Russia, but he was convinced that the war in the east would be over in two months, or three at the most. He not only said this, but acted on it, refusing to make any preparations for a winter campaign. A series of sharp defeats, and he was certain that Stalin's Government would fall. 'Hopes of victory,' Field-Marshal von Kleist said after the war, 'were largely built on the prospect that the invasion would produce a political upheaval in Russia . . . and that Stalin would be overthrown by his own people if he suffered heavy defeats.'[1] 'We have only to kick in the door,' Hitler told Jodl, 'and the whole rotten structure will come crashing down.' Hitler was not blind to the numerical superiority of the Russians, but he was certain that the political weakness of the Soviet régime, together with the technical superiority of the Germans, would give him a quick victory in a campaign which he never expected to last much longer than that in which he had overrun France the year before.

Once he had extended his power to the Urals and the Caucasus, Hitler calculated, he would have established his empire upon such solid foundations that Britain, even if she continued the war and even if the United States intervened on her side, would be unable to make any impression on it. Far from being a desperate expedient forced on him by the frustration of his plans for the defeat of Britain, the invasion of Russia represented the realization of those imperial dreams which he had sketched in the closing section of *Mein Kampf* and elaborated in the fireside circle of the Berghof. At one and the same time he would be able to guarantee German victory in the war and the creation of that European New Order which was to be the permanent memorial to his genius. This was the prize – and it was to be had, so he convinced himself, at the cost of no more than a single campaign which would be over before the winter came.

The opening of the campaign seemed to justify Hitler's optimism. The German armoured divisions struck deep into Russian territory. By 5 July they had reached the Dnieper, by the 16th Smolensk, little more than two hundred miles from Moscow and four hundred and fifty miles from the starting point of Bialystok. On 14 July Hitler issued a directive in which he spoke of considerable reductions in the strength of the Army in the near future, and the diversion of the main effort in armaments to the Air Force for the conduct of the war against the last remaining enemy, Britain.

But, although the German troops rapidly gained ground, they did not succeed in destroying the Russian armies by the huge encircling movements which Hitler had envisaged. However many Russian troops were taken prisoner, there were always

1. Quoted by B. H. Liddell Hart: .op. cit., p. 259.

more ready to defend the next line – and all the time the German Army was being drawn deeper in.

At this point a divergence began to appear between Hitler's and the Army High Command's views of the objectives to be gained. Hitler – as his first directive of 18 December 1940 shows – laid the greatest stress on clearing the Baltic States and capturing Leningrad; once the initial battles were over, the Centre Army Group was to support this northerly drive through the Baltic States and not to press on to Moscow. At the same time the Southern Army Group was to drive south-east towards Kiev and the Dnieper, in order to secure the agricultural and industrial resources of the Ukraine.

Brauchitsch and Halder took a different view. They believed that the best chance of catching and destroying the Russian forces was to press on to Moscow, along the road to which they would find the bulk of those forces, including the new armies which were being rapidly formed. They were in favour of concentrating, not dispersing, the German effort. This view was supported by Bock, the Commander-in-Chief of the Centre Army Group, and by his two panzer commanders, Guderian and Hoth, but it was rejected by Hitler, who insisted on ordering part of Bock's mobile forces to assist the northern army group's drive on Leningrad and the rest to wheel south and support the advance into the Ukraine.

Brauchitsch temporized on the grounds that time was needed to overhaul the tanks and bring up replacements. The time thus gained was used to renew the arguments against Hitler's orders, and the dispute rumbled on throughout August while the Centre Army Group remained halted east of Smolensk.

By September Hitler was beginning to lose interest in Leningrad, but he was still opposed to the drive on Moscow and much more excited by the possibility of a huge encirclement in the Ukraine. Angered by the opposition of the Army High Command, he rejected a memorandum drawn up by the General Staff with the remark that only minds set in the mould of outworn theories could fail to notice the opportunities in the south. In the end he agreed that the Centre Army Group should send only limited forces to assist in the attack on Leningrad and that it should prepare to launch a major offensive against Moscow, but he insisted that the battle of encirclement in the Ukraine must be put first and that Bock's army group must make the fullest possible contribution to this before being freed to resume its advance eastwards.

Reluctantly the General Staff were forced to assent, but General Halder has since argued that this was the turning-point of the campaign and that Hitler threw away the chance of inflicting a decisive defeat on the Russians for the sake of a prestige victory and the capture of the industrial region of the Ukraine.

For not only had this dispute seriously worsened the relations between Hitler and his generals, it also led to the waste of valuable time. The southern encirclement proved a great success and over six hundred thousand Russians were taken prisoner east of Kiev, but it was late in September before the battle was ended. The onset of the autumn rains, which turned the Russian countryside, with its poor roads, into a quagmire, promised ill for the attack on Moscow, which the Army High Command had wanted to launch in August. The Balkan campaign and the bad weather in the early summer of 1941 had already cut short the campaigning season, and beyond the autumn there loomed the threat of the Russian winter. Hitler, however, elated by his success in the south, now pushed forward the attack on Moscow which he had held back for so long.

On 2 October the advance of the Centre Army Group was resumed, after a halt of two months. On the 3rd Hitler spoke in Berlin, boasting that 'behind our troops there already lies a territory twice the size of the German Reich when I came to power in 1933. Today I declare, without reservation, that the enemy in the east has been struck down and will never rise again.' On 8 October Orel was captured, and the next day Otto Dietrich, the Reich Press Chief, caused a sensation with the announcement that the war in the east was over. 'For all military purposes, Soviet Russia is done with,' Dietrich declared. 'The British dream of a two-front war is dead.' Between Vyazma and Bryansk, another six hundred thousand Russians were trapped and taken prisoner. A week later the German spearheads reached Mozhaisk, only eighty miles from the Russian capital.

Yet even now Hitler could not make up his mind to concentrate on one objective. In the north Leeb was ordered at the same time to capture Leningrad,[1] link up with the Finns and push on to cut the Murmansk railway. In the south Rundstedt was ordered to clear the Black Sea coast (including the Crimea) and

1. The military directive of 29 September announced: 'The Führer has decided to have St Petersburg wiped off the face of the earth . . . the problem of the survival of the population and of supplying it with food is one which cannot and should not be solved by us' (N.D. C-124).

strike beyond Rostov, eastwards to the Volga and south-eastwards to the Caucasus. 'We laughed aloud when we received these orders,' Rundstedt later declared, 'for winter had already come and we were almost seven hundred kilometres from these cities.'[1]

Thus, with forces which were numerically inferior to the Russians, throughout the campaign of 1941 Hitler swung between a number of objectives, losing time in switching from one to another, stretching his resources to the limit and fanning out his armies across a thousand-mile front, while always falling short of the decisive blow which would knock Russia out of the war. He had fallen into the trap against which he had warned his generals before the invasion began, that of allowing the Russians to retreat and draw the Germans farther and farther into the illimitable depths of their hinterland. When the dreaded winter broke over them, the German armies, despite their victories and advances, had still not captured Leningrad and Moscow, or destroyed the Russian capacity to continue the war.

Once the attack on Russia had been launched, the war on the Eastern Front absorbed all Hitler's thoughts and energies. The greater part of his time was spent in the east, at his permanent headquarters, Wolfsschanze, near Rastenburg in east Prussia or at such field headquarters as Werwolf (near Wyniza in the Ukraine) with only occasional visits to Berlin or Bavaria. Not content with fixing the strategic objectives of his armies in the east, he began to interfere in the detailed conduct of operation. 'What had been comparatively infrequent in previous campaigns,' General Halder writes, 'now became a daily occurrence.'[2]

It was not only the military operations in the east which absorbed him: true to the conception of Germany's future which he had formulated in *Mein Kampf* – *Lebensraum* in the east – he saw himself about to realize his historical destiny by the foundation of a new German Empire in the lands conquered from the Russians. The prospect gripped and excited his imagination. From this period, the summer of 1941, date the records of his conversations taken under Bormann's supervision and subsequently published as his table talk.[3] They give a vivid impression

1. Field-Marshal von Rundstedt's interrogation, July 1945; Milton Shulman: *Defeat in the West*, p. 68.
2. Halder: *Hitler as War Lord*, p. 43.
3. *Hitler's Table Talk, 1941–4* (London, 1953). Another version has been published by one of the reporters, Dr Henry Picker, *Hitler's Tischgespräche* (Bonn, 1951).

of Hitler's mood at the peak of his fantastic career, the peer as he saw himself of Napoleon, Bismarck, and Frederick the Great, pursuing, to use his own words, 'the Cyclopean task which the building of an empire means for a single man'.[1]

What India is for England [he declared at an after-dinner session early in August], the territories of Russia will be for us. If only I could make the German people understand what this space means for our future! . . . We must no longer allow Germans to emigrate to America. On the contrary, we must attract the Norwegians, the Swedes, the Danes, and the Dutch into our Eastern territories. They'll become members of the German Reich. . . .

  The German colonist ought to live on handsome, spacious farms. The German services will be lodged in marvellous buildings, the governers in palaces. . . . Around the city, to a depth of thirty to forty kilometres, we shall have a belt of handsome villages connected by the best roads. What exists beyond that will be another world in which we mean to let the Russians live as they like. It is merely necessary that we should rule them.[2]

On the evening of 17 October, with the Russians (as he believed) already defeated, and Todt and Sauckel to provide an appreciative audience, Hitler let his imagination ride:

This Russian desert, we shall populate it. . . . We'll take away its character of an Asiatic steppe, we'll Europeanize it. With this object we have undertaken the construction of roads that will lead to the southernmost part of the Crimea and to the Caucasus. These roads will be studded along their whole length with German towns and around these towns our colonists will settle.

  As for the two or three million men whom we need to accomplish this task, we'll find them quicker than we think. They'll come from Germany, Scandinavia, the Western countries, and America. I shall no longer be here to see all that, but in twenty years, the Ukraine will already be a home for twenty million inhabitants, besides the natives. . . .

  We shan't settle in the Russian towns and we'll let them go to pieces without intervening. And above all, no remorse on this subject! We're absolutely without obligations as far as these people are concerned. To struggle against the hovels, chase away the fleas, provide German teachers, bring out newspapers – very little of that for us! We'll confine ourselves, perhaps, to setting up a radio transmitter, under our control. For the rest, let them know just enough to understand our highway signs, so that they won't get themselves run over by our vehicles.

  For them the word 'liberty' means the right to wash on feast days . . . There's only one duty: to Germanize this country by the immigration of Germans and to look upon the natives as Redskins.[3]

1. *Hitler's Table Talk*, p. 41 (27–8 September 1941).
2. ibid., pp. 24–5 (8–9, 9–10, 10–11 August 1941).
3. ibid., pp. 68–9 (17 October 1941).

Ten days later he declared:

Nobody will ever snatch the East from us!... We shall soon supply the wheat for all Europe, the coal, the steel, the wood. To exploit the Ukraine properly – that new Indian Empire – we need only peace in the West....

For me the object is to exploit the advantages of continental hegemony.... When we are masters of Europe, we have a dominant position in the world. A hundred and thirty million people in the Reich, ninety in the Ukraine. Add to these the other states of the New Europe and we'll be 400 millions as compared with the 130 million Americans.[1]

It was in this mood that Mussolini found his brother dictator when he visited Hitler at his East Prussian headquarters towards the end of August 1941. Wolfsschanze ('Wolf's Lair') was hidden in the heart of a thick forest, miles from any human habitation. Its buildings resembled Alpine chalets, elaborately fitted with central heating, telephone exchanges, a wireless station, and a cinema, protected by powerful A.A. batteries and surrounded by a triple ring of guards. Only later did Hitler move, under the threat of air attacks, to the concrete bunker in which he passed the last years of his life, but from the beginning the dim light of the forest produced a feeling of gloom in everyone who went there.

Two conversations took place between the Führer and the Duce on the 25th, and Mussolini's records of both have been preserved. The first meeting was taken up with an exposition of the military situation in the east, during which Mussolini was reduced to the role of admiring listener. Hitler, he noted, spoke with great confidence and precision, but admitted that faulty intelligence work had completely misled him as to the size and excellence of the Russian forces as well as the determination with which they fought. In their second talk, the same evening, the two dictators ranged over the rest of the world. Hitler spoke bitterly of Franco and was evasive on the subject of the French, who were, as always, the object of jealous complaints by Mussolini. He showed some embarrassment at the Duce's pressing offer of more Italian troops for the Eastern Front, but 'concluded by expressing the most lively desire to come to Italy – when the war is over – in order to pass some time in Florence, a city dear to him above all others for the harmony of its art and its natural beauty.'[2]

The next day Hitler and Mussolini flew to Field-Marshal von

1. *Hitler's Table Talk*, pp. 92–3 (26–7 October 1941).
2. *Ciano's Diplomatic Papers*.

Kluge's H.Q. at Brest-Litovsk, and later in the week to Rundstedt's at Uman in the Ukraine. There Mussolini inspected an Italian division and lunched with the Führer in the open air, surrounded by a crowd of soldiers. At the end of the meal Hitler walked about among the crowd talking informally, while Mussolini, to his annoyance, was left with Rundstedt. The Duce took this as a deliberate slight, and remarked to his ambassador that Hitler in the middle of his troops looked anything but a soldier. Mussolini had his revenge, however, on the return flight, when he insisted on piloting the plane in which he and Hitler were flying. Hitler's own pilot, Bauer, remained at the controls all the time, but Hitler never took his eyes off Mussolini and sat rigid in his seat until Mussolini left Bauer to his job. The Führer's congratulations were mingled with undisguised relief. Mussolini was childishly delighted and insisted on his performance being recorded in the communiqué.

The visit appears to have been organized more for propaganda purposes than to provide an occasion for serious discussions. Earlier in August, Churchill and Roosevelt had met off the coast of Newfoundland and from there issued the joint declaration of war aims known as the Atlantic Charter. The meeting of Hitler and Mussolini and the final communiqué, with the prominence which it gave to the slogan of the 'European New Order', was designed as a counter-demonstration. The dictators pledged themselves to remove the causes of war, eradicate the threat of Bolshevism, put an end to 'plutocratic exploitation', and establish close and peaceful collaboration among the peoples of Europe. This was an expansion of Hitler's earlier idea of a 'Monroe doctrine for Europe' directed against the Anglo–Saxon powers. When Ciano visited Hitler's headquarters towards the end of October 1941, he was much struck by the way in which this idea had taken root.

In the past [he wrote to Mussolini] we have seen in turn the flowering and decline of a series of slogans which are born in the mind of the Führer and are repeated all the way down to the lowest-ranking of his collaborators. Now the fashionable slogan is that of 'European solidarity'. Europe – the Führer said – besides being a geographical expression is a cultural and moral concept. In the war against Bolshevism the first signs of continental solidarity have shown themselves. . . . This is what all those near him repeat.[1]

1. *Ciano's Diplomatic Papers*, pp. 455–60. Ciano's letter to the Duce, 26 October 1941.

A fortnight after receiving Ciano in East Prussia Hitler was in Munich for the traditional celebration of the 8 November anniversary. In his speech Hitler developed an argument which was to provide a companion theme to the European New Order in Nazi propaganda – Germany as the society in which class divisions and privileges had been abolished, the New Germany in the New Europe.

What distinguishes the present from what went before [he said at Munich] is simply this: then the people were not behind the Kaiser. . . . Then the leaders had no roots in the people, for when all is said and done it was a class state. Today we are in the midst of the completion of what grew out of that (First) War. For when I returned from the war, I brought back home with me my experiences at the front; out of them, I built my National Socialist community of the people at home. Today the National Socialist community of the people takes its place at the front, and you will notice how the Armed Forces from month to month become more National Socialist, how they increasingly bear the stamp of the New Germany, how all privileges, classes, prejudices and so on are more and more removed; how, from month to month, the German national community gains ground.[1]

At the end of November Hitler and Ribbentrop staged a demonstration of the European solidarity which, they claimed, had come into existence under Germany's benevolent leadership. Representatives of nine European countries,[2] together with those of Japan and Manchukuo, were summoned to Berlin to renew the original Anti-Comintern Pact. Ciano wrote in his diary: 'The Germans were the masters of the house, and they made us all feel it, even though they were especially polite to us. There is no way out of it. Their European hegemony has now been established. Whether this is good or bad is neither here nor there; it exists. Consequently, it is best to sit at the right hand of the master of the house.'[3]

What the New Order would mean in practice can best be judged from a conversation which Ciano had with Göring in Berlin. Reporting this to Mussolini, Ciano explained that they had been discussing Greece and the fear that the Greeks might soon be suffering from famine. Göring showed little interest:

We cannot worry unduly about the hunger of the Greeks [he said]. It is a misfortune which will strike many other peoples besides them. In the camps for Russian prisoners they have begun to eat each other. This

1. Speech at Munich, 8 November 1941 (Prange: pp. 117–18).
2. There were: Italy, Spain, Hungary, Rumania, Slovakia, Croatia, Bulgaria, Finland, and Denmark.   3. *Ciano's Diary*, p. 402.

year between twenty and thirty million persons will die of hunger in Russia. Perhaps it is well that it should be so, for certain nations must be decimated. But even if it were not, nothing can be done about it. It is obvious that if humanity is condemned to die of hunger, the last to die will be our two peoples.[1]

Throughout this same month of November the German armies had been fighting their way nearer to Moscow under steadily worsening weather conditions. For now the autumn rains were followed by the dreaded Russian winter. Guderian noted the first snowfall on the night of 6–7 October, at the moment when the drive on Moscow began again, an early start for the cold weather. Confident that the campaign would be finished before the snows, Hitler and his staff had made no provision for winter clothing to be issued to the troops. From early November the Germans were fighting in sub-zero temperatures, intensified by a bitter wind, the few hours of daylight and the long nights, and fighting in an unfamiliar land far from home against an enemy inured to the conditions, warmly clothed and equipped for winter operations. 'Only he who saw the endless expanse of Russian snow during this winter of our misery and felt the icy wind that blew across it,' Guderian later wrote, '. . . can truly judge the events that now occurred.'[2]

But Hitler insisted that the Russian resistance was on the verge of collapse. When Ciano saw him at his East Prussian headquarters towards the end of October, Hitler kept on repeating that Russia was already 'virtually' defeated. Russian dead, wounded, and prisoners he put at the fantastic figure of ten millions; the armoured divisions had been decimated; the corps of non-commissioned officers wiped out almost in its entirety.

Warnings and appeals were of no avail. Hitler categorically refused to admit that he had been wrong. Whatever the cost in men's lives, his armies must make good his boasts, and he drove them on relentlessly. On 2 December Kluge's Fourth Army made a last desperate effort to break through the Russian defences in the forests west of Moscow. There was light only until three o'clock in the afternoon, snow was thick on the ground and the earth was frozen to a depth of several inches. A few parties of troops from the 258th Infantry Division actually reached the outskirts of the capital and saw the flashes of the A.A. guns defending the Kremlin, but they could not hold these outlying positions and had to be pulled back.

1. *Ciano's Diplomatic Papers*, pp. 464–5.
2. Heinz Guderian, *Panzer Leader*, pp. 254–5.

At that moment, on 6 December, to the complete surprise of Hitler and the German High Command, the Russians launched a major counter-offensive along the whole Central Front with one hundred fresh divisions, and swept away the German threat to Moscow. The German troops, already driven to the limit of endurance, wavered; for a few days there was great confusion and the threat of a Russian break-through. Hitler was faced with the most serious military crisis of the war so far. Even if he surmounted it, one thing was already clear: the great gamble had failed and 1941 would end without the long-heralded victory in the east.

II

On 7 December, the day after the Russians opened their offensive to relieve Moscow, the Japanese took the American Fleet by surprise in Pearl Harbour. At the beginning of the month, Oshima, the Japanese ambassador in Berlin, received instructions to inform the German Government that Japanese–American relations had reached a crisis and that war might be imminent: he was to ask Ribbentrop for a formal commitment on Germany's part to declare war on the United States under the Tripartite Pact. This was the first direct news the Germans had received of the possibility of immediate war between Japan and America. In fact the Japanese task force had already sailed for Pearl Harbour on 25 November, but taking a leaf out of Hitler's book, the Japanese kept their own counsel and the news of the attack on Pearl Harbour came as a surprise to Hitler.

At the time of Matsuoka's visit to Berlin in the spring of 1941 Hitler had urged the Japanese Foreign Minister to attack Singapore. After the invasion of the Soviet Union Ribbentrop made persistent attempts through the German Ambassador in Tokyo to persuade the Japanese to take the Russians in the rear.[1] The one course, however, which Hitler had never recommended to the Japanese had been to attack the U.S.A.: indeed, he had constantly repeated to Matsuoka in the spring that one of the beneficial results of seizing Singapore would be to deter the Americans from entering the war.

It might have been expected therefore that the Führer would

1. cf. Ribbentrop's telegram to Ott, 10 July 1941, and Ott's reply: 'I am trying with all means possible to work towards Japan's entry into the war against Russia as soon as possible.' N.D. 2,896 and 2,897-PS.

show some irritation at the independent course adopted by the Tokyo Government in face of his advice. On the contrary, he agreed to give the formal guarantee for which the Japanese asked and appears to have been delighted with the news of Pearl Harbour. The Japanese tactics appealed to him and he told Oshima: 'You gave the right declaration of war. This method is the only proper one . . . one should strike – as hard as possible – and not waste time declaring war.'[1] He rapidly decided to follow the Japanese example by declaring war on the United States himself. When Ribbentrop pointed out that the Tripartite Pact only bound Germany to assist Japan in the event of an attack on her by some other Power, and that to declare war on the U.S.A. would be to add to the number of Germany's opponents, Hitler dismissed these as unimportant considerations. He seems never to have weighed the possible advantages of deferring an open breach with America as long as possible and allowing the U.S.A. to become involved in a war in the Pacific which would reduce the support she was able to give to Great Britain.

Hitherto, Hitler had shown considerable patience in face of the growing aid given by the U.S. Government to the British. But he was coming to the conclusion that a virtual state of war already existed with the U.S.A.[2] and that there was no point in delaying the clash which he regarded as inevitable. The violence of Hitler's attack on President Roosevelt in his speech of 11 December suggests the force of the resentment accumulating under the restraint he had so far practised in his relations with America.

Two other factors affected Hitler's decision. The first was his disastrous underestimate of American strength. He knew nothing of the United States. The mixture of races in its population, as well as the freedom and lack of authoritarian discipline in its life, predisposed him to regard it as another decadent bourgeois democracy, incapable of any sustained military effort. The ease with which the Japanese struck their blow at Pearl Harbour confirmed these prejudices. Hitler certainly never supposed – any more than Hindenburg and Ludendorff in 1917 – that he would have to reckon with a major American intervention in the European war, nor did he foresee the possibility of an invasion on

1. Hitler's remarks to Oshima, 14 December 1941, N.D. 2932-PS.
2. In the second half of October 1941, there were two engagements between U.S. destroyers and German U-boats. On the second occasion, an American destroyer was sunk and a hundred of her crew lost.

the scale of that which the British and the Americans mounted two and a half years later.

The second factor is more difficult to assess. When Mussolini learned of the possibility of war between Japan and the United States, in expressing his satisfaction he made the remark: 'Thus we arrive at the war between continents which I have foreseen since September 1939.'[1] The prospect of such a war embracing the whole world excited Hitler's imagination with its taste for the grandiose and stimulated that sense of historic destiny which was the drug on which he fed. Elated by the feeling that his decisions would affect the lives of millions of human beings, he declared in the speech of 11 December, in which he announced Germany's declaration of war on America: 'I can only be grateful to Providence that it entrusted me with the leadership in this historic struggle which, for the next five hundred or a thousand years, will be described as decisive, not only for the history of Germany, but for the whole of Europe and indeed the whole world. ... A historical revision on a unique scale has been imposed on us by the Creator.'[2]

Most of Hitler's speech on 11 December was devoted to abuse of the America of President Roosevelt, whom he depicted as the creature of the Jews. He drew a comparison between the success of National Socialism in rescuing Germany from the Depression and what he described as the catastrophic failure of the American New Deal: it was the desire to cover up this failure which led Roosevelt to divert American attention by a provocative foreign policy. The old demagogic tricks were employed to underline this comparison between Nazi Germany, a 'have-not' nation, and the wealthy United States:

I understand only too well that a world-wide distance separates Roosevelt's ideas and mine. Roosevelt comes from a rich family and belongs to the class whose path is smoothed in the democracies. 1 was only the child of a small, poor family and had to fight my way by work and industry. When the Great War came, Roosevelt occupied a position where he got to know only its pleasant consequences, enjoyed by those who do business while others bleed. I was only one of those who carried out orders as an ordinary soldier and actually returned from the war just as poor as I was in the autumn of 1914. I shared the fate of millions, and Franklin Roosevelt only the fate of the so-called upper ten thousand.[3]

At the end of his speech Hitler announced that a new agreement had been concluded between Germany, Italy, and Japan,

1. *Ciano's Diary*, p. 405.   2. Prange: p. 97.   3. ibid., p. 368.

binding them not to conclude a separate armistice or peace with the U.S.A. or with England, without mutual consent.

It was with Russia, however, far more than with the United States or Great Britain, that Hitler was still concerned in the winter of 1941–2. The Russian counter-offensive, launched on 6 December, faced him with a crisis, which, if mishandled, might well have turned to disaster. 'At the critical moment,' says one of the divisional commanders on the Eastern Front, 'the troops were remembering what they had heard about Napoleon's retreat from Moscow, and living under the shadow of it. If they had once begun a retreat it might have turned into a panic flight.'[1]

Hitler rose to the occasion. By a remarkable display of determination he succeeded in holding the German lines firm. Whatever his responsibility for the desperate situation in which the German Army now found itself, and whatever the ultimate consequences of his intervention, in its immediate effects it was his greatest achievement as a war-leader.

Hitler's method of dealing with the crisis was simple. In face of the professional advice of his generals and in total disregard of the cost to the troops, he ordered the German armies to stand and fight where they were, categorically refusing all requests to withdraw. This order was enforced in the most ruthless fashion. Officers who failed to obey were dismissed or court-martialled. Field-Marshal von Rundstedt was ordered to hand over his command for withdrawing after the failure of the attack on Rostov; Guderian, who commanded one of the panzer armies on the Moscow front, was relieved of his command; Höppner, another outstanding panzer general, was dismissed the service, stripped of his rank and decorations, and forbidden to wear his uniform.

The toll taken by the Russians, and even more by the terrible winter, was high. Thousands of German soldiers died of the cold, for Hitler had obstinately refused to consider the possibility of a winter campaign or to provide adequate clothing. In certain places it proved literally impossible to carry out Hitler's orders, and he had reluctantly to accept the withdrawal of the German positions after divisions had been decimated by the Russian attacks and frost-bite. But the Russians did not break through, and when the spring came to thaw the snows the German Army still stood on a line deep in the interior of Russia. More than this, by drawing on his own country and his allies, Hitler brought up

1. General von Tippelskirch, quoted by Liddell Hart: op. cit., p. 289.

the forces on the Eastern Front to sufficient strength to enable him to propose a resumption of the offensive in 1942.

The importance of the winter crisis of 1941–2 is not, however, adequately represented by its immediate military results. It marks a decisive stage in the development of Hitler's relations with the Army which was to have considerable consequences for the future.

After the invasion of Russia there was no longer a High Command or General Staff in Germany comparable with that over which Hindenburg and Ludendorff had presided in the First World War. Hitler ordered the C.-in-C. of the Army and his Staff (O.K.H.) to confine themselves to the conduct of the war in the east (excluding Finland). The other fronts were to be left to his own Supreme Command of the Armed Forces (O.K.W.). But the O.K.W. was in turn excluded from the Eastern Front, and in any case lacked the independent authority which the High Command of the Army traditionally possessed in Germany. The responsibility for the conduct of operations was thus divided, and the strategic picture of the war as a whole remained the concern of Hitler alone.

Hitler was far from being a fool in military matters. He had read widely in military literature and he took an eager interest in such technical matters as the design of weapons. His gifts as a politician gave him notable advantages in war as well. He was a master of the psychological side, quick to see the value of surprise, bold in the risks he was prepared to take and receptive of unorthodox ideas. The decisive support he gave to the expansion of Germany's armoured forces, his adoption of Raeder's proposal for the occupation of Norway, and of Manstein's for the thrust through the Ardennes, have already been mentioned as illustrations of these gifts. Nor was Hitler far from the truth when he argued that if he had listened to the High Command he would never have pushed through German rearmament at the pace he wanted, or have dared to take the risks which brought the German Army its sensational triumphs of 1940–1.

His faults as a military leader were equally obvious. He had too little respect for facts, he was obstinate and opinionated. His experience in the First World War, to which he attached undue importance, had been extremely limited. He had never commanded troops in the field or learned how to handle armies as a staff officer. He lacked the training to translate his grandiose conceptions into concrete terms of operations. The interest which he took in technical details, instead of compensating for these deficiencies, only made them clearer. He was far too interested in such matters as the precise thickness of the concrete covering a line of fortifications for a man whose job was to think clearly about the over-all pattern of war. Moreover, he allowed himself to become intoxicated with figures, with the crude numbers of men or of armaments production, which he delighted to repeat from memory without any attempt to criticize or analyse them.

These were precisely the faults which the professional training of the generals qualified them to correct. A combination of Hitler's often brilliant intuition with the orthodox and methodical planning of the General Staff could have been highly effective. But this was ruled out by Hitler's distrust of the generals.

Well aware of the unique position which the Army held in German history, and its unrivalled prestige as the embodiment of the national tradition, he was quick to suspect its leaders of a lack of enthusiasm, if not active disloyalty, towards the new régime. On several occasions Hitler expressed his envy of Stalin, who had been able by his pre-war purge of the Red Army to secure a High Command completely loyal to Communism. The German generals, Hitler complained, had no such faith in the National Socialist idea. 'They have scruples, they make objections and are not sufficiently with me.'[1] The German Officer Corps was the last stronghold of the old conservative tradition, and Hitler never forgot this. His class-resentment was never far below the surface; he knew perfectly well that the Officer Corps despised him as an upstart, as 'the Bohemian corporal', and he responded with a barely concealed contempt for the 'gentlemen' who wrote 'von' before their names and had never served as privates in the trenches.

To political distrust and social resentment was added Hitler's inveterate suspicion of the expert, the professional staff officer who, like the professional economist, saw only difficulties. Nothing so infuriated Hitler as the 'objectivity' of the trained mind which refused to accept his own instinct for seeing all problems in the simplest possible terms and his insistence on will-power as a universal answer. Hitler was a man who found it difficult to take advice and intolerable to listen to criticism. It required great tact to get him to accept a view which differed from his own, and this was a quality which few of the German generals possessed. He

1. Quoted by B. H. Liddell Hart: op. cit., p. 299.

was naturally arrogant, and he quickly bridled at any suggestion that he was being talked down to by men who claimed to know more than he did and did not recognize his genius. Thus, far from welcoming the very different talents of his military advisers as complementary to his own, he despised them as men hidebound by tradition, as much his inferiors in the understanding of war as Papen and Hugenberg had been in their grasp of politics.

So long as the German Army was successful the underlying lack of confidence between Hitler and his generals could be papered over. But the moment Hitler found himself faced with a situation like that on the Eastern Front in the winter of 1941–2 he made it only too clear that he had no faith at all in the High Command's ability to deal with it, and felt that he could rely solely on himself. Brauchitsch, feeling that he was placed in an impossible position, offered his resignation on 7 December. After brusquely telling him he was too busy to give an answer, ten days later Hitler accepted his offer, and on the 19th announced that he would himself take over the command-in-chief of the German Army in the field.

This step was the logical conclusion to the policy of concentrating all power in his own hands which Hitler had steadily pursued since 1933. In 1934, on the death of Hindenburg, he had become the Head of the State and Supreme Commander of the Armed Forces as well as Chancellor. In 1938, with the suppression of the War Ministry, he had arrogated the functions of the former Minister of War to his own High Command of the Armed Forces (O.K.W.). Now he took over the High Command of the Army (O.K.H.) as well.

In 1934, at the time of the Röhm Purge, the generals congratulated themselves on the deal they had made with Hitler. In 1938, when Blomberg and Fritsch were removed, they were brought to realize too late that they had acquired not a servant nor even a partner, but a master. Now that master formally extended his authority from the conduct of the affairs of the State to the conduct of military operations. To General Halder Hitler remarked

This little affair of operational command is something that anybody can do. The Commander-in-Chief's job is to train the Army in the National Socialist idea, and I know of no general who could do that as I want it done. For that reason I've decided to take over command of the Army myself.[1]

1. Halder: op. cit., p. 49.

So, seven years after his death, Röhm's object was realized, and the Army *gleichgeschaltet* – by the man who had had Röhm murdered.

Another consideration did not escape that sly politician. To Brauchitsch Hitler explained that, to save the situation, 'he had put in the scales the entire confidence which he enjoyed in the Army'.[1] But to the German people Brauchitsch was made to appear as the man responsible for such a situation ever having arisen, and this belief was carefully cultivated by Hitler himself. The Führer could do no wrong. If the promise of victory by the autumn had proved illusory, it was because the High Command, not the Führer, had failed. After visiting Hitler's headquarters three months later, Goebbels wrote in his diary:

> The Führer spoke of Brauchitsch only in terms of contempt. A vain, cowardly wretch who could not even appraise the situation, much less master it. By his constant interference and consistent disobedience he completely spoiled the entire plan for the eastern campaign as it was designed with crystal clarity by the Führer. The Führer had a plan that was bound to lead to victory. Had Brauchitsch done what was asked of him and what he really should have done, our position in the east today would be entirely different.[2]

Supremely confident in his own powers, Hitler did not stop to reflect that, in his new position, it would be less easy to find scapegoats in the future. For even when he had been most calculating in his exploitation of the image of the inspired Führer, Hitler had never lacked belief in the truth of the picture he was projecting. But as success followed upon success the element of calculation was completely overshadowed by the conviction that he was what he had so long claimed to be, a man marked out by Providence and endowed with more than ordinary gifts. The image he had himself created took possession of him.

This conviction was immeasurably strengthened by the experience of the winter months of 1941–2. In the speech which he delivered on 30 January 1942, at the height of the crisis, he spoke of his 'unbounded confidence, confidence in myself, so that nothing, whatever it may be, can throw me out of the saddle, so that nothing can shake me'.[3]

Goebbels was shocked, when he saw Hitler in March, at the toll which those months had taken of Hitler's health: 'I noted

1. Brauchitsch's evidence at Nuremberg; N.P., part XXI, p. 35.
2. *The Goebbels Diaries*, p. 92.   3. B.B.C. Monitoring Report.

that he had already become quite grey and that merely talking about the cares of the winter makes him seem to have aged very much....'[1] He complained of bouts of giddiness and told Goebbels that he never wanted to see snow again: it had become physically repulsive to him. None the less the ordeal had not broken Hitler, and the success of his intervention in checking the Russian counter-offensive exalted his sense of mission and his confidence in his military genius. After the winter of 1942 he was less prepared than ever to listen to advice – or even information – which ran contrary to his own wishes. This was the reverse side of the strength which he derived from his belief in himself – and it was the weakness which was to bring him down, for in the end it destroyed all power of self-criticism and cut him off from all contact with reality.

This can already be seen in 1941. For, if Hitler saved the German Army in the winter of that year, it was principally as the result of his miscalculation that it had ever been placed in such a position. Not only was the decision to invade Russia his, as naked an act of aggression as even Hitler ever committed; but he had refused, in the face of his generals' advice, to concentrate his forces against Moscow until it was almost the end of the campaigning season, and he then obstinately persisted in prolonging the attempt to capture the capital up to and beyond the danger point.

It was inevitable that a man in Hitler's position should refuse to admit in public that he had made mistakes and seek a scapegoat in Brauchitsch; but he refused to make such an admission even to himself, and so lost the chance to learn from his mistakes. His fatal facility for convincing himself of the truth of whatever he wanted to believe soon created the unshakeable conviction that the failure of 1941 had been due to the shortcomings of the Army High Command, and that, now he had taken over the direction of operations himself, 1942 would infallibly produce the knock-out blow which had eluded him the previous year. Thus, as belief in Nazi victory claims weakened in Germany under the ineluctable pressure of events, it only grew stronger in Hitler's own mind, in defiance of events, until he became the last victim of his own propaganda.

1. *The Goebbels Diaries*, p. 92.

III

This same sense of confidence was equally marked in Hitler's private conversation during these months.

Most of the conversations took place after the midday or evening meal at Wolfsschanze in East Prussia, although there are also records of talks in the Reich Chancellery, at field head-quarters, or on the Führer's special train. Interruptions were rare, apart from the occasional remark to provide the next topic or draw Hitler out.

Sometimes Hitler was in a reminiscent mood and would recall the early struggle and triumphs of the Party. Politics and war formed the staple subjects of his conversation and his discussion of these showed his familiarity with European history. The historical character he most admired was Frederick the Great. He criticized Napoleon for accepting the imperial title and for forwarding the interest of his family so blatantly. 'Despite all Napoleon's genius, Frederick the Great was the most outstanding man of the eighteenth century.'

One problem to which Hitler returned several times was how to choose the head of a state, the problem, in fact, of succession. In the course of history, he declared, two constitutions had proved themselves in this respect: the Papacy, despite the pre-posterous doctrine on which it was based, and the Venetian Republic.

Hitler was impressed by the achievements of the British (a Nordic people) in creating their Empire. 'If the British Empire collapsed today, it would be thanks to our arms, but we'd get no benefit, for we wouldn't be the heirs. . . . If the English are clever, they will seize the psychological moment to make an about-turn – they will march on our side. By getting out of the war now, the English would succeed in putting their principal competitor, the United States, out of the game for thirty years.'[1] 'England,' he declared on another occasion,[2] 'can continue to be viable only if she links herself to the Continent. She must be able to defend her imperial interests within the framework of a continental organi-zation. It's only on this condition that she'll keep her Empire.' The obvious partner for Britain, in Hitler's view, was Germany, and more than once he argued that German relations with

1. *Hitler's Table Talk*, pp. 92–3 (26–7 October 1941).
2. ibid., pp. 264–5 (31 January 1942).

Britain were like those which existed between Prussia and the Hapsburg Monarchy in 1866: after Bismarck had defeated Austria, she was prepared to accept alliance with Prussia, and so it would be with Britain if she had the good sense to recognize her real interests.[1]

The Englishman is superior to the German in one respect – that of pride. Only the man who knows how to give orders has pride. . . . The basic reason for English pride is India.

What India had been to the British, Hitler declared, the empire in the east which he was founding at Russia's expense would be to the Germans. This was still the theme which stimulated his imagination most and he compared his work as an empire builder, on a larger scale, with that of Bismarck.[2]

These reflections of mine [he remarked in a lunchtime session on 29 June 1942] are inspired by my own experience with the difficult piece of history to which I have had to put my hand. The generations which follow us will no doubt accept without comment the unification of Europe which we are about to accomplish, in the same way as the majority of our contemporaries regard the foundation of the Bismarckian Empire as a simple fact of history. The immense labour involved in the welding together of northern, western, central and eastern Europe into one entity will be quickly forgotten. . . .
  There is one point I must stress in this connexion – and I cannot stress it too often or too strongly – and that is, that this welding together of Europe has not been made possible by the efforts of a number of statesmen devoted to the cause of unification, but by FORCE OF ARMS.[3]

Hitler's contempt for the Slav peoples was unvarying, but his appreciation of Stalin rose sharply in face of the unexpected Russian power of defence. 'He must command an unconditional respect. In his own way he is a hell of a fellow! He knows his models, Genghiz Khan and the others very well, and the scope of his industrial planning is exceeded only by our own Four-Year Plan.'[4] A few days later, he described the Russian leader as 'half beast, half giant. The people can rot for all he cares. If we had given him another ten years, Europe would have been swept away, as it was at the time of the Huns'.[5] Towards Churchill and Roosevelt, on the other hand, he displayed a virulent scorn: the British were fools not to see their advantage in making peace, and the

1. cf. *Hitler's Table Talk*, pp. 46 and 264–5.   2. ibid., pp. 11 and 23.
3. ibid., p. 541 (29 June 1941).   4. ibid., p. 587 (22 July 1942).
5. ibid., p. 624 (9 August 1942).

Americans, 'half Judaized, half negrified', were a decadent nation, corrupted by materialism.

Hitler's conversation, in fact, provides an illuminating anthology of his hatreds and prejudices, from smoking, hunting, and eating meat all the way to Christianity and the Jews. Amongst those for whom he had a particular dislike were civil servants, lawyers, and judges who believed in 'objective' justice; diplomats and anyone else from the traditional upper classes; monarchs and their courts (especially the Italian); the middle classes and their bourgeois conventions; schoolmasters and academic education, a subject to which he returned again and again with many references to his own schooldays.

Indeed, the first impression left by reading the *Table Talk* is of the remarkable extent to which Hitler's ideas in 1941–2 remained the same as in the 1920s when he wrote *Mein Kampf*, or when he talked to Rauschning in the 1930s. The struggle for existence is a law of Nature; hardness is the supreme virtue; the key to history lies in race; power is the prerogative of a racial élite. There is the old scorn for the Christian virtues, dismissed as the attempt of the underdog to impose shackles on the strong; there is the old belief in force as the decisive factor in politics and the basis of the new empire which he was founding; there is the old hatred of the Jew as the eternal enemy of Aryan 'culture' and the Germanic peoples.

No other themes recur with such regularity in Hitler's conversation as Christianity and the Jews, and it is characteristic of the pathological state of his mind that the two are inextricably connected. Half a dozen brief quotations in proof of this must suffice to represent the hundred or more which could be selected from the pages of Bormann's record.

The heaviest blow that ever struck humanity was the coming of Christianity. Bolshevism is Christianity's illegitimate child. Both are inventions of the Jew. The deliberate lie in the matter of religion was introduced into the world by Christianity[1]. ... Taken to its logical extreme, Christianity would mean the systematic cultivation of the human failure.[2]

The reason why the ancient world was so pure, light, and serene was that it knew nothing of the two great scourges: the pox and Christianity.[3] ... The Jew who fraudulently introduced Christianity into the ancient world – in order to ruin it – re-opened the same breach in modern times, taking as his pretext the social question. Just as Saul became St Paul, Mardochai has become Karl Marx.[4] ... The decisive falsification of

1. *Hitler's Table Talk*, p. 7. 2. ibid., p. 51. 3. ibid., p. 75. 4. ibid., p. 314.

Jesus's doctrine was the work of St Paul. . . . For the Galilean's object was to liberate His country from Jewish oppression. He set Himself against Jewish capitalism, and that's why the Jews liquidated Him. . . . The Jews, by the way, regarded Him as the son of a whore and a Roman soldier.[1] . . . Christ was an Aryan and St Paul used his doctrine to mobilize the criminal underworld and thus organize a proto-Bolshevism. . . . Christianity is an invention of sick brains. . . . The war will be over one day. I shall then consider that my life's final task will be to solve the religious problem.[2]

If it's possible to buy the high dignitaries of the Church with money, let's do it. And if one of them wanted to enjoy his life, and for this purpose put his hand into the till, for the love of Heaven let him be left in peace. The ones we have to fear are the ascetics, with rings under their eyes, and the fanatics. . . .[3] I'll make these damned parsons feel the power of the state in a way they would never have believed possible. For the moment I am just keeping my eye upon them: if I ever have the slightest suspicion that they are getting dangerous, I will shoot the lot of them. This filthy reptile raises its head whenever there is a sign of weakness in the State, and therefore it must be stamped on. We have no sort of use for a fairy story invented by the Jews. The fate of a few filthy lousy Jews and epileptics is not worth bothering about.[4]

The most lasting impression left by the 700 pages of the *Table Talk* is of the vulgarity of Hitler's mind, cunning and brutal in its sophistries, forceful but devoid of human feeling, as unabashed as it was ignorant. There is not a hint in the dogmatic expression of his opinion on every conceivable subject – art, religion, women, history, economics, law – that on some he might be less well informed than other people or that a different view might also be possible.

When allowance is made for the gain in confidence and experience of twenty years, the Hitler of the *Table Talk* is still recognizably the same harsh, intolerant figure already familiar from the pages of *Mein Kampf* or the speeches of the 1920s. Success had altered little of the essential Hitler, and as for the set-back of the winter, it left his belief in his own cocksure genius strengthened rather than impaired.

This was the mood in which Hitler began to draw up his plans for the new campaigning season of 1942. When Goebbels saw him at his headquarters in March, he reported:

1. *Hitler's Table Talk*, p. 76.   2. ibid., pp. 142–4.
3. ibid., p. 411.   4. ibid., p. 625.

The Führer again has a perfectly clear plan of campaign for the coming spring and summer. He does not want to over-extend the war. His aims are the Caucasus, Leningrad, and Moscow. . . . Possibly this may mean a hundred years' war in the east, but that need not worry us.[1]

When Halder told him that the Army Intelligence Service had information that six or seven hundred tanks a month were coming out of the Russian factories, Hitler thumped the table and said it was impossible.

The Russians were 'dead'. This winter offensive had consumed the last of their strength, and it was only a question of giving a push to what was already tottering. Nietzsche and Clausewitz were quoted in support of his 'heroic' decision.[2]

The German Army had come through the winter without a major disaster, but at a heavy price. Casualties numbered 1,168,000, not counting the sick; out of the 162 divisions on the Eastern Front, only eight were ready for offensive operations at the end of March and the sixteen armoured divisions could only count on 140 serviceable tanks between them.

Despite these losses, Hitler issued emphatic orders to prepare for a resumption of the offensive, with the south as the principal theatre of operations and the oil of the Caucasus, the industries of the Donbass and Stalingrad on the Volga as the objectives.

The Home Front, no less than the Army, needed its faith in the Führer's leadership restored, and in the first four months of 1942 Hitler found time to make three big speeches.

Of the first, delivered on the anniversary of 30 January, Goebbels wrote: 'The meeting was as successful as those in 1930, 1931, and 1932. . . . The Führer has charged the entire nation as though it were a storage battery. . . . As long as he lives and is among us in good health, as long as he can give us the strength of his spirit, no evil can touch us.'[3]

At the second, delivered on Heroes Memorial Day, in March, Hitler declared: 'We feel all at this moment the grandeur of the times in which we live. A world is being forged anew.'[4]

But it was in his speech of 26 April that Hitler, with the winter now behind him, gave the fullest expression to his renewed faith in Germany's eventual triumph. This time he made no attempt to conceal how near the German Army had been to disaster. He deliberately exaggerated the seriousness of the situation on the Eastern Front in order to throw into more effective contrast his

1. *The Goebbels Diaries*, pp. 92–3.　　2. Halder: op. cit., p. 54.
3. *The Goebbels Diaries*, p. 27.　　4. B.B.C. Monitoring Report.

own decision to assume personal responsibility and the news that the crisis had been mastered. 'Deputies,' he told the packed and excited meeting of the Reichstag in the Sportpalast, 'a world struggle was decided during the winter. . . .' Then, picking up the allusion to Napoleon's Retreat from Moscow, so often invoked during the winter, he added: 'We have mastered a destiny which broke another man a hundred and thirty years ago.'[1]

Hitler's picture of the conditions under which the Army had fought in the east during the past few months was a prelude to a demand for still greater powers to be vested in himself, the counterpart on the Home Front to his decision to take over the personal conduct of operations on the Eastern Front.

The law, duly passed by the Reichstag without discussion, proclaimed:

The Führer must have all the rights demanded by him to achieve victory. Therefore – without being bound by existing legal regulations – in his capacity as Leader of the Nation, Supreme Commander of the Armed Forces, Head of the Government and supreme executive chief, as Supreme Justice and Leader of the Party – the Führer must be in a position to force, with all the means at his disposal, every German, if necessary, whether he be common soldier or officer, low or high official, or judge, leading or subordinate official of the Party, worker or employer, to fulfil his duties. In case of violation of these duties the Führer is entitled, regardless of rights, to mete out punishment and remove the offender from his post, rank, and position without introducing prescribed procedures.[2]

Hitler's request for a confirmation of the arbitrary power which he already possessed is at first sight puzzling. The explanation of the decree of 26 April 1942 is to be found in Goebbels's diaries, in which the Minister of Propaganda continually complains of the shortcomings of the state and party administration, and of the failure to organize German economy and civilian life to meet the demands of 'total' war. During his visit to headquarters in March, Goebbels pressed Hitler to adopt much more drastic measures to control war-profiteering and the black market, to increase production, reduce the swollen staffs of overgrown ministries, and provide additional manpower.

Goebbels and Hitler laid the blame for these shortcomings on the conservatism of the German Civil Service and judiciary. But they were only paying the penalty for treating the administration

1. B.B.C. Monitoring Report.   2 . N.D. 1,961-PS.

of the State as 'spoils' for the Nazi Party once it had come to power. The boasted totalitarian organization of the National Socialist State was in practice riddled with corruption and inefficiency under the patronage of the Nazi bosses, from men like Göring and Himmler down to the Gauleiters and petty local racketeers of every town in Germany. At every level there were conflicts of authority, a fight for power and loot, and the familiar accompaniments of gangster rule, 'protection', graft, and the 'rake-off'. The Nazis did not change their nature when they came to power, and they remained what they had always been, gangsters, spivs, and bullies – only now in control of the resources of a great state. It is astonishing that they had not ruined Germany long before the end of the war. The fact that they did not was due to the stolid virtues and organizing ability of the permanent officials of the civil service, of local government and industry, who, however much abused, continued like the German Officer Corps to serve their new masters with an unquestioning docility.

Hitler was the last man to remedy this situation. Without administrative gifts, disliking systematic work and indifferent to corruption, Hitler was at the same time far too jealous of his authority to make any effective delegation of his powers.

In the 1930s Hitler spoke of the Party as 'a chosen Order of Leadership' whose task was 'to supply from its membership an unbroken succession of personalities fitted to undertake the supreme leadership of the State'. On closer inspection the new élite was far from impressive. Even amongst the Reich leaders of the Party there were few men of ability, integrity, or even education. One of the exceptions was Goebbels. Göring, too, undoubtedly displayed ability in 1933–4, but by 1942 this had long been overlaid by the habits of indolence and the corruption of power. Men like Ley, Ribbentrop, Funk, Darré, and Rosenberg were wholly unfitted to hold positions of responsibility, not to speak of lesser figures like Frank, the notorious Governor-General of Poland, or Viktor Lutze, the Chief of Staff of the S.A., killed in a motor accident while on his way back from a black-marketing expedition, but accorded a hero's funeral by the Führer on his way to the Nazi Valhalla. As for the Gauleiters, those gross and seedy Pashas of the thousand-year Reich, some of them were incapable of appearing in public without scandal, while all, almost without exception, lined their pockets, ran the local rackets, and, as Goebbels remarked, 'had only to be given the old *ius primae noctis* to enjoy powers greater than those of the most absolute princes of the seventeenth and eighteenth centuries'.[1]

In February 1942, however, Hitler had the luck to make one of the few good appointments he ever made. Albert Speer, whom he chose as Minister for Armaments and Munitions in the place of Dr Todt (killed in an air accident), was a young architect who had attracted Hitler's attention and had been set to complete the new Reich Chancellery. Disinterested as well as able, he soon showed himself to be an organizer of remarkable powers and was entrusted with one job after another until he became virtual dictator of the whole of German war production. Finding himself faced with great difficulties in the way of procuring manpower from the obstruction of the Gauleiters, Speer shrewdly suggested that one of them should be made responsible for increasing Germany's labour force. This led in March 1942, to the appointment as Plenipotentiary-General for Manpower of Fritz Sauckel, a former sailor and a Party Member since 1921, who was Gauleiter of Thuringia. These measures, in particular the powers given to Speer and the use he made of them, produced a sensational rise in German war-production in 1942 and 1943 without which Hitler could never have continued the war at all.

To make good the German losses in manpower, Hitler demanded more of the satellite states. Keitel was sent to Budapest and Bucharest to procure more divisions: the O.K.W. counted on fifty-two allied divisions for the 1942 campaign, a quarter of the total force available.

The bulk of these divisions were to come from Rumania (twenty-seven) and Hungary (thirteen). But Hitler now began to ask for the Italian troops which he had scorned to accept the year before, and in February Göring was sent on a visit of several days to Rome. 'As usual', Ciano commented, 'he is bloated and overbearing . . . at the station he wore a great sable coat, something between what motorists wore in 1906 and what a high-grade prostitute wears to the opera.'[2] Hitler had not seen the Duce since August 1941 and, now that the winter crisis was over, he thought it desirable to remove any doubts in Mussolini's mind and to revive his flagging faith in an Axis victory. Accordingly the Duce and Ciano again set out for the north at the end of April 1942, and spent two days with Hitler at Salzburg.

1. The diary of Rudolf Semmler: *Goebbels, the Man Next to Hitler*, p. 86.
2. *Ciano's Diary*, p. 430.

They were entertained this time not at the Berghof, but in Schloss Klessheim, the former Baroque palace of the Prince Bishops of Salzburg, tastefully furnished with hangings, carpets, and furniture brought from France. Ciano reported that Hitler looked tired and grey, but he was even more impressed by his loquacity.

Hitler talks, talks, talks, talks. Mussolini suffers – he, who is in the habit of talking himself, and who instead has to remain silent. On the second day, after lunch, when everything had been said, Hitler talked uninterruptedly for an hour and forty minutes. He omitted absolutely no argument: war and peace, religion and philosophy, art and history. . . . Only Cavallero, who is a phenomenon of servility, pretended he was listening in ecstasy, continually nodding his head in approval. The Germans, poor people, have to endure it every day, and I am certain there isn't a gesture, a word or a pause they don't know by heart. General Jodl, after an epic struggle, finally went to sleep on the divan. Keitel was yawning, but succeeded in keeping his head up. He was too close to Hitler to let himself go as he would have liked to do.[1]

The discussions followed familiar lines. There was the usual *tour d'horizon*, the familiar appeasement of Italian suspicions of France. But most of the time Hitler talked about Russia, freely comparing himself to Napoleon – to the latter's disadvantage and Mussolini's chagrin. He told the Duce in private: 'I believe that I am in the protection of Providence,' and cited the escape from catastrophe in the winter as proof.

On the way back Mussolini complained that he could not see why Hitler had asked them to make the journey. Resentment at his own reduced role was beginning to be tinged with the uneasy fear that he, as well as the Germans, would have to pay for the mistakes of an overconfident Hitler.

IV

For two years after the invasion of Russia Hitler's time was almost completely taken up with the direction of the war on the Eastern Front, which he obviously regarded as the decisive theatre of operations. His interest in other theatres was intermittent until, in 1943, the loss of North Africa and the collapse of Italy forced him to recognize that it was a world alliance with which he was at war and that he must fight on the south and west as well as in the east, on the sea and in the air no less than on land.

1. *Ciano's Diary*, pp. 462–3.

The fundamental weakness of Hitler's strategy was this failure to grasp in time the unity of the war, the neglect until too late of the Mediterranean and the Atlantic, the underestimate of Britain's recuperative powers and America's strength. Much has been written of the inadequacy of Hitler's strategy in the later stages of the war, but by then the disparity between Germany's and her opponents' resources was so great that inevitably he was on the defensive. Hitler's real failure as a strategist was earlier, in the years before the United States and Russia had begun to develop their full strength, or Britain had fully recovered from the setbacks of 1940. It was then that he still enjoyed the initiative and still possessed a superiority in force. Instead of using these to the best effect, he threw away his temporary advantages, in the first place, by the decision to attack Russia; and in the second place, as a consequence of this first mistake, by his neglect of those other theatres in which the British and the Americans were eventually to make their own powerful contribution to his defeat.

Before the attack on Russia Hitler had evaded Raeder's proposals for intensifying the war in the Mediterranean, with the promise to take up these plans after Russia was defeated. Although Hitler was forced to send stronger forces to the Mediterranean theatre, throughout 1941 and the winter of 1941–2, the sole purpose behind these moves was defensive, to prevent an Italian collapse in North Africa. At the end of the winter, however, Raeder returned to the attack and succeeded in rousing Hitler's interest in the Mediterranean, largely because of the grandiose way in which the plan (known as the 'Great Plan') was dressed up as a drive through the Middle East to join the Japanese in a vast encirclement of Britain's Asian Empire. Hitler agreed to a two-fold operation for the summer of 1942 – 'Operation Hercules' for the capture of Malta (the key to the security of Rommel's supply route), and 'Operation Aida', the renewal of the desert offensive against Egypt, Suez, and beyond to Persia. These two operations were to serve as the prelude to the 'Great Plan', and they were among the subjects Hitler discussed with Mussolini at Salzburg in April.

The operations began well with Rommel's capture of Tobruk and the invasion of Egypt. By 30 June 1942, a month after the offensive had opened, the Afrika Korps reached the El Alamein line, only sixty-five miles from Alexandria. But Hitler showed a curious reluctance to undertake the second part of the plan, the assault on Malta. He refused to see the force of Raeder's and Kesselring's argument that without the capture of the island Rommel's supply position must remain precarious. He had already postponed 'Operation Hercules' until Rommel could capture Tobruk and clear Cyrenaica: now he postponed it again, proposing to starve and bomb Malta into submission and arguing that its capture was no longer necessary with Rommel on the verge of occupying Egypt.

Thus the impetus of the opening weeks of the campaign was lost. As the summer passed, the British had time to build up their forces in Egypt and to strengthen Malta; the losses on the Italy–North African run began to mount again. By the autumn the Afrika Korps was still at El Alamein and Malta still unsubdued.

At the beginning of September Hitler saw Rommel (who was on sick leave) and reassured him: 'I mean to give Africa all the support needed. Never fear, we are going to get Alexandria all right.'[1] But in fact Hitler's interest in the Mediterranean and North Africa, never more than fitful, was beginning to waver again. In 1941 he sacrificed the chance of sweeping victories in the south to the dream of defeating Russia in a single campaign. In 1942, while agreeing to the 'Great Plan', he never once displayed that energy and singleness of purpose in forcing it through which had held the Eastern Front firm in the winter. To Hitler, until he was about to lose it for good, North Africa remained a sideshow by comparison with the real war in the east. He never grasped its importance in the total picture of the war, as Churchill had done even when Britain's power was reduced to its lowest ebb.

In fact, for all his talk of a war between continents Hitler showed little understanding of sea-power, the element which bound together the alliance which opposed him. As lòng as he held the initiative he went on thinking in terms of war as he had known it on the Western Front in 1914–18, as a land war. The unique series of the Führer Conferences on Naval Affairs thus represents in fact a record of failure on the part of the Naval High Command in its dealings with the Supreme Commander of the German Armed Forces.

For years Admiral Raeder had tried to persuade Hitler that Germany's most dangerous enemy was Great Britain, and that the one certain way of defeating her was by attacking her trade routes and blockading her ports. Even after the directive for 'Barbarossa' had been issued, Raeder argued: 'There are serious

1. Quoted by Desmond Young: *Rommel*, p. 171.

doubts as to the advisability of "Operation Barbarossa" before the overthrow of Britain. . . . What is being done for U-boat and naval-air construction is much too little. . . . Britain's ability to maintain her supply lines is the decisive factor for the outcome of the war.'

This was in December 1940. Hitler's reply was to promise Raeder – as in the case of the Mediterranean – that once Russia had been defeated he should have all he asked for. The Army's demands could then be cut down, and German war production concentrated on the needs of the Navy and Air Force. Meanwhile the Navy had to be content with what it could scratch together in face of the competition of the Army and the Air Force. Raeder was not allowed to establish a naval air force, nor was he able to secure the effective cooperation of the Luftwaffe in attacks on British shipping, harbours, and shipyards. Göring, who was on bad terms with the Commander-in-Chief of the Navy, was a law unto himself, and Hitler simply let the quarrel between the two Services drag on.

The Navy was short of U-boats as well as of aircraft. Up to February 1941, Raeder found it impossible to keep more than some six U-boats at sea at a time. By the end of 1941 this had been increased to sixty. With these limited forces the U-boats achieved remarkable successes in 1942, sinking over nine hundred vessels, of six and a quarter million gross tons, nearly three times the figure for 1941. These results were so striking that Hitler was converted and began to talk of the U-boats as the factor which would decide the outcome of the war. In May 1942 Dönitz, the Flag Officer U-boats, was summoned to attend the Führer conferences for the first time. When Raeder demanded that no workman engaged on U-boat construction or repair should be drafted for military service, Hitler at once agreed, and more than three hundred U-boats were in fact completed during 1942.

But Hitler's interest in the possibilities of the U-boats came too late. Although the shipping losses between the beginning of 1942 and the spring of 1943 taxed the Allies to the limit, they now had at their disposal resources which Hitler, deeply committed in Russia, could not hope to equal. By the middle of 1943 Britain and the U.S.A. were on the way to establishing a superiority in methods of defence (both by sea and air) which neither the German Navy nor the Luftwaffe was able to reduce and which was steadily reinforced during the later years of the war. The great hopes which Hitler began to entertain of the U-boats and which

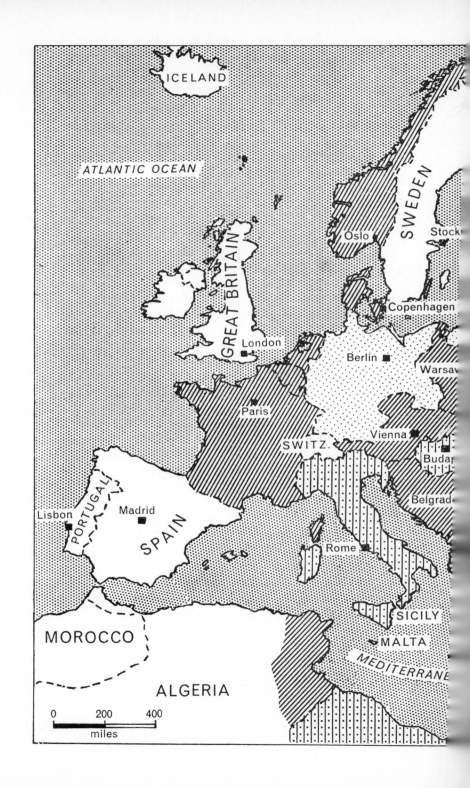

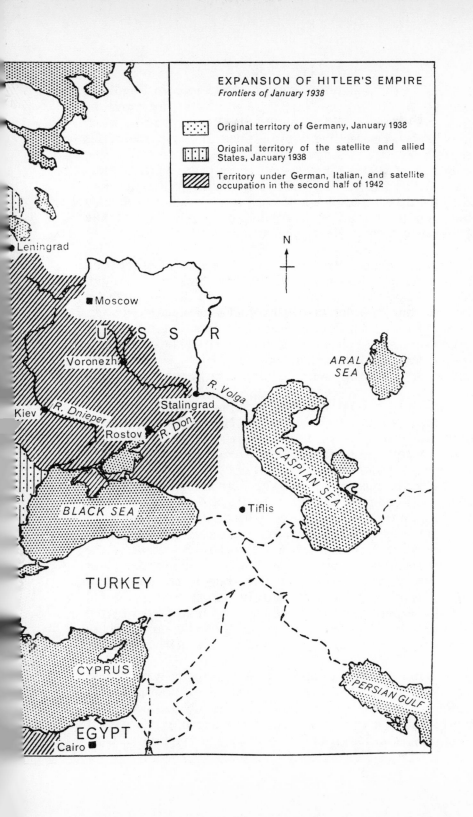

EXPANSION OF HITLER'S EMPIRE
Frontiers of January 1938

Original territory of Germany, January 1938

Original territory of the satellite and allied States, January 1938

Territory under German, Italian, and satellite occupation in the second half of 1942

N

Leningrad

Moscow

U S S R

Voronezh

ARAL SEA

R. Volga

Kiev

R. Dnieper

Stalingrad

Rostov *R. Don*

CASPIAN SEA

st

BLACK SEA

Tiflis

TURKEY

CYPRUS

PERSIAN GULF

EGYPT

Cairo

he signalized by the appointment of Dönitz to succeed Raeder as Commander-in-Chief of the Navy were stultified. In the end the Battle of the Atlantic, which might – as Raeder had so often argued – have been decisive, was destined to prove one of his greatest failures. It was a failure which, like that to exploit the opportunities of 1940–2 in the Mediterranean, sprang from Hitler's defective grasp of the war as a whole and which was confirmed by the decision to invade Russia, a campaign into which a disproportionate amount of Germany's resources in men and machines was drawn at the expense of every other front.

On the third front, the western seaboard of Europe and Northern Africa, Hitler was not blind to the threat of an Anglo-American landing, but the problem of how to defend so vast a coastline was one to which he never found a satisfactory answer. Moreover, in 1942 he badly misjudged the direction in which to look for an attack. For, from the autumn of 1941, he displayed a growing conviction that Britain and the U.S.A. – possibly in cooperation with Russia – were planning a large-scale assault on Norway.

There was little enough evidence to support such a view, but Hitler insisted in oracular fashion that 'Norway is the zone of destiny in this war.' Troops, heavy artillery, aircraft, and naval forces were accordingly dispatched to strengthen the Norwegian coastal defences. So impressed was Hitler by his intuition that he refused Raeder permission to send the German surface fleet into the Atlantic on commerce raiding, and insisted on the risks of a passage through the Strait of Dover in broad daylight in order to get the battle-cruisers *Scharnhorst* and *Gneisenau* and the cruiser *Prinz Eugen* from Brest to Norway. Virtually the whole of the German surface fleet was concentrated in Norwegian waters. Not until 1943 was Hitler prepared tacitly – but never openly – to admit that he had been wrong. By then the Allied armada had safely landed an army in North-west Africa, unmolested by the German naval forces a thousand miles away to the north, where they remained vainly keeping guard against an attack which never came.

Against a much more ominous threat from the west which began to develop in 1942 Hitler found himself without adequate defences. The German Air Force, already roughly handled in the Battle of Britain, never recovered from the demands made on it in Russia. It was no longer able to prevent the bombing of German industrial towns by the R.A.F. with forces of up to and over a thousand planes. The first thousand-bomber raid, on Cologne, took place on the night of 30–31 May 1942, and it was a portent for the future. The war was beginning to come home to Germany.

V

In dealing with these other fronts we have been talking of the later months of 1942 and even anticipating the events of 1943. But at the time when the Germans renewed their Russian offensive in the summer of 1942 few of the difficulties which were to become apparent by the end of the year had yet appeared. The U-boat war was going well, Rommel had resumed his offensive in North Africa, and a big Russian attack at Kharkov in May had been defeated.

Hitler had chosen the south as the main theatre for his operations on the East Front in 1942, and powerful German forces drove fast down the corridor between the Don and Donetz rivers. While one wing pushed east towards the Volga at Stalingrad, the other drove past Rostov and, covering another four hundred and fifty miles, reached the Caucasus and the more westerly oilfield round Maikop in the first half of August.

Hitler moved his H.Q. to Winniza, in the Ukraine, during July, and from here he followed the progress of his armies with mounting excitement. Now, he declared, his faith and determination in the winter had been justified: Russia was on the verge of defeat.

Hitler, however, made exactly the same mistake he had made the year before. Overestimating the German strength, he did not limit himself to his original objective, to reach the Volga and capture Stalingrad, but tried to break into the Caucasus with its valuable oilfields as well, thus dividing his forces and ending by gaining neither Stalingrad nor the oil. At the end of July, when the 4th Panzer Army could probably have taken Stalingrad without much difficulty, it was diverted south to support Kleist's drive for the Caucasus. When it was freed to return north the Russians had gathered sufficient strength to hold Stalingrad. A more methodical attempt had then to be made to take the city, and by September the battle for Stalingrad was beginning to assume proportions which made Halder doubt whether its capture was worth the effort or the risks. For the city's name and its historical association with Stalin during the Civil War made the Russians as eager to defend it as Hitler was to take it. A battle of prestige was thus joined between the two régimes. As the Germans fought their way forward they exposed their long-drawn-out northern flank to grave danger from a Russian counter-attack across the Don. The German forces were so stretched that the last reserves had to be committed, and by September the greater part of this northern flank running from Voronezh to Stalingrad and covering several hundred miles, was held by Hungarian, Italian, and Rumanian divisions.

Halder's attempts to point out the dangers of the situation led to a repetition of the scenes of the previous autumn and winter. Hitler accused the General Staff of cowardice, ridiculing the Intelligence reports of growing Russian strength in preparation for a massive counter-attack.

When a statement was read to him [Halder recalls] which showed that Stalin would still be able to muster another one to one and a quarter million men in the region north of Stalingrad (besides half a million more in the Caucasus), and which proved that the Russian output of first-line tanks amounted to twelve hundred a month, Hitler flew at the man who was reading, with clenched fists and foam in the corners of his mouth, and forbade him to read such idiotic twaddle.[1]

Even a child could see the use Stalin was likely to make of the armies he was building up behind the front, but Hitler refused categorically to admit that such forces existed. As Halder justly remarks, 'his decisions had ceased to have anything in common with the principles of strategy and operations as they had been recognized for generations past. They were the product of a violent nature following its momentary impulses, a nature which acknowledged no bounds to possibility and which made its wish the father of its deed'.[2] When Halder recommended the breaking off of the attack at the end of September, Hitler dismissed him. 'You and I have been suffering from nerves,' Hitler told him. 'Half my nervous exhaustion is due to you. It is not worth it to go on. We need National Socialist ardour now, not professional ability. I cannot expect this of an officer of the old school such as you.'[3] Halder's successor as Chief of the Army General Staff (O.K.H.) was General Zeitzler, a younger man without Halder's experience or authority, a fact which recommended him to Hitler.

1. Halder: op. cit., p. 57.   2. ibid., pp. 55–6.
3. It is a fascinating study to compare the relationship between Hitler and Halder with that between Churchill and the Chief of the Imperial General Staff, Alanbrooke, Cf. Arthur Bryant: *The Turn of the Tide* and *Triumph in the West*.

Meanwhile, the thrust into the Caucasus had been halted short of the main oilfields by stiffening Russian resistance. Hitler, beside himself with impatience, sent Jodl to investigate. When Jodl, on his return, ventured to defend the Commander-in-Chief in the Caucasus, Field-Marshal List, Hitler flew into another of his fits of fury. What particularly angered him was Jodl's citation of his own earlier directives to prove that List had only been obeying orders.

From that day on Hitler refused to eat any more with his staff officers at the common table. An S.S. officer was ordered to be present at every conference and stenographers were to take down every word. For several months Hitler declined to shake hands with Jodl, and on 30 January 1943 he sent word that he was to be replaced. By a rare stroke of irony, Paulus, the man Hitler chose as Jodl's successor, the next day surrendered to the Russians at Stalingrad, a fitting comment to the end of this chapter in the history of Hitler's relations with his generals.

By the autumn of 1942 all Hitler's urging could not alter the fact that the German advance at Stalingrad, as well as in the Caucasus and North Africa, had been brought to a standstill. This time it was more than a temporary interruption; it was the end of Hitler's offensives. The climacteric had been passed, and for the first time since he proclaimed Germany's rearmament in 1935, more than seven years before, the initiative passed out of Hitler's hands, never to return. It had been a remarkable career while it lasted. At the moment when the tide turned in the autumn of 1942 Hitler was undisputed master of the greater part of continental Europe, with his armies threatening the Volga, the Caucasus, and the Nile. For the man who had begun by peddling third-rate sketches in the back-streets of Vienna this was no small achievement. But now the price had to be paid for the methods of treachery and violence by which it had been accomplished – and it was relentlessly exacted.

On the night of 23 October 1942 the British 8th Army under General Montgomery attacked the German lines at El Alamein and after twelve days' heavy fighting broke out into the desert beyond.

On the night of 7–8 November British and American troops landed along the coast of Morocco and Algeria, and within a few days occupied the whole of French North Africa as far as the Tunisian frontier.

On 19 and 20 November three Russian Army Groups under the command of Generals Vatutin, Rokossovsky, and Eremenko attacked on a huge front north and south of Stalingrad and within five days succeeded in encircling twenty-two Germans divisions between the Volga and the Don.

Taken together, these three operations mark the turning-point in the war and the seizure of the initiative by the Allies. Henceforward Hitler was forced to stand upon the defensive.

The Führer was slow to recognize, and even slower to admit, the importance of the operations now begun. On 8 November, after the break-through at El Alamein and on the actual day of the Allied landings in North-west Africa, he appeared in Munich for the customary celebration of the 1923 putsch. Drawing the familiar contrast between the Imperial Germany of 1918 and the Third Reich, he declared:

He who was then the Kaiser was a man lacking the strength to resist his enemies. But in me they have found an adversary who does not even think of the word 'capitulation'. Ever since I was a boy it has always been my habit – originally perhaps a bad one, but in the final resort a virtue – to have the last word. All our enemies may rest assured that while the Germany of that time (1918) laid down its arms at a quarter to twelve, I on principle have never finished before five minutes past twelve.[1]

None the less, despite his confident tone, it was noticeable that Hitler was already arguing on the defensive, and at the end of his speech he went out of his way to answer those who criticized him for not speaking more frequently. Underneath the boasting and the sarcasm a note of anxiety was clearly to be detected.

Hitler's very success in halting a German retreat in the winter of 1941–2 now proved a fatal legacy. His one idea was to stand firm at all costs. He telegraphed to Rommel (who had been summoned from hospital to take over the Afrika Korps): 'There can be no other consideration than that of holding fast, of not retracting one step. . . . You can show your troops no other way than that which leads to victory or death.'[2] When Rommel flew back to Germany at the end of November and told Hitler that Africa was lost, and the only course was to get the Afrika Korps out to fight in Italy, Hitler shouted at him that he was a defeatist and his troops cowards. Generals who had made the same sort of suggestion in Russia, he added, had been put up against a wall

1. B.B.C. Monitoring Report.
2. *The Rommel Papers*, ed. by B. H. Liddell Hart, p. 321.

and shot. Despite his categorical orders, however, neither Rommel nor anyone else could halt the Allies' advance.

The Allied landings in French North Africa in November took Hitler completely by surprise. He immediately summoned Laval, as well as Ciano, for a meeting at Munich. Laval's efforts to be friendly were coldly rebuffed. When Laval hedged, Hitler bluntly informed him that the Germans would occupy Tunisia at once, together with the rest of Unoccupied France. At last Mussolini had his way over France, but he was no longer in a position to derive much satisfaction from it: Italy was too obviously the Allies' next target after North Africa.

After his long neglect of the Mediterranean Hitler began to pour troops and supplies into Tunisia in order at all costs to hold a bridgehead covering Tunis and Bizerta. Even a part of these forces, had they been made available earlier, would have been sufficient to capture Egypt and Suez: now they were to be thrown away in vain. In something of a panic Mussolini urged Hitler to come to terms with Russia, or at least shorten his lines on the Eastern Front, so that the greatest number of divisions could be moved to the Mediterranean and the west. These suggestions, which Ciano repeated to the Führer during a meeting at Rastenburg in December, were ignored. Hitler refused to yield a foot of ground anywhere: he was determined to hold Tunisia and so deny the Allies the free use of the Mediterranean, but he was equally determined not to give up anything elsewhere. The results of such a strategy were neither difficult to see nor long in coming.

Meanwhile the Russians methodically tightened the net round the German Sixth Army at Stalingrad. The formula which had proved successful the previous winter was monotonously repeated: Stand and fight to the last man. Manstein's efforts to open a corridor from the outside were thrown back, but Hitler refused to let von Paulus attempt to break the ring from the inside. No conceivable military purpose was served by holding the German troops in their positions, but Hitler's personal prestige as a leader was now engaged, and in comparison with that the lives of the three hundred and thirty thousand men of the 6th Army were nothing.

Towards the end of January 1943 Paulus reported that the suffering of the troops, through cold, hunger, and epidemics, was no longer bearable, and that to continue fighting in such conditions was beyond human strength. Hitler was unmoved. For answer he sent Paulus the message:

Capitulation is impossible. The 6th Army will do its historic duty at Stalingrad until the last man, in order to make possible the reconstruction of the Eastern Front.[1]

Hitler did not hesitate to stoop to bribes: at the last moment he promoted Paulus to the rank of Field-Marshal in order to buy the loyalty of the commander whose troops he had deliberately condemned to death. 'There is no record in military history,' he remarked to Jodl, 'of a German Field-Marshal being taken prisoner.' To the Italian Ambassador he compared the German Army at Stalingrad with the Three Hundred at Thermopylae. They would show the world, he declared, the true spirit of National Socialist Germany and its loyalty to its Führer.

The outcome was a far worse blow to Hitler's prestige than any order to withdraw could ever have been. On the night of 31 January, the Russians announced that they had completed the capture or annihilation of the remainder of the 6th Army and the 4th Panzer Army, adding that among the officers who had surrendered was Field-Marshal von Paulus himself, his Chief of Staff, General Schmidt, and the Commander of the II Army Corps, General von Seydlitz.

At noon on 1 February, the day after the Russian communiqué, Hitler held his usual military conference, the minutes of which have been recovered since the war. Totally oblivious of his own responsibility for what had happened, the Führer spared no thought for the men he had driven to death or captivity. He could think only of the commanders who had capitulated: such ingratitude and disloyalty, he declared, were beyond his comprehension.

The man should have shot himself just as the old commanders who threw themselves on their swords when they saw their cause was lost. That goes without saying. Even Varus gave his slave the order: 'Now kill me!' . . .

You have to imagine, he'll be brought to Moscow. There he will sign anything. He'll make confessions, make proclamations. You'll see: they will now walk down the slope of spiritual bankruptcy to its lowest depths. . . . The individual must die anyway. Beyond the life of the individual is the Nation. But how anyone could be afraid of this moment of death, with which he can free himself from this misery, if his duty doesn't chain him to this Vale of Tears. No!

What hurts me most, personally, is that I promoted him to Field-Marshal. I wanted to give him this final satisfaction. That's the last

1. Von Paulus's evidence at Nuremberg, N.P., Part VI, p. 262.

Field-Marshal I shall appoint in this war. You mustn't count your chickens before they are hatched. I don't understand that at all. So many people have to die, and then a man like that besmirches the heroism of so many others at the last minute. He could have freed himself from all sorrow and ascended into eternity and national immortality, but he prefers to go to Moscow. What kind of choice is that? It just doesn't make sense.[1]

It was the comment of a supreme egotist, the complaint of a man who was to see in the sufferings and defeat of a nation only his own betrayal by a people unworthy of their Führer.

V

The battle of Stalingrad marked the peak of the German attempt to subdue Russia, and with the summer of 1943 the Soviet counter-offensive, launched on a massive scale, put an end to German hopes of doing anything more than defend their positions on the Eastern Front. The empire in the east was to remain unachieved.

Amongst the reasons for the German failure one is of particular interest: Hitler's neglect of the political possibilities of weakening Russian resistance. At an earlier stage – for instance, in preparing to attack France – Hitler had shown a brilliant understanding of how war could be waged with other than military weapons. But, although he repeatedly described the war with Russia as an ideological conflict and counted on the overthrow of the Soviet Government by the Russian people, the harsh policy he adopted in the east worked in the opposite direction.

There is evidence to show that when the German armies entered the Ukraine and the Baltic States they were looked upon as liberators. The treatment the local population received from the civil administration and the S.S. who moved in behind the armies rapidly destroyed these illusions. Ignoring all that might have been done to drive a wedge between the people and the Soviet Government, especially in the Ukraine, Hitler preferred to treat the inhabitants of Eastern Europe indiscriminately as Slav *Untermenschen*, fit only for slave labour. The proposals put forward by Rosenberg's Ministry for the Eastern Territories to win support by the abolition of the collective farms, the establishment of

1. Felix Gilbert (ed.): *Hitler Directs His War* (New York, 1950), pp. 17–22. This is a volume of the records of Hitler's military conferences discovered at the end of the war and put together with the help of the stenographer.

religious freedom, and the grant of a measure of self-government under local Quisling régimes had no interest for Hitler. The
spirit of German policy was better expressed by Erich Koch, the
Gauleiter of East Prussia whom Hitler appointed Reich Commissioner for the Ukraine. Speaking to a German audience at
Kiev on 5 March 1943, Koch proclaimed: 'We did not come here
to serve out manna. We have come here to create the basis for
victory. We are a master race, which must remember that the
lowliest German worker is racially and biologically a thousand
times more valuable than the population here.'[1]

The protests of Rosenberg's ministry against this brutal and
short-sighted attitude were unavailing. The men who shaped
German policy in the east were not the ineffectual Rosenberg and
his officials, but Koch; Himmler, and the S.S.; Sauckel, whose
job was to import slave labour into Germany, and Bormann, who
used his influence with Hitler to support Koch and discredit
Rosenberg.

Goebbels was quick-witted enough to see the opportunities
that were being lost. In September 1941 he dictated a lengthy
memorandum on political plans for handling the Russian peoples,
and the next year tried to get Hitler to issue a proclamation
promising the Russians greater freedom and some relief from the
oppressive exactions of the Soviet Government. But Goebbels
had no more success than the officials in Rosenberg's ministry.
Hitler, whose political interests had waned as he became absorbed
in his new role of military genius, was set upon clear-cut victory
in the field and remained indifferent to the possibility of winning
support in the east. In the summer of 1943 Goebbels was driven
to complain in his Diary:

We are doing too much on the military and too little on the political side
of the war. At this moment, when our military successes are none too
great, it would be a good thing if we knew how to make better use of the
political instrument. We were so great and resourceful in that way at the
time of our struggle for power; why shouldn't we achieve mastery in
this art now?[2]

Goebbels put his finger on a fundamental weakness, but his
analysis did not go far enough. For the neglect of political possibilities was due to something more than the demands of the war.
Hitler's policy in Eastern Europe was no hasty improvisation: it
was the calculated expression of a mind which could conceive of

1. N.D. 1,130-PS.
2. *The Goebbels Diaries* (28 July 1943), p. 333.

politics only in terms of domination and could understand the exercise of power solely in terms of the whip.

The proof of this is to be found in the records of a number of discussions between the Nazi leaders which go back at least to 1940, and in which Hitler explained his plans for the future not only of Russia but of the two other Slav countries of Poland and Czechoslovakia.

One such discussion took place on 2 October 1940 after a dinner in Hitler's apartments at the Reich Chancellery. Hans Frank, the Governor-General of Poland; Koch, then Gauleiter of East Prussia; Baldur von Schirach, the Gauleiter of Vienna; and Martin Bormann were the Führer's guests, and the conversation turned to the future of the Polish Government-General.

Hitler's ideas were perfectly clear.

The Poles [he declared], in direct contrast to our German workmen, are especially born for hard labour. We must give every possibility of advancement to our German workers; as to the Poles, there can be no question of improvement for them. On the contrary, it is necessary to keep the standard of life low in Poland, and it must not be permitted to rise. . . . The Government-General should be used by us merely as a source of unskilled labour. . . . Every year the labourers needed by the Reich can be procured from the Government-General. It is indispensable to bear in mind that the Polish landlords must cease to exist, however cruel this may sound, they must be exterminated wherever they are. . . .

There should be one master only for the Poles – the Germans. Two masters, side by side, cannot and must not exist. Therefore all representatives of the Polish intelligentsia are to be exterminated. This, too, sounds cruel, but such is the law of life.

The Poles will also benefit from this, as we look after their health and see to it that they do not starve, but they must never be raised to a higher level, for then they will become anarchists and Communists. It will therefore be proper for the Poles to remain Roman Catholics: Polish priests will receive food from us and will, for that very reason, direct their little sheep along the path we favour. . . . If any priest acts differently, we shall make short work of him. The task of the priest is to keep the Poles quiet, stupid, and dull-witted. This is entirely in our interests. Should the Poles rise to a higher level of development, they will cease to be that manpower of which we are in need. . . . The lowest German workman and the lowest German peasant must always stand economically ten per cent above any Pole.[1]

About the same time Hitler was presented with a number of

1. Bormann's notes, quoted in N.P., Part VI, pp. 219–21.

plans for the future of the Protectorate of Bohemia-Moravia. After deliberation he accepted one which provided for the settlement of an increased number of Germans in the Protectorate where they would assimilate that part of the Czech population which was of racial value.

The other half of the Czechs must be deprived of their power, eliminated and shipped out of the country by all sorts of methods. This applies particularly to the racially Mongoloid part and to the major part of the intellectual class. The latter can scarcely be converted ideologically and would become a burden by constantly making claims for the leadership over the other Czech classes, and thus interfering with a rapid assimilation. Elements which counteract the planned Germanization ought to be handled roughly and eliminated.[1]

These were the precedents for Hitler's policy in Russia, and they were faithfully followed. On 16 July 1941, less than a month after the invasion of the Soviet Union, Hitler held a conference at his Führer Headquarters which was attended by Göring, Rosenberg, Bormann, Keitel, and Lammers, the head of the Reich Chancery. Rosenberg's attempts to plead for a friendly policy towards the Ukrainian people had no effect; the note which Hitler struck was in a wholly different key. Under cover of military occupation of the areas seized, plans for a permanent settlement were to be introduced. 'Nobody,' he warned his audience, 'must be able to recognize that it initiates a final settlement, but this need not prevent our taking all necessary measures – shooting, resettling, etc. – and we shall take them.'

Bormann's notes of Hitler's remarks continue:

On principle we have now to face the task of cutting up the giant cake according to our needs, in order to be able:
    First, to dominate it;
    Second, to administer it, and
    Third, to exploit it.
The Russians have now ordered partisan warfare behind our lines. This partisan war again has some advantage for us: it enables us to eradicate everyone who opposes us.
Principles:
    Never again must it be possible to create a military power west of the Urals, even if we have to wage war for a hundred years in order to attain this goal. Every successor of the Führer should know: security for the Reich exists only if there are no foreign military forces west of the Urals. It is Germany which undertakes the protection of this area against all

1. Report on Hitler's views by Karl Hermann Frank, State Secretary for the Protectorate, at a conference on 9 October 1940. N.D. 862-PS.

possible dangers. Our iron principle is and has to remain: *We must never permit anybody but the Germans to carry arms.*

This is especially important. Even when it seems easier at first to enlist the armed support of subjugated nations, it is wrong to do so. In the end this will prove to be to our disadvantage. Only the Germans may carry arms, not the Slav, not the Czech, not the Cossack, nor the Ukrainian. On no account should we apply a wavering policy such as was done in Alsace before 1918.[1]

The first need was to exploit the occupied eastern territories for the strengthening and relief of the German war economy. This had been foreseen in the economic directives drawn up before the invasion,[2] and was continually reaffirmed by Göring and others. In a conference on 6 August 1942 Göring, as Plenipotentiary for the Four-Year Plan, told the commissioners for the occupied regions: 'It used to be called plundering. But today things have become more genteel. In spite of that, I intend to plunder and to do it thoroughly.'[3]

As the bombing of German industry and the losses of manpower and equipment began to exert a greater strain on the German economy, so the demands on the eastern territories mounted. These demands were not limited to raw materials, food, and machinery, but extended to manpower as well. Russia, like Poland and the other occupied countries in the west, France, Belgium, and Holland, was turned into a vast labour camp to provide the human material which German industry and agriculture needed. The organization of this new slave traffic was in the hands of Sauckel, and the brutality of the methods by which men, women, and children were rounded up, shipped to Germany and forced to work, often under unspeakable conditions, beggars description. By the end of 1944, 4,795,000 foreign workers had been recruited for work in Germany, of whom 1,900,000 were Russians, 851,000 Poles, 764,000 French, 274,000 Dutch, 230,000 Yugoslavs, and 227,000 Italians.[4] Sauckel himself admitted (at a Central Planning Board meeting on 1 March 1944) that 'out of five million foreign workers who have arrived in Germany, not even two hundred thousand came voluntarily'.[5] Regular man-hunts were organized, men and women seized from their homes or on the streets, flung into cattle-trucks, and transported hundreds of miles. On the way many died of privation.

1. N.D. L-221. 2. cf. above, pp. 642–3. 3. N.P., Part IX, pp. 322–4.
4. N.D. 2,520-PS, using German official figures.
5. N.P., Part II, p. 314.

The most fortunate were those who were detailed for work on farms. Those who were sent to the heavily bombed industrial centres suffered cruelly: they were commonly housed in camps without the most primitive facilities, exposed to epidemics, underfed, and frequently beaten.[1]

The figure of five million workers did not satisfy Hitler. He constantly increased his demands on Sauckel, who in turn urged the local authorities to apply the most ruthless measures to secure more manpower. The realization that the large numbers of prisoners of war captured in the east might be used for this purpose led the Germans to reconsider the treatment which these had hitherto received. As Himmler explained in a speech at Posen in 1943:

At that time [1941] we did not value the mass of humanity as we value it today, as raw material, as labour. What after all, thinking in terms of greatness, is not to be regretted but is now deplorable by reason of the loss of labour, is that the prisoners died in tens and hundreds of thousands of exhaustion and hunger.[2]

3,800,000 Russian prisoners were taken in the opening campaign of 1941. Great numbers of them were deliberately left to die from hunger or cold in the cruel winter of 1941–2. The change of policy meant that three-quarters of a million Russians were working in factories, mines, and farms by the end of 1944. But it could not bring the dead to life again: of more than five million Russian soldiers captured by the Germans during the war, two million are known to have died in captivity and another million are unaccounted for.[3]

Hitler's policy in the eastern occupied territories, however, was only in part determined by Germany's immediate economic needs. As he explained in the conference of 16 July 1941, under cover of the occupation he was determined to lay the basis of a final settlement in the lands between the Vistula and the Urals. Colonies of settlers from Germany and from the German

1. cf., for instance, the report of Dr Wilhelm Jäger, who was responsible for the medical supervision of the foreign workers at Krupps; N.D. D-288; N.P., Part II, pp. 319–23.

2. Himmler's speech at Posen, 4 October 1943. N.D. 1919-PS. See further below, pp. 697–8.

3. These figures are taken from Alexander Dallin, *German Rule in Russia, 1941–45*, pp. 426–7, a remarkably thorough investigation of the whole question of German occupation policy in Russia.

minorities in other countries (*Volksdeutsche*) were to be established in Poland and European Russia, each settlement being linked by a network of military roads and protected by S.S. garrisons set up at key points, whose task was not only to guarantee the new frontiers after the war but to keep the native population in permanent subjection. Part of this native population was to provide slave labour for the industries and agriculture of the new German Empire, and was to remain in a status of total inferiority, without rights and without education, treated literally as a sub-human race at the arbitrary disposal of their overlords. The surplus – including all those of education, property, and position whc might provide a nucleus of leadership – was to be exterminated to make room for the new colonists, or left to die of starvation. The task of carrying out this nightmarish programme was the special privilege of Himmler and the S.S.

Hitler had appointed Himmler as Reich Commissioner for the Strengthening of German Folkdom on 7 October 1939. His tasks were defined as the elimination of such alien groups as represented a danger to the Reich and the German Folk Community, and the formation of new German settlements from returning German citizens and racial Germans abroad.[1] To carry out these duties Himmler set up special departments of the S.S. and outlined his programme in a number of speeches to his S.S. commanders which give an authoritative picture of Hitler's plans for the future.

The most interesting of these speeches of which we have a record is one which Himmler made to his S.S. Obergruppenführers at Posen on 4 October 1943. He began by insisting on the need for ruthlessness.

One basic principle must be the absolute rule for the S.S. men: we must be honest, decent, loyal, and comradely to members of our own blood and nobody else. What happens to a Russian and a Czech does not interest me in the slightest. What the nations can offer in the way of good blood of our type we will take, if necessary, by kidnapping their children and raising them here with us. Whether nations live in prosperity or starve to death interests me only in so far as we need them as slaves for our *Kultur*: otherwise it is of no interest to me. Whether ten thousand Russian females fall down from exhaustion while digging an anti-tank ditch interests me only in so far as the anti-tank ditch for Germany is finished. We shall never be rough and heartless when it is not necessary, that is clear. We Germans, who are the only people in the

1. Hitler's secret Decree of 7 October 1939; N.D. 686-PS.

world who have a decent attitude towards animals, will also assume a decent attitude towards these human animals. But it is a crime against our own blood to worry about them and give them ideals, thus causing our sons and grandsons to have a more difficult time with them. When somebody comes to me and says: 'I cannot dig the anti-tank ditch with women and children, it is inhuman, for it would kill them,' then I have to say: 'You are the murderer of your own blood, because if the anti-tank ditch is not dug German soldiers will die, and they are the sons of German mothers. They are our own blood. . . .' Our concern, our duty, is our people and our blood. We can be indifferent to everything else. I wish the S.S. to adopt this attitude to the problem of all foreign, non-Germanic peoples, especially Russians.

In passing, Himmler mentioned the extermination of the Jews:

Most of *you* know what it means when a hundred corpses are lying side by side, or five hundred or one thousand. To have stuck it out, and at the same time – apart from exceptions caused by human weakness – to have remained decent fellows, that is what has made us hard. This is a page of glory in our history which has never been written and is never to be written. . . . We had the moral right, we had the duty to our people to destroy this people [the Jews] which wanted to destroy us.

Towards the end of his speech Himmler turned to the future:

If the peace is a final one, we shall be able to tackle our great work of the future. We shall colonize. We shall indoctrinate our boys with the laws of the S.S. . . . It must be a matter of course that the most copious breeding should be from this racial élite of the Germanic people. In twenty to thirty years we must really be able to present the whole of Europe with its leading class. If the S.S., together with the farmers, then run the colony in the east on a grand scale without any restraint, without any question about tradition, but with nerve and revolutionary impetus, we shall in twenty years push the frontiers of our Folk Community five hundred kilometres eastwards. . . .[1]

A few months earlier, in April 1943, Himmler was at Kharkov, and there he spoke to his S.S. officers in the same strain.

We know [he declared] that these clashes with Asia and Jewry are necessary for evolution. . . . They are the necessary condition for our race and for our blood to create for itself and put under cultivation in the years of peace (during which we must live and work austerely, frugally, and like Spartans) that settlement area in which new blood can breed as in a botanical garden. . . . We have only one task, to stand firm and carry on the racial struggle without mercy. . . . We will never let that excellent weapon, the dread and terrible reputation which preceded us in the battles for Kharkov, fade, but will constantly add new meaning to it. They can call us what they like in the world; the main thing is that we

1. N.D. 1,919-PS.

are the eternally loyal, obedient, steadfast, and unconquerable fighting men of the Germanic people and of the Führer, the S.S. of the Germanic Reich.[1]

This vision of the S.S. Empire of the future remained unrealized, but the preliminary work of preparation was put in hand from the beginning of the war, and certain characteristic institutions of the S.S. State were well established – the Waffen (Armed) S.S., the Concentration Camps, and the Einsatzkommandos (Extermination Squads). By 1944, the extermination of the Jews, the first item on the programme, was well on the way to being accomplished.

The Waffen S.S. divisions numbered only three at the beginning of the war, but by the end this figure had risen to thirty-five, over half a million men. They were designed as an alternative military force to the Army and one upon which Hitler could rely implicitly. The Waffen S.S. was also to have important functions after the war. These were set out by Hitler on 6 August 1940, when the S.S. division Leibstandarte Adolf Hitler was set up. His remarks were later circulated to Army officers as an authoritative view of the future of the S.S.

The Greater German Reich [Hitler pointed out] in its final form will include within its frontiers national entities who are, from the beginning, not well disposed towards the Reich. It is therefore necessary to maintain, outside the German core of the Reich, a State military police capable of representing and imposing the authority of the Reich within the country in any situation.

This task can be carried out only by a State Police which has within its ranks men of the best German blood and which identifies itself unreservedly with the ideology at the base of the greater German Reich. Only a formation composed in this way will resist disintegrating influences even in critical times. Such a formation – proud of its racial purity – will never fraternize with the proletariat and with the underworld which undermines the fundamental idea. . . . Returning home after having proved themselves in the field, the units of the Waffen S.S. will possess the authority to execute their tasks as State Police.[2]

An interesting feature of the Waffen S.S. was the high percentage of racial Germans from outside the Reich, and even of foreigners, taken into it. Of the nine hundred thousand (including all losses) who passed through the Waffen S.S., less than half were Reich Germans.[3] The Aryan was a type Hitler and Himmler

1. N.D. 1,919-PS.   2. N.D. D-665.
3. The figures given at the Nuremberg Trial for the end of 1944 were: 410,000 Reich Germans; 300,000 Racial Germans (*Volksdeutsche*); 50,000 from other Germanic races; 150,000 foreigners.

hoped to find in other nations than the German and to recruit for an élite which was to be international in character.[1]

Among the particular duties of the S.S. was that of organizing the concentration camps. Between 1937 and 1945, 238,980 prisoners were sent to one of these camps alone, Buchenwald, near Weimar, where 33,462 are recorded as having died. In a circular letter of 28 December 1942, an official of the S.S. Main Office complained that out of 136,870 new arrivals in concentration camps between June and November 70,610 were already dead: this, he pointed out, seriously reduced the numbers available for armaments work in the concentration-camp factories.[2]

Before the war, the concentration camps had been used for the 'preventive detention' of opponents of the régime in Germany. During the war great numbers of Jews and of members of the Resistance movements from the occupied countries were transported to them. Then in 1942, Himmler, with Hitler's agreement, began to use the concentration camps as a source of labour for armaments work, and the S.S. established its own factories. By agreement between Himmler and the Reich Minister of Justice, Thierack, certain categories of prisoners were agreed upon as suitable 'to be worked to death'.[3] Among other uses to which concentration-camp prisoners were put was to serve as the raw material for medical experiments by S.S. doctors. None of the post-war trials produced more macabre evidence than that at the so-called 'Doctors' Trial'.[4] All the experiments were conducted without anaesthetics or the slightest attention to the victims' sufferings. Amongst the ordeals to which they were subjected were intense air pressure and intense cold until the 'patient's' lungs burst or he froze to death; the infliction of gas gangrene wounds; injection with typhus and jaundice; experiments with bone grafting; and a large number of investigations of sterilization (for 'racial hygiene'), including castration and abortion. According to a Czech doctor who was a prisoner at Dachau and who personally performed some seven thousand autopsies, the usual results of such experiments were death, permanent crippling, and mental derangement.[5]

The work of guarding the concentration camps and carrying

1. Cf. above, p. 400.   2. N.D. 2,171-PS.   3. N.D. 654-PS.
4. The official title was United States *v.* Brandt *et al.*, the first of the twelve trials conducted at Nuremberg before U.S. military tribunals.
5. Deposition of Dr Franz Blaha; N.D. 3,249-PS.

out the brutal sentences of flogging, torture, and execution which were everyday occurrences was alloted to the S.S. Death's Head Units (Totenkopfverbände). In a speech which he delivered to S.S. leaders at Metz in April 1941, Himmler described such work as 'fighting the sub-humanity (*Untermenschentum*). This will not be a boring guard duty, but, if the officers handle it right, it will be the best indoctrination on inferior beings and the sub-human races.'[1]

More terrible even than the concentration camps were the extermination camps. The largest of these was Auschwitz in Poland, where the four large gas chambers and crematoria were capable of a rate of extermination far above that of the others like Treblinka. To illustrate what this meant it is worth printing an extract from the affidavit of Rudolf Höss, the Commandant of Auschwitz. According to his own testimony, Höss, who was born in 1900, had been a member of the Party since 1922 and of the S.S. Totenkopfverbände since 1934. For eleven years he served in concentration camps, and from May 1940 to December 1943 at Auschwitz. In his affidavit he says:

I was ordered to establish extermination facilities at Auschwitz in June 1941. At that time there were already three other extermination camps in the Government-General: Belzek, Treblinka, and Wolzek. I visited Treblinka to find out how they carried out their extermination. The Camp Commandant told me that he had liquidated eighty thousand in the course of one half year. He was principally concerned with liquidating all the Jews from the Warsaw ghetto. He used monoxide gas and I did not think that his methods were very efficient. So at Auschwitz I used Cyclon B, which was a crystallized prussic acid dropped into the death chamber. It took from three to fifteen minutes to kill the people in the chamber, according to climatic conditions. We knew when the people were dead because their screaming stopped. We usually waited about half an hour before we opened the doors and removed the bodies. After the bodies were removed, our special commandos took off the rings and extracted the gold from the teeth of the corpses. Another improvement that we made over Treblinka was that we built our gas-chambers to accommodate two thousand people at one time. . . .[2]

The gold fillings from the teeth were melted down and shipped with the other valuables, such as wedding rings and watches, taken from the Jews to the Reichsbank. Under a secret agreement between Himmler and the Nazi president of the Reichsbank,

1. N.D. 1,918-PS.   2. N.D. 3,868-PS.

Funk, the loot was deposited to the credit of the S.S. in an account with the cover name of Max Heiliger.

Even the facilities at Auschwitz could not meet the demands made on them in 1944. In forty-six days during the summer of that year, between two hundred and fifty thousand and three hundred thousand Hungarian Jews alone were put to death at the camp and the S.S. resorted to mass shootings to relieve the pressure on the gas chambers.

When the invasion of Russia began Hitler and Himmler recruited four special units known as Einsatzkommandos to carry out the extermination of the Jewish population and also of Communist functionaries. Otto Ohlendorff, the Chief of the Security Police (SD), who commanded Einsatzgruppe D in southern Russia for a year, estimated that ninety thousand men, women, and children were liquidated by his formation during that period. At first the victims were made to dig mass trenches into which they were thrown after execution by shooting: the scenes described of terrified children and distracted mothers are without pity. In the spring of 1942, however, the efficient Main Office in Berlin began to supply gas vans for mobile extermination. Another formation, Einsatzgruppe A, in northern Russia, killed a hundred and thirty-five thousand Jews and Communists in its first four months of operations.[1]

The subsequent capture and trial by an Israeli court of Eichmann, the head of the Jewish Office of the Gestapo, has provided further evidence of the sufferings inflicted on the Jewish people by the S.S. How many Jews perished in the extermination camps and at the hands of the Einsatzkommandos will never be known precisely. The best calculation that can be made of the cost of 'the Final Solution' in human lives puts the figure between 4,200,000 and 4,600,000.[2]

It has been widely denied in Germany since the war that any but a handful of Germans at the head of the S.S. knew of the scope or savagery of these measures against the Jews. One man certainly knew. For one man they were the logical realization of views which he had held since his twenties, the necessary preliminary to the plans he had formed for the resettlement of Europe on solid racial foundations. That man was Adolf Hitler.

1. Otto Ohlendorff's Affidavit; N.D. 2,620-PS.
2. This is taken from the exhaustive study by Gerald Reitlinger: *The Final Solution*, to which (and his subsequent book: *The S.S. – Alibi of a Nation*) the reader may be referred for further details and documentation.

Himmler organized the extermination of the Jews, but the man in whose mind so grotesque a plan had been conceived was Hitler. Without Hitler's authority, Himmler, a man solely of subordinate virtues, would never have dared to act on his own. This was the subject of those secret talks '*unter vier Augen*' between the Führer and the Reichsführer S.S. at which no one else (save occasionally Bormann) was allowed to be present and of which no records survive. There are few more ghastly pages in history than this attempt to eliminate a whole race, the consequence of the 'discovery' made by a young down-and-out in a Vienna slum in the 1900s that the Jews were the authors of everything that he most hated in the world.

At a meeting of the entire Party leadership at Berlin in May 1943, Goebbels records, Hitler declared that 'the anti-Semitism which formerly animated the Party must again become the focal point of our spiritual struggle'.

At the same time he added: 'All the rubbish of small States still existing in Europe must be liquidated as fast as possible. The aim of our struggle must be to create a unified Europe: the Germans alone can really organize Europe.'[1]

Here is the true picture of that European New Order of which Hitler had spoken to Hermann Rauschning as long ago as 1932–3, with the extermination of the Jews as the first step in the establishment of the imperial rule of the *Herrenvolk* over the whole Continent. With such plans in mind, it was entirely logical on Hitler's part to treat talk of European cooperation as a fit theme for propaganda, but nothing more. Such an empire could be won and maintained by force alone: there was no room for cooperation.

It is all too easy to dismiss such a conception as the fantasy of a diseased brain: it is well to remember, however, that in the sinister sites of Auschwitz and Buchenwald, and the well-kept records of the S.S., there are the proofs of how near the fantastic came to being realized.

1. *The Goebbels Diaries*, p. 279.

CHAPTER THIRTEEN

TWO JULYS

1943-4

I

THE immediate consequences of the Stalingrad disaster were not so great as might have been expected, and did not lead to a collapse of the German front in the east. The Russian attempt to cut off the army in the Caucasus was defeated by a skilfully conducted retreat. Moscow, it is true, was relieved, but Leningrad remained under German shell-fire. The Russians drove the Germans out of the Donetz Basin and Kharkov during February, but a German counter-offensive in March recaptured them, and when the winter fighting came to an end the German line, although withdrawn in the centre and the south, was still deep in Russian territory. It was not until the late summer of 1943 that the Russians renewed their attacks. By that time Hitler was faced with an even graver situation in Italy.[1]

Hitler's rapid decision to seize Tunisia in November 1942 proved effective in balking the Allies of victory before the end of that year. He was even hopeful of holding Tunisia indefinitely, and so barring the use of the Mediterranean sea-route to Britain. The news from Italy, however, made him anxious: the Duce was ill, dislike of the Germans was widespread, and the one ambition of the Italian people was to get out of the war as soon as possible. Changes in the Italian High Command and Government at the beginning of 1943 increased German suspicions, and when Ciano left the Foreign Ministry to become Ambassador to the Vatican, the Germans were sure that he had gone there to negotiate a separate peace.

Something must clearly be done to stiffen his failing ally, and at the end of February 1943 Hitler sent Ribbentrop on a visit to Rome with a long personal letter to the Duce. Hitler did not mention Stalingrad, and his references to the Eastern Front, which were relegated to the end of the letter, betrayed considerable embarrassment. But he insisted that the war in the east must

1. For the history of German–Italian relations in the later years of the war, the reader should consult the authoritative account (with much new material) in *The Brutal Friendship*, by F. W. D. Deakin.

go on until the Russian giant was destroyed: until that was accomplished Europe would never know peace.

I know as well as you, Duce, how difficult it is to take historic decisions, but I am not certain that after my death another will be found with the necessary force of will. . . . I consider that it is by the grace of Providence that I have been chosen to lead my people in such a war.[1]

The rest of the letter was taken up with an encouraging survey of the war situation, in which Hitler laid particular stress on the success of the U-boats.

Ribbentrop's visit was followed by Hitler's agreement to allow the Italian workmen in Germany to return home – a considerable concession at a time when Sauckel was mobilizing the labour resources of the rest of Europe to work for Germany. But neither encouragement, repeated in further letters from the Führer, nor concessions, had any effect. Mussolini, ageing, sick, and disillusioned, was fast losing control of the situation. Mass strikes in Turin and Milan, with the slogans 'Peace and Liberty', were a pointer to the impending collapse of the régime. A few days later the Allies began their final drive to clear Tunisia. All that Mussolini could think of was a renewed appeal to Hitler to make a separate peace with Russia. Hitler's reply was to press Mussolini to come to Salzburg, where they met in the middle of April.

Mussolini promised his lieutenants that this time he would stand up to Hitler: he was determined to urge peace with Russia, and the withdrawal of the Italian armies from abroad to defend their homeland. But, face to face with the dynamic Führer, he succumbed and sat silent while Hitler talked.

By putting every ounce of nervous energy into the effort [Hitler told Goebbels] he succeeded in pushing Mussolini back on the rails. In those four days the Duce underwent a complete change. When he got out of the train on his arrival the Führer thought he looked like a broken old man; when he left again he was in high fettle, ready for anything.[2]

On this occasion Hitler overrated his powers as a faith-healer. Mussolini returned to Rome leaving unsaid all he had meant to tell the Führer, but at heart already a defeated man, no longer able to convince himself of the part he had to play. His despair was soon justified. On 7 May Tunis and Bizerta were captured by the Allies and within a week the entire Axis forces in Africa,

1. *Les Lettres secrètes échangées par Hitler et Mussolini* (Paris, 1946), pp. 143–63.
2. *The Goebbels Diaries*, pp. 274–5.

which Hitler, against Rommel's advice, had built up to more than two hundred and fifty thousand men, were taken prisoner with all their equipment. In less than six months Stalingrad and Tunisia together had cost the Axis the loss of well over half a million men.

It was obvious that the Allies would not be content to stay in Africa, but would attempt a landing on the northern shores of the Mediterranean – and equally obvious that, with the loss of the troops in Tunisia, Hitler and Mussolini would be hard pressed to prevent them. The first problem was: where? In the summer of 1943 the choice was felt to lie between Sicily and Sardinia, with Mussolini favouring the former and Hitler the latter. The second was the technical problem of how best to dispose the forces available. But the most difficult of all was the third: whether the Italians could be relied on to fight.

Cooperation between the Italian and German Armed Forces was increasingly strained. Report after report from German officers in Italy left Hitler in no doubt of the danger of the situation but he feared to take drastic action lest this should drive the Italians into open revolt.

In this uneasy state of mind, foreseeing what might happen but unable to prevent it, Hitler waited for the Allied attack. It came on 10 July, in Sicily, and the Allies at once made good their landings.

Nine days later Hitler summoned Mussolini to meet him at Feltre, in northern Italy. It was their thirteenth meeting, and a repetition of the April talks at Salzburg. In a last effort to put new life into the alliance, Hitler talked for three hours on end before lunch. There was one course open to them, he declared, to fight and go on fighting, on all fronts – in Russia as well as Italy – and with a fanatical will to conquer. In Germany, he boasted, boys of fifteen were now manning the A.A. batteries.

If anyone tells me that our tasks can be left to another generation, I reply that this is not the case. No one can say that the future generation will be a generation of giants. Germany took thirty years to recover; Rome never rose again. This is the voice of History.[1]

After lunch Hitler summoned up his energies for a second performance. Once again, as Ciano had so often noted, he talked, talked, talked; and once again the Duce sat silent to the end. He even failed to get a promise of reinforcements from the Germans.

1. *Hitler e Mussolini*, Italian minutes of the discussions at Feltre, pp. 165–90.

Immediately after the Feltre meeting Italian discontent with the German alliance and with the Duce as its representative came to a head. The Fascist Grand Council (which had not been summoned since December 1939) met on the night of 24–25 July, and Mussolini had to listen to violent criticism of his conduct of the war. The following evening the Duce was dismissed by the King and placed under arrest. The veteran Marshal Badoglio formed a non-Fascist government; the party itself was dissolved, and Fascist officials expelled from their posts. The basis of the new Government's authority was the Crown and the Army.

The news of Mussolini's fall, though it had long been foreseen by Hitler, came as a profound shock to the Führer's Headquarters. Hitler had never wavered in personal loyalty to Mussolini. In private he constantly referred to him as the one man to be trusted in Italy, and in public he repeatedly identified the Nazi and Fascist Revolutions as the twin foundations of the New Order. Now, at one blow, after more than twenty years in power, the Roman dictator had been deprived of office, unceremoniously bundled into an ambulance and driven off under arrest – without a shot being fired or a voice raised in protest.

The precedent was too obvious for even the least political of Germans to miss. The Führer's own prestige was directly involved, and the Nazis' embarrassment was shown by the silence of the German Press after the brief announcement that Mussolini had resigned on grounds of ill-health. Hitler at once ordered Himmler to take severe measures to prevent trouble in Germany, but he declined to make any speech, despite reports that the German people were anxiously expecting him to explain what had happened. In fact, Hitler was not anxious about the repercussions in Germany; his concern was with Italy, and how to prevent the change of government in Rome leading to the loss of the peninsula. If that could be accomplished not only would the military situation be saved, but the events in Rome would have less effect on the other satellite states, who were eagerly watching to see whether Italy would succeed in getting out of the war.

As soon as the news reached his headquarters Hitler summoned an immediate conference of all the Nazi leaders, together with Rommel, Dönitz, and other military figures. The fact that a situation he feared had at last materialized relieved rather than depressed Hitler. Despite the strain, intensified by heavy fighting

on the Eastern Front, he kept his head, showing not only determination and energy in dealing with the crisis, but considerable
skill as well. This, combined with the slowness of the Allies in
taking advantage of the situation, enabled him to make a brilliant
recovery.

Hitler did not wait for his lieutenants to arrive before taking a
number of key decisions on the spur of the moment. The first and
most important was that the new Italian Government under
Badoglio, however much it might protest its loyalty to the Axis,
was only playing for time in order to make a deal with the Allies
and must be treated accordingly. The second was to move in
every man he could find in order to seize control and hold Italy
when the time came.

In a conference with his generals between 9.30 and 10.15 on the
evening of 25 July, only a few hours after Mussolini's dismissal,
Hitler brushed aside Jodl's argument that they ought to wait for
exact reports.

Certainly [he replied], but we have to plan ahead. Undoubtedly, in their
treachery, they will proclaim that they will remain loyal to us; but this is
treachery. Of course they won't remain loyal. . . . Although that so-and-
so Marshal Badoglio declared immediately that the war would be continued, that won't make any difference. They have to say that. But we'll
play the same game, while preparing everything to take over the whole
area with one stroke, and capture all that riff-raff.[1]

Hitler's first thought was to stage a second putsch with the help
of the 3rd Panzergrenadier Division stationed outside Rome, and
to capture the new Government, the King and the Crown Prince
by force. When Hewel, Ribbentrop's man at F.H.Q., asked if the
exits of the Vatican should be blocked, Hitler answered: 'I'll go
right into the Vatican. Do you think the Vatican embarrasses
me? We'll take that over right away. It's all the same to me. That
rabble [the Diplomatic Corps] is in there. We'll get that bunch
of swine out of there. Later, we can make apologies.'

Subsequently, under pressure from Ribbentrop and Goebbels,
Hitler agreed to spare the Vatican, but for some days he still
played with the idea of an immediate *coup*.

By the time Goebbels and the rest arrived on the 26th, Hitler
had prepared four sets of plans, and the forces to carry them out
were steadily being collected. The first, known by the code word

1. These and the following remarks by Hitler are all taken from the
stenographers' records printed in Felix Gilbert: pp. 39–71.

Eiche ('Oak'), was a plan for the rescue of Mussolini; the second, *Student*, provided for the occupation of Rome and the restoration of the Fascist régime; the third, *Schwarz* ('Black'), covered the military occupation of Italy; and the fourth, *Achse* ('Axis'), dealt with measures for the capture or destruction of the Italian fleet.

Hitler attached great importance to securing Mussolini in person to lead a restored Fascist government, and he used the occason of the ex-Duce's sixtieth birthday on 29 July to demonstrate his loyalty. Laudatory notices were published in the German Press, together with the news that the Führer had sent the Duce a special edition of Nietzsche's works in twenty-four volumes with a personal dedication. The others were less sure. While Göring and Ribbentrop supported Hitler, Goebbels, in his diary, described Hitler as 'over-optimistic about the Duce and the possibilities of a Fascist come-back'. Dönitz, Rommel, and Jodl thought the same and said so. 'These are matters which a soldier cannot comprehend,' was Hitler's retort. 'Only a man with political insight can see clearly.'

The practical question was one of timing. Hitler, Göring, and Goebbels wanted to act at once: the King, Crown Prince, and Badoglio's Government should be seized and brought to Germany, while Mussolini was restored to power in Rome. Rommel (whom Hitler had appointed Commander-in-Chief in Italy) and the other soldiers wanted to wait until the situation became clearer. They feared that precipitate action would drive Badoglio, whom they hoped to keep on their side, into the arms of the Allies; they were highly sceptical about the authority of Mussolini or the popularity of a revived Fascist régime, and they were impressed by the risks involved at a time when the German forces in Italy were still weak.

No clear decision was taken either way: instead, Hitler continued to defer final orders from day to day, much to his advantage. For Badoglio was in a difficult position. Hitler was right in supposing that he would at once begin negotiations for a separate peace, but until he could reach agreement with the Allies he had to keep up the pretence of cooperation with the Germans. Hitler, realizing the game that was being played, made the most of the Allies' long delay to strengthen his forces in Italy before the showdown came. At the end of the six weeks which the Allies allowed to elapse between Mussolini's fall (25 July) and the publication of the armistice with the Badoglio Government (8 September)

Hitler was in a very much stronger position to put his plans into effect.

II

The announcement of the Italian armistice again took Hitler by surprise. He was away at Zaporozhe in the Ukraine, dealing with the situation on the southern sector of the front, and arrived back at his headquarters shortly before the news came in. The Italians kept up appearances to the last moment and succeeded completely in deceiving the Germans. There was only time to send the code-word for action to Kesselring, who was in command in southern Italy; thereafter, communication became difficult and information scarce. At Hitler's request Goebbels flew out to Rastenburg on a grey, wet autumn morning. He found Hitler in a bitter mood, full of indignation with the Italians, not least because they had tricked him. 'The Duce will enter history as the last Roman,' Goebbels wrote, 'but behind his massive figure a gypsy people has gone to rot.'[1]

Goebbels pleaded as persuasively as he could with the Führer to speak over the radio. Hitler had not spoken since the occasion of Heroes Memorial Day in March, and on that occasion he read his speech so badly and made so poor an appearance that it left the worst impression on those who were present. At the time of Mussolini's fall he had declined to say anything in public and it was only with difficulty that Goebbels succeeded in overcoming his objections now.

The speech contains little that is of interest. Hitler paid an impressive tribute to Mussolini, 'the greatest son of Italian soil since the collapse of the Roman Empire', and laid stress on his own loyalty: 'I have not learned to change my views from time to time according to circumstances, or merely to deny them.'

By contrast, the treachery of the Italians would be a matter of national shame for generations to come. But its results would not affect the war:

The struggle in Italy has for months been carried on mainly by German forces. We shall now continue the struggle free of all burdensome encumbrances. . . . Tactical necessity may compel us once and again to give up something on some front in this gigantic fateful struggle, but it will never break the ring of steel that protects the Reich.

Lest there should be illusions abroad, Hitler added:

1. *The Goebbels Diaries*, p. 349.

Hope of finding traitors here rests on complete ignorance of the character of the National Socialist State; a belief that they can bring about a
25 July in Germany rests on a fundamental illusion as to my personal
position, as well as about the attitude of my political collaborators and
my field-marshals, admirals and generals.[1]

The speech was broadcast on the evening of 10 September, and
even before it went out a special bulletin reported striking successes for the Germans in Italy. Hitler had raised the German forces
there to some sixteen divisions, and these now proceeded to disarm the much more numerous Italian formations and to seize the
key positions, including control of Rome, without meeting any
serious resistance. The King and Badoglio fled from the capital,
and within a matter of hours the Germans were masters of the
greater part of the country.

Simultaneously with the announcement of the armistice, the
Allied Fifth and Eighth Armies had landed on the Italian mainland
and begun to fight their way north. To Kesselring's relief, however,
the Allies landed much farther south than he had dared to hope,
not in the neighbourhood of Rome as he had feared, but at Salerno, to the south of Naples. Hitler and his military advisers had
already written off the south of Italy, and the German defence
plans were based on positions well to the north of Rome. Kesselring was under orders to retreat to the Apennines above Florence,
and it was there that Rommel had established his headquarters
as Commander-in-Chief. But when Kesselring succeeded in
holding up the Allied advance – even by the end of the year they
had advanced no more than seventy miles from Salerno –
Hitler agreed to recast his plans and allow Kesselring to fight
on the Winter Line drawn across the peninsula not far to
the north of Naples. This left more than two-thirds of Italy,
including the industrial north, in German hands, and it was
not until June 1944 that the Allies succeeded in reaching
Rome.

After his fall Mussolini was moved by the Badoglio Government from one place to another until he was finally taken to a
small hotel at the Gran Sasso, high up in the Abruzzi Mountains.
Hitler took a close personal interest in Mussolini's movements,
and once he had been located a spectacular rescue from the air
was planned. On 12 September this was carried out with success
by an S.S. detachment under the command of Otto Skorzeny,

1. Prange: pp. 381–6.

and Mussolini was brought to the Führer's Headquarters at Rastenburg.

The first meeting between the two men was cordial, but a rapid disenchantment followed. Hitler's plan was to re-establish the Fascist régime in Italy. A small number of former Fascist leaders, Pavolini, Farinacci, and Mussolini's son, Vittorio, had reached Germany and were already at work. But these were minor figures: to be successful the new Fascist Republic must have Mussolini at its head. The Duce, however, had changed out of all recognition: he was a shrunken figure, an ageing man without political ambition, whose real wish was to be allowed to go home to the Romagna. Under Hitler's urging – and scarcely veiled threats – he agreed to play the part for which he had been cast, but it was without enthusiasm and, as it soon appeared, only with the help of vigorous prompting from the producer.

Hitler's disillusionment touched him deeply. When Goebbels visited his headquarters towards the end of September, Hitler took him for a walk and poured out his pent-up feelings.

The Duce [Goebbels recorded in his diary] has not drawn the conclusions from Italy's catastrophe which the Führer expected. He was naturally overjoyed to see the Führer and to be at liberty again. But the Führer expected that the first thing the Duce would do would be to wreak full vengeance on his betrayers. He gave no such indication, however, which showed his real limitations. He is not a revolutionary like the Führer or Stalin. He is so bound to his own Italian people that he lacks the broad qualities of a world-wide revolutionary and insurrectionist.[1]

This unwillingness to treat his enemies as Hitler had treated Röhm in 1934 was beyond the Führer's comprehension: he was particularly incensed that Mussolini refused to take action against his son-in-law, Ciano, who had taken refuge in Germany and whom the Nazis had long wanted to be shot.

There could be no question, however, of considering the Duce's personal feelings. He must do as he was told. On 15 September Mussolini's restoration to the leadership of Fascism was proclaimed, and the new Italian Social Republic came into being. Its 'Government' followed a squalid and undistinguished career until the end of the war in Italy. Even when Mussolini returned to Italy and settled at Gargnano, on Lake Garda, he remained the prisoner of the Germans, and his villa was surrounded by S.S. Guards, ostensibly as a bodyguard. The new régime possessed

1. *The Goebbels Diaries*, p. 378.

neither independence nor authority: it was despised by the Germans and hated by the Italians.

As for Mussolini himself, the last phase of his life was the most degrading of all. He was reduced to the rank of a puppet dictator who despised even himself. In October Mussolini had to surrender Trieste, Istria, and the South Tyrol to Germany, and there was even talk of incorporating Venetia in Greater Germany. In November he was obliged to hand over Ciano to the Germans, and he shut himself up with his mistress, refusing to see his daughter Edda. But Hitler exacted the full humiliation. In January 1944 Ciano was shot by a Fascist firing squad acting under the nominal authority of his father-in-law. The fascination which Hitler had once exerted over Mussolini was turned to hatred. The Duce made few appearances in public, and left decisions largely to his 'Ministers', who intrigued incessantly against each other and against him. But he could not escape from the destiny he had forged for himself in making his pact with Hitler and, when the end came, his body, side by side with that of his mistress, was hung up on a gibbet in that same city of Milan in which he had proclaimed the Axis on 1 November 1936.

Hitler's conviction that Fascism could be revived in Italy proved as insubstantial as his belief in Mussolini as a brother Superman superior to the blows of Fate. But the Italian Social Republic served his purpose: it enabled appearances to be preserved, at least for a time. Taken with the German success in occupying the greater part of Italy and holding the Allies well south of Rome, the restoration of Mussolini could be presented as a triumphant ending to the crisis which had threatened in the summer to leave the southern frontiers of the Reich directly exposed to Allied attack.

Moreover, the Germans were successful not only in securing most of Italy, but also in taking over the Italian zones of occupation in the Balkans, in Yugoslavia, Albania, and Greece, where Hitler had for some time been apprehensive of a British landing. Considering the course of events in the Mediterranean theatre since El Alamein and the landings in North-west Africa fourteen months before, Hitler might well congratulate himself at the end of 1943 on the effective way in which, by energy, determination, and luck, he had retrieved a disastrous situation.

Even so, what had happened in Italy could scarcely be considered a victory, and the position in the south was very much weaker than it had been at the end of 1942. Now the war was being fought on the mainland of Europe, not in North Africa, and, however slow might be the Allied advance, all that Kesselring could do was to fight a skilful rearguard action. If this was true of Italy, the prospect elsewhere was still darker.

In the east, after throwing back the Russians in March 1943, in July the Germans launched a new offensive against their lines round Kursk. Half a million men, the finest troops left in the German Army, including seventeen panzer divisions equipped with the new heavy Tiger tanks, were used to carry it out. After heavy and costly fighting the Russians not only succeeded in bringing the German attack to a halt, but on 12 July themselves opened an offensive (for the first time in the summer) farther north. Gradually their attacks spread along the whole front. On 4 August they retook Orel, and on 23 August Kharkov. On 23 September they recaptured Poltava, and on the 25th Smolensk, from which both Napoleon and Hitler had directed their invasions of Russia.

However hard the Germans fought, they were borne back by the sheer weight of the attack. No sooner had one thrust been sealed-off or thrown back than fighting would flare up on another sector. The Donetz Basin was lost, the Crimea cut off. On 6 November the Russians entered Kiev, and on the last day of 1943 recaptured Zhitomir for the second time. The sole result of Hitler's inflexible orders to stand and fight, without giving a yard, was to double the German losses and deprive his commanders of any chance of using their skill in defence. There had been no pause for the autumn, and now there was none for the winter. As the year ended the Red Army was steadily pushing the Germans back through the scenes of their victories in 1941, back to the Polish and Rumanian frontiers.

The Russian advances, especially in the south, had political as well as military repercussions. As the Red Army drew nearer to their frontiers, fear began to spread among the satellite states, Rumania, Hungary, and Slovakia, whose loyalty to the Axis had been badly shaken by events in Italy. Hitler, already worried about the Balkans and the possibility of landings there, watched Turkey too with anxiety.

It was for these political as much as for military reasons that he rejected any suggestion of withdrawal on the southern sector of the Eastern Front, and obstinately refused to give up the Crimea at the cost of losing well over a hundred thousand men, mostly Rumanian troops. When Field-Marshal von Weichs and Admiral Dönitz urged him to evacuate the German garrisons in the Aegean and on Crete he gave the same reply. He could 'not order the proposed evacuation of the islands on account of the political repercussions that would necessarily follow. The attitude of our allies in the south-east, and also of Turkey, is determined exclusively by their confidence in our strength. To abandon the islands would create the most unfavourable impression. To avoid such a blow to our prestige, we may even have to accept the eventual loss of the troops and material.'[1]

In the west, although the Allies had not yet attempted an invasion, 1943 saw two heavy blows to Hitler's hopes, the defeat of the U-boats and the intensification of the air war against Germany. In January 1943 Raeder was replaced as Commander-in-Chief of the Navy by Dönitz. So angry was Hitler at the Navy's failure to sink the Allied convoys on their way to Russia by the Arctic route and at the heavy German losses that, in a furious outburst on New Year's Day, he ordered the German High Seas Fleet to be decommissioned and its ships broken up for scrap. On 6 January he accused Raeder and the Navy of lacking the will to fight and run risks. Raeder at once asked to be relieved of his command. Hitler appointed the Navy's U-boat specialist, Dönitz, in his place, but the successes of 1942 were not repeated. As the Allies strengthened their defences against submarine attack, the figures for U-boat losses began to rise, and at the end of May Dönitz was driven to withdraw all his vessels from the North Atlantic.

Hitler was no longer blind to the importance of the Battle of the Atlantic, but he lacked the resources to support it. He might promise Dönitz increased production of U-boats, but it could only be at the expense of other equally urgent needs, while the Luftwaffe could no longer defend Germany, let alone spare planes for the Atlantic. Although the U-boat crews returned to the convoy routes in September, they succeeded in sinking no more than sixty-seven ships in the last four months of 1943, during which their own losses amounted to sixty-four vessels, a rate of loss which could not be sustained for long. By the end of 1943 the Battle of the Atlantic was lost.

The U-boat war was secret and remote: it was difficult for the ordinary man in the German street to know whether it was being

1. *Führer Conferences on Naval Affairs*, 24 September 1943.

lost or won. But the war in the air touched him directly, and here there was no doubt who was in the ascendant. During the year the American day-bombers joined the R.A.F. in keeping up an almost continuous offensive against targets in Germany and Western Europe. The scale of the raids began to rise too. In July Hamburg was devastated by a series of attacks, while between mid-November 1943 and mid-February 1944 the R.A.F. dropped twenty-two thousand tons of high-explosive on Berlin.

Hitler was beside himself with fury at the failure of Göring and the Luftwaffe to fend off the attacks or to satisfy his demand for reprisals on Britain. At conference after conference he cursed the Air Force representatives for their incompetence. Yet he took care never to go to a single one of the devastated cities apart from Berlin, to which his visits were increasingly rare. He was indifferent to the loss of life; what worried him most was the effect on German war production.

In 1938 and 1939 Hitler had been warned by Schacht and others that Germany had not the economic resources to wage another major war. By 1943 the accuracy of these warnings was obvious. Scarcely a single issue was discussed at Hitler's conferences which was not affected, by Germany's increasing shortage of everything – shortage of manpower, of raw materials, of transport, of oil, of food, of steel, of armaments and planes. Even had her own industries remained untouched, Germany would have found it beyond her strength to wage a long war with the three most powerful nations in the world, the U.S.A., Great Britain, and the Soviet Union. But to the natural inequality of her resources and the slow, unrelenting pressure of the blockade was added the disorganization of her industries and communications by attack from the air. Systematically the Allied air forces raided one after another of Germany's industrial centres, and, as soon as the damage was repaired, returned to drop more bombs. Even if the German people could withstand the strain of the air war, the effect on war production was such that it must in the end place Germany in a position of permanent inferiority.

Thus, if the last months of 1942 mark the turning-point of the war, 1943 may be taken as the year of Germany's defeat.

Towards the end of 1943 at the latest [writes General Halder, once Chief of Staff to the German Army] it had become unmistakably clear that the war had been lost. . . . Would it not have been possible even so to beat off the invasion and thus provide the basis for a tolerable peace? Had the 'Fortress Germany' no hope of consuming the enemy's strength on its walls? No! Let us once and for all have done with these fairy tales. Against a landing fleet such as the enemy could muster, under cover of a complete and undisputed air superiority, Germany had no means of defence. . . .

By the sacrifice of German blood and at the cost of exposing the homeland to the enemy Air Forces, the war could still be kept going for a little longer. But were the results to be gained by such a course worth the sacrifice?[1]

III

The man with whom alone rested the answer to this question was now in his fifty-fifth year. The strain imposed upon him by the war, particularly since the winter of 1941–2, had begun to leave its mark. Göring thought he had aged fifteen years since the beginning of the war. During the course of 1943 Hitler began to suffer from a trembling of his left arm and left leg, which – apart from the period immediately after the bomb explosion in July 1944 – became steadily more pronounced and refused to yield to any treatment. In an effort to control this tremor, Hitler would brace his foot against some object and hold his left hand with his right. At the same time he began to drag his left foot, as though he were lame. Professor de Crinis, of the Charité Hospital in Berlin, believed that these were the symptoms of Parkinson's disease (*Paralysis agitans*), but he never had the opportunity of examining Hitler, and other specialists believed that they had an hysterical origin like the stomach-cramps from which he had suffered for some time. It has also been suggested that Hitler's physical as well as psychological symptoms in the last years of his life may have been those of a man suffering from the tertiary stages of syphilis.

To meet the demands which he made upon himself between 1930 and 1943 Hitler must have had an iron constitution, and during this time the only operation he underwent was for the successful removal of a polyp on his vocal cords. He was inclined to fuss about his health, believing that he had a weak heart and complaining of pains in his stomach and occasional bouts of giddiness. But his doctors found nothing wrong with his heart or his stomach, and until 1943 he actually suffered very little from ill-health.

Under the stress of war, however, Hitler began to take increasing quantities of drugs to stimulate his flagging energies. Since

1. Halder: op. cit., p. 64.

1936 he had kept as his personal physician in constant attendance on him a Professor Morell, a quack doctor who had once practised as a specialist in venereal disease in Berlin. Morell, who was introduced to Hitler by the photographer Hoffmann, won Hitler's confidence by curing him of eczema of the leg, and used his position to make a fortune by manufacturing patent medicines under the Führer's patronage. He is described by Professor Trevor-Roper after the war as 'a gross but deflated old man, of cringing manners, inarticulate speech, and the hygienic habits of a pig'. Even in Hitler's circle Morell added a touch of the grotesque, and he was bitterly attacked by the other doctors who attended the Führer. Hitler himself never trusted Morell, trying constantly to trip him up and threatening him with ejection or worse. He evidently resented his dependence upon him, but the fact of this dependence was incontestable. At every meal Hitler took a considerable number of tablets prepared by Morell and had frequent injections as well every day during the last two years of his life.

According to Trevor-Roper, the list of drugs which Morell admitted having used on Hitler contains the names of twenty-eight different mixtures of drugs, including his own proprietary brand of sulphonamide (which was condemned by the pharmacological faculty of Leipzig University as harmful to the nerves), various fake medicines, narcotics, stimulants, and aphrodisiacs.[1] When Dr Giesing examined Hitler after the attempted assassination in July 1944, he found that, to relieve the pains in his stomach, Morell had been giving him for two years at least a drug known as Dr Koester's Antigas Pills which was compounded of strychnine and belladonna. Giesing believed that Hitler was being slowly poisoned by these pills and that this accounted both for the intensification of the pains and for the progressive discoloration of Hitler's skin. The only result, however, of telling Hitler was the dismissal of his other doctors, who supported Giesing, and the end of Dr Giesing's own visits to the Führer's Headquarters. During the last two years of the Third Reich, not only Hitler but practically all the other members of his entourage kept themselves going on the drugs obligingly dispensed by Dr Morell.

To the strain of responsibility and the evil effects of Morell's ministrations must be added the effects of the life Hitler was now

1. H. R. Trevor-Roper: *The Last Days of Hitler* (2nd edition, London, 1950), p. 69.

leading. From the summer of 1941 Hitler made his permanent headquarters at Wolfsschanze, in East Prussia. Apart from a period at Werwolf, near Winniza, from July to October 1942, brief visits to the front or Berlin, and rather longer visits to Salzburg and his house on the Obersalzberg, Hitler lived the greater part of the years between June 1941 and November 1944 in one of the most remote provinces of the Reich, increasingly cut off from the life of the country over which he ruled.

Even when the Führer's Headquarters were housed in wooden chalets above ground, the sense of isolation in the gloom of this northern forest was felt by most visitors to be oppressive. But under the threat of air-raids Hitler soon moved to one of the massive concrete bunkers embedded in the ground, and made his home in a suite of two or three small rooms with bare, un-decorated concrete walls and the simplest wooden furniture. After the lofty spaciousness of the Reich Chancellery, or of the Berghof with its superb mountain views, the rich carpets and the bowls full of flowers – in all of which he had delighted – the contrast was striking.

The austerity of Hitler's life at his headquarters matched the bleakness of the surroundings. General Jodl, who spent much time there, described it as 'a mixture of cloister and concentration camp. There were numerous wire fences and much barbed-wire. There were far-flung outposts on the roads leading to it, and in the middle was the so-called Security Zone No. 1. Permanent passes to enter this security zone were not even given to my Staff. Every guard had to inspect each officer whom he did not know. Apart from reports on the military situation, very little news from the outer world penetrated this holy of holies.'[1]

The main event of each day was the Führer's Conference at noon. To describe these as conferences is actually to misrepresent their character: they were a series of reports on the military situation, in which decisions were taken solely by the Führer. A certain number of officers were nearly always present: Generals Keitel and Jodl, from the Führer's own Supreme Command of the Armed Forces; the Chief of Staff of the Army; the Chief of Staff of the Air Force, or his deputy; the representative of the Commander-in-Chief of the Navy; the permanent representatives of Himmler (S.S. Gruppenführer Fegelein) and of Ribbentrop (Ambassador Hewel). Other commanders or ministers would attend intermittently: sometimes Göring or Speer would be

1. N.P., Part xv, p. 283.

there, or the Commander-in-Chief of the Navy, less frequently
Himmler. Each of these officers was accompanied by his adjutants,
who carried the maps to be spread out on the big centre table, or
the memoranda and diagrams to be presented. As each report
was made – Eastern Front, Italy, air war, and so on – Hitler
would announce his decision, and the officers concerned would
leave the room to send off the necessary instructions. There was
no general discussion of the situation as a whole: only the
Führer was allowed to concern himself with the over-all picture.

The length of the conference varied. It might go on for one,
two, or three hours. After September 1942 stenographers were
always present to prepare a record of what was said. Another,
more restricted military conference sometimes followed late in
the evening, and there were frequent private meetings between
Hitler and his chief lieutenants, Himmler, Bormann, the powerful
head of the Party Chancery, or Goebbels on a flying visit from
Berlin.

Hitler's day was almost entirely taken up with meetings of this
kind. He rose late, breakfasted alone, and after the noon conference took lunch, often with some of the visitors to the conference,
at any time between 2 and 5 p.m. Usually he rested in the late
afternoon, resuming his talks at six or seven o'clock. Dinner
might be served at any time between 8 p.m. and midnight. There
followed further discussions and his day ended with tea in the
company of his secretaries – possibly Morell and Julius Schaub,
his adjutant, as well – at four o'clock in the morning.

Apart from a short walk with his Alsatian bitch, Blondi, which
had been given him by Bormann to raise his spirits after Stalingrad and to which he became very attached, Hitler took no exercise and enjoyed no form of relaxation. As the war went on he
dropped the habit of seeing films after dinner, apart from newsreels. Up to the time of Stalingrad, he sometimes spent an evening
listening to gramophone records, Beethoven, Wagner, or Wolf's
Lieder. After Stalingrad, however, he would hear no more music,
and his sole occupation as they drank their tea in the early hours
of the morning was to recall the past, his youth in Vienna and
the years of struggle. This was interspersed with reflections on
history, on the destiny of man, religion, and other large subjects.
Soon, his secretary complains, his remarks became as familiar as
the records; they knew exactly what he would say and kept awake
only with the greatest difficulty. On no account was the war or
anything connected with it permitted as a subject of discussion

during the tea-hour. For similar reasons Hitler gave up inviting guests to his meals and finally ate alone with his secretaries, who were under strict instructions not to mention the war.

The dominant impression derived from accounts of life at the Führer's Headquarters in 1943 and 1944 is one of intense boredom, punctuated by the excitement of crises like that caused by Mussolini's fall and by Hitler's unpredictable outbursts of rage, usually directed against the generals.

'It is tragic,' Goebbels wrote after a talk with Göring, 'that the Führer has become such a recluse and leads such an unhealthy life. He never gets out into the fresh air. He does not relax. He sits in his bunker, worries, and broods. If one could only transfer him to other surroundings! . . . The loneliness of General Headquarters and the whole method of working there naturally have a depressing effect upon the Führer.'[1]

The long days spent idling and talking up at the Berghof were gone for ever. Hitler saw few of his old Party comrades now, and little even of Eva Braun, who remained on the Obersalzberg. Occasionally his interest in the arts revived, as when he talked of making his home-town Linz into a German Budapest, with a great art gallery and opera-house. But his chief motive in this, as he repeated several times to Goebbels, was to reduce the cultural pre-eminence of Vienna, the city which had once rejected him. Sometimes he roused himself on Goebbels's visits to talk of the days when he would be able to get out of uniform and 'visit theatres and cinemas again, go to the Wintergarten with me in the evening, or drop in at the K.d.d.K. [the Artists' Club] and be a human being again among humans'.[2] But, so long as he remained at his headquarters, Goebbels thought that his dog, Blondi, was closer to him than any human being.

Hitler's ostensible reason for shutting himself up in this way was the demands made on him by the war. But there was a deeper psychological compulsion at work. Here he lived in a private world of his own, from which the ugly and awkward facts of Germany's situation were excluded. He refused to visit any of the bombed towns, just as he refused to read reports which contradicted the picture he wanted to form. The power of Martin Bormann, Hitler's personal secretary and head of the Party Chancery, was built up on the skill with which he pandered to

1. *The Goebbels Diaries*, p. 200.
2. ibid.. p. 289.

this weakness, carefully keeping back unpleasant information and defeating the attempts of those who tried to make Hitler aware of the gravity of the situation.

Hitler had always hated an 'objective' attitude towards facts, and this prejudice became more marked as the facts became more unpalatable. In the last eighteen months of his life, the refusal to see or admit what was happening outside the magic circle of his headquarters was the essential condition of his ability to continue the war. The concrete bunker in which he immured himself was a refuge against something far more threatening than bombs, against the intrusion of a harsh reality into the world of fantasy in which he preferred to live.

A symptom of this attitude was his unwillingness to make a speech in public. In the last years of his life Hitler deliberately refused to exercise the extraordinary powers he had once displayed as a mass-orator. After Stalingrad, apart from the funeral addresses for Lutze and Dietl, Hitler delivered only two more speeches in public. In this same period he made no more than five broadcasts, while at the Munich anniversary celebrations of February 1943, 1944, 1945, and November 1944, his speech was read for him in his absence.

Goebbels did everything he could to overcome the Führer's reluctance. Hitler's excuse was always the same: he was waiting for a military success. But again one may suspect a deeper reason. Hitler's gifts as an orator had always depended on his flair for sensing what was in the minds of his audience. He no longer wanted to know what was in the minds of the German people; at all costs he must preserve his illusions. Until he could force events to conform to the pattern he sought to impose and reappear as the Magician Vindicated he hid himself away in his headquarters.

As the Allied armies began to press in on Germany in the course of 1944, some of the Nazi leaders began to look around for ways to disappear or make private deals with the enemy. This, if inglorious, may be regarded as a normal human reaction to such a situation. Hitler's was wholly different. He was fighting for something more than his power or his skin; he was fighting to preserve intact that image he had created of himself as one of Hegel's 'World Historical Individuals'. The unforgivable sin was to fail, as Mussolini had failed, to rise to the measure of events. Hitler's faith was crystallized in the belief that if only he could survive the buffetings of the waves which were breaking over him he would be saved by some miraculous intervention and still triumph over his enemies. Everything depended upon the will to hold out.

This belief in turn depended upon the fundamental belief which he never abandoned to the end of his life – that he was a man chosen by Providence to act as the agent of the 'World Historical Process'.[1] Every incident in his life was used to support the truth of this assertion: the number of times he had escaped attempts at assassination, which he placed at seven, culminating in his extraordinary escape from serious injury on 20 July 1944; or the fact that the Russians had not broken through in the winter of 1941–2. Anything, however trivial, which went right in the last two years of the war served Hitler as further evidence that he had only to trust in Providence and all would be well.

Inevitably he turned to the past history of the Party and his own rise from obscurity to justify his belief. In the early 1920s he had been laughed at, too – and been proven right. Had not the autumn of 1932 seen the Nazis at their lowest ebb, losing votes, without money and badly split by the quarrel between Hitler and Gregor Strasser? Yet within six weeks they were in power. Had not the experts said that Germany's economic situation was hopeless, just as the generals said her military situation was hopeless, and had he not shown the economists, as he would show the generals now, that if the will was there, nothing was impossible?

There were other, more material factors on which Hitler based his hopes of a dramatic reversal of the war in his favour. In his speech of 8 November 1942, after declaring that he would never lay down his arms until five past twelve, Hitler referred to the new secret weapons which Germany was building and promised the Allies an answer to their bombing raids 'which will strike them dumb'. The weapons he had in mind were the V1, the flying bomb, and the V2, the rocket. To these must be added the new jet fighter-planes, with which the Luftwaffe was to sweep the enemy from the skies, and new types of U-boats, with which the Navy was to cut the Allies' supply lines.

The secret weapons were not an invention of Hitler's imagination; they actually existed, and, in the case of the V1 and V2, were to play some part in the final stages of the war. But the hopes which Hitler and Goebbels placed upon them were exaggerated. Ignoring the almost insuperable difficulties of mass-production under the Allied air-attacks, they expected of them

1. cf. the quotation from Hegel above, pp. 383–4.

not merely increased losses for the enemy, but a transformation of the strategic situation, a miracle which would set at naught rational calculations of manpower, economic resources, and military strength. This was a hope to which Hitler clung until the very end, it was his unfailing answer to every objection, yet it was a hope built upon the slenderest foundation, and the secret weapons, too – at least as they figured in Hitler's mind – soon belonged more to the realm of fantasy than that of fact.

More substantial, it may now appear, was the parallel set of hopes which he built up of a split between the partners in the Grand Alliance. No one, looking back at German anti-Bolshevik propaganda from the era of the Cold War, can fail to be struck by the aptness of much of the argument.

'It is no longer a question,' Hitler declared in his broadcast of 30 January 1944, 'whether the present war will maintain the old Balance of Power or re-establish it, but of who will predominate in Europe at the end of this struggle – the European family of nations, represented by its strongest State, Germany, or the Bolshevik colossus. ... There can only be one victor in this war, either Germany or the Soviet Union. Germany's victory means the preservation of Europe: Soviet Russia's means its destruction.'[1]

The speciousness of such an argument in the mouth of Hitler, the man who had signed the Nazi–Soviet Pact in 1939 and who did more than any other to destroy Europe, does not alter the fact that subsequent events have shown how precarious was the basis of the wartime alliance between the Western Powers and the U.S.S.R. German propaganda, constantly repeating the theme of the Bolshevik threat to European civilization, was quick to pick on any hint of friction between the Allies, and Goebbels as well as Ribbentrop urged Hitler to follow this up with diplomatic action to split the alliance.

One difficulty was to decide which of the Allies, Great Britain and the U.S.A., or the U.S.S.R., was more likely to listen to German overtures for a separate peace. Precisely the same question, it is worth noting, divided German opposition circles in their discussions of how to get rid of Hitler and end the war.

On general grounds Goebbels preferred London to Moscow. 'One can always make a better deal with a democratic State,' he reflected cynically, 'and, once peace has been concluded, such a

1. B.B.C. Monitoring Report.

State will not seize the sword for twenty years to come.'[1] But the Anglo-American formula of 'unconditional surrender' forbade much hope in this direction. After a long talk with Hitler at his headquarters on 23 September 1943, Goebbels wrote in his diary: 'He does not believe that negotiations with Churchill would lead to any result as he is too deeply wedded to his hostile views and, besides, is guided by hatred and not by reason. The Führer would prefer negotiations with Stalin, but he does not believe they would be successful.'[2] Hitler gave the same reason to Goebbels as he gave to Ribbentrop: nothing could be achieved by negotiation until a decisive success had been won in the east. Only then would the Russians be in the right frame of mind to consider the terms Hitler was determined to exact. As this condition continued to elude Hitler, the proposal lapsed.

It can, of course, be argued that Hitler was right in believing that a deal between any German Government, of which he was the head, and either the Western Powers or Russia was out of the question. This did not, however, prevent him from expressing the firm conviction until the last week of his life that the Allies were certain to fall out and building the most extravagant hopes on such a quarrel, hopes which he kept alive in those around him by spreading rumours that negotiations were about to begin through a third party, or had already begun.[3]

But all these hopes – the secret weapons and the break-up of the Grand Alliance – were subsidiary to the central pillar of Hitler's faith, the belief in himself, in his destiny and consequent ability to master any crisis. It was from this belief alone that he derived the strength of will to continue the war long after it had been lost, and to persuade not only himself, but many of those around him, against the evidence and their own common sense, that all was not yet hopeless. To the 'historic' image of the Führer, Hitler was prepared to sacrifice the German Army, the German nation, and in the end himself. From this course he never deviated: the only question was whether the German Army and the German nation were prepared to let him.

IV

Little in the way of dissuading Hitler, still less of opposing him, could be expected from the other Nazi leaders. Of the original

1. *The Goebbels Diaries*, p. 387.   2. ibid., p. 386.
3. cf. Speer's evidence; N.P., Part XVII, pp. 26–7.

group with which Hitler had secured power, Röhm and Strasser had been murdered, while Frick had subsided into obscurity, losing the Ministry of the Interior to Himmler in 1943 and being kicked upstairs to the titular office of Reich Protector of Bohemia and Moravia.

Göring, still Hitler's successor, Reichsmarshal, Commander-in-Chief of the Air Force, Minister for Air, Plenipotentiary for the Four-Year Plan, Chairman of the Council of Ministers for the Defence of the Reich, Minister President of Prussia, President of the Reichstag and holder of a score of other offices, had steadily lost authority since the beginning of the war. In 1933–4 he was unquestionably the second man in Germany; by 1942, sloth, vanity, and his love of luxury had undermined not only his political authority but his native ability. He took his ease at Karinhall, hunting and feasting, amassing a fabulous collection of pictures, jewels, and *objets d'art* for which the cities of Europe were laid under tribute, and amusing himself by designing still more fantastic clothes to fit his different offices and changing moods. When he appeared in Rome or at the Führer's H.Q. in a new white or sky-blue uniform, surrounded by a retinue of aides-de-camp and carrying his bejewelled Marshal's baton, he still blustered loudly and claimed a privileged position. But it was a hollow show, with nothing behind to support it.

In 1942 and 1943 Goebbels tried to build up a group around Göring to capture influence with the Führer, urging the Reichsmarshal to bestir himself and make use of his formidable paper authority to resist the growing ascendancy of Bormann. A series of secret meetings was held between Göring, Goebbels, Speer, Ley, and Funk, but Goebbels was reluctantly forced to recognize that Göring was no longer the man he had been, and that his credit with the Führer was seriously weakened. Hitler was tolerant of Göring's weaknesses, he still summoned him to all important conferences, and as late as the time of Mussolini's overthrow (July 1943) he was prepared to say: 'At such a time one can't have a better adviser than the Reichsmarshal. In time of crisis he is brutal and ice-cold. I've always noticed that when it comes to the breaking point he is a man of iron without scruples.'[1] But Hitler was not blind to what was happening to Göring, and the failure of the Air Force finally discredited the Reichsmarshal in his eyes. There were angry scenes between the

1. Hitler's Conference on 25 July 1943, after the news of Mussolini's overthrow; Felix Gilbert: op. cit., p. 44.

two men, Hitler accusing the Luftwaffe of cowardice as well as incompetence, and blaming Göring for letting himself be taken in by the Air Force generals. Some personal feeling for Göring remained until the end, but Hitler had no longer any confidence in him, and Göring kept out of his way.

In any case, Göring never had the moral courage to act independently of Hitler or to go against him. Intelligent enough to realize the hopelessness of Germany's position in the last year and a half, he chose to turn a blind eye to what was only too plain, to hope that something would turn up and to disown responsibility. Only at his trial after the war did he reveal something of the cunning and force which he had once possessed.

The last of the original leadership, Joseph Goebbels, was both able and tough. A genius as a propagandist, he claimed that no one since Le Bon had understood the mind of the masses as well as he – forgetting Hitler for the moment. But his cynical intelligence and caustic tongue did not make him popular in the Party. In the early years of the war, Hitler became very cool towards Goebbels, partly because of the scandal caused by his love affairs, partly out of mistrust of his malicious wit, but the later years, which marked the eclipse of Göring, saw Goebbels steadily rise in favour.

As early as 1942 Goebbels began to campaign for a more drastic mobilization of Germany's resources. This was a clever line to adopt when, as Goebbels was quick to see, many people in responsible positions were beginning to hedge. Goebbels was the man, not Hitler or Göring, who visited the bombed cities in the Rhineland, and who won high praise for his conduct as Gauleiter of Berlin during the heavy bombing of the capital. The idea of creating a more radical group round Göring failed, and Goebbels had to come to terms with Himmler and Bormann, but he won back the confidence of a Hitler who was himself becoming more and more radical. He was one of the few men with whom Hitler could still exchange ideas, and he was Hitler's choice for the office of Reich Chancellor in the Government he bequeathed to Admiral Dönitz.

Goebbels saw well enough the disaster which threatened Germany, and in 1943 and 1944 tried to persuade Hitler to consider a compromise peace. When this came to nothing he was too intelligent to suppose that there was any future for himself apart from Hitler, and instead of turning against the Führer he began to out-Herod Herod in his demands for still more drastic measures. It was Goebbels who, in 1945, proposed that Germany should denounce the Geneva Convention and shoot captured airmen out of hand, and who persuaded Hitler not to leave Berlin. His passion for self-dramatization was aroused by the idea of fighting on to the end, however hopeless the position, and he was the one member of the original group who joined Hitler in the Berlin bunker and, disdaining capture, killed his wife, children, and himself when Hitler committed suicide.

Of those who became prominent after 1933 only three are worth more than cursory mention: Himmler, Bormann, and Speer. Himmler's rise dated from 1934; in the following ten years he acquired sole power over the whole complex structure of the police state. As Minister of the Interior, Himmler controlled the Secret Police, the Security Service (SD) and the Criminal Police. As Reichsführer S.S. he commanded the political corps d'élite of the régime and, in the Waffen (Armed) S.S., possessed a rival army to the Reichswehr, numbering half a million men by the summer of 1944. Through the concentration camps, which he also controlled, he organized his own labour corps, which was set to work in factories run by the S.S. In the east he was in charge of all plans for the resettlement of the conquered territories. Himmler's Reichssicherheitshauptamt (the Reich Security Main Office), in effect, administered a state in miniature, the embryonic S.S. State of the future, jealously defending its prerogatives and ceaselessly intriguing to extend them.

The year 1944 added considerably to Himmler's empire. The functions of military counter intelligence, hitherto conducted by the O.K.W. through the department known as the Abwehr, were turned over to Himmler, who established a unified Intelligence Service. After the unsuccessful plot of July 1944 he became Commander-in-Chief of the Home Army, took over all prisoner-of-war camps from the Armed Forces and, before the end of the year, assumed the active command of an army group at the front.

Here was an organization which, if its ruler could have been persuaded to act, represented a concentration of power which even Hitler could not ignore. At one time, in 1943, an approach was made to Himmler by two members of the anti-Hitler opposition, Dr Langbehn, a Berlin lawyer, and Johannes Popitz, the Prussian Minister of Finance, in the hope of persuading him to take independent action.[1] This led nowhere: Himmler was the

1. See A. W. Dulles: *Germany's Underground*, c. 11.

last man of whom any such action could be expected, for two very good reasons.

Apart from the efficiency with which he built up his organization, he was a man of undistinguished personality and limited intelligence. He lacked the initiative to strike out a line for himself, particularly if it meant any conflict with the Führer, nor had he sufficient grasp of the situation to understand the gravity of Germany's position or to conceive of alternative courses.[1]

Moreover – the second reason – Himmler unquestioningly believed in the doctrines of Nazism, especially its racial doctrines, with a single-minded faith. He spent much time and money in developing such activities as those of the S.S. Institute for Research and the Study of Heredity (the *Ahnenerbe*), and the Foundation for the Study of Heredity, whose tasks were defined as research into 'the area, spirit, and heritage of the Indo-Germanic race, which is a Nordic race'.[2] A racist crank, he was passionately interested in all sides of *völkisch* and Aryan 'culture', from astrology and the measurement of skulls to the interpretation of runes and prehistoric archaeology.[3] To Himmler the Nazi *Weltanschauung* was the literal, revealed truth, and his humourless pedantry, which rivalled that of Rosenberg, bored and irritated Hitler.

This was poor material out of which to make the leader of an opposition, and only in the last days of the collapse was Himmler brought, with the utmost difficulty, to admit the possibility of acting on his own initiative to end the war.

The last of the great feudatories of the Nazi Court to carve out his demesne was Martin Bormann. It was Hess's flight to Scotland in May 1941 which gave him his chance. Himmler's empire was the S.S. and the police; Göring's, the Four-Year Plan and the Luftwaffe; Ley's, the Labour Front – Bormann's was the Party. Succeeding to Hess's position as Head of the Party Chancery, as

1. For an illuminating account of Himmler's personality see the memoirs of Felix Kersten, Himmler's doctor: *The Kersten Memoirs* (London, 1956).

2. N.D. 488-PS: Bye-Laws of the Institute, drawn up by Himmler in 1940.

3. Among the captured German records is a lengthy and embittered correspondence between Himmler's *Ahnenerbe* and Rosenberg as the Führer's Delegate for the Ideological Indoctrination of the N.S. Party over the responsibility for the archaeological collections dealing with East European prehistory which had been captured in Russia.

early as January 1942 he was able to secure a directive laying down that he alone was to handle the Party's share in all legislation; 'personnel questions of civil servants' (in plainer terms, jobs for Party members in the State administration), and all contacts between the various ministries and the Party. Direct communication between the supreme authorities of the Reich and other offices of the Party was not permitted.[1]

This could be made into a powerful position, and Bormann was indefatigable in working to enlarge his claims. His agents were the Gauleiters, who were directly responsible to him. In December 1942, when all Gaue became Reich Defence Districts, the Gauleiters, now Reich Defence Commissioners as well, gained an effective control over the whole of the civilian war effort. The decentralization of administration made necessary by the heavy bombing concentrated still further power in their hands. After Himmler became Minister of the Interior in 1943 a clash between the two empires of the S.S. and the Party was inevitable. To the surprise of most people, Bormann not only held his own against the powerful Reichsführer S.S., but by the end of 1944 had gained a lead in the struggle for power.

While both men controlled powerful organizations, Bormann grasped the importance of making himself indispensable to Hitler. In constant attendance on him, he succeeded in drawing most of the threads of internal administration into his hands. Hitler, preoccupied with the war, was glad enough to be relieved of the burden of administration which he had always disliked, and in April 1943 Bormann was officially recognized as Secretary to the Führer. It was Bormann who decided whom the Führer should and should not see, what he should or should not read, who was present at nearly every interview and drafted the Führer's instructions. The importance of this position can scarcely be overestimated, for, as Weizsäcker, the State Secretary in the Foreign Office, says: 'Ministerial skill in the Third Reich consisted in making the most of a favourable hour or minute when Hitler made a decision, this often taking the form of a remark thrown out casually, which then went its way as an "Order of the Führer".'[2]

In this way Bormann, a brutal and much-hated man, acquired immense power. It was a power, however, which he exercised not in his own right, but solely in the name of Hitler. 'A few critical words from Hitler,' Speer said after the war, 'and all Bormann's

1. N.D. 2,100-PS.   2. Weizsäcker: op. cit., p. 164.

enemies would have jumped at his throat.'[1] Like his great rival Himmler, once separated from Hitler, Bormann was a political cypher. For all these men the road to power lay through acquiring Hitler's favour, not in risking its loss through opposition, and Bormann's voice, like that of Goebbels, was always raised in advocacy of more extreme measures.

As for the others, Ribbentrop still occupied the post of Foreign Minister, but had ceased to be taken seriously by Hitler or anyone else. Ley, when he was sober, ran anxiously from one group to another, trying to curry favour. The rest, such men as Funk, Rust, Backe, Seldte, Frank, Sauckel, and Seyss-Inquart, were minor figures, gratified by a nod of recognition from the Führer and wholly excluded from any share in, or even knowledge of, major decisions of policy.

Until the last few days of his life when Himmler and Göring made their last-minute attempts to negotiate with the Allies – and were promptly expelled from the Party – Hitler's hold over his Party remained intact. Its leaders were his creatures: had it not been for Hitler not one of them – with the possible exception of Goebbels and Göring – would ever have risen from the obscurity which was their natural environment. The position and wealth they enjoyed they had secured by his favour; their power was derivative, their light reflected. To turn against Hitler, to question his decisions, would have been to destroy the thread of hope to which they still clung. If Hitler failed, they would fall with him. If nothing else, the common crimes in which they had shared bound them together. But there was something more than fear.

They were all under his spell, blindly obedient to him, and with no will of their own – whatever the medical term for this phenomenon may be. I noticed during my activities as architect, that to be in his presence for any length of time made me tired, exhausted and void. Capacity for independent work was paralysed.[2]

The man who gave this account – Albert Speer – is perhaps the most interesting case of them all, precisely because it is so different from that of the others.

Speer only came into prominence in the spring of 1942, when Hitler suddenly nominated him as Minister for Armaments Production, but his rise in the next two years was rapid. By August 1944 he was responsible for the whole of German war

1. Quoted by Trevor-Roper: op. cit., p. 45.
2. ibid., p. 85.

economy, with fourteen million workers under his direction. It was Speer who, by a remarkable feat of organization, patched up the bombed communications and factories, and somehow or other maintained the bare minimum of transport and production without which the war on the German side would have come to a standstill. Without Speer Hitler would have lacked the power to stage his fight to the finish.

The Führer was generous in his praise of Speer's achievement, put increased responsibilities on him, and showed a warm personal regard for him. For his part Speer was not unaffected by the spell Hitler was still able to cast over those near him, but he stood apart from the contest for power which absorbed the energies of men like Bormann. He was interested far more in the job he had to do than in the power it brought him. Preserving a certain intellectual detachment, he disinterested himself in politics. A long illness kept him away from the Führer's Headquarters from February to June 1944, but on his return he became disquieted at the price which Germany was being made to pay for the prolongation of the war and – more disquieting still – realized that Hitler was determined to destroy Germany rather than admit defeat.

Having arrived at this conclusion, Speer systematically set about frustrating Hitler's design, and eventually, early in 1945, planned an attempt to kill Hitler and the men around him by introducing poison-gas into the ventilation system of his underground bunker. The plan had to be abandoned for technical reasons. Thereupon Speer continued his efforts to thwart Hitler's orders and to salvage something for the future. Yet he never again attempted to remove the man who was the author of the policy he opposed. The reason is interesting. Speer did not lack the physical courage to make a second attempt, but, as he admitted later, in the conflict of loyalties which divided his mind, he could not rid himself of the belief that Hitler was, as he claimed to be, the only leader who could hold the German people together, that he was, in von Brauchitsch's phrase at the Nuremberg Trial, Germany's destiny, and that Germany could not escape her destiny.

Here, in the self-confessed failure of the one man among the Nazi leaders who retained the intellectual independence to see clearly the course on which Hitler was set and the integrity to reject it, is the clearest possible illustration of the hold which Hitler kept until the end over the régime he had established and the Party he had created.

V

If little had ever been expected of the Party by those Germans who saw in Hitler the evil genius of their country, much had been hoped of the Army. So far the Army had disappointed those hopes. For a moment in the autumn of 1938 it had seemed possible that the Army High Command might lead a revolt against Hitler to avoid war,[1] but the conspiracy came to nothing, and thereafter, however great their misgivings (at least in retrospect), however little the enthusiasm they felt for 'the Corporal' and his régime, the generals obeyed his orders, fought his battles for him and accepted the titles, the decorations and the gifts he bestowed on them.

In the strained relations which developed between Hitler and the Army after the invasion of Russia it was Hitler, not the generals, who took the offensive. Again and again he reversed the decisions of his senior commanders, ignored their advice, upbraided them as cowards, forced them to carry out orders they believed to be impossible to execute, and dismissed them when they failed. According to Field-Marshal von Manstein's evidence at Nuremberg, of seventeen field-marshals only one managed to get through the war and keep his command: ten were dismissed. Of thirty-six colonel-generals eighteen were dismissed and only three survived the war in their positions.[2] Manstein offered these figures as proof of the Army's opposition to Hitler; on the contrary, they would seem to illustrate the docility with which the generals submitted to treatment such as no previous German ruler had ever dared to inflict on the Army.

Hitler's criticism of the German Officer Corps was directed against its conservatism and its 'negative' attitude towards the National Socialist revolution. In practise, the revolutionary spirit meant willingness to carry out Hitler's orders without hesitation and without regard for the cost, the sort of spirit Paulus so lamentably failed to show at Stalingrad by his failure to prolong a useless resistance until the last man was dead. In March 1943 Goebbels wrote: 'The Führer is making every effort to inject new blood into the Officer Corps. Slowly but surely the basis of selection for officers is being changed.'[3] Meanwhile, although he could not continue the war without the generals, those who

1. See above, c. 8.   2. N.P., Part XXI, pp. 60–61.
3. *The Goebbels Diaries*, p. 220.

retained office or secured promotion were the compliant, the ambitious who concealed their doubts, or rough-and-ready soldiers like Model and Schörner, who went up to the front, drove their men to the limit and did not worry their heads too much about the strategic situation.

As the war went on Hitler came to rely more and more on the Waffen S.S. divisions, who were provided with the best equipment, given priority in recruitment and reserved for the most spectacular operations. Towards the end of the war the number of these divisions had risen to more than thirty-five. The growth of this rival S.S. Army was a particular grievance with the Regular Army officers. Knowing this, Hitler delighted to praise the S.S. troops and to give their exploits special mention in his communiqués. This was the way in which he kept his promise of 1934 that there should only be one bearer of arms in the State – the Army.

After the fall of Mussolini, Hitler congratulated himself upon having no monarchy in Germany which could be used, as the royal authority had been used in Italy, to turn him out of office. The thorough process of Nazification to which he had subjected the institutions of Germany, from the Reichstag to the Law Courts, from the trade unions to the universities, had destroyed, he believed, the basis for an organized opposition. The process was not, however, complete: two institutions in Germany still retained some independence.

The first was the Churches. Among the most courageous demonstrations of opposition during the war were the sermons preached by the Catholic Bishop of Münster and the Protestant pastor, Dr Niemöller. Nazi zealots, like Bormann, regarded the Churches with a venomous hostility, while Catholic priests as well as Protestant pastors were active in the anti-Nazi opposition. Neither the Catholic Church nor the Evangelical Church, however, as institutions, felt it possible to take up an attitude of open opposition to the régime. Yet without the support of some institution, any Opposition appeared to be condemned to remain in the hopeless position of individuals pitting their strength against the organized power of the State. It was natural, therefore, that those few Germans who ventured to think of taking action against Hitler should continue to look with expectation to the Army, the only other institution in Germany which still possessed a measure of independent authority, if its leaders could be persuaded to assert it, and the only institution which commanded the armed force needed to overthrow the régime. The triumphs to which Hitler led the German Army in 1940–1 silenced such hopes. But they revived when the Russian campaign began to go wrong, when Hitler quarrelled with and humiliated his generals and when his refusal to listen to their advice threatened greater disasters in the future.

There is some danger in talking of the 'German Opposition' of giving altogether too sharp a picture of what was essentially a number of small, loosely connected groups, fluctuating in membership, with no common organization and no common purpose other than their hostility to the existing régime. Their motives for such hostility varied widely: in some it sprang from a deeply felt moral aversion to the whole régime, in others from patriotism and the conviction that, unless he were halted, Hitler would destroy Germany. To diversity of motives must be added considerable divergence of aims, about the steps to be taken in opposing Hitler as well as the future organization of Germany and Europe. It would be hard, for instance, to imagine a greater contrast than that between the radical Stauffenberg, who carried out the attempted assassination on 20 July, and Moltke, the leader of the Kreisau Circle, on the one hand, or between either of these and Karl Goerdeler, the conservative Prussian monarchist of an older generation, who was to be Chancellor in the post-Hitler government, on the other.

Among those who continued to meet and discuss the chances of action against the régime were the two older men generally regarded as the leaders of the conspiracy – General Ludwig Beck, the former Chief of Staff of the Army, and Dr Karl Goerdeler, a former Oberbürgermeister of Leipzig – and the ex-Ambassador to Rome, Ulrich von Hassel. A key figure since 1938 had been Colonel (later General) Hans Oster, the chief assistant of the enigmatic Admiral Canaris in the Abwehr, the counter-intelligence department of the O.K.W. The Abwehr provided admirable cover and unique facilities for a conspiracy, and Hans Oster – 'a man such as God intended men to be'[1] – gathered a small group of devoted men around him of whom the outstanding members were Hans von Dohnanyi and Justus Delbrück; two Berlin lawyers, Joseph Wirmer and Claus Bonhöffer, and the latter's

1. This is the phrase used of him by Fabian von Schlabrendorff, who almost alone of the leading conspirators survived the plot of 20 July and subsequent arrest. See his account of Oster in *Officers against Hitler*, p. 39.

brother Dietrich Bonhöffer, a Protestant pastor and professor of theology who had once been minister of the Lutheran Church in London.

One of the uses to which the conspirators put the facilities of the Abwehr was to try and make contact with the British and Americans in the hope of securing some assurances as to the kind of peace the Allies would be willing to make if Hitler's government was overthrown. Thus in May 1942 Dietrich Bonhöffer travelled to Stockholm and met Bishop Bell of Chichester on forged papers prepared by Hitler's own counter-intelligence service. Bishop Bell passed on all that he learned of the conspirators' plans to the British Government, and other contacts were made through Allen Dulles, the head of the American O.S.S. in Switzerland. None of these approaches, however, elicited any positive response. The Allies were sceptical about any German opposition and (particularly after the demand for an 'Unconditional Surrender' expressed at the Casablanca Conference in January 1943) the conspirators had to face the need to act on their own without any encouragement from outside.

The conspirators devoted much time and energy to discussing how Germany and Europe should be organized and governed after the overthrow of Hitler. Goerdeler, for example, who was indefatigable in travelling to and fro to urge those in authority to take a stand against Hitler, left behind a large number of memoranda on these topics.[1] Discussion of such questions was the purpose of the group which Count Helmuth von Moltke, thirty-eight years old, a former Rhodes Scholar at Oxford and bearer of one of the most famous names in German military history, brought together on his estate at Kreisau in Silesia. The Kreisau Circle was drawn from a cross-section of German society: amongst its members were two Jesuit priests, two Lutheran pastors; conservatives, liberals, and socialists, landowners and former trade unionists. The discussions at Kreisau were concerned, not with planning the overthrow of Hitler, but with the economic, social, and spiritual foundations of the new society which would come into existence afterwards. Moltke, who died for his beliefs with great courage, was strongly opposed to any active steps to get rid of Hitler. In his last letter to his wife from prison Moltke pointed to the fact that his arrest had prevented him from being drawn into the July plot as an example of Divine

1. See Gerhard Ritter: *Carl Goerdeler und die Deutsche Widerstandsbewegung* (Stuttgart, 1955; abridged English translation, *The German Resistance*).

intervention. In another letter he wrote that the course his trial had taken 'sets us poles apart from the Goerdeler faction and its sordid aftermath, right apart from all practical activity'.[1]

An analysis of the different groups and shades of opinion represented in the German Opposition lies outside the scope of this study. From the point of view of Hitler their activities were only important in so far as they led to action.

At first, Goerdeler and Beck pinned their hopes on persuading one or other of the commanders in the field – amongst them Field-Marshal von Kluge, the commander of Army Group Centre in the East – to arrest or get rid of Hitler. All such hopes proved illusory and after Stalingrad the more active conspirators accepted the fact that they would have to assassinate Hitler first before anyone in authority would be willing to move. The first such attempt was planned in February and March 1943. A recent convert to the plot was General Olbricht, chief of the General Army Office (Allgemeine Heeresamt) who held the post of deputy to the commander of the Home or Replacement Army (Ersatzheer). The Home Army was, in fact, not an active command but the organization for mobilizing and training recruits who were sent as drafts to the different fronts. The only armed men of which it disposed were a number of garrison troops in Berlin and other German cities. But Olbricht was willing to use the resources of the Home Army to try and carry out a *coup* in the confusion which would follow Hitler's assassination. This was to be undertaken by General Henning von Tresckow, G.S.O.1 at Kluge's Army Group Centre, and Schlabrendorff, a young lieutenant on his staff.

The attempt was made on 13 March 1943, when Hitler paid a visit to Kluge's headquarters at Smolensk. Tresckow and Schlabrendorff succeeded in placing a time-bomb on the plane which carried him back to East Prussia. By the devil's own luck – a not inappropriate phrase – the bomb failed to explode. With remarkable coolness, Schlabrendorff flew at once to the Führer's Headquarters, recovered the bomb before it had been discovered – it had been hidden in a package of two bottles of brandy to be delivered to a friend – and took it to pieces on the train to Berlin.[2]

As many as six more attempts on Hitler's life were planned in

1. *A German of the Resistance: The Last Letters of Count Helmuth von Moltke* (London, 1946), p. 21.
2. Fabian von Schlabrendorff: op. cit., c. 6.

the later months of 1943, but all for one reason or another came to nothing. In the meantime Himmler's police agents, although singularly inefficient in tracking down the conspiracy, were beginning to get uncomfortably close. In April 1943 they arrested Dietrich Bonhöffer, Joseph Müller, and Hans von Dohnanyi. Too many threads led back to the Abwehr, which the rival S.S. Intelligence Service was eager to suppress, and in December 1943 General Oster, the key figure in the Abwehr, was forced to resign.

Fortunately, just as the Abwehr circle was being broken up, a new recruit joined the conspiracy who promised to bring to it the qualities of decision and personality which the older leaders lacked.

Klaus Philip Schenk, Count von Stauffenberg, born in 1907, came of an old and distinguished South German family. He was a brilliant creature, with a passion not only for horses and outdoor sports but for literature (he was a favourite of Stefan George, the poet) and for music, at which he excelled. To his friends' surprise, he made the army his career. After several years in a famous cavalry regiment, he was selected for the General Staff and served with distinction as a staff officer in Poland, France, and Russia. It was while in Russia that his doubts about Hitler hardened into a conviction of the need to rid Germany of his rule and he was initiated into the conspiracy by Tresckow and Schlabrendorff. Stauffenberg's new purpose was not altered by the wounds which he suffered in the Tunisian campaign and which cost him his left eye, his right hand, and two fingers of the other hand. As soon as he had recovered, he secured appointment to Olbricht's staff in Berlin and threw himself into preparations for a renewed attempt at a *coup d'état.*

Stauffenberg used the pretext of the dangers of a revolt by the millions of foreign workers in Germany to prepare plans for the Home Army to take over emergency powers in Berlin and other German cities. 'Operation Valkyrie' was worked out in detail and a series of orders and appeals drawn up to be signed by Beck as the new head of state and Goerdeler as chancellor.

With the help of men on whom he could rely at the Führer's headquarters, in Berlin and in the German Army in the west, Stauffenberg hoped to push the reluctant Army leaders into action once Hitler had been killed. To make sure that this essential preliminary should not be lacking, Stauffenberg allotted the task of assassination to himself despite the handicap of his injuries.

Stauffenberg's energy had put new life into the conspiracy, but the leading role he was playing also roused jealousies. So did his views. Stauffenberg was by temperament a radical, highly critical of Goerdeler's old-fashioned conservatism and much closer to the socialist wing of the conspiracy round Julius Leber, Adolf Reichwein, and Wilhelm Leuschner.[1] These differences were heightened by the knowledge that they were now working against time. Further arrests were made early in 1944, including that of von Moltke: in February, the greater part of the Abwehr functions were transferred to a unified Intelligence Service under Himmler's control, and Himmler told Admiral Canaris, now deprived of his office as head of the Counter-Intelligence, that he knew very well a revolt was being planned in Army circles and that he would strike when the moment came.

At this moment came the news that the Allies had landed in Normandy. Stauffenberg had not expected the invasion so soon and he, Beck and Goerdeler were at first so taken aback that they hesitated whether to go on. With the Anglo-American armies as well as the Russians pressing the Germans back, was there any longer a chance of securing a compromise peace, even if Hitler were removed? Would they not simply incur the odium of a second stab in the back without being able to alter the course of events? It was Tresckow who spoke out firmly and steadied Stauffenberg's and the others' purpose.

The assassination [he replied to a message from Stauffenberg] must be attempted at any cost. Even should it fail, the attempt to seize power in the capital must be undertaken. We must prove to the world and to future generations that the men of the German Resistance dared to take the decisive step and to hazard their lives upon it. Compared with this object, nothing else matters.[2]

Tresckow's advice was heeded, and by good luck Stauffenberg was now placed in a position from which he could put his plans into operation more easily: at the end of June he was promoted to full colonel and appointed Chief of Staff to the Commander-in-Chief of the Home Army. This not only allowed him to send out orders in the name of his Commander, but also gave him frequent access to Hitler who was particularly interested in finding replacements for his losses in Russia.

1. Leuschner was to have been Vice-Chancellor and Leber to have held the key position of Minister of the Interior in the coalition government to be headed by Goerdeler.
2. Schlabrendorff, op. cit., p. 131.

Time, however, was now more pressing than ever. On 4 July Julius Leber and Adolf Reichwein were arrested following an attempt (to which Stauffenberg had reluctantly agreed) to get in touch with an underground German Communist group. On 17 July a warrant was issued for the arrest of Goerdeler. The plot was now in danger of being wrecked by further arrests within a matter of days, if not hours.

Stauffenberg had already made two attempts to carry out the assassination of Hitler. On 11 July he attended a conference at Berchtesgaden with a time-bomb concealed in his brief-case, but in the absence of Himmler and Göring he decided to wait until there was a better chance of killing all the leaders at one blow. A second chance came on 15 July when he was again summoned to a conference at the Führer's Headquarters in East Prussia. This time, in order to be sure of success, General Olbricht gave the order for 'Valkyrie' and started troops moving into the centre of Berlin two hours before the conference began. Stauffenberg made a telephone call to check with Olbricht before returning to the conference-room to set off the bomb. When he got back he found that Hitler had unexpectedly cut the meeting short and gone. A second hurried telephone call to Berlin gave Olbricht the chance to halt 'Operation Valkyrie' with the explanation that the troops had simply been called out on a practice exercise. But at a meeting with Beck the following day Stauffenberg agreed that whatever happened the attempt must be made on the next occasion. Four days later, on 20 July, he flew to East Prussia determined that his third chance should be decisive.

For Hitler the first six months of 1944 had brought nothing but an intensification of all the familiar problems. In January the Russians freed Leningrad from its German besiegers; in February they crossed the old Polish frontier, and in March the Rumanian. After a pause for the spring thaw, the Red Army renewed its attacks on 20 June. This time the German armies, stretched out in defence of lines which Hitler refused to shorten, could not withstand the weight of the Russian advance. Over large sections the German front ceased to exist, and in the first half of July Minsk, Vilna, Pinsk, and Grodno all fell. The German divisions Hitler insisted on holding in the Baltic States were threatened with encirclement, while the Russians were already thrusting towards the province of East Prussia, the first German territory to be threatened with invasion. On 20 July Hitler was at the height of one of the worst crises he had had to face on the Eastern Front, a front which had shifted its position several hundred miles nearer to Germany since July 1943.

During the same six months the Allied air forces continued to bomb German towns and communications with monotonous regularity and in March the Americans made their first day raid on Berlin. In Italy Kesselring held the Gustav or Winter Line until the beginning of the summer, but in May he was driven out of his positions and forced to retreat. The Allies entered Rome, the first European capital to fall to them, on 4 June.

Two days later at dawn the British and Americans began the long-awaited assault from the west. In preparation for the invasion, Hitler had recalled Rundstedt to act as Commander-in-Chief in the west. Considerable effort had been expended in building defences along the western coastline of Europe, but the length of that coastline as well as shortages of material and man-power made the Atlantic Wall less strong and much less complete than German propaganda represented it to be. Only after Rommel's appointment to inspect the coastal defences at the end of 1943 and subsequently to the command of Army Group B (Holland, Belgium, and northern France) was a determined drive made to strengthen the obstacles in the way of a landing. Sharp differences of opinion persisted among the commanders on the best way in which to defeat an attempted invasion and about the disposition of forces. In June 1944 sixty German divisions were available to hold a front which extended from Holland to the south of France; few were of first-rate quality, and only eleven of them were armoured formations. These were barely adequate forces with which to hold the west, especially when account was taken of their dispersal and of the air supremacy enjoyed by the Allies.

German Intelligence was badly at fault in forecasting the date, place, and strength of the invasion. Hitler rightly guessed that Normandy would be the part of the coast chosen by the Allies – against the advice of Rundstedt and other generals, who expected the landing farther north in the Pas de Calais. Hitler, however, also believed, as did Rommel, that a second landing would take place in the narrower part of the Channel, where the sites for the V1s were situated, and the elaborate deception planned by the British to encourage this belief was accepted at face value. As a result powerful German forces – the Fifteenth Army, numbering fifteen divisions – were stationed north of the Seine and held there, on Hitler's orders, when their intervention in the fighting in Normandy might have had great effect.

The actual landing in the early hours of 6 June caught the Germans unawares. Rommel was visiting his home near Ulm on his way to see Hitler at Berchtesgaden. Hitler's insistence that major decisions must all be referred to him imposed further delays, and so the opportunities of the first few hours were missed. Once the bridgehead had been made good, Hitler refused to give his commanders a free hand, constantly intervened to dictate orders which were out of keeping with the situation at the front, and persisted in believing that the Allies could still be thrown back into the sea. Relations between Hitler and the generals on the spot rapidly became strained, and on 17 June he summoned both Rundstedt and Rommel for a conference at Margival, near Soissons.

The meeting was held in an elaborate Command Headquarters which had been prepared for the invasion of Britain in 1940. Hitler had flown to Metz and motored across France. General Speidel, who was present, describes him as looking 'worn and sleepless, playing nervously with his spectacles and an array of coloured pencils which he held between his fingers. He was the only one who sat, hunched upon a stool, while the Field-Marshals stood'.[1]

The Führer was in a bitter mood. The fact that the Allied landings had succeeded he ascribed to the incompetence of the defence. When Rommel answered with an account of the difficulties of the situation, which were only increased by Hitler's rigid insistence on defending every foot of territory, Hitler went off into a monologue on the subject of the V-weapons which, he declared, would be decisive. Rommel's attempt to make him grasp the seriousness of the German position failed. Hitler talked of 'masses of jet-fighters' which would shatter the Allied air superiority, described the military situation in Italy and on the Russian front as stabilized, and lost himself in a cloud of words prophesying the imminent collapse of Britain under the V-bombs. When Rommel finally urged him to consider ending the war in view of the desperate situation in which Germany found herself, Hitler retorted: 'Don't you worry about the future course of the war. Look to your own invasion front.'

At lunch, Speidel reports, Hitler ate his plate of rice and vegetables only after it had been tasted for him. Two armed S.S.

1. Hans Speidel: *We Defended Normandy* (London, 1951), p. 106.

men stood behind his chair throughout and a selection of pills and medicines was ranged before him. The same night Hitler left again for Berchtesgaden without going near the front: one of his own V-bombs which exploded near his headquarters hastened his departure.[1]

Further efforts to make Hitler realize that the attempt to defeat the landings had already failed proved no more successful. After a visit to Berchtesgaden at the end of June, when the two Field-Marshals again tried to persuade Hitler to give them a free hand in the west and to end the war, Rundstedt was relieved of his command. Hitler offered his place to Field-Marshal von Kluge. But Kluge was no more able than Rundstedt or Rommel to stem the Allied advance, and by 20 July, although he still refused to recognize the fact, Hitler was confronted with as serious a military crisis in the west as in the east. For the first time he was being made to realize the meaning of 'war on two fronts'.

VI

Hitler spent the first two weeks of July 1944 on the Obersalzberg, and returned to his Headquarters in East Prussia in the middle of the month. Mussolini was due to visit him there on the 20th, and for that reason the conference had been moved to 12.30 p.m.

Stauffenberg flew from Berlin during the morning and was expected to report on the creation of new Volksgrenadier divisions. He brought his papers with him in a brief-case in which he had concealed the bomb fitted with a device for exploding it ten minutes after the mechanism had been started. The conference was already proceeding with a report on the East Front when Keitel took Stauffenberg in and presented him to Hitler. Twenty-four men were grouped round a large, heavy oak table on which were spread out a number of maps. Neither Himmler nor Göring was present. The Führer himself was standing towards the middle of one of the long sides of the table, constantly leaning over the table to look at the maps, with Keitel and Jodl on his left. Stauffenberg took up a place near Hitler on his right, next to a Colonel Brandt. He placed his brief-case under the table, having started the fuse before he came in, and then left the room unobtrusively on the excuse of a telephone call to Berlin. He had been gone only a minute or two when, at 12.42 p.m., a loud explosion shattered the room, blowing out the walls and the roof,

1. Speidel: op. cit., 8.

and setting fire to the debris which crashed down on those inside.

In the smoke and confusion, with guards rushing up and the injured men inside crying for help, Hitler staggered out of the door on Keitel's arm. One of his trouser legs had been blown off; he was covered in dust, and he had sustained a number of injuries. His hair was scorched, his right arm hung stiff and useless, one of his legs had been burned, a falling beam had bruised his back, and both ear-drums were found to be damaged by the explosion. But he was alive. Those who had been at the end of the table where Stauffenberg placed the brief-case were either dead or badly wounded. Hitler had been protected, partly by the table-top over which he was leaning at the time, and partly by the heavy wooden support on which the table rested and against which Stauffenberg's brief-case had been pushed before the bomb exploded.

Although badly shaken Hitler was curiously calm, and in the early afternoon he appeared on the platform of the Headquarters station to receive Mussolini. Apart from a stiff right arm, he bore no traces of his experience and the account which he gave to Mussolini was marked by its restraint.

As soon as they reached Wolfsschanze Hitler took Mussolini to look at the wrecked conference room. Then, as he began to re-enact the scene, his voice became more excited.

'After my miraculous escape from death today I am more than ever convinced that it is my fate to bring our common enterprise to a successful conclusion.' Nodding his head, Mussolini could only agree. 'After what I have seen here, I am absolutely of your opinion. This was a sign from Heaven.'[1]

In this exalted mood Hitler went with Mussolini to his own quarters, where an excited group had gathered for tea. Göring, Ribbentrop, and Dönitz had joined Keitel and Jodl, and sharp recriminations began to be exchanged over the responsibility for the war. Hitler sat quietly with Mussolini in the middle of this scene until someone mentioned the Röhm 'plot' of 1934. Suddenly leaping to his feet in a fury, Hitler began to scream that he would be revenged on them all, that he had been chosen by Providence to make history and that those who thwarted him would be destroyed. This went on for half an hour. When he had exhausted his rage Hitler in his turn relapsed into silence, sucking an occasional pastille and letting the protestations of loyalty and a

1. Paul Schmidt: op. cit., p. 582.

new quarrel which had begun between Göring and Ribbentrop pass over his head.[1]

In the confusion after the bomb had exploded Stauffenberg had succeeded in bluffing his way through the triple ring of guard-posts and had taken a plane back to Berlin. Some time passed before anyone at the Führer's headquarters realized what had happened – at first Hitler thought the bomb had been dropped from an aeroplane – and it was longer still before it was known that the attempted assassination had been followed by an attempted putsch in Berlin.

There, in the capital, a little group of the conspirators had gathered in General Olbricht's office at the General Staff Building in the Bendlerstrasse. Their plan was to announce that Hitler was dead and that an anti-Nazi government had been formed in Berlin, with General Beck as Head of State (Reichsverweser) Goerdeler as Chancellor, and Field-Marshal von Witzleben as Commander-in-Chief of the Armed Forces. Orders were to be issued in their name declaring a state of emergency and transferring all power to the Army in order to prevent the S.S. seizing control. The entire state administration, the S.S. itself, the police, and the Party were to be subordinated to the Commanders-in-Chief of the Army, in Germany to the Commander-in-Chief of the Home Army, and in the occupied countries to the Commanders-in-Chief of the different theatres of operations. The Waffen S.S. was to be incorporated in the Army, and all senior Party, S.S., and police officials to be placed under arrest. In Berlin plans had been concerted to bring in troops from barracks outside the city in order to surround the Government quarter, secure the Gestapo headquarters and the radio station, and disarm the S.S.

Whether these orders would be obeyed was a gamble, but it was hoped that – once Hitler himself had been removed – those officers who had hitherto refused to join the conspiracy, whether out of fear or scruples about the oath of allegiance, would support the new Government. The smouldering hostility of the Army to

1. An eye-witness account of the scene was given by Dollmann, the S.S. leader accompanying Mussolini, and has been caustically re-told by H. R. Trevor-Roper: op. cit., pp. 35–7. Göring who tried to direct attention from the failures of the Air Force to the bankruptcy of Ribbentrop's foreign policy, threatened to smack the Foreign Minister with his marshal's baton. 'You dirty little champagne salesman,' Göring roared at him. 'Shut your damned mouth.' 'I am still Foreign Minister,' Ribbentrop shouted back, 'and my name is *von* Ribbentrop.'

the S.S. and the Party, the desperate position of Germany unless she could make a compromise peace, and, most important of all, the knowledge that the assassination had been successful, would, it was hoped, overcome all hesitations, and a number of sympathizers ready to act had already been secured in the different commands.

Everything depended upon two conditions, the successful assassination of Hitler and prompt, determined action in Berlin. The first of these conditions had already been invalidated but this was not known to Stauffenberg, who left the Führer's Head-quarters convinced that no one could have survived the explosion in the conference room. The first reports of the explosion to reach the Bendlerstrasse, however, not long after 1 p.m., made it clear that Hitler was not dead, and Olbricht therefore decided not to issue the order for 'Valkyrie'. Thus the second condition failed too. It was not until Stauffenberg reached Rangsdorf airfield after a three-hour flight from East Prussia that he was able to get through by telephone to Olbricht and – believing, as he still did, that Hitler had been killed – to persuade him to start sending out orders for action. This was at 3.45 p.m. and it took Stauffenberg another three-quarters of an hour to get to the centre of Berlin and at last supply the drive which had been lacking at the centre.

Even Stauffenberg's energy and determination, however, could not make good the three to four hours which had been lost. Everything still remained to be done. Even in Berlin no move had been made to seize the radio station or the Gestapo headquarters in the Prinz Albrechtstrasse, which was virtually unguarded and where several of the conspirators, including Julius Leber, could have been released. Nor was any attempt made to arrest Goebbels, the Gauleiter of Berlin, although Graf von Helldorf, the Berlin chief-of-police, was deep in the conspiracy and eager to act.

So was General von Hase, the Berlin Commandant, but it was not until after 4 o'clock that he was told to bring in troops to occupy the government quarter. Hase called in the Guard Battalion Grossdeutschland, under Major Remer, from Döberitz. Remer (who was not in the plot) acted promptly, but the suspicions of a National Socialist guidance officer, Dr Hans Hagen, a self-important young man from the Propaganda Ministry who was lecturing to the battalion, were aroused. Hagen got in touch with Goebbels and when Remer arrived to arrest the Propaganda Minister, he was persuaded instead to speak on the telephone to Hitler's headquarters in East Prussia. The unmistakable voice over the wire convinced Remer that the Führer was not dead, as he had been told: the major was promptly promoted to colonel on the spot, and personally ordered by Hitler to use his troops to suppress the putsch.

After Stauffenberg's return, orders had been hurriedly sent out to the chief army commands to carry out 'Operation Valkyrie', and action was already in train in Paris, Vienna, and Prague when shortly after 6.30 p.m. the German radio broadcast an announcement, telephoned by Goebbels, that an attempt had been made to kill Hitler but had failed. Once this became known, fear of Hitler's revenge and eagerness to re-insure became the dominant motives in the minds of that large number of officers who had hitherto sat on the fence and waited to see if the putsch was successful before committing themselves.

In accordance with the plan, General Fellgiebel, the Chief Signals Officer of Hitler's headquarters, had succeeded in interrupting communications with the outside world for a considerable time after the bomb had exploded.[1] But this isolation could not be maintained and, once Hitler had realized that an attempt was being made at a *coup d'état*, he ordered immediate counter-measures.

The broadcast from Berlin in the early evening had already warned the wary. Soon after 8 o'clock Keitel sent out a message by teleprinter to all commands countermanding the instructions issued from the Bendlerstrasse, and directing all commanding officers to ignore orders not counter-signed by himself or by Himmler, whom Hitler had appointed Commander-in-Chief of the Home Army and placed in charge of the security of the Reich. An hour later the radio put out an announcement that Hitler would broadcast to the German people before midnight.

The plan to capture Berlin had totally miscarried and the situation of the little group of conspirators was now hopeless. In the course of the evening a group of officers loyal to Hitler, who had been placed under arrest in the Bendlerstrasse earlier in the day, broke out of custody, released General Fromm (whose office as Commander-in-Chief of the Home Army had been taken over by Höppner) and disarmed the conspirators. Fromm's own

1. I accept the argument of Mr Shirer (*The Rise and Fall of the Third Reich*, p. 1052, n. 2) that Fellgiebel could hardly have been expected to destroy the communications centre at headquarters and that my earlier version of these events was unkindly critical of General Fellgiebel. I also accept his view (p. 1050, n. 1) that the decision to hold the conference in the Lagebaracke was nothing exceptional and that Hitler's life was not saved by a sudden decision to change from the bunker.

behaviour had been equivocal and he was now only too anxious to display his zealous devotion by getting rid of those who might incriminate him. When troops arrived to arrest the conspirators, Fromm ordered Stauffenberg, Olbricht, and two other officers to be shot in the courtyard, where the executions were carried out by the light from the headlamps of an armoured car. Beck was allowed the choice of suicide. Fromm was only prevented from executing the rest by the arrival of Kaltenbrunner, Himmler's chief lieutenant, who was far more interested in discovering what could be learned from the survivors than in shooting them out of hand, now that the putsch had failed. Himmler, reaching Berlin from East Prussia in the course of the evening, set up his head-quarters at Goebbels's house, and the first examinations were carried out that night. The man-hunt had begun.

In one place only were the conspirators successful – in Paris. There they had been able to count on a number of staunch supporters, headed by General Heinrich von Stülpnagel, the Military Governor of France. As soon as he received the code word from Berlin Stülpnagel carried out the orders to arrest the 1,200 S.S. and S.D. men in Paris, and the Army was rapidly in complete command of the situation.[1] But here, too, the conspirators were dogged by the same ill-luck that had pursued them throughout the day.

In the early months of 1944, Field-Marshal Rommel, then recently appointed to a command in the west, had been brought into contact with the group around Beck and Goerdeler, by Karl Stroelin, the Oberbürgermeister of Stuttgart. Rommel was a man of action, not much given to reflection, but he needed little convincing at this stage of the war that, if Germany was to be saved, Hitler must be got rid of. Rommel was opposed to an assassination of Hitler on the grounds that they must avoid making a martyr of him. He proposed instead that Hitler should be seized and tried before a German court. He accepted the leadership of Beck and Goerdeler, however; he was willing to take over command of the Army or Armed Forces – his popularity would have been a considerable asset – and he proposed to initiate armistice negotiations with General Eisenhower on his own authority, on the basis of a German withdrawal from the occupied territories in the west in return for the suspension of the Allied air-raids on Germany. In the east the fighting was to be continued, with the

1. See Wilhelm von Schramm: *Der 20 Juli in Paris* (Bad Wörishofen, 1953; English translation, *Conspiracy among Generals*).

German forces defending a line running from Memel to the mouth of the Danube.

Hitler's handling of the invasion only stiffened Rommel's attitude. On 15 July, after the two meetings with the Führer in June and the removal of Rundstedt, Rommel sent him an urgent memorandum in which, after outlining the grave situation in the west, he forecast an Allied break-through in two to three weeks. 'The consequences will be immeasurable. The troops are fighting heroically everywhere, but the unequal struggle is nearing its end. I must beg you to draw the conclusions without delay. I feel it my duty as Commander-in-Chief of the Army Group to state this clearly.'[1]

After sending the memorandum by teleprinter, Rommel told his Chief of Staff, General Speidel, who was fully involved in the conspiracy, that, if Hitler refused this last chance, he was resolved to act. On 17 July, however, while returning from the front, Rommel's car was attacked by British fighters and the Field-Marshal severely injured. Thus, on 20 July, Rommel was lying unconscious in hospital, and the command of Army Group B, as well as the command-in-chief in the west, was in the hands of Field-Marshal von Kluge, a horse of another colour.

Kluge knew just as well as his predecessor, Rundstedt, what was being planned; he had been approached by the conspirators as long ago as 1942, while commanding in the east, and he had endorsed the view expressed in Rommel's memorandum to Hitler. But when the attempt on Hitler's life failed, he refused to consider taking independent action in the west. Without the support of the commander in the field, Stülpnagel could do nothing: he had created an opportunity which there was no one to exploit. So, by dawn on the 21st, the putsch had collapsed in Paris as well as in Berlin, and Stülpnagel was summoned home to report. Now it was Hitler's turn to act, and his revenge was unsparing.

VII

Half an hour after midnight on the night of 20–21 July all German radio stations relayed the shaken but still recognizable voice of the Führer speaking from East Prussia.

If I speak to you today [he began] it is first in order that you should hear my voice and should know that I am unhurt and well, and secondly that you should know of a crime unparalleled in German history. A very

1. Speidel: op. cit., pp. 126–7.

small clique of ambitious, irresponsible, and at the same time senseless and stupid officers had formed a plot to eliminate me and the High Command of the Armed Forces.

The bomb placed by Colonel Graf von Stauffenberg exploded two metres to my right. One of those with me has died; other colleagues very dear to me were severely injured. I myself sustained only some very minor scratches, bruises, and burns. I regard this as a confirmation of the task imposed upon me by Providence. . . .

The circle of these conspirators is very small and has nothing in common with the spirit of the German Wehrmacht and, above all, none with the German people. I therefore give orders now that no military authority, no commander and no private soldier is to obey any orders emanating from this group of usurpers. I also order that it is everyone's duty to arrest, or, if they resist, to shoot at sight, anyone issuing or handling such orders.

I am convinced that with the uncovering of this tiny clique of traitors and saboteurs there has at long last been created in the rear that atmosphere which the fighting front needs. . . .

This time we shall get even with them in the way to which we National Socialists are accustomed.[1]

Hitler's threats were rarely idle, and this time he was moved by a passion of personal vindictiveness. No complete figure can be given for the number of those executed after 20 July: a total of 4,980 has been accepted as the best estimate that can be made. Many thousands of others were sent to concentration camps. The investigations and executions of the Gestapo and S.D. went on without interruption until the last days of the war, and the sittings of the People's Court under the notorious Nazi judge, Roland Freisler, continued for months. The first trial, held on 7 August, resulted in the immediate condemnation of Field-Marshal von Witzleben, Generals Höppner, Hase, and Stieff, together with four other officers, and they were put to death with great cruelty, by slow hanging with a noose of piano wire from a meat-hook, on 8 August. The executions as well as the trial were filmed from beginning to end for Hitler to see the same evening in the Reich Chancellery.[2]

With a handful of exceptions, saved largely by luck, all those who were at all active in the plot, on the civilian as well as the military side, were caught and hanged. This was to be expected, but Hitler and Himmler used the opportunity to imprison or kill

1. B.B.C. Monitoring Report.
2. The film of the executions appears to have been destroyed, but the film of the trial was captured intact and gives a vivid impression of the indignities inflicted on the defendants and of their courage.

many who had only the flimsiest connexion, or none at all, with the conspiracy, but who were suspected of a lack of enthusiasm for the régime. In some cases whole families, such as those of Goerdeler, Stauffenberg, and Hassell, were arrested. Among others sent to concentration camps were Dr Schacht and General Halder, both of whom had been living in retirement. Few who had ever shown a trace of independence of mind could feel safe.

By the autumn sufficient evidence had been collected to rouse Hitler's suspicions of Rommel. After a slow recovery from his injuries, in October, Rommel received a brief message from the Führer offering him the choice between suicide and trial before the People's Court. For the sake of his family, Rommel chose the former. The cause of his death was announced as heart failure, due to the effects of his accident, and the Führer accorded him a State funeral. Hitler was not prepared to admit that the most popular general of the war had turned against him: 'His heart,' declared the funeral oration, which Rundstedt was called upon to read, 'belonged to the Führer.'[1]

It was against the Officer Corps that Hitler's resentment was most sharply directed. To the defeatism, cowardice, and conservatism which – as he convinced himself – had balked him of victory, the generals had now added the crime of treason. Had Hitler been free to give full rein to his anger, he would have made a clean sweep and imprisoned or shot every general within sight. But in the middle of a grave military crisis this was more than he could afford to do. However reluctant he was to concede it, he still needed the Officer Corps to win the war for him. Nor would his own prestige allow him to admit that the Army no longer had complete faith in his leadership. In public, therefore, elaborate measures were taken to conceal the split between the Army and its commander-in-chief. In his broadcast of 20–21 July Hitler insisted that only a small clique of officers was involved, and this was repeated by Goebbels in the report to the nation which he broadcast a few days later. Goebbels described the plot as a stab in the back aimed at the fighting front and crushed by the Army itself.

The Order of the Day issued by the new Chief of Staff of the Army, General Guderian, on 23 July, followed the same line. Pledging the loyalty of the Officer Corps and Army to the Fuehrer, Guderian spoke of 'a few officers, some of them on the retired list, who had lost courage, and out of cowardice and weakness

1. Speidel: op. cit., 159.

preferred the road of disgrace to the only road open to an honest soldier, the road of duty and honour'. The next day Bormann issued a directive to the Party ordering that there should be no general incrimination of the Army and that the reliability of the Armed Forces during the attempt should be stressed. To preserve the formal 'honour' of the German Army, a Court of Honour was set up which expelled the guilty officers from the Army and handed them over, as civilians, to the People's Court.

But in fact the humiliation of the Army was complete. The generals who in 1934 had insisted on the elimination of Röhm and the S.A. leadership had now to accept the Waffen S.S. as equal partners with the Army, Navy, and Air Force, with Himmler himself as Commander-in-Chief of the Home Army and soon as the active commander in the field of an Army Group. On 24 July the Nazi salute was made compulsory 'as a sign of the Army's unshakable allegiance to the Führer and of the closest unity between Army and Party'.[1] On the 29th General Guderian issued a further order which insisted that henceforth every General Staff Officer must actively cooperate in the indoctrination of the Army with National Socialist beliefs and publicly announce that he accepted this view of his duties.[2] So far as is known not a single officer expressed his disagreement with Guderian's order. To make quite sure National Socialist Political Officers were now appointed to all military headquarters in imitation of a Russian practice much admired by Hitler, but abandoned by the Soviet Government during the war

The effects of 20 July on Hitler's relations with the Army were not limited to the final destruction of the once powerful position of independence enjoyed by the Army in Germany. Despite the measures taken to ensure loyalty, and despite the purge of the Officer Corps which followed the attempt, Hitler's distrust of the Army was henceforward unconcealed. This was bound to affect the desperate effort which had now to be made to hold the enemy outside the German frontiers. There was little enough hope of doing that in any case; there was less still when the Commander-in-Chief's attitude towards his own commanders was governed by invincible suspicion and vindictive spite.

1. N.D. 2,878-PS, quoting *Das Archiv*.
2. For the text, see J. W. Wheeler-Bennett: *The Nemesis of Power*. pp. 679–80. It is interesting to note that General Guderian, who has much to say in his memoirs about the character of the German General Staff, neither quotes nor refers to this document.

CHAPTER FOURTEEN

THE EMPEROR WITHOUT HIS CLOTHES

I

BY the end of July 1944 the Russian armies had cut off the German Army Group North by a thrust to the Baltic; had destroyed Army Group Centre and reached the Vistula; and had driven Army Group South (Ukraine) back into Rumania. Great efforts by Model, who was sent to command on the Centre Front in Poland, and by Guderian, the new Army Chief of Staff, succeeded in checking the Russian advance. But the Russians were only temporarily halted after advancing close on four hundred miles since the last week in June, and on the southern front, in Rumania, there was no pause at all.

Hitler was forced to commit all his reserves in order to hold any line in the east, but he stubbornly refused to withdraw his troops from the Baltic States, where Schörner's Army Group North, numbering some fifty divisions, was left to fight a local war which had no bearing on the main battle for the approaches to Germany. Hitler's reasons for this refusal, in which he persisted, were the possible effect of such a withdrawal on Sweden (with the all-important iron-ore supplies), and the loss of the Baltic training grounds for the new U-boats on which he set great store. He argued that Schörner was engaging a large number of Russian divisions which would otherwise be used on other and more vital fronts. The Russians, however, were not short of manpower, while the Germans were. Guderian protested strongly against the decision, but in vain. In fact, after the big German defeats of the summer in the east, Hitler was still trying to hold with much-reduced forces a longer line than that through which the Russians had already broken. The man who had once proclaimed mobility as the key to success now rejected any suggestion of mobility in defence in favour of the utmost rigidity.

The Russian break-through in Poland was followed at the end of July by an American break-through in France. On 28 July the Americans captured Coutances, and two days later Avranches; by the 31st they were into Brittany. The German left flank collapsed, and the war of movement in the west began. Patton's Third Army striking eastwards for Le Mans, and the threat of encirclement at Falaise, were the plainest possible indication that

the time had come for an immediate German withdrawal behind
the Seine. Hitler, remote from the battle in his East Prussian
headquarters, and ignorant of the massive superiority of the Allied
forces, especially in the air, refused to consider such a course.
Kluge was ordered to counter-attack at once and close the
American corridor through Avranches and Mortain.

Hitler's distrust of his generals, to which we have referred, was
amply illustrated on this occasion.

The plan came to us [General Blumentritt, Kluge's Chief of Staff, says]
in the most minute detail. It set out the specific divisions that were to be
used. . . . The sector in which the attack was to take place was specifically identified and the very roads and villages through which the forces
were to advance were all included. All this planning had been done in
Berlin from large-scale maps and the advice of the generals in France
was not asked for, nor was it encouraged.[1]

The S.S. generals at the front were the loudest in their protests
against the folly of gambling the few remaining armoured
divisions on an attack which, if it failed (as seemed almost
certain), would leave the German Army in the west fatally weakened. Kluge's only reply was that these were Hitler's orders and
that the Führer would tolerate no argument.

When the operation failed Hitler peremptorily ordered the
attack to be renewed. To General Warlimont, who visited the
front and returned to report, Hitler remarked: 'Success only
failed to come because Kluge did not want to be successful.'[2] On
15 August, when Kluge, up at the front, was out of touch with his
headquarters for twelve hours, Hitler leaped to the conclusion
that the Field-Marshal was trying to negotiate a surrender. 'The
15th of August,' he said subsequently, 'was the worst day of my
life.'[3] The next day he summoned Model from the Eastern Front
and ordered him to take over Kluge's command at once. On his
way back to Germany Kluge committed suicide: he closed a long
letter of self-defence to Hitler with the advice to end the war.

Model, who was now called on to perform the same task of
rescuing the German Army in France as he had already carried
out in Poland, was one of the few generals whom Hitler trusted
and whom he allowed to argue with him. A rough, aggressive
character, who had nothing in common with the stiff caste conventions of the German military tradition, Model had identified
his fortunes with those of Hitler's régime, and was promoted to
the rank of Field-Marshal at the age of fifty-four. But neither

1. Shulman: pp. 145–6.   2. Liddell Hart: p. 421.   3. Gilbert: p. 102.

Model nor anyone else could prevent the collapse of the German front in France.

While Patton struck out boldly for the east, and Paris was liberated, the German Army in the west was streaming back across the Seine in headlong retreat, harried by the Allied forces in pursuit and subjected to incessant attack from the air. In the circumstances Model did well to preserve anything from the rout. On 29 August, as the last of his men were crossing the Seine, he reported to Hitler that the average strength of the panzer and panzer-grenadier divisions which had fought in Normandy was five to ten tanks each, and that out of the sixteen infantry divisions which he had got back over the Seine he could raise sufficient men to form four, but was unable to equip them with more than small arms. Another seven infantry divisions had been totally destroyed, while of some two thousand three hundred German tanks and assault guns committed in Normandy, according to Blumentritt only a hundred to a hundred and twenty were brought back across the Seine. These were the fruits of Hitler's direction of the battle from a headquarters a thousand miles away and in defiance of the advice of his commanders in the field.

France was lost. It was now a question of whether the line of the German frontier and the Rhine could be held. In the first few days of September Patton's Third Army reached the Moselle, and the British Second Army, covering two hundred and fifty miles with its armour in four days, liberated Brussels, Louvain, and Antwerp. On the evening of 11 September an American patrol crossed the German frontier: five years after the Polish campaign, the war had reached German soil.

In a conference with three of his generals on the afternoon of 31 August Hitler made it clear that, whatever happened and whatever the cost to Germany, he was determined to maintain the struggle.

The time hasn't come [he declared] for a political decision. . . . It is childish and naïve to expect that at a moment of grave military defeats the moment for favourable political dealings has come. Such moments come when you are having successes. . . . But the time will come when the tension between the Allies will become so great that the break will occur. All the coalitions have disintegrated in history sooner or later. The only thing is to wait for the right moment, no matter how hard it is. Since the year 1941 it has been my task not to lose my nerve, under any circumstances; instead, whenever there is a collapse, my task has been to find a way out and a remedy, in order to restore the situation. I really think one can't imagine a worse crisis than the one we had in the east this year. When Field-Marshal Model came, the Army Group Centre was nothing but a hole.

I think it's pretty obvious [Hitler continued] that this war is no pleasure for me. For five years I have been separated from the world. I haven't been to the theatre, I haven't heard a concert, and I haven't seen a film. I live only for the purpose of leading this fight, because I know if there is not an iron will behind it this battle cannot be won. I accuse the General Staff of weakening combat officers who join its ranks, instead of exuding this iron will, and of spreading pessimism when General Staff officers go to the front. . . .

If necessary we'll fight on the Rhine. It doesn't make any difference. Under all circumstances we will continue this battle until, as Frederick the Great said, one of our damned enemies gets too tired to fight any more. We'll fight until we get a peace which secures the life of the German nation for the next fifty or hundred years and which, above all, does not besmirch our honour a second time, as happened in 1918. . . . Things could have turned out differently. If my life had been ended (i.e. on 20 July) I think I can say that for me personally it would only have been a release from worry, sleepless nights, and great nervous suffering. It is only a fraction of a second, and then one is freed from everything, and has one's quiet and eternal peace. Just the same, I am grateful to Destiny for letting me live, because I believe . . .[1]

In this mood, strangely compounded of inflexible determination and self-pity, Hitler called on the German people for one more effort, and for the last time the German people responded. They no longer saw, or even heard, the man whose orders they obeyed, but the image of the Führer was still strong enough to carry conviction, and conviction was powerfully reinforced by fear.

It was to fear that Goebbels now openly appealed: the régime and the German people were indissolubly linked, they must sink or swim together. The news of the Morgenthau Plan, which provided for the dismemberment of Germany, the destruction of her industrial resources, and her conversion into an agricultural and pastoral country, appeared to offer proof that Goebbels was right when he declared that the Allies intended the extermination of a considerable proportion of the German people and the enslavement of the rest. The grim picture which Goebbels had been drawing for months of the German people's fate under a Russian occupation was now supplemented by the prospect of an equally terrible revenge at the hands of the Western Allies. 'The Jew Morgenthau', Berlin Radio proclaimed, 'sings the same tune as the Jews in the Kremlin.' With the Red Army on the threshold of

1. The transcript is incomplete; Gilbert: op. cit., pp. 105–6.

East Prussia, and the British and Americans on the edge of the Rhineland, the argument had an urgency it had never possessed before. To add point to it, Himmler announced on 10 September that the families of those deserting to the enemy would be summarily shot.

The Allies' plan was to burst into Germany before the winter came, and to strike at the basis of her war economy in the Ruhr and Rhineland. Bad luck, bad weather, difficulties of supply, and differences of opinion within the Allied High Command, combined to defeat their hopes. To these must be added the unexpected recovery of the German Army. At the end of August this had been a broken force on the run; by the end of September it had rallied along the line of the German frontier and succeeded in forming a continuous front again west of the Rhine, a front which the Allies pushed back but failed to break throughout the winter. Behind it the Siegfried Line was hastily restored and manned. The British attempt to breach the river line at Arnhem and turn the German defences from the north was defeated, while the stubborn rearguard action of the German Fifteenth Army holding the Scheldt Estuary denied the British and Americans the use of the vital port of Antwerp until the end of November, nearly three months after its capture. Field-Marshal von Rundstedt, whom Hitler had recalled to be Commander-in-Chief in the west at the beginning of September, had few illusions about the future, yet the measures taken by him and by Model, as the Commander of Army Group B, won for Hitler the breathing space of the winter before the Allies could bring their full weight to bear in the battle for Western Germany.

Hitler used this respite to build up as hurriedly as possible new forces with which to fill the gaps left by the summer's fighting. In the west alone 1944 had cost him the loss of a million men. Immediately after the 20 July attempt he agreed to give Goebbels the sweeping powers he had asked for more than a year before,[1] and on 24 August Goebbels announced a total mobilization which went far further than any previous measures. With this last reserve of manpower Hitler hoped not only to re-form the divisions which had been broken up on both the Western and Eastern Fronts, but to create twenty to twenty-five new Volksgrenadier divisions, eight to ten thousand men strong, under

1. The Propaganda Minister's own comment was: 'It takes a bomb under his backside to make Hitler see reason.'

Himmler's direction. This was partly bluff, for units which had been reduced to the fighting value of no more than a battalion were retained as divisions in the German Order of Battle. Rather than use the men he had available to rebuild these to their full strength, or break them up completely, Hitler preferred to set up new divisions and retain the old formations in being at a half or a quarter of their strength. In this way he could keep up the illusion that he was still able to increase his forces to meet the crisis. As a final measure Hitler proclaimed a *levée-en-masse*. A proclamation of 18 October 1944 called up every able-bodied man between the ages of sixteen and sixty to form a Volkssturm, a German version of the British Home Guard, placed under the orders of Himmler and organized by Bormann and the Party.

At the beginning of September 1944 the total paper strength of the German Armed Forces was still over ten million men, of whom seven and a half million were in the Army and Waffen S.S. It was Hitler's own decision that kept these very considerable forces scattered over half the Continent, holding hopeless positions in the Baltic States, the Balkans, and Scandinavia, instead of concentrating for the defence of the Reich itself. He refused to admit how desperate the situation had become, or to abandon hope of reversing the situation by a dramatic stroke. Thus Western Holland must be held to allow the V2s to be directed against London; Hungary and Croatia for the bauxite supplies necessary for the jet aircraft; the Baltic coast with its training-grounds; and the naval bases in Norway for the new U-boats on which he built so much.

Thanks to Speer, German armaments production had not yet been crippled by the bombing. The German aircraft factories, which in January 1944 produced 1,248 fighter-planes, in September achieved the record figure of 3,031. Figures for other arms showed the same ability to maintain, and in some cases even to increase, the rate of production over that for the first half of 1944. The big exception was the output of tanks, but even this was off-set by a sharp rise in the production of assault guns.

The greatest material difficulty was the desperate shortage of oil and petrol, due to the systematic Allied bombing of the synthetic oil plants, refineries, and communications. By September German stocks of petrol, which had been no more than one million tons in April, had been cut to 327,000 tons, and at the end of September the Luftwaffe had only five weeks' supply of fuel left. Moreover, Speer maintained arms production only by drawing heavily on supplies of raw materials and components which could scarcely be replaced, and by efforts which could neither be maintained nor repeated. Germany made a remarkable recovery in the last three months of 1944, but it was the last reserves of men, materials, and morale on which Hitler was now drawing; if he squandered these there was nothing left.

II

Everything turned upon the use which Hitler proposed to make of the forces which he had scraped together. The momentary calm encouraged his illusions. In the west the Allied successes of the summer dwindled into stalemate west of the Rhine. In Italy Kesselring halted Alexander's armies south of the Po. In Poland the Vistula still stood between the Russians and the old German frontier. A lull settled over the greater part of the front north of the Carpathians during the later months of 1944, and a Russian attempt in October to break into East Prussia at the northern end was repulsed. But the resumption of the Allied attacks on all fronts was only a question of time, and the real weakness of the German position was shown by the success of the Red Army's autumn offensive in the Balkans.

For the Russians, having forced Hitler to throw in all his reserves on the Centre Front in the summer, now reaped their advantage in the south. On 20 August a new offensive opened with the invasion of Rumania and continued without remission to the end of the year. In the first few days Rumania capitulated, and the Russians were able to occupy the oilfields without opposition. On 8 September the Red Army began the occupation of Bulgaria, and the loss of Germany's two Balkan satellites was accompanied by the withdrawal of Finland from the war. The position which Hitler had established in the Balkans in 1941 collapsed like a pack of cards. In October the British freed Athens, and the Russians reached Belgrade, where they joined hands with Tito's partisan forces. By the beginning of November the Germans were fighting desperately to hold the line of the Danube in Hungary; by the beginning of December they were besieged in Budapest, less than a hundred and fifty miles from Vienna.

Hitler did not ignore the danger from the south-east. Part of the meagre reserve in hand for the defence of the Eastern Front was sent south of the Carpathians, and the Germans succeeded in prolonging the battle for the Hungarian capital into February

1945, only giving ground street by street. But Hitler had already made up his mind in the autumn that the new divisions and those which were being reformed were to go to the west, not to the Eastern Front. This decision was put into effect in the last three months of 1944, when eighteen out of twenty-three new infantry (Volksgrenadier) divisions were sent to the Rhine. At the same time the panzer and panzer-grenadier divisions already stationed in the west were re-equipped, and over two-thirds of the Luftwaffe's planes deployed in their support.

In deciding for the west against the east, Hitler was not thinking in terms of defence of the German frontiers; he thought solely of an offensive which would take the Allies by surprise, enable him to recapture the initiative and so gain time for the development of the new weapons and of the split between the members of the Grand Alliance upon which he counted to win the war. If the basis of this calculation was slender, it was natural for Hitler to think along these lines. For him at least the only choice lay between victory or death. A defensive campaign could defer a decision, but would not alter the situation. The one chance of doing that was to stake what was left on the gamble of attack. With this purpose in mind he saw a greater possibility of success in the west than in the east. Distances were shorter, less fuel would be needed, and strategic objectives of importance were more within the compass of the forces of which he disposed than in the open plains of the east, where the fighting was on a different scale. Nor did he believe the Americans and British were as tough opponents as the Russians. The British, he soon convinced himself, were at the end of their resources, while the Americans were liable to lose heart if events ceased to go favourably for them.

Accordingly, at the end of September, Hitler and Jodl set to work in great secrecy to plan a counter-offensive in the west for the end of November. The object of the attack was the recapture of the principal Allied supply port of Antwerp by a drive through the Ardennes and across the Meuse, which would have the effect of cutting Eisenhower's forces in two and trapping the British Army in the angle formed by the Meuse and the Rhine as they turn westwards towards the sea. Letting his imagination race ahead, Hitler was soon talking of a new break-through in the Ardennes comparable with that of 1940 and leading to a new Dunkirk from which this time the British Army would not be allowed to escape.

The idea was excellent. The last thing the Allied commanders expected was a German attack, and they were caught completely off their guard. The Ardennes sector was the weakest point in their front, held by no more than a handful of divisions, and the loss of Antwerp would have been a major blow at the supply lines of the Anglo-American Armies. But the idea bore no relation to the stage of the war which had been reached in the winter of 1944–5. The permanent disparity between the resources of Germany in 1944 and those of the three most powerful states in the world could not be redressed by a single blow with the forces which Hitler was able to concentrate in the west. Even if the Germans took Antwerp – a feat which every one of the German commanders in the field believed to be beyond their strength – they could not hold it. The utmost Hitler could hope to inflict on the Allied armies was a set-back, not a defeat, and in the process he ran the heavy risk of throwing away the last reserves with which the defences of the Reich could be strengthened.

The attempt of the men in command to argue with Hitler, and to persuade him to accept more limited objectives, proved as unsuccessful as all the other previous attempts.[1] To have admitted that the generals were right would have meant admitting that the war was lost. Hitler's confidence is well illustrated by his rebuke to the Chief of the Army General Staff, Guderian, when the latter ventured to argue that he was leaving the Eastern Front dangerously weak.

There's no need for you to try to teach me [Hitler shouted back]. I've been commanding the German Army in the field for five years, and during that time I've had more practical experience than any 'gentleman' of the General Staff could ever hope to have. I've studied Clausewitz and Moltke and read all the Schlieffen papers. I'm more in the picture than you are.[2]

By the beginning of December Hitler had collected twenty-eight divisions for the Ardennes attack and another six for the thrust into Alsace which was to follow. The main brunt of the offensive was to be carried by two panzer armies, the Sixth S.S. Panzer Army under Sepp Dietrich and the Fifth Panzer Army under Manteuffel, which between them disposed of some ten

1. Rundstedt's subsequent comment was: 'If we reached the Meuse we should have got down on our knees and thanked God – let alone try to reach Antwerp.' Shulman: op. cit., p. 228.
2. Guderian: op. cit., p. 378.

armoured divisions. The final plans, drawn up at Hitler's head-quarters, were sent to Rundstedt with every detail cut and dried down to the times of the artillery bombardment, and with the warning in Hitler's own handwriting: 'Not to be altered.' In order to keep even tighter control over the handling of the battle Hitler moved his headquarters from East Prussia to Bad Nauheim, behind the Western Front.

Four days before the attack was due to begin, on 12 December, Hitler summoned all the commanders to a conference. After being stripped of their weapons and brief-cases and bundled into a bus, they were led between a double row of S.S. troops into a deep bunker. When Hitler appeared with Keitel and Jodl, he was later described by Manteuffel as 'a stooped figure with a pale and puffy face, hunched in his chair, his hands trembling, his left arm subject to a violent twitching which he did his best to conceal.
. . . When he walked he dragged one leg behind him'.[1] He made a long, rambling speech which lasted for two hours, during which S.S. guards stood behind every chair and watched every move-ment that was made.

Much of what Hitler said was a justification of his career and of the war. He laid particular stress on the incongruity of the alliance with which Germany was faced.

Ultra-Capitalist states on the one hand; ultra-Marxist states on the other. On the one hand, a dying empire, Britain; on the other, a colony bent upon inheritance, the United States. . . . America tries to become England's heir; Russia tries to gain the Balkans, the narrow seas, Iran and the Persian Gulf; England tries to hold her possessions and to strengthen herself in the Mediterranean. . . . Even now these States are at loggerheads, and he who, like a spider sitting in the middle of his web, can watch developments, observes how these antagonisms grow stronger and stronger from hour to hour. If now we can deliver a few more heavy blows, then at any moment this artificially bolstered com-mon front may collapse with a gigantic clap of thunder. . . . Wars are finally decided by one side or the other recognizing that they cannot be won. We must allow no moment to pass without showing the enemy that, whatever he does, he can never reckon on a capitulation. Never! Never![2]

With this exhortation Hitler dismissed the soldiers, and at dawn on 16 December the attack was launched.

Hitler at least achieved the satisfaction of taking his opponents

1. Quoted in S. Friedin and W. Richardson (eds.): *The Fatal Decisions*, p. 266.
2. Führer Conferences, Fragment 28, 12 December 1944, p. 578.

by surprise, and in the first few days the German Army made considerable gains which the German radio and press puffed up into one of the greatest victories of the war. Yet never for a moment were the Germans within sight of reaching Hitler's objective of Antwerp. On the contrary, as soon as the Allies had recovered their balance the Germans found themselves thrown back on the defensive, fighting hard to hold the gains they had made. By Christmas it was evident that, if they wanted to avoid heavy losses, they would be well advised to break off the battle and withdraw.

Hitler furiously rejected any such suggestions. Twice Guderian, who was responsible for the defence of the Eastern Front, visited Hitler's headquarters and tried to persuade him to transfer troops to the east, where there were ominous signs of Russian preparations for a new offensive. Hitler impatiently rejected Guderian's reports. The Russians, he declared, were bluffing. 'It's the greatest imposture since Genghis Khan. Who's responsible for producing all this rubbish?'[1] After reinforcements had been sent to Budapest, the reserves for a front of seven hundred and fifty miles in the east totalled no more than twelve and a half divisions. Yet Hitler refused to write off the Ardennes offensive. Not only was Model ordered to make another attempt to reach the Meuse, but a new attack was to be launched into northern Alsace.

As a preliminary to this Hitler again assembled the commanders concerned on 28 December. He depicted the results of the fighting in the Ardennes in the most exaggerated terms – 'a transformation of the entire situation such as no one would have believed possible a fortnight ago'. He would not listen to the argument that they were not yet ready.

Gentlemen, I have been in this business for eleven years and during those eleven years I have never heard anybody report that everything was completely ready. Our situation is not different from that of the Russians in 1941 and 1942 when, despite their most unfavourable situation, they manoeuvred us slowly back by single offensive blows along the extended front on which we had passed over to the defensive. . . .

The question is . . . whether Germany has the will to remain in existence or whether it will be destroyed. . . . The loss of this war will destroy the German people. . . .

For me the situation is nothing new. I have been in very much worse situations. I mention this only because I want you to understand why I pursue my aim with such fanaticism and why nothing can wear me down.

1. Guderian: op. cit., p. 383.

If we succeed [he added], we shall actually have knocked away one half of the enemy's Western Front. Then we shall see what happens. I do not believe that in the long run he will be able to resist forty-five German divisions which will then be ready. We shall yet master fate.[1]

Once again the German attack fell short of Hitler's objective – this time Strasbourg – while Model's second attempt to break through the Ardennes was no more successful than the first. On 8 January Hitler reluctantly agreed to the withdrawal of the German armour on the Ardennes front. It was a tacit admission that he had failed. He continued to claim that he had inflicted a heavy defeat on the enemy, but the figures do not bear him out. The First and Third U.S. Armies fighting in the Ardennes lost 8,400 killed, with 69,000 wounded and missing. The total German casualties were around 120,000, in addition to the loss of 600 tanks and assault guns and over 1,600 planes. Most important of all, while the Americans easily made good their losses, Hitler's were irreplaceable. The consequences of his unsuccessful gamble in the west, when added to the policy of 'no withdrawal' on every front, were not long in appearing.

While Hitler still disposed of 260 divisions on paper (twice as many as in May 1940), 10 were pinned down in Yugoslavia and 17 in Scandinavia; 30 were cut off in the Baltic States; 76 engaged in the west and 24 in Italy. A further 28 divisions were fighting to hold Budapest and the remnant of German-occupied Hungary. Only 75 divisions were left to guard against the most dangerous threat of all, the possibility of a Red Army thrust across the northern plains directed at the industrial districts of Silesia, Saxony, and Berlin itself. The divisions and equipment so laboriously scraped together in the closing months of 1944 had been expended without strengthening the defences in the east, and there were no more reserves to replace them. When Guderian tried to point out the dangers to Hitler at a conference on 9 January he was met with an hysterical outburst of rage. 'He had,' says Guderian, 'a special picture of the world, and every fact had to be fitted into that fancied picture. As he believed, so the world must be: but, in fact, it was a picture of another world.'[2]

Reality, however, was to prove stronger than fantasy. Hitler still insisted that priority must be given to the west and told Guderian he must make do with what he had in the east. But, on

1. Gilbert: op. cit., pp. 157–74.
2. Guderian's interrogation by the Seventh U.S. Army, quoted by Chester Wilmot: *The Struggle for Europe*, p. 622.

12 January, the Red Army opened its offensive in Poland and the German defences went down like matchwood before the on-slaught of a hundred and eighty Russian divisions attacking all along the line from the Baltic to the Carpathians. By the end of the month Marshal Zhukov was within less than a hundred miles of the German capital, and the Berlin Home Guard (Volkssturm) was being sent to hold the line of the Oder.

III

Hitler had now left his East Prussian headquarters for good. He had stayed there for another four months after the bomb attempt, and only in November was he persuaded to go to Berlin, where he remained from 20 November to 10 December, before moving to Adlershorst ('Eagle's Nest'), his field headquarters in the west.

During the late summer and autumn his health became worse and for considerable periods he was confined to his bed. The most serious effect of the bomb explosion had been the damage to his ears: the tympanic membranes on both sides were broken and he suffered from irritation in the labyrinths of the ears. After a period of rest in bed these healed. But the effects of his unhealthy life, shut up in his bunker without exercise, fresh air or relaxation – not to speak of the effects of Morell's drugs – could only be cured if he was prepared to change his way of living entirely and begin by taking a holiday. His doctors urged him to go to the Ober-salzberg, but he refused. So long as he remained in East Prussia, he declared, it would be held, but if he left it would fall to the Russians.

In the middle of September, however, he broke down com-pletely and had to return to bed. Apart from continual headaches and an aggravation of his stomach cramps, he was troubled by his throat. Professor von Eicken, who had removed the polyp on his vocal cords in 1935, operated to remove another in October: he had also to treat him for infection of the maxillary sinus. For a time Hitler's voice was scarcely recognizable, so weak had it become.[1] His secretary, who visited him while he was laid up in September, came away with the impression that he had reached the limit of his strength. Lying on a camp-bed between the naked concrete walls of the bunker, he appeared to have lost all desire to go on living.

1. These medical facts were collected by H. R. Trevor-Roper during his investigation in 1945 and are given in his book, pp. 72–4.

Yet Hitler never relaxed his control of operations, and by one more effort of will he recovered sufficiently to get up and resume work. The attempt of the doctors who were called in to destroy Hitler's faith in Morell failed completely and recoiled on their own heads. Brandt, who had been his personal surgeon for twelve years, was abruptly dismissed from all his offices. Not content with this, Hitler waited for an opportunity to have him imprisoned and condemned to death a few months later. Thereafter Morell's position remained unchallenged to the end of Hitler's life, while he continued to provide the drugs and injections on which the Führer was now wholly dependent.

Although Hitler was able to leave his bed and move about, all those who saw him in the last six months of his life agree in their description of him as an old man, with an ashen complexion, shuffling gait, shaking hands and leg. Guderian, who was frequently in his company, writes:

It was no longer simply his left hand, but the whole left side of his body that trembled. . . . He walked awkwardly, stooped more than ever, and his gestures were both jerky and slow. He had to have a chair pushed beneath him when he wished to sit down.[1]

This was his state of health when he returned from the west in the middle of January, shortly after the beginning of the Russian offensive, and moved into the Reich Chancellery.

The vast pile which Hitler had built to overawe his tributaries was now surrounded by the ruins of a bombed city. Jagged holes had appeared in the Chancellery's walls; the windows were boarded up; the rich furnishings removed – except from Hitler's own quarters. For, by some odd chance, the wing in which Hitler had his rooms was still undamaged at the beginning of 1945. The windows in the large room used for the daily conference retained their glass and their grey curtains; the thick carpet and deep leather chairs were undamaged, the telephones in the ante-room still worked. During the frequent air-raids Hitler moved to the massive concrete shelter built in the Chancellery garden. He took no risks, and on one occasion at least, in February, when the attack was concentrated on the area of the Reich Chancellery, showed undisguised anxiety at the possibility of being trapped underground.

Hitler rarely moved out of the Chancellery building, and in the last month lived almost entirely in the deep shelter. One of the

1. Guderian: op. cit., p. 443.

few visits he paid was in January, shortly after his return to Berlin, when he drove out to Goebbels's home and took tea with his wife and family. It was the first visit he had paid them for five years, an indication of Goebbels's return to favour in the latter part of the war. Hitler was accompanied by a bodyguard of six S.S. officers, his adjutant and his servant, the last carrying a brief-case in which were contained the Führer's own vacuum-flask and a bag of cakes. They spent the afternoon reviving memories of 1932 and discussing the plans for rebuilding Berlin. When Hitler left, Frau Goebbels expressed her satisfaction with the remark: 'He wouldn't have gone to the Görings.'[1]

Two other descriptions of Hitler at this time have been given by the young orderly officer to General Guderian and by one of Hitler's secretaries.

Captain Gerhard Boldt had never met Hitler before February 1945, when Guderian took him to an afternoon conference in the Reich Chancellery. The military guard, which was still stationed outside the entrance, presented arms as the Chief of Staff drove up; inside, however, they were subjected to a thorough examination by the S.S. guards and obliged to hand over their revolvers and cases. In the ante-room they found sandwiches and drinks laid out on the sideboard, though the air of hospitality was again tempered by the presence of more S.S. officers armed with tommy-guns in front of the door leading to Hitler's study.

When the group summoned for the conference was finally allowed to enter, Hitler met them in the centre of the room. Boldt was the last to be introduced. He noticed that Hitler's handshake was weak and soft.

His head was slightly wobbling. His left arm hung slackly and his hand trembled a good deal. There was an indescribable flickering glow in his eyes, creating a fearsome and wholly unnatural effect. His face and the parts around his eyes gave the impression of total exhaustion. All his movements were those of a senile man.[2]

Hitler sat down behind his desk, on which a pile of maps had been laid, and the conference began.

The first to make his report was General Jodl, who described the situation on the fronts for which the O.K.W. was responsible. Boldt was impressed by the practised way in which he slipped in

1. Semmler: op. cit., pp. 174–5.
2. Gerhard Boldt: *Die letzten Tage*; English translation, *In the Shelter with Hitler* (London, 1948), c. 1.

brief references to the withdrawal of divisions under cover of colourful accounts of individual actions.

At the end of the conference, on Guderian's insistence, Admiral Dönitz raised the question of evacuating by sea the half-million men cut off in the Baltic States. Hitler rose from his desk and took a few paces up and down the room before shouting: 'I have said once before, a withdrawal of these forces is out of the question. I cannot give up the material and I have to take Sweden into consideration.' The most he would concede was the evacuation of a single division.

With that Hitler dismissed his officers, keeping only Bormann in attendance. The rest trooped out into the ante-room, and while the adjutants began to telephone instructions orderlies brought in drinks and cigars for the principals. The conference had lasted nearly three hours and it was dark when Boldt drove back with the Chief of Staff through the silent and deserted streets of the capital to the Army's H.Q. at Zossen. The day's work, however, was not over. Later they were summoned to a further conference in the Chancellery shelter at 1 a.m.

This time they met in a small underground room, less than twenty feet square. A single bench, a table, and a desk-chair were the only furniture. Guderian took the opportunity to make a strong plea for the withdrawal of troops from all fronts to form a concentration of forces in Pomerania and so relieve the pressure from the east. Hitler allowed him to speak without interruption; only his hands clenched nervously together showed his feelings. When Guderian finished a long silence followed, punctuated by the noise of exploding time-bombs. Then Hitler slowly stood up, staring into space, and took a few shuffling steps forward. Without a word he signalled to them to go; once again only Bormann remained behind.

This was Hitler at his clumsiest: unable to answer Guderian, he fell back on the oldest of his tricks – or was he sincere in seeing himself as the genius surrounded by pygmies who failed to rise to the level of his vision? Both explanations are necessary: neither the element of calculation nor the element of conviction can be left out.

The second picture is from the middle of March. His secretary, who was lunching alone with him, was kept waiting until nearly three o'clock before he came. Hitler was in an angry mood, kissed her hand in perfunctory fashion, and at once began to complain that he could trust no one. Now his personal adjutant, Albrecht

Bormann (the brother of Martin Bormann), had failed to carry out his express orders about strengthening the shelter.

I am lied to on all sides [he continued], I can rely on no one, they all betray me, the whole business makes me sick. If I had not got my faithful Morell I should be absolutely knocked out – and those idiot doctors wanted to get rid of him. What would become of me without Morell was a question they didn't ask. If anything happens to me Germany will be left without a leader. I have no successor. The first, Hess, is mad; the second, Göring, has lost the sympathy of the people; and the third, Himmler, would be rejected by the Party.

In any case, he added, Himmler was unacceptable because of his lack of artistic feeling. The question of a successor preoccupied him throughout the rest of the meal. After telling his secretary not to talk rubbish, he apologized for bringing political problems to the table. When he finished he stood for a few minutes lost in thought and then turned to go with the parting words: 'Rack your brains again and tell me who my successor is to be. This is the question that I keep on asking myself without ever getting an answer.'[1]

From the period between September 1942 and the beginning of 1945 only a few scattered records of Hitler's table talk have survived. But there has recently come to light the transcript of seventeen conversations (or rather, monologues) which Bormann arranged to be recorded in February 1945.[2] Unlike the earlier table talk, which ranged over every subject from Hitler's views on marriage to the part played by Christianity in the destruction of the Roman Empire, these excerpts have a single theme: the war and Hitler's analysis of the mistakes which had brought Germany to the position in which she then found herself. It was one of the few times in his life when Hitler was prepared to admit that he had made any mistakes at all, and this alone would endow these talks with interest, quite apart from the fact that whenever Hitler discussed politics – as distinct from art or religion – he never failed to show the power of his twisted mind.

Had it been wrong to go to war? No, he had been jockeyed into war: 'It was in any case unavoidable; the enemies of German National Socialism forced it upon me as long ago as January 1933.'[3] The same was true of the attack on Russia. 'I had always

1. Zoller, *Hitler Privat*, pp. 203–5.
2. Published as *The Testament of Adolf Hitler* (London, 1961).
3. ibid., p. 41.

maintained that we ought at all costs to avoid waging war on two fronts, and you may rest assured that I pondered long and anxiously over Napoleon and his experiences in Russia. Why, then, you may ask, this war against Russia, and why at the time I selected?'[1]

Hitler gave several answers to this question. It was necessary to deprive Britain of her one hope of continuing the war; Russia was withholding the raw materials essential to Germany; Stalin was trying to blackmail him into concessions in Eastern Europe. But the reason to which he always returned,

and my own personal nightmare, was the fear that Stalin might take the initiative before me. . . . If I felt compelled to settle my accounts with Bolshevism by force of arms. . . . I have every right to believe that Stalin had come to the same decision even before he signed the pact [of 1939].[2] War with Russia had become inevitable, whatever we did and to postpone it only meant that we should later have to fight it under conditions far less favourable.[3]

Had the Japanese attack on the United States been a fatal error? No, for Roosevelt and his Jewish masters had already made up their minds to bring America into the war. Japan was a good friend and ally, although 'it is of course regrettable that the Japanese did not enter the war against Russia and at the same time as ourselves'.[4]

'The disastrous thing about this war is the fact that for Germany it began both too soon and too late.'[5] He needed, Hitler declared, twenty years in which to bring his new élite to maturity. Instead the war came too soon:

We lacked men moulded in the shape of our ideal . . . and the war policy of a revolutionary state like the Third Reich has of necessity been the policy of petty bourgeois reactionaries. Our generals and diplomats, with a few, rare exceptions, are men of another age, and their methods of waging war and conducting our foreign policy also belong to an age that is passed.[6]

But the war also came too late. From a military point of view, it would have been better to fight in 1938 not 1939. Czechoslovakia was a better issue than Poland; Britain and France would never have intervened, and Germany could have consolidated her position in Eastern Europe before facing world war several years later. 'At Munich we lost a unique opportunity of easily and swiftly winning a war that was in any case inevitable.'[7] It was all

1. *The Testament of Adolf Hitler* p. 63.
2. ibid., p. 65 and p. 99.   3. ibid., p. 66.   4. ibid., p. 78.
5. ibid., p. 58.   6. ibid., p. 59.   7. ibid., p. 84.

Chamberlain's fault: he had already made up his mind to attack Germany, but was playing for time and by giving way all along the line robbed Hitler of the initiative.

Once the war had begun, 'I must admit that my unshakable friendship for Italy and the Duce may well be held to be an error on my part.' The Italian alliance had been a disaster. Not only had the Italians lost every campaign on which they had embarked, but by stirring up the Balkans they cost Germany six vital weeks' delay in the attack on Russia.

Our Italian ally has been a source of embarrassment to us everywhere. It was this alliance which prevented us from pursuing a revolutionary policy in North Africa. . . . All Islam vibrated at the news of our victories. The Egyptians, the Iraqis, and the whole of the Near East were all ready to rise in revolt. Just think what we could have done to help them, even to incite them. . . . But we missed the bus, thanks to our loyalty to our Italian allies.[1]

Arab contempt for the Italians and the Duce's 'ridiculous pretensions' of an Italian empire robbed Germany of her opportunity.

Our greatest political blunder has been our treatment of the French. We should never have collaborated with them . . . our obvious course should have been to liberate the working classes and help the workers of France to implement their own revolution.[2]

A similar opportunity had been lost in the French empire where it should have been German policy to rouse the Arabs and other colonial peoples to throw off the French yoke. 'These Latin countries bring us no luck' – neither Italy, nor France, nor Franco's Spain.

But the greatest mistakes, Hitler concluded, had been made by Britain and the United States. Britain ought to have seen that it was in her interests to ally with Germany, the rising continental power, in order to defend the imperial possessions which she was now certain to lose.

If fate had granted to an ageing and enfeebled Britain a new Pitt instead of this Jew-ridden, half-American drunkard [Churchill], the new Pitt would at once have recognized that Britain's traditional policy of balance of power would now have to be applied . . . on a world-wide scale. Instead of maintaining . . . European rivalries, Britain ought to do her utmost to bring about a unification of Europe. Allied to a united Europe, she would then still retain the chance of being able to play the

1. pp. 70–1.   2. ibid., p. 60.

part of arbiter in world affairs . . . [But] I had underestimated the power of Jewish domination over Churchill's England.[1]

If Britain ought to have allied with Germany, the United States ought to have realized that she had no quarrel with the Third Reich and preserved her isolation. 'This war against America is a tragedy. It is illogical and devoid of any foundation of reality.'[2] Once again it was due to the same sinister influence, the Jewish world conspiracy against Nazi Germany.

Never before has there been a war so typically and so exclusively Jewish. I have at least compelled them to discard their masks . . . I have opened the eyes of the whole world to the Jewish peril.[3]

I have always been absolutely fair in my dealings with the Jews. I gave them one final warning. I told them that, if they precipitated another war, they would not be spared and that I would exterminate the vermin throughout Europe, and this time once and for all. . . . Well, we have lanced the Jewish abscess; and the world of the future will be eternally grateful to us.[4]

Such was Hitler's reasoning as he faced the possibility of defeat. There was not even a passing thought for the millions of deaths, the untold suffering, and the destruction he had brought on Germany and Europe. If he admitted to errors of judgement, they sprang from insufficient hardness, from his own too great tolerance; and the blame for war and for defeat rested not on himself, but on others, above all the Jews and their tools Churchill and Roosevelt who had sacrificed the true interests of their countries by making war on Germany.

To this Hitler added a postscript. On 2 April, prompted by Bormann, he delivered the last of his table talk monologues, in effect a political testament to the German nation. 'I have been Europe's last hope,' he had declared in February.[5] If Germany was to suffer defeat after all, it would be utter and complete, and a tragedy for Europe as well as the German people. Then with a last burst of prophetic power he drew his picture of the future:

With the defeat of the Reich and pending the emergence of the Asiatic, the African, and perhaps the South American nationalisms, there will remain in the world only two Great Powers capable of confronting each other – the United States and Soviet Russia. The laws of both history and geography will compel these two powers to a trial of strength, either military or in the fields of economics and ideology. These same laws make it inevitable that both Powers should become enemies of

1. *The Testament of Adolf Hitler*, pp. 30–2. 2. ibid., p. 87.
3. ibid., p. 52. 4. ibid., p. 57. 5. ibid., p. 101 (26 February 1945).

Europe. And it is equally certain that both these Powers will sooner or later find it desirable to seek the support of the sole surviving great nation in Europe, the German people.[1]

Those who dismiss Hitler's political gifts as negligible may well be asked how many in the spring of 1945, with the war not yet over, saw the future so clearly.

As the façade of power crumbled, Hitler reverted to his origins; there is a far closer resemblance between the early Hitler of the Vienna days and the Hitler of 1944–5 than between either and the dictator of Germany at the height of his power. The crude hatred, contempt, and resentment which were the deepest forces in his character appeared undisguised. They found expression in the increasing vulgarity of his language. It was the authentic voice of the gutter again.

The man who had made it his first principle never to trust anyone now complained bitterly that there was no one he could trust. Only Eva Braun and Blondi were faithful to him, he declared, quoting Frederick the Great's remark: 'Now I know men, I prefer dogs.'[2]

His rages became more violent and more frequent. On one occasion Guderian's aide-de-camp felt so alarmed that he pulled the general back by his coat for fear that Hitler might make a physical attack on him. On another occasion Guderian had an argument with him which lasted two hours.

His fists raised, his cheeks flushed with rage, his whole body trembling, the man stood there in front of me, beside himself with fury and having lost all self-control. After each outburst of rage Hitler would stride up and down the carpet-edge, then suddenly stop immediately before me and hurl his next accusation in my face. He was almost screaming, his eyes seemed about to pop out of his head and the veins stood out on his temples.

When he found, however, that Guderian was not to be shifted from his opinion, Hitler suddenly gave way, and added, with his most charming smile: 'Now please continue with the conference. Today the General Staff has won a battle.'[3]

Years before, Hermann Rauschning, describing Nazism as the St Vitus's Dance of the twentieth century, had diagnosed its essential element of nihilism. In his conversations with Hitler during the years 1932–4 he records many remarks that betray the

1. ibid. p. 107.   2. Zoffer: op. cit., p. 230.   3. Guderian, pp. 414–15.

underlying passion for destruction which was only cloaked during the period of his success.

In talking to Rauschning, Hitler frequently became intoxicated with the prospect of a revolutionary upheaval which would destroy the entire European social order. After the Röhm purge of 1934 Hitler is reported to have said: 'Externally, I end the revolution. But internally it goes on, just as we store up our hate and think of the day on which we shall cast off the mask, and stand revealed as those we are and eternally shall remain.'[1]

Earlier in 1934, when Rauschning asked him what would happen if Britain, France, and Russia made an alliance against Germany, Hitler replied: 'That would be the end. But even if we could not conquer them, we should drag half the world into destruction with us, and leave no one to triumph over Germany. There will not be another 1918. We shall not surrender.'[2]

This was the stage Hitler had now reached, and he was as good as his word. Goebbels shared Hitler's mood, and Nazi propaganda in the final phase has a marked note of exultation in the climax of destruction with which the war in Europe ended. But Hitler's determination to drag Europe down with him was not limited to propaganda. It was most clearly expressed in his insistence on continuing the war to the bitter end and in his demands for a 'scorched earth' policy in Germany. Speer did his best to dissuade Hitler on the grounds that the German people must still go on living even if the régime were to be overthrown. On 15 March Speer drew up a memorandum in which he set out his case. Within four to eight weeks, he wrote, Germany's final collapse was certain. A policy of destroying Germany's remaining resources in order to deny them to the enemy could not affect the result of the war. The overriding obligation of Germany's rulers, without regard to their own fate, was to ensure that the German people should be left with some possibility of reconstructing their lives in the future.[3]

Hitler was adamant. On 19 March he issued categorical and detailed orders for the destruction of all communications, rolling-stock, lorries, bridges, dams, factories and supplies in the path of the enemy.[4] Sending for Speer, he told him:

If the war is to be lost, the nation also will perish. This fate is inevitable. There is no need to consider the basis even of a most primitive existence

1. Rauschning: *Hitler Speaks*, p. 176.   2. ibid., p. 125.
3. N.D., Speer Document, 026.
4. N.D., Speer Documents, 027, 028, 029.

any longer. On the contrary, it is better to destroy even that, and to destroy it ourselves. The nation has proved itself weak, and the future belongs solely to the stronger eastern nation. Besides, those who remain after the battle are of little value; for the good have fallen.[1]

From this policy Hitler never wavered. In these senseless orders to destroy everything and to shoot those who failed to comply with his directive he found some relief for the passion of frustrated anger which possessed him, and it was only thanks to the devotion of Speer that these orders were not fully carried out. But, as General Halder remarks, this mood was something more than the product of impotent rage. 'Even at the height of his power there was for him no Germany, there were no German troops for whom he felt himself responsible; for him there was – at first subconsciously, but in his last years fully consciously – only one greatness, a greatness which dominated his life and to which his evil genius sacrificed everything – his own Ego.'[2]

In order to keep alive the will to go on fighting, Hitler made desperate efforts to conceal the hopelessness of the situation. As soon as he came across the words: 'The war is lost,' in Speer's memorandum, he refused to read another line and locked it away in his safe. Guderian was present on another occasion when Speer requested Hitler to see him alone. Hitler refused:

All he wants is to tell me again that the war is lost and that I should bring it to an end. Now you can understand why it is that I refuse to see anyone alone any more. Any man who asks to talk to me alone always does so because he has something unpleasant to say to me. I can't bear that.[3]

Hitler turned for comfort to the example of Frederick the Great, who in 1757, when Prussia was invaded by half a dozen armies and all hope seemed gone, won his greatest victories of Rossbach and Leuthen and routed his foes. He kept Graff's portrait of Frederick hanging above his desk and told Guderian: 'When bad news threatens to crush my spirit I derive fresh courage from the contemplation of this picture. Look at those strong, blue eyes, that wide brow. What a head!'[4]

His private conversation in the early hours of the morning, however, was increasingly pessimistic in tone. Before the war he had strongly condemned suicide, arguing that if only a man would hold on something would happen to justify his faith. Now he announced his conversion to Schopenhauer's view that life was

1. Speer's evidence at Nuremberg, N.P., Part XVII, p. 35.
2. Halder, pp. 69–70.   3. Guderian, p. 407.   4. ibid., p. 416.

not worth living if it brought only disillusionment. He was depressed by his own ill-health. 'If a man is no more than a living wreck, why prolong life? No one can halt the decay of his physical powers.'

His secretary, who had to endure many such outbursts, records that after his return to Berlin in January his conversations became entirely self-centred and was marked by the monotonous repetition of the same stories told over and over again. His intellectual appetite for the discussion of such large subjects as the evolution of man, the course of world history, religion, and the future of science had gone; even his memory began to fail him. His talk was confined to anecdotes about his dog or his diet, interspersed with complaints about the stupidity and wickedness of the world.[1]

These early morning sessions grew later and later. Hitler frequently continued interviews and conferences well after midnight and often did not go to bed till dawn. He cut down his sleep to little more than three hours, rising again about noon, occasionally strolling round the Chancellery garden in the afternoon and usually taking a brief nap in the evening.

Yet he still maintained his hold over those who were in daily contact with him: the sorcerer's magic was not yet exhausted. In March 1945, Forster, the Gauleiter of Danzig, came to Berlin determined to make Hitler realize the desperate situation of his city. This time, he told the secretaries in the ante-room, he would not be fobbed off with promises; they could count on him to speak out and tell the brutal truth. But when Forster came out of his interview with Hitler he was a changed man.

The Führer has promised me new divisions for Danzig [he declared]. I was not at all clear where he would find them, but he has explained to me that he means to save Danzig and that there is no further room for doubt.[2]

Sustained by these promises, Forster returned to continue the fight.

Forster, it is worth remembering, was a man who had known Hitler for many years, yet he was still susceptible to his charm and conviction. The same is true of the other old Party members – Goebbels, Göring, Himmler, Bormann, Ribbentrop – every one of whom clung despairingly to the hope that the man to whom they owed everything would yet find a way out.

Himmler was unquestionably the second man in the rapidly

1. Zoller, pp. 230–1.   2. ibid., pp. 29–30.

dwindling Nazi empire and the most obvious heir to Hitler. But Himmler's position was not undisputed. In accepting the active command of an Army Group, first on the Rhine, later on the Vistula and the Oder, Himmler made the mistake of removing himself from the Führer's court, while his failure to halt the Russian advance much reduced his standing with Hitler. In the last six months of the Third Reich it was Bormann, rather than Himmler, who was the rising power at the Führer's Headquarters.

For Bormann, content to keep in the background and appear solely as the devoted servant of the Führer, took care never to leave Hitler's side. He adjusted his way of life in order to go to bed and rise at the same time as Hitler, and he strengthened his control over access to him. Bormann was still not powerful enough to keep out Himmler, Speer, and Goebbels. But Himmler came little to headquarters now, and Bormann soon made sure of Himmler's permanent representative with Hitler, Hermann Fegelein. He took every opportunity to undermine Hitler's confidence in Speer, while with Goebbels, whose position had been much strengthened in the past year, he concluded a tacit alliance. They joined in advocating extreme measures and constituted the leaders of a radical group, the other members of which were Fegelein, Ley, and General Burgdorf, the Führer's chief military adjutant, who had presented Rommel with Hitler's message and the phial of poison in October 1944.

In the middle of these rivalries Hitler's own position remained unchallenged, nor did anyone, except Speer, dare to question the wisdom of his decision to continue the war. The intrigues were aimed not at replacing him, but at securing his favour and a voice in the nomination of his successor. No more striking testimony to Hitler's hold over those around him can be imagined than the interest they still showed in the unreal question of who was to succeed him.

I V

As day succeeded day in the isolated world of the Reich Chancellery and its garden shelter, the news grew steadily worse. Between 12 January, the day on which the Russians opened their offensive in Poland, and 12 April, the day on which the U.S. Ninth Army crossed the Elbe, the Allies inflicted a total defeat upon the German Army.

In January the Russians overran Poland and reached the Oder. They broke into Silesia, the one German industrial district which had escaped major damage from air attack, and by February were threatening Berlin and Vienna.

For a time the Germans checked the Russians on the Oder, only to see their western defences crumble. In March the Americans and the British crossed the Rhine, and, one after another, the famous names of the Rhineland cities appeared in the Allied communiqués. Hitler brought in Kesselring to replace Rundstedt as Commander-in-Chief West, but Kesselring could no more stem the tide than anyone else. On 1 April Model's Army Group was encircled in the Ruhr. Less than three weeks later they had joined the rest of the two million prisoners captured in the west since D-day, while Model in despair committed suicide in a wood near Duisburg. An organized front no longer existed in the west, and on the evening of 11 April the Americans reached the Elbe near Magdeburg, in the very heart of Germany.

On 9 April Königsberg, the capital of East Prussia, fell; on the 13th the Russians captured Vienna, and on the 16th they broke the defence line on the Oder. The way to Berlin was open, and it was now only a question of time before the armies advancing from the west met those coming from the east and cut Germany in two.

Hitler had lost all control over events, and by April he had the greatest difficulty in discovering what was happening. The Germans went on fighting – in the east, with the courage of despair – but there was no longer any organized direction of the war. This is amply confirmed by such records as survive of the conferences Hitler held from the beginning of January onwards. Once the operations in the Ardennes had failed, all sense of purpose was lost. The discussions of the military situation in the early months of 1945 are rambling, confused, and futile. The leadership was not only morally, but intellectually, bankrupt. Hours were wasted in discussion of questions of detail and local operations, interrupted by reminiscences and recriminations. Hitler no longer showed any grasp of the situation. His orders became wilder and more contradictory, his demands more impossible, his decisions more arbitrary. His one answer to every proposal was: No withdrawal. By his refusal to let his commanders make their stand behind the Rhine, and his insistence that they must fight to the west of the river, he flung away a score of divisions needlessly. As late as 10 March he rejected a request to withdraw from northern Norway, and still would not agree to the evacuation of the troops cut off along the eastern shores of the Baltic.

Hitler had long scorned the belief that war can be waged without resort to terrorism. A succession of orders from his headquarters – such as the notorious 'Commissar' and 'Commando' orders – demanded deliberate brutality in dealing with the enemy. In February 1945 there were prolonged discussions of a proposal made by Goebbels and eagerly seized on by Hitler that the German High Command should denounce the Geneva and other international conventions, shoot all captured enemy airmen out of hand and make use of the new poison gases, Tabun and Sarin. Characteristically, the argument that most attracted Hitler was the effect this would have on the German soldier. Sweeping aside the legal argument, he declared:

To hell with that. . . . If I make it clear that I show no consideration for prisoners but treat them without any consideration for their rights, regardless of reprisals, then quite a few [Germans] will think twice before they desert.[1]

Only with the greatest difficulty was he restrained from taking this desperate and irresponsible step.

Without bothering to investigate the facts he ordered the dismissal, degradation and even execution of officers who, after fighting against overwhelming forces, were forced to give ground. Even the Waffen S.S. was not exempt from his vicious temper. When Sepp Dietrich, once the leader of his personal bodyguard and now in command of the Sixth S.S. Panzer Army, was driven back into Vienna, Hitler radioed:

The Führer believes that the troops have not fought as the situation demanded and orders that the S.S. Divisions Adolf Hitler, Das Reich Totenkopf, and Hohenstauffen, be stripped of their arm-bands.

When Dietrich received this he summoned his divisional commanders and, throwing the message on the table, exclaimed: 'There's your reward for all that you've done these past five years.' Rather than carry out the order, he cabled back, he would shoot himself.[2]

Hitler still tried to buoy himself up with the belief that the new weapons, of which he never ceased to talk, would work a miracle. But gradually these hopes too faded and his continued references to them became no more than the mechanical repetition of ritual

1. Gilbert, Appendix, p. 179.
2. Shulman, pp. 316–17.

phrases. The V1s and V2s had come and gone. The Ardennes offensive had been launched and failed. The jet fighters never took the air. The U-boat fleet, reinforced by the new types on which Hitler and Dönitz had built the most extravagant expectations, put to sea but were routed.

The last hope of all was a split in the Grand Alliance. At his conference on 27 January Hitler suddenly asked:

Do you think that, deep down inside, the English are enthusiastic about the Russian developments?

GÖRING: They certainly didn't plan that we hold them off while the Russians conquer all of Germany. If this goes on we will get a telegram in a few days. . . .

JODL: They have always regarded the Russians with suspicion.

HITLER: I have ordered that a report be placed into their hands that the Russians are organizing two hundred thousand of our men, led by German officers and completely infected with Communism, who will then be marched into Germany. . . . That will make them feel as if someone had stuck a needle into them.

GÖRING: They entered the war to prevent us from going into the east, not to have the east come to the Atlantic.[1]

Hitler's political instinct was still keen, but time was against him. Churchill, Roosevelt, and Stalin, meeting at Yalta in February, patched up their differences and contrived an agreement which, however impermanent, outlasted Hitler. The demand for unconditional surrender was reaffirmed, and the Allied armies never paused in their advance.

The level to which the hopes of the German leaders were now reduced is well illustrated by their reception of the news of Roosevelt's death on 12 April. The story is recounted by Schwerin von Krosigk, Hitler's egregious Finance Minister, and confirmed by other eye-witnesses.

A few days before the 12th (Goebbels told Schwerin von Krosigk), in order to comfort the Führer, he had read him the passage in Carlyle's *History of Frederick the Great* in which the author describes the difficulties confronting the Prussian king in the winter of 1761–2:

How the great king himself did not see any way out and did not know what to do; how all his generals and ministers were convinced that he was finished; how the enemy already looked upon Prussia as vanquished; how the future appeared entirely dark, and how in his last

1. Gilbert, pp. 117–18

letter to the Minister Graf Finckenstein[1] he set himself a time limit: if there was no change by 15 February he would give up and take poison. 'Brave king!' Carlyle writes, 'wait but a little while, and the days of your suffering will be over. Behind the clouds the sun of your good fortune is already rising and soon will show itself to you.' On 12 February the Czarina died; the Miracle of the House of Brandenburg had come to pass. The Führer, Goebbels said, had tears in his eyes.[2]

Thereupon Goebbels sent for the horoscopes of the Führer and of the Weimar Republic, both of which, he claimed, had been astonishingly right about the war and now predicted a great success for Germany in the latter half of April, followed by peace in August.

Goebbels was so taken with this historical parallel that on 12 April, while paying a visit to the headquarters of the Ninth Army at Kuestrin, he tried to convince General Busse and his Staff that

for reasons of Historical Necessity and Justice a change of fortune must occur now just as it did in the Seven Years War with the Miracle of the House of Brandenburg. One of the officers present asked somewhat sceptically which Czarina was to die this time. To this Goebbels replied that he did not know either, but that Fate held all sorts of possibilities in her hands. He then went back home and received the news of Roosevelt's death. Immediately he telephoned to Busse and said: 'The Czarina is dead.' Busse told him that this made a great impression on his soldiers; now they saw another chance.[3]

In his excitement Goebbels called for champagne and rang up Hitler:

'My Führer, I congratulate you! Roosevelt is dead. It is written in the stars that the second half of April will be the turning-point for us. This is Friday 13 April. It is the turning-point.'[4]

Goebbels's mood was fully shared by Hitler, but the sense of relief did not last long. When reports from the front showed that Roosevelt's death had not affected the enemy's operations, Goebbels remarked disconsolately: 'Perhaps Fate has again been cruel and made fools of us.'[5]

In the middle of April the Nazi Empire which had once

1. As Professor Trevor-Roper points out, neither the facts nor the quotation are accurate. The Minister to whom Frederick wrote was not Finckenstein but the Count d'Argenson.

2. Schwerin von Krosigk's diary (unpublished).

3. ibid.

4. Evidence of Frau Haberzettel, one of the secretaries in the Propaganda Ministry, quoted by H. R. Trevor-Roper, pp. 112–13.

5. Semmler, p. 193.

stretched to the Caucasus and the Atlantic was reduced to a narrow corridor in the heart of Germany little more than a hundred miles wide. Hitler had reached the end of the road.

V

Shortly after Hitler's hopes had been raised and dashed by Roosevelt's death, Eva Braun arrived unexpectedly in Berlin and, defying Hitler's orders, announced her intention of staying with him to the end. For some time Goebbels had been urging Hitler to remain in Berlin and make an ending in the besieged city worthy of an admirer of Wagner's *Götterdämmerung*. Goebbels scorned any suggestion that by leaving the capital he might allow the two million people still living there to escape the horrors of a pitched battle fought in the streets of the city. 'If a single white flag is hoisted in Berlin,' he declared, 'I shall not hesitate to have the whole street and all its inhabitants blown up. This has the full authority of the Führer.'[1]

None the less Hitler's mind was not yet made up. Preparations were in train for the Government to leave Berlin and move to the 'National Redoubt' in the heart of the Bavarian Alps, round Berchtesgaden, the homeland of the Nazi movement, where the Führer was expected to make his last stand. Various ministries and commands had already been transferred to the Redoubt area, and the time had come when Hitler himself must follow if he was still to get through the narrow corridor left between the Russian and American armies.

Hitler's original plan was to leave for the south on 20 April, his fifty-sixth birthday, but at the conference on the 20th, following the reception and congratulations, he still hesitated. For the last time, all the Nazi hierarchs were present – Göring, Himmler, Goebbels, Ribbentrop, Bormann, Speer – together with the chiefs of the three Services. Their advice was in favour of his leaving Berlin. The most Hitler would agree to, however, was the establishment of Northern and Southern Commands, in case Germany should be cut in two by the Allied advance. There and then he appointed Admiral Dönitz to assume the full responsibility in the north, but, although Kesselring was nominated for the Southern Command, Hitler left open the possibility that he might move to the south and take the direction of the war there into his own hands.

1. Semmler, p. 190.

On the 21st Hitler ordered an all-out attack on the Russians besieging Berlin. 'Any commander who holds back his troops,' Hitler shouted to the Luftwaffe General Koller, 'will forfeit his life in five hours. You yourself will guarantee with your head that the last man is thrown in.'[1] The direction of the attack Hitler confided to an S.S. general, Steiner, and he built the most exaggerated hopes on the success which he anticipated from the operation. It was the disappointment of these hopes which led him finally to make up his mind and refuse to leave the capital.

For Steiner's attack was never launched. The withdrawal of troops to provide the forces necessary allowed the Russians to break through the city's outer defences in the north, and Hitler's plan foundered in confusion. Throughout the morning of the 22nd a series of telephone calls from the bunker failed to elicit any news of what was happening. By the time the conference met at three o'clock in the afternoon there was still no news of Steiner, and Hitler was on the verge of one of his worst outbursts.

The storm burst during the conference, which lasted for three hours and left everyone who took part in it shaken and exhausted. In a universal gesture of denunciation Hitler cursed them all for their cowardice, treachery, and incompetence. The end had come, he declared. He could no longer go on. There was nothing left but to die. He would meet his end there, in Berlin; those who wished could go to the south, but he would never move. From this resolution he was not to be moved. Telephone calls from Himmler and Dönitz, and the entreaties of his own Staff, had no effect. Acting on his decision, he dictated an announcement to be read over the wireless, declaring that the Führer was in Berlin and that he would remain there to the very last.

The implications of Hitler's declaration were more far-reaching than may appear at first sight. For, since 1941, Hitler had taken over the immediate day-to-day direction of the war as the active Commander-in-Chief of the German Army. Now that he was forced to admit the fact of defeat, however, the man who had insisted on prolonging the war against the advice of his generals refused to take any further responsibility. Instead, he instructed his two chief assistants, Generals Keitel and Jodl, to leave at once for Berchtesgaden and declined to give them further orders. All the grandiloquent talk of dying in Berlin cannot disguise the fact that this petulant decision was a gross dereliction of his duty to

1. Karl Koller: *Der letzte Monat*, p. 23.

the troops still fighting under his command and an action wholly at variance with the most elementary military tradition.

Jodl later described to General Koller, the Luftwaffe Chief of Staff, their unavailing efforts to persuade Hitler to change his mind.

Hitler declared that he had decided to stay in Berlin, lead its defence, and then at the last moment shoot himself. For physical reasons he was unable to take part in the fighting personally, nor did he wish to, for he could not run the risk of falling into enemy hands. We all attempted to bring him over from this decision and even offered to move troops from the west to fight in the east. His answer was that everything was falling to pieces anyway, and that he could do no more: that should be left to the Reichsmarshal [Göring]. When someone remarked that no soldier would fight for the Reichsmarshal, Hitler retorted: 'What do you mean, fight? There's precious little more fighting to be done and, if it comes to negotiating, the Reichsmarshal can do better than I can.' The latest development of the situation had made the deepest impression on him, he spoke all the time of treachery and failure, of corruption in the leadership and in the ranks. Even the S.S. now told him lies.[1]

By the time Jodl and Keitel left Hitler on the evening of 22 April he had recovered his self-control and talked calmly to Keitel of the possibility of the Twelfth Army, then fighting on the Elbe under General Wenck, coming to the relief of Berlin. But his decision to stay in the capital was irrevocable; as a logical consequence he began to burn his papers and invited Goebbels, the advocate of a 'world-historical end', to join him in the Führerbunker.

VI

The setting in which Hitler played out the last scene of all was well suited to the end of so strange a history. The Chancellery air-raid shelter, in which the events of 22 April had taken place, was buried fifty feet beneath the ground, and built in two storeys covered with a massive canopy of reinforced concrete. The lower of the storeys formed the Führerbunker. It was divided into eighteen small rooms grouped on either side of a central passageway. Half of this passage was closed by a partition and used for the daily conferences. A suite of six rooms was set aside for Hitler and Eva Braun. Eva had a bed-sitting-room, a bathroom, and a dressing-room; Hitler a bedroom and a study, the

1. Koller, op. cit., p. 31 – his diary entry for 23 April.

sole decoration in which was the portrait of Frederick the Great. A map-room used for small conferences, a telephone exchange, a power-house, and guard rooms took up most of the rest of the space, but there were two rooms for Goebbels (formerly occupied by Morell) and two for Stumpfegger, Brandt's successor as Hitler's surgeon. Frau Goebbels, who insisted on remaining with her husband, together with her six children, occupied four rooms on the floor above, where the kitchen, servants' quarters and dining-hall were also to be found. Other shelters had been built near-by. One housed Bormann, his staff and the various Service officers; another Mohnke, the S.S. commandant of the Chancellery, and his staff.

The physical atmosphere of the bunker was oppressive, but this was nothing compared to the pressure of the psychological atmosphere. The incessant air-raids, the knowledge that the Russians were now in the city, nervous exhaustion, fear, and despair produced a tension bordering on hysteria, which was heightened by propinquity to a man whose changes of mood were not only unpredictable but affected the lives of all those in the shelter.

Hitler had been living in the bunker for some time. Such sleep as he got in the last month appears to have been between eight and eleven o'clock in the morning. As soon as the mid-morning air attacks began, Hitler got up and dressed. He had a horror of being caught either lying down or undressed.

Much of the time was still taken up with conferences. The midday or afternoon conference was matched by a second after midnight which sometimes lasted till dawn. The evening meal was served between 9 and 10 p.m., and Hitler liked to drag it out in order not to be left alone during a night air-raid. Sometimes he would receive his secretaries at six in the morning, after a late-night conference. He would make an effort to stand up and greet them, but rapidly sank back exhausted on to the sofa. The early morning meal was the one he most enjoyed, and he would eat greedily of chocolate and cakes, playing with Blondi and the puppies which she produced in March. To one of these puppies Hitler gave his own old nickname, Wolf, and brought it up without anyone's help. He would lie with it on his lap, stroking it and repeating its name until the meal was over and he tried to get some sleep.

Between 20 and 24 April a considerable number of Hitler's

entourage – including Göring; Hitler's adjutant, Schaub; and Morell – left for the south. In the last week of his life Hitler shared the cramped accommodation of the Führerbunker with Eva Braun; the Goebbels and their children; Stumpfegger, his surgeon; his valet, Heinz Linge; and his S.S. adjutant, Günsche; his two remaining secretaries, Frau Christian and Frau Junge; Fräulein Manzialy, his vegetarian cook; and Goebbels's adjutant. Frequent visitors to the Führerbunker from the neighbouring shelters were Bormann; General Krebs, who had succeeded Guderian as the Army's Chief of Staff; General Burgdorf, Hitler's chief military adjutant; Artur Axmann, the leader of the Hitler Youth (a thousand of whom took part in the defence of Berlin), and a crowd of aides-de-camp, adjutants, liaison officers and S.S. guards.

On Monday 23 April, having at last come to a decision, Hitler was in a calmer frame of mind. Keitel, who talked to him in the afternoon, reports that he appeared rested and even satisfied with the position.[1] This was borne out by his reception of Speer, who flew back from Hamburg to say farewell, and made a full confession of the steps he had taken to thwart Hitler's orders for scorching the German earth. Hitler undoubtedly had a genuine affection for Speer, but it is surprising that he was moved, rather than incensed, by his frankness. Speer was neither arrested nor shot, but allowed to go free, and like everyone else who saw Hitler that day he was impressed by the change in him, the serenity which he appeared to have reached after months of desperate effort to maintain his conviction, in the face of all the facts, that the war could still be won. Now that he had abandoned the attempt to flog himself and those around him into keeping up the pretence he was more philosophical and resigned to facing death as a release from the difficulties which overwhelmed him. He repeated to Speer what he had told Jodl and Keitel the day before, that he would shoot himself in the bunker and have his body burned to avoid its falling into the hands of the enemy. This was stated quietly and firmly, as a matter no longer open to discussion.

While it is true, however, that Hitler never varied this decision, his moods remained as unstable as ever, anger rapidly succeeding to resignation, and in turn yielding to the brief revival of hope. This is well illustrated by the incident of Göring's dismissal, of

1. Keitel's interrogation at Nuremberg, 10 October 1945.

which Speer was also a witness before he left the bunker for good in the early hours of the 24th.

When Göring flew to the south he left behind as his representative General Koller, the Chief of Staff of the Air Force. On 23 April Koller appeared at the Obersalzberg and reported the decisions of the fateful conference in the bunker the day before. Hitler's intentions appeared to be clear enough: 'if it comes to negotiating the Reichsmarshal can do better than I can.' But Göring was afraid of the responsibility, afraid in particular of Bormann. 'If I act now,' he said to his advisers, 'I may be stamped as a traitor; if I don't act, I shall be accused of having failed to do something in the hour of disaster.'[1] Sweating with anxiety, he sent for Lammers, the State Secretary of the Reich Chancellery and fetched from the safe the decree of June 1941 which named him as the Führer's successor. Finally he decided to wireless Hitler for confirmation:

My Führer,
    In view of your decision to remain at your post in the fortress of Berlin, do you agree that I take over, at once, the total leadership of the Reich, with full freedom of action at home and abroad, as your deputy, in accordance with your decree of 29 June 1941? If no reply is received by ten o'clock tonight I shall take it for granted that you have lost your freedom of action, and shall consider the conditions of your decree as fulfilled, and shall act for the best interests of our country and our people. You know what I feel for you in the gravest hour of my life. Words fail me to express myself. May God protect you and speed you quickly here in spite of all.

Your loyal
Hermann Göring[2]

When Göring's message reached the bunker it did not take long for Bormann, Göring's sworn enemy, to represent it as an ultimatum. Speer, who was present, reports that Hitler became unusually excited, denouncing Göring as corrupt, a failure, and a drug addict, but adding: 'He can negotiate the capitulation all the same. It does not matter anyway who does it.'[3]

The addition is revealing. Hitler was clearly angry at Göring's presumption – the habits of tyranny are not easily broken – he agreed to Bormann's suggestion that Göring should be arrested

1. Koller, op. cit., p. 37.
2. Quoted by Trevor-Roper, p. 145.
3. Speer's evidence at Nuremberg, N.P., Part XVII, p. 57.

for high treason, and he authorized his dismissal from all his offices, including the succession – yet 'it does not matter anyway'. As Speer pointed out at Nuremberg, all Hitler's contempt for the German people was contained in the off-hand way in which he made this remark.

To try to make too much sense out of what Hitler said or ordered in those final days would be wholly to misread both the extraordinary circumstances and his state of mind. Those who saw him at this time and who were not so infected by the atmosphere of the bunker as to share his mood regarded him as closer than ever to that shadowy line which divides the world of the sane from that of the insane. He spoke entirely on the impulse of the moment, and moods of comparative lucidity, such as that in which Speer had talked to him on the 23rd, were interspersed with wild accusations, wilder hopes and half-crazed ramblings.

Hitler found it more difficult than ever to realize the situation outside the shelter, or to grasp that this was the end. Conferences continued until the morning of the day on which he committed suicide. On the 24th he sent an urgent summons for Colonel General Ritter von Greim, in command of Air Fleet 6, to fly from Munich to Berlin. Greim made the hazardous journey into the heart of the capital, with the help of a young woman test-pilot, Hanna Reitsch, at the cost of a severe wound in his foot. To get there they had to fly at the level of the tree-tops, in the face of heavy A.A. fire and constant fighter attacks which cost the escorting planes considerable losses. When Greim arrived it was to find that Hitler had insisted on this simply in order to inform him personally that he was promoting him to be Commander-in-Chief of the Luftwaffe in succession to Göring, an appointment that he could perfectly well have made by telegram. The only result of Hitler's action was to imprison the new Commander-in-Chief in the bunker for three days and to cripple him with a wounded foot.

The scene when Hitler greeted Greim and Hanna Reitsch was marked by the theatricality of Hitler's behaviour. Hanna Reitsch describes the tears in his eyes as he referred to Göring's treachery:

His head sagged, his face was deathly pallid, and the uncontrolled shaking of his hands mad e the message [from Göring] flutter wildly as he handed it to Greim.

The Führer's face remained deathly earnest as Greim read. Then every muscle in it began to twitch and his breath came in explosive puffs; only with effort did he gain sufficient control to shout: 'An ultimatum! A crass ultimatum! Now nothing remains. Nothing is spared to me. No allegiances are kept, no honour lived up to, no disappointments that I have not had, no betrayals that I have not experienced – and now this above all else. Nothing remains. Every wrong has already been done me.'[1]

Later that night Hitler sent for Hanna Reitsch and gave her a vial of poison. 'Hanna, you belong to those who will die with me. Each of us has a vial of poison such as this. I do not wish that one of us falls into the hands of the Russians alive, nor do I wish our bodies to be found by them.' At the end of a highly emotional interview Hitler reassured her: 'But, my Hanna, I still have hope. The army of General Wenck is moving up from the south. He must and will drive the Russians back long enough to save our people. Then he will fall back to hold again.'

Hitler's resentment found expression in constant accusations of treachery, which were echoed by Goebbels and the others. Hanna Reitsch describes Eva Braun as 'raving about all the ungrateful swine who had deserted their Führer and should be destroyed. It appeared that the only good Germans were those who were caught in the bunker and that all the others were traitors because they were not there to die with him.'[2] Eva regarded her own fate with equanimity. She had no desire to survive Hitler, and spent much of her time changing her clothes and caring for her appearance in order to keep up his spirits. Her perpetual complaint was: 'Poor, poor Adolf, deserted by everyone, betrayed by all. Better that ten thousand others die than that he should be lost to Germany.'[3]

On the night of the 26th the Russians began to shell the Chancellery, and the bunker shook as the massive masonry split and crashed into the courtyard and garden. Resistance could scarcely last much longer. The Russians were now less than a mile away, and the Army which had once goose-stepped before Hitler's arrogant gaze on the Wenceslas Square of Prague, through the ruins of Warsaw, and down the Champs Élysées was reduced to a handful of exhausted companies fighting

1. Hanna Reitsch's interrogation by the U.S. Army, 8 October 1945, N.D 3,734-PS. Fräulein Reitsch has since repudiated parts of this interrogation. The American authorities, however, have confirmed its substantial accuracy as a record of what she said in October 1945. Cf. Trevor-Roper: op. cit., 2nd edition, pp. xlvii–liv.
2. N.D., 3,734-PS.   3. ibid.

desperately street by street for the barely recognizable centre of Berlin.

Hitler was still waiting for news of Wenck's attack. On the 28th he wirelessed to Keitel:

I expect the relief of Berlin. What is Heinrici's army doing? Where is Wenck? What is happening to the Ninth Army? When will Wenck and Ninth Army join us?[1]

Hanna Reitsch describes him pacing up and down the shelter 'waving a road map that was fast disintegrating from the sweat of his hands and planning Wenck's campaign with anyone who happened to be listening'.[2]

The answer to Hitler's questions was simple: Wenck's forces like the Ninth Army had been wiped out; Heinrici's army was in retreat to the west to avoid surrender to the Russians.

The climax came on the night of Saturday–Sunday, 28–9 April. Between nine and ten o'clock on the Saturday evening Hitler was talking to Ritter von Greim when a message was sent to him which determined him to end at last the career which had begun twenty-seven years before, at the end of another lost war. Brought by Heinz Lorenz, an official of the Propaganda Ministry, it consisted of a brief Reuter report to the effect that Himmler had been in touch with the Swedish Count Bernadotte for the purpose of negotiating peace terms.

VII

Since the beginning of 1945 Himmler had been secretly urged by Walter Schellenberg, the youngest of his S.S. generals, to open negotiations with the Western Powers on his own initiative, and when Count Bernadotte visited Berlin in February to discuss the release of Norwegian and Danish prisoners on behalf of the Swedish Red Cross, Schellenberg arranged for Himmler to meet him in the hope that this might provide the opportunity he sought. At that stage the reluctant Reichsführer S.S., much troubled by his loyalty to Hitler, had been unwilling to commit himself. Even when Bernadotte paid a second visit to Berlin in April Himmler could not make up his mind to speak out. But reports of the dramatic scene at the conference of 22 April and Hitler's declaration that the war was lost, and that he would seek death in the ruins of Berlin, made much the same impression on Himmler that

1. Keitel's interrogation, NCA., Supp. B., pp. 1281–2.
2. N.D. 3,734-PS.

it had made on Göring. 'Everyone is mad in Berlin,' he declared. 'What am I to do?' Both men concluded that loyalty to Hitler was no longer inconsistent with steps to end the war, but while Göring telegraphed to Hitler for confirmation of his view, Himmler more wisely acted in secret.

On the night of 23–24 April, while Hitler was raging at the disloyalty of Göring, Himmler accompanied Schellenberg to Lübeck for another meeting with Count Bernadotte at the Swedish Consulate. This time Himmler was prepared to put his cards on the table. Hitler, he told Bernadotte, was quite possibly dead; if not, he certainly would be in the next few days.

In the situation that has now arisen [Himmler continued] I consider my hands free. I admit that Germany is defeated. In order to save as great a part of Germany as possible from a Russian invasion I am willing to capitulate on the Western Front in order to enable the Western Allies to advance rapidly towards the east. But I am not prepared to capitulate on the Eastern Front.[1]

On condition that Norway and Denmark were included in the surrender, Bernadotte agreed to forward a proposal on Himmler's lines through the Swedish Foreign Minister, although he warned the two Germans that he did not believe there was the least chance that Britain and the U.S.A. would agree to a separate peace.

While Bernadotte left for Stockholm, Himmler began to think of the ministers he would appoint to his Government when he assumed power, and to discuss with Schellenberg the new Party of National Union which was to take the place of the Nazi Party.

On 27 April, however, Bernadotte returned from the north with the news that the Western Allies refused to consider a separate peace and insisted on unconditional surrender. This was a heavy blow especially to Schellenberg. But worse was to follow: on the 28th the fact that Himmler had been taking part in such negotiations was reported from London and New York. Himmler was now to discover, as Göring had before him, that it was unwise to discount Hitler before he was really dead.

Hitler was beside himself at the news. 'His colour rose to a heated red and his face was unrecognizable. . . . After the lengthy outburst, Hitler sank into a stupor, and for a time the entire bunker was silent.'[2] Göring had at least asked permission first before beginning negotiations; Himmler, *der treue Heinrich*, in

1. Count Folke Bernadotte: *The Curtain Falls* (N.Y., 1945), pp. 106–13.
2. Reitsch: N.D. 3734-PS.

whose loyalty he had placed unlimited faith, had said nothing. That Himmler should betray him was the bitterest blow of all, and it served to crystallize the decision to commit suicide which Hitler had threatened on the 22nd, but which he had not yet made up his mind to put into effect. This final decision followed the pattern of all the others: a period of hesitation, then a sudden resolution from which he was not to be moved. So it had been before the decision to stay in Berlin; and so it had been in the succeeding week over the question of suicide. Throughout the week Hitler spoke constantly of taking his own life, and on the night of the 27th – if Hanna Reitsch's report is to be believed – he held a conference at which the plans for a mass suicide were carefully rehearsed and everyone made little speeches swearing allegiance to the Führer and Germany. But still he waited and hoped – until the night of the 28th. That was the night of decisions.

Shortly after he received the news from Lorenz, Hitler disappeared behind closed doors with Goebbels and Bormann, the only two Nazi leaders in whom he now felt any confidence. Hitler's first thought was revenge, and Bormann had at least the satisfaction of removing Himmler as well as Göring before the Third Reich crumbled into dust.

Himmler's representative with the Führer, Fegelein, had already been arrested after it had been discovered that he had slipped quietly out of the bunker with the apparent intention of making a discreet escape before the end. The fact that he was married to Eva Braun's sister, Gretl, was no protection. He was now subjected to a close examination on what he knew of Himmler's treasonable negotiations and then taken into the courtyard of the Chancellery to be shot. Himmler was more difficult to reach, but Hitler ordered Greim and Hanna Reitsch to make an attempt to get out of Berlin by plane and entrusted them with the order to arrest Himmler at all costs. 'A traitor must never succeed me as Führer,' Hitler shouted in a trembling voice. 'You must go out to ensure that he will not.'[1]

Greim and Hanna Reitsch left between midnight and 1 a.m. on the morning of Sunday 29 April, and Hitler now turned to more personal matters. One human being at least had remained true and she should have her reward. Now that he had decided to end his life, the argument he had always used against marriage – that

1. Hanna Reitsch's interrogation, N.D. 3,734-PS.

it would interfere with his career – no longer carried weight. So, between 1 a.m. and 3 a.m. on the 29th, Hitler married Eva Braun. The ceremony, performed according to civil law, was hurriedly carried out by a municipal councillor, Walter Wagner, then serving in the Volkssturm and called in by Goebbels. The Führer's marriage took place in the map-room of the bunker which was used for small conferences. Both bride and bridegroom swore that they were 'of pure Aryan descent'; Goebbels and Bormann were present as witnesses and signed the register after the bride and bridegroom. Eva began to write her maiden name of Braun, but struck out the initial B and corrected her signature to 'Eva Hitler, *née* Braun'. Afterwards the bridal party returned to their private suite, where a few friends – Bormann, Goebbels and his wife, Hitler's two secretaries, his adjutants, and his cook – came in to drink champagne and to talk nostalgically of the old days and Goebbels's marriage at which Hitler had been one of the witnesses before they came to power.

The celebration went on while Hitler retired to the adjoining room with his secretary, Frau Junge. There, in the early hours of 29 April, he dictated his will and his political testament. Both documents are of such interest as to justify quotation at length.[1]

Facing death and the destruction of the régime he had created, this man who had exacted the sacrifice of millions of lives rather than admit defeat was still recognizably the old Hitler. From first to last there is not a word of regret, nor a suggestion of remorse. The fault is that of others, above all that of the Jews, for even now the old hatred is unappeased. Word for word, Hitler's final address to the German nation could be taken from almost any of his early speeches of the 1920s or from the pages of *Mein Kampf*. Twenty-odd years had changed and taught him nothing. His mind remained as tightly closed as it had been on the day when he wrote: 'During these years in Vienna a view of life and a definite outlook on the world took shape in my mind. These became the granite basis of my conduct. Since then I have extended that foundation very little, I have changed nothing in it.'[2]

The first part of the Political Testament consists of a general defence of his career:

More than thirty years have now passed since in 1914 I made my modest

1. The two documents are contained in N.D. 3,569-P S.
2. *Mein Kampf*, p. 32.

contribution as a volunteer in the First World War, which was forced upon the Reich.

In these three decades I have been actuated solely by love and loyalty to my people. . . .

It is untrue that I, or anyone else in Germany, wanted the war in 1939. It was desired and instigated solely by those international statesmen who were either of Jewish descent or worked for Jewish interests. I have made too many offers for the control and limitation of armaments, which posterity will not for all time be able to disregard, for the responsibility for the outbreak of this war to be laid on me. I have further never wished that, after the fatal First World War, a second against England or against America, should break out. Centuries will pass away, but out of the ruins of our towns and monuments hatred will grow against those finally responsible for everything, International Jewry, and its helpers. . . .

I have also made it plain that, if the nations of Europe are again to be regarded as mere shares to be bought and sold by those international conspirators in money and finance, then that race, Jewry, which is the real criminal of this murderous struggle, will be saddled with the responsibility. . . .

Hitler then turned to defend his decision to stay in Berlin and to speak of the future.

After six years of war, which in spite of all set-backs will go down one day in history as the most glorious and valiant demonstration of a nation's life-purpose, I cannot forsake the city which is the capital of the Reich . . . I have decided, therefore, to remain in Berlin and there of my own free will to choose death at the moment when I believe the position of Fuehrer and Chancellor can no longer be held. . . .

I die with a happy heart aware of the immeasurable deeds of our soldiers at the front. . . . That from the bottom of my heart I express my thanks to you all is just as self-evident as my wish that you should, because of that, on no account give up the struggle, but rather continue it against the enemies of the Fatherland. . . . From the sacrifice of our soldiers and from my own unity with them unto death will spring up in the history of Germany the seed of a radiant renaissance of the National Socialist movement and thus of the realization of a true community of nations. . . .

. . . I beg the heads of the Army, Navy, and Air Force to strengthen by all possible means the spirit of resistance of our soldiers in the National Socialist sense, with special reference to the fact that I myself, as founder and creator of this movement, have preferred death to cowardly abdication or even capitulation.

To this Hitler could not refrain from adding a gibe at the Officer Corps:

May it at some future time become part of the code of honour of the German officer – as it already is in the case of our Navy – that the surrender of a district or of a town should be impossible and that the leaders should march ahead as shining examples faithfully fulfilling their duty unto death.

The second part of the Testament contains Hitler's provisions for the succession. He began by expelling Göring and Himmler from the Party and from all offices of State. He accused them of causing immeasurable harm to Germany by unauthorized negotiations with the enemy and of illegally attempting to seize power for themselves. As his successor he appointed Admiral Dönitz President of the Reich, Minister of War, and Supreme Commander of the Armed Forces – and promptly proceeded to nominate his Government for him. Goebbels and Bormann had their reward, the first as the new Chancellor, the second as Party Minister. Hitler's choice for Foreign Minister was Seyss-Inquart, once a key figure in the annexation of Austria and since 1940 Reich Commissioner for the Netherlands. Himmler's successor as Reichsführer S.S. was Hanke, the Gauleiter of Lower Silesia, and, as Minister of the Interior, Paul Giesler, the Gauleiter of Upper Bavaria. The influence of Bormann is evident in the appointment of Party Gauleiters to both posts. Ley, Funk, and Schwerin-Krosigk kept their offices; Speer was replaced by Saur, his chief assistant at the Ministry for Armaments; while the last Commander-in-Chief of the German Army was Field-Marshal Schörner, who commanded the undefeated Army Group in Bohemia.

The last paragraph returned once more to the earliest of Hitler's obsessions: 'Above all I charge the leaders of the nation and those under them to scrupulous observance of the laws of race and to merciless opposition to the universal poisoner of all peoples, international Jewry.'

The Testament was signed at four o'clock in the morning of Sunday 29 April, and witnessed by Goebbels and Bormann for the Party, by Burgdorf and Krebs, as representatives of the Army. At the same time Hitler signed his will, which was again witnessed by Goebbels and Bormann, with the additional signature of Colonel von Below, his Luftwaffe adjutant. This was a shorter and more personal document:

Although I did not consider that I could take th e responsibility during the years of struggle of contracting a marriage, I have now decided, before the end of my life, to take as my wife the woman who, after many years of faithful friendship, of her own free will entered this town, when it was already besieged, in order to share my fate. At her own desire she goes to death with me as my wife. This will compensate us for what we have both lost through my work in the service of my people.

What I possess belongs – in so far as it has any value – to the Party, or, if this no longer exists, to the State. Should the State too be destroyed, no further decision on my part is necessary.

My pictures, in the collection which I have bought in the course of years, have never been collected for private purposes, but only for the establishment of a gallery in my home-town of Linz on the Danube.

It is my heartfelt wish that this bequest should be duly executed.

As my executor I nominate my most faithful Party comrade, Martin Bormann. He is given full legal authority to make all decisions. He is permitted to hand to my relatives anything which has a sentimental value or is necessary for the maintenance of a modest standard of life [*eines kleinen bürgerlichen Lebens*]; especially for my wife's mother and my faithful fellow-workers who are well known to him. The chief of these are my former secretaries, Frau Winter, etc., who have for many years helped me by their work.

I myself and my wife choose to die in order to escape the disgrace of deposition or capitulation. It is our wish to be burned immediately in the place where I have carried out the greater part of my daily work in the course of my twelve years' service to my people.

Hitler's choice of Dönitz as his successor is surprising, and to no one did it come as more of a surprise than to Dönitz himself. Since Dönitz had replaced Raeder as Commander-in-Chief, however, Hitler had come to look upon the Navy with different eyes. He attached the greatest importance to the U-boat campaign, and contrasted the 'National Socialist spirit' of the Navy under Dönitz with what he regarded as the treachery and disaffection of the Army and Air Force. In the last year of his life Hitler showed more confidence in Dönitz than in any of his senior commanders, and this was repaid by an unquestioning loyalty on the Admiral's part. With Göring and Himmler excluded, Goebbels was the obvious choice as Hitler's successor, but Goebbels would never have been accepted by the soldiers. To command the Armed Forces – which, in effect, meant to negotiate a surrender – someone else, preferably a serving officer, must become Head of the State and Minister for War. Goebbels was thus to succeed Hitler as Chancellor, but Dönitz was to become Head of the State and Supreme Commander. By choosing an officer from the Navy, rather than from the Army, Hitler offered a last deliberate insult to the military caste on whom he laid the blame for losing the war.

Hitler knew very well that the war was lost, but, as the political testament shows, he was making a clumsy attempt to save something for the future. As a legacy to a new generation of National Socialists, however, it was a singularly unimpressive document. The game was played out and when the prestige of power was stripped away nothing remained but the stale and unconvincing slogans of the beer-hall agitator of the 1920s.

Characteristically, Hitler's last message to the German people contained at least one striking lie. His death was anything but a hero's end; by committing suicide he deliberately abandoned his responsibilities and took a way out which in earlier years he had strongly condemned as a coward's. The words in the Testament are carefully chosen to conceal this; he speaks of his 'unity with our soldiers unto death', and again of fulfilling his duty unto death. It is worth noting that when General Weidling, the Commandant of Berlin, discovered that Hitler had committed suicide shortly after refusing the garrison permission to fight its way out of the city, he was so disgusted that he at once released his soldiers from their oaths. None the less the fiction was maintained in the official announcement, and Dönitz, in his broadcast of 1 May, declared that the Führer had died fighting at the head of his troops.

After he had finished dictating the two documents Hitler tried to get some rest. Goebbels too retired, but not to sleep. Instead, he sat down to compose his own last contribution to the Nazi legend, an 'Appendix to the Führer's Political Testament'.

For days Goebbels had been talking in extravagant terms of winning a place in history. 'Gentlemen,' he told a conference at the Propaganda Ministry on 17 April, 'in a hundred years' time they will be showing a fine colour film describing the terrible days we are living through. Don't you want to play a part in that film? ... Hold out now, so that a hundred years hence the audience does not hoot and whistle when you appear on the screen.'[1] Goebbels's genius as a propagandist did not desert him. Despite Hitler's order, he declined to leave his leader's side and finished his apologia with the promise 'to end a life which will have no further value to me if I cannot spend it in the service of the Führer'.

1. Semmler, p. 194.

In the course of Sunday, the 29th, arrangements were made to send copies of the Führer's Political Testament out of the bunker, and three men were selected to make their way as best they could to Admiral Dönitz's and Field-Marshal Schörner's headquarters. One of the men selected was an official of the Propaganda Ministry, and to him Goebbels entrusted his own appendix to Hitler's manifesto. At midnight on 29 April another messenger, Colonel von Below, left carrying with him a postscript which Hitler instructed him to deliver to General Keitel. It was the Supreme Commander's last message to the Armed Forces, and the sting was in the tail:

The people and the Armed Forces have given their all in this long and hard struggle. The sacrifice has been enormous. But my trust has been misused by many people. Disloyalty and betrayal have undermined resistance throughout the war. It was therefore not granted to me to lead the people to victory. The Army General Staff cannot be compared with the General Staff of the First World War. Its achievements were far behind those of the fighting front.[1]

The war had been begun by the Jews, it had been lost by the generals. In neither case was the responsibility Hitler's and his last word of all was to reaffirm his original purpose:

The efforts and sacrifice of the German people in this war [he added] have been so great that I cannot believe they have been in vain. The aim must still be to win territory in the east for the German people.[2]

VIII

During the 29th, while the messengers were setting out from the bunker, the news arrived of Mussolini's end. The Duce, too, had shared his fate with his mistress; together with Clara Petacci, he had been caught by the Partisans and shot on the shore of Lake Como on 28 April. Their bodies were taken to Milan and hung in the Piazzale Loreto. If Hitler made any comment on the end of his brother dictator it is unrecorded; but the news can only have confirmed him in the decision he had taken about his own end. Even when dead he was determined not to be put on show.

He now began to make systematic preparations for taking his

1. The original text of the message has been destroyed: the version quoted was reconstructed by Colonel von Below and is given by Trevor-Roper, p. 214.
2. ibid.

life. He had his Alsatian bitch, Blondi, destroyed, and in the early hours of Monday 30 April assembled his staff in the passage in order to say farewell. Walking along the line, he shook each man and woman silently by the hand. Shortly afterwards Bormann sent out a telegram to Dönitz, whose headquarters was at Plön, between Lübeck and Kiel, instructing him to proceed 'at once and mercilessly' against all traitors.

On the morning of the 30th Hitler was given the latest reports on the situation in Berlin at the usual conference. The Russians had occupied the Tiergarten and reached the Potsdamer Platz, only a block or two away from the Chancellery. Hitler received the news without excitement, and took lunch at two o'clock in the afternoon in the company of his two secretaries and his cook. Eva Hitler remained in her room and Hitler behaved as if nothing unusual were happening.

In the course of the early afternoon Erich Kempka, Hitler's chauffeur, was ordered to send two hundred litres of petrol to the Chancellery Garden. It was carried over in jerrycans and its delivery supervised by Heinz Linge, Hitler's batman.

Meanwhile, having finished his lunch, Hitler went to fetch his wife from her room, and for the second time they said farewell to Goebbels, Bormann, and the others who remained in the bunker. Hitler then returned to the Führer's suite with Eva and closed the door. A few minutes passed while those outside stood waiting in the passage. Then a single shot rang out.

After a brief pause the little group outside opened the door. Hitler was lying on the sofa, which was soaked in blood: he had shot himself through the mouth. On his right-hand side lay Eva Braun also dead: she had swallowed poison. The time was half past three on the afternoon of Monday 30 April 1945, ten days after Hitler's fifty-sixth birthday.

Hitler's instructions for the disposal of their bodies had been explicit, and they were carried out to the letter. Hitler's own body, wrapped in a blanket, was carried out and up to the garden by two S.S. men. The head was concealed, but the black trousers and black shoes which he wore with his uniform jacket hung down beneath the covering. Eva's body was picked up by Bormann, who handed it to Kempka. They made their way up the stairs and out into the open air, accompanied by Goebbels, Günsche, and Burgdorf. The doors leading into the garden had been locked and the bodies were laid in a shallow depression of sandy soil close to the porch. Picking up the five cans of petrol, one after another, Günsche, Hitler's S.S. adjutant, poured the contents over the two corpses and set fire to them with a lighted rag.

A sheet of flame leapt up, and the watchers withdrew to the shelter of the porch. A heavy Russian bombardment was in progress and shells continually burst on the Chancellery. Silently they stood to attention, and for the last time gave the Hitler salute; then turned and disappeared into the shelter.

Outside, in the deserted garden, the two bodies burned steadily side by side. It was twelve years and three months to the day since Hitler had walked out of the President's room, Chancellor of the German Reich.[1]

The rest of the story is briefly told. Bormann at once informed Dönitz by radio that Hitler had nominated him as his successor, but he concealed the fact of Hitler's death for another twenty-four hours. During the interval, on the night of 30 April, Goebbels and Bormann made an unsuccessful effort to negotiate with the Russians. The Russian reply was 'unconditional surrender'. Then, but only then, Goebbels sent a further cable to Dönitz, reporting Hitler's death. The news was broadcast on the evening of 1 May to the solemn setting of music from Wagner and

---

1. What happened to the ashes of the two burned bodies left in the Chancellery Garden has never been discovered. That they were disposed of in some way remains a possibility, since an open fire will not normally destroy the human body so completely as to leave no traces, and nothing was found in the garden after its capture by the Russians. Professor Trevor-Roper, who carried out a thorough investigation in 1945 of the circumstances surrounding Hitler's death, inclines to the view that the ashes were collected into a box and handed to Artur Axmann, the leader of the Hitler Youth. There is some slight evidence for this and, as Trevor-Roper points out (in the Introduction to his second edition, pages xxxii–xxxiv), it would have been a logical act to pass on the sacred relics to the next generation. The simplest explanation may still be the correct one. It is not known how thorough a search was made by the Russians, and it is possible that the remains of Adolf Hitler and his wife became mixed up with those of other bodies which have been found there, especially as the garden continued to be under bombardment until the Russians captured the Chancellery on 2 May.

The question would scarcely be of interest had the failure to discover the remains not been used to throw doubt on the fact of Hitler's death. It is, of course, true that no final incontrovertible evidence in the form of Hitler's dead body has been produced. But the weight of circumstantial evidence set out in Trevor-Roper's book, when added to the state of Hitler's health at the time and the psychological probability that this was the end he would choose, make a sufficiently strong case to convince all but the constitutionally incredulous – or those who have not bothered to study the evidence.

Bruckner's Seventh Symphony: the impression left was that of a hero's death, fighting to the last against Bolshevism.

An attempt at a mass escape by the men and women crowded into the network of bunkers round the Chancellery was made on the night of 1–2 May, and a considerable number succeeded in making their way out of Berlin. Among them was Martin Bormann: whether he was killed at the time or got away has never been established. Goebbels did not join them. On the evening of 1 May, after giving poison to his children, Goebbels shot his wife and himself in the Chancellery Garden. The bodies were set fire to by Goebbels's adjutant, but the job was badly done, and the charred remains were found next day by the Russians. After Goebbels's death the Führerbunker was set on fire.

In the following week Dönitz attempted to negotiate terms of surrender with the Western Allies, but their reply was uncompromising. The German Army in Italy had already capitulated and the British and Americans refused to be drawn by Dönitz's clumsy efforts to secure a separate peace and split the Grand Alliance. On 4 May Admiral von Friedeburg signed an armistice providing for the surrender of the German forces in north-west Europe, and early on the morning of the 7th General Jodl and Friedeburg put their signatures to an unconditional surrender of all the German forces presented to them jointly by the representatives of the U.S.A., Great Britain, the U.S.S.R., and France at Rheims.

The Third Reich had outlasted its founder by just one week.

EPILOGUE

EPILOGUE

MANY attempts have been made to explain away the importance of Hitler, from Chaplin's brilliant caricature in *The Great Dictator* to the much less convincing picture of Hitler the pawn, a front man for German capitalism. Others have argued that Hitler was nothing in himself, only a symbol of the restless ambition of the German nation to dominate Europe; a creature flung to the top by the tides of revolutionary change, or the embodiment of the collective unconscious of a people obsessed with violence and death.

These arguments seem to me to be based upon a confusion of two different questions. Obviously, Nazism was a complex phenomenon to which many factors – social, economic, historical, psychological – contributed. But whatever the explanation of this episode in European history – and it can be no simple one – that does not answer the question with which this book has been concerned, what was the part played by Hitler. It may be true that a mass movement, strongly nationalist, anti-Semitic, and radical, would have sprung up in Germany without Hitler. But so far as what actually happened is concerned – not what might have happened – the evidence seems to me to leave no doubt that no other man played a role in the Nazi revolution or in the history of the Third Reich remotely comparable with that of Adolf Hitler.

The conception of the Nazi Party, the propaganda with which it must appeal to the German people, and the tactics by which it would come to power – these were unquestionably Hitler's. After 1934 there were no rivals left and by 1938 he had removed the last checks on his freedom of action. Thereafter, he exercised an arbitrary rule in Germany to a degree rarely, if ever, equalled in a modern industrialized state.

At the same time, from the re-militarization of the Rhineland to the invasion of Russia, he won a series of successes in diplomacy and war which established an hegemony over the continent of Europe comparable with that of Napoleon at the height of his fame. While these could not have been won without a people and an Army willing to serve him, it was Hitler who provided the indispensable leadership, the flair for grasping opportunities, the boldness in using them. In retrospect his mistakes appear obvious, and it is easy to be complacent about the inevitability of his defeat; but it took the combined efforts of the three most power-ful nations in the world to break his hold on Europe.

Luck and the disunity of his opponents will account for much of Hitler's success – as it will of Napoleon's – but not for all. He began with few advantages, a man without a name and without support other than that which he acquired for himself, not even a citizen of the country he aspired to rule. To achieve what he did Hitler needed – and possessed – talents out of the ordinary which in sum amounted to political genius, however evil its fruits.

His abilities have been sufficiently described in the preceding pages: his mastery of the irrational factors in politics, his insight into the weaknesses of his opponents, his gift for simplification, his sense of timing, his willingness to take risks. An opportunist entirely without principle, he showed both consistency and an astonishing power of will in pursuing his aims. Cynical and calculating in the exploitation of his histrionic gifts, he retained an unshaken belief in his historic role and in himself as a creature of destiny.

The fact that his career ended in failure, and that his defeat was pre-eminently due to his own mistakes, does not by itself detract from Hitler's claim to greatness. The flaw lies deeper. For these remarkable powers were combined with an ugly and strident egotism, a moral and intellectual cretinism. The passions which ruled Hitler's mind were ignoble: hatred, resentment, the lust to dominate, and, where he could not dominate, to destroy. His career did not exalt but debased the human condition, and his twelve years' dictatorship was barren of all ideas save one – the further extension of his own power and that of the nation with which he had identified himself. Even power he conceived of in the crudest terms: an endless vista of military roads, S.S. garrisons, and concentration camps to sustain the rule of the Aryan 'master race' over the degraded subject peoples of his new empire in the east.

The great revolutions of the past, whatever their ultimate fate, have been identified with the release of certain powerful ideas: individual conscience, liberty, equality, national freedom, social justice. National Socialism produced nothing. Hitler constantly exalted force over the power of ideas and delighted to prove that men were governed by cupidity, fear, and their baser passions. The sole theme of the Nazi revolution was domination, dressed up as the doctrine of race, and, failing that, a vindictive destructive-ness, Rauschning's *Revolution des Nihilismus*.

It is this emptiness, this lack of anything to justify the suffering he caused rather than his own monstrous and ungovernable will which makes Hitler both so repellent and so barren a figure. Hitler will have his place in history, but it will be alongside Attila the Hun, the barbarian king who was surnamed, not 'the Great', but 'the Scourge of God', and who boasted 'in a saying', Gibbon writes, 'worthy of his ferocious pride, that the grass never grew on the spot where his horse had stood'.[1]

The view has often been expressed that Hitler could only have come to power in Germany, and it is true – without falling into the same error of racialism as the Nazis – that there were certain features of German historical development, quite apart from the effects of the Defeat and the Depression, which favoured the rise of such a movement.

This is not to accuse the Germans of Original Sin, or to ignore the other sides of German life which were only grossly caricatured by the Nazis. But Nazism was not some terrible accident which fell upon the German people out of a blue sky. It was rooted in their history, and while it is true that a majority of the German people never voted for Hitler, it is also true that thirteen millions did. Both facts need to be remembered.

From this point of view Hitler's career may be described as a *reductio ad absurdum* of the most powerful political tradition in Germany since the Unification. This is what nationalism, militarism, authoritarianism, the worship of success and force, the exaltation of the State, and *Realpolitik* lead to, if they are projected to their logical conclusion.

There are Germans who reject such a view. They argue that what was wrong with Hitler was that he lacked the necessary skill, that he was a bungler. If only he had listened to the generals – or Schacht – the career diplomats – if only he had not attacked Russia, and so on. There is some point, they feel, at which he went wrong. They refuse to see that it was the ends themselves, not simply the means, which were wrong: the pursuit of unlimited power, the scorn for justice or any restraint on power; the exaltation of will over reason and conscience; the assertion of an arrogant supremacy, the contempt for others' rights. As at least one German historian, Professor Meinecke, has recognized, the catastrophe to which Hitler led Germany points to the need to re-examine the aims as well as the methods of German policy as far back as Bismarck.

1. Gibbon: *Decline and Fall of the Roman Empire*, c. 34.

The Germans, however, were not the only people who preferred in the 1930s not to know what was happening and refused to call evil things by their true names. The British and French at Munich; the Italians, Germany's partners in the Pact of Steel; the Poles, who stabbed the Czechs in the back over Teschen; the Russians, who signed the Nazi–Soviet Pact to partition Poland, all thought they could buy Hitler off, or use him to their own selfish advantage. They did not succeed, any more than the German Right or the German Army. In the bitterness of war and occupation they were forced to learn the truth of the words of John Donne which Ernest Hemingway set at the beginning of his novel of the Spanish Civil War:

No man is an Iland, intire of it selfe; every man is a peece of the Continent, a part of the maine; If a clod bee washed away by the Sea, Europe is the lesse, as well as if a Promontorie were, as well as if a Mannor of thy friends or of thine own were; Any man's death diminishes me, because I am involved in Mankinde; And therefore never send to know for whom the bell tolls; It tolls for thee.

Hitler, indeed, was a European, no less than a German phenomenon. The conditions and the state of mind which he exploited, the *malaise* of which he was the symptom, were not confined to one country, although they were more strongly marked in Germany than anywhere else. Hitler's idiom was German, but the thoughts and emotions to which he gave expression have a more universal currency.

Hitler recognized this relationship with Europe perfectly clearly. He was in revolt against 'the System' not just in Germany but in Europe, against the liberal bourgeois order, symbolized for him in the Vienna which had once rejected him. To destroy this was his mission, the mission in which he never ceased to believe; and in this, the most deeply felt of his purposes, he did not fail. Europe may rise again, but the old Europe of the years between 1789, the year of the French Revolution, and 1939, the year of Hitler's War, has gone for ever – and the last figure in its history is that of Adolf Hitler, the architect of its ruin. '*Si monumentum requiris, circumspice*' – 'If you seek his monument, look around.'

BIBLIOGRAPHY

THIS revised bibliographical note takes account only of first-hand sources including journals and memoirs; it includes secondary works only where these make use of original material unpublished before. The best periodical in which to follow new publications is the *Vierteljahrshefte für Zeitgeschichte*, published by the Munich Institut für Zeitgeschichte. The interested student should also consult the separate parts of the catalogue of the Wiener Library, London. Two valuable sources, not normally available to the historian, on which I have been able to draw are the German newsreels of these years and the recordings of Hitler's speeches in his own voice.

1. WRITINGS AND SPEECHES OF ADOLF HITLER

Mein Kampf (English translation by James Murphy), London, 1939.
Hitler's Secret Book (English translation of *Hitlers Zweite Buch*), New York.
Adolf Hitlers Reden, edited by Dr Ernst Boepple, Munich, 1934.
Die Reden des Führers nach der Machtübernahme, Berlin, 1939.
My New Order (Hitler's Speeches, 1922–41), edited by Count Raoul de Roussy de Sales, New York, 1941.
The Speeches of Adolf Hitler, 1922–39, edited by Norman H. Baynes, 2 vols., Oxford, 1942.
Hitler's Words (Speeches, 1922–43), edited by Gordon W. Prange, Washington, 1944.
Hitler: Reden und Proklamationen, edited by Max Domarus, vol. I (1932–8), Munich, 1962.
Hitler's Table Talk, 1941–4, London, 1953.
Hitlers Tischgespräche im Führerhauptquartier, 1941–2, edited by Dr Henry Picker, Bonn, 1951.
The Testament of Adolf Hitler: The Hitler-Bormann Documents, February–April 1945, London, 1961.

2. DOCUMENTARY COLLECTIONS

(*a*) The most important collection is that prepared for use in the Nuremberg Trials after the war. The complete version of the proceedings of the main trial and the full text of the documents presented in evidence have been published as:

> *The Trial of the Major War Criminals before the International Military Tribunal, Proceedings*, vols. I–XXIII, Nuremberg, 1947–9.
> *Documents in Evidence*, vols. XXIV–XLII, Nuremberg, 1947–9.

Translations of most of the documents used by the British and American Prosecuting Counsel, together with translations of certain of the defence documents and of the most important affidavits and interrogations, have been published by the United States Government Printing Office under the title *Nazi Conspiracy and Aggression*, 8 vols. plus 2 supplementary vols., A and B, Washington, 1946–8. A verbatim record of the trial proceedings has been published by H.M.S.O. *The Trial of German Major War Criminals*, 22 parts, London, 1946–50.

All three publications retain the document numbers used at the trial, and the same system of reference has been used in this book.

For subsequent trials, see

1. *Trials of War Criminals before the Nuremberg Military Tribunals*, 14 vols., Washington, 1951–3.
2. *Law Reports of Trials of War Criminals*, vols. i–xv, H.M.S.O., London, for the U.N. War Crimes Commission, 1947–9.
3. *Das Urteil im Wilhelmstrassen-Prozess*, edited by R. W. M. Kempner and Carl Hänsel, Munich, 1950.

(*b*) *Documents on German Foreign Policy*
Series C: 1933–7 and Series D: 1936/7–40. This is a comprehensive selection in translation of captured material from the German Foreign Office and other archives, published under the auspices of the British, French, and U.S. Governments.

(*c*) *Documents on British Foreign Policy*
2nd series, 1929–38; 3rd series, 1938–9.

(*d*) *Other documentary material*
Wille und Macht 5 (1937). *Heft 17* contains a number of documents for the events of 8–9 November 1923.
Völkischer Beobachter, Special number of 8 November 1933, containing reminiscences of 8 November 1923 by Rosenberg, Ulrich Graf, Weiss, Röhm, and Rossbach.
Der Hitler Prozess, the record of the Court Proceedings in Munich in 1924, Munich, 1924.
Hitler und Kahr, Aus dem Untersuchungsausschuss des bayerischen Landtags. Landesausschuss der S.P.D. in Bayern, Munich, 1928.
Feder, Gottfried: *Das Programm der N.S.D.A.P. und seine weltanschaulichen Grundgedanken*, Munich, 1932. (English translation, London, 1934.)
Rosenberg, Alfred: *Das Parteiprogramm, Wesen, Grundsätze und Ziele der N.S.D.A.P.*, Munich, 1930.
Hitler's Auseinandersetzung mit Brüning, Munich, 1932.
Protokoll der Mündlichen Verhandlung in dem Entnazifizierungsverfahren gegen den Generalleutnant a.D. Oscar von Hindenburg, at Ülzen, 14 March 1949.
Weissbuch über die Erschiessungen des 30 Juni 1934, Paris, 1934.
Protokoll des Schwurgerichts in dem Strafverfahren gegen Josef Dietrich und Michael Lippert, at Munich, 6–14 May 1957.
Dokumente der deutschen Politik, vol. i (1933–8), and for subsequent years down to 1940, Berlin, 1935–43.

Ciano's Diplomatic Papers, London, 1948.

Hitler e Mussolini – Lettere e documenti, Milan, 1946.

Les Lettres secrètes échangées par Hitler et Mussolini, Paris, 1946.

Documents and Materials Relating to the Eve of the Second World War.
vol. I, *November 1937–8*; vol. II, *The Dirksen Papers, 1938–9*, Moscow, 1948.

German Foreign Office Documents: Turkey, Moscow, 1948.
Hungary, Moscow, 1948.

Documents Concerning German–Polish Relations and the Outbreak of Hostilities between Great Britain and Germany, London, 1939, Cmd. 6106.

The French Yellow Book, Diplomatic Documents, 1938–9, London, 1939.

Official Documents concerning Polish–German and Polish–Soviet Relations, 1933–9, The Polish White Book, London, 1939.

Polnische Dokumente zur Vorgeschichte des Krieges, German F.O., Berlin, 1940. (Translation, New York, 1940.)

Nazi–Soviet Relations, 1939–41. From the Archives of the German Foreign Office, Department of State, Washington, 1948.

Le Procès du Maréchal Pétain, 2 vols., Paris, 1945.

Pétain et les Allemands, Memorandum d'Abetz, Paris, 1948.

The Spanish Government and the Axis, Department of State, Washington, 1946.

The Führer Conferences on Naval Affairs, reprinted in *Brassey's Naval Annual* for 1948.

Hitler Directs his War, edited by Felix Gilbert. New York, 1951. Records of Hitler's military conferences.

A German of the Resistance. The last letters of Count Helmuth James von Moltke, London, 1946.

Der lautlose Aufstand. Bericht über die Widerstandsbewegung, 1933–45, Hamburg, 1953.

3. MEMOIRS AND DIARIES

Alfieri, Dino: *Deux Dictateurs face à face, Rome–Berlin 1939–43*, Geneva, 1948.

Assmann, Kurt: *Deutsche Schicksalsjahre*, Wiesbaden, 1950.

Baur, Hans: *Hitler's Pilot*, London, 1958.

Bernadotte, Fulk: *The Curtain Falls*, New York, 1945.

Best, S. Payne: *The Venlo Incident*, London, 1950.

Boldt, Gerhard: *In the Shelter with Hitler*, London, 1948.

Bonnet, Georges: *Fin d'une Europe*, Geneva, 1948.

The Bormann Letters, London, 1954. (Correspondence with his wife, 1943–5).

Brandmayer, Balthasar: *Meldegänger Hitler*, Überlingen, 1933.

Ciano's Diary, 1937–8, London, 1952.

Ciano's Diary, 1939–43, London, 1947.

Coulondre, Robert: *De Staline à Hitler, 1936–9*, Paris, 1950.

Dahlerus, Birger: *The Last Attempt*, London, 1947.

Diels, Rudolf: *Lucifer ante Portas*, Stuttgart, 1950.

Dietrich, Otto: *Mit Hitler in die Macht*, Munich, 1934.

Dietrich, Otto: *The Hitler I Knew*, London, 1957.

Dirksen, Herbert: *Moskau – Tokio – London*, Stuttgart, 1949.

Ambassador Dodd's Diary, 1933–8, London, 1941.

Drexler, Anton: *Mein Politisches Erwachen*, Munich, 1923.

Duesterberg, Th.: *Der Stahlhelm und Hitler*, Wolfenbüttel, 1949.

Flandin, P. E.: *Politique française 1919–40*, Paris, 1948.

François-Poncet, André: *The Fateful Years*, London, 1949.

Gamelin, General Maurice Gustav: *Servir*, 3 vols., Paris, 1946–7.

Geyr von Schweppenburg: *The Critical Years*, London, 1952.

Gilbert, G. M.: *Nuremberg Diary*, London, 1948.

Gisevius, Bernd: *To the Bitter End*, London, 1948.

The Diary of Josef Goebbels, 1925–6, London, 1962.

The Goebbels Diaries, 1942–3, London, 1949.

Goebbels, Josef: *Kampf um Berlin*, Munich, 1934.

Goebbels, Josef: *My Part in Germany's Fight*, London, 1935.

Greiner, Joseph: *Das Ende des Hitler Mythos*, Vienna, 1947.

Guderian, Heinz: *Panzer Leader*, London, 1952.

Halder, Franz: *Hitler as Warlord*, London, 1950.

Hanfstängl, Ernst: *The Missing Years*, London, 1957.

The Von Hassell Diaries, 1938–44, London, 1948.

Henderson, Sir Nevile: *Failure of a Mission*, London, 1940.

Heusinger, Adolf: *Befehl im Widerstreit*, Stuttgart, 1950.

Hoffmann, Heinrich: *Hitler was my Friend*, London, 1955.

Hossbach, Friedrich: *Zwischen Wehrmacht und Hitler*, Hanover, 1949.

Kallenbach, Hans: *Mit Adolf Hitler auf Festung Landsberg*, Munich, 1933.

Kesselring, Albert: *A Soldier's Record*, New York, 1954.

The Kersten Memoirs, 1940–45, London, 1956.

Kleist, Peter: *Zwischen Hitler und Stalin*, Bonn, 1950.

Koller, Karl: *Der letzte Monat*, Mannheim, 1949.

Kordt, Erich: *Wahn und Wirklichkeit*, Stuttgart, 1947.

Kordt, Erich: *Nicht aus den Akten*, Stuttgart, 1950.

Krause, K. W.: *Zehn Jahre Kammerdiener bei Hitler*, Hamburg (no date).

Krosigk, Graf Lutz Schwerin von: *Es geschah in Deutschland*, Tübingen, 1951.

Kubizek, August: *Adolf Hitler, Mein Jugendfreund*, Graz, 1953.

The Diary of Pierre Laval, New York, 1948.

Lossberg, General Bernhard von: *Im Wehrmachtführungsstab: Bericht eines Generalstabsoffiziers*, Hamburg, 1950.

Ludecke, Kurt: *I Knew Hitler*, London, 1938.

Manstein, F. M. Eric von: *Verlorene Siege*, Bonn, 1955.

Meinecke, Friedrich: *Die deutsche Katastrophe*, Wiesbaden, 1947.

Meissner, Otto: *Staatssekretär unter Ebert–Hindenburg–Hitler*, Hamburg, 1950.

Mend, Hans: *Adolf Hitler im Felde*, Munich, 1931.

Mussolini, Benito: *Memoirs, 1942–3*, London, 1949.

Oven, Wilfred von: *Mit Goebbels bis zum Ende*, Buenos Aires, 1949.

Papen, Franz von: *Memoirs*, London, 1952.

Rahn, R.: *Ruheloses Leben*, Dusseldorf, 1949.

Rauschning, Hermann: *Hitler Speaks*, London, 1939.

Remer, Otto: *20 Juli 1944*, Hamburg, 1951.

Reynaud, Paul: *La France a sauvé l'Europe*, Paris, 1947.

The Ribbentrop Memoirs, London, 1954.

Röhm, Ernst: *Die Memoiren des Stabchefs Roehm*, Saarbrucken, 1934.

The Rommel Papers, London, 1953.

Rosenberg's Memoirs (ed. Serge Lang and Ernst von Schenck), New York, 1949.

Schacht, Hjalmar: *Account Settled*, London, 1948.

The Schellenberg Memoirs, London, 1956.

Schlabrendorff, Fabian von: *Revolt against Hitler*, London, 1948.

Schlange-Schöningen, Hans: *The Morning After*, London, 1948.

Schmidt, Paul: *Statist auf diplomatischer Bühne*, Bonn, 1949.

Schultz, Joachim: *Die Letzten 30 Tage – aus dem Kriegstagebuch des O.K.W.*, Stuttgart, 1951.

Schuschnigg, Kurt von: *Ein Requiem in Rot-Weiss-Rot*, Zurich, 1946. (English translation: *Austrian Requiem*, London, 1947.)

Semmler, Rudolf: *Goebbels, the Man next to Hitler*, London, 1947.

Severing, Carl: *Mein Lebensweg*, vol. ii., Köln, 1950.

Shirer, William L.: *A Berlin Diary*, London, 1941.

Sommerfeldt, Martin H.: *Ich war dabei*, Darmstadt, 1949.

Speidel, General Hans: *We Defended Normandy*, London, 1951.

Stahremberg, E. R. von: *Between Hitler and Mussolini*, London, 1942.

Strasser, Otto: *Hitler and I*, London, 1940.

Suñer, R. Serrano: *Entre les Pyrénées et Gibraltar*, Geneva, 1947.

Thyssen, Fritz: *I Paid Hitler*, London, 1941.

Wagner, Friedelind: *The Royal Family of Bayreuth*, London, 1948.

Ward Price, G.: *I Knew these Dictators*, London, 1937.

Weizsäcker, Ernst von: *Memoirs*, London, 1951.

Westphal, General Siegfried: *The German Army in the West*, London, 1951.

Zoller, A. (ed.): *Hitler Privat*, Düsseldorf, 1949.

4. SECONDARY WORKS WHICH CONTAIN OR MAKE USE OF ORIGINAL MATERIAL

Abshagen, K. H.: *Canaris*, Stuttgart, 1949.

Bénoist-Méchin, Jacques: *Histoire de l'armée allemande depuis l'Armistice*, Paris, 1936–8

Bracher, K. D., W. Sauer, and G. Schulz: *Die Nationalsozialistische Machtergreifung*, Cologne, 1960.

Castellan, G.: *Le Réarmament clandestin du Reich, 1930–5*, Paris, 1954.

Dallin, Alexander: *German Rule in Russia, 1941–4*, London, 1957.

Deakin, F. W.: *The Brutal Friendship*, London. 1962.

Dulles, Allen: *Germany's Underground*, New York, 1947.

Feiling, Keith: *The Life of Neville Chamberlain*, London, 1946.

Förster, Wolfgang: *Ein General kämpft gegen den Krieg* (Beck's papers), Munich, 1949.

Franz-Willing, Georg: *Die Hitler-bewegung.* I: *Der Ursprung, 1919–22*, Hamburg, 1962.

Gordon, Harold J.: *The Reichswehr and the German Republic*, Princeton, 1957.

Greiner, Helmuth: *Die oberste Wehrmachtsführung 1939–43*, Wiesbaden, 1951.

Heiden, Konrad: *Der Führer*, London, 1944.

Hilger, Gustav, and Alfred Meyer: *The Incompatible Allies, German–Soviet Relations, 1918–41*, New York, 1953.

Hofmann, H. H.: *Der Hitler Putsch*, Munich, 1962.

Jetzinger, Franz: *Hitler's Youth*, London, 1958.

de Jong, Louis: *The German Fifth Column in the Second World War*, London, 1956.

Kielmannsegg, Graf: *Der Fritzsch Prozess*, Hamburg, 1949.

Kochan, Lionel: *Pogrom, November 10 1938*, London, 1957.

Köhl, Robert L.: *R.K.F.D.V., German Resettlement and Population Policy, 1939–45*, Cambridge, Mass., 1957.

Langer, W. L.: *Our Vichy Gamble*, New York, 1947.

Liddell Hart, B. H.: *The Other Side of the Hill* (3rd edn), London, 1951.

Martiensen, Anthony, K.: *Hitler and his Admirals*, London, 1948.

Matthias, Erich, and Rudolf Morsey (eds.): *Das Ende der Parteien*, Düsseldorf, 1960.

Olden, Rudolf: *Hitler the Pawn*, London, 1936.

Pechel, Rudolf: *Der Deutsche Widerstand*, Zürich, 1947.

Rabenau, Lt-Gen. Friedrich von: *Seeckt, aus seinem Leben*, 2 vols., Leipzig, 1940.

Reitlinger, Gerald: *The Final Solution*, London, 1953.

Reitlinger, Gerald: *The S.S.: Alibi of a Nation*, London, 1956.

Ritter, Gerhard: *Carl Goerdeler und die deutsche Widerstandsbewegung*, Stuttgart, 1955.

Schramm, Wilhelm von: *Der 20. Juli in Paris*, Bad Woerishorn, 1953.

Shirer, William L.: *The Rise and Fall of the Third Reich*, London, 1960.

Shulman, Milton: *Defeat in the West*, 2nd edn, London, 1949.

Tobias, Fritz: *Der Reichstagsbrand: Legende oder Wirklichkeit?*, Rastadt, 1962.

Trevor-Roper, H. R.: *The Last Days of Hitler*, 2nd edn, London, 1950.

Waite, Robert G. L.: *Vanguard of Nazism, The Free Corps Movement*, Cambridge, Mass., 1952.

Wheatley, Ronald: *Operation Sea-Lion*, Oxford, 1958.

Wheeler-Bennett, J. W. (Sir John): *Hindenburg, The Wooden Titan*, London 1936.

Wheeler-Bennett, J. W. (Sir John): *The Nemesis of Power. The German Army in Politics, 1918–45*, London, 1953.

Wilmot, Chester: *The Struggle for Europe*, London, 1952.

Zeller, Eberhard: *Geist der Freiheit: Der 20 Juli 1944*, Munich, 1954.

5. ARTICLES

Angress, W. T., and Bradley F. Smith: 'Diaries of Heinrich Himmler's Early Years', in *Journal of Modern History*, vol. XXXI, No. 3, September 1959.

Brüning, Heinrich: 'Ein Brief', in *Deutsche Rundschau,* July 1947.

Castellan, G.: 'Von Schleicher, von Papen et l'avènement de Hitler', in *Cahiers d'Histoire de la Guerre*, No. 1, January 1949.

Craig, Gordon A.: 'The Reichswehr and National Socialism; The Policy of Wilhelm Groener, 1928–32', in *Political Science Quarterly*, vol. LXIII, No. 2, June 1948.

   'Briefe Schleichers an Groener', *Die Welt als Geschichte*, vol, XI, 1951.

Fodor, M. W.: 'The Austrian Roots of Hitlerism', in *Foreign Affairs*, vol. XIV, 1935–6.

Hale, Oron J.: 'Adolf Hitler, Taxpayer', in *American Historical Review,* vol. LX, No. 4, July 1955.

'Hitlers Eintritt in die Politik und die Reichswehr', in *Vierteljahrshefie für Zeitgeschichte*, vol. VII, 2, 1959.

Kempner, R. W. M.: 'Blueprint of the Nazi Underground'. *Research Studies of the State College of Washington*, vol. XIII, No. 2, June 1945.

Landauer, Carl: 'The Bavarian Problem in the Weimar Republic, 1918–23', in *Journal of Modern History*, vol. XVI, 1944.

Poole, De Witt C.: 'Light on Nazi Foreign Policy', in *Foreign Affairs*, vol. XXV, 1946.

Whiteside, A. G.: 'Nationaler Sozialismus in Österreich vor 1918', in *Vierteljahrshefte für Zeitgeschichte*, vol. IX, 4, 1961.

INDEX

The only unusual abbreviation is H., which stands for Hitler.